Rivall Friendship

by Bridget Manningham

Medieval and Renaissance
Texts and Studies

Volume 575

Rivall Friendship
by Bridget Manningham

Edited by

Jean R. Brink

with Mary Ellen Lamb
and William F. Gentrup

Arizona Center
for Medieval &
Renaissance Studies

Tempe, Arizona
2021

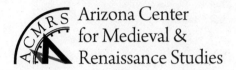
Arizona Center
for Medieval &
Renaissance Studies

Published by ACMRS (Arizona Center for Medieval and Renaissance Studies)
Tempe, Arizona
©2021 Arizona Board of Regents for Arizona State University.
All Rights Reserved.

ISBN 978-0-86698-633-5

*This book has received the Weiss-Brown Publication Subvention Award from the
Newberry Library.*

*The award supports the publication of outstanding works of scholarship that cover
European civilization before 1700 in the areas of music, theater, French or Italian
literature, or cultural studies.*

It is made to commemorate the career of Howard Mayer Brown.

∞
Printed in the United States of America

In memory of
Daniel Theodore Brink
May 26, 1940 – October 17, 1997

TABLE OF CONTENTS

ACKNOWLEDGMENTS

I wish to acknowledge the many substantial contributions to this edition of Mary Ellen Lamb. It was she who crystalized the insight that the transition from the romance to the novel was related to the connection between Artabella's romance and Arthenia's history. She also drafted early versions of the appendices on historical names and places and on characters' names and assisted in checking my transcription against the manuscript and microfilm. More than that, she sorted out recto and verso for the folios and always responded promptly and in good humor to my many emails. To William Gentrup, I also owe many debts. He copyedited this edition, making invaluable recommendations on typesetting. His proofreading contributed to the quality of the transcription. In addition, he is responsible for the observation that because the manuscript ends precisely at the bottom of the page and is right justified, there may have been additional pages that are missing.

I have been very fortunate in having the support of two Directors of the Arizona Center for Medieval and Renaissance Studies: Robert Bjork, who initially contracted this edition for ACMRS Press and Ayanna Thompson, who oversaw the completion of this edition as General Editor. Thanks as well to Roy Rukkila, Managing Editor, and to Todd Halvorsen, Manager of Design and Production at ACMRS Press.

I am indebted to the Newberry Library, Chicago, IL for permitting me to transcribe and edit this manuscript. At my request, Jill Gage, Custodian of the John M. Wing Foundation on the History of Printing and Bibliographer for British Literature and History, oversaw the foliation of *Rivall Friendship*. Lia Markey, Director of the Renaissance Center, has encouraged this project. Arizona State University, the National Endowment for the Humanities, and the Newberry Library helped in financing my research on this transcription.

My thanks also to my gifted graduate students, Teresa Tinkle and Margaret Sullivan, and to my sons, Robert and Peter Brink, for their assistance in transcribing *Rivall Friendship*. I acknowledge as well the support and assistance of Dan Brink, to whom this edition is dedicated, and who more than once retrieved this transcription of *Rivall Friendship* from the innards of a computer.

ILLUSTRATIONS

INTRODUCTION

In the summer of 1981, I attended an NEH Paleography Institute at the New-berry Library led by Anthony G. Petti, author of *English Literary Hands from Chaucer to Dryden,* and directed by John Tedeschi.[1] I was and am fascinated by manuscripts. To satisfy that fascination and to practice my developing paleo-graphical skills, I decided to examine all of the early modern manuscripts in the Newberry's collection. I thought that my search for buried treasure ought to include anonymous manuscripts, such as commonplace books and paleographi-cal documents, neither of which might be cataloged under an author or a title. So, I started with the chronological file, and I supplemented this by consulting the shelf list. Either this approach was magic, or serendipity guided the search because, using these procedures, I turned up the second part of Lady Mary Wroth's *Urania* before its existence was widely known and the then anonymous *Rivall Friendship.*

I was immediately attracted to the language and style of *Rivall Friend-ship.* The artfully balanced clauses reminded me of Sir Philip Sidney's *Defence of Poetry* and Roger Ascham's *Schoolmaster,* two of my touchstones for Renaissance prose. In 1981 I read enough of *Rivall Friendship* to discover that there was a first-person narrative of the English Civil War and Restoration inserted into the account of Artabella's courtship by Phasellus and Diomed.

On and off during the past decades, I have continued to check bibliographies and catalogs to see if *Rivall Friendship* might have been printed or even adapted from a French, Spanish, Italian, or other source. While we cannot rule out the possibility that *Rivall Friendship* was indeed printed under a variant title or that a source or another copy may exist somewhere, I now think it most likely that *Rivall Friendship* survives in only one copy, the manuscript located at the New-berry Library and cataloged as Case MS fY 1565.R52.

---

[1] Anthony G. Petti, *English Literary Hands from Chaucer to Dryden* (Cambridge, Massachusetts: Harvard University Press, 1977).

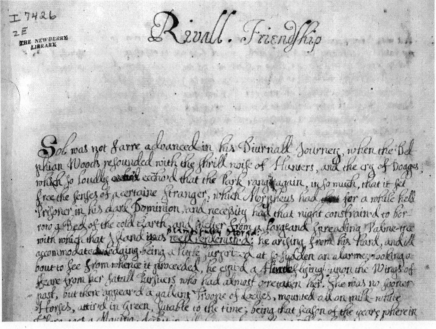

Figure 1. Predominant hand, possibly a professional scribe.

Description of the Manuscript

Rivall Friendship has no title page. The beginning of the narrative, "Sol was not farre advanced in his Diurnall Journey when the Delphian Woods resounded with the shrill noise of Hunters," immediately follows the title *Rivall Friendship*. The call number in the upper left-hand corner suggests that this manuscript was part of a private library prior to its acquisition by the Newberry. The folio manuscript is divided into two parts: Part 1 contains 214 folios and Part 2, 165. The 379 folio pages measure 28 by 17 cm. with writing on 23 by 13.5 cm. and approximately forty lines on each page. To suggest the size and length of the manuscript, each of these folio pages transcribes roughly to two typewritten pages or four handwritten 8 × 11-inch pages.

The manuscript seems to be written in two identifiable hands, both seventeenth-century italic (Figures 1 and 2); the predominant hand is written with sufficient elegance so that it was probably the work of a professional scribe. The manuscript was paginated in the upper right and left margins, but the Newberry has foliated the manuscript, and all references will be to this foliation.[2]

---

[2] References to the manuscript will specify Part 1 or 2, Book number, and foliation,

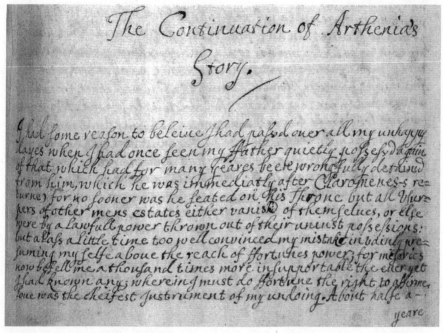

Figure 2. Secondary Italic hand.

Signatures are also noted at the bottom of the first page of each gathering until the latter part of the manuscript. Catchwords are given in the lower right corner of each page.

A third, primarily correcting, hand is reproduced as Figure 3. This hand uses a distinctive brown ink, underlines words or letters to be deleted, and writes above the line words or letters to be inserted. Deletions and insertions using this specific procedure are identified in textual footnotes. The changes made early in the manuscript are primarily substantive, but as the manuscript progresses, the correcting hand focuses more on spelling. The large number of substantive changes suggests that this hand is probably not scribal and that it may even be authorial. The correcting hand suggests no emendations after folio 165^v in the continuation of Arthenia's narrative in Part 2 of *Rivall Friendship*.

The writing on 140 folios (1.8.94^v to 2.Cont.165^r) is difficult to decipher because the ink seems to have faded. The manuscript was very handsomely bound in leather, and the leather cover was mended at some point. As a conservation

e.g., Part 2. Book 3. 134^v will be listed as 2.3.134^v. In Part 2, Arthenia's experiences are not divided into books but designated as "The Continuation of Arthenia's Story" (Cont.). Jill Gage, Custodian of the John M. Wing Foundation on the History of Printing at the Newberry Library, graciously oversaw this foliation.

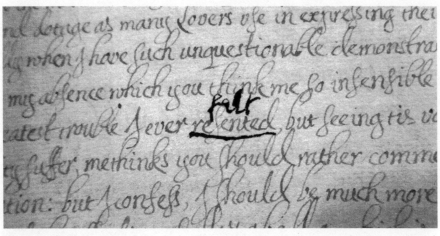

Figure 3. Correcting hand.

measure, the staff of the Newberry Library has taken the manuscript out of this cover and rebound the manuscript. The original binding is preserved in an attached envelope and folder.

Provenance

We know how this seventeenth-century manuscript came to be located at the Newberry Library. *Rivall Friendship* is one of three manuscript seventeenth-century prose romances purchased by the Newberry in the 1930s. In 1926 Frederick Ives Carpenter (1861–1925), a Spenserian scholar and a Trustee of the Library, left the Newberry his collection of printed romances with a bequest for future acquisitions. The Newberry already owned a printed edition of the *First Part of Lady Mary Wroth's Urania* (1621) and in 1936 purchased the only surviving manuscript of Part Two (Newberry, Case MS fY 1565.W95).[3] The Newberry also purchased "The Lady Alice Oldfieild Her Kallicia and Philaedus" (Newberry, Case MS fY 1565.H635, formerly Phillipps MS 10596). This romance,

---

[3] For modern editions, see *The First Part of the Countess of Montgomery's Urania*, ed. Josephine A. Roberts (Binghamton, New York: MRTS at Center for Medieval and Renaissance Studies, 1995) and *The Second Part of The Countess of Montgomery's Urania*, ed. Josephine A. Roberts, completed by Suzanne Gossett and Janel Mueller (Tempe, AZ: ACMRS Press at the Arizona Center for Medieval and Renaissance Studies, 1999).

apparently a holograph, has been attributed to the royalist George Hitchcock by John D. Hurrell.[4]

In 1937 the Newberry purchased from Pickering and Chatto its third seventeenth-century manuscript romance, *Rivall Friendship*. The sales catalog used by Pickering and Chatto has survived and is entitled *A Catalogue of / English Novels / and Romances / 1612–1837*. A note indicates that Pickering and Chatto tried to ascertain if these novels and romances had been previously cataloged: "The novels and romances printed before 1740 listed in this Catalogue have been checked with the entries in 'A List of English Tales and Prose Romances Printed before 1740' by Arundell Esdaile, 1912." If romances, such as *Rivall Friendship*, were not previously recorded in bibliographies, we have a note to that effect. The Pickering and Chatto catalog also records the existence of marginalia and enclosures. The description of *Theophania* (1655), for example, observes that "this copy has inserted after the title-page two printed leaves (4 pp.) 'The Clavis to Theophania' and contains contemporary MS. Marginalia giving a key to pseudonyms" (#761, page 82).[5]

In the Pickering and Chatto catalog, the description of *Rivall Friendship* is numbered 623 and appears on page 68:

> 623. *Rivall Friendship.* A MS. Romance in two parts, neatly written on 379 pages, folio (c. 1660–1690), bound in contemporary calf, back neatly repaired. 20 pounds. An allegorical romance interspersed with a few poems. As far as we can ascertain unpublished; complete mss. of these xvii. century romances must be of the utmost rarity.

The sales catalog also reprints but does not comment upon a note regarding provenance pasted inside the front cover of the bound manuscript.

After the Newberry acquired *Rivall Friendship*, a description was prepared for the 1937 *Newberry Book List*, No. 25, 4 March 1937, that reads as follows:

> An unpublished manuscript of a seventeenth-century prose romance selected from Pickering and Chatto's Catalogue no. 623 by Dr. Forsythe and recommended for purchase from the Carpenter Fund. 18 £

---

[4] For a description of this manuscript, see John D. Hurrell, "An Unpublished Novel of the Seventeenth Century: George Hitchcock's 'The Lady Alice Oldfeild Her Kallicia and Philaedus,'" *The Newberry Library Bulletin*, 6, No. 10 (May 1979), 345–52. Hurrell identifies the author as George Hitchcock, son of John Hitchcock, Esq., a barrister at Grey's Inn.

[5] Anon., *Theophania: Or, Several Modern Histories Represented by Way of Romance, and Politicly Discours'd Upon*, Publications of the Barnabe Riche Society 10, ed. Renee Pigeon (Ottawa, Canada: Dovehouse Editions, 1999). For the seemingly unsubstantiated attribution to Sir William Sales, see 12.

Figure 4. Drawing of the watermark.

On 13 March 1937, the following information and dates were added to the description recorded in the *Newberry Book List*:

> 2 parts: 214 and 165 folio pages with 40 lines to a page. Faded ink in Part 8 of Part 1 f. 188 to f.114 of Part 2. Contemporary calf binding (1650–1675)

According to the *Newberry Library Book-List*, which also serves as an accession catalog, the handwriting of the manuscript dates from around 1650–1675. The watermark of a horn is found throughout the manuscript of *Rivall Friendship* (Figure 4). Similar watermarks seem to have been used between 1665 and 1680, making it likely that the manuscript was copied near the conclusion of the dates (1650–1675) suggested by the Newberry's analysis of the handwriting.[6] In addition, it has been possible to date the end papers around 1760. They bear Britain's coat of arms and the garter motto: *Honi soit qui mal y pense* ("Shame to him who thinks evil of it," popularly rendered as "Evil to him who evil thinks") as a water mark with G R (George Rex) as a secondary mark.[7] It is likely that these papers were added when the manuscript was bound or rebound in the eighteenth century.

---

[6] This watermark resembles the horn on a shield identified as No. 2670, part of the group consisting of 2668–71 and dated c. 1665–80, as well as No. 2779 (dated 1650) in Edward Heawood, *Watermarks, Mainly of the Seventeenth and Eighteenth Centuries.* Monumenta Chartae Papyraceae Historiam Illustrantia (Hilversum, Holland: Paper Publications Society, 1950), PL 340 and PL 357.

[7] The watermark, appearing only in the endpapers, seems to reproduce exactly the coat of arms, No.450 (dated 1760) in Heawood, *Watermarks, Mainly of the Seventeenth and Eighteenth Centuries,* PL 76.

External Evidence of Authorship

Both the Newberry Library and Pickering and Chatto, the bookseller, call attention to the note pasted inside the manuscript cover signed M. A. L. The handwriting of the note, particularly its use of a long "s," suggests that this note was written prior to the twentieth century; it is possible that the note was pasted inside the cover of *Rivall Friendship* when end papers dating approximately 1760 were added to the manuscript. M. A. L, who is neither a Manningham, nor an Ellis, has yet to be identified. M. A. L. states suggestively that the manuscript became the property of the Ellis family because of a marriage into this family of a Miss Manningham.

> This manuscript came to the Ellis family by the marriage of one of them to a Miss Manningham either sister or daughter to Dr. Thos: M. Bp of Chichester 1696 by one of whose family this work was composed. (See Figure 5.)

Although not hitherto recognized, this clue to authorship indicates that the manuscript passed through the female line.

Thomas Manningham's will survives, and in it he specifies that his books, scribal manuscripts, and other papers will not pass with his major estate to his eldest son.[8] He explains that he has departed from primogeniture and bequeathed his books and papers to another son, who has pursued a career in the church. One of Thomas Manningham's family wrote the manuscript, but unlike his books and other papers, *Rivall Friendship* descended to a Miss Manningham who married into the Ellis family.[9] Genealogists exhibit little interest in female descendants because they do not retain the family name and can be difficult to trace. Even George Agar Ellis, who edited a collection of the Ellis family letters and who included a genealogical chart of his family history, ignores the descendants of women except in the case of his own female ancestor.[10]

---

[8] For Manningham's will, see The National Archives: PRO, PROB 11/587. Sig. 176.

[9] For the transmission of pictures and embroidered caskets through the female line, particularly in royalist households, see Mihoko Suzuki, *Subordinate Subjects: Gender, the Political Nation, and Literary Form in England, 1588–1688* (Aldershot: Ashgate, 2003), 170–73.

[10] *The Ellis Correspondence: Letters written During the Years 1686, 1687, 1688, and Addressed to John Ellis, Esq. Comprising many Particulars of the Revolution*, ed. Hon. Agar Ellis, 2 vols. (London: Henry Colburn, New Burlington Streets, 1829), I: xii–xxiii. The original letters are preserved in the Birch Collection, British Library. For a brief history of the Ellis family, who may have owned the manuscript in the eighteenth century, see Appendix 1.

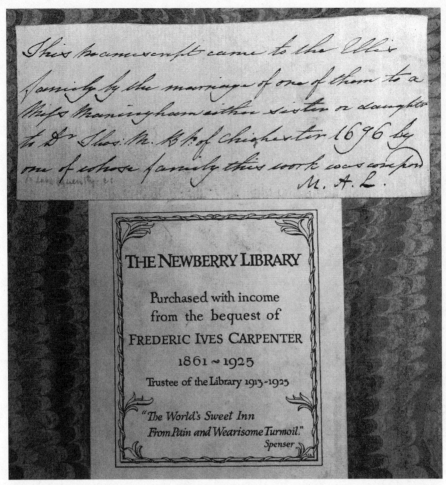

Figure 5. Note indicating provenance. Previously pasted inside the front cover of the manuscript.

Dating

Thomas Manningham is identified by name in the one clue to provenance, and so we need to refine the dating so as to eliminate the possibility that *Rivall Friendship* was authored by his offspring. As noted above, the Newberry *Book-List* dates the handwriting to 1650–75. *Rivall Friendship* was written after the Restoration of Charles II in 1660 because his procession into London is described at length in Book 8 of Part 1. In Part 2, there is also a likely reference to James Butler, Duke of Ormond, who served as Lord Lieutenant of Ireland, 1660–69 and 1677–85.

Because Thomas Manningham's two eldest sons were not baptized until 1683 and 1685, they could not have authored *Rivall Friendship* unless it was written in the eighteenth century. The extensive commentary on the Civil War and the entertainments marking the progress of Charles II into London would have become less interesting politically as time passed. Taken together, the handwriting and the political references suggest that *Rivall Friendship* was completed prior to or during the last quarter of the seventeenth century, sometime between 1665 and 1685. For these reasons, it seems likely that *Rivall Friendship* was written by someone belonging to the immediate generation of Thomas Manningham rather than by his offspring, i.e., a sister rather than a daughter.

Thomas Manningham

The authorship of Thomas Manningham, the only person referenced in the note concerning provenance, must be seriously considered.[11] Manningham (d. 1722) was born in St. George's Southwark, the son of Richard Manningham (d. 1682), rector of Michelmersh, Hampshire, and Bridget Blackwell. Little is known about Richard Manningham except that he was sequestered during the Civil War and lost Bradbourne House, the family estate. In spite of these financial hardships, Richard managed to give his son an excellent education at Winchester and at New College, Oxford, where Thomas matriculated with a scholarship on 12 August 1669. In 1681 Thomas was presented with the comfortable living of East Tisted in Hampshire. Anthony Wood describes him as "a high flown" preacher and "passionately desirous to collect himself, to be known to few, and to be envied by none."[12]

There are indications that Thomas Manningham was confident of his own worth. When Queen Anne was ill and confined to her chamber, it was suggested that he pray in an adjoining room, but he refused saying that "he did not chuse to whistle the prayers of the church through a key hole."[13] He is described by Donald Gray in his *Oxford Dictionary of National Biography* article as a Hanoverian Tory with high church sympathies and as intolerant of dissent.[14] After he

---

[11] In the note signed by M. A. L., Bishop Thomas Manningham's name is followed by the date 1696, but this date, unless it indicates flourished, does not appear significant in his life.

[12] Anthony Wood, *Athenae Oxonienses, An Exact History of All the Writers and Bishops Who Have Had their Education in the University of Oxford*, new edition with additions by Philip Bliss, 4 vols. (London: Thomas Davison, 1820), 4:5555

[13] John Nichols, *Literary Anecdotes of the Eighteenth Century, Comprizing Biographical Memoirs of William Bowyer, Printer, F. S. A. and Many of his Learned Friends*, 6 vols. (London: Nichols, Son, and Bentley, 1812), 1: 208.

[14] Donald Gray, Thomas Manningham," *ODNB*, online 3 Jan 2008.

was appointed Bishop of Chichester in 1709, he found that Whigs predominated in his chapter and reported to the archbishop on the dangers of dissenters in his diocese. He dutifully supported the succession laid down by the Act of Settlement rather than the Jacobite cause. In 1715, he was one of the bishops who signed a declaration condemning the Jacobite rebellion of that year.

His published sermons indicate that he had the background and learning but not the sense of humor to have written *Rivall Friendship*. He describes with obvious distaste the Interregnum as a period when innovation was rampant, and "[e]very conceited Politician sent forth his new System of Civil Government: Every illuminated Brother, his new Models of Christs Kingdom: every one was for erecting an Empire for himself, and a Platform wherein his own Imaginations might rule."[15] More an Anglican than a classicist, Manningham disparagingly dismisses Platonists as "a Sect of People who were generally of a soft and Amorous Nature, who plac'd their Happiness in the Speculation of Ideas; and who rarely consider'd God, as a Righteous Punisher of Sin, but chiefly as a most amiable Being for them to contemplate; they usually entertain'd very good Opinions of themselves, and of their own Perfections."[16]

Manningham's attitudes toward wit also make his authorship of *Rivall Friendship* unlikely. In *A Sermon Preached at the Hampshire Feast on Shrove-Tuesday, February 16, 1685/6*, he states that "Man was not made for *Levity*, but for grave and weighty Affairs."[17] He is concerned about "lasciviousness and its pervasiveness," describing it as the "very Character of the Age . . . the nauseous repetition of almost every great Table, and every private Club; 'tis the Song and Poetry of the Young, and the filthy Jest of the Aged." His views on wit and comedy suggest that some passages in *Rivall Friendship* might have offended his sense of decency: "We must not countenance the least *Uncleanness* by an ambiguous word, by a complyant Smile, by a wanton Metaphor: but when others talk *Lewdly*, let us pray *inwardly*; what they call *Comedy*, let us represent to our selves as the *deepest Tragedy*." Thomas Manningham does not appear to be the sort of

---

   [15] Thomas Manningham, *A Solemn Humiliation for the Murder of Charles I. With some Remarks on those Popular Mistakes, Concerning Popery, Zeal, and the Extent of Subjection, which had a fatal Influence in our Civil Wars.* (London: Printed by F. Collins for W. Crooke, 1686), D2^r, p. 19. [D.M. 509]. From the Huntington Library copy RB 223650.

   [16] Sermon No. 30 in a collection of thirty-three sermons. See *"The Nature and Effects of Superstition." In a Sermon. Preached before the Honourable House of Commons, on Saturday, the Fifth November 1692.* By Thomas Manningham, D.D. and Chaplain in Ordinary to their Majesties. (London: Thomas Braddyll and Robert Everingham, 1692), C1^v, p. 10. [E-PV]. From the Huntington Library copy RB 439690–722.

   [17] Sermon No. 5 in *Six Sermons preached on the Occasions Following:* . . . *A Sermon on Shrove-Tuesday, at the Feast of the Natives of Hampshire.* (London: Printed by F. Collins, for W. Crooke, 1686), D1^r, p. 17 and D4^v, p. 24. [D.M. 508]. From the Huntington Library copy RB 316383.

person who could envision Phasellus's swooning for love, like Chaucer's Troilus, and then sticking a mysterious weed up his nose to hasten his demise. Likewise, Phasellus's suicide would be unacceptable to Bishop Manningham.

If we turn to Manningham's personal life, he and his wife Elizabeth (1657–1714) had ten children. When Elizabeth died in 1714 at age 57, Manningham buried her in Chichester Cathedral and wrote an epitaph emphasizing her godliness:

> She was comely in her person, meek in her temper, most humble in her behaviour, prudent in all her actions, and pious through her whole life. She had a mind improved by a good share of useful learning, but that appeared only in her judgement. She never took one step into the vanities of the world; but . . . she employed her time chiefly in the exercise of her constant devotion, and in giving her children their first instructions in Religion.[18]

Judging from the tone of Elizabeth's epitaph, Thomas was not an advocate for female learning. He valued Elizabeth's docility and commented that her mind had been improved by "useful learning," thus suggesting that she was brought up to be a good housewife rather than liberally educated in the classics. Manningham's assertion that [her learning] "appeared only in her judgement" suggests that he would have been unlikely to encourage either his wife or his daughters to write a romance.

Of Thomas and Elizabeth's ten children, five are identified in Thomas Manningham's will: three sons, Thomas, Richard, and Simon, and two married daughters, Mary Rawlinson and Dorothea Walters.[19] Of these two daughters, it was the elder, Mary Manningham Rawlinson, who inherited *Rivall Friendship*. Mary Manningham married Reverend Dr. Robert Rawlinson of Charlwood in Surrey, becoming his second wife in 1716; she did not die until 1752 in the parish of St. Leonard, Shoreditch, on October 24. Her will dated August 6, 1750 was proved on October 26, 1752.[20] Her only heir was a girl named Mary, who was the younger half-sister of Sir Thomas Rawlinson who became Lord Mayor of London in 1754.[21] This Mary Rawlinson, whose mother's family name was

---

[18] Nichols, *Literary Anecdotes*, 1:208.

[19] *Notes and Queries: A Medium of Intercommunication for Literary Men, General Readers, etc.*, 8th series, vol. 5, January-June 1894 (London: Office Bream's Bldgs., Chancery Lane by John C. Francis, 1894), 411.

[20] Ibid., see also PCC, 261, Bettesworth.

[21] *Publications of the Thoresby Society, For the year 1908: A History of the Parish of Barivich in Elmet, York*, ed. F. S. Colman, vol. 17 (Leeds: Knight and Forster, 1908), 257–58. The marriage is not recorded in *The Parish Registers of St. Michael, Cornhill, London Containing Marriages, Baptisms, and Burials From 1546 to 1754*, ed. Joseph Lemuel Chester (London: 1882), but it is likely that Mary Rawlinson would have been married by her father, Rev. Dr. Robert Rawlinson of Charlwood, Surrey.

Manningham, married Francis Ellis, a well-to-do woolen draper. He was born on October 4, 1709, and married Mary at St. Michael's, Cornhill, in 1736/7.[22] Mary (Rawlinson) Ellis and Francis Ellis are described as having had two sons, Robert and William, who died without issue.

In summary, the physical evidence of the manuscript, the Newberry's dating of the handwriting and the likely dating of the watermarks in the paper as well as the provenance outlined in the note signed M. A. L suggest that *Rivall Friendship* was written by someone belonging to Thomas Manningham's generation. Thomas Manningham himself had the rhetorical skill to have written *Rivall Friendship,* but his temperament, as reflected in his published sermons and as assessed by his contemporaries, indicates that he is unlikely to have been the author of this seventeenth-century prose romance. Based on its provenance, specifically its transmission through the female line, it seems probable that the author of *Rivall Friendship* was a woman belonging to Thomas Manningham's own generation.

Internal Evidence:
Gender, Narrative Structure, Psychology

The author of *Rivall Friendship* articulates anti-patriarchal positions on marriage and inheritance. These proto-feminist views do not necessarily suggest the gender of the author, but we might expect the experiences of educated women to lead them to question gender hierarchy and the impact of primogeniture on inheritance laws. In Part 1 of *Rivall Friendship,* the conventional dominance of men over women in marriage is questioned: "not that I account all wemen slaves, or think all men are Tyrants to their Wives; but if they are not they are at least capable of becoming so when ere they please" (1.7.83ᵛ). In Part 2, the author comments on the contemporary inheritance practice of favoring men over women. In Delphos, we are told, there is the practice "not to be found in any kingdom of the world but this" of giving the "scepter in succession to the eldest child, preferring the daughter before the son, if she be born first" (2.4.164ʳ).

In addition, the events in *Rivall Friendship* are for the most related through the eyes of women. After an omniscient author briefly sets the stage at the beginning of the action, the two major narratives are narrated by women. In Books 1–4 of Part 1, Celia, a companion and attendant to Queen Ermilia, relates the story of Princess Artabella (Queen Ermilia's mother) and her courtship by Diomed and Phasellus. This narration is introduced by Celia to explain to Arthenia, who was washed up on the shores of Delphos disguised as a man, why there is a law on Delphos condemning to death lowborn men who enter the palace grounds

---

[22] *Publications of the Thoresby Society,* 17: 258.

without the queen's permission. In Books 5–8 of Part I, Arthenia, who becomes the next female narrator, explains to Celia and Queen Ermilia how she came to be washed up on the shores of Delphos. She uses first-person narration to relate her own history which she describes as inextricably involved with the English Civil War:

> I was yet but an infant, when I beheld my Country cruelly embroil'd in a Civ-
> ill, and most unnaturall War; and terribly wasted, and destroy'd with Fire
> and sword, not of strangers, but even of those very People she had bred . . . so
> much dependance has my owne perticuler story on this Warre, that I cannot
> give a perfect account of my misfortunes without relating it; since my unhap-
> piness derives its originall from that of my country. (I.5.61ᵛ)

The narrative structure of Part 2 of *Rivall Friendship* employs a similar pattern of female narration. Books 1–4 continue the account of Artabella's story and are narrated by Celia. Arthenia continues her history now situated in Restoration London in a section labeled "The Continuation of Arthenia's Story."

Perhaps even more telling than the prominence of female narrators, there is persuasive psychological evidence that the author of *Rivall Friendship* was a woman. Both narratives portray Artabella and then Arthenia as victimized women. These women, in spite of Artabella's protestations to the contrary, are not brought down by fortune or fate; rather, they suffer misfortune because they are betrayed by their lovers. Not only does Phasellus betray Artabella to advance himself by marrying Queen Oriana, he also deceitfully persuades his best friend Diomed to relinquish his suit for Artabella. An unmitigated villain, Phasellus arranges for the kidnapping of Artabella by his henchmen and imprisons her. After conveniently disposing of Artabella, he then tricks Queen Oriana into marriage by pretending that he is her father's choice. Likewise, in Arthenia's history, the actions of Loreto are devoid of conscience where women are concerned. Even though he proclaims his eternal devotion to Arthenia, he woos one woman for her fortune and then marries a wealthy heiress. Even after this marriage, he continues to pursue Arthenia, presumably to seduce her. In Part 2, Arthenia is pursued and compromised by Issodorus, who is depicted as manipulative and mendacious. Arthenia's story is not finished in the present manuscript, but it seems likely that Issodorus is responsible for her being abandoned and washed ashore in Delphos.

Clues in the Historical Allegory

The historical allegory also invites us to associate *Rivall Friendship* with the Manninghams and their family home in Kent, Bradbourne House (Figure 6). In Part 1, Book 5, Arthenia describes her birth as "neer to the Citie Agrigentum"

Figure 6. Bradbourne House.

(1.5.62^r). When the city of Agrigentum appears in Arthenia's history of the Civil War, the topical details identify Agrigentum as East Malling, where Bradbourne House, the Manningham family estate, is situated. We are also told that Agrigentum is located in the province of Nota (Kent) and that in May 1648 it served as a place of temporary retreat for the forces of the royalist *Gerandus* (George Goring, first Earl of Norwich). When the parliamentarian general *Faragenes* (Sir Thomas Fairfax) approached, *Gerundus* sought sanctuary for his troops in Enna (Maidstone) and afterward ferried his troops across the river to Colchester (1.6.72^v –73^r).

The dating of the manuscript, its transmission through the female line, the pervasive feminist critique of patriarchy by female narrators, the prominence of victimized women abused by unsatisfactory and disloyal lovers, and clues in the historical allegory, specifically the correspondence of the setting of Agrigentum to East Malling, the Manningham family seat, suggest that the author of *Rivall Friendship* was very likely to have been Bridget Manningham, the older sister of Thomas Manningham, a Caroline and Hanoverian bishop, and the granddaughter of John Manningham, the diarist who recorded performances of Shakespeare's plays.

Manuscript Transmissions: The Sidneys and the Manninghams

Sir Philip Sidney is a canonical author whose works were printed in edition after edition. Manuscripts, however, differ from printed texts. The history of the manuscript of the Old *Arcadia* illustrates the vulnerability of all manuscript texts. However popular the printed *Arcadia* unquestionably was, the manuscript of the Old *Arcadia* remained unprinted for over three centuries. In 1926, it was printed by Albert Feuillerat for Cambridge University Press, but the Old *Arcadia* did not receive an accurate text until 1973, fifty years later.[23] Sir Philip's brother, Robert Sidney, Earl of Leicester, also authored a manuscript collection of poems that was not published until the twentieth century.[24]

Lady Mary Wroth printed the first part of the *Urania* in 1621, but the second part, like her uncle's Old *Arcadia*, was preserved only in manuscript.[25] Moreover, if Wroth had not printed the first part and so insured that her authorship of the *Urania* was widely known, then the authorship of the second part, surviving in one holograph copy at the Newberry, would have been unclear. This manuscript has no title page and no indication of the author's name. Thus, if it were not for the 1621 printed edition of Part 1, Part 2 of the *Urania*, like *Rivall Friendship*, would be an anonymous text preserved in a single manuscript at the Newberry Library!

Bridget Manningham belonged to a family, like that of the Sidneys, who valued authorship and preserved manuscripts. She was the granddaughter of the witty John Manningham, member of the Middle Temple and celebrated Jacobean diarist. John Manningham's diary was not printed during his lifetime; it was preserved by the Manningham family, an indication of familial respect for manuscripts. The *Diary* passed into the British Library (becoming Harleian MS 5353) before it was finally edited and printed in 1868.[26] Significantly, property records safely stored away in a muniment room are more likely to survive than diaries, memoirs, or literary manuscripts. The Manningham family shared the Sidneys' values, preserving the manuscript *Diary* of their ancestor until it was printed generations later. Bridget Manningham's *Rivall Friendship*, like John Manningham's *Diary*, was preserved and seems to have passed through the female line into the Ellis family until it was sold to Pickering and Chatto, the booksellers, who sold it to the Newberry Library.

---

[23] See *The Countess of Pembroke's Arcadia* [The Old Arcadia], ed. Jean Robertson (Oxford: Clarendon Press, 1973), v–vii and xlii–lxvi. See also H. R. Woudhuysen, *Sir Philip Sidney and the Circulation of Manuscripts, 1558–1640* (Oxford: Clarendon Press, 1996).

[24] *The Poems of Robert Sidney*, ed. P. J. Croft (Oxford: Oxford University Press, 1984).

[25] For Lady Mary's biography, see Margaret P. Hannay, *Mary Sidney, Lady Wroth* (Burlington, VT: Ashgate, 2010).

[26] *Diary of John Manningham, of the Middle Temple, and of Bradbourne, Kent, barrister-at-law*, Camden Society, os. 99, ed. John Bruce (Westminster: J. B. Nichols and Sons, 1868). Bruce seems to have been responsible for the attribution of the manuscript to John Manningham of Bradbourne House, Kent. For a modern edition, see *The Diary of John Manningham of the Middle Temple, 1602–1603*, ed. Robert Parker Sorlien (Hanover, New Hampshire: University Press of New England, 1976), 265.

Bridget Manningham

To begin the history of the literary Manninghams, we can start with John Manningham, the diarist and frequenter of Shakespeare's plays, who grew up in Fen
Drayton, Cambridgeshire.[27] After his father Robert died in 1588, he became
the adopted son and heir of his relative, Richard Manningham of Kent, a retired
member of the Mercers' Company of London. This Richard Manningham was
prosperous enough to have purchased the fine manor house of Bradbourne in
East Malling, near Maidstone in Kent. John Manningham named his first son
Richard (1608–1682) in honor of his foster father, whom he described as his
father-in-love. He married Anne Curle, the sister of Edward Curle, his chamber
mate at the Middle Temple. Curle's father, William, was a retainer of Sir Robert
Cecil and also quite prosperous.

John Manningham's son Richard Manningham married Bridget Blackwell of Broxbourne, Hertfordshire in 1636. In 1637 Bridget gave birth to her
first child, Anne Manningham, who seems to have been named Anne after her
husband's grandmother. Anne is not mentioned in her father's will and so is
likely to have predeceased her father. Bridget, who was her parents' surviving
daughter, was named after her mother. In May 1638, Richard became the Rector of Michelmersh, Hampshire, a parish located near property belonging to the
Sidney family. He retained that position until he was sequestered in 1646. His
sequestration may account for his having had the leisure to oversee his daughter's
extraordinary education. She is familiar with Plutarch as well as Shakespeare
and knows the fine points of classical mythology. When she uses "admire" as a
synonym for "wonder" (rather than adore or appreciate), she makes the kind of
connection a classical scholar might make.

During the Interregnum, Richard Manningham lost Bradbourne House in
Kent to Thomas Twisden.[28] Thomas was the younger son of Sir William Twisden of Roydon Hall, East Peckham, and, more significantly, the brother-in-law
of the Cromwellian officer, Matthew Thomlinson. Under Cromwell's influence,
Twisden was installed as Recorder and Town Clerk of Maidstone and built up a
successful law practice during the Interregnum. With his fortune, he purchased
Bradbourne, the Manningham family estate. It seems unlikely to be a coinci-
dence that one of the female figures featured in the Civil War sections of *Rivall
Friendship* has a change in financial fortunes that causes her fiancé to repudiate
her, break the engagement, and cancel the wedding plans.

After the Restoration, Richard Manningham was restored to his rectory
at Michelmersh, which he held until his death on June 12, 1682, but he never

---

[27] For this information, see the genealogical appendices to *The Diary of John Manningham*, ed. Sorlien.

[28] For Thomas Twisden, see J. R. Twisden, *The Family of Twysden and Twisden:
Their History and Archives* (London: John Murray, 1939).

regained Bradbourne House. His will was probated the following November. In it, he mentions three sons: Richard, Nicholas, and Thomas, later Bishop of Chichester, and a daughter, Bridget. We do not know when Bridget Manningham was born; she seems never to have married and later entrusted *Rivall Friendship* to her niece, Mary (Manningham) Rawlinson, Thomas Manningham's daughter. There is thus substantive external evidence, confirmed by documentary records, that *Rivall Friendship* was authored by a member of the Manningham family who belonged to Thomas Manningham's generation and plausible internal evidence that this was the work of Bridget Manningham who was living in 1682.

Literary and Historical Contexts

Rivall Friendship is remarkable in two significant respects: first, Bridget Manningham juxtaposes Artabella's romance with Arthenia's history explicitly labeled a history in her text, giving this unprinted manuscript text a pivotal position in the transition from the early modern romance to what will later be called the novel.[29] Second, *Rivall Friendship,* a post-Civil War romance, examines protofeminist issues, such as patriarchal dominance in the family and marriage, in an almost modern manner. The literary transition from the romance to the novel may be related to this feminist thrust because after the English Civil War, social norms were in flux in a way that they were not to be again until after World War I.[30] In consequence, Bridget Manningham depicts the romance of Artabella as giving way to the verisimilitude of Arthenia's narration of battles in the Civil War and to Restoration courtships in which love is subordinated to the interests of money and property. All of this is handled with stylistic elegance. Passionate feelings pour out in finely balanced sentences with an insistent parallelism.

In Artabella's romance, birth is of the utmost importance. The female protagonists, Artabella and Oriana, are both princesses and intensely aware of their

---

[29] The terms, "romance" and "novel," refer to prose fiction in general. On early modern usage, see Christine S. Lee, "The Meanings of Romance: Rethinking Early Modern Fiction," *Modern Philology* (2014), 287–311. See also James Grantham Turner, "Romance and the Novel in Restoration England," *Review of English Studies*, 63.258 (2011): 58–85. For more general studies, see Helen Hackett, *Women and Romance Fiction in the English Renaissance* (Cambridge: Cambridge University Press, 2000) and the Introduction (xviii-xix) to *Prose Fiction in English from the Origins of Print to 1750,* ed. Thomas Keymer (Oxford: Oxford University Press, 2017).

[30] Feminism, like education of the lower classes, is not a progressive history. After the English Civil War, reformers hesitated to educate the lower classes because they feared that the overproduction of intellectuals might breed social unrest. Lawrence Stone concludes that in quantitative terms, it was not until after World War I that English higher education was as egalitarian as it was in the 1630s. See Stone, "The Educational Revolution in England, 1560–1640," *Past and Present* 28 (1964), 41–80, esp. 69.

rank and position in society. Diomed, the romantic hero, spells out his lineage in some detail, explaining that he is Prince Lucius and descended from Augustus Caesar and that he is by birth heir to a kingdom (1.2.28ʳ). Prince Lucius has disguised himself as Diomed so that he can win renown and merit, wanting to be worthy of ruling an empire because of "vertue" as well as "birth" (1.2.28ᵛ). Only in retrospect does it seem important that we are told that Diomed's friend "was not born a Prince" (1.2.28ᵛ).[31]

In the class-structured society of Artabella's romance, obedience to the father or to parental figures is required because familial bloodlines are the source of status and rank. Unaware of his noble birth, Princess Oriana tells Diomed, "if you can gain *Achemenes* [her father] to favour your desires, I shall not oppose them, for his Will must ever be my Law" (1.2.35ʳ). Manningham portrays both Oriana and Artabella as acknowledging the importance of their fathers' wills in determining whom they should marry. To emphasize that obedience and duty are patriarchal obligations, Manningham makes King Achemenes and his brother Menzor unmarried widowers so that no wives complicate the issue of paternal authority. Even before Achemenes and Menzor are aware of Diomed's birth, his military prowess makes him the preferred husband for the daughters of both patriarchs. The villainy of Phasellus is not immediately apparent, and we, as readers, sympathize with Artabella's attraction to him until he betrays Artabella and then tricks Oriana into marriage.

Oriana's fate tests the legitimacy of patriarchy. After marrying Phasellus whom she despises, Oriana contemplates suicide in the "face of Phasellus" because he will not release her from "that engagement Achemenes laid on her" and plans to stab her own heart "for its disobedience to the King my Fathers will" (2.3.143ᵛ). Oriana explains to Diomed that Phasellus had continued "still urging me with my Duty, and my Engagement to *Achemenes*, which (he said) if I would have a Dispensation from, I must fetch him from the Dead to absolve me." (2.4.154ʳ). When Phasellus, the villain, argues in favor of paternal authority, it becomes clear that Manningham is using the convention to interrogate patriarchy. When Oriana later learns that Phasellus has tricked her into marriage by using her filial obedience against her, she repudiates her filial duty as "blind obedience to my Fathers Will" (2.3.143ᵛ) and still considers suicide but only as a means of depriving Phasellus of her crown. Far from being rewarded for her

---

[31] In a passage suggesting that Manningham may have known Plutarch as well as Shakespeare, we are told that Phasellus was descended from Marc Antony, "one who though he never bare the burden of a Crown" had "the satisfaction to behold many puissant Kings his Vassalls prostrate their Crowns and Scepters at his Feet" (1.2.28ᵛ). Fortune was kinder to "*Augustus* with whom he disputed the Empier of the World" (28ᵛ) or he [Marc Antony] would have "questionless worn that Empieriall Diadem which his Predescessor *Julius Caesar* onely fancied, never really put on; being by treachery cut off ere he could bring his design to maturity" (28ᵛ).

"blind obedience to her Fathers Will," it is clear that she would have fared better if she had followed her own heart; she dies a virgin and her cousin's son inherits the crown of Persia.

Artabella's story tests patriarchal authority in another way. In contrast to Oriana, who follows what she thinks is her father's directive, Artabella ignores her father Menzor's preference for Diomed and commits herself to Phasellus. When she later discovers the full extent of his villainy, she exclaims:

> tis onely unhappie *Artabella* that has been the cause both of her owne misfortunes, and poor Prince *Lucius*'s too; for had I not so blindly ty'd my heart to a fond dotage on *Phasellus*, I had not (questionless) oppos'd my Father^'s^ Will. (2.4.158^r^)

Artabella thus recognizes that her "fond dotage on Phasellus" was mistaken and that she should not have opposed her "Father's Will." In contrast, Oriana marries Phasellus because it seems to be her duty, but after both Diomed and Phasellus die, she does not remarry. Artabella, who disobeys her father Menzor, later marries King Alcander of Delphos, and lives happily with him. It is their son who inherits Achemenes' and Oriana's throne.

The moral of Artabella's romance is thus far from a simplistic endorsement of patriarchy. Manningham shows that Oriana's efforts to follow her father's behests make her susceptible to the machinations of the villainous Phasellus. Artabella, in contrast, pays lip service to her duty to her father while she is deceiving him. In spite of Artabella's rejection of her father's will, she is rewarded. Her life ends happily when she is united in marriage to the worthy Alcander. Prior to the marriage, Artabella tests his fidelity by entering a convent while he tests himself by going on a grand tour seemingly structured by visits to eligible marriage partners. Alcander passes his test with flying colors; his loyalty assured, he marries Artabella, and they live happily ever after on Delphos.

If Artabella's romance interrogates patriarchy, it all the more absolutely reifies the importance of class. Diomed, who is really Prince Lucius, represents all that is admirable in a friend, lover, and warrior. Artabella, presumably as a result of her experience with Phasellus, establishes a law in Delphos condemning to death lowborn unauthorized male intruders into the royal presence.

> This law prohibits all Persons (Princes, and Ambassadours excepted) from coming into the Queens presence, or within the precincts of the Palace (upon any account whatever) under pain of Death, without a Warrant first obtain'd from the Queen, sign'd with her owne hand, and seal'd with the Privie Signet. (1.1.3^v^)

This law, which cannot be altered without the consensus of all the nobles, would have allowed Diomed, born a prince, access to the Palace and banned the ignoble Phasellus from its precincts.

Manningham seems to have imagined the two narratives together as part of a whole. She links the romance of Artabella with the history of Arthenia in a striking *in media res* beginning in which a young man sees a troop of ladies, attired in green, pursuing a hind. A young woman (later revealed to be Celia) catches sight of him and urges him to fly, but before he can respond, the queen and her ladies arrive. Queen Ermilia asks what "ill Fate hath conducted thee hither to thy Death," but it is not until the next day that Arthenia (disguised as a man) learns the nature of her offense. Celia explains that there is a law condemning lowborn men to death if they enter the palace grounds without royal authorization. Rather than protesting his fate, the unknown person asks that his death may occur as soon as possible. He is saved from death only when an ambassador reveals his identity as a woman named Arthenia! This dramatic introduction links the narratives of Artabella and Arthenia, which are then related retrospectively by two female narrators, Celia, who relates Artabella's romance, and Arthenia, who tells her own history. Arthenia's presence in the opening scene and her position as principal auditor for Celia's account of Artabella's romance demonstrates that Manningham wants the reader to link these two narratives. The generational divide between Artabella's romance (its narrative concerns events occurring before the present Ermilia, Queen of Delphos, was born) and Arthenia's history reinforces the reader's perception of Arthenia's history as similar to the novel, an emerging literary form.

The English Civil War and its aftermath is the setting for Arthenia's history. This distinctly royalist narrative begins with a retelling in classical dress and personages of battles in the Civil War, describes the execution of Charles I (Clearchus), and concludes with a description of Charles II's (Claromenes's) progress into London for his coronation (Figure 7). In Part 1, Arthenia fends off the advances of a rake named Loreto. In the second part of Arthenia's history, set in post-Civil War London, the relationship between the sexes has changed into the kind of battle depicted in Restoration comedies. In Part 2, Issodorus explicitly justifies his romantic deceits as a strategy to win the war between the sexes:

> But why Madam should you count that so crimenall in matters of love (continu'd he) which in War is daily practiced uncondemn'd; for you well know tis allow'd to those who besiege a Towne to have recourse to strategems to get, what by force, or treaty they cannot hope to gain, and using that litle artifice to inhance the value of my love, by endeavouring to perswade you 'twas sacred to your selfe alone without any others having had an interest in it. (2.Cont.186^r)

The narrative shifts from a description of the battles of the English Civil War to accounts of embattled Arthenia's attempts to withstand advances from Loreto in Part 1 and Issodorus in Part 2.

Figure 7. Charles II's Progress into London.

The difference between the romance of Artabella and Arthenia's history is suggested by the handling of war and kingship, themes present in both narratives. In Part 2, Book 3, Mexaris, Diomed's squire, supplies a tribute to Diomed's prowess that identifies him as the hero of a romance:

> Though the Scythians trymph'd over the life of *Achemenes* (said *Mexaris*) they cannot boast they did so over my Masters; for after he had died their Fields with the blood of thousands of them, subdu'd the whole Kingdome, taken *Oruntus* Prisoner and reduced him to that estate as to impose on him what Conditions he pleas'd, established a perpetuall League of Amitie between both the Kingdomes, and returned a victorious Conquerour into Persia. (2.3.134$^\text{v}$)

The exaggeration of Diomed's having "died their Fields with the blood of thousands" in Artabella's romance can be juxtaposed with the more realistic descriptions of war in Arthenia's historical narrative:

> Having perform'd all the duties of a Generall he gave the onset, charging so fiercely on the right wing of the enemy, consisting of *Faragene*'s Cavalarie in the van, and the Corsicans in the Reere, that they fell back in such disorder on their owne infantry that they broke their ranks, treading many of them under their horses Feet. (1.5.65$^\text{v}$)

Arthenia explains that the cavalry became so disorganized that they rode down their own infantry while Mexaris' romanticizes Diomed's having "subdu'd the whole kingdom" of Scythia.

Mexaris supplies an account of Diomed's death and that of his rival and erstwhile friend Phasellus (hence the title *Rivall Friendship*). Concluding his description of Diomed's death with an elegant antithesis, he observes: "He there (instead of those Tryumphs his renouned Valour merited) found his death; not from the sword of a professed Enemy, but from the secret treachery of a perfidious Friend" (2.3.134$^\text{v}$). Rhetorical polish of this kind is not absent from Arthenia's history, but it is rarely used to describe battles or laud the heroic achievements of a protagonist; it is reserved for the philosophical core of the narrative, the speeches and reflections of Clearchus (King Charles I).

Manningham's Charles is endowed with reason and insists that reason, rather than "humour" should monitor his actions, particularly in dealing with the Senate:

> I will not, to gratifie my owne humour, deny any thing that my reason allows me to grant, so, on the other side, I will never yeeld to more then Reason, Justice, and Honour obliges me too in refference to my Peoples good. I'le study to satisfy the Senat in what I may, but I will never for feare, or flattery gratifie any Faction how potent soever. (1.5.67$^\text{v}$)

Like Aphra Behn and Margaret Cavendish, Bridget Manningham is a royalist. Charles I defends not divinely appointed kingship but law and liberty. He is portrayed as eloquently affirming the importance of reason: "But though I am not so confident of my owne abilities as not willingly to admit of the Councells of others; so neither am I so doubtfull of my selfe as brutishly to submit to any mans Dictates: for that were to betray the soveraignity of Reason in my Soule, and the majesty of my Crowne and Dignity, which gives me power to deny what my Reason tells me I ought not to grant" (1.6.67^v). In spite of this emphasis upon reason and law, Manningham fully accepts the premise that a king's position sets him apart from his subjects and that they owe him obedience: Charles also remarks: "they may remember, they set in Senat as my subjects, not superiors; call'd thither to be my Councellours, not Dictators" (1.5.67^v).

Like Arthenia's history, Artabella's romance also treats the topics of reason and absolute kingship. After his proposal of marriage to Achemenes's daughter Oriana is rejected, Octimasdes of Scythia invades Persia and loses his life. His brother Oruntus becomes king of the Scythians, and he, too, invades Persia, but is vanquished by Diomed and the Persian army. Oruntus is so wicked, so much the epitome of an evil king, that he poisons his own daughter for facilitating Diomed's escape from prison. Diomed, who now has control over Oruntus' fate, acknowledges the absolute power of kings:

> I am not ignorant Madam of that power which belongs to Kings; I know it absolute, not to be controul'd by any; but I know withall that Good and just Princes never make their Will their Law; none but a Tyrant does do soe, and such your King shew'd himself, when he with so much inhumanity murther'd his onely Daughter; had he put her to death Legally, he had been much more excusable. (1.4.57^v)

Here Diomed seems to take the legalist position too far in stating that Oruntus' murder of his daughter would seem "more excusable" if it were within the law. It is noteworthy, however, that in her treatment of kingship Manningham uses the principles of reason and law to connect Artabella's romance with Arthenia's history.

The romance of Artabella is set in ancient Persia and makes use of conventional romance motifs including kidnapping by sinister figures, a rescue which leads to another kidnapping by pirates, an oracle, a sojourn at the temple of Diana, a deadly potion which simulates death, passionate affirmations of love by a lover likely to die if rejected, and even a romantic hero, Diomed, who turns out to be a descendant of Augustus Caesar. Arthenia's first-person narrative, which looks forward to the novel, rejects the marvelous and instead relates the history of battles in the English Civil War and then depicts the difficulties faced by a single woman as she negotiates the drawing rooms, public houses, and communal gardens of Restoration Britain.

Manningham's description of the Restoration court and its "ruffling braveries" displays her talent in setting a scene:

> the ruffling braveries of the Court with all its perfum'd Gallants who spend their time in nought but in debauching each other, or else in studying which way they may easiest beguile poore woemen by their trifling courtships; pretending much of love but intending nothing save their delusion or abuse. (2.Cont.165ʳ)

In Arthenia's history, once the battles are concluded, little happens. Neighbors visit and become friends. Arthenia and Bellamira eat at the public house, Lavernus. After the war, except for the triumphant progress of Charles II into London, Arthenia's history turns upon her courtship by two suitors: Loreto, who marries for money seemingly under parental pressure, and Issodorus, who lies to Arthenia about his dead wife, and whose friends seem to think that he also needs to marry for money. Restoration Britain is a world in which the possession of money and property, or lack thereof, has become a serious matter.

In Artabella's romance, Bridget Manningham is quite scrupulous about maintaining the verisimilitude of historical detail. Unlike more fantastical romances that feature monsters, giants, and magic, this romance aspires to a level of probability in its historical and geographical details. Artabella's uncle, the Persian king Achemenes corresponds to an historical Achaemenes, the possibly legendary founder of the Persian dynasty in the seventh century BC.[32] When Artabella is abducted, she is transported across Bactrian sands at night to Zarispe by the Caspian Sea. These geographical details are confirmed by Peter Heylyn's contemporary atlas.[33] Plausible foreign customs are also introduced. At Delphos, Artabella and her company dine not on tables but on carpets (1.2.39ᵛ). Some elements in Artabella's romance, such as the pirates, mysterious potions, Delphic oracle, and becoming a votary of Diana's, are also conventional in heroic romances by Philip Sidney, Robert Greene, and others, and may have been influenced by Heliodorus's *Aethiopian History* which was translated from the Greek in 1577.[34]

---

[32] Herodotus, *Histories, Books V–VII: The Persian Wars*, trans. A.D. Godley, Loeb Classical Library (Cambridge, Mass.: Harvard University Press, 1922), 7, 11.

[33] Peter Heylyn, *Cosmographie* (London, 1652), 175.

[34] Steve Mentz, *Romance for Sale in Early Modern England* (Aldershot: Ashgate, 2006), 33, 77–83, 105–122, 152–161. For a translator of French heroic romances who may have influenced Manningham, see Joseph E. Tucker, "John Davies of Kidwelly (1627? -1693), Translator from the French: With an Annotated Bibliography of his Translations," *The Papers of the Bibliographical Society of America*, 44, No. 2 (1950), 119–52. For example, Davies, like Manningham, uses the verb "resent" and the noun "resentment" to signify deep feelings as well as a grudge against someone.

For Arthenia, Manningham creates a very different world from that of Artabella. Money and property are more important than class in Restoration Britain. Arthenia is not royal; she reports that she was born into "a Family noble enough" (1.5.62ʳ) and assures her listeners that she does not want to promote herself by calling attention to the deeds of her ancestors; it is her own virtue and deeds that are important. She also reveals that she is not an authority on the Civil War, since she was a child when it began, but adds that she has educated herself as to its history. Arthenia's "misfortunes," her loss of fortune and property, resulted from the Civil War.

> Multitudes were imprison'd, and compell'd to purchace their liberties at such excessive ransomes, as prov`d the ruines of their families. Many others who might have boasted larg Possessions (either left them by their provident Predessessors, or gain'd by their owne laborious industry) suddenly torne from them, their houses rifled, and their whole estates confiscate to the Senats use. (1.5.68ᵛ)

She dwells poignantly on the fate of well-to-do royalists when "divers who were wealthy to a superfluity, in the space of one poore day have been reduced to such necessity, as that they have not known where to seeke their next nights Lodging" (1.5.62ʳ).

In Restoration England, the fate of a single woman without fortune is described by Marione, a friend who warns her to make an advantageous marriage because after her parents' death, her condition will become "deplorable . . . destitute of Friends, support, or maintenance; subject to all the blowes of Fortune, and miseries that necessity (that cruell Mistress) can overwhelme you with" (1.7.86ʳ). Arthenia's view of seventeenth-century marriage is almost as bleak as the fate awaiting a spinster. In response to a wooer, she says: "nor do I prize my liberty at so low a rate as to exchange it for slavery, or prefer the tyranique yoak of marriage before it; not that I account all wemen slaves, or think all men are Tyrants to their Wives; but if they are not they are at least capable of becoming so when ere they please" (1.7.83ᵛ). Bridget Manningham resists patriarchal structures and takes a very bleak view of the position of women in seventeenth-century Britain. Arthenia, even more than the royal Oriana and Artabella, has limited choices.

Loreto, Arthenia's first wooer, is introduced as a young Cavalier who distinguishes himself by holding a bridge and then "when the souldiers under his command wanted Bullets, he instantly caus'd all the mony he had brought with him for his owne perticuler expences, to be cut in pieces" (1.6.73ᵛ) and then used as bullets. Later, he becomes the Restoration gallant bent on seducing her but conceals his intentions by vowing eternal love. Although he acknowledges that her beauty first attracted him, he claims, "t'was that Vertue that I am perswaded you are absolute Mistress of which made my heart your willing Prisoner" (1.7.83ʳ) and then assures her that his intentions are honorable:

> Then think not Madam that my respects for you are attended with ought but
> honour; nor that I have any other design then to lay both my self and Fortune
> at your Feet, wishing no greater glory, nor satisfaction then to make my selfe
> yours by Hymens sacred tye. (1.7.83ʳ)

In spite of these protestations, Loreto proves false.

Until his aunt dies, Loreto is dependent on his mother for support. He woos
the aged Madona, whom Manningham describes as a "Golden Bait" (I.7.88ᵛ), and
then marries the wealthy Belissa. After he marries Belissa, Arthenia describes
her as "more noble" in birth, more "courtly" in education, more beautiful, and,
perhaps most important, possessed of a fortune far exceeding her own (1.7.94ʳ).
Loreto, however, continues to pursue Arthenia after his marriage, indicating that
he has no compunctions about seducing her and sacrificing her virtue to his pleasure.

In the "Continuation" of Arthenia's adventures in Part 2, she encounters
Issodorus, whose passionate avowals of utter devotion prompt her, like Artabella,
to commit herself. Issodorus, making a solemn vow to be hers forever, appeals, as
did Loreto before him, to "Hymens sacred tye" and insists that she also pledge herself to him (2.Cont.185ᵛ). Arthenia pledges herself "to be yours and onely yours
so long as you are mine" (185ᵛ). In her role as narrator in the frame, Arthenia
candidly admits that this commitment was a mistake ("how willingly do we close
our passion blinded eyes; and stop our Eares" [185ᵛ]), but in the narrative she
remains unaware of her own peril. Issodorus, like Loreto, is a predator. Falsely
claiming that Arthenia is the first woman he has loved in the seven years since
his wife's death, Issodorus is not contrite when his lies are exposed. He remarks
only that love, like war, allows "strategems to get, what by force or treaty" one cannot hope to gain (185ᵛ). Arthenia, however, remains constant to him even when
she attracts the attentions of a wealthier suitor, Silisdes.

Arthenia's narrative concludes almost immediately after her virtue is compromised. Issodorus arrives limping from a hunting injury. Since he needs to rest
before an engagement, Arthenia accompanies him to a room where he can relax
and even locks the door. As she begins to leave, he begs her to stay, laying his
head on her lap; they both fall asleep. When the door opens exposing Arthenia
and Issodorus, Silisdes excuses the compromising situation by assuring the company that Issodorus is her brother. Almost immediately, Arthenia and her real-life
brother leave town. Issodorus meets her for a private conference, and she expresses
her regret that Issodorus has not given her his picture as he had promised. In the
final, seemingly unfinished sentence of the manuscript, Issodorus apologizes and
hopes to "make amends for this my first offense which I am" (2.Cont.190ʳ). This

165

hand with an unnecessary griefe (replyd he) for that which fate may possibly proue kinder then to permit, I onely spake of my Death as asking that might
happen. But to put these sad thoughts out of your mind which I haue raisd pray toll
me where you had this Ring (pursud he looking on that his Mother gaue me) twas
Perisanas present to me (answerd I) when I took my leaue of her yesterday, and a
happines beyond expression should I count it were, but sure she would make good
what the Motto of it promises. What may it be (demanded he) Nothing shall proue
my constant loue (replyd I) but. I doubt when she once comes to the knowledge of
yours to me, it will be a meanes to depriue me of hers, which I so highly value as I
can neuer quit the interest I haue in it without an infinite concern. Neuer feare
you shall be put to that trouble said he since I dare assure you the kindnes she
has for you is so firmly rooted in her heart that there is not any thing that can be
capable of depriuing you of it If that I mentiond does not (replyd I) I am certaine nothing else euer shall. By this time my Brother being ready calld on me to
go, which I sought most to obey with a heauy heart, as supposing the time of our seperation to be come; but Theodorus resolud to let me be as happy in his company a
litle longer, telling me he would go with me to the next Towne which was that we
where we designd to rest at Noon. It was night two houres that we stayd there;
and hauing Dind, Melliantes to giue us the more freedome of converse left us a-
lone, saying he would go and giue order for the Horses to be brought forth; but no
sooner was his back turnd ere I burst out into a most violent passion, weeping
most bitterly, though I did all I could to fetter up my griefe within the confines of my
Brest; but so unruly was it, that the more I thought to restrain it, with the greater violence did it break forth. This Theodorus being a spectator of, for a while followd
my example, but assoon as his passion would suffer him to speak he cryd for the Gods
sake Deare Arthenia do not break my heart with griefe to see you in wast so many
of those precious teares in vain, in deploring what necessity confines us too; I
shall leaue you with the pressure of such a heauy weight of sadness on my soule as
needs not yours to be an addition to my Burthen: Then since tis so decreed that our
persons must unauoidably be seperated, let not our sorrows be united, suffer
the whole load then to remain on me, who am fitter to sustain it then you are. Ah
Theodorus said I how great an argument of my discretion it might be counted I
cannot tell, but sure it would be but a litle one of my loue if I could part from you
with dry eyes, when I consider to how long an absence I am confind doomed. I must confess
this testimony of your kindnes is very obliging (replyd he) yet would I rather choose to
haue been denied this satisfaction then to read it in your teares, which I once more beg
you to drye, and no longer suffer those watery cloudes to eclips the luster of your eyes. It
would haue much aleviated my trouble (said I) had you been as good as your word in giue-
ing me your Picture ere I went out of Towne for your Maiesty must know (pursud Arthenia
to the Queen) he had a good while since promisd it me, but had so long delayd to set for it
as it could not possibly be finishd though it was begun before I came away, that I might haue
found a pleasing diuersion for my eyes (continud I) in veewing your shaddow, when they
had lost the satisfaction of beholding the substance any longer. But tis no matter (went q
on with a sigh) you cannot hinder me from bearing away your image so deeply engrauen
in my heart as no length of time shall ere be able to deface it. And there foreuer shold I were
yours (replyd he) but though I haue been very much to blame in so long neglecting to
to get it dispatchd (as not thinking your departure would so soon haue happned) yet
by my future diligence I hope to make amends for this my first offence which I am.

Figure 8. Last page of the manuscript.

last sentence breaks off, and the narrative ends without giving any explanation of why Arthenia washed up on the shore of Delphos dressed as a man.[35]

In Arthenia's history, Manningham weaves the accounts of her wooing by Loreto and then by Issodorus into her descriptions of the historical figures and battles of the Civil War, employing a transparent topicality that may have owed something to literary fashion.[36] The anonymous *Theophania*, printed in 1655 but written around 1645, for example, also uses Sicily to represent England, Corsica Scotland, Sardinia Ireland, Palermo London, Nicosa Nottingham; the name Clearchus, however, is used for the Duke of Buckingham rather than Charles I.[37] This veiled topicality, according to Stephen Zwicker, satisfied readers who "had an appetite for hidden things."[38]

A political romance might also aspire to counsel the informed reader. The author of *Theophania* offers diplomatic advice to the royalist party. Since help from abroad is unlikely, the host Synesis (Robert Sidney, Earl of Leicester) counsels Alexandro (Prince Charles) to advise his father to negotiate a peace with Corastus (Cromwell), and Alexandro pledges to do so.[39] In some romances, the topicality may be included to enhance its seriousness. Sir George Mackenzie's *Aretina: A Serious Romance* (1660), for example, inserts a spate of topical allegory distinctly different from the rest of the romance and concludes with the bonfires and bells accompanying the reinstatement of Theopemptus (Charles II).[40] In Sir Percy Herbert's *Cloria and Narcissus* (1653 and 1654), later expanded into *Princess*

---

[35] See Figure 8. I am indebted to William Gentrup for suggesting that the manuscript may not have been finished because the manuscript concludes at the very bottom of the folio page, rather than mid-page (Figure 8). The final pages may have been lost.

[36] Pertinent discussions include Paul Salzman, *English Prose Fiction, 1558–1770*, 148–201; Paul Salzman, "Royalist Epic and Romance," *The Cambridge Companion to Writing of the English Revolution*, ed. N. H. Keeble (Cambridge: Cambridge University Press, 2001), 215–30; Nigel Smith, *Literature and Revolution in England, 1640–1660* (New Haven: Yale University Press, 1994), 233–49, esp. 234.

[37] *Theophania* (1655), ed. Pigeon, 37, 287.

[38] Steven N. Zwicker, "Royalist Romance?" *Prose Fiction in English from the Origins of Print to 1750*, 243–259, esp. 252; vol. 1 of the *Oxford History of the Novel in English*, ed. Thomas Keymer (Oxford: Oxford University Press, 2018). See also Aemilia Zurcher, *Seventeenth-Century English Romance: Allegory, Ethics, and Politics* (New York: Palgrave Macmillan, 2007). For the suggestion that romance became a genre from which much could be learned, see Lois Potter, *Secret Rites and Secret Writing: Royalist Literature, 1641–1660* (Cambridge: Cambridge University Press, 1989), 73–90, esp. 75.

[39] *Theophania* (1655), ed. Pigeon. Cenodoxius (2nd Earl of Essex), who commands the Parliamentarian army, claims that he had no intent to uncrown the king.

[40] George Mackenzie, *Aretina: A Serious Romance* (London: Robert Broun, 1660), Book 3.

Cloria (1661), the author addresses an elite audience whom he pointedly elevates above the "vulgar sort" who read his *Princess Cloria* only for entertainment. [41]

The Civil War is not only the backdrop to Arthenia's narrative. While astutely recognizing that money and property are beginning to supersede the importance of birth and class in Restoration Britain, Bridget Manningham also understands that the Civil War may change the type of romance that will be written. The frame and the narrative symbolically interact as Arthenia relates the story of the execution of a king. On the day appointed for his execution, Charles I acts with Christlike dignity, even forgiving those who have humiliated him and sought his death. Charles "with a greater Patience than ever Mortall was before endued" (1.6.74^v) submits to the executioner who severs his head and exposes "it to the view of all such as had the heart to behold so dismall, and afflicting an Object" (74^v). Arthenia brands the execution a "heinous Crime without example" (74^v). Queen Ermillia, who is part of the audience listening to Arthenia's narrative, significantly exclaims:

> I am ~~most~~ strangly amaz'd (repli'd the Queen) at what you tell me, that I should scarce take this story for any other then a Romantick Fiction, did you not assure me tis a reall truth. (1.6. 74^v)

Arthenia's narrative is rooted in fact, and when Queen Ermillia, who is herself a figure in a fictional romance, exclaims that Charles's execution must be a fiction, we recognize that Manningham has moved from Artabella's romance to Arthenia's history; exotic locales have receded in favor of everyday experiences, and a new literary form has begun to emerge.

Editorial Principles of this Edition

Theories of textual editing have identified two central areas of debate, attribution and modernization. Attribution remains controversial especially when dealing with 1) anonymous works; 2) works extant in two or more texts but attributed to different authors; and 3) works, widely understood to be scribal publications, which may have been composed by their authors in different formats or languages, or may have been modified by readers or copyists who actively revise texts during the transmission process. The value of attribution itself has also been questioned. For example, there has recently been a call for recogniz-

---

[41] Preface to Sir Percy Herbert, *Princess Cloria* (London: Ralph Wood, 1661). For commentary on the political romance, see Paul Salzman, "The Princess Cloria and the Political Romance in the 1650s: Royalist Propaganda in the Interregnum," *Southern Review* (1981): 236–46.

ing anonymity as a category of authorship. [42] The Modern Language Association awarded a prize to an edition of Sir Walter Ralegh's poetry in which the editor identifies when and where a poem was attributed to Ralegh but takes no stand on these attributions. [43] Attributions of poems to major authors frequently provoke controversy, and, in some instances, these discussions can be productive. [44]

Rivall Friendship was considered to be anonymous when it was acquired by the Newberry Library from the bookseller, Pickering and Chatto. The case for the authorship of Bridget Manningham is presented above in the Introduction. Additional evidence, of course, might surface and be used to make a case for another author. Rather than dwelling on such uncertainties, this edition makes the best possible case for the attribution of *Rivall Friendship* to Bridget Manningham.

On the issue of modernization, there is no consensus concerning how to edit early modern texts as witnessed by the tradition of modernizing Shakespeare and printing Edmund Spenser's works in old spelling editions. It could be argued that Shakespeare's prominence in the school curriculum has been maintained by the availability of modernized texts, but then we need to keep in mind excesses such as the modernization of Hamlet's famous soliloquy to "To be or not to be" from "that is the question" to "that is what is the matter." Few old spelling texts can claim to be printed from an author's holograph manuscript. As Jean Robertson and Victor Skretkowicz, editors respectively of Sir Philip Sidney's Old and New *Arcadias*, have pointed out, if no manuscript in the author's hand is extant, an old spelling edition merely preserves the "idiosyncrasies of one particular scribe" or, in the case of printed texts, its compositor or compositors. [45] On the other hand, even those who favor modernization recognize that something is lost when we make a sixteenth- or seventeeth-century narrative read like its modern equivalent. Addressing this very point from an historical perspective, Maurice Evans, who modernizes spelling in his edition of Sidney's *Arcadia*, observes:

---

[42] See, for example, Marcy L. North, *The Anonymous Renaissance: Cultures of Discretion in Tudor-Stuart England* (Chicago: University of Chicago Press, 2003); see also North's "Amateur Compilers, Scribal Labour, and the Contents of Early Modern Poetic Miscellanies," *English Manuscript Studies* 16 (2011): 82–111.

[43] *The Poems of Sir Walter Ralegh: A Historical Edition,* ed. Michael Rudick, Renaissance English Texts Society, 23 (Tempe, AZ: Medieval and Renaissance Texts and Studies, 1999).

[44] Don W. Foster, *Elegy by W. S.: A Study in Attribution* (Newark, DE: University of Delaware Press, 1989). See also Foster's argument that each author has a literary fingerprint in *Author Unknown: On the Trail of Anonymous* (New York: Henry Holt, 2000).

[45] *The Countess of Pembroke's Arcadia* [The Old Arcadia], ed. Robertson, lxix and *The Countess of Pembroke's Arcadia* [The New Arcadia], ed. Victor Skretkowicz (Oxford: Clarendon Press, 1987), lxxx.

I have made no attempt to modernize the vocabulary since Sidney himself used deliberately archaic language appropriate to the decorum of a Romance and designed to raise the style above the colloquial level in accordance with the best Heroic theory.[46]

No easy answer exists for the editor of an early modern text.

Succinctly stated, the editorial dilemma facing an editor of *Rivall Friendship* is whether to transcribe *verbatim*, regularize, or modernize this two part seventeenth-century romance. In *A Continuation of Sir Philip Sidney's "Arcadia"* by Anna Weamys, Patrick Colborn Cullen reprints the 1651 printed edition and also supplies a modernized text.[47] The length of *Rivall Friendship* makes a printed transcription accompanied by a modernization impractical.

Transcription

My editorial decision to transcribe *Rivall Friendship* with minimal regularization and modernization was influenced chiefly by the consideration that this manuscript appears to be unique and so an accurate transcription is of the first importance. Second, even without modernizing spelling and syntax, the language of *Rivall Friendship* is accessible to most modern readers, particularly to those students and scholars accustomed to working with seventeenth-century texts.[48] Even the general reader of Malory's *Knights of King Arthur* or Chaucer will not find the syntax or vocabulary impenetrable. In the interest of assisting that general reader, Appendix 2 identifies historical figures and places, and Appendix 3 lists the names of characters.

Rivall Friendship survives in one manuscript copy, and this manuscript preserves a readable text; therefore, this edition attempts to reproduce this manuscript as faithfully as possible. The single intervention in the direction of modernization has been to introduce paragraphing to distinguish speakers and to indicate major breaks in the narrative such as changes of location or time of day. In instances when spelling may render meaning unclear, a modern orthography is suggested in brackets, for example "mene" [mien]. These editorial decisions

---

[46] Sir Philip Sidney, *The Countess of Pembroke's Arcadia*, Penguin Classics, ed. Maurice Evans, (London: Penguin, 1977), 47.

[47] *A Continuation of Sir Philip Sidney's "Arcadia" by Anna Weamys*, Women Writers in English 1350–1850, ed. Patrick Colborn Cullen (Oxford: Oxford University Press, 1994).

[48] Modernization also opens the door to issues such as whether to prefer British to American spelling (favour to favor; rigour to rigor; colour to color; humour to humor). *Rivall Friendship* sometimes uses spelling now associated with American rather than British spelling.

are motivated by the desire to "intervene no more than necessary for the sake of reasonable clarity."[49]

Two features of *Rivall Friendship* may be useful to point out: 1) *handwriting*: there are at least three identifiable hands (Figures 1–3). In contrast to the other two hands that cross out a word to be deleted, the correcting hand underlines a word for deletion and then inserts a correction. As noted previously, the correcting hand initially makes substantive changes but later concentrates on correcting spelling--always in the direction of modernity. These emendations are pointed out in textual footnotes. 2) *vocabulary*: the words "resent" (v) and "resentment" (n), deriving from *resentir* in French, are used to refer to sentiments or intense feelings as well as the feeling of indignation or having a grudge. It is useful to point out that the word "resentment" is corrected by the correcting hand to "sentiments" (1.1.14^{r}).

Conventions of this Transcription

1) Obvious errors such as missing parentheses to indicate a speaker or missing close parentheses have been silently corrected, e.g., "my name (repli'd he)."

2) Names of characters have been regularized and italicized throughout except in instances in which the manuscript indicates that only the name is to be italicized, not the possessive marker, "s", e.g. "*Artabella*s" in which Artabella is italicized but "s" is not.

3) If there are possibilities of two readings (e.g., "Silvan sports" or "Silvah sports"), then the reading is selected which is closer to normal usage in modern English.

4) No attempt has been made to correct either to/too or then /than when comparisons are indicated, e.g., "by the advantage of her dress, which was much more becoming then the Persian habit"; or "certain it is, he thought her more faire and Excellent then the Sea-born Goddess."

5) The periphrastic possessive, "the Prince his quarrel," for "the Prince's quarrel," has been retained throughout.

6) Regularization of spelling, capitalization, and abbreviations:
   • i/j, u/v. have been normalized throughout.
   • Capitalization has been modernized for double consonants, e.g., "flying upon the wwinges of ffeare" becomes "Wings of Feare."

---

[49] Cullen, ed. Weamys, lxvii.

• Slash marks showing word or line divisions have been removed, as well as catch words indicating the first word of the following page.

7) Abbreviations expanded without textual notes:
   • Matie = Majestie
   • Mat^{ies}= Majesties
   • M^{rs} = Mistress
   • S^{r} = Sir
   • W^{ch} = which
   • W^{t} = with
   • Y^{e} = the
   • Y^{r} = your
   • Y^{t} = that
   • Y^{ou}r = your
   • the[n] above the line has been silently expanded
   • The tilde [~] or macron [-] to indicate m or n has silently been completed

Rivall Friendship

THE FIRST PART

The First Book

Sol was not farre advanced in his Diurnall Journey when the Delphian Woods resounded with the shrill noise of Hunters, and the cry of Dogges, which so loudly eccho'd that the Park rang again, in so much, that it set free the senses of a certaine stranger, which Morpheus had ~~thus~~ for a while held Prisoner in his dark Dominion, and necessity had that night constrain'd to borrow a Bed of the cold Earth, and shelter from a large and spreading Palme-tree with which that Island was ^plentifully stored^ well replenished:[1] he arising from his hard, and ill accommodated lodging being a little surprized at so sudden an alarme; looking about to see from whence it proceeded, he espied a Hinde flying upon the Wings of Feare from her fatall Pursuers who had almost o'retaken her. She was no sooner past, but there appear'd a gallant Troope of Ladies, mounted all on milk-white Horses, atir'd in green, sutable to the time; being that season of the yeare wherein Flora goes a Maying, deck't in all her verdant glories. These Ladies could not so fitly be compar'd to any, as the goddess Diana, and her Nymphes; for they bare each of them a Horn of Bugle by their sides, a sheafe of Arrows at their backs, and Bowes in their hands; and thus attir'd, they proceeded in their Silvan sports, not minding ought but that. But one of them (whose name was *Celia*) who pursu'd the Game more earnestly than the rest, was advanced forwards before the other about five, or six hundred paces; and casting her eye aside, she saw the stranger who stood intentively viewing these gallant Hunt-resses whose beauties cast a greater splendor thorough those Woods then Phebus brightest beames.

Celia no sooner beheld him, but she knew him to be a stranger to that coun-trey by the habit which he wore; and believing his youth uncapable of any ill intent, she rode up to him crying, fly Sir fly, if you love your life.

He approaching her with a very great respect, answer'd. I never was so much a Coward Madam to fly from Death in my highest prosperity; but it would worse

---

[1] Well replenished is underlined and "plentifully restored" inserted above; it is pos-sible that this substantive change in a darker ink could be authorial.

become me now, to turn my back on that, which I have left my Native Countrey
to find. But however Madam, I am oblig'd to pay you my humblest acknowledgments for that noble care you are generously pleas'd to shew for the preservation
of an unfortunate Strangers life.

She had not time to reply, for the Queen and all the other ladies were come
up to them. The Queen no sooner saw him, but arming her Brow with an unusuall severity, on which naturally dwelt nothing but sweetness, she thus spake to
him.

Rash young man what ill Fate hath conducted thee hither to thy Death.

He hearing nought but Death denounced against him, was nothing startled;
nor did he put on so much as a discomposed look at that which certainly had
strook a terrour into the heart of any other, less acquainted with the miseries of
Life.

You tell me of Death Madam (said he addressing himselfe to the Queen)
[fol. 1ᵛ] but may I not have leave to enquire what Crime I have committed that
can merit so fatall a sentence; for I can safely protest I do not know that I have
offended any person so much as in a thought, since misfortune cast me on this
shore. If I have offended I shall not refuse willingly to resign my life; but if I must
dy, I shall (I confess) find more satisfaction in falling an innocent Victime, then
a guilty Sacrifice.

Yes said the Queen, you shall have leasure to be made acquainted with your
offence, which is unpardonable that I'le assure you, unless you are of Royall
birth; which I suppose you are not, having no equipage, nor any to attend you.

Were I sure to obtain my life (and that it were as considerable to me, as it is
the contrary) or something yet more precious (said he) I would scorn to purchase
it at so base a rate, as by owning of a falsehood: tis therefore Madam I declare
ingenuously you ere not in your opinion of my birth, yet is it not ignoble: but yet
you cannot justly ground that beliefe on my being unattended; for the same Fate
which took from me all but my unfortunat life, might as well have despoiled me
of my servants, as it has of all things else, except these few Clothes I weare: But
those two Unconstant Deities (Fortune and Neptune) were but seemingly kind,
to be the more really cruell: they have indeed preserv'd my Life on the Sea, but
to make me loose it with more horrour (perhaps) upon the Land.

With that, he foulded his armes, and stood for awhile in the posture of a
person oppress'd with griefe. But of a sudden erecting his eyes to Heaven, he
cry'd out. O you Celestiall powers, I must adore your Justice, a thousand times
have I wisht for Death, far have I gone to seeke it, and shall I now repine that I
have found my desire, though in another manner then I design'd; what though
the way be different; the end is still the same.

He had scarce finish'd this speech, ere the Queen commanded one of her
Ladies to give the Signall for the coming of her guard which were not farre distant; which being given, there came in thirty Gentlemen well hors'd, and Arm'd,
and presented themselves to the Queen to know her pleasure.

Here (said she) take that man (pointing to the stranger) and carry him to Prison, and let him be securely kept till you receive further order.

With that some of them went to him with an intent to bind him; which he perceiving, streaching out his Armes said. Here, bind these hands which were ne're bound by any man before; I would to Heaven my heart had been as free, then had I never been expos'd to this Ignominy.

Nor shall not now (repli'd the Queen). You may guard him securely enough (said she to her servants) without binding since you see he is not in a condition to make any resistance; and tis enough to inflict on him the penalty of the law, without treating him with rigour; which may induce him to believe us cruell, more then just. Let him be civilly us'd I command you.

With that, bowing to the Queen as an acknowledgment of her favour to him, he willingly resigned himselfe to the conduct of his Guard, as unconcernedly as if he had been going to the freedome of a Palace, rather then the confinment of a Prison. The gatehouse belonging to the Palace Royall (for so was that place call'd where the Queen as all her Predecessors usually resided) was the Prison for Persons of quality; and thither was our unfortunate Stranger led by those to whose custody he was committed. But as he pass'd along, The Thracian Ambassadour (who was just then going to his Lodging) chanced to espie him: he no sooner cast his Eye on him, but he commanded his Chariot to stay; and viewing him intentively, was strook with [fol. 2ʳ] wonder, strongly fancying he beheld a Face he was no stranger too; and not being able to pass further till he had made an enquirie who that person was, and whether they were carrying him: he was told, he was a Stranger, and that none knew either his name or Countrey; and that they were by the Queenes especiall command carrying him to Prison. He then ask'd what his offence might be; they replyed, they were as ignorant of that, as his condition; onely they believed his being a stranger was his greatest crime.

That, in my opinion is a very small one (said Gentillus for so was the Ambassadour call'd).

We are not to dispute that with your Lordship, answer'd one of them, passing on.

Stay said Gentillus, may I not be permitted to speak with the Prisoner.

No my Lord (said they) without leave from the Queen.

Hearing that, he gave order for his Chariot to go on, and the Prisoner went to the Place assign'd him: which bateing his restraint, relish'd nothing of a Prison. He was led up staires, into a larg Chamber neatly furnish'd, and fitly accommodated with all things needfull. As soon as he was enter'd, those who brought him thither retir'd, leaving him alone; which solitude was much more pleasing then their Companies; where we will leave him, and returne to the Queen, who after his departure, began seriously to consider his undaunted deportment.

It cannot be (said she to Celia, who of all her Ladies she honour'd with a perticuler esteeme) but that this man is endued with an extraordinary courage, or has been persecuted by more then ordinary misfortunes, which either makes him scorne to beg his life, or renders it inconsiderable to him.

I am of the opinion (reply'd *Celia*) tis misfortune makes him receive the tydings of his Death with so little concern.

Be it what it will (answer'd the Queen) I am perswaded, Fortune, not design brought him hither; and tis on that account, I am more troubled at his disaster, then angry at his fault: and I could wish, I had forborne taking my pleasure to day in this Park, that I might not have met with this adventure, which gives me more discontent then satisfaction; since I must be necessitated to sacrifice an unfortunat (perhaps an innocent and vertuous) person to the rigour of the Law. Oh who would be a Soveraign Princess, to have her hands so bound up by Justice, that she cannot extend mercy to Offenders though it be her desire.

Why should your Majesty be so concern'd for this Unknown (repli'd another of the Queens Ladies) as to resent [feel] anything for the Loss of his Life: tis better a thousand such Lives as his should be Lost, then you be displeas'd or the Laws violated: besides, tis possible in doing Justice, you will conferre on him a more acceptable favour then in giving him his Life, were it in your power. Nay perhaps he may be some notorious Crimenall, who for some horrible offence, may have been banish'd, or fled his Countrey, and still may retaine the sting of a guilty mind, which may so terrifie him, as Death may be rather a mercy, then a Justice to him.

Forbeare *Procentia* said the Queen, you are too rash, in censuring one you know not; and till you do, Charity should make you judge the best: his Face speakes too much Innocence to leave a suspition in us, of ought in him but misery, and that may clame compassion both from me, and you.

This was their discourse as they rode homeward; for the Queen would no longer follow the Chace, but for that day gave it off, having her mind otherwise employ'd:

[fol. 2ᵛ] and besides, the Sun being mounted to the top of the ^Hemisphere^ ~~Zodiack~~ rendred that time of the day unseasonable for that exercise. Being return'd to the Palace, Dinner was presently serv'd up with all due Pompe, and Ceremony; and having din'd, she went to her Appartment for a while, and then descended into the great Hall, where she alwayes spent the Afternoones, in hearing the complaints of her Subjects, and doing them Justice; where she sate on a Throne of Parian Marble, under a Cannopie of state, of Crimson-velvet, richly embroidred with Pearle, supported on each side with Pillars of Green Jasper.

On the one hand of her stood the image of Justice, with a Sword in one hand, and Ballances in the other; on his head a Coronet of Gold, his eyes blinded with a Scarfe of White, and his Robe of a Scarlet Colour. On the other Peace, seting in a Chaire, her Atire white, girt with a Girdle of Starres, a Wreath of Olive on her head, and on her shoulder a Silver Dove; in her left hand she held forth a handfull of ripe Eares of Corne, as Emblemes of peace and plenty. In this place the Queen continu'd till the Evening approach'd, and then retired to her rest, after she had taken her repast.

The next morning the brightness of ^Phebus^ ~~Aurora~~ (who being newly risen from faire Thetis watrey bed) darted his resplendant beames just on the Face of the Unknown; and therewith awak'd him from his disturb'd repose; for his mind being diversly aggitated with severall Cogitations had rendred his sleep full of confused, and troublesome fancies.

But opening his eyes he cast them on that bright Intruder, crying out with precipitance, O Phebus thou beholdrst me alike unhappy here, as in my owne Countrey: the change of Climats cannot change my Destiny; misery I see, attends me in all places. Ah pittyless Fortune (my implacable Enemy) art thou yet satisfi'd, or hast thou any disaster left to throw on this Unhappy one, whom thou makest the Mark of all thy cruelties. No, (continu'd he smiling) thankes be to Heaven, the date of thine, and Cupids tyranie is almost expir'd, who has so proudly tryumpht o're a heart, that has these many yeares laine prostrate at his mercy; but now the time is come, I can defie ye both; my Death will put an end, both to the power of Love and Fate.

Scarce had he cloth'd these thoughts in Airey Garments, ere he heard the Dore of his Chamber unlock, and drawing the Curtain of his Bed to see who enter'd, he saw it was one of his Keepers, who by the Queens command came to let him know, he might have the Liberty to walk in the Palace-Gardens when ever he desir'd it, attended by two of his Keepers.

Her Majesty is too generous (said he to the man who brought him the Message) to a person destined for Death: this noble treatment will make me receive my death with more regreet, since I have been so unfortunat to deserve it from the hands of so gracious a Princess, who is so obliging, that she has rendred me more a Prisoner to her gooddness, then her power; for the one can but inthrall my body, but the other binds my soule: but seeing she has been pleas'd so freely to offer me this favour, I will by no meanes refuse it, lest she think I slight it. You may attend me about an houre hence (continued he) and I shall be ready to walk for one halfe houre.

The man departing, he instantly arose and dress'd himselfe, and calling for his Keepers, he was by them conducted into the garden; whether being come, he carelessly walk'd on, without somuch as once considering the beautie, or the rarities of it: but being guided by his pencive thoughts, he pass'd on, till he came into a Close Walk set on both sides with cypress-trees, which walk he [fol. 3ʳ] thought more agreeable to his humour then any in the Garden. He had not took many turnes in it, when casting up his Eyes (which were before steadfastly fix'd on the ground) he saw two Woemen coming towards him; the little desire he had to be seen, made him desirous to avoid meeting them: but while he consider'd how he might do it, they were come so neer, that he perceiv'd the one of them to be the Lady, who the day before endeavour'd his saftie: which when he saw, he chang'd his intention of shunning, into a desire of meeting her, that he might (as in civility he thought himselfe oblig'd) renew his thankes for her generosity to him.

He was no sooner come up to her, and going to speak, but she prevented him, saying, had you taken my advice yesterday, you needed not to have been waited on by such Servitors as these, nor had you fallen into that Danger, from which you are never like to escape.

I cannot at all repent that I made no better ~~advice~~ use of your Friendly advice Madam (said he) then to render it fruitless, since I have thereby an opportunity once more to see a person so infinitly obliging; which happiness I value at a higher rate then the preservation of an unfortunate Life.

The sight of me can in no way countervaile the loss of your life Sir (repli'd she) and I am sorry I could oblige you no otherwise then in designe; but were it in my power, I would not onely restore you that Liberty you have lost, but secure your Life from that Law, by which it is justly forfeited. But lest you should think I have some other motive besides pity to induce me to it, I protest tis no other then a compassionate sensibility of the miseries of Unfortunate persons (in which number I believe you one) incites me to it.

Since you are so infinitly good (repli'd he) as undeservedly to concerne your selfe in my mishaps, soe farre as to give me an interest in your pity, I must humbly beg you will compleat the obligation by the addition of one Favour more. Tis onely Madam that you would let me understand whom I have offended, or what crime I have committed that could be of so hainous a quality as to deprive me of Life, or ~~dep~~ reduce me to this condition wherein now I am.

This will I willingly do (answer'd she) if it may give you any satisfaction; but this is no place for discourse, retire with me into one of the Arbours here at hand, and I will fully satisfie your request. Then turning to his Keepers, you may trust this Gentleman with me (said she) I will engage for his returne to yee, and my life shall answere for his escape.

They knowing the power she had with the Queen, durst not refuse, but retireing to the further part of the Walk, Left the Stranger with *Celia*, who with her Charge (attended with her Maid) withdrew into the next Arbour; whether being come, she sate downe on one of the seates, inviting the Vnknown by her example to do the like, which at her intreaty he did.

To tell you (said she) what fault you have committed, I need say no more, then that you have violated the Law of this land, which prohibits all Persons (Princes, and Ambassadours excepted) from coming into the Queens presence, or within the precincts of the Palace (upon any account whatever) under pain of Death, without a Warrant first obtain'd from the Queen, sign'd with her owne hand, and seal'd with the PrivieSignet. Nor is it here, as in other Kingdomes, where Princes retaine a power of pardoning Offenders, be their crimes never so hainous; but here it is not so, for Kings, nor Queenes [fol. 3ᵛ] have no more power to forgive Capitall Offendors in this Kingdome, then Judges who in other places condemne them. But *Ermillia* the Queen that now reignes, is of so mercifull, and gentle a disposition, and so much detests all things that rellish of cruelty; that she has oft condemn'd the severity of some of our lawes, and in perticuler this: though tis not in her power to abolish that, or any other, without the consent of her Nobles; which never meet in a generall Session (unless some urgent occation intervene) but once in seven yeares: which has never happen'd since the Queen was invested with the Regall Diadem. But seeing she could not of herselfe take away a Law which she never approv'd of; fearing ~~some~~ some person or other might through ignorance fall under the penalty of it; which as it seemes was your selfe, who were decreed to be the first; but her feare was not greater then her princely care to prevent any sinister accident that thereby might accrew. And to that intent, she caus'd this Law, together with the penallty of it, to be ingraven on Marble Pillars, in faire Characters in all Languages, and plac'd in the most conspicuous places in every Citty of this Kingdome, that it might be known by all, and consequently avoided. And now that I have fully acquainted you with the severity of our Lawes, I trust you will do the Queen that justice, as not censure her of cruelty, or rigour, in taking away your Life for such a slight offence (as perhaps you believe yours to be) since tis not in her power to save it. This I dare confidently assure you, she is more concern'd for your misfortune, then you are your selfe; and could she by any meanes preserve you, you should find her no less mercifull then just.

I ever held the Royall dignity in so sacred a veneration (said he) that I durst never call in question their Justice in punishing Offendors: that they are just, tis no more then what they are oblig'd too, if mercifull, tis wholly from their good-ness. That I must dy is not more certain, then that I am not concern'd for it; and if at my death I resent [feel] anything that may render it displeasing, it will be onely that I must dy a Debtour to your generosity, having not the least capacity left me of making any other returne, more then a bare acknowledgment of all your noble favours.

I am glad Sir (repli'd she) to heare you owne your selfe my Debtour, not that I think you so in the least; but because I hope by the intercession of that opinion in you, I may obtain ^the^ a Satisfaction of a desire I am possess'd with; which if I may, it will not onely Satisfie your supposed Debt, but make me farre more your Debtour, then you can believe your selfe mine.

O, Madam (cry'd he) why do you not let me know wherein I may serve you, or indeed my selfe, by furnishing ^me^ with an occation to gratify your transcen-dant civility to this unhappy wretch.

Tis onely (said she) that you would acquaint me with your name and Coun-trey, and what misfortune brought you where we found you.

My name (repli'd he) is *Mellidorus*, my Countrey Sicilia, from whence I was bound by Sea for Sardinia: but Fortune (that unconstant Deity) thought She could not exhibit that implacable enmity She has ever born me, without pursu-ing me with her persecutions on Neptunes watry Element. After She had drove me from the Land, She stir'd up Eolus to let loose the most impetious of his

Stormes, by the violence whereof I was driven on this Coast, (farre distant from my intended Harbour) where I suffer'd shipwrack with the Loss of [fol. 4^r] all things my Life excepted, but of all my Losses none grieves me so much as the Loss of a faithfull Servant I had, of whose fidelity I have had so ample testimony, that it invited me to make him the onely Companion in my intended Voiage. Perhaps Madam (continu'd he) you expect a more full relation of my Life, and were I to Live, I should at Larg give it you; but since it is decreed that I must dy, I desire my follies and misfortunes, may be buried with me in the Grave of Oblivion: therefore I must humbly beg your pardon that I give you no clearer a discovery of my selfe.

I would not have you (said *Celia*) esteeme me so uncivilly importunate as to desire ought that may be contrary to your resolves.

After some other discourses of indifferent matters, Possibly (said she) you may admire why so strict a Law should be inacted in this Land, being a place of such resort for Strangers, from all parts, which come hither to consult Apollo's Oracle so famous thorow the Universe.

Indeed Madam (he repli'd) I should very much have wondred at that so strict a prohibition, had my thoughts been at Leasure to contemplate ought but my owne miseries: but I presume it was not establisht without some very weighty reason.

You judge aright (answer'd she) for so there was, as I could make it appeare, had I but time to tell you upon what account it came first to be made; and thereby let you see, that in other Ages there have been those who have been persecuted no less by Fortune then your selfe. But I cannot now stay to tell it you, because tis much about the time of the Queens rising, at which I am this day oblig'd to be present; but if you please to meet me here about this time to morrow, I will give you the relation, which perhaps you will not esteeme unworthy of your knowledge.

I believe Madam (said he) you are very highly in the Queenes fauour, and being so, you may do me a very acceptable kindness in letting her know, tis my humble, and earnest desire she would vouchsafe to put a period to my sufferings by a speedy death; which with raptures of Joy I shall embrace, if I may be but so happy as to know she is not offended with me for a fault my ignorance onely made me commit.

Since you desire it (she repli'd) I shall acquaint the Queen with your request; but I had much rather find out a way (if it were possible) to preserve you from this inevitable danger.

To which friendly expression he made a sutable reply; and rising up, was taking his leave, whilst she sent her Maid to call his Keepers, who upon her sommons came into the Arbour. Here said she I return you my Charge. Then turning to *Mellidorus* she bid him farewell, after he had promised to meet her on the morrow, and went to the Queen, and he to his Prison where he spent part of the day in his ordinary disquiets.

Celia being come to the Queen told her how by accident she had met the Stranger, and what discourse she had with him. Just as *Ermillia* was come out into the Chamber of State, came the Thracian Ambassadour to entreat her permission to see and speak with the Prisoner: to which request the Queen answer'd, he might have that liberty in the Afternoon in her presence; for she intended to send for him to come before her, to give him his sentence. To which intent Dinner being past she sent one of her Gentlemen [fol. 4ᵛ] to fetch him, who soon after brought him in. Being perswaded he knew for certaine for what end he was sent for, he approach'd the Queen with an assured Look, nothing daunted with the feare or apprehension of his ensuing Death.

The Queen seeing him; *Mellidorus* said she (for so I understand you are call'd) I suppose you are ere this enform'd both of the nature and quality of your Offence, with the punishment due unto it; from which it lies not in our power to exempt you: but all the fauour we can shew you, you shall assuredly find from our Royall bounty; which is onely to give you the choice of three deathes, which you will elect you may (being those to which Offenders of quality are always condemned) Which is either to be sacrificed to the great Apollo, who is the Deity that of all others we in Delphos do most peculierly adore. Or else to be devour'd by a Lion, or strangled by the hands of two Eunuchs destin'd for that purpose.

I shall not long stand to determine (answer'd *Mellidorus*) which of the three to make my choice: for did I believe the Gods took delight in humane blood, or that it were a sacrifice acceptable to them, I should prefer that before all others: but being of a contrary Faith I shall by no meanes elect that. Nor shall I give up my selfe to the cruell embraces of a Savage, although the King of Beasts; nor make my Grave within his bowells. No Madam, since you are graciously pleas'd to leave it to my choice, I shall chuse to receive my death from the hands of your Eunuchs.

Well, said the Queene seeing you have made that your choice, that you have: and I here pronounce your sentence. You must within three days prepare so to dye. I had destin'd you to a longer reprieve, had you not by *Celia* requested the contrary.

Ah Madam (repli'd he) you are too gracious to this Unfortunate; your goodness, were I to continue neere you, would undoubtedly make me as enamour'd of Life; as now I am of Death. But if a Crimenall may have leave to implore one favour more (continu'd he, casting himselfe at the Queens Feet) it should be my humble supplication that your Majesty would vouchsafe my Body may be conveied (when my Soule has left its habitation) back to Sicilia there to be interred in the Monuments of my Ancestors.

Rise *Mellidorus* said the Queen your request is granted; and if you have ought else to aske demand it freely, and if we can grant, you shall obtain it.

I have no more to beg (repli'd he) but onely that this day may conclude both my miseries and me. No great Queen I beseech you permit me not here to Languish three dayes more; but give me my Pasport to the Haven of rest, and Port of happiness, by Lisenceing me immediatly to embrace Death, now the most wellcomest of Friends, and my most kind Conducter to Elizium; where in those Shades of bliss, and Plaines of pleasure I shall forever walk [fol. 5ʳ] cloth'd with a Robe of immortality and no more know what sorrow meanes.

If I gave you three more dayes to Live (said the Queen) it was no more then I thought necessary to prepare you for the other Life; but since by your expressions you seem so fit for Deaths entertainment, you shall to morrow be presented with your Fatall Attendants. There was not a person present that beheld the innocent Countenance of *Mellidorus*, and how unconcernedly he receiv'd the sentence of death; but was so concern'd for him, that they could not refraine from commiserating his sad misfortune with teares of pity: nor was there any there who would not presently have thrown themselves at *Ermillias* Feet to have implor'd his pardon, had there been any possibility of obtaining it; especially *Celia* who wholy melted into teares of pity for him.

But scarce was he gone out of the Presence, when *Gentillus* (who had stood moveless as a Statue ever since he heard *Mellidorus* speak of Sicilie, at mentioning whereof he was confident he was the person that he took him for) addressing himselfe to the Queen, I beseech you Madam (said he) does your Law extend it selfe to all persons; are no Sex, nor condition exempted from the penalty of it.

Yes (said the Queen) Woemen, and all Men of Royall birth are no way lyable to it.

Then *Mellidorus* must not dy (repli'd he).

How (said the Queen) know you any reason that will be sufficent to free him from it.

Yes Madam (answer'd he) *Mellidorus*'s Sex will free him, for on my word he is not what his Habit speakes him; but a disguis'd Lady whom I have long since had the honour to be acquainted with. If you distrust my words (continu'd he) behold this assurance (continu'd he pulling forth a Picture and presenting it to the Queen) and compare but the Lines of this dead Figure, with the Lively Features of *Mellidorus*'s Face, and you will undoubtedly perceive Madam as great a resemblance as their habits will permit.

The Queen haveing view'd it, found in it so great a Likeness of *Mellidorus*'s face that she concluded it could not possibly be the Pourtracture of any other: which perswasion had no sooner possest her, but she sent for him once more to come before her. He dreaming of nothing less then a discovery, instantly return'd, and presented himselfe to her to know for what intent she had sent for him.

I charge you *Mellidorus* (said the Queen) resolve me one question faithfully which I shall aske you.

I trust your Majesty (repli'd he) has a more charitable opinion of me then to believe I will be guilty of an untruth in your presence; but if I would, certainly I durst not be so impious as to appeare before the Face of Heaven with a Lye in my mouth.

That, then (said the Queen) which I desire to [fol. 5ᵛ] know of you is, whether your Habit and your Sex agree, or in fine whether you are not a Woman.

At this demand, *Mellidorus* was ready to sink downe with griefe; having his Eyes cover'd with teares, and his Cheekes with blushes.

Ah Madam cry'd he, I am I confess a Woman; but the most Unfortunate that ever breath'd: and the rather soe, having this new affliction added to the weight of my other miseries. Since I must dy, oh how much better had it been to have died in obscurity, then thus to be discover'd; before, your Majesty believ'd me onely unfortunate, and on that score perhaps esteem'd me worthy of your pity; but now I must be oblig'd wholy to the Charity both of you, and all here present, if ye account me not an Object worthy onely of contempt, and scorn to appeare before ye in a Garb so unsutable to me; and whereby I may seem to have divested my selfe of that Modesty which is the chiefest Ornament (and ought to be an insepparable Companion) of our Sex. But I beg most gracious Queen you would a while suspend your censure till I acquaint you with those reasons I had to take on me a habit so disagreeable to that Modesty I ever made a most severe profession of.

I shall not censure you for your habit (repli'd the Queen) but I must tell you, you have very much displeas'd me by this concealment of your selfe, since thereby you almost rendred me guilty of the death of an innocent person, such as you now appeare to be; which you had inevitably done, had not this noble Lord (pointing to *Gentillus*) prevented it by discovering you to be a woman.

At which, looking about to see who had given the Queen this Intelligence, *Gentillus* presented himselfe to her, saying, behold Madam before you a person whom though time has worn him out of your memory, yet has it not wrought that effect on him: nor was your disguise able to conceale you from the knowledge of him who once passionately ador'd you; but though those Flames have been long since quench'd in the waters of dispaire, yet I have still retain'd for you an intire Friendship, which I will carry with me to my Grave.

Whilst he was speaking in this manner, *Mellidorus* earnestly look'd on him; and being exceedingly surpriz'd with wonder, she could no longer refrain, but cry'd with transport, Good Heavens who is this I see. Are you my Lord *Gentillus* whom I have seen in Sicilie.

Yes Madam (answer'd he) I am; and the happy *Gentillus* since I have bin so fortunate to redeeme you from a Death so certaine, as nothing but a Miracle could have rescued you from.

Why (said she) I must not dy then.

No Madam (answer'd he) Ladies are exempted from the penalty of this Law by which you were condemn'd.

Ah my Lord (repli'd she sighing) how much more acceptable a kindness had you done me, had you not reveal'd my condition, but let me now have ended my dayes in quiet, and not have call'd me from the Gates of [fol. 6ʳ] Death into which I was entering; to endure more misery.

Scarce was *Mellidorus* known to be a Woman, ere all those Ladies who stood bewailing her misfortune had their teares of compassion turn'd to those of joy, to see her so happily, and timely discover'd; and would instantly have flown to testifie their joy by their embraces, had not the Queens presence restrain'd them; but though respect with held the others, it had not that power on *Celia* who was no longer able to forbear (transported with joy as she was) to run with open Armes to embrace her.

Ah Madam cry'd she, how much beyound expression am I glad to find my selfe so happily deceiv'd.

But as the disguised Lady was going to answer, the Queen prevented her by giving *Celia* a command to conduct her to a more agreeable Lodging then that she late^ly^ appointed her. Goe (said she to the Unknown) along with *Celia*, and divest your selfe of those Garments, and assume others more sutable to your sex: she will accommodate you with all things necessary.

Fain would she have given the Queen those humble acknowledgments she believ'd due to her generous bounty, but shame stop'd the Current of her words, and left her no other language but blushes to speak her thankes; and turning about to follow *Celia*, *Gentillus* came and presented her his hand to lead her out, which she courteously accepted.

And as she pass'd along, my Lord (said she) I beg your stay awhile till I return (which shall not be long first) that I may have the satisfaction to know how it was possible for you to know me under this disguise, which I believ'd sufficent to conceale me from the eyes of my owne Brother had he seen me in it.

Yes Madam (answer'd he) I shall obey your Commands: with that, kissing her hand he retir'd to the Queen to wait her returne.

When *Celia* had brought her to her Chamber, she presented her with severall garments, desiring her to chuse those she best lik'd, which she did, after she had view'd them all, making choice of those which were worn constantly by all the Ladies of the Court that were Virgins. Which was a Peticote of blushcolour, a Gowne of white, open before, and pin'd back, with hangingsleves of the same: the Sleeve which cover'd her Arme came no further then the Elboe, being very wide, turn'd back and button'd on each shoulder with a rich Orientall Pearle thorow a Loope of Gold. A Scarfe of Watched tied cross; and knit on the left shoulder; her Haire part bound up with Hairelaces of Blushcolour, Watched, and White Riben: the [fol. 6ᵛ] other part hung downe in Curles shaddowing her Neck which was quite bare, onely she had round the edge of her gowne a row of Puffes of Lawne; and over all she put on a Vaile of Tyffany which reach'd from head to foot.

The Sicilian Lady being thus attir'd, had not the patience to continue longer in her Chamber, but quited it to go learne from *Gentillus* what she most ardently long'd to know. *Celia* perceiving her desire, took her by the hand and leading her back into the Queenes presence at whose Feet she cast herselfe, as well to give her thankes for her Princely favours, as to implore her pardon for those faults ignorance only had made her guilty of.

Ermillia giving her, her hand to kiss as a testimony of her favour, raised her up; we have pardon'd you (said she) and wholy banisht all thoughts of your supposed crime, as we trust you have all resentments [feelings] for the ill usage you did, and worse, you were like to receive from us: but as your Ignorance was the sole cause of your supposed fault, so is it ours that our reall injuries ought to be imputed.

Your Majesty (repli'd the Unknown) has treated me far more generously then I could expect, even then when you deem'd me worthy of death; but since my discovery you have multiplied your royall bounties on me so infinitly above my desert; that had I by my Death purchaced the least of those transcendant favours, I should have esteem'd the price but inconsiderable; nor could my sufferings have been imputed to ought but my disguise, which rendred me an apparent Offender. But I shall henceforth account this the onely happie day that ever I beheld, since I have liv'd to tast the goodness of so gracious a Queen; nor will I any more repent my preservation; nor look on it otherwise then as a Providence from Heaven and an eternall obligation to you my Lord *Gentillus* (continu'd she turning to him).

The saving your Life Madam (said he) is not so great an obligation to you, as tis a satisfaction to me if I have had the honour of doing it.

Many other words of Complement having pass'd between them, she again intreated him to let her know by what meanes he came to know her. That he told her he would presently satisfie her in if the Queen would vouchsafe to permit him that liberty in her presence: which being granted, in these words he began, addressing his speech to the Sicilian Lady.

I confess Madam (said he) you may very well admire, how it should be possible for me to retaine your Idea so perfectly in my mind, as to know you (especially in such a disguise) after almost ten yeeres absence: indeed it would have been no easie matter still to have retained you so fresh in memory, had I been oblig'd to nothing but the Charactar which that passion I had for you; once ingrav'd in my mind; for I confess 'twas very probable time (that great distroyer of all things) would ere [fol. 7ʳ] this have defaced it. But I must acknowledge Madam, I always carry that about me, which will never suffer me to loose that Impression which the hand of Love first wrought. Tis this Madam (continued he pulling forth her Picture which not long before he had shewne *Ermillia*) tis this I say which has preserv'd you so fresh in my mind. Perhaps this confession may as much offend as surprize you; but I cannot beg your pardon for what I did, since it has been the happie Instrument of your preservation.

Ah *Gentillus* (said she) for Heavens sake rid me quickly out of this astonishment whereinto the sight of this Picture has cast me; that it somuch resembles me as all the World must needs believe it mine I cannot deny; but how, or by what meanes you came by it, is that I somuch wonder at. I am certaine I never yet bestow'd my Picture on you, nor any man breathing.

No Madam (answer'd he) I declare I receiv'd it not from you, nor am I oblig'd to any, but my owne artefice for the favour of it which I thus effected. It was my fortune to see you at your Cousin *Tellimurs* in Palermo, whether you came to see a Funurall which was to pass by his house in state: that was the first time I ever saw you; and indeed I may truly say the last of my Liberty: for I no sooner beheld you, but my heart which preserv'd it selfe from the assaults of all our Thracian beauties, that very instant resign'd its freedome at your Shrine, and laid it selfe a prostrate Vassall at the mercy of a Beauty whom I knew not, nor was Like to doe. But it chanced not long after, I obtain'd the acquaintance of your Cousin at whose house you then were; with whom I contracted a very great Friendship: nevertheless I conceal'd from him as well as others the passion I had for you. But at Last, perceiving by my change of humour, and an unusuall penciveness which accompanied me (so contrary to that pleasant disposition I was naturally of) that something more then ordinary disturb'd my quiet: which he seem'd much concern'd for, and beg'd me with many earnest intreaties to let him know the cause of my alteration. A long while I oppos'd his intreaties, pretending severall feigned causes, which to say truth seem'd no other to him. Soe that at last, overcome by his pressing importunities (fearing he might impute my privisie to a want of Friendship) I unlock't the Closet of my brest intirely to him, and laid before him the greatness of my passion, desireing his assistance and advice. Which when he had heard, seeming to wonder at it, he said, he could not but admire what I saw in you more then in others, to be tai'ne Captive at the first assault. Ah *Tellamour* (said I) misprize not those bright powers that conquer'd me; she carries Charmes sufficent to inthrall all those that dare resist the puisant power of that Deity who knowes no limits to his Soveraignity.

If it be so (repli'd he looking very sadly) I am really sorry for your sake, that you should soe [fol. 7ᵛ] unhappily fix your love on a person from whom I cannot give you the least incouragment to hope for a recipprocall esteeme; nor lies it in my power to serve you any otherwise then with my Councell, which if you would take, you should immediatly pluck from your Brest a passion which has already given you somuch discontent, and from which you must never expect to reap any satisfaction. But perhaps my discourse would be more pleasing should I agreeably flatter your desires with the hopes of obtaining them; but I cannot do that, and be what I profess my selfe; or without being guilty of base flattery, and dissemulation, which I never yet knew how to act towards any, much less my Friend: being so well acquainted with my Cousins humour as I am; for I know her to be of so severe a vertue that she would rather dy then suffer a thought to harbour in her soule that may in the least be prejudiciall to that duty she believes due to those whom Heaven and Nature have given the disposall of her. And from the concession of her Parents you can hope as little; for I have oft heard them protest they would assoon wed her to a [her] grave, as to any person that should carry her out of Sicilie. But besides these difficulties, there is one obstacle more which will undoubtedly prove greater then the other: which is, that she is already disposed of, and her affectiones questionless preingag'd to *Loreto* the Duches of Verona's youngest son, to whom I am confident she is speedily to be united by the Hymeneall bond of Marriage: and knowing this, I cannot but be ingenious with you, and let you know it too; if you may without delay teare from your heart that, which if longer retain'd will prove more difficult, if not impossible to be avoided. Therefore deare *Gentillus* (pursu'd he imbraceing me) let me conjure you if you Love your owne repose cashiere [dismiss] from your breast what will enevitably be the ruine of it. It grieves me that I cannot serve you which if I could, or that there were any possibility of gaining her favour for you, I protest I would endeavour though with the hazard of my Life to purchace you that content; but where I cannot serve you, I shall beare a larg share in what you suffer by sympathizing with you.

This, and much more did he say, and thereby left me not the least foundation to erect my tottering hopes on. When I had seriously weigh'd, and consider'd all those arguments he had used, I found them all so well grounded on reason that they left me nothing to reply. And then I began to consider, seeing I could never hope to possess you, how, or by what meanes I might obtaine what might give me satisfaction, and you no prejudice. Which I had no sooner thought on, but I addrest me to my friend *Tellamour*, beging him that he would permit me to give you an entertainment or two at his house, that I might have the happiness to see you once again before you left Palermo, promising him faithfully no way to importune you with my unfortunate passion. But though [fol. 8ʳ] he would not permit me the honour to treat you at his house, yet he promis'd however I should have the satisfaction to wait on you there, which he accordingly perform'd; for you were invited as you may remember Madam.

Yes my Lord (interrupted she) I very well remember that invitation; but had I known upon what score t'was made, I believe I should scarce have come.

I believ'd so too answer'd he, and t'was to your ignorance I imputed that favour: but to proceed, at Dinner I had the good fortune to be placed opposite to you, where I might feast my eyes with viewing you, as well as my body with the variety of those Viands that *Tellamour* had provided. I had then waiting on me a Page, excellent in Apelles's Art; whom I commanded to take your Picture as you set at Dinner; which he might conveniently enough do standing behind me. I charg'd him to shew to best of his skill; and truly I think he did, for the excellency of the Work, sufficently speakes the praises of the Workman: but that one time being not enough to finish it, I was constrain'd to beg of my Friend once more to favour me with such another courteous opportunity; which he willingly consented too, and accordingly performed; so that by the second siting the Picture was fully compleated, and with it ended my happiness: for the very next day you left Palermo, and return'd your Fathers; since which time I never saw you till I had the happiness so unexpectedly to meet you here: for I was presently after calld home by the command of my Father, upon a designe to marry me, then the most unpleasing thing in the World; ~~being~~ and indeed the most unseasonable; being (as I then was) prepossest with a passion for another.

For a long time I found inventions to evade his Propositions: but at last I was faine to force my inclinations to a seeming obedience; who otherwise might have look'd on me as a contemner of his paternall authority: wherefore to satisfie his desires I made my addresses to *Vindecia* (for so was that Lady call'd) but after so cold, and indifferent a manner, that all persons that saw my deportment perceiv'd they were rather feign'd than reall. My Father was one of the first that took notice of it, and rebuk'd me for it in such termes that it greev'd me I could not submit to his Will. But whilst I acted the pretended Lover to *Vindecia*, I many times addrest my reall courtship to your Shaddow, seting it before me, and importuning it with the most amorous, the most passionat complaints that the violence of my Passion could suggest; vainly imagining that the liveless Image of what I so ador'd had a power to mittigate my griefes, or redresse those torments that I then resented [felt].

For more then three yeeres, sighes and teares were my constant Companions; and thousands of extravagant actions did I commit, which nothing but the transports of Love could render excusable. But at last, time, with the help of my reason [fol. 8 ^{v}] (which began to reascend the throne from whence it had so long been banish'd) by degrees made me consider how vainly I pursu'd an impossibility, and for an imaginary felicity slighted a reall one; for no other but I would have esteem'd the affection of *Vindecia* so. In fine after much strugling I made it my resolution to adore you no longer as a Mistress (since I was certaine I must ne're enjoy you) but forever to love and esteeme you as a Sister: which resolution when I had once assum'd, I made it my earnest endeavour to comply sincerely with the Will of my Father to marry *Vindecia*; which in a short time after I did. But before I made her mine, I resolv'd to make my selfe intirely hers, by a perfect resignation to her of that heart which I once laid prostrate at your Feet Madam (continu'd he) which I found not halfe so difficult as I apprehended I should, for she carried Charmes both in her face and conversation so invinceable, as has since made me oft admire how I was able so long to resist them. But at length we were of two, made one, by the sacred bond of marriage, to the great satisfaction of both our Parents: and tis nere six yeares since which we have continu'd our affections in their primative ardour. So that now Madam (pursu'd he) you see I am not in a condition to implore ought from you but to be enroll'd in the number of your Friends, which I will never cease to be till I cease to live.

Gentillus having thus ended his story, the Unknown made this reply. The latter part of your relation my Lord (said she) gives me as high a satisfaction, as the begining gave me a feare I must have been necessarily guilty of a Crime I have alwayes abhorred more then the cruellest of Deathes: for had you continu'd that kindness (soe unfortunate to you) which you declare you once had for me; which has put you to the deare expence of so much griefe and trouble, I must notwithstanding have been ungratfull. For to have lov'd you as a servant, Vertue would have forbid it; and to have lov'd you for a Husband, those bands of Love which are never to be dissolved, that have knit my heart indissolubly to another till the hand of Death unties the Knot would have oblig'd me to the contrary; yet is it not *Loreto*.

Did you not marry *Loreto* then Madam (said he) as I was enform'd you would,

No *Gentillus* (repli'd she) I never married him; nor yet no other, nor is it he that I esteeme so deare, but another farre more ungratfull, though he was to too much tainted with that Stigian vice.[2] But seeing tis onely my Friendship you require, it shall be paid you with a zeale worthy the Object, and for duration be as lasting as your owne. And I assure you I shall account my selfe (although unfortunate in althings else) infinitly happy in this, that I may by a thing so inconsiderable as my Friendship but gratifie you in the least, for what you have done and suffer'd for my sake.

But may I not beg Madam (answer'd he) to know [fol. 9ʳ] who that happie, yet unworthy person is that has prov'd so ungratfull to you, since you assure me tis not *Loreto*; and what strange accident has made you turne travellour, especially to pass the Sea, which I have heard you had ever a great aversion too.

I did intend to make it my request to her (said *Ermilia*) to give me the relation of her life and fortunes if you had not prevented me.

That shall I willingly do (answer'd the Unknown) whenever your Majesty shall command me; though I know I cannot recount my miseries without renewing my griefes at recalling them into my mind but I shall wave those thoughts if I may give you any diversion by my relation.

Well (said the Queene) I will sommon you of your promise to morrow, for this day is too farre spent to begin your story; and besides I am willing my Lord *Gentillus* should be present at the audition of it, for I perceive he is unaquainted with the greatest part of those things which compose your misfortunes.

Your Majesty gesses right (said he) for the truth is I know very little of this Ladies adventures; for when I left Sicilie I believ'd her so happie, that I thought none had less cause to complain of Fortunes unkindness.

Ah *Gentillus* (repli'd the Unknown with a sigh drawne from the very Center of her heart) how much were you mistaken in your beliefe: tis very certaine I was then seemingly happie enough; and tis as true that that was the happiest time that ever I saw in my whole life; but even then was I far enough from that condition you thought me to be in, as you will understand by the Sequell of my story.

Gentillus kindly accepting the Queenes proffer of being present when the Sicilian Lady was to begin her ensuing discourse, took his leave both of *Ermilia* and her for that night, and departed to his Lodging; and the Sicilian by the Queens permission to her Appartment. But *Celia* would by no meanes let her

---

[2] Stigian vice refers to the forgetfulness of the dead after they cross the river Styx.

go alone; but besought the Queene she might be her Bed Fellow for that night, which request *Ermilia* having granted, they retir'd together into the Chamber appointed for the Unknown, whether being come, she minded *Celia* of the prom- ise she had made ~~her~~ to give her the relation upon what account that severe Law against Strangers came first to be made: which *Celia* after a little silence to rec- ollect what she had to say began: and taking a seat by the Unknown she thus assum'd her discourse [fol. 9ᵛ].

The Story of Artab^e^lla, Queen of Delphos

In my opinion none ought to account themselves, nor are they to be esteem'd by others, either happy, or unfortunate, till they have acted their last part on this Worlds Theatre: for many have the begining of their days most prosperous, yet end them miserably. On the otherside diverse persons live many yeares, nay almost their whole lives in perpetuall sufferings and sorrows, yet at last receive a happie period to all their miseries, and end their dayes in happiness. These are the secret Decrees of Providence; that none, how ~~happie~~ miserable soever might dispaire; nor no happie person should presume good Fortune will perpetually attend them. The truth of this assertion, what I have to relate will certainly tes- tifie; for none I really think ever underwent a larger share of misfortunes then *Artabella* our late Queene (who was the occation of that Law being enacted) yet found she at last a more propitious Fate.

She was born in Persia, Daughter to *Menzor* a Brother of *Achemenes's* King of that Countrey. No sooner was she born but she beheld herselfe unfortunate (had she been sensible of so great a loss) in the death of her Mother, a most Vertuous Princess: but her Father ~~seing~~ seeing *Eudora* dead, thought it his duty to take on him a double care for his little *Artabella* the onely Pledge of their marriage. Assoon as she was capable of it he sent her to the Court, to be educated with the Princess *Oriana* the Kings onely Daughter, and Heire apparant to the Crowne of Persia. The Princesse *Oriana* was elder then her Cousin *Artabella* by two yeares; but likeness of humour, and disposition, together with their education infused into the Soules of these two young Princesses such an intire affection, that the Relation that was between them was not so neere as their Friendship was great. They sweetly pass'd away their Infant dayes in all those pleasures and delights, wherewith great Princes Courts are for the most part still replenish'd, not once being sensible of the least of discontents. And as they increas'd in yeeres, so did they in beautie; for before the twelfth yeere of their ages they were become the marvels of the world; for Fames Shrill Trump had loudly proclam'd their praises in all parts of the Universe, though t'was but then the dawning of those morning beauties, the noon whereof shone with so great [fol. 10ʳ] a luster.

Oriana had receiv'd from Nature a more rarer tincture of red and white then *Artabella*, which made her be accounted the more beautifull: but in requitall, *Art-*

abella had something in her face so infinitly taking, and such a pleasing sweetness as nothing could be comparable to it; so that although *Oriana* was more faire, *Artabella* was the more lovely. Severall Kings and Princes were become their Vassalls, and at their Shrines had offer'd up their hearts: and secretly did they pine away their lives in pencive sadness for those Beauties which they could onely adore, but never hope to enjoy. *Artabella* had from her Infancy the greatest aversion to a passionate Love, or any thinge of that nature; that asmuch as in her lay she avoided the society of all men; that she might not be seen, nor be belov'd by any: esteeming it a cruelty to make mens torments the witnesses of her beautie, since she could returne no love againe. *Oriana* was not somuch averse to Love, or marriage as she; but made it indifferent to her, wisely resolving to submit to her Fathers Will, to be dispos'd by him as he thought fit. These were the inclinations of these two Princesses.

Amongst those Princes that sued to *Oriana*, *Octimasdes* King of Scythia was one: but it was generally believ'd it was the Kingdome rather then her he was ambitious of. He was a person of so ill a humour, and such a horrid aspect, that he was fitter to create feare in the heart of a young Lady then any other passion. And when he came to demand her of *Achemenes* in marriage, he did it in such an imperious manner, as if he would command rather the intreat his consent: but somuch was *Oriana* displeas'd at his deportment, that she detested him more for his insolence then for his deformity: nor was the King her Father's aversion to him much less then hers. Besides he saw many inconveniences must of necessity accrew to Persia by that alliance; as thereby bringing it into subjection to the Scythian Crowne, which he knew the Persians would never submit too: so that after he had conferred with his Councell, he found ^them^ all generally somuch against it, that he resolv'd *Oriana* should never be his: which when she knew, she was not a little joy'd. However the King though[t] fit to treat him with all imaginable respect, giving him all the opportunities that might be to make his addresses to the Princess, being secure enough that he could never prevaile to gain her. This he thought the best way in pollicie that he might not appeare openly to slight, or disoblige so potent a Monarch: soe that if he obtain'd not his desires, he might blame *Orianas* disdaine, not his dislike. But when *Octimasdes* saw that all his endeavours were fruitless, and that he could not with all his flatteries, and dissemulations [fol. 10ᵛ] gain the heart of *Oriana*, he would have perswaded *Achemenes* to make use of his paternall power, and royall authority to force her inclinations.

But the King answer'd, for that he must excuse him; for if his Daughter could not affect him, he should account himselfe rather a Tyrant, then a Father to compell her for any Maxime of State whatever, to give her person to one who had no interest in her heart. Nor should you (*Octimasdes* said he) methinks desire to be united to a Princess that loves you not: you see I have given you all opportunities, and meanes conducing to the wining her affection; but you see her aversion to you is such, as she will not be perswaded fairely to be yours, and truly I shall use no force.

Octimasdes being highly insenc'd at this resolution of the Kings, presently took his leave both of him and the Princess: but before he went away, he told her, perhaps when t'was too late she might repent her scorne. But being glad she was freed from his importunities she minded not his threatnings. No sooner was he return'd to Scythia, but he sent a Herald to *Achemenes* to let him know, that if he would not consent to make the Princess *Oriana* his; he would come with an Armie of threescore thousand Scythians, and destroy his Kingdome with Fire and Sword, and make *Oriana* kneell to obtain that which she had scornfully refused.

Tell your Master (answer'd *Achemenes*) the heart of *Oriana* is to be wonne by serviceses not threatnings. I shall not carry either Fire or Sword into his Dominions, but I shall endeavour to defend my owne from the invasion of soe ill a Neighbour.

And from me (said the Princess with a disdainfull smile) you may tell that proud King, he does much deceive himselfe in believing *Oriana* to be of such a poor base spirit to stoop so low to kneel to him; no, let him know I scorn to beg my life (were it in his power) much less his favour: and sooner would I imbrace Death in the most terriblest of shapes that ever the cruelest of Tyrants ere invented then render my selfe his: and did I distrust the puissance of my Fathers power were insufficent to defend me from him, I would fly to the protection of some other Prince; and make my selfe the reward of his services. In fine let him never expect ought from me but hatered and disdaine, since he has so farre provok'd me.

The Herald having receiv'd these answers, denounced Warre against Persia, and returned to Scythia; where he related to the King his Master the bad success of his message: which when *Octimasdes* understood, he presently caus'd a mighty Armie to be raised to carry into Persia. But whilst he was preparing in Scythia, *Achemenes* was not idle; for in little more then three monethes space he had rais'd a Force equall to the Scythian Kings. He, who was elected Generall of the Persians, was *Menzor*, *Artabellas* Father; [fol. 11ʳ] a valiant and well experienced Commander.

But that I may not trouble you Madam (said *Celia*) with these Warlike affaires which may seeme tedious to you, I will pass them over as succinctly as I can, without injuring the truth of my relation. Know then, after some short time these two great Bodies met upon the Frontires of Persia neere Scythia, where on a larg Plaine not farre distant from the Citty Bilbina, the King of Scythia, and *Menzor* joyn'd Battell. Victory was a long time nobly disputed on both sides, though with little advantage to either: but at last after many turnings, she utterly abondon'd the Persians Standards; to perch upon the Scythian Ensignes. Yet had they not much cause to brage; for they lost ~~that day~~ the best part of their Cavallrie, with all the chiefest of their Commanders. The Persians lost that day above 40000 men, but the Scythians not above 20000; but questionless they had not purchaced the Victory at so cheap a rate, had not the Valiant *Menzor* been so sorely wounded that he was carried out of the Field for dead.

The Fight being ended, the Persians retir'd to Bilbina to wait for a recrute which *Achemenes* sent them by that time *Menzor* was well recover'd of his Wounds; and that very day they arriv'd he left his Chamber, resolving no longer then the next day to deferre trying his Fortune a second time. But Fortune who is many times no less unjust then she is unconstant, prov'd herselfe so now by taking the part of those who fought on an unjust score; for she had almost been as unkind to the Persians in this Battell as in the former; by giving away the Victory againe; had she not beene stopt by the prodigious valour of two Cavalliers richly arm'd, and gallantly mounted: the Armes of the one was Azure colour set thick with starres of Gold; his Cask richly gilt, shaded with a Plume of Watched Feathers; on his Arme he bore a Shield wherein was portraid Mars the God of War. The Armes of the other were Coale black inlaid with Silver; his Casque of the same, with a Plume of Black and White Feathers, and in his Shield he bare the Sun eclipst.

These two Heroes came to the Fight just as the Persians were turning their backs upon their enemies; which when they saw (he in the Blew Armour cri'd out to them). Oh degenerate Persians whether do you runne; do you not blush to abandon your valiant Generall: whilst he is hewing you out a Path to victory, will you so shamefully turne your backes upon her when she is coming to salute you: and will you somuch belie that report which Fame gives of your Valours, which has been heretofore so unmatchable that it has brought us from the furthest part of the World to be pertakers of your renoune; and shall we find our selves deceiv'd. You may belie your Fames, and fly like Cowards, but we will take yon galant Mans part, and either bring him off victorious, or dy with him.

With that they flew into the [fol. 11ᵛ] thickest of the enemies Squadrons making all fly before them, rallying again the Persian scattered Troopes, and dispersing the Scythians; till at last with much paines haveing got up to the Generall, where he was nobly disputing his life singly against more then thirty of his Foes, without the least hopes of a reliefe.

Courage brave *Menzor* (said these Strangers to him) we are come to thy rescue, or to dye by thee.

These words they seconded with as many happie blows which gave death where e're they lighted: so that they soon freed him from that iminent danger which so highly threatned him. When they had done that they left him, and flew with the greatest speed imaginable to all those places where their assistance was most necessary. All that beheld their actions thought they saw somewhat in them more then mortall: as for *Menzor,* he believ'd they were the Tutelar Gods of Persia who had put on humane shapes to preserve vertue, and innocence from oppression, which must have suffer'd in their overthrow. But e're he was aware *Menzor* had engag'd himselfe so farre amongst his enemies againe, that he fell into a danger much greater then that he lately scap'd; for they had unhors'd him, thrown him to the grownd; and one of them after he was fallen, was searching the defect of his Armour that he might kill him; but was happily prevented by the coming of him who wore the blew Armes, who by accident seeing the danger he was in, flew to rescue him from the hands of those who sought by number more then valour to destroy that gallant person: the sight of his distress inspir'd him with a rage so furious, as all the Scythian Forces had been too little to resist: soe that coming up to him just as they were going to strike their Swords into his Breast; he cut off with one blow that Villans Arme that would have murder'd him, and with a second, sent another headless to the earth.

It were incredible should I tell you (said *Celia*) all those wonders he perform'd for the preservation of *Menzor*s life which without his assistance had question-less there expir'd; but let it suffice to tell you Madam, at length, though with much danger, and many wounds he brought him off safe; and presenting him with another Horse, he besought him not to precipatate himselfe into so high a danger any more. Having thus sav'd the Generalls life againe he left him, to goe seek his Friend, whom in little space he found acting gallantly for the honour of Persia. In short, these two Valiant Strangers so chang'd the face of things, that of almost conquer'd Persians, they became the Conquerours; for in such a man-ner they behaved themselves, that the cowardliest person in their Armie began to raise their spirits with the hopes of victory, and fell on more vigorously then ever, having such valiant Leaders: which when *Octimasdes* saw, he was so inrag'd at those two Strangers; especially him in the Blew Armes, that he vow'd his death; and that all the power of Persia should not shield him from his Vengeance. In this transported fury did he run to find him out; which at last he did: the [fol. 12ʳ] brave Stranger perceiving his intent came up to him;

King of Scythia (said he to him) if it is I you seek, know that I scorn to fly thee; for I esteeme it more honour to vanquish thee, then to overcome thy whole Armie.

Stay (repli'd *Octimasdes* netled with these words) I am not conquer'd yet: nor shalt thou find it so easie as thou believ'st it to overcome me; though thou hast disorder'd my Troopes, slaughter'd my Subjects, and almost wrested from me an assured Victory; yet shall I find a time to chastise thee for thy insolence. With that *Octimasdes* came up to him like a Lion enrag'd, giving him no time to reply. But the Unknown soon cool'd his courage; for with three blowes he sent him ~~grov~~ to the earth, grovelling in the Dust, in as bad a condition as *Menzor* was the last battell: and questionless he had there ended his life, had it not been prevented by a vast number of the Scythians who convei'd him to his Tent. The King being carried off a retreat was sounded by the Scythians, which was read-ily obey'd; the Persians pursuing them unto their Trenches, which were so well fortifi'd that they could not enter, but were constrain'd to retire. The Battell being ~~almost~~ thus ended, and the almost dying hopes of the Persians reviv'd by the sole valour of those strange Champions, they all return'd to the Campe:

whether being come, *Menzor* commanded a sumptuous Tent to be immediatly erected for the Strangers; which being accordingly perform'd, he himselfe waited on them thither, though they would by no meanes have permitted him. Having brought them in and embraced them with much affection, which the sight of those galant actions they perform'd for the honour of his Countrey had created in him:

Tis to you brave men (said he) that we must attribute the prosperous success of this days enterprise; and to your valours alone that we are all indebted for our lives, and liberties, and perhaps the King my brother his Crowne and Kingdome; wherein if there be ought to be found that may any way recompence so great a benefit, I dare engage you shall have no cause to repent your generosities, or belive ye have oblig'd an ungratefull Prince. And for my owne part Sir (said he to him in the Blew) I must ever owne my selfe your Debtor for my life in perticuler since you so generously sav'd it with the hazard of your owne; and as I hold it of you, so will I never scruple to loose it for your service.

We have done nothing Sir (repli'd the valiant Stranger) that can in the least merit these expressions from you; nor have we perform'd anything but what in Justice all generous persons are oblig'd too, going in quest of Glory as we did; to take part with those who have right on their side, as we were assur'd you had: though we are both Strangers here, not having been more then three dayes in this Kingdome; yet was it long enough to enforme our selves of the occation of this Warre, which told us you had Justice on your side; and that was a suffcent invitation to us to joyne with you: and if therein we have had the good fortune to do you any service, we shall account it reward enough that you [fol. 12ᵛ] esteeme it soe. And for my selfe my Lord (continu'd he) for what I had the happiness to performe for you, if I may obtain the honour of your Friendship, I shall value it at a higher rate then I would the gift of a Crowne; and for my Friend here I humbly beg the same.

If that be all you aske (answer'd *Menzor*) let me never receive favour more from any person if I refuse it you; and if in the highest degree I study not occations to evince how much I am your Friend, and yours Sir too (said he) to the other, who assur'd him he should never have cause to account his Friendship misplaced.

By this time the Chirurgion was come to dress their Wounds, which were no small number that they had receiv'd in the Fight: and till he saw them dress'd, he would not leave them, nor take the least care of his owne. But when they were disarm'd to have their Wounds search'd (for they had not till then put off their Armes) they appear'd so exceeding ~~lovely~~ gracefull and lovely, both for their shapes and features, that they seem'd as worthy of admiration for their handsomness, as for that generous valour whereof they had given such notable proofes. He who wore the Blew Armes (and seem'd by the respect the other paid him to be the more noble of the two) had a Face so full of Majesty, and Martiall too withall, that he might well have pass'd for that Deity he carried in his Shield: besides he had such a Princely deportment in all his actions, that all that saw him were strongly perswaded he was descended of no less then royall blood. The other was of so sweet and pleasing a countenance, and so extreame beautifull, that he had been in Femalle habit he might well have pass'd for one of the Fairest Ladies that e're was seen in Persia: and such, doubtless he had been taken for, had not his strength, and valour cleer'd the mistake, and told them by experience, he was none of that softer sex. *Menzor* having seen the strangers dress'd, and receiv'd from the Chirurgion an assurance that their wounds were nothing dangerous, which made him extreame joyfull, took his leave of them for that night, and departed to his owne Tent.

The next morning the Valiant Unknown calling his Squire to him, sent him to enquire how *Menzor* did; and how he had rested that Night; which he accordingly did. *Menzor* causing him to be brought into his presence, ask'd of him the same questions concerning his Master and the other, as he came to be resolv'd concerning him. To which (he answer'd) they were in as good a condition as could possibly be expected. *Menzor* supposing he might from the Squire learne who those two galant persons were, ask'd of him some questions to that intent. To which (he repli'd) he was sorry he could not satisfie his desire; for he had receiv'd a command from his Master before he left his Countrey, not to discover to any person who he, nor his companion were; neither their names, nor Countrey.

But what reason he had (added he) to [fol.13ʳ] conceale them is unknowne to me. But my Lord you may be pleas'd to know him who wore the Azurecolour'd Armour (who is my Master) by the name of *Diomed*, and the other by that of *Phasellus*. But thus much I will presume to tell you, that he I serve is of no ordinary or meane extraction; nor yet the other though much his inferior. He was bred up with my Master, who took such an intire affection to him even from his very Infancy; and *Phasellus* to him, that I really believe there was never greater Friendship between Brothers, then is between these two Friends. *Diomed* lives not but in *Phasellus*'s love, nor *Phasellus* but in his. This is all at present I dare tell your Highness, but if you please to permit me to aquaint my Master with your desires, possibly he may dispence with his resolution not to discover himselfe, and give me a command to satisfie you.

If your Master (said *Menzor*) has any reason to conceale himselfe, I would not seeme so uncivily importunate as for the satisfaction of my curiosity to desire the knowledge of ought that he intends to keep a secret; tis enough that I know him to be both generous and valiant, which qualities are sufficent to give me a higher esteeme for him then if I were assur'd he were the greatest Prince on earth and wanted those excellencies that render him so accomplish'd; for I ever preferred Vertue before the highest birthes; and count it farre better to be good then great: and if I desir'd to know who your Master is, it was on no other score than that I might give him that respect which is his due; but seeing he thinks fit not to be known, I ~~shall hens~~ shall henceforth give him the respects his merits justly challenge and that is as much as if I were certaine he were born a Prince.

That day, and the next were spent wholy in consultations what was most expedient to be done concerning the carrying on of the Warre. Some were of one opinion, and some of another: but the result of all was, that the Persians should (if it were possible) force their enemies to fight againe before such time as they could receive any new supplies: or in case they refused to fight, that they should storme their Campe, though it were a matter of great difficulty, and much danger. To this intent the Persian Generall sent one prively the third Night after the Battell to spie the enemies Trenches; and where they might with the most facillity be surpriz'd. But when they came into the Campe (which was not till the dead of Night) he found no Guard as he expected, onely many Tents, with some Colours standing, and some few men to maintaine the Fires: which when he had seen, admiring what might be the occation of the Scythians flight, he return'd to his Generall with this intelligence: who musing at it no less then he that brought it, knowing the enemy to be in no such extreamity as to force them ignominiously to fly from a Foe, whom not long before they seem'd rather to dispise then apprehend.

Notwithstanding he commanded a Troop of Horse to go into the Scythian Campe and Ceaze on those who were left behind, and bring them to him; which was accordingly done: for those few accounting it rather madness then Valour to resist [fol. 13ᵛ] a five times greater number then their owne, yeelded themselves Prisoners to the Persian Troop ~~who~~ being presented to *Menzor*, he asked of them the cause of their Armies sudden departure; which they upon the hopes of freedome (as he upon the word of a Prince promis'd they should have if they discover'd to him the the truth) ingeniously confest, that their King died of those woundes he receiv'd from the hands of him who wore the blew Armes immediatly after he was brought into his Tent: which unfortunate disaster (as they said) had struck such a terrour into all their hearts, that they had as little the power as the Will any longer to continue a Warre, the begining had prov'd so fatall, and disadvantagious to them; though some of the more dareing Spirits perswaded him who had the supreame power after the Kings disease to stand it out one battell more; that they might revenge their Soveraigns death, and their owne disgrace. But the wiser Partie concluded t'was better to ~~dest~~ desist now then further to exasperate the King of Persia whom they had already but too much provok'd, by entering his Kingdome in a Hostile, and invasive manner, without any just cause that might excite them to it: and therefore they suppos'd it far better to depart his Teritories whilst they retained a power to continue in them, then stay till they were driven out; which might be a meanes to obtain a peace from *Achemenes*: and besides, they found themselves reduced to so low a condition that they were utterly disabled from fighting againe, till they receiv'd some supplies; which they fear'd would be so long ere they arriv'd that it was more then probable they must be reduced to great necessities. Thus after they had weigh'd all considerations, they concluded without delay to depart that very night; leaving their Tents as they were, and some few souldiers to keep in the Fires on purpose to delude the Persians; that they might not suspect their flight till they were farre enough from their pursute. Withall they told him, that the ensuing night they had also departed for Scythia had they not been prevented; but they would not dispaire of a returne since they had the good Fortune to fall into the hands of so gracious a Prince: and the rather, since he could derive no advantage either from taking away their lives, or detaining them Prisoners.

No (said *Menzor*) seeing you have been so ingenious in what I demanded of you, you have my promise for your release, and are free to depart when ever ye will. But (continu'd he) you may see the Heavens have took on them the protection of Innocence, by the ill success of your Designe; and that the Gods are no favourers of an unjust cause: and notwithstanding ye have done enough to excite the Persian King to a continuance of that Warre, which you, not we began: yet I know he so much detests any thing of wronge or injustice, that he will never make an ill example his president. Goe therefore and perswade your Country to sue for peace; which if they speedily do, I dare [fol. 14ʳ] engage they shall obtaine it: but if not, they will repent when tis too late. For believe it you will find it farre more difficult then your late King expected to conquer Persia; possibly his Successors passion may not somuch blind his reason as to refuse such an advantagious proffer as this I make you.

After they had told *Menzor* if it were in their power, to effect it, Scythia should henceforth be as much a Friend to Persia, as of late it had been an enemie, they departed to their own countrey. The War being thus finish'd, which was fear'd would have cost a much larger expence both of blood, and time. Finish'd did I say, ah no, it was but for a while suspended: for as hidden Fire, which may for a time be conceal'd, yet at last breakes out into a more violent Flame, so did this War. But *Menzor* having quieted all disturbances for the present; assoon as his wounds would permit him, and that his two valiant Assistants (*Diomed* and *Phasellus*) were in a condition fit for travell, took his march with the remainder of his Army toward Susa. But before he arriv'd there, Fame had carri'd thither the report of his success; with the Magnanimous Valour and Gallantry of *Diomed* and *Phasellus*, which inflam'd *Achemenes* with an ardent longing to see those two persons which had done such brave things for the honour of Persia.

But being at length arriv'd at that proud City, *Menzor* tryumphantly enter'd it under a Canopie of state, of cloath of Tissue, supported by twelve of the chiefest of the Nobility. On each side of him rode *Diomed* and *Phasellus*, who were admir'd by all the people as they pass'd along, no less for their beautie, and comly proportion, then for their valiant actions, and follow'd with loud praises, and acclamations even to the Palace gates: but as they alighted to enter, they were met by the Faire *Artabella*, who hearing of her Fathers returne, was come downe into the great Court of the Palace to meet him, and to congratulate his safe return. She was waited on by *Saparilla* (one of her Maids) and two Pages who carried up

her Traine. She no sooner saw her father, but she flew to him on the Wings of
Love, and Duty; and flinging herselfe at his Feet, he reach'd her his hand to raise
her up, which she kiss'd, and embraced with teares of Joy.

Ah my Lord (cry'd she with transport) ah my deare Father am I so happie as
to see you here againe in saftie; not being able to say more, excess of joy stifleing
her words: but these few expressions (though confus'd) were more emphaticall
then a much larger speech.

Menzor having rais'd her up, and embraced her with a most tender affection;
yes my deare Child (said he) your Father is return'd in saftie, and with victory
too: but if the honour of your Countrey or my life be dear to you (as I have no
reason to believe the contrary) returne your thankes to those Celestiall Powers
that rule our Destinies, and then to these brave Men (continu'd he pointing to
Diomed and his Friend) to whose noble valour you must ever acknowledge your
selfe oblig'd (next to the [fol.14ᵛ] goodness of Heaven) for so transcendant a
favour; and in a more perticuler manner to this generous person (said he takeing
Diomed by the hand and presenting him to her) without whose assistance you
had had no Father to have wellcom'd home. *Diomed* being presented to her by
Menzor, saluted her with an infinite respect, and stooping to kiss her Robe, she
gave him her hand very graciously, saying is it to you Sir that I am indebted for
my Fathers Life; sure then, the highest, and most signall favour I can shew you,
you have more then merited from me.

Prince *Menzor* and your selfe Madam (answer'd he) are pleas'd to set too
high a value on a service so inconsiderable, that it deserves not the owning; since
I have done nothing more then what Justice oblig'd me too: but had I known
he had been the Father of so much perfection, or been the bestower of so rich
an Ornament on the World to adorne it, as such an incomparable beauty as you
(most Excellent Princess) are Mistress of; that alone had been a sufficent invitation to me to espouse his quarell.

This complement call'd up a scarlet blush into the Face of *Artabella*, which
added more lustre to that beauty which of it selfe was sufficent to ravish all
that beheld it: and this effect it had on the heart of *Phasellus*, who stood as one
b[e]reav'd of all sense, or motion (while *Diomed* paid her his respects) having
his eyes fix'd on her into whose breast his heart was flowne: for Love no sooner
made an assault but that he won the Fort.

Perhaps Madam (said *Celia*) you may think it strange or indeed scarce credible, that Love should make so absolute a conquest in so short a time: but had
you seene those charming Graces, and attracting Beauties she was owner of,
you would not think it soe: for in the opinion of all that ever saw her, she was
without comparisson the most accomplish'd Piece that ever the hand of Nature
drew: and therefore tis no wonder that *Phasellus* who was extreame amorous,
should be caught (in those snares which are aptest to take a heart susseptable of
Loves impressions) at the first view. After *Diomed* had left her; *Menzor* presented
Phasellus to her that she might take a perticuler notice of him too. After which,

Menzor (accompanied with his two Friends) went to give *Achemenes* an account of the Warre whom he met at the top of the Staires, attended by severall persons of honour belonging to the Court: for the King having just then heard of his Brothers arrivall, was coming to meet him. *Menzor* no sooner saw the King; but he threw himselfe at his Feet; but *Achemenes* quickly rais'd him up, and embraced him with the most tender ^sentiments^ <u>resentments</u>[3] that the affection for so good a Brother could inspire him with.

Wellcome my dearest Brother (said he to him) the Victory and Peace you have brought with you gives not so high a satisfaction to my People, as your safe returne gives me a joy.

The Peace I bring Sir (repli'd *Menzor*) I wish may be as lasting, as the Fame of those who purchaced it: for my owne part I pretend no title to it; for had it not been for the noble effects that the (never sufficently) admired Valour of these brave Strangers has produced, I had certainly lost my life, and you that benefit you now enjoy. I will not question your justice somuch, as to implore ought from [fol. 15ʳ] you in their behalfes, but expect Sir you should requite them with the greatest of your royall favours.

No, Brother (said the King) Vertue needs no other intercessor besides its merit; which shines so bright in these persons who have oblig'd me, that the highest recompence Persia can present them will (I feare) fall short of their deserts, and be too little to express my gratitude. Then turning to *Diomed* and *Phasellus* he embraced them likewise with as affectionate a kindness as if they had been Sons rather then Strangers to him; expressing an infinit esteeme for them both: to which they made each of them a sutable reply.

After this the King retired with *Menzor* to his Cabinet, where he told *Achemenes* so many hansome things of *Diomed*, that the bare recitall of them created in him a greater value for him then he had for any man in his Dominions *Menzor* excepted. He presently setled on him a Revenue for so long as he should make Persia his aboade sufficent to maintaine him an equipage, and port answerable to the greatest Prince in the Realme. *Achemenes* and *Menzor* being retired, some of the Gentlemen belonging to the King, conducted *Diomed*, and *Phasellus* to lodgings appointed for them; which were both stately, and in all respects befitting the magnifficence of so mighty a Monarch. The Chambers were severall, yet nere neighbours one to the other: but as nigh as they were, *Diomed* thought the single Particion of a Wall too great a distance; not enduring that any thing should separate betwixt him and his deare *Phasellus*; nor would he be perswaded to let him absent himselfe from him in the night, but made him the constant partner of his Bed, as he had made him the chiefest possessor of his Friendship. The Gentlemen which waited on them thither, having perform'd that civility departed, leaving them to enjoy that repose they thought necessary after their

---

[3] The word <u>resentments</u> is underlined but not crossed out; carets indicate that ^sentiments^ is intended to replace "resentments."

toylsome travell; to which rest, *Diomed* soon dispos'd himselfe, after some discourses of severall theames: as of *Menzors* galantry, and the Kings kindness: but that which they chiefeliest insisted on, was the lustre of those two bright Starres (*Oriana* and *Artabella*) whose beauties were as blazing Comets to attract the eyes of all beholders with wonder to admire them. But these rare Objects wrought no other effect on the mind of *Diomed* then an equall admiration, and esteeme for both: but though *Phasellus* admir'd the Princess asmuch as *Diomed*, yet he adored *Artabella* with so intire a reverry, that the growing Idea of her inchanting graces which presented themselves to his fan^c^ie permitted him not that night to close his eyes, or take one minutes rest.

But if *Phasellus* was that night disturb'd in his repose; the Innocent *Artabella* was no less disquieted with the thoughts of him: for (as afterwards she confest to *Saparilla*) she was not able to banish him from her mind one moment after she first saw him, nor could she fancy she ere saw ought that in her eyes appear'd so lovely. After making fruitless [fol. 15ᵛ] endeavours to shake off those Cogitations which she as little k̶n̶e̶w̶ approv'd as knew the reason of; she began to mistrust by the character she had heard given of it, that it was some infection proceeding from one of Cupids shafts, which undiscern'd had strook her to the heart; which disease she had alwayes dreaded more then death:

[W]ith this apprehension she being exceedingly surpriz'd suddenly started up in her bed; and fetching a deep sigh, ah *Artabella* (said she to herselfe). What is the matter; or what reason hast thou to confine thy thoughts to one object more then another: certainly none, tis blind passion, and not reason that provokes thee to it; and shall I yeeld my selfe a servant to what I have hitherto made my slave: What strange extravagant madness is this in me to tye my thoughts to the Image of a stranger, and he perhaps of obscure birth when divers Kings, and Princes which have been my vasalls, could ne'er obtaine from me the least regard. Perchance (continu'd she) tis thus *Cythere's* Son intends to punish me for my contempt of his authority, and neglect of those who were in all respects my equalls, by making me affect one who may be much my inferior: but if this be thy aime, Believe it Cupid thou shalt miss thy marke; for sooner will I die then submit to a yoke I have hitherto so much dispis'd: well may'st thou knock at my breast (as now thou doest) but never shalt thou find an enterance to robbe the heart of *Artabella* of that quiet it has ever yet enjoy'd.

If thou wouldst give away thy liberty fond girle (pursu'd she) why did'st thou not chuse to bestowe it on *Diomed* who has highly oblig'd thee by the preservation of thy Fathers life (rather then on *Phasellus*) and then thy folly might be stil'd gratitude, not passion; which might a little extenuate thy fault: but if thou givest admittance to this blind Guest, thou wilt leave thy selfe no Advocate to plead on thy behalfe, but all the world must needs condemne thee both of lightness, and indiscretion, so easily to abandon thy freedome to one who as little dreames of love for thee, as thou ought'st to thinke of conferring thine on him. O never give the World occation to loose that opinion it has of thy vertue, nor by a compliance with this traitorus passion (which seekes to rebell against thy reason) blemish thy reputation which is so pure a Tincture, that the least staine will never be defaced. But why (said she after a Little silence) should I endeavour to withstand what possibly the Heavens have decreed the Destinies may be have so ordain'd it, that my former aversion to Love should be a meanes of preserving my affections intire for him: besides, I know not, but he may be a person every way worthy of me; which if he be, what prejudice can it be for me to follow in that Track where many greater, and wiser woemen then my selfe have led the way.

Then after a little pause, fie *Artabella* fie (said she), art thou not asham'd to give admittance to ~~so~~ such guilty thoughts as these: if thou wilt needs list thy selfe under Loves Standerd, yet stay till thou mayest do it on honourable termes; stay for shame till thou art conquer'd by the [fol. 16ʳ] services of him to whom thou desirest to resigne thy freedome, and do not basely prostitute thy heart to one to whom thy person is a stranger too; and one who does not, nor possibly never will sue for that favour from thee; either banish these crimenall desires from thy soule, or cloister up thy selfe in darkness, and never more look on that Light which presented thee with so troublesome an object which is like to prove the ruine of thy repose.

It was almost break of day ere she could make a truce with these inquietudes, or could admit slumber to close her eyes: but at length o'ercome with watching (a thinge, which till that night she had never been acquainted with) she fell into a sound a sleepe, as *Saparilla* found it no easie matter the next day to awake her; which she had not presum'd to do, if her kindness to her mistress had not made her apprehend something of ill in that unseasonable sleep. After *Saparilla* had wak'd her, she arose, and dress'd her; but stir'd not out of her Chamber that day, nor many other that succeeded; pretending an indisposition for her confinement, that she might put in practice what she had resolv'd. But soe was *Oriana* concern'd for her dissembled illness, that she was never from her; making herselfe a Prisoner rather then she would want her deare *Artabellas* company.

The Princess perceiving her Cousins to be rather an indisposition of the mind, then body; made it her designe to divert her by all manner of pleasant discourses; and one day, feigning more mirth then her reserv'd temper was wont to allow in rallery (she ~~sh~~ said) laughing; introth Cousin I thinke thou art in Love, thy humour is so suddenly, and strangly alter'd.

Why Madam (repli'd *Artabella* with a very serious tone) will Love make one mellancholy.

Soe I have heard (said the Princess) but know nothing of it by experience.

I believe Madam (answer'd she) you are not ignorant of my hatered to that idle passion and therefore I cannot think you really believe me guilty of so great a folly, as volluntarily to fall into a snare I have hitherto diligently avoided: you know Madam no person is ever in one and the same temper.

Tis very true (repli'd *Oriana*) I know they are not, but for you who were alwayes so free from mellancholy that I never saw you in my life put on a discontented look; now to be sad; especially in this time of so universall a joy, to what cause but Love can I impute it.

You will do me Justice (answer'd she) to impute my ill humour to anything rather then that; tis certaine I was never ceaz'd on by so deep a sadness in my life; but the reason is unknown to me; and therefore I cannot but apprehend it ominous; and dread something of misfortune in it; but I hope ere long to reasume my former temper.

This discourse was broaken off by the coming in of *Menzor* who brought with him *Diomed*, and *Phasellus* to visit *Artabella*, in whose company, and *Orianas* they spent that afternoon. If the Princess before fanci'd *Artabella* to be an Amorist, she might have chang'd her suspition into a certaintie upon the enterance of *Phasellus*, had she but observ'd her change of countenance; for no sooner did she see him come into the Chamber but [fol. 16ᵛ] her Face was painted with a Vermillion blush. *Phasellus* saw it, and took notice of it too, but knew not whether to impute it to displeasure, or a more obliging cause. This second enterview perfected the victory on both sides; for they were both conquerours, yet knew they not that either of them were overcome. A thousand sighes did *Phasellus* send that afternoon to *Artabella* as tokens of his passion, and would have had those dumbe messengers have told ^her^ that, which his tongue had not the confidence to disclose.

Severall were the discourses that pass'd in this noble society; but being nothing pertinent to my story (said *Celia*) I shall pass them by. Many times after this had *Phasellus* the satisfaction of seeing *Artabella* though never no opportunity of converse with her (but what diverse persons were witnesses too) though he diligently sought it; but she so carefully avoided, as gave him not the liberty to acquaint her with what she dreaded to know, yet could not keep her heart from desiring. All other meanes being deni'd him, he resolv'd his Pen should be the Ambassadour of his thoughts, and thereby let her understand the passion hee had for her: which he thus effected.

Every day did *Artabella* usually walk in the Gardens belonging to the Palace, attended with her Maids (and sometimes accompani'd with the Princess) to take the Aire, and tast the pleasure of the Evenings coolness; that Countrey being exceeding hot for the greatest part of the yeare. An houre before *Phebus* left the earth was the time she most commonly destin'd for that excercise, and oft when she was weary would she retire into an Arbour that stood in the center of a Little Wilderness which was encompass'd with a Mote in such a manner as made it a perfect Island: this place, of all other in the Garden was that in which she most delighted; which *Phasellus* had observ'd by her constant frequenting it. [T]hither stole he one day prively, not long before he expected she would take her walk; and on a Table of black Marble which stood there, he laid a Letter where he was sure she could not miss of seeing it when ever she came thither: this having done, he departed, trembling with feare for the success; yet he went not out of the Wilderness, but secretly conceal'd himselfe there; which he might easily enough do, the

Trees standing so very thick that he might without being discover'd both heare, and see all that was done, or said in the Arbour.

His designe answer'd his wishes for that Evening *Artabella* came thither onely with her Favourite (*Saparilla*) and entering in; she perceiv'd a Paper lye on the Table; curiosity at first led her to look on it, supposing it might be something that *Oriana* might have writ for her owne diversion, and carelessly left there, not suspecting any would come thither to peruse it, unless herselfe, from whom she believ'd the Princess had not any thing conceal'd; so that she thought, she might without a breach of Friendship, or civility see what it was: but having taken it up, she soon perceiv'd her errour, finding it to be a Letter seal'd, with a Superscription directed to herselfe. The hand she was utterly a stranger too, nor could she imagine how it [fol. 17ʳ] came thither: calling *Saparilla* to her, she ask'd her if she could resolve her whose hand it was; but she repli'd she knew not, nor did she ever see any like it. This assurance rais'd in *Artabella* a suspition that it was convei'd thither by the subtilty of some pretended Lover; which apprehension perplex't her with a thousand fancies; nor could she readily determine whether she had best peruse it or no. One while she resolv'd to teare, or burne it without seeing what it contain'd; but then she thought, he that had given her that trouble would find meanes to renew it; and if it were any thinge of Love, she believ'd she might better frustrate their designes by her knowledge, then by her ignorance of it. Many times did she take it up, and as often throw it from her with disdaine, as one divided between feare, and desire: but at last, catching it up; what said she, shall I so much distrust my owne strength, as not to dare look on a piece of Paper. With that, she unript the Seale and read these words.

To the Princess Artabella

> *Were I possessor Madam of as many Crownes as you of beauties, I should account it more glorious to be your slave, then to weare those glittering Diadems: and at the feet of her would I prostrate them with a joy not to be express'd, on the Altar of whose beauty I have offer'd up my heart. I confess the meaness of the Votary may render the Offering despicable; but since those Divinities we reverence are not offended with the addoration of the poorest Mortall, my hopes are, that you who are so resembling to those Powers in all things, will not scorne a Devotion of the same nature: which I am confin'd to pay you with a zeale equall to that I pay the Diety I adore. But if my presumption makes me soare so high, that the Wings of my too to ambitious desires are sing'd at the Sunne of Beautie, so that I find poor Icarus's[4] fate to be drown'd in the Ocean of dispaire; I shall however receive this satisfaction, if I must not live your Adorer, I shall dy your Martyre. This declaration (Divine Princess) possibly may displease you; but if it does, remember*

---

[4] In Ovid's *Metamorphoses* (Book 8, ll. 185–235), Icarus and his father Daedalus escape Crete by flying with wings made of feathers and wax. Daedalus warns his son that if he flies too near the sun, the wax will melt and he will fall to earth.

Madam tis the vastness of your owne perfections which are the occation of my Crime: and if for giving admittance to a passion which is attended with so sacred a respect, you believe you have reason to be offended with me; I have certainly more to complaine of you; who insteed of a reward for that service I had the honour to performe for your Countrey, instantly ceaze me your Prisoner; from which Captivity I can never hope for a redemption, unless by Death, except your favour pay my ransome. But so far am I ^from^ repining at this condition, that I esteeme it more glory to weare the Princess Artabellas Chaines ^then^ the Crowne of the Universe accounting those the greater Ornament. I dare not Madam acquaint you with his name [fol. 17ᵛ] *who is the perfectest of your Adorers Lest he receive the sentence of death by an eternall banishment, but live in hope the Fates will one day furnish him with an opportunity of evincing by the greatness of his future services the vastness of his passion who is the humblest of your Slaves, and*

Your Eternall Vassall

But if she were perplex'd when she onely suspected what it was, she was even confounded with vexation now that she was certaine ~~who it was~~ of it. A good while she stood seriously considering this adventure; at last fetching a deep sigh, and letting the Letter fall out of her hand, she sate down, leaning her Arme on the Table, and her Cheek on her hand, musing on one passage of the letter; wherein he who had writ it, had mention'd the services her Countrey had receiv'd from him; which made her confident it came either from *Diomed* or *Phasellus*; but whether of the two she could not determine, which rendred her trouble the greater.

Saparilla who stood by observing her Princesses disturbance by her deportment, threw herselfe at her Feet, beging her with teares, that she might not be a stranger to those thoughts that she aparently saw gave her so great a disquiet. At this action of *Saparillas*, *Artabella* being come a little to herselfe; ask'd her what t'was that she would know.

What tis that afflicts you Madam (repli'd she) if I am not more unworthy to be a pertaker of your concernes then hitherto you have thought me. *Artabella* loving her intirely, could not deny ought to her intreaties, much less her teares, but took up the letter, and gave it her to read. See there (said she) the occation of my discontent.

Saparilla having read it o're and o're repli'd, I cannot for my life apprehend Madam why this should disquiet you so highly as I see it does; since this is not the first person that has discover'd a passion for you; and yet I never saw you somuch concern'd at it, as now you are at this. Perchance you know him to be a person infinitly beneath your Illustrious extraction, and that may excite your displeasure: but pardon me Madam if I presume to say, tis a trouble that proceeds from some other cause then anger, the effects whereof appeare so legible in your face.

Thou gessest right (said *Artabella*) for anger is not that passion that disturbes me most.

Ah Madam (cry'd *Saparilla*) will you not tell me what it is. I protest tis no vaine curiosity that make me thus inquisitively to enquire into the occation of your discontent; but onely an earnest desire to find out some remedy for your maladie.

Yes (said she sighing) I would tell thee, did not shame tye up my tongue.

I cannot think you capable (repli'd *Saparilla*) of a thought you need blush to owne. [fol. 18ʳ]

Time was (said the Princess) I had a Soule so pure, that if the most crimi-nall of my thoughts had been written here (pointing to her forehead) I need not to have blush'd' though read by the severest Critticks; but now alass it is not soe (continu'd she letting fall some Christall drops from her faire eyes) I am no lon-ger the innocent *Artabella*, and for that I hate my selfe: tis needless for me to say more when I have told thee that I haue which I could have wish'd I had still been ignorant of my selfe. I love, is not that enough to make thee wonder; if it be not I will tell ^thee^ more to aggravate my crime, I love *Phasellus*; who possibly not once throwes away a thought on me: or admit his passion equall'd mine; yet can-not that exempt me from being guilty of the highest folly, or at best the greatest fraility; in suffering my selfe to be led Captive by that insulting passion: Must I who have sworne allegiance at Dianas Shrine[5] turne Rebell and submit my selfe a subject to blind Cupid her greatest Foe: but if I must, and that the Forces of my reason proves too feeble to defend me from the allconquering power of this Assailant, I'le dye ten thousand deathes rather then suffer this unwilling Subjec-tion to transport me to ought that may prejudice my duty or my honour.

That you love Madam (said *Saparilla*) I confess is to me a wonder, because I always believ'd your Breast impenitrable; but since you are capable of Loves impressions, I do not at all admire you love *Phasellus*; seeing he is certainly the most admirable, the most lovely person (in the opinion of all that see him) that ever was look'd on by mortall eye. But if you think your selfe blameable in your kindness for him; give me leave Madam to tell you; that there is no action but the intention renders either good or ill; and therefore your passion being grounded on Vertue (as I am confidently assur'd it is) you need not exclame against your selfe for giving admittance to that which the wisest could ne're resist; and for which you have the example of many vertuous Princesses to plead on your behalfe. Besides, Love being not simply evill in it selfe, unless it makes us transgress those limits which Vertue prescribes it; in my Judgment then tis no such hainous crime for you to love, nor yet to love *Phasellus* neither: though perhaps you may feare a check from discretion for making an unknown person the object of your pas-sion, and one for ought you know of obscure birth or meane extraction: but let

---

[5] Diana is the goddess of the hunt, moon, and chastity, but here the allusion seems to be to virginity.

not this apprehension perplex you, since he may as well be thought to be sprung from some Royall branch, seeing the grandure of his renouned actions seemes as if they silently proclaim'd as much. Or admit he be as low as we can fancy him, yet Vertue alone retaines a power to raise her Followers to that sublime condition, from whence persons that have not such Heroick Soules oft tumble downe. But if your trouble springs from a feare, that you have not vanquish'd his heart who has conquer'd yours; methinkes this letter may expell that doubt: for who but *Phasellus* can it come from.

My doubt of that (repli'd *Artabella*) is it which creates my trouble; for I find nothing in it that gives me any assurance that it came not from *Diomed* rather then him: and then do but think, how more then unhappie my condition will be should *Diomed* love me; since I know my [fol. 18ᵛ] Father has so high ^an esteeme^ of his Vertue, such a reall Friendship for his person, and so great a desire to requite his gallantry by some very extraordinary favour; as I have oft heard him say, there is not any thing in his power to give, which he accounts not too meane a recompence for that assistance he receiv'd from him when his life lay at stake. Then seeing tis so, have I not all the reason in the world to feare, if he had but the confidence to demand me of my father, that he would assoon obtaine as aske; and when once his passion is seconded by the authoritie of a Father; what have I left to defend my selfe against it; but must rellish either of Ingratitude, or want of duty, or both. I confess *Diomed* may justly merit the esteeme of the greatest Princess on earth; and oft have I admir'd why my fancie should lead me to affect *Phasellus* rather then him, since my obligations are farre greater to *Diomed* then to *Phasellus*: I know no reason for it, but must conclude, tis the uncontrolable power of my Destiny that will have it so, from whence there is no appeale.

Cease deare Madam (said *Saparilla*) to afflict your selfe; and do not I beseech you anttedate your troubles; tis time enough to greeve when you have just cause; which now you have not, unless you will torment your selfe with an apprehension, which has no other originall then a bare suspition. I will not say but *Diomed* may love you, but I dare pawne my life *Phasellus* does. ·

What makes you think so (hastily repli'd *Artabella*, interrupting her)

That, said *Saparilla*, which would have made you, or any other certaine of it; had you but taken notice of his deportment that time your Father brought him with *Diomed* to waite on you: he entered your Chamber in the highest disorder that ever I beheld one in my life; he blush'd, look'd pale, and approach'd you with a trembling which sufficently express'd the aggitation of his Soule. For my part I admire all there present did not observe it as well as I.

All this might be (answer'd *Artabella*) and yet I no cause of it, for there was the Princess with me at the same time; and why might not her presence worke that alteration which thou observedst in *Phasellus*.

No, Madam (repli'd she) all his actions assur'd me the contrary: for whilst he was there, his eye was perpetually on you; and as you may very well remem-

ber, he appli'd himselfe wholy to you in all his discourses, not once regarding the
Princess after he had paid her his repects at his coming in.

This may be too (said *Artabella*)] yet may it onely be a personated part, the
better to disguise his love to her, thinking it not safe (perhaps) to disclose to the
World a passion for the Daughter of so great a King: and therefore possibly he
had rather have me suspected for the Object of his Love, then *Oriana*.

Though I doubt not in the least (repli'd *Saparilla*) that you are she whom
Phasellus adores, and consequently that this letter came from him; yet will I not
beg you to be of the same opinion, till I have convinced you by some undeniable
demonstration; which [fol. 19ʳ] ere to morrow night I question not to do; therefore good Madam lay aside all disquiet thoughts, and hope the best till then.

Artabella (repli'd not, onely sigh'd) and rising up was going away: but before
she had stir'd three steps from her seat *Phasellus* came in from that place where he
had stood all this while conceal'd; and throwing himselfe at her feet.

It is too long Divine Princess (said he) for you to be held in suspence till to
morrow night, since you may this very moment be resolv'd who that presumptious person is, that has assum'd the confidence to present you his addresses in
that crimenall paper, for such I must terme it, since it has disturb'd your quiet:
tis no other then *Phasellus* is guilty of it; Late the Unfortunate, now the happie
Phasellus: for to that sublime condition has your confession rais'd me by acknowledging to *Saparilla* that I am not indifferent to you; which is a blessing I prize so
highly, that to have obtain'd it, I would have despised the Empier of the World,
and all the felicities that the most happie Creatures ever knew: but if the violence
of my passion has carried me beyond the limits of my duty, engaging me to stay
here to make a discovery of your inclinations (which else I should never have
been able by any other meanes to have understood) and thereby learne my destiny
from the Oracle of my Fate; which otherwise I must still have continu'd ignorant
of: pardon me Madam I beseech you this one offence, and I vow by those bright
eyes of yours which took me Prisoner the first moment they encounter'd mine,
ne're to displease you more: and for what is past, inflict on me never so severe a
Pennance for the expiation of my fault, and by all that's sacred I'le inflict it on
my selfe without a murmur; onely forgive but this, and permit me to adore you.

Assoon as *Artabella* saw him enter the Arbour, she was confident he had
overheard what she had said to *Saparilla* concerning him; which so surpriz'd her
that she was even confounded with shame: not having confidence to look *Phasellus* in the face, but with a downe cast look she stood as one convicted of some
horrible offence. Long it was ere she recover'd out of her amaize, but much longer ere she could returne an answere to what *Phasellus* had said: for shame and
resentment strove so in her breast (to find her most secret thoughts laid open to
him, whom of all men she least desir'd should know them) that for a good space
it utterly depriv'd her tongue of its faculty: but at last, anger proving more powerfull in her then shame she thus repli'd.

It were invain to deny, what your inquisitiveness has rendered soe intelligible; I must confess I have lov'd you; but your incivility, or your rashness call it which you will; has lost you that place in my esteeme, which somthing that I fancied excellent in you had gain'd: and believe it, you shall derive little advantage from your discovery; for I command you if you have any respect for her, to whom you have shewn so little, evince it by [fol. 19ᵛ] never coming in my presence more; since I cannot behold you without proclaming to the World my shame, by those blushes which the sight of you will paint upon my face. Nor do I this so much to punish you as my selfe; for foolishly doating on a person who by his temerity, has rendred himselfe unworthy of the conquest of *Artabellas* heart.

Ah Madam (answer'd he flinging himselfe again at her feet and embraceing her knees) are you then determin'd to be cruell; and must poor *Phasellus*, who even now believ'd himselfe the happiest person breathing, be thrown from that height of felicity downe to an Abiss of misery: and must one offence (and that not wholy unexcusable, if the irresistable power which compell'd me to it, may be impartially consider'd) merit so rigorous a doome, that the severest death were a mercy to it. Oh either revoke your cruell sentence, or give me leave to expire in your presence.

Artabella made him no answer, but loosing his armes, went away; leaving him in as great a confusion, as she herselfe had been in a little before.

But no sooner had she turn'd her back, but he ris up; and drawing his Sword cry'd, yes Madam I will obey you; but it shall be by death, for tis impossible to live and performe your to too cruell command: this sword will at once teach me obedience, and revenge you for my unadvized rashness. I will not live Madam to make you blush for any sin of mine: and when I have wash'd away my crime with my heart blood, perhaps you will pitty him whom once you lov'd, though now you hate.

Finishing these words he let the Pumell of his sword to the ground, and going to fling himselfe upon it, he suddenly felt himselfe stay'd by one, who clasping him about the waist hinder'd him from his intended purpose. He hastily turning his head to see who had rendred him that Friendly, though then unwellcome office, found himselfe in the Armes of *Diomed*; who impatient of so long an absence, had been to seek him in all places he could imagine he might be in. There was no Walk, no Arbour in the Garden where he had not sought him, and was just then returning to the Palace, supposing he might be gone in some other way unknown to him: but being guided by his good Genius he came unawares into the Wilderness, a place which he had never seen before: and hearing some voices, he came neer the Arbour just as *Artabella* quited it. He came thither time enough to heare the fatall resolution of his deare *Phasellus*, and as the Gods would have it, to prevent the execution of it. But when he saw it was *Diomed* that had frustrated his dire intent, he was even ready to dye with vexation.

Oh Heavens *Phasellus* (said he to him) what is it you intend: or what madness is it has possest you; and hurried you on to this dispaire: have I deserv'd so little from you as to be made a stranger to your thoughts; I have not us'd you at this rate.

Phasellus finding this reproofe justly to taxe him with a breach of Friendship, was not able to refraine from sheding teares as a testimony of his griefe, that *Diomed* should to that impute his silence.

O *Diomed* (said he) be not so unkind as to censure me ^as^ difficent in my Friendship; but as you have done me the honour to believe me hitherto your [fol. 20ʳ] Friend, so assure your selfe you shall never have just cause to account me other; for I will to the last minute of my breath preserve those sacred Bonds uncancel'd: then do not load my Soule with a heavier weight of misery, which is already too to much oppress'd. My silence which I know you do account my crime; was occation'd meerly through a feare of your displeasure (which I knew I should have incurr'd had I acquainted you with my passion; which your insensibility of that power to which I have submitted, would have term'd my folly) and not through any disrespect: then banish all such misapprehensions deare Sir I beseech you: and do me the justice as to believe, though I am unfortunate, I am not ingratefull; which I should be in the highest degree, if I were wanting in that duty I owe you, to whom I am indebted for all that I have, or am; and forgive me this supposed fault, which onely seemes, but is no reall one; since my intentions may protest my Innocence.

Oh say not so (repli'd *Diomed*) lest you force me to entertaine a worse opinion of you then that I lately had: for tis impossible your intentions should speak you innocent and at the same time your actions express you guilty of the most irreparabled breach of Friendship by seeking to take away my life.

Now you are no less cruell then unkind (answer'd *Phasellus*) to charge me with a Crime, I am so farre from being guilty of, that had I ten thousand lives, freely would I sacrifice them all, rather then you should suffer the least of ills: no, first let me be buried quick ere I think a thought that may be to your prejudice.

Mistake me not (said *Diomed*) I know thou do'st not actually seek to deprive me of life; but yet thou art asmuch to blame, if thou art accessary to my death by procuring thy owne distruction. I know thou art not ignorant of my affection to thee: thou know'est that tis in thee alone my life consists; my vitall Threed being twin'd with yours, did you imagine you could cut the one, and leave the other whole. No my *Phasellus* if thou hast a mind to die, make thy passage to Death thorow my brest, and pierce that heart with thy Sword, which thou would'st have pierced with a more painfull sorrow for thy loss; and then follow me if thou wilt: but believe it, if I can hinder thee, thou shalt never lead me the way.

Ah (said *Phasellus* deeply sighing) did you but know what prompts me to this deed, I am perswaded you would not all condemne me; but rather repent you kept me from puting my selfe into a condition which onely can render me happie.

No (repli'd *Diomed*) I shall never repent I hinder'd you from being your owne Executioner: but if your condition be so sad as you pretend, pray let me understand wherein and what it was induced you to act this tragicall part; and be sure, if there be any possibility of it, I'll find out a cure for your dispaire: but if not, I shall be an equall sharer in your sufferings, and then your griefe when tis divided, will be the more supportable: therefore I once more charge, and conjure you by our Friendship to let me know it, or never expect that I will pardon you the injury you would have done me.

Well (answer'd *Phasellus*) since you ~~will~~ so strictly [fol. 20^v] enjoyn me to give you the trouble of my Concernes, I will at larg declare them to you; onely I must implore your pitty: and that you will be so charitable as not to keep me any longer from a death as necessary as that which makes me desire it is intollerable: but if you do, my resentments [sentiments] will ere long give me that cure, which you will not permit me to receive from my resolution. Then siting downe together, he declar'd to *Diomed* all the perticulers of his discontent. As how long he had been in love with *Artabella*, what course he took for the discovery of his passion to her, and how he had conceal'd himself in that Wilderness, to find how she resented [felt] it; and perceiving by her discourse to her Maid it was not displeasing to her, he unadvizedly ventur'd to present himselfe before her; flattering himselfe with a hope to gain a more perfect assurance of her favour. But that unseasonable discovery of my selfe (continu'd he) prov'd my utter ruine; for she appear'd so highly insenced at me, for surprizing her in that manner, that the favourable opinion she had of me was turn'd into a perfect resentment, which concluded in an utter banishment, without the least hopes of a repeale.

And is this all (said *Diomed*) O Foolish *Phasellus* I could not imagine thou had'st had so little of reason in thee, as to kill thy selfe for a womans peevishness. If she had a reall kindness for thee (as her words seeme to import) she cannot so divest herselfe of it, but that it will again returne to plead on thy behalfe after the storme of her anger is a little over; and then thinke what a griefe it will be to her, to find she was the occation of your death. You could not (in my judgement) expect less in the height of her displeasure, to see herselfe betray'd into a revealing of her most private thoughts, contrary to her intentions you may be sure: but passion, never askes advice of reason, if it did; discretion would have told you, then was no convenient season to gain assurances of her esteeme; but after you had thus rashly runne your selfe into this errour, would you repaire it by committing a greater absurdity. No *Phasellus* (pursu'd he) you should wait with patience till the storme were over blown, and then questionless your banishment will be recall'd: but to destroy your selfe, you render your selfe uncapable of that which you most passionatly desire.

Then after a little silence, he went on. But that you may not thinke, what I have said proceeds from an insensibility of what so neerly touches you; know that I do as truly sympathize with you as if we had but one Soule, to animate two bodies. Thou wert mistaken *Phasellus*, when thou thought'st me ignorant of that power which has reduced thee to this condition; for I will tell thee, and believe it for a truth: that very Flame which burnes so bright in thee, has also sing'd my heart. I love as well as you; and tis that faire Princess that has made you her slave, has likewise captiv'd me. Did you imagine I could look on such vast perfections, and be unconcern'd for her that ow^n^es them; nay, start not to heare me say I am your Rivall.

How (cry'd *Phasellus*) do you love *Artabella*, nay then there is no hope for me; tis time, nay more then time that I were dead.

Yes (repli'd *Diomed*) I do love her but yet you shall not dy; no, you shall live and enjoy her for all me, for I promise you I will be no obstruction to it. You [fol. 21ʳ] deeme your selfe unhappy, but if you seriously consider, I am much more so; for your advantages are far greater then mine (were I disposed to oppose you) haveing already gain'd an interest in her heart whom we both love, which I can never hope to do: for by her owne confession the feare of my affection, was that which did somuch perplex her. But as you have the advantage of me one way, so have I no less of you another, would I make use of it. For this very morning *Menzor* met me in the Cypress Grove whether I was gone to walk: and after a Friendly salutation (as a parenthesis to his discourse) he embraced me saying, I am both sorry and asham'd Sir, to see, you and your noble Friend should receive no other reward for the services you have done this Kingdome, then the honour that attends heroick deeds. I am afraid ye either think us forgetfull, or ungratfull, especially my selfe who am more perticulerly oblig'd to you dear sir (continu'd he embraceing me again). Then after many other obliging expressions he told me, there was not any thing in his power to bestow, which he did not think infinitly short of what I had deserv'd from him: but since he had nothing better, he would present me with the dearest jewell that he was possest of, which was his Daughter, if I could think her worthy my esteeme; promising me all the assistance I could expect from him both as her Father, and my Friend, protesting if he could (without a prejudice to the Princess *Oriana*) present her to me as the Heire of Persia, he should not thinke her too deare for me.

Really I stood amaiz'd at this generous proffer; but I suppose you do not question whether or no I embraced it, since t'was the onely happiness I was ambitious of. But now do not imagine I tell you this to adde to the burden of your griefe; believe it your content is dearer to me then soe, my intention is rather to convince you that my Friendship is not to be equall'd; and that I can be content to wave my owne satisfaction if I may thereby establish yours. Yes my *Phasellus* for thy sake I'll pluck this passion from my brest; which is not of so long continuance, not yet so deeply rooted, but that in time I hope to master it; for I will never cherish ought in me that may be to thy prejudice: nay, I will do more for thee then this, if thou wilt not be thine owne enemy.

Did you ever heare of a higher gallantry then this of *Diomeds* (said *Celia* to the Unknown).

Yes Madam (answer'd she) I know a person of our owne sex that can equall, I [Aye] and surpass him too; for t'was a little kind of Justice that he should cease from being Rivall to *Phasellus*, because his owne passion bare the later date: and besides, it was not half so difficult at first to quench a Flame which was but newly kindled, as to extinguish one of long continuance: but this Excellent Lady whom I mention'd (and of whom I must more fully give a Character when I recite my misfortunes) declin'd a passion for her Rivalls sake which had been of many yeeres standing: but I confess the generosity of *Diomed* is to be admir'd and I should think it yet more admirable were I not so well acquainted with the others; which I know to be such, (and so your selfe will acknowledge when once you have heard her story) as the earth never bare her equall; and were that brave man living in this age [fol. 21 ᵛ] I know none that could match his Vertue but herselfe; or were so worthy of him as she would be.

Well (repli'd *Celia*) I will not stand to oppose your opinion, but proceed in my story; for I feare I shall scarce finish it before the Queen challenges of you the performance of your promise. Know then (continu'd she) that every word which *Diomed* spake of his love to *Artabella* was as a Dagger at *Phasellus's* heart; but when he came to the period of his story: *Phasellus* was so amaized at his kindness to him, that he knew not in what language to cloth his resent^i^ment^s^ [sentiments] of it.

At last, fetching a sigh, you are too Generous a Friend to poor *Phasellus* (said he) to purchase his content, with the price of your owne. Your generosity is to me a Glasse wherein I clearly view my owne unworthiness; for if before, passion alone excited me to dy, now reason will much more: for how can I endure to see you condescend somuch beneath your selfe as to yeeld ought to him, who is no other then your servant, though you are pleased to honour him with the most ambitioned title of your Friend. Shall I suffer *Diomed* to robbe himselfe of the most transcendent felicity the Heavens can give to enrich *Phasellus*. No no (pursu'd he) it will be ten thousand times more satisfaction to me to dye, then live and deprive you of so great a bliss.

I robbe my selfe of nothing (answer'd *Diomed*) nor yet do you deprive me of ought, if it be my owne free act to resign it to you.

These arguments which he [*Diomed*] made use of to testifie his Friendship, and those which preceeded to divert him [*Phasellus*] from his dispaire could not perswade him to lay aside his desire of dying; for *Artabella's* anger, together with the griefe he conceiv'd to see himselfe travers'd in his passion by him whom of all men living he had most reason to apprehend, both for the merit of his person, and the power he had with her Father; notwithstanding his protestations to make no use of it to his prejudice; yet weighing *Diomeds* affection in the scailes of his owne passion, he believ'd it impossible for him to performe that promise. These considerations so possest him, that they left no place for any perswasions to enter; and in such a sort did they work upon his Spirits, that with the violence of his griefe he burst out a bleeding, in so excessive a manner, that *Diomed* fear'd he would bleed to death if it were not suddenly stanch'd; for the blood flow'd out of both his Nostrills like two little Rivers.

He [Diomed] appli'd to him all those remedies he had formerly known to do him good (for *Phasellus* was often subject to that distemper, though never in that extreamity before) but when he saw all his endevours fruitless, he was even driven to his wits end, and what to do in that case he knew not: loath he was to leave him in that condition, and to stay and see him dy for want of help he could less endure: but seeing him bleed faster and faster, he found it would prove but a fruitless charity to stay longer with him: so taking away his sword (that he might leave him nothing to do himselfe a mischiefe with in his absence) he ranne to the Palace to call some other more expert in that cure then himselfe.

In the mean time *Phasellus*⁶ seeking for something wherewith to act his design ere *Diomed* return'd, found a certaine Weed growing in the wilderness, which would at any time provoke one to bleed that did but smell of it though they were not apt to it of themselves; as he was. This did [fol. 22ʳ] he gather, and thrust up into his Nose, to the intent that way to draw out his life: and such effect it took, that by the time that *Diomed* and the Chirurgion came, he had lost so great a quantity of blood that he was fallen on the Ground almost sense-less. But when he [*Diomed*]came and saw his friend in that case, he seem'd even distracted; he stamp'd and tore his haire, with all the gestures of a madman (for indeed he was little better seeing him he lov'd so deare, reduced to that extream-ity) vowing most desperatly if he died, not to outlive him a minute. *Phasellus* seeing this, began to repent what he had done, and suffer'd the Chirurgion to endevour his preservation: but had he been minded to oppose him, his weakness doubtless would have rendred him unable.

But we will leave them for awhile, and returne to *Artabella* whom we left in great disorder said *Celia*, but perceiving it grew very late she thought it con-venient to deferre the remaining part of the story till the next day, and for that night to go to their rests. *Celia* took hers very quietly, having nothing to disturbe her repose; but the Sicilian Ladies was much interrupted with divers troubled fancies, and Mallancholy Dreames, which tormented her no less sleeping, then her thoughts did when she was awake. But both of them awaking early the next morning, and having given each other the good morrow, they arose and drest themselves that they might be in areadyness when ever *Ermillia* should call for them: but in the meane time at the Sicilians request, *Celia* (calling to mind where she left off) reasum'd her former discourse in these words.

---

⁶ The MS reads Diomed, but Phasellus is intended.

Rivall Friendship

THE FIRST PART

The Second Book

You may remember Madam (said *Celia*) we were going to see what was become of the Princess *Artabella*; who when she departed from the Willderness, went with an intent to go to her Chamber; but as she was going *Menzor* met her, having been there to seek her; He perceiving something of disorder in her lookes, and seeing her go with a more then ordinary hast call'd her to him; and taking her by the hand, what is the matter (said he) that you seeme so troubled; whether go you so fast.

This question being asked her on the sudden, she had no answer ready: but *Saparilla* who was not so much surpriz'd as she, had one by good fortune at her Finger sends, whereby she sav'd her the trouble of a reply. Nothing Sir ailes the Princess [fol. 22ᵛ] (said she) but that she was extreamly scar'd with a Viper which lay lurking in the Grass, hard by where she sate, which was like to have stunge her ere she was aware:

(Ah poor *Saparilla* continu'd *Celia*, thou told'st a Lye, but yet it prov'd a truth).

Where was it (repli'd *Menzor*) ~~we will~~ that you saw it, we will go kill it if we can, to prevent any further danger.

No Sir (repli'd *Artabella*, having a little ralli'd her discomposed spirits, and being glad of her Maides excuse) let it live; perhaps it meant me not the harme I fear'd from it: besides t'will be invain to seek it now, for I suppose tis gone from thence ere this; I'le take more care henceforwards to prevent such frights.

But whether were you going (said *Menzor*),

To my Chamber (she repli'd).

You shall walk a turne or two with me (said he) and then you shall go in, but before you go I must impart somewhat of concernment to you. It has alwayes been my prayers (continu'd he) that I might live to see thee happily match't, as may be both to thy content, and my satisfaction; and my chiefest care of late has been to find out one to bestow thee on, every way worthy of thee: long did I seek, ere I could find, on whom to fix my choice; but at last, Fortune presented to me a person as well accomplish't as my heart could wish; a man so farre above all others that yet I ever saw, that I can never enough admire his excellencies. But you cannot but be so well acquainted with him, that whatever I say, will rather detract from his worth, then give him his due praise. I suppose after this that I have said, tis needless to tell you tis *Diomed* I intend you, then whom the World has not a braver man.

All the while he spake *Artabella* was so troubled that she could scarce lend an eare to what he said without shewing how much it displeas'd her. But when she heard who t'was her Father had design'd for her, she was not able to forbeare interrupting him, though she knew not what Arguments to have reco^u^rse too, to evade his intentions; for well she knew, she could alledge no reason to justi-fie her dislike of *Diomed*, but would reflect on *Phasellus* (who in despight of all her anger still retain'd an interest in her heart) and be injurious to his pretences. Great was the straite to which she was reduced; but she chose rather to embrace a single life forever, then consent to be any ones if she might not be *Phasellus*'s; and to that intent she thus refus'd *Menzors* proffer.

I confess Sir (said she) *Diomed* is a person truly worthy of those praises you have given him, and possibly as worthy of me as any of those that have pretended to me; but being so neere alli'd to the Crowne, do you believe the King will not take it amiss that you should give me to a private person, without his consent, or approbation: or admit he leave to you the sole power of my disposall, can you your selfe Sir value me at so low a rate as to bestow me on one you know not.

Though his extraction be unknown to me (repli'd *Menzor*) his vertues are not; those he has given sufficent testimony of: and I, ever in my Judgment, gave Vertue the preheminence of [fol. 23^r^] dignity; but I have a strong perswasion I shall find both in him: but if in the latter I am deceiv'd, and that he be not born to a Crowne, I make no question he may acquire one by his Valour to present you, and that is more noble. However I am assur'd you will be happy in him, and I desire no more. And as to your objection, concerning the Kings consent, I feare it not; having never yet oppos'd my designes in ought: nor do I believe he will in this; since his interest, no less then my owne desires incites me to it: for we have all the reason in the World to apprehend a second invasion from Scythia; for tis not long since I was credibly enform'd, that *Oruntus* has vow'd to revenge on us his Brothers death: and think you then, the assistance of such Valiant men may not be as needfull as before; and I verily perswade my selfe, if we can but engage the one to stay, the other will not leave us: then sure *Achemenes* cannot take it ill from me, if I am willing to dispence with those advantages I might pretend too by matching you elsewhere, to purchace him so powerfull an Assistant: but the truth is, my chiefest aime is my owne satisfaction; which I cannot desire more compleat, then to see you *Diomeds*.

I must ever acknowledge with all due thankfullness (answer'd she) your ten-der care of me; but if you wish my happiness, permit me to continue as I am; and give me leave to end my days in Virgin innocence: I confess I have been long since devoted to a single life, and pleas'd my selfe with the hopes that I should find from you no opposition as to that resolution, seeing you never urg'd me to the acceptance tion of any of those proffers that have been made me (though you could not be ignorant Sir how highly I might have been advan[c]'d by some of them) but always left it to my owne free choice.

How (said he) did you imagine I left it to your choice whether ever you would marry or no; truly if you did, you were deceived: but if you have been hitherto pleas'd with such a mistaken fancy, pray disabuse your selfe; and believe, that I intended nothing less. Do you think I can be perswaded with you to bury the hopes of all posterity. Had the Heavens blest me with any more but you, I might perchance have been content to indulge in you this desire: but since thou art my onely Child, I never will; for who, but my *Artabella* can preserve my name alive, when I am dead.

Your vertues Sir (repli'd she) will preserve your memory much better then any Successour.

Talk no more (said he) nor seek not arguments to oppose my Will; which is, that you ma marry *Diomed*, but dispose your selfe to receive his Addresses with all kindness whenever he shall tender them: and believe it I shall judge of your duty to me, by the respect you shew to this command.

With that, he was going away, but she fell on her knees, catching hold of his hand, beging [him] to stay and heare her speak once more before he went. Taking her up, he ask'd what t'was she had to say.

I have ever from my Infancy (said she) had such an aversion to Love, that I have asmuch as in civility I could avoided the society of all men: [fol. 23ᵛ] but those I have been constrain'd to admit a converse with, I have regarded with such an indifferency, that I could never in my esteeme prefer one before another; but alwayes look'd on those that were excellent, as I should on a rare Picture; onely to admire it: and this effect *Diomeds* perfections has produced in me. I do admire him above all other of his sex, but pardon me if I say, I do not love him any further then gratitude obliges me, and feare I never shall: which grieves me to the Soule that I cannot willingly comply with your desires. But I will do what lies in me, to bend my inclinations that way which you intend them. I onely beg (Sir) you will not force my affection to the ruine of my content; but give me leave to take a more perticuler survey of *Diomeds* worth, that if possible, I may bring my heart to affect him: but if I cannot obtain that of my selfe, let me beseech you deare Father (continu'd she falling on her knees again) and conjure you by these teare[s] (which witness my unwillingness to disobey you) and by the memory of my Deare Mother, not to compell me to give my person where I cannot give my Heart; lest in aiming to make me happy, you render me most miserable. I am very sensible how much you are indebted to him, and what he has deserv'd from you upon that score; but if you can find nought else to cancell that Obligation with, adopt him for your Heire, and disinherit me; I shall not account it too larg a reward for the services I have receiv'd from him; nor look on him with envie, though he enjoy my right; leave me sir nothing but the possession of my self, and I shall be content.

I did not think I should have found you so refractory (repli'd he) to that which I expected you would have embraced with a satisfaction correspondent to your Duty, since you know it is my Will: but however, I shall give you a day or two, to consider of this proposall: perhaps when you have thought better on't you will be of another opinion: but remember *Artabella*, if you expect to find me an Indullgent Father, I look you should shew your selfe an obedient Child.

Assoon as he was gone she hasted to her Apartment, where she might uninterruptedly breath forth her complaints against her Fathers severity: whether being come, she threw herselfe on her Bed, abandoning herselfe to such an excess of weeping, that any one that had seen her, would have believ'd she had intended to have drown'd herselfe in those Floodes of griefe. Her inexorable cruelty to *Phasellus* came then into her mind to afflict her; which made her repent that severe command she had imposed on him: for since he had two such mighty oppositions to encounter (as *Diomeds* affection, and *Menzors* power) she could bu not but thinke it too to much for her disdaine to fight against him any longer.

Saparilla seeing her Lady so dejected would have said somewhat to asswage her griefe; but as she was about to speake, she receiv'd a charge from *Artabella* to the contrary: for such is my condition (said she) as can admit no consolation; nor canst thou say any thing, that will not rather aggravate, then mittigate my discontent.

The faithfull servant hearing her say so, durst not disobey, but answer'd her laments in the same language she express'd them in. After *Artabella* had tir'd her eyes with teares, [fol. 24ʳ] and her heart with sighes; finding no redress from any thing, she rose from her Bed, and withdrew to a Window which look'd into the Garden; and leaning her cheek on her hand, she fell into a serious consideration of her misfortune, and what way she had left to escape it: but as she stood there, in that mellancholy muse, she cast her Eyes on an Object which was like to have prov'd fatall to her. It was *Phasellus*, who was just then carried by to his Lodging: for though the Chirurgion had try'd the uttmost of his skill, yet was it more then two houres before he could stop the Current of his blood. But at last, having anointed his Temples, and Nostrills with an Ointment of most excellent Vertue against that Distemper, with much adoe he prevail'd: but with the excessive loss of blood *Phasellus* was so weakned, that when he went to rise, he stager'd, and fell backward; nor was he able to go one step towards his Lodging, so that they were constrain'd to call some to carry him in a Chaire.

And in this condition it was that *Artabella* chanced to espie him, all pale, and bloody as he was; which made her imagine him dead, and that by the hands of *Diomed* too: supposing he had by some accident discover'd *Phasellus*'s passion for her, and on that score had fought with him, and reduced him to that deplorable estate wherein she beheld him: this thought no sooner came into her mind, but she shreekt out, and sunk downe dead. There was at that instant none of her Maides with her; for she had commanded them all forth, that she might the more freely vent her griefe: nor was *Saparilla* with her then, for she was some minuts before gone into her owne Chamber: but when when she return'd, and found her Lady stretch'd on the Floore, cold, and senseless; she was so affrighted, that she stood as it had been one Planet strook: but *Artabellas* danger soon rous'd her

[*Saparilla*] from those dumps, and made her cry out for help; whilst she herselfe did all she could to call back Life, which seemingly had abandoned that faire habitation; which at last she effected, though it was a long time ere *Artabella* recover'd so much sense as to speak: which assoon as she could (casting a languishing look on *Saparilla*, and ^with^ her hand lifting up hers with which she held her head, and puting her from her) preethee said she let me alone, I would faine dy, if thou lovest me, thou wilt not hinder me.

For heavens sake (cry'd *Saparilla*) what new griefe is it that hurries you on to this extreamity of dispaire, so willfully to give up your selfe to Deathes cold embraces: your condition Madam is not yet so desperate, but you may find divers wayes to felicity, and yet not tread that Path the violence of your passion leads you to.

Alass (repli'd she) thou know'st not the greatest of my misfortunes; nor can I tell thee, since to pronounce it would stricke a new terrour to my Soule; thou soon, too soon alass (pursu'd she with a sigh) wilt learne it from the mouthes of others.

With this she was begining to faint again, which *Saparilla* perceiving, she was going to send one of the other Maides to call the Kings Phisician who was always resident in the Palace; but she [Artabella] commanded the contrary, charging her [fol. 24ᵛ] withall not to let *Menzor* know any thing of her indisposition; vowing if she did; not to take any thing that the Phisician prescrib'd her. *Saparilla* having receiv'd such an absolute command, durst not disobey as long as she had any way, or meanes left to preserve her; but stept into the Princess her mistress's Closet, and fetcht from thence a Cordiall of Soveraign vertue against all fainting Distempers: (for *Artabella* was ever adicted to the study of Phisick; and never was without many rare, and admirable things; which she always dispos'd of (by the hands of her Servants) to such poor persons as beg'd, or stood in need of remedies for their Diseases: and never was she better pleas'd, then when she found some whereon to excercise her Charity.) which Cordiall *Saparilla* beg'd her with so pressing an importunity to drink, that she could not refuse it, but took and drank it off: which when she had done, she likewise perswaded her to go to bed; which *Artabella* was not much averse too, knowing she might there take the greater liberty to indulge her sorrowes.

But as she was going to be undress'd, *Diomed* came to the Chamber dore, desiring admission to speak with her: she admiring what occation should produce such an unseasonable visit (for night had spread its sable Canopie over the Face of Heaven) that she might know what brought him thither, for a while gave a truce to her teares, and gave him leave to enter; though she scarce had patience to look on him whom she suppos'd the Murtherer of *Phasellus*. But resolving not to discover her griefe to him, she put on a serene countenance far different from that she lately wore. But her resolutions were but vaine, for all her cunning could not conceale from him those markes of griefe which visibly appear'd in her Face: but taking no notice of it, he approach'd her with a garb so majestick, and yet with such respect, that she had as much reason to admire, as she had cause to be satisfi'd with it: And puting one knee to the ground, in this manner he made his address. Perhaps madam (said he) you wonder to see me here at so unfit a time; but that necessity which compells me to it, must make my Apollogie for this incivility; unpardonable I confess on any other score.

Rise (answer'd *Artabella*) or I will not heare you.

This posture Madam (he repli'd) is most sutable to an humble Petitioner, and such at this time am I; and unless I may be so happy as to obtain my sute I'll never rise: for if I must dye, I cannot find a more glorious place then at your feet to offer up my life.

But she protesting not to give eare to any thing that he said, but to quit the place unless he arose, he to obey her stood up. Now *Diomed* (said she) what is it you desire.

My life (repli'd he) I come to beg, which lyes at your mercy; and tis from that alone I must implore it.

Your life (said she) I do not know that it can any way depend on me; but if it did; I should account my selfe [fol. 25^r] both ungratfull and unjust should I take life from him who gave my Father his, or at least preserv'd it to him: but tis neither in my power to give or take.

Yes Madam (answer'd he) tis as absolutely in your power to destroy me, if you refuse to shew mercy to a Wretch that lies even drown'd in a Sea of griefe for your displeasure, as if immediatly you struck a Dager to my heart.

If (repli'd she very coldly) you had been as apprehencive of my displeasure as you seeme, sure you would have had a greater respect for me, then to do that which you could not but be confident would mortally offend me.

He was amazed to heare her speak after this manner, and standing silent awhile to bethinke him what he had done that could be capable of displeasing her, but was not able to conceive the cause; unless she were angry that he had hindred *Phasellus*'s designe. She hearing him returne no answer, construed his silence as a signe of guilt, and was about to leave him and retire to her Closet: but he stay'd her by crying out with transport. Have I offended you Madam, the Heavens can testifie my innocence and that I do not know wherein, unless it were a crime to save the life (of one, he would have said, which you have sentenced to death, by destining him to a banishment, more insupportable) but she interrupted him assoon as ever she heard him mention the saving of a life, supposing it was her Fathers he meant to reproach her with: but giving him not time to end his speach.

Upbraid me not with that (she said) for I acknowledge my obligation is as great to you upon that score as you can believe it: but yet I did not think your presumption had aimed at me for your reward; bate but that *Diomed* and there is not any thing wherein my honour is not concern'd which I will not condescend to gratifie you in.

Keep but that promise Madam (repli'd he) and I will aske no greater happiness: for all the reward I'll beg, shall be your pitty for *Phasellus*, and that you will render him back that heart you lately with somuch cruelty depriv'd him of.

She being confirm'd by this discourse that he had kill'd *Phasellus*, and that their quarell arose from his overhearing their discourse in the Arbour; for she could not imagine he would court her in his Rivalls behalfe if he were in a condition to reape any benefit by it: wherefore being thus perswaded, she fanci'd he came with no other intent then to circumvent her, and sound her inclinations, and accordingly fram'd her reply. I know not to what end (said she) you implore my pitty for *Phasellus*; I confess his condition sufficently deserves it: but you know, and so do I, that he can receive no satisfaction from it: therefore to what end would you have me love a shade, or bestow my heart upon a senseless Carkase.

But I will meet your designe (continu'd she with a shower of teares [fol. 25ᵛ] which she was no longer able to restraine) by acknowledging that, which had *Phasellus* liv'd I never would have done, for fear of prejudicing him as well as my owne reputation by this confession; but since he lives not, I'le make no scruple to declare I lov'd him: he was the onely person that ever made me know affections power; with him my love began, and with him it shall end. Then flatter not your selfe with a hope so vaine, that you shall by his death be ever the neerer to the obtaining my esteem; no no, believe it I'le bury in his Grave all passion that excepted which will serve to send me after him: nor shall you, or any other ever revive my dying Flame. Go barbarous man (pursu'd she) cruell to thy Friend, and treacherous to me, go and compleat thy mischiefes by telling *Menzor* of this Declaration; and thereby move him to sacrifice me to his fury and send my Soule to Elizium to beg pardon of *Phasellus* for being the innocent occation of his death. But now I think better on't, do not incence my Father by acquainting him with this Confession; nor provoke not the author of my life to give me death: but stay awhile, and you shall see my griefe act both his revenge and yours.

Diomed being joyfull he had made a discovery which could not but prove very satisfactory to his Friend; but yet withall being troubled at *Artabella's* injurious opinion of him; but fancying it proceeded (as indeed it did) from a false beliefe of *Phasellus*'s death; thinking t'was probable she might have seen him carried to his Lodging: and distance not permitting a perfect view, might possess her with a perswasion that he was dead; which induced him to excuse all her ill language to himselfe since it proceeded from no other cause then the transports of her love.

I am glad Madam (said he) to find your mistake so advantagious to my wishes, and that the prejudice you conceiv'd against me has no other originall then that. But I am sorry withall that I have been so unfortunate as to create in you such hard thoughts of me, as to be accounted the Murtherer of my dearest Friend, and a Traitour to your selfe; but ere many minutes pass I question not to make it appeare that I am neither. *Phasellus* lives Madam.

It is impossible (repli'd she) you cannot make me give my eyes the lye which saw him dead.

Would I were as certaine you would not scorne his passion (answer'd he) nor refuse his services, as I am sure he lives to pay you them. But if you yet want Faith to credit what I affirme, do me but the honour to let me conduct you to his Chamber, where your Eyes may convince you of the truth of this ascertion [fol. 26ʳ] and their owne mistake: but had it not been for this Barbarous man, this ~~this~~ treacherous person, ther had ere this indeed been nothing for you to love, or pitty of *Phasellus* but the bare name or memory. But I have onely repriev'd him, tis you must give him life, by sealing of his pardon, and repealing his banishment.

If this be true you tell me (reply'd she) I will with the greatest submission imaginable beg your pardon for the wronge I have done you in my thoughts: but if you are somuch *Phasellus*'s Friend as you pretend, what mov'd you to incite my Father to force me to accept you for a Husband, especially before you had made any addresses to me upon that account.

If I had ever su'd to *Menzor* (said he) without your permission you might justly charge me Madam with the highest presumption, the greatest arrogance that ever any was guilty of. But I had never vanity enough in me to imagine that ought that I have done, or any thing that ever I shall be able to do could any way merit such a super excellent felicity as the possession of you who are a recompense too high for vertue; then certainly much too high for me to pretend too.

Did you not then solicite my father on that score (repli'd she)

Never (answer'd he) but it was his owne free proffer to conferre so rich a blessing on me: which should I have refused, the World undoubtedly would have condemn'd me of madness. Nor can you justly charge it on me as a crime either to *Phasellus* or your selfe that I with joy accepted the tender of so trancendant a happiness, since I was ignorant of his passion for you, or your kindness for him; till going to seek him after my departure from *Menzor* I found him in those despaires to which your severity had reduced him.

Then did he relate to her the desperate condition wherein he had found him, and with what difficulty he had kept him from killing himselfe; and what an inconvenience the violence of his griefe had brought upon him.

I must confess Madam (continu'd he) I have long since ador'd you with a respect I never yet pai'd any Mortall, though I had not confidence enough to owne it to you: but when I beheld poor *Phasellus* in that plight, and learn'd from him the occation of it, my passion gave place to Friendship; for I could not live, and see him die who was far dearer to me then my life. I had not a recourse to that which Rivalls use to fly too, though I knew him the chiefest obstacle to my desired happiness: I took another course, farre different, for I resolv'd for his sake to abandone all pretences to your esteeme; and if I could not absolutely banish you my heart, yet to be silent in my passion; and conceale it so closely in my breast that it should never trouble any but unhappie *Diomed*. But if I found that it would prove too powerfull for me to keep under I would endeavour to divert it, by fixing it on some other object not unworthy my esteeme. Perhaps you may thinke my passion less then *Phasellus*'s that I could so easily divest my self of it: but [fol. 26ᵛ] alass tis not so soon done as resolv'd on; t'will cost me many a bitter conflict yet before I vanquish it: but what ere I suffer neither he nor you shall ever know: nor shall you ever Madam be troubled with its importunities.

She had not patience to heare him further, but with exclamation cry'd; O the the most Generous of men, the best of Friends; I beg your pardon for those unjust suspitions I had of you, in the same posture that you lately implor'd my pitty for *Phasellus*.

With that she was falling on her knees, but he prevented her by staying her up, and saying. It is too much beneath you Madam to stoop so low to me. I willing excuse the injustice you did me, and would if it were a thousand times a greater injury upon the score you did it.

I am amazed (said she) at your gallantry, and so infinitly griev'd that I must be ungratfull, that you cannot wish me a severer punishment then that consideration will prove; and could any thing make me repent my love to *Phasellus*, or deeme my affection misplaced this noble carriage of yours would worke that effect: but since it is impossible to take that heart from him which I did but seemingly deprive him of, accept all that I am able to bestow; which is a Friendship equall to that you have for him; and if you can oblige me in any thing more, tis in accepting it, and confering on me yours.

Ah (repli'd he sighing) is that all I must expect; and must I never hope for more.

I have now so great a confidence in your vertue (said she) as to believe you do not hope for ought from me but that; if you do, you soon forget your resolution.

Tis true Madam I confess it (answer'd he) but I will be more mindfull for the future.

Well repli'd she you shall see how great a confidence I repose in you; for I will henceforth have no other Councellour but your self, and from your advice alone will I take precepts how to order my concerns. That I love *Phasellus* it would be a rediculous folly to deny, since tis to you so known a truth: but that I will never condescend to the least perticuler in favour of him to the prejudice of that duty I owe *Menzor* is as certaine: therefore I think it requisite not to let him know the interest he has in me; but to permit him still to continue in his opinion of my severity, since tis impossible I feare for him ever to gain my fathers consent to make me his.

No Madam (said he) if he must perish, let his ruine rather proceed from *Menzors* cruelty then yours: for sure you cannot see your self the cause of his death without recenting [feeling] the greatest of griefes.

Tis sure (answer'd she) should I occation his death, I should in that procure my owne: but I hope that opinion which I desire to confirme him in will produce a better effect, as the changing his love into recentment.

Alass (repli'd he) you cannot make me believe you really wish that, which tis contrary to reason that you should: for can it be possible for any one to desire to be hated by those they love.

Yes (said she) I had rather he should hate me then that his passion should do him that prejudice you speak of.

There is not any thing (repli'd *Diomed*) but he would easily dispence with, were he but certaine he were not banish'd your favour; nor no misfortune which he would not despise had he but the satisfaction to know as much as I. But I see the disquiet of your mind much better then you can express it. You say you love him, and I believe it [fol. 27ʳ] but will not any way oblige him till you have a Lysence from your duty; and you dread your fathers displeasure; but that fear is in a manner needless, for I dare undertake not onely to appease him should he be offended with you ^but^ to gain his consent likewise for *Phasellus*; nor do I believe you will find him so inexorable as you fancie; and I question not but in a short time to find such powerfull inducements as shall perswade him to accept him for his Son with as high a satisfaction as he seem'd to express to make me soe. Though by birth I confess he is somewhat my inferior, yet is he such a one as a Princess needs not blush to owne a passion for: but as I surpass him in one perticuler, he has the good Fortune to excell me in many other.

I shall be very well pleas'd (said she) to find him such as you say: but give me leave to tell you, that I believe you will not find it so easie as you imagine to perswade my Father to give me to him, though he was so free to bestow me on you who have done so many gallant things to merit his esteeme, which *Phasellus* cannot any further pretend too then he is pleas'd to allow him a place in it.

That I have oblig'd him more then *Phasellus* is my happiness (repli'd he) but though Fortune was more propitious to me then him I dare answere his ambition was as great, and his design as reall to serve him as mine; and therefore I am perswaded your Father is too just not to value his intentions at as high a rate as he has priz'd my actions. But whilst I plead for my friend I seeme to forget him, or at least the sad condition wherein I left him: therefore madam let me humbly beg the favour of a visit for him, since you may perform it with the greatest security from a surprize that may be; and give me but the honour to waite on you to his Chamber with *Saparilla* to attend you.

Were it as convenient (answer'd she) as the time of Night renders it unseasonable I should not grant your request; for do you imagine I have the confidence to see him so soon after an acknowledgment so injurious to that severe vertue I have ever made a proffession of: tell him what you please concerning me, but spare me the confusion it would throw on me to repeat that Folly to him which I have declar'd to you: but remember whatever assurances you give him of my esteeme, to assure him withall, that I will suffer him to dy, nay dy my self rather then ever be guilty of any thing that may detract from my obedience to my Father.

Such a transcendant felicity ^as^ the Princess *Artabellas* affection (said he) will be too great to be credited from any but her self: he will rather fancy it a Fiction devized by me to perswade him to live, unless I bring him some testimony more pregnant then my asserting it.

If he will not believe it (repli'd she) let him come and see whether it be a truth or no.

Alass Madam (answer'd he) *Phasellus* is not in a capacity to wait on you; or if he were, I know he durst not come; he is too inviolable a performer of your commands to appear in your presence since you thought fit to banish him your sight, till he is well assur'd you have revers'd that sentence.

Aske any thing (said she) as a witness to my favour to him but that you last demanded, and I'le not deny it.

I'le onely beg the favour of one line from your faire hand (repli'd he) but to assure him of his repeal, and I will sue for no more at this time.

You are too importunate (said she smiling) [fol. 27ᵛ] but I'le excuse it upon the score of Friendship. Then calling for Pen and Paper she writ these words.

The Princes Artabella to Phasellus

If you are really what you seem evince it by a speedy recovery; if you do not, I
shall look on you as no other ^then^ the enemy of my repose as much as Diomed
has shewn ~~himf~~ himself a Friend to yours: live then, if for no other cause but to
testifie your gratitude to him to whom you are no less oblig'd for this, then to the
inclinations of

Artabella

When she had writen it she gave it *Diomed*: you see (said she) how willing I am to gratifie your Friendship, since for your satisfaction I force my selfe to those things most contrary to my humour. But before you go (continu'd she) you may give me a very great satisfaction if I may obtain of you one request without a prejudice to your self. Which is onely to let me know both your owne extraction and *Phasellus*'s that I may not still be ignorant who I have given my heart too.

This madam (he repli'd) I shall in few words resolve you; neither indeed can I discover his condition and conceale my owne, though I have some reasons that oblige me not to be known to any person whilst I make my residence abroad: but since it may conduce to the advantage of my Friend, I shall not scruple to declare that to you, which I desire may be a secret to all others; for I question not Madam but you are indued with that vertue which few of your sex can boast, though much to be admir'd for all other excellent qualitites.

The confidence (said she) that you repose in me shall never be deceiv'd.

Know then most Excellent Princess (repli'd he) that I am Nephew to
A^u^gustus C̶e̶aaesar[1] by his only Daughter the Princess *Julia*, who after the
death of the brave *Marsellus* (to whom she was first married) was again given by
the Emperour in marriage to his peculier Favouret *Agrippa*, as a person by him
believ'd more worthy of that honour then any Prince in Europe: from this second marriage I had the honour to proceed; and by my Royall Grandfather nam'd
Lucius Octavius (which name of *Octavius* himself was always call'd by, before he
took on him that of *Augustus*, which he assum'd not till such time as he joyn'd to
it that of Emperour) and by him declar'd his Successor in that mightie Empier:
two Brothers I have, both younger then my self, and one onely Sister call'd *Juliana*, who though she had attain'd but the twelfth year of her age when I left
Rome, yet were she not my sister I would say she Farre excel'd the fairest of our
Romane Dames; and such attractive charmes she carried in her lookes (young as
she was) that she might have [28ʳ] had the satisfaction (if her innocence could
have taken any in it) to have seen severall Princes (who were sent to Rome to
receive an education worthy of their births) weare her Fetters: this Sister did I
from her Infancy design for *Phasellus*, that I might by so neer an alliance tye him
no less strictly to me by the bands of Affinity then by those of Friendship: and
with her I intended to bestow on him soe larg a share of my Dominions (if I liv'd
my self to take possession of them) as he should have no reason to complain he
was not born a Prince, as I must confess he was not; yet is he descended from
one who though he never bare the burden of a Crown, yet did he ^en^throne
and un^de^throne[2] Princes at his pleasure, and had the satisfaction to behold
many puissant Kings his Vassalls prostrate their Crowns and Scepters at his Feet;
and had Fortune been but as propitious to him as she was kind to *Augustus* with
whom he disputed the Empier of the World, he had questionless worn that Empieriall Diadem which his Predecessor *Julius Caesar* onely fancied, never really
put on; being by treachery cut off ere he could bring his design to maturity. I
suppose Madam the Charactar I have given you sufficently speakes him to be the
great *Mark Antonie*, no less famous for his misfortunes then his Valour; whose
eldest Son *Julius Antonius*, was Father to *Phasellus*, or rather *Julius*, for so was he
call'd after his Fathers name; taking on him that of *Phasellus* (onely to oblige me)
as I did that of *Diomed* the better to disguise my true condition.

This I tell you madam (continu'd he) possibly may seeme so strang as scarce
worthy of credit since I am so meanly attended, without any equipage sutable to
my quality: but those reasons that invited me to travaile, induced me likewise to
go unattended to the end that I might ~~th~~ keep my self unknown till my return
which I intend not till I have gained so faire a reputation in the World as to have

----

[1] The lineage initially cited is inconsistent. Diomed seems to be the grandson, not
the nephew, of Augustus.

[2] Throne and unthrone are corrected to ^en^throne and ^dethrone^; "un" is underlined and "de" is inserted above.

no less a title to the Empire by vertue then by birth: and withall to fit my selfe
for so great and weighty an employment as I am one day to take on me. And
this I knew no better way to improve my self in then by travaile, which I knew
I should never obtain the Emperours consent for; which made me resolve to
depart in private. Unknown to any but my Sister I stole from Rome, waited on
onely by one Squire, and accompani'd with *Julius* to whom alone I had imparted
my designe, which he approv'd of, resolving likewise to take the same cou^r^se,
which I believ'd he would readily embrace; for oft had I heard ^him^ say (with
griefe) that the Gods had given him a courage much greater then his birth; and
complain (all things being in such tranquility and peace at home) that he wanted
a subject to employ his Courage on, which it was probable he might meet with in
other Countreys. I was not ignorant that by this action I incen'st the Emperour
against me: but I hope ere I see Rome again to performe something that may
invite him to pardon that liberty I took, when he considers upon what score I
assum'd it. Thus Madam have I declar'd that to you, which I will not discover to
any other: and since you were pleas'd to say you would be adviz'd by me, I deeme
it convenient [fol. 28^v^] for a while to hide from *Menzor* that respect you have for
Phasellus (for so we will call him still if you please, I desire (said she) he may have
no other name then that, since it was by that I knew him mine) as also his passion for you (continu'd *Diomed*), till he has ^had^ the good Fortune to performe
some such additionall generous acts as may induce your Father to pardon him,
and excuse your passion by the knowledge of that vertue which created it.

I [Aye] but (said she) my Father has so strictly charg'd me to receive your
addresses, that he will not admit of any pretence, or excuse to the contrary, if he
be not told my heart is already prepossest with an affection for another.

No madam (he repli'd) that would be the ready way to ruine your desires,
and incurre his displeasure, when he shall find your aversion to me has no other
cause then a preposession: no, rather give me leave to make some seeming Overtures to you, which you may ~~be~~ before him receive with kindness; and I will
assure him I find as much content in my Amours as I can in reason expect; and
withall desire him to keep it secret till I have oblig'd *Achemenes* to entertaine such
an advantagious opinion of me, as he may not oppose my felicity: this I propose
onely as a meanes to gain time till *Phasellus* has found an opportunity to ingrati-
ate himself with *Menzor*, and interesse himselfe further in his favour.

Against this advice *Artabella* had nothing to reply, but that she feared she
should not act the dissembler well; or if she did, she doubted it might raise some
^little^[3] Jealousie in *Phasellus*, lest that which was done in rallery, might be
reallity: which scruple he having clear'd, and made her understand there was no
better way to divert that Storme she apprehended, and dispose all things to her
content: which when she had a while consider'd on, she acknowledg'd her obli-

---

[3] The word "little" is inserted in what appears to be darker ink.

gation to him for this Councell. Then wishing her as much true Joy as he said he knew her letter would conveigh to his Friend, he bid her good night, after he had assur'd her, that he would for her sake no less then *Phasellus's* raise him to that height assoon as he ascended the Emperiall Throne, that she should have no cause to think she had made a choice below her birth, or he no reason to envie the most mi mighty Monarch, protesting Rome should see none greater in it (himself excepted) then *Phasellus*.

She would have given him her thankes for so Princely a promise, and made her excuse for not giving him that respect the granduer of his quality might have challeng'd, but he gave her not the leasure, but return'd to *Phasellus* whom he found in the greatest anxieties imaginable for feare he should return without success; but seeing him enter, he rais'd himself up in his bed, and turning to *Diomed*, what do you bring me Sir (said he) Life, or Death. I am resolv'd to obey what commands soever that Divine Princess has impos'd on me.

Then you must live (repli'd *Diomed*) if you love her, since she has commanded it as an evidence of your passion.

Yes (answer'd *Phasellus*) I will live since she injoynes it; but to what end should she desire me to live if she resolve to kill me hourly by a thousand deaths which her cruelty will inflict if she refuse my love.

An obedient Lover ought to obey, and not dispute (said *Diomed*) seeing tis her Will: but if you will put on patience but a little space, I shall make it appeare you have more reason to extoll her goodness, then exclame against her cruelty. See here (continu'd he pulling forth the Letter) behold what a comfortable Cordiall she has sent you: then calling for a Candle, *Phasellus* took it with a trembling, yet greedy hand, and [fol. 29ʳ] read it; which when he had done, he kiss'd it, and imbraced *Diomed*.

Oh dearest of Friends (cry'd he) how many thousand obligations have you conferr'd on me in this one.

Speak not of that (said *Diomed*) this is the least of that which I have done, and will do for thee; but prepare with Joy wit to heare what I have yet to tell thee.

Then seting down he related to him perticulerly all that had pass'd between *Artabella* and himselfe concerning him: as also the agreement they had made for awhile to delude *Menzor*, and thereby fill'd him with a Joy not to be express'd. But when he came to tell him of that resolution she had made, never to be his without *Menzor's* consent, he allai'd much of his precedent Joy.

Ah (said he sighing) to what a height of felicity did you raise me; but t'was too high for me to rest on; for I see such a Barre to my hop'd happiness as I doubt I shall never be able to remove. But yet, why should I dispaire, seeing I have overcome the greatest difficulty by vanquishing *Artabellas* resentments [sentiments], I will not fear the less; but assume a hope that in time I may through your assistance overcome that other obstruction to my happiness; and by your meanes obtain *Menzor's* permission to make my Addresses to his excellent daughter.

You need not doubt (answer'd *Diomed*) but I will contribute the uttmost of my endeavours to build your content, since I have not stuck to lay its Foundation upon the ruines of my owne. But we will talk no more of that, go you to sleep, and setle your disturb'd fancie; and regain that strength which you have too much impair'd by your rash and violent humour; that you may be able to go throw your selfe at the Feet of your Princess, to pay your thankes for that favour she has shewn you; and I will study how to accomplish that designe which I have contriv'd to render your happiness compleat.

Fain would *Phasellus* have repli'd, but *Diomed* would not suffer him, but injoyn'd him silence; desiring him not to disturbe his quiet, but wholly leave the care of his concernes to him. *Phasellus's* indisposition was quickly nois'd about the Court; insomuch that it came to *Achemenes's* and *Menzors* eare, who both of them appear'd sensibly concern'd for him. That very night ere *Diomed* return'd from *Artabella* the King had sent one to see him and bring him an account of his health: and the next morning *Menzor* gave him the honour of a visit, expressing a great deall of trouble for his illness. But so much did the repose of his mind contribute to the wellfare of his body, that the next day he was able to quit his bed, and the day after, his Chamber; which assoon as he was in a capacity of doing, he went with ~~Artabella~~ *Diomed* to wait on *Artabella* to pay her his Devotions, as to a Deity he had receiv'd a blessing from, much more precious then his life.

When they came in, they found there the Princess *Oriana* which *Phasellus* was a little troubled at, le^a^st her presence might deprive him of an opportunity of converse with his Princess: but *Diomed* soon freed him from that feare by leading *Oriana* to the Window, pretending [fol. 29 ᵛ] something of a private discourse with her: she being not unwilling to shew him any civill courtesie refus'd him not, but withdrew with him; for it was certaine she had a more then ordinary respect for him, far beyond what she ever had for any man before; yet nothing more then what Friendship might allow. *Phasellus* took notice of this obliging actions of *Diomeds*, and was highly pleas'd with it; and accordingly after thank'd him for it. But that he might not render fruitless his Friends officious care, he address't himself to his Princess; and taking one of her faire hands (which she with a little unwillingness permitted him) and joyning it to his lips with an action wholy passionate. Were it as convenient my adorable Princess (said he) as it is requisit, I would upon my knees implore your pardon for that errour, (nay that crime, for so I'le stile it, since it was such esteem'd by you) which the transports of my passion forced me to commit; as also in that posture pay those retributions which I owe for that unmerited clemencie you have been graciously pleas'd to shew your poor servant, when he was even overwhelm'd with dispaire.

As for your fault (repli'd she) I have wholy remitted it; and as for that which caus'd it, it likewise occation'd your punishment; and that a ~~much~~ more severe one, then I did, or should have imposed on you, had your offence been of a much more hainous quality: then speak no more of that, since I have done enough to assure you I have expell'd all thoughts of it.

But may I not feare Madam (answer'd he) I am still too indifferent to you, or that you may in time recall that transcendant felicity of your affection wherewith at present you pleas'd to honour me.

I know not (repli'd she casting down her eyes, and blushing) what to say, for I should thinke my actions had suffcently testified my esteeme; and ~~that~~ ^what^ I have condescended too in favour of you, might have clear'd all scruples concerning it: but if what I have already done, does not content you, let this protestation that I now make, give you satisfaction: that nothing but infidelity in you, shall ever have power to make me preferre any other before you; nor shall time, nor any other consideration whatever, rob *Phasellus* of the heart of *Artabella*, nor force her to be any mans, if she may not be his. After this engagement I suppose you have no reason to be dissatisfi'd; but expect no more promises from me.

I aske no more Madam (said he) and I beg of Heaven to invent new Plagues, and greater punishments for me, then have hitherto been inflicted on the most impious Offenders, if ever I give you cause to repent this favour, or any other you shall please to conferre on your *Phasellus*: for so I presume to stile my self since you vouchsafe not to disowne me.

He had not time to proceed, for *Diomed* and the Princess came and joyn'd company with them, and for a while pass'd away the time in severall pleasant discourses. After this *Phasellus* went to wait on *Achemenes*, and as he was going he met *Menzor*, who much congratulated his recovery; testifying abundance of joy to see him so soon in a capacity of leaving his Chamber; and went along with him to the King who seem'd to take no less [fol. 30ʳ] a content in his wellfare then his Brother had done.

Now had *Diomed* nothing more to do in the behalf of his beloved Friend, but absolutely to banish from his mind all thoughts of *Artabella*: but alas poor Prince, he found it much more ~~di~~ difficult then he expected: but notwithstanding he put on a resolution either to dye, or conquer; which at length (though not without many a painfull conflict between his generous Friendship and his passion) he effected. But questionless his resolution would have stood him in little stead, had he not had so faire an invitation to decline his affection for *Artabella* to place it on *Oriana*, who was no less beautifull, then the other was lovely: and one from whom he might derive those advantages which he could no way pretend too from *Artabella*. Besides, being incourag'd by the greatness of his birth not to fear a refusall from *Achemenes*, or herself, when he should once acquaint them with it. These considerations mov'd him to turn his eyes on the admirable perfections of that Princess. But now he had a harder Game to play then ever, being oblig'd to demean himself in such a manner to *Artabella*, that *Menzor* might believe him as happy as he knew himself the contrary upon that score: and yet he fear'd, that pretended kindness would ruine his designe upon *Oriana*, by giving her cause to suspect his passion for her was but feign'd: or else that he gave her but the reversion of a heart which another had rejected; as indeed he did, but was not willing she should know it. But so discreetly did he carry himselfe, that *Oriana* never had the least suspition of his love to *Artabella*; and yet, before *Menzor* he acted so well the passionat Lover, that he believ'd it reall: nay, *Artabella* herselfe was sometimes apprehensive that his heart and tongue too well agreed; and was often greev'd to see the trouble that for her sake he underwent. But when she was convinced that what he did was onely to delude her Father, and that although his passion was not extinct, yet the Object of it was chang'd, she was so well pleas'd, that she treated him with all the kindness, and respect that perfect Friendship could oblige her too; which gave *Menzor* as high a satisfaction as it was possible for him to conceive.

But this obliging deportment of hers to *Diomed*, infused some little feares into the mind of *Phasellus*, lest he should have a larger share in his Princesses esteeme then he could admitt of; notwithstanding she gave him daily many innocent testimonies of her vertuous, and unfeigned love; yet were they not sufficent to preserve him from Jealousie (that Poison of the Soule, and baine of all content) which so farre infected him, that it rendred his Addresses more cold, his visits less frequent to *Artabella* then usuall. *Diomed* was the first that perceiv'd it; and being confirm'd by severall circumstances that he was the Object of his Jealousie, he was very much [fol. 30ᵛ] concern'd that he for whose sake he had done somuch should give way to such unworthy thoughts of him, or such causeless suspitions of a Princess whose purity and candor was a sufficent guard against Detraction it self. At first he hoped that a little time would rectifie his errour; but seeing him still persevere in it, he took an occation one day to tell him of his fault, and represent to him the injury he did, both him, and *Artabella*. Fain would *Phasellus* have perswaded him he was mistaken in thinking there was any alteration in him; but alass it was to visible to be deni'd.

No no *Phasellus* (said *Diomed*) think not by this arteficiall dissemulation to disguise the wrong thou dost thy Friend, and Mistresse cans't thou be so unjust to imagine me capable of such a degenerate baseness as to seek by treachery to undermine thee, when I might (had it been my desire, or design) have oppos'd thee fairly: or if you can have such ignoble thoughts of me, yet methinkes that incomparable Vertue wherewith *Artabella* is indu'd, might have secur'd you from the least doubt or apprehension of disloyalty in her.

This reproofe being no less just then reasonable, forced him with shame to acknowledge his crime, but yet withall, he would have extenuated it by saying, his diffidence proceeded from no other cause then a sense of his owne unworthiness to possess so Divine a person, who could not be ignorant of her owne worth and merit (he said) which might excite her to esteeme him who best deserv'd her: and then, that which in others might be stil'd inconstancie, in her might be term'd Justice.

I know not (repli'd *Diomed*) what you call Justice, but certainly in the opinion of all reasonable men, infidelity was ever counted the highest injustice that could be done to any one; for admit you were as unworthy as you fancie, or as you may make your selfe indeed by these groundless mistrusts; or that I had done more to deserve her love then I have, or ever shall; yet neither the one consideration, nor the other can exempt her from the title of faithless, and unjust, should she for me, or any other, decline her affection, or violate the least tittle of her promises to you: then think not by a pretended feare of a want of merit, to paint over a Vice that appeares so detestable to your Friends, and ruinous to your owne repose, but go, and implore a pardon from your Princess whose Vertue and Innocence you have as highly wrong'd, as my integrity and Friendship.

At this *Phasellus* seem'd very penitent, beging *Diomed* both to forgive and forget his fault, which he said he so hated, and himself for being guilty of it, that he vow'd rather to rip his heart from out his brest, then harbour the least conjecture that might be capable of displeasing him, or offending his Princess.

With this Protestation *Diomed* was as well satisfi'd as he was the contrary before, and for *Phasellus*'s pardon, it was no sooner ask'd then granted. But this unexpected indifferency in his carriage had extreamly troubled *Artabella*, and the rather in regard she knew not what cause to impute it too. She [fol. 31ʳ] sommon'd all her actions before the Barre of a strict inquirie, but could find none but what might pass for innocent in the account of the severest Censurer, and then, what prejudice he could conceive against her, the more she sought, the further she was from finding. But alass this trouble was but a tast of that sorrow whereof ere long she was to drink so deep a draught; for this soon pass'd away by the returne of *Phasellus* to his accustom'd duty, and respect, which he pai'd her with a much greater assiduity then before, to make amends for his late neglect. But no sooner was this discontent over, but the Fates threw on her a much greater affliction then ever she was sensible of before, by depriving her of a most dearly beloved, and no less loving Father; snatching him away by the irresistable power of a violent Feavour, in less then ten days space.

Tis not possible for me (said *Celia*) to draw the true resemblance of her in her sorrow; but certain it is, that to such a height of griefe did that insupportable loss transport her, that those that saw her believ'd (and not without reason) that she would speedily follow him. All the perswasions that *Oriana* or the King could use, wrought nothing on her, but rather serv'd as aggravations of her griefe; which indeed none could justly blame considering how ~~ligitimate~~ it was: nor was she the onely, though the chiefest person concerned in his Death; all Persia in generall, lamented her perticuler loss; but especially *Achemenes* bewail'd him with all ^the^ tenderest ~~resentments~~ [feelings] that the death of a Brother, and such a Brother as the World could not shew a more affectionate one, was able to produce: oft was he heard to say with teares, that the chiefe Pillar of his Kingdome was fallen, and wish that he had parted with his Crown to save his life; and to testifie the kindness he had for him living, he shew'd it to that part of him which yet surviv'd, the disconsolate *Artabella*: for no sooner had the Universall Conqueror tryumph'd over her Father, by leading him to that Prison whence no ransome could redeeme him, but he gave her an equall interest in his Princely care with that he had for the Princess: ~~of her~~ and in all respects treated her as a

Daughter: so that if her wound could have admitted of any cure but that of time, she needed not to have felt so great a smart as she long endured: but at length, Time, that universall cure of griefes, wrought that effect on hers; and made her cease from sheding those fruitless teares, which she so long invain had been too prodigall of; that she might give permission to *Phasellus* to waite on her, which Favour she had denied him a great while after *Menzor*'s death; confining herself to her Chamber for above a quarter of a year, suffering none to see her, but those she durst not refuse a visit from, as the King, and Princess: and though *Phasellus* had often beg'd the favour of her sight, yet would she not condescend to it, that she might debarre herself the enjoyment of all things that might affoard her either comfort, or content: and indeed, *Phasellus*'s company was all that she could find a satisfaction in; and on that score it [fol. 31ᵛ] was that she refused to see him. And besides to take from him all hopes that she would so soon (as possibly he expected) assume that liberty which her Father at his death bequeath'd her, leaving her wholy (as he did) to her owne dispose.

But now that she had found from the hand of time a little ease for her tormented mind; and that those Clouds of griefe wherewith sorrow had so long orecast the heaven of her beautie were a little disperced, she resolv'd no longer to suffer *Phasellus* to languish for the enjoyment of her sight, nor debarre herself that innocent freedome she formerly had taken. All the Court was extreamly joy'd to see her abroad once more, whom they lately fear'd would have buried herselfe alive by abandoning all society. But above all, *Phasellus* seem'd so transported that he was scarce able to contain his Joy within the bounds of moderation, but was thorow the excess of it like to discover that, which prudence told him ought as yet to be preserv'd a secret: for although *Menzor* left *Artabella* at liberty to make her owne choice, yet was the Kings consent no less necessary now, then her Fathers was before: not that she beleiev'd the King would find any reason to disapprove of *Phasellus* for a Husband for her; but the onely thing she apprehended was, le^a^st he might be displeas'd that she should presume to chuse any one without his knowledge or approbation, which persons of her quality (being so neer alli'd to the Crowne as she was) seldome or never do, without incur^r^ing a reproofe from their Soveraign. This consideration made her unwilling *Achemenes* should be acquainted with her passion, till he might be perswaded to allow of it; which she hop'd would be a matter of no great difficulty if *Diomed* once undertook to effect it; which she could not at all doubt of, considering his Friendship to *Phasellus*, and *Achemenes*'s to him: for after *Menzor* died, he possest the Kings favour in so high a degree, that he appear'd the onely man in Persia that *Achemenes* honour'd with a perticuler esteeme: and though Envie does alwayes attend on Favourits, yet such an influence had his Vertues on the hearts of all in generall, that there was not any that bare a noble Soule, or had the least sense of Vertue, that once repin'd, or thought his Fortune greater then his merit.

These things she represented to *Phasellus* as oft as he prest her to perfect his felicity, which he said, could never be compleat till Hymen had united their hands, as well as Love their hearts. But this she would not as yet be perswaded too, but endeavour'd by reason to convince him that there was a kind of nessesity for this delay; which she assur'd him should be no way to his prejudice; for his she would be; nor should all the powers on earth (now that she was freed from her Fathers) force her to anothers, or detain her from him: but as she told [fol. 32ʳ] him, she thought it more discretion if she could obtain the Kings consent, then for her openly to declare what he might possibly look on as a disrespect to that duty she ow'd him as her Soveraign. But notwithstanding she carried herself so reserv'd towards him in publick, yet in private she allow'd him all the freedom that Vertue and honour would permit; and daily gave him such unquestionable demonstrations of her fidelity, and reall esteeme; that he could not but be as well satisfi'd with his condition, as if he had been possest of what he most desir'd.

But though *Phasellus* was arriv'd at almost as great a height of happiness as fancy could imagine, yet *Diomed* poor Prince, made but a slow progress in his Amours to *Oriana*. For as oft as he sought opportunities of disclosing his passion, she still found evasions to prevent him; yet alwayes demean'd herselfe with so great a civility, and respect that she gave him no just cause to be dissatisfi'd with her: but yet small comfort was it to him to live between hope and dispaire: so that he resolv'd no longer to deferre a declaration, which could not be much more injurious to him then his silence was.

But as he was upon the point openly to profess himself a Servant to the Princess (from whom he could not feare a scorn as to his birth, if she did not disdaine his person) Persia rang with the certaine intelligence of a new invasion from *Oruntus* (the King of ~~Persia~~ ^Scythia^) in revenge of his Brothers death: which when *Achemenes* was assur'd of, he resolv'd to prevent him, by carrying the Warre home into his owne Country; for seeing he delighted in it, he would so farre oblige him as to present him with his owne desires: and to this end he speedily caus'd an Armie of no less then fourscore thousand men to be rais'd to send into Scythia. The noise of this ensuing Warre for a while gave a stop to *Diomed's* intentions; in hope this War (which he intended to be an Actor in) might present him with some occations of acquiring more glory, and new opportunities of further obliging *Achemenes*. Never till now was Persia truly sensible of the loss of their valliant Generall; and when all men were big with expectation who the King would confer that honour on, he declar'd, he thought none so well worthy of it as *Diomed*; who (as he said) had once before by his sole vallour freed Persia from the invading Scythian. This choice was highly approv'd on by all but *Praxaspes* (a Persian Prince) who having some relation to the Crowne, thought scorn a wandring stranger (as he term'd *Diomed*) should be preferr'd before him, or intrusted with an affaire of so high a concernment: but for all his resentment [feelings], he was fain to comply with the Will of the King, which he well knew was not to be opposed. All else but he, were farre better pleas'd to be commanded by *Diomed*, then he was to command them; for when *Achemenes* gave him his Commission he would modestly have declin'd it, desiring him to give that honour to some other whose yeares and experience might render him fitter to undertake [fol. 32ᵛ] so great an enterprize. But all he said rather heightned the Kings esteeme then any way alter'd his resolves; which when *Diomed* saw, he took on him to be Generall, more out of compliance to *Achemenes* his desires then his owne inclinations: though he was not ignorant how advantagious it might be to his designes, by affording him all the opportunities that might be of gaining a greater increase of glory; which was the onely thing his desires aim'd at, as being the ready way to obtain the Princesse's affection, who could value none but such as the highest Vertue gave a title to her Love.

This Warre was a new affliction to poor *Artabella*, when she consider'd it must of necessity separate her and *Phasellus* for some considerable time, if not for ever, the events of War being doubtfull: and he, she knew, or at least beleiv'd, had too much of gallantry to continue in the pleasures of a Court, whilst his Friend underwent those many dangers that attend on War. Nor was she less a Friend to his Fame, then a Lover of his person; and on that score it was, she would not court his stay so much as with a wish; being sensible how prejudiciall it would be to that which she priz'd highest in him if he should not accompany *Diomed* in this expedition.

The time preceeding their departure, *Diomed* spent in excercising his Souldiers, and in all the duties of a discreet Commander; which his wise conduct, rather then his age, or experience spake him to be: and so well did he instruct all his Officers, that a more exact dissipline was never seen at Rome, then in the Persian Campe as it afterwards appear'd. *Phasellus* might have made choice of what Place, or Command in the Armie he was most ambitious of; but he was so farre from desiring, that he would not accept of any; protesting he had rather be at liberty to fight there where his assistance was most necessary. But about two days before the Armie was to begin their march, there came to Susa (where the King was then resident) 500 young Gentlemen of the noblest Families in the Kingdome, and volluntarily proffer'd their service to *Diomed*, beging him to appoint a Captain over them, whom unanimously they desir'd might be *Phasellus*, since they could not have the honour (as they said) to be commanded by himself in perticuler. An imployment fitter for *Phasellus* then this; *Diomed* could not have wish'd (since they were men whose courages seem'd equall to their births,) and therefore yeelded to their requests. Nor could *Phasellus* civilly refuse it, seeing they had so far oblig'd him, as to nominate him in perticuler. These Gallants were all, exceedingly well hors'd and Arm'd: their Horses being of the breed of Sparta, and their Armour of the purest Lydian Steel pollish'd as bright as Silver.

All things being now in a readiness, *Diomed* thought it best, not any longer to delay time (that he might take from the enemie all those advantages that delays might give them) but sent away the whole [fol. 33ʳ] body of his Armie under the command of *Barsarnes* his Lieutenant Generall, onely he detain'd *Phasellus*'s Troope in Susa to wait on their Captain, and himselfe, who stay'd a day or two behind to receive the Kings orders for the management of this

great affaire; which he had no sooner receiv'd but he went to take his leave of
Achemenes, who imbraced him with as great a kindness as *Menzor* could have
expected had he been living.

Goe *Diomed* (said he) and make good your title to what I do designe you;
and let the Scythians know, though I have lost a Brother, yet Persia still retaines
a Person that can repaire that loss.

To this expression of the Kings he made a reply, no less gratfull, then his was
obliging, and departed to kiss the Princess's hand, whilst *Phasellus* went to bid
adue to *Artabella*. She finding herself unable to think that *Phasellus* must leave
her, without a mortall disquiet, knew she was much less able to beare his departure without a visible griefe; which that she might the better conceale, for a week
before, she fain'd herselfe not well; nor did she much dissemble, for the trouble
of her mind made her really almost ill as she pretended. When *Phasellus* came in,
he found her siting in the most Melancholy posture imaginable; and so deeply
musing, that she perceiv'd him not till he was come almost to her: but when she
saw him, she gave a sudden start.

And are you come *Phasellus* (said she) to tell me that you must be gone: alass
I know it but too well, then spare me the trouble of hearing you speake it: but
notwithstanding tis to me a griefe so great, so bitter to part with you, that I had
rather dye (did not Death forever deprive me of your company) then beare it, yet
I will not use one Argument to stay you here, nor once desire it of you. The onely
thing that I will beg of you shall be, not to let your high courage transport you to
actions beyond ~~the reach~~ your capacity; I mean, that you be not too prodigall of a
life that is not at your owne disposal and that you may do nothing rashly, consider
Phasellus each drop of blood you shed, is drawn from the heart of *Artabella*. With
that, a floud of teares fell from her eyes, which drown'd the passage of her words
that she could say no more.

For Heavens Sake Madam (he repli'd) dry up those precious drops: the sight
of so much griefe in you, wounds me farre deeper then any enemies sword can do;
I know ere long I shall returne in saftie, for I cannot doubt any ill fate attends a
person that weares the glorious title of *Artabella's* Servant.

To tell you (said *Celia* to the Sicilian Lady) all the expressions that *Artabella*
made, both of griefe and affection to *Phasellus*; and all that he said to passifie
her, would be but tedious; and much better Madam may you conceive (if you
have ever been in the like condition) what pass'd between them then I relate it:
therefore if you please we will leave them for a while, and follow *Diomed* [fol.
33ᵛ] to *Oriana's* Chamber whether he was gone. You may well imagine it was no
small trouble to him to leave her (loving her passionately as he then did) without
knowing what to hope or feare; having never made any perticuler address to her,
nor ever made other discovery of his passion then what his sighes might give.
This, when he reflected on, imprinted such a sadness in his lookes, that any
one that saw him might easily perceive it; especially when he came to take his
leave of *Oriana* for then he seem'd so disorder'd that she could not forbear tak-

ing notice of it saying, were I not assur'd both of your fidelity to my Father, and your generous courage sufficently enough, not to leave in me the least doubt of your continuing the same, this discontent that sets upon your Brow would breed a suspition in me, that you are dissatisfi'd with your employment, or else that you doubted your success; which can never be fear'd so long as *Diomed* maintaines our quarell.

You will oblige me Madam (repli'd he) to impute this sadness (which in despight of my endeavour to the contrary will shew it self) to any cause rather then a dissaffection to the King your Fathers service: for such is the respect I owe him, that had I as many lives to loose as I have liv'd minutes; or were each drop of blood that runs in my Veines a River; I would freely sacrifice those lives, and draw those rivers dry, with a joy not to be express'd, to purchace him that peace, and prosperity I wish him. Nor it it any feare of a misfortune as to the Kings concerns that does afflict me, neither the sword of an enemie that I dread; for their united Force I can, and do dispise. No Madam, tis onely a feare that has possess'd me (which prints these Charactars of sadness which you read in my Lookes) that when I have subdu'd those barbarous Scythians (which I question not through the assistance of the Gods to do) and brought home Victory along with me, that then I must be condemn'd to suffer death, or banishment.

I cannot think the Noble *Diomed* (said she) capable of contracting any guilt, that may in the least deserve so severe a punishment; yet admit you could, certainly you know my Father but a little, if you imagine cruelty has any acquaintance with his disposition: for great indeed must be your crime, which so many obligations as he has, and may yet receive from you, cannot move him to forgive.

It is not Madam (answer'd he) from *Achemenes* that I apprehend that severe sentence, but from the Oracle of my Fate his faire Daughter, on whose permission to adore her, depends my life, or death. This presumption Madam you may esteem unpardonable; but that which makes my offence, must likewise plead my excuse: your unequall'd perfections being the cause that has produced an effect, which I can no more repent of, then endeavour to recover a freedome, which the irresistable influence of your divine graces made me so long since most willingly resigne, though till this minute I retain'd the power not to importune you with my passion: nor had I as yet unvail'd my heart, till by some noble actions I might have hop'd to gaine some little title to your esteeme, had I been but certain I should [fol. 34ᵛ] ever again behold those Eyes which have enspir'd me with a Flame so lasting, as, the coldness of the Grave can never tryumph over, nor extinguish.

I am sorry (repli'd *Oriana* very mildly) that you should now give me cause to be displeased with you, since I have hitherto highly esteem'd you, and alwayes valu'd you at as high a rate as I thought you could any way pretend too; but since you have abused those favours I have shewn you by making them a rise to your ambitious pretences, you must not thinke it strange if I henceforth let you see the difference there is between the Daughter of *Achemenes* and your selfe.

If you meane Madam (answered he) betwixt our births, perhaps hereafter when I have the honour to be known to you, there will not be so vast a disproportion found as you suppose; but I confess between your merits and my deserts, there is so great a one as nothing can be more: but if none but a person that can equall your perfections must possess you, there lives not a man upon the earth that can be worthy of that honour. But that you may see Madam I am not ambitious of ought, but of the glory of being yours, I wish you were the meanest Lady in Persia, that then you might perceive the passion I have for you, proceeds not from selfe interest, but springs onely from the acquaintance I have with those pe divine excellencies that render ^you^ the Merrour of your age, and sex: or if you esteeme the Crown of Persia to rich an Ornament for *Diomed* to weare, bestow it on some other more deserving; give me but your person, and let who will enjoy your Fathers Throne; I shall find a Diadem to empale your Temples with, no less glittering then this that you are born too, and an Empier of as larg an extent to make you Empress of.

If you (the Princess answer'd) will have me credit so great an improbability, as that a Prince, and such a Prince as you speak your selfe to be; should remaine incognito so long as you have done, you must give me some testimony more convinceing then your bare assenting it; yet I must needs say, I have observ'd somewhat in your meen [mien], and actions that seem'd silently to declare your nobility.

If I may be but so happy Madam (he repli'd) as to gain a beliefe from you of what I have declar'd but till the end of this War, I'le aske no greater favour now; at which time, if I do not give you undeniable demonstrations of what I now averre, inflict on me the punishment due to a dissembler, and to a person that would go about to betray you with a falshood.

If you are such (said she) as your discourse seemes to inferre, I have not so much reason to be offended with you as I late suppos'd I had; but were you yet much greater then you are, I must tell you, I cannot approve of a discourse I understand not; and therfore must desire you not to give me the trouble of hearing it repeated.

Your desires Madam (said he) shall ever be commands to me, and as such, religiously observ'd; then seeing tis your Will I suffer in silence, I will obey you: but Death I trust will proove more kind then you, in healing those wounds your beauty made, but you refuse to cure. But when I have^[n]'t^ found remedy that ^which^ now I go to seek, and that I [fol. 34^v^] am fallen your Victime, let me conjure you Madam (continu'd he throwing himselfe at her Feet) not to hate the memory of him ^who^ would live onely to adore you, and di'd to obey you.

These words he pronounced with so serious, and mournfull an accent, that *Oriana's* heart which was not composed of Adamant relented; and giving him her hand to raise him up. No (*Diomed* said she) your offence is not so hainous as to deserve death for the expiation of it: but if you are such an obedent servant as you would make me believe, do not vainly throw away your life; and to encourage you to the performance of this Command, I'le tell you, that perhaps Fortune may be more propitious to you at your returne then you now expect, for if you can gain *Achemenes* to favour your desires, I shall not study to oppose them; for tis his Will, must ever be my Law.

She had much adoe to bring out these last words; but when she spoke them, she was somuch out of countenance that she could not stay to heare what answer he would make, but bid him farewell, wishing him happie success, and a prosperous returne, and retir'd to her Closet.

You may imagine (said *Celia* to the Sicilian lady) that *Diomed* went away very well satisfi'd, for a more favourable answer he could not have wish'd. The next morning early he and *Phasellus*, together with his Vollunteres left Susa, and in few dayes o'retook the whole body of their Armie, and by great marches came to Maran the chiefe Citty of Margiana a Province of Persia, not farre from the River Araxes over which they were to pass into Scythia. When they came thither, *Diomed* made there some litle stay to rest his Troopes, that they might march unharras'd into Scythia, which after some small repose they did made all possible speed to do.

But ere they could pass the Araxes (which separates the two Kingdomes) *Oruntus* had sent an Armie not much inferior to the Persian. These Forces he intended should have enter'd Persia before they had enter'd his Dominians, but *Diomed* was too nimble for them, for he was assoon at the one side of the River, as they were at the other; whether being come, he try'd all wayes imaginable to gain the opposite Bank, but was a long time kept off by their Arrowes: but the difficulty, and danger he found in the attempt rais'd his courage (if possible) to a higher pitch; for after having sounded the River to find where it was easiest to be Fourded, he clasp'd downe the Vizour of his Helmet, and relying somewhat on the goodness of his Armour, he rush'd into the water, animating his Cavallry by his perswasion, but more by his example to follow. The next that went in after him was *Phasellus* and his Troop, and after them the rest; so that in fine there stay'd not one Horseman behind. This was no petty enterprize that *Diomed* [fol. 35ʳ] undertook, for the Araxes running swiftly, they had much adoe to beare up against the Current: but at last, though with much difficulty they got safe over, except some few that were slain with the Arrowes which were incessantly shot at them as they swame.

The Scythians terrifi'd at such a prodigie of courage as they beheld in *Diomed*, had not enough left them to stand the first assault: he perceiving the confusion, whereinto their feare, and astonishment had thrown them, gave them not leasure to rally their discomposed spirits, but charg'd them so vigorously, that thereby he gave his Infantry time to pass over in those Boates they had provided for that purpose; and they coming up fresh to his assistance, with an inconsiderable loss, he put the Scythians to the route, killing above 40000 upon the place, besides a considerable number of Prisoners which they took; the rest fled to Eupateria the next Citty, whether *Diomed* meant first to direct his march: which

he thought best ^to do^ assoon as conveniently he could, that he might not give
time to the enemy by their recrutes to relieve that Citty, which once being taken,
he knew would be of no small consequence to him upon any occation to retire
too. But when he drew neer it, he found it seated soe amongst the Rocks, that it
seem'd almost inaccessable; and as strongly fortified by Art, as Nature: but this,
^instead^ of disheartning, rather inflam'd this fierce young Prince with a more
fervent desire of improving his glory, by interprizing things not easily gain'd.

But whilst he besieg'd this Place (which was as well victuall'd for a siege, as
fortifi'd) *Oruntus* was not employ'd like him, who sate devizing a Net to catch
Flyes whilst his Citty was in danger to be taken; but with all cellerity rais'd
another Armie farre greater then the former; over which he appointed *Cydarius*
(Prince of Issedon) Generall; a person of the greatest valour, and conduct in his
Kingdome. This was so speedily perform'd, that they came and camp'd at the
Persians backs ere *Diomed* imagin'd there could be any appearance of an Armie;
for though he kept Scoutes on all sides to bring him intelligence, yet *Cydarius*
march'd with that secricy, and through such bye, and unfrequented places, that
the Scoutes discover'd them not till they surrounded the Persians, leaving them
no way to escape (having the Citty before, and they behind) unless they could
hew themselves a passage thorow their Armie: so that of besigers, the Persians
were now become the besieged.

Diomed soon found the errour, the little knowledge he had in that Countrey
made him commit; and therefore to rectifie it, he resolv'd to raise the siege: and
supposing, darkness would most savour his design, he order'd his Armie to be
ready for a march about the dead [fol. 35ᵛ] of night; which being come, he sent
a small Partie to allarum that side of the Campe where *Astianax* the Lieutenant Generall of the Scythians was quarter'd, and whilst the Enemy thought the
greatest danger to arise from thence, he broke with all his Force upon that part
where *Cydarius* lay, not dreaming of any such surprize; and gave them so sudden,
and hot a charge, being assisted by Nights black shades (which alwayes represents
dangers in the most horrid shape) and their feares, which had in a manner infatuated them, and put them in so great a disorder, that ere Aurora could discover
what they had done, they found they had safely pass'd the Campe, and retreated
to the top of an high Hill at a good distance, leaving the Scythians to lament the
deaths of 5000 of their Fellows.

This exploit of *Diomeds* so frighted the enemie, notwithstanding the valour
of their Captain, that instead of offering to fight him (as he expected they would)
they pass'd thorow Eupateria which open'd her gates to receive them, and went
and encamped on the other side; as well to cuccour [succor] the Citty, as to
secure themselves till further supplies should come, which they daily look'd
for: but before they came, *Diomed* had 10000 Foot, and 5000 Horse sent him
by *Achemenes* to augment his strength, wherewith he so strongly rebesieg'd
Eupateria, as in despight of all the opposition they could make, he in ten dayes
space carri'd it by storme; and with such a heroick courage march'd to encounter

his enemies, that it utterly destroy'd theirs, and made them timerously retire to a place where t'was impossible to constraine them to fight; nor could he by any meanes provoke them to it (though he had oft made it his endeavour) till after the arrivall ^of^ 8000 to increase their number. Yet was it not out of cowardice that *Cydarius* declin'd the battell, but out of prudence: having already receiv'd two great losses, and therefore was unwilling to put the third to a hazard, or stand to the curtesie of Fortune, till he knew himself strong enough to dispute the Victorie; which now he knew he was, and therefore would no longer delay, but drew out his Forces into Batailia on a larg and spacious Plain on the right side of Eupateria.

Diomed though much fewer in number, with joy accepted *Cydarius*'s summons, and ranging his men to the best advantage, advanced to the Battell as to an assured victory. After the Charge was mutually sounded the Fight most fiercely began on all sides; and thorough all the Ranks Death walk'd in tryumph, nor knew he a long time on which side to boast his greatest Trophies, nor could that day deside it, though there was slain above 50000 on both sides, besides 10000 wounded. Nothing but the approach of night could make the valliant leaders to retire; but that compell'd them to a cessation till the next Morning: when early they renew'd the Fight more vigorously then before, and *Phasellus* and his Followers did so many gallant things, that should I undertake to [fol. 36ʳ] relate them (said *Celia*) I should but injure the Acters: but notwithstanding all his valour he was one time very neer being taken; the danger he was in soon flew to the eares of *Diomed*, who was himself at the same instant almost in as bad a condition, for advanceing too farre amongst his enemies, he could not retreat, but was even overwhelm'd with those multitudes, that presst him so closely that he had no small taske to defend himselfe: but the newes of his deare Friends danger transported him to that height of rage, that the effects of it fatally discharg'd it self with a fury so impetuous, that in an instance he laid 4^00^0 of his enemies dead at his Horses Feet, and through their bodies made a Lane to pass to *Phasellus*'s assistance: but when he got up to him he saw it needless, for the courage of his Generous Companions had freed him, which haveing with Joy beheld, he left him to go seek out *Cydarius*, who was bravely performing the duty of a Generall. *Diomed* finding him truly valliant, thought him the worthiest of his sword which had too long imbrew'd it self in common blood. And besides, he saw him the onely person that supported the now drooping spirits of the Scythians; and therefore (not without good reason) he concluded, if he could either kill, or take him Prisoner, the Bataile would quickly be at an end.

But whilst he was searching after *Cydarius*, *Phasellus* had the good Fortune to kill *Astianax* with his owne hand, which very much discourag'd that part of the Armie which he commanded; which when *Cydarius* understood, he ranne with a desire equall to *Diomeds*, to find him out, knowing it was his life alone that could raise again those fainting spirits, which the loss of one of their Generalls had so disheartned, that they were ready to quit the Field. But far he had not gone, ere (according to his wish) he found him; whom he no sooner saw, but he cry'd out, defend thy self. *Diomed* not giving him leasure to say more, met him with his sword advanced in the Aire, which he discharg'd so fully on his head that it made him reel in his Sadle; but the goodness of his Armour so well resisted the Blows, that he receiv'd not much prejudice by it: but setling himself faster, he quickly requited *Diomed* with another, no less forceable; but being nimble, he started aside, so that the blow that was intended for his head, lit on his left shoulder: but he repay'd it with another that cut in sunder the Braces of *Cydarius*'s Helmet. His head being thus unarm'd, he cover'd it with his Shield, and so well defended himself, that *Diomed* confest he never met a braver man: which made him rather desirous to take, then kill him, and on that score he proffer'd him his life, on condition he would yeeld himself Prisoner.

This he being displea[s]ed at, repli'd, I scorn a Life that must be purchaced with my freedome, let Cowards accept life on such conditions, a generous spirit ever prefer'd [fol. 36ᵛ] a noble death before a base captivity, or mercy from an enemy.

With this he renew'd the Combate with so fresh a vigour, that *Diomed* saw it was invain longer to spare him, but laid him on so briskly, that in a short time he dismounted him, and laid him at his Horses Feet for dead. When the Scythians saw their Generall dead, their hopes expir'd with him, and staying not so much as to fetch off his body; but basely abandoning him, they turn'd their backs and fled, whilst the Persians persu'd them as long as day would permit, and gain'd a victory as intire as they could wish it; for of those vast numbers that came into the Field, there was scarce 3000 left alive (and of those, divers were taken Prisoners) to go carry to Sinope the sad tydings of ther defeat: nor had those Troopes so scap't, had not the darkness of the night befriended them.

No sooner was *Diomed* return'd from the pursute, but he went himselfe by the light of many Torches to search for the body of *Cydarius* that he might be carried from amonge those heapes of Carkases wherewith he was inviron'd, that he might either conveigh his body to Issedon (the chiefe Citty of his Princepality) or else give it there those Funurall Exequies his Vertue merited. Being come where he lay weltring in a sea of blood, he caus'd him to be taken up, and carried to his owne Tent; whether being brought they laid him on a Bed, and going to disarme him, they heard him grone, which gave them an assurance life had not quite forsaken him. This *Diomed* being enform'd of, commanded his Chirurgions (who were dressing his owne Wounds that he had receiv'd in the Fight) to leave him, and view *Cydarius* his body, promising them great rewards if they could cure him (for as he said, it griev'd him very much so gallant an enemy should perish by his sword) this they promis'd to do, if it were in the power of Art to performe. When they had search'd his wounds, they found not any that they could think mortall, only the loss of somuch blood made them doubtfull of their success: notwithstanding haveing first dress't his wounds, they then made it

their business to recall those spirits which were taking their last farewell; which
at last they effected.

When he first open'd his eyes, he cast them with a languishing look about,
and perceiving himself in a strang place, and not one Face present that he had
ever seen, he presently conjectur'd what his condition was; and fixing his eye on
Diomed, as on a person that deserv'd a more perticuler notice then any of the
rest; when he had recover'd his speech, he address't himself to him with a faint
voice saying. I am your Prisoner Sir I see, but Death will set my better part at
liberty ere long, and deprive you of that satisfaction you pretend too in sending
Cydarius shakled to your King, and free me from the shame I suffer in seeing my
selfe o'recome.

Tis true (*Diomed* repli'd) you are my Prisoner by the Law of Armes, which
gives me a right to stile you so; but yet, such shall your usage be, as you shall have
but little reason to believe you are soe: and were I absolute Master of my actions,
I soon would render you that liberty you so generously disputed; nor [fol.37ʳ]
should any thing detain you here, but an incapacity to go hence: though I am
not ignorant that in giving you your freedome, I restore the King your Master
more then the fortune of this day has taken from him: but being oblig'd to give
an account of my proceedings to *Achemenes*, I dare not presume without his permission to give you what I wish I could. Then think not *Cydarius* I so dilligently
sought you to insult over, or to reserve you as a Trophie to adorne my tryumphs
with; but rather with a designe to save your life if there were any possibility of it:
which if I may be a meanes of preserving, believe it tis the onely satisfaction that
I aime at; and shall esteeme it the greatest I derive from this success.

These high expressions of civility strook *Cydarius* dumbe, but when he had
regain'd his speech (he cry'd out) Great Gods is it possible so much Vertue lives
on earth. I will no longer account my selfe wholy miserable since you have let me
be vanquish'd by no other then the most generous of men (and streaching out his
Armes to embrace *Diomed* who did the like to him) I am not troubled now to live
(continu'd he) nay I shall eagerly court my cure, that I may be in a condition to
find out some way more then by words, to express my gratitude, and the sense I
have of your galantry; it onely troubles me that I am bound by my alleageance to
my Prince to be your enemie; but though I am confined to be so to your Partie,
yet no consideration whatsoever, shall make me an enemy to your person: for
against all men breathing my King excepted, I will ever take your part.

After *Diomed* had renew'd his assurances to *Cydarius* of a treatment worthy
of him, he wish'd him good rest; and leaving him to his repose, he retir'd to his
owne, after he had caus'd those hurts he had receiv'd in the Fight to be dress't,
which were so inconsiderable that they deserv'd not the name of wounds. *Phasellus* scap'd not altogether so well, but though his Wounds were many, yet were
they in such places as they did not much prejudice him, nor at all confine him to
his bed, longer then was necessary for that rest that Nature requir'd. Some days
ensuing were spent in burying the dead, lest those vast number of Carcasses by

their stench should infect the Aire. Assoon as *Cydarius* was in a condition to be remov'd *Diomed* caus'd him to be conveigh'd to Eupateria which he strongly fortifi'd placeing in it a considerable Garrisson to defend it against the Scythians in case they should attempt the recovery of it; for no sooner was the Battell wone but they yeelded themselves to the mercy of the Conquerour.

Here left he *Cydarius* with servants to attend him sutable to his quality (not as a Prisoner, but as a Prince) and advanced like a tryumphant Conquerour, finding but little opposition; for so formidable was his very name to the Scythians, that he no sooner summon'd their Citties then they yeelded: so that in foure moneths space he subdu'd three of the most considerable Provinces of Scythia; which were the Sacans, Sogdians, and Massigets. *Achemenes* constantly receiv'd the tydings of *Diomeds* successfull [fol. 37ᵛ] proceedings with an infinite satisfaction, and was per[pe]tually busied in raising new leavies to send him as often as he should stand in need of them. Nor was *Oruntus* less solicitus for the providing for the defencive, then *Achemenes* was for the offencive part of war; and to that end he had drawn together all the Force that he could possibly raise, intending to march in person at the head of them, to try if by his presence he could regain what he had lost; or if his ruine was decreed, he resolv'd to fall like himself. This resolve of his *Diomed* was not a little joy'd at hoping that this one Battell more, would deside the controversie, and end the war, the finishing whereof he passionatly long'd for, that he might be at leasure to attend his owne concernes; and wait on his Princess, from whose sight he had in his conceit been absent whole ages; so tedious is time to an impatient Lover.

This designe of *Oruntus's* he gave *Achemenes* an account of by Letters; which he having receiv'd, dispatch'd away with all expedition 60000 to aide him against that day which was destin'd to be the last to such an infinite of men. This *Oruntus* having intelligence of, made all the hast he could to meet *Diomed* that he might fight him before that supply could joyne with him. But *Diomed* to incommode him as much as might be, would not stir from the place where he was, that he might put him to the trouble of a longer march, but encamp'd neer Issedon, intending to wait his coming, which he had not long expected ere they came. He would willingly have declin'd fighting till the arrivall of these additionall numbers that he daily look'd for, who were coming to him with all the hast they could possibly make; for knowing his Armie to be far less then the Scythians, he was not willing wholy to depend on Fortune, who for the most part failes those that relie upon her.

But notwithstanding his endeavour to the contrary, *Oruntus* constrain'd him either to fight, or retire: but when he [Diomed] saw there was no way to avoid it without a prejudice, he accepted of the Battell; trusting to the protection and goodness of the Gods who had thitherto carried him on so properously in all his undertakings: and in hopes that they would not now abandon him, he began the Battaile with such an undaunted look that it startled the most valourous of his enemies, and rais'd his owne Partie to that height of courage that nothing could along time withstand their force: but the Scythians Arrowes did so gall, and vex their Horses, that they were more troubled to rule them then overcome their Foes. Twice *Diomed* encounter'd *Oruntus* hand to hand, and questionless the second time he had found his Brothers Fate had it not been for some of the most dareing of his men; who seeing the [fol. 38ʳ] danger he was in threw themselves between and parted them; but many of them paid no less a price then their lives for his rescue.

But to contract this relation in as narrow a compass as possibly I can, because it would require a larger time then I am alow'd to recite each perticuler, and besides having so many things of greater consequence then the perticulers of a Battell to relate, I shall pass over these tragicall events as briefly as I may. Let it suffice then Madam (continu'd *Celia*) that I tell you that in this Battell the Sceane chang'd thrise; for Victory was three times won, and lost: but after all her various traverses she stay'd herselfe upon the Persian Banners: though I know not whether they account'd not this victory worse then a defeat, since they unfortunately lost their valliant Leader (the noble *Diomed*) who eagerly chaceing the flying Scythians, had by misfortune his Horse kill'd by an Arrow. For the Bow is a weapon those People are so skillfull at, that they can shoot with no less dexterity backward then Forward. The falling of his Horse dead under him being perceiv'd by some of the hindmost of them, with a shout they turn'd back and run upon him in such multitudes that all his strength was too little to defend him; and so far was he advanced before the rest, that ere they could come up to his assistance, they so incompass'd him round, that being o're power'd by their numbers, he was taken: which they had never done, had they not press'd him so closely, that they left him not roome to use his sword.

And now the Fight began again afresh; for the foremost of the Scythians hearing their Fellows shout, immediatly conjectur'd it was for some advantage they had gain'd, which invited them once more to make head against the Persians, and face about on those they lately fled before. This latter part of the Fight was much more bloody then the former: nor am I able to express (said *Celia*) the rage where with the Persians were inspir'd when they knew their valliant Leader was taken; insomuch that they fell on upon their enemies with a fury equall to that of Lyons: But for *Phasellus*'s part, he was even mad with rage, and the rather when he saw him [*Diomed*] past recovery: for the Scythians if they could make good their retreat t'was all they could hope for, once more turn'd their backs and fled to Issedon with winged speed, and in that Citty shut up themselves. *Oruntus* having heard of *Diomed's* being taken, gave immediate command he should be put in Irons, and secur'd in a Prison of that excessive strength as t'was altogether impossible for him to escape; intending (as he said) after the War was ended, to put him to a most ignominious death, in revenge of *Octimasdes*'s, and those many thousands of his subjects as by his meanes had lost their lives.

These menases [menaces] being told to *Diomed*, did [fol. 38ᵛ] not at all startle him, nor ~~wh~~ were *Oruntus* threatnings half so terrible as his Chaines were insupportable: but seeing there was no remedy, he resolv'd to beare his captivity with so heroick a patience, as that his greatest Foes should be driven to acknowledge, though Fortune had reduced him to the condition of a slave, he did not merit to be such. But the Joy that was in Issedon that they had taken him, was surpass'd by the Persians griefe that they had lost him. But lest the disorder they were in for want of their Generall (being now like a body without a head) might give the Scythians any advantage, with an universall consent they made choise of *Barsarnes* their Leiutenant Generall to execute his Office till they might be happie in his restoration; which they vow'd suddenly to accomplish, or every man of them to loose their lives.

Fames winged Pursevant soon flew to *Achemenes* with the tydings of the Victory, and *Diomeds* mishap, which quite destroy'd the Joy it was to heare his affaires were in so prosperous a condition; and in its stead, fill'd him with so great a trouble, and discontent as he had never felt for any thing but his deare Brothers death. The Princess was not much less concern'd then he, though she was fain to conceale part of her resentment [sentiment], lest it should be imputed to a more obliging cause then meerly an esteeme for that gallantry which had so bravely signaliz'd it selfe in all his actions.

And no doubt but *Artabella* would have born her part in the generall griefe had she not been ignorant of it, being then absent from Court, having left it soon after *Phasellus*'s departure, and retir'd to a Castle of her owne neer to Shiras; the Citty which was founded on Persepolis that once renouned Citty, which was built for the most part of Cypresswood; the walls of the houses being of Marble. But its chiefest Ornament was the Palace Royall, built on a Hill, and encompass'd with a treble wall; the first sixteen cubits high, the second thirty, and the third sixty, all of them of black pollish'd Marble, with stately Battlements; and in the circute of the Palace a 100 Turrits, which presented to the beholders view a most goodly prospect. Nor was the inside of less beauty; then the outside was of majesty: the Roofes thereof shining with Silver, Gold, Ivory, and Amber. The Kings throne being all of massie Gold, inlaid with the richest Pearles. But neither its riches, nor its state could secure it from its ruine: for *Alexander the great*, in a drunken Fit consum'd it with Fire, at the request of *Lais* an infamous strumpet. But the downfall of that, was the rise of Shiras: Seated it is in a larg Plain encompass'd round with Mountaines, under one of which tis built, and beautified with dellicate Gardens, and stately Temples; two whereof are [fol. 39^r] much larger then the rest; and made more admirable by the addition of two Spires cover'd with a painting of Mosaick work; as light almost by night as day, by reason of a thousand Lampes burning Nightly in them. And in fine, such a Citty it is, that for good wine, pretty woemen, and pleasant Fruits it may compare with the best in Persia. Here *Artabella* drew her first breath (it being the chiefest Citie belonging to her Fathers principality) and on that score she chose it for the place of her retirement till the return of *Phasellus*: or if the Fates had so ordain'd, that she must never see him more, she there resolv'd to end her dayes in solitude.

The sound of a Bell made *Celia* break off her discourse and the Sicilian enquire the cause of its ringing; which *Celia* having told her it was a sommons to dinner, she led her downe staires into a very spacious Roome in which the Queens wemen alwayes dined: but here they eat not their meat as in other Countries seting at Tables, but on the ground on rich Persian Carpets; which custome was intraduced in the Delphian Court by *Artabella*, who being a Persian Princess, would needs follow the fashion of her owne Country in that perticuler. After they had dined, they pass'd away the time together for the space of half an houre, every one desiring to out vie each other in their civilities to the strang Lady, who was not backward in her requitall. But *Celia* being enform'd by *Amena* (one of the Court Ladies) that the Queen was at present employ'd in hearing a title pleaded to an estate by two kinsmen (who pretended each of them a right to it) which she was to determine that afternoon: this information she no sooner receiv'd, but knowing *Ermillias* concern to be such for her subjects as she would rather chuce to dispence with any pleasure or diversion how great soever, then neglect the least thing tending to their good or benefit; she told her new companion that if she pleased to take a turne or two in the Garden she would pursue what she had begun till such time as the Queen should be at leasure to send for her.

This proposall was no sooner made then accepted; and making her [Arthenia's] excuse to the Ladies for quiting their companies so soon: which nothing but that passionate desire she had to know the conclusion of their late Queens adventures (she said) could have made her guilty of so great a rudeness, she follow'd *Celia* into the Garden, where she had not been since that morning she met her there: at which time she was so wholy taken up with the considerations of her miseries, and that death which so neerly seem'd to threaten her, as she never so much as once look'd on or regarded any of those rarities that offer'd themselves to her view. The most remarkable whereof were two dellicate Fountains; one in the [fol. 39ᵛ] midst of the Garden which she now took a perticuler notice of being paved with White Marble spoted with black; the Water it contain'd being so purely cleare as rendred the bottom visible, which presented to the beholder a most delightfull Object. In the midle of it was a Statue representing Neptune with a Trident in his hand and a Wreath of Corall on his head, seated in a Chariot of Fishes shells so curiously cemented as it appear'd but one intire shell of Mother of Pearle; and drawn by Sea Horses. The other, which deserv'd no less a regard, was seated in the remotest part of the Garden, and surrounded in that manner with Trees as rendred it so shady as the Suns hotest Beames could not be offencive to any that reposed themselves by it: in the midst of this Fountain stood A a fig a Figure resembling *Arion* mounted on a Dolphins back: and towards the brime of it six Tritons on the one side, and over against them on the other a like number of Sirens, their humane parts only appearing above the Water, standing as it were in maze at the mellody of Arions Harp:[4] neer to the edge of this Fountain, under the shady covert of those Trees *Celia* invited the Sicilian Lady to repose herself whilst she prosecuted her Naration in these words.

---

[4] Arion, a virtuoso harpist, was rescued by a dolphin when he jumped into the sea rather than be murdered by sailors (Herodotus, *Histories* 1.23–4).

Rivall Friendship

THE FIRST PART

The Third Book

I will not question your memory so much, said Celia to the Unknown [*Arthenia*], as to repeat ought that I have already declar'd; onely mind you Madam that we left *Artabella* in the Castle of Shiras, and *Diomed* imprison'd in Issedon. No sooner had *Achemenes* heard the unhappy tydings of his being taken Prisoner, but he dispatch'd away a Messenger to *Oruntus* to make him an offer of all those Prisoners he had in his power together with *Cydarius*, in exchange for *Diomed*: but so far was he from hearkning to that proposall, that he return'd him answer. That if the Gods had bless'd him with a Son, and that Son had bin [fol. 40^r] in *Cydarius's* condition, he would rather chuse to let him continue in it, then loose the satisfaction of being reveng'd on *Diomed*; nor should half his Empier (would he give it) pay his ransome, nor all the Forces of it rescue him from a death then which nothing could be more certaine.

Divers there present, whom *Cydarius's* vertues had made his Friends (especially the Princess *Clazomena*) were very much concern'd at *Oruntus* his cruell determination; because there was no other way of possibility for him to be set at liberty: knowing full well they were not in a condition to free him by force: and since their King so slighted the King of Persias proffer, they had all the reason in the World to believe, *Cydarius's* life would depend on *Diomeds* Fate. For by the Law of Justice they could expect no other then that the same rigour wherewith he was us'd, *Cydarius* would be treated. These considerations mov'd them to sue to *Oruntus* to accept *Achemenes* his Proposition; representing how prejudiciall ^to him^ it might prove to sacrifice himself and kingdome to the fury of a powerfull and enraged enemy, from whom he must never hope any reconsiliation if he should proceed th to take away the life of a person whom he had shewen so great a Concerne for, as to take a perticuler care for him. But so displeasing was this advice to *Oruntus* that he commanded them not to speake one word more touching *Diomeds* release, or in his behalf: and remaining obstinatly unalterable in his resolution, he dismist the Messenger with an absolute deniall; who returning to *Achemenes* gave him an account of his fruitless embassie: which he having with impatience heard, he sent out his sommons into all parts of his mightie Empier for the raising such numerous multitudes of men as had been suffic^i^ent to make a conquest of the World; then what could Scythia now expect being in so declining a condition. This galant Armie which was composed out of all the Provinces of his Kingdome, being of Susianians 12000, of Margianians 20000, of Bactrians 10000, of Carmanians 30000, of Persians properly so call'd 40000:

he resolv'd in person to command; leaving *Oriana* to governe as Regent in his absence; of whose wisdome he was so well assur'd that he would joyne no other with her, but left her absolute in her power.

You must know Madam, said *Celia*, the Persians worship the Fire with the greatest devotion of any of those Gods they adore; for in the time of peace in the Temple of the Sun whom they stile *Orosmades* they daily offer a perticuler sacrifice to it, and carry it with them in the Warres (if the King be their in person) as their tutuler Deity; at which time tis carried before them in the Front of the Armie, attended by their Priests, and follow'd by a Traine of Boys, in number 365, all cloth'd in [fol. 40ᵛ] Scarlet: and in this equipage *Achemenes* march'd on towards Scythia; vowing if they took away the life of *Diomed* to speak his griefe in bloudy accents, and write his revenge in Crimson Charactars, where we will leave him for a while and returne to Issedon.

Many, though vain were the attempts of the Persians to set their Generall free; but neither pollicie, nor strength could effect it: for *Oruntus* sent them word that when ever they should go about to storme the Citty, the head of *Diomed* should be immediatly struck off in their sight, and tumbled to them over the Wall; nay further, he threatned them, that if in three days space they did not raise their siege, he should be torne a pieces with foure Horses. This threatning of *Oruntus* as it assur'd them his condition was almost desperate, so it fill'd them with a feare that the Tyrant would make use of his power whilst it lasted, to act his revenge, though it could be of little availe to him; and so distracted were they between various resolutions that they knew not which to pitch upon. For they thought if they should continue the siege, they might thereby be accessary to *Diomeds* death; and in case they rais'd it they had no assurance he should live, so that what to do they knew not. But whilst they were in this dubious condition not knowing what to resolve, there came one from *Cydarius* with a letter to *Oruntus* in the behalf of *Diomed*, desiring leave of *Barsanes* that he might be permitted to carry it to the King: there was no question but this request was granted assoon as ask'd, and the Messenger dispatch'd away with speed, and till his returne they would conclude of nothing. This letter being presented to *Oruntus*, he found it contain'd these words.

Cydarius to his Soveraign the great Oruntus

The generous treatment I receiv'd from Diomed when Fortune put me in his power, and the experience of his Heroique and noble disposition, constraines me to become his Advocate to your Majesty, and present you this Humble Petition ^in the behalfe^ of a person to whom I am indebted for my life, and perhaps had bin so for my liberty ere this, had he not been confin'd in his owne. Therefore I most humbly beseech your Majesty to spare his life since he has no otherways disoblig'd you then by faithfully discharging the trust imposed on him by that King he serves. But if Sir you object the death of our late King your royall Brother, and say that it would be injustice to spare the life of him [fol. 41ʳ] that took away his, I confess

my resentments [sentiments] *fall little short of yours when I reflect upon that loss:*
but on the other side when I consider, he slew him not basely, or treacherously; but
that Octimasdes assail'd him with an intention to give him death if Fortune had
been propitious to him, I must impute that disaster rather to Destiny that had so
decreed it, then account it as a crime in Diomed worthy so severe a revenge as I
am enform'd you designe to take on him: then do not Sir for your owne sake so
farre provoke the Gods to punish us, (who are I feare already but too much incen'st
against us) for a thing so cruell as that which you intend against that Gallant
man, that lyes at your mercy; whom did you but know, I am perswaded you
would rather esteeme then hate. Besides Sir, consider you do not onely sacrifice an
enemy, but a loyall Subject to your revenge: for to be sure I must inevitably suffer
the like severity from the King of Persia as you inflict on him: and if a Subject can
merit ought from his Soveraign, I would say I have deserv'd not to be given up
to destruction when tis in your power to preserve me from it. But if this Liberty I
take great Sir displeases you, it is neerness of blood which encourages me to assume
a greater freedome then perhaps your Majesty would excuse in another; not that
*I ground my presumption so much on that neither, as on the favour ^wherewith^*
you have been hitherto pleas'd to honour

Cydarius

But *Oruntus* as little regarded this as he did the Petitions of others which not
long before had on the same score su'd to him; for haveing perused *Cydarius's*
letter he tore it in pieces before the Face of him that brought it, biding him tell
him that sent it, he ought to have known his humour better then to believe his
resolutions were to be altered by importunity, or any consideration whatsoever.
This was all the Answere he could get, and with this he return'd: Whereupon a
Councell was again assembled to consult what to doe: the greater part were of an
opinion the siege ought to be continu'd; for as they said, if *Oruntus* could bring
them to that which he demanded, he might as well afterwards enjoyne them to
relinquish their conquests and depart out of his Dominions. But on the other side
Phasellus and some of them by whom *Diomed* was most esteem'd (among whom
Barsarnes was one) advised for a while to withdraw their Forces, till they might
find some [fol. 41ᵛ] meanes or opportunity to get *Diomed* out of the enemies
power, alleidging it could be no great disadvantage to their affaires, considering
to how low a condition *Oruntus* was reduced.

But whether Party would have prevail'd (said *Celia*), I know not; the dispute
being ended by a rumour which was on a sudden spread thorow all the Campe
of two men being taken wearing Scythian colours as they ^were^ passing the
Watch which was but newly set, who without any resistance yeelded themselves,
desiring to be carried to the Generalls Tent; which was the place where the chiefe
Officers of the Armie were set in Councell: whether being brought, and admitted in, the one of them pulling off his Casque quickly made himself known to be
Diomed; which sight they were so much surpriz'd at, that they knew not whether
they might credit their eyes or no: but being confirm'd by his voice that it was

really him they beheld, I cannot tell (said *Celia*) which was greatest their Joy, or their astonishment at his escape. *Phasellus* was the first that ran to receive him with open Armes, wherein he kept him so long lock'd in close embraces as the others thought he intended to ingross him wholy to himself: but assoon as he had (though unwillingly) got loose from his Deare *Phasellus*'s armes, where he could much rather have stay'd forever; he turn'd to *Barsarnes* who came with Joy to give up his Commission.

The Heavens can witness for me Sir (said he) that I resign my power with as great a satisfaction as I receiv'd it with griefe; and as I am beyond measure glad to see you here again in a condition to make use of it, so not any thing ever ^was^ so great a trouble to me, as that I could not serve you any otherways then in desire, nor act nothing towards the regaining your liberty, though none more passionatly wish'd it then my selfe.

I have ever found you so truly generous (repli'd *Diomed*) and somuch my Friend, that I have not the least reason to question the truth of what you protest; but if you esteeme my freedome a benefit worthy the acknowledging, give this Gentleman thankes (added he pointing to him that came with him) to whom I shall ever owne my self redevable [obligated] as to the chiefe Instrument of my preservation and escape; which how it was effected I must referre you to him, since he can much better enforme then my self.

Diomed having declar'd his obligation to this Stranger, they all carress'd him with abundance of kindness, expressing their thankfullness to him in such a manner as made him know the great concerne they all had in their Generalls safty. There was not a person there but would willingly have known the manner of his escape, had it been seasonable then to request it; but when they consider'd from what place *Diomed* so lately came, where it was likely he had not been very well accommodated with any thing ~~tough~~ touching his repose, they silenced their desires and waited on him to his Tent, where they left him with *Phasellus* (who alwayes was his Bedfellow as well in War as Peace) and return'd to *Phileno* (for so was he call'd that came along [fol. 42^r] with *Diomed*) to whom *Barsarnes* (as well to satisfie his owne curiosity, as to oblige those that were with him) made it his request to let them understand the manner of *Diomeds* escape; which desire of his being known to *Phileno*, in these words he gave him the relation of it.

I have Sir (said he addressing his speech to *Barsarnes*) the honour to belong to *Clazomena* Daughter and Heire to *Oruntus*, heaven having bless'd him with no ~~th~~ other Child. A Princess she is, so richly blest with all the gifts of Nature, that none could ever boast a larger share: nor ^are^ ~~has~~ the beauties of her mind less to be admired then her outward perfections; and of a nature so compassionate that it has bin the wonder of many besides my selfe, that such Clemency and goodness should be in ^the Daughter of^ a Father so severe and rigid. This mercyfull disposition of hers, set her on work to save the life of a person, who though her enemy, she could not but admire. But though her generosity would have incited her to do much on his behalf, yet she must pardon me if I believe she had some other inducement to invite her to what she did, more then barely the score of gallantry, or pity: for in what she has done, she has expos'd her owne life to the hazard of her Fathers fury, which is like enough to be fatall to her if ever it be known to him. But whatever it was that incited her to it; she had no sooner resolv'd to free *Diomed* but she acquainted me with her designe, conjuring me by all the power she had over me to assist her in it. I must confess I was at first a little startled at her intention, as knowing the hazard she might run thereby, and the difficulty I found to get that done which she enjoyn'd me (but I may with truth averre my owne life was the least of my cares) however, knowing it was my duty to obey, and not dispute, I waved all opposing Considerations, and bent my mind to study how to performe my Princesses command, which I thus effected. *Iros* to whose custody he was committed, knowing the interest I had with the Princess above any of her other servants, never question'd me what my business was with *Diomed* at any time when I went to him, which I never did but twice, lest I might give occation of suspition.

The first time I went to him I had on two sutes of Clothes, the one whereof I left with him (after I had acquainted him with my intent) which he conceal'd till he might have occation to use them. The windows of his Chamber were all bar'd cross with Iron Barres, so that I knew there was no way for him to get out, though I could have procur'd a Poison which in time would have eate those Barres in sunder; but that would have taken up more time then I had to spend; and besides it might perhaps have been discover'd by some or other: but I took a more speedy course, for I had brought with me an Iron Instrument, wherewith he might in short time dig thorough the Wall. I told him on which side to make his breach, and the Night following when sleep had summon'd all to rest, he began it; and in a short space made one wide enough to creep out at; which when he had done, he fastned a Cord which I had also brought him, to a Beame which went cross his Chamber, and by it slid downe into my Armes where I stood ready to receive him. But now the day [fol. 42ᵛ] being too farre advanced for us to proceed any further till the next night, I led him to my Chamber, where I conceal'd him till the ensuing night might afford us a conveniency of pursuing our design, knowing none would in the least suspect his being there.

But many houres had not pass'd ere some of *Iros's* servants told him *Diomed* was gone, whereat he was most ex[t]reamly troubled, as well he might, knowing on him *Oruntus* would discharge the uttmost of his fury; nor knew he whether it were his best way to go and acquaint *Oruntus* with it, or conceale it as long as he might from him, in hope he might find out who were his Assistants; for without some being privie to it he was perswaded he could not have made an escape: but at last he resolv'd to make no words of it for a day or two; and happie for us it was he did not; for had it been known, it would questionless have been more difficult, if not impossible for me to have got him out of Towne. Assone as darkness had extinguish'd the brightness of the day, I led him downe into a Garden which was full half a mile in length, at the end whereof was a Gate which opened into cer-

tain Fields, the Key of which I had receiv'd of the Princess. On the back side of
the Gate I had tide two Horses, on which we mounted, and fetching a compass
round about the City, we came (after many turnings and windings, to avoid the
danger of a pursute) to your Campe, where we were ceaz'd on as Prisoners and
brought hither.

Phileno having finish'd his relation, *Barsarnes* desired one of those Officers
that were present to make him his Bedfellow for that night, which he with willingness haveing consented too, they all wish'd him good rest, and retir'd to their
owne. The next dayes news was brought that *Achemenes* was within a days march
with all that mighty Armie that he brought with him; which when *Diomed* heard,
he made all possible preparation to receive him; and being come he went to meet
him; and falling on his knees and embraceing the Kings, who raised him up, and
pressed him in his Armes with a most tender affection. I am glad (said *Achemenes*
to him) to find my feares were vaine, and that Heaven has taken such a perticuler
care for your saftie and deliverance as has rendred mine unnecessary. But had the
Gods suffer'd the Tyrant to have taken away your life, you see I come prepared
for a revenge which nothing could have equal'd but his cruelty.

This is not the first time Sir (repli'd *Diomed*) that I have been oblig'd to your
Majesty, for in so high a manner have you multipli'd your unmerited Favours on
me, that my whole life could I live *Nestors* age would be too little to study for an
expression of my gratitude: but for this last effect of your goodness tis somuch
to be admir'd, that I want words to express that deep sense I have of it. But if I
might not seeme importunate, I would humbly sue Sir, that *Oruntus's* rigour to
me, might not provoke you to treat *Cydarius* ill, who is a person (if my judgment
deceives me not) truly generous, and not guilty of any thing that may be term'd
a crime, for if performing the duty of a loyall subject be his greatest Crime, what
must his Vertues be.

It troubles me said *Achemenes* that *Diomed* should think any argument more
prevalent with me then his desires, and tis to those I give *Cydarius*, from this
minute he is yours to dispose of as you [fol. 43ʳ] please, if you thinke good to give
him his freedome, you may freely do it.

Diomed having given the King thankes, dispatch'd a Messenger to *Cydarius*
to come to him with all speed, which he did; with a Guard, not dreaming of his
freedome: but when he came to *Diomed* he quickly gave him to understand he
was no longer under a restraint for I have obtain'd that of *Achemenes* for you (said
he) which your inexorable King would not consent too on my behalf; this gratitude would have bound me too had Friendship no share in the Obligation; but
being oblig'd by two such tyes I could not do less, and to do more is not in my
power: I will not court you to stay with us, though I should be extreamly glad to
enjoy you longer, that I might have time to tell you how much I am your Friend:
but I cannot desire that of you, which I would not my self consent too, for I know
Cydarius is too noble to desert his King at such a time as his assistance is most

requisite, and when all the strength that he can make will be too little to oppose us.

Though I had much rather stay with you (repli'd *Cydarius*) then returne to Issedon, yet since my honour calls me I must goe; but this I will assure you ere we part, I'le sooner turne the point of my owne Sword to my brest then unsheath it against so true a Friend: with this protestation, after he had embraced *Diomed* he took his Leave and went to Issedon.

But the third day after he return'd again, desiring to be admitted to the Kings presence. There was with *Achemenes* at that present, *Diomed* and divers of the Persian Nobility who all admir'd what brought him back so suddenly: but assoon as *Diomed* had notice of his being without, he went immediatly to fetch him in; but when he saw him, he thought he had beheld the Picture of Sorrow rather then *Cydarius*: for so strangly was he chang'd, that had not his Face been very fresh in his memory it would have been no easie thing to have known him. He seeing *Diomed* look so amazedly on him, told him he had reason to admire [wonder] at his dejected lookes.

But your wonder (said he) will quickly cease when once you know the cause of my returne, and the sad occation of my alteration, or if it still continues, it will rather be that I have liv'd to tell it you: but I have prolong'd my unhappy life for no other end then onely to come and implore your King and you, to revenge the death of a Princess whose Vertue and innocence loudly calls for vengeance.

What Princess (said *Diomed* hastily interrupting him)[?]

The faire *Clazomena* (repli'd he) who has been sacrificed to the brutish rage of an inhumane Father, both upon your account and mine.

Oh Heavens (said *Diomed* with an action full of transport) is it possible that any Father should so far divest himselfe of all sentiments of pitty, or that any humane shape should harbour such a Flinty heart, that so much beauty, and so clearly a Vertue (as report spake her to be endued with) could not melt into compassion. Come (added he taking *Cydarius* by the hand, and leading him to the King) feare not to obtain of *Achemenes* all you can desire.

Being come up to the [fol. 43ᵛ] Chaire where the King was seated, he threw himself down before him. It is not more my misfortune then my griefe dread Sir said he, that I am constrain'd to sue for Justice from another King against my owne; which no concerne of mine how deare soever should have compell'd me too, had not his unheard of, and most detestable cruelty cancel'd all those bonds of Alleigance that ty'd me to him: but now I can no longer look on him as my Soveraign, but as the Murtherer of Vertue it selfe in the person of the vertuous *Clazomena*, in whose behalf I now presume to beg most gracious King you will take on you to revenge the most deplored death of that poor Princess; for none on earth I know to whom more fittly to appeale for vengeance then to the great *Achemenes*.

I doe not at all admire (said *Achemenes*) at the severity of your King towards his enemies, since he has been so cruell to his neerest Relation, his onely Child:

but assure your self *Cydarius* if the Gods permit, he shall find from my hand a
punishment worthy of him. But in the meane time, pray let me heare the manner
of this horrid Tragedy.

After I had from your Royall bounty receiv'd the favour of my Freedome
(said *Cydarius*) I went immediatly to Issedon where I was wellcom'd by all, and
receiv'd by *Oruntus* with seeming expressions of no ordinary Joy: for seeing me,
he rose from his seat, and embraceing me, he declar'd, he knew not whether was
greater, his Joy or wonder to see me safe in Issedon again.

And infinitly do I long (said he) to be resolv'd how you got free; for I cannot
imagine, unless *Achemenes* has given you your liberty in hopes that I will be so
generous as to act by his example, and give *Diomed* his; but if he has done it upon
that account, I shall laugh to see how much I shall deceive his expectations; for he
must dy, since I have vow'd it, and nothing but my concerne for you, could have
prevail'd with me to protract so deare a satisfaction as his death will be to me: but
now that you are here in saftie, I will no longer delay it. Goe presently (said he to
some that stood neer him) goe, and give order a Scaffold be immediatly erected
on the Citty Wall, where in the sight of all the Persians he may loose his head.

I seeing him so eager in the pursute of an imaginary revenge which he was
never like to take, could not forbear smiling to my selfe, though I was very much
concern'd to see how obstinatly he was bent upon the distruction of my Noble
Friend: but not to interrupt him, I let him go on till he came to a period, and then
I told him. Sir (said I) to him. *Diomed* must dy, tis very certain, but the date of
his life is not so neer an expiration as you suppose, since it depends on Heavens
decree, not yours.

You are mistaken *Cydarius* (said he) Heaven has not a Miracle great enough
to adde one day more to his life; for ere the Sun descends into the Western shades
he shall have breath'd his last.

Were you not my Soveraign (I repli'd) I should presume to say you did
amiss, to limmit the puissance of the Gods, or measure an infinite by a Finit
power: think not sir, but that the Gods can by some meanes or other, (although
unknown to you) if so they please, rescue him from you even at that very moment
when you believe his Destiny the neerest. [fol. 44^{r}]

With that there came one running in, and told *Oruntus* that having been at
the Prison to bid *Diomed* prepare for his ex^e^cution he could not find him there:
which when he heard, he fell into a rage I am not able to express; he stamp'd,
and tore his haire, for madness, with other extravagant actions unbeseeming the
Majestie of a King: at last coming to me, and casting a look on me so terrible,
that all except my selfe trembled to see him; but innocence is never terrifi'd with
frowns, and therefore being guiltless of any thinge that could be thought crimenall, I receiv'd him with asᵑ undesturb'd a countenance as his was fierce.

But fixing an eye on me which sparkled with fury, Villain (said he), tis thou
hast rob'd me both of the glory, and satisfaction of my revenge that I design'd to
have taken on that Homocide: didst thou imagine (Traitour as thou art) that thy

being the first Prince of the blood should excuse thee or move me to pardon thee:
but I perceive thou art so far from accounting what thou hast done, a Crime, that
thou rather gloriest in it, and comest to upbraid me, as even now thou didest,
with my want of power to punish a Malefactoures, which thou, not the Gods
hast ravisht from me: and after the contrivance of thy treachery, and the accomplishment of it, thou hast the impudence to appeare in my presence; for which,
thy life alone shall be a recompense: nay, I am onely sorry thou hast but one, to
satisfie my just anger with.

Sir (repli'd I) if I had any way deserv'd this wellcome, or done any thing
that justly might displease you, I should most willingly embrace Death as the
due desert of that treachery, and impudence you are pleas'd to charge me with;
but till I am convicted of a crime that may deserve it your Majesty must excuse
me if I cannot somuch injure my owne Innocence as to beg pardon for what I am
not guilty of. That *Diomed* has escap'd those tortures you threatned him withall,
and is at present in the Persian Campe, is not a greater truth, then that I had no
hand in his escape nor ever contriv'd, or in the least assisted him in it or once
so much as knew of it, till that very day he sent me home by the permission of
Achemenes, and therefore Sir if it can be prov'd by the testimony of any one Witness that what I say is false, inflict on me the severest of your punishments: but
if I am worthy to dy meerly because I know he is at liberty, all here are now no
less culpable then my self.

I question not (answer'd *Oruntus*) since you had so much subtilty to act your
Treason undiscover'd, but you still retaine cunning enough to conseale it, but
what you so confidently deny, the Rack shall instantly force you to confess.

Such a thing (repli'd) I was never heard before, that a free born Prince
should be exposed to the ignominious punishment of a Gally Slave: but you
are my King, and I your Slave it seemes; you may inflict, and I must suffer: but
tis not all your Torments shall make me belie my innocence. I have serv'd you
faithfully Sir; nor in the course of my whole life have I ever let a thought into my
So^u^le that misbecame a faithfull Subject; and am I thus rewarded: however I
cannot repent my Loyalty, since Heaven I know will recompense it.

At *Oruntus*'s command they were going to lay hands on me to lead me to that
Torture he had so unjustly condemn'd me too: but the faire [fol. 44ᵛ] *Clazomena*
(with a Face all bathed in Teares, falling on her knees) besought him to give her
leave to speake. He seeing her in that posture, remitted something of his passion;
and raising her up, demanded what she had to say. I come Sir (said she) to cleare
Cydarius, and withall to put into your hands the offendor, who is no other then
the unhappie *Clazomena* your unfortunate Daughter, who has been so unhappie
as to displease you in so high a manner. I will not beg my life, for should you give
it me without a pardon, the sense of your displeasure would be much more griev-
ous then any other punishment I can suffer. The onely thing that I'le implore,
shall be (continu'd she falling on her knees again) that when by death I have
expiated my offence, that then you will forgive Sir what t'was not in my power to

help; for the Gods can witness for me, that had there been any hopes for me to save what was far dearer to me then my life, by any other way then that I took; I never would have ventur'd to provoke your anger.

Oruntus having hearkned to her with astonishment, assum'd again that fury wherewith his Visage was so lately painted: whilst we that were there present were strook with a terrible apprehension what would be the event of that Storme which we saw rising. Twise, or thrise did he walk two and fro about the Roome with hasty steps; and then coming to her with a look so full of terrour that it was able to have daunted a stouter courage then *Clazomenas*. And was it you then Traitoress (said he) that durst presume not only to oppose, but absolutely to hinder the design both of your Father, and your King, upon that Murtherer of your Royall Uncle; for whom if thou hadst any kindness whilst living, or any spark of pitty remaining for his unfortunate death, or any sense of duty towards me, thou wouldst sooner thy self have pierced his heart with a Dagger, then contriv'd a meanes to save his life. You imagine you have done a glorious Act; yes no question you have gain'd an everlasting Fame, by obliging your Fathers utter enemy; to the sole ruine of that content which he aim'd at in his distruction. Degenerate Girle, (pursu'd he) unworthy of the title of *Oruntus* Daughter, whom I shall never think on more without a blush, when I reflect upon thy crime, which renders thee so odious to me, that I repent thou hadst thy being from me: but since thou art become a Rebell against nature, I will not give so ill a president to any Parent as to indulge rebellion though in his owne blood: for I will rather chuse to be counted cruell, then unjust; which I should be, should I pardon that in you which I would punish in another. Thy crimes being of so deep a dye, nothing but thy blood can wash away the staines, or give me a sufficent reparation for what thou hast depriv'd me of. I will therefore, that thou immediatly, in the same place, and manner pay downe thy life, as he whom thou hast wrested from me should have done.

With that a shower of Teares fell from faire *Clazomena's* eyes able to have mollifi'd a heart of Adamant, and infused pitty into the fiercest Tiger: but this remorceless King was more obdurate.

Think not (said he) that thou canst move me by these Crocodilian teares to pitty thee, no, since [fol. 45ʳ] thou hast forgot the duty of a Child, I can forget the compassion of a Father. Goe, try if you can suffer for your treason as bravely as you acted it: it will rejoyce me rather to dye childless, then to leave such a one as you behind me.

Seeing I must dye (said she) I will not scruple to declare the cause of my offence; which were I to live, those Racks you threatned *Cydarius* with, should never have compell'd me to confess: t'was Love sir that constrain'd me to do what I have done; but yet, a love so pure, so innocent that I can no otherwayes repent it then as it has been the occation of incurring your displeasure, which to appeaze (I declare) I embrace death more willingly then you condemne me to it.

Something more she was about to say, but he prevented her by saying: art thou not content to do amiss, but thou must agravate thy crime by a declaration of thy Folly; which it would better have becom'd thee to conceale, then publish with thy almost dying breath. I'le heare no more; take her away: this night let her be confin'd to her Chamber, and to morrow on the Scaffold let her loose her head.

This cruell sentence past, he went away, leaving her (poor unhappy Princess) to lament her destiny, which I resolv'd to hinder, or beare her company to the other World: to which intent, my self, with many other of the Nobility follow'd *Oruntus*, and threw our selves at his Feet; beseeching him to spare our Princesse: and if his wrath could not be pacifi'd without a sacrifice, we beg'd that he would sacrifice us all to his anger, so he would be but so mercifull as forgive her. But he was no less inexorable upon her account then yours sir (said *Cydarius* to *Diomed*) but when I saw no intreaty could prevaile, I resolv'd to try the rethorick of Force. I was not ignorant it was a crime unpardonable in me to oppose my King: and had it been on any other score, I would sooner have died then resisted the least of his commands; but I could not suffer this cruell Decree of his against the Princess to be put in execution, without doing my utmost to prevent it; really believing when the height, and violence of his Cholour was a little over, he would esteeme it ^rather^ an obligation, then an Offence that I hindred him from per-petrating so horrid a cruelty.

But I confess I did not then consult with duty, somuch as with somewhat else which then began to take possession of my Soule. I found how ill the sever-ity of *Oruntus* was resented [felt] by all in generall; which gave me no small hopes I should be seconded in my design: however I resolv'd to be quiet till the last, hoping the King would of himselfe revoke his sentence when he had a little consider'd what he had done: but alass my hopes were but Flatterers, for he still held his resolution; for the next day was not many houres old when he gave order for *Clazomena* to be led to Execution. All that night I never clos'd my eyes, but spent it in going from one place to another; making it my business to see how many I could perswade to joyne with me; and indeed Fortune was so propitious to me, that I found so considerable a number that would take my part (and most of them men of quality) that I did not dispaire of accomplishing my design of rescuing *Clazomena*. There was above a 100 that I had gain'd in that short time; and more I question'd not but would assist us if [fol.45 ᵛ] occation shoule [should] invite them: these all devoted their lives intierly to the Princesses service, vow-ing every man of them to dye in the place ere she should: but I enjoyned them to make no ressistance, nor stir till such time as they should see me draw my sword, and then, I gave them order what to do.

No sooner was *Oruntus*'s command given concerning his Daughter but she was brought forth of her Chamber by those appointed to guard her to the Place of execution, which were not many, *Oruntus* not apprehending any would be so hardy as to offer any opposition to his Will. I was just going to her Chamber when I met one of her servants that waited on her coming to seek me out, to tell me the Princess desir'd to speak with me: I following him, met her just as she was coming out of her chamber; she espying me came towards me, whilst those about her withdrew at a little distance out of that respect which they could not but still acknowledge due to the granduer of her birth. I seeing her come towards me hasted to meet her; whilst she looking on me with an Eye so sweet, and yet so sad, as would have inspir'd pitty into the heart of the most savage Creature: I am sure it so far pierced mine that I could not refrain from teares; but some drops in despight of me stole from my eyes: which she perceiving, fetching a sighe, and earnestly looking on me. *Cydarius* (said she) you are now by just succession to sway this Scepter, if the valour of the conquering Persian leave you any thing to rule: then let me conjure you by that Vertue which has hitherto shin'd bright in all your actions, when my Father has by death put off his Crowne, and you have put it on, never, oh never let cruelty dim the splendour of it: for believe it the richest, and most glorious Diadem if once soil'd with that, looses its luster, and becomes contemptable; for nothing so well sutes with Majesty as mercy.

With that, taking me by the hand, with an obliging freeness (which she had never us'd before; and which I could not but admire at, knowing the reservedness of her humour) farewell *Cydarius* (said she) I dy most willingly since I leave you behind me to possess my Fathers Throne; which that you may live to enjoy, and with it all true felicity, is the last wish of *Clazomena*.

With that she put a Paper in my hand, charging me not to open it till Death had closed her eyes, and was turning about to go away; but ere she went, I told her, that then I must never see what it contain'd. For you must live Madam (said I) or I must dy as well as you; tis not the treasure of *Oruntus*'s Crowne shall hire me to survive you; for that would be a burden so intollerable when I should reflect on that fatall occation that preserved it to me, that I could ne're be able to support it.

Whether or no she heard me I know not, for she was gone a good distance from me ere I had done speaking: but seeing her gone I followed after till she mounted the scaffold, which she look'd on as the Stage whereon she was to act her lives last part. But seeing her prepare for the reception of the fatall blow, I saw it was then no time to dally, or expect any mercy for her from her cruell Father: I mounted the Scaffold (none opposing me, not knowing, but I had authority so to do) and snatching out my Sword, I run the Ex^e^cutioner through, crying out, he that seeks to take the Princesses life away, must first take mine; for [fol. 46ʳ] whilst I have strength to weild my sword, I will defend hers against the World.

The suddeness of the action, and the vehemence of my words amaz'd all that either heard, or saw me; which I perceiving, told them. Till now, I could not have believ'd that Scythia had bred so many base unworthy men, as tamely to stand and see their Princess put to death meerly to saciate the cruelty of their King: who though he has at present suffer'd his passion to insult over his reason so farre as to compell him causelessly to condemne ^her^ to this ignominious death; yet, when his anger is a little over (as questionless it will, ere long) he then will curse us all, for suffering that to be done, which his passion, not himself commanded: and then I dare promise you he will rather thanke then be offended with us, that we thus prevented the exterpation of his royall Family; which you all know in *Clazomena* is extinct. I think none of you heare are ignorant how I oppose my owne interest in seeking to preserve her: and therefore certainly you cannot deeme it rebellion, but rather love to my King, that forces me to draw my sword in opposition of his injustice; that I might thereby hinder him from doing that, which will not onely render him hatefull to all good, and vertuous Princes, when Fame has once proclaim'd him to be the Murtherer of a Princess surpass'd by none for Vertue; ~~and~~ ^but^ pull downe on him the just Vengeance of heaven.

Having done speaking, I heard a murmuring amongst the multitude, which at last brake forth into loud shoutes: the greatest part of them crying, long live our Princess; let the Princess *Clazomena* live. But in the meane time, some pick-thanks (who had seen what I had done) ranne with open mouthes to *Oruntus* to acquaint him with it; which, with a strang impatience having heard, he gave order for his Guards (which were 200 horse) to go immediatly and hew in pieces all that made resistance. This Order being given, the Guards soon appear'd, to execute the Kings command; which that Party which I had gain'd perceiving, met them with undaunted resolutions; between whom, began a most bloody skirmish, which *Clazomena* seeing. Oh *Cydarius* (said she) what have you done: you have a little while detain'd me here, but alass ^that^ short reprieve will onely render my death more terrible to me, since it will be accompani'd with the slaughter of many of my Fathers subjects, and my Friends, who will unavoidably loose their lives in the quarell of an unfortunate Creature.

Feare not Madam (I repli'd) the Gods I trust will yet preserve you; but if it be decreed that you now must enter the Gates of Death, *Cydarius* will lead you the way, not stay to follow you: but I must leave you for a while, and either pur-chace your saftie, or my owne death.

With that, I left the scaffold to joyne with my Party, which I found increas'd to a far greater number then I could have hop'd; so that I did not doubt but to make conditions with *Oruntus* ere the Fray was ended. Greater advantages I might have gain'd, durst I have pursu'd them; for the adverse Party began to retreat, but I durst not follow very far, lest *Clazomena* should be taken from me by a surprize, and so I might thereby loose the onely Prize for which I fought: but at last, taking the Princess in my ~~hand~~ Armes, halfe [fol. 46^v^] dead with feare, I carried her to the house of one *Adrastus* (my assured friend) where I left her with a sufficent Guard to defend her, and return'd to renew the Fight, which now began to be more bloody then before; for *Oruntus* hearing of the ill success of his Guards, was coming towards us with the remaines of what souldiers he had left, which were more numurous by far then those we had; but what we lack'd in number, was suppli'd with courage: as for *Oruntus* Partie, they were not want-ing in that perticuler neither; but the badness of their cause, and the goodness of ours, took off much of that height of courage wherewith they fought, though the King did all he could to animate them. But those men I had (which were very few in number, in comparison of the other) though they did as much as it was possible for men to do, yet doubting, thorough inequality of number I should at last be overcome, I seemingly retreated, and drew back till I came to one of the Citty Gates; and ceazing on the guard which kept it, I put others in their places: which when I had done, I vow'd to set open the Gate for the Persians to enter, if *Oruntus* would not consent to let the Princess live.

This resolute determination being told the King (fearing as it seemes, that I would do what I had vow'd; and knowing force would be in vain to hinder me, since I had proceeded so far) he advanced towards me, and ^calling^ me by my name. *Cydarius* (said he) I could not have believ'd (had not my eyes as well as eares assur'd me) you would ere have been so base a Traitor to your lawfull Soveraign, not onely to oppose him in his commands, but to threaten also, to deliver him up to his enemies: which I have now cause to suspect you design'd when you were a Prisoner, and that you obtain'd your liberty on that score, though you make the rescue of *Clazomena* the pretence to palliate your treachery.

The name of a Traitor Sir (repli'd I approaching him with a reverend respect) I have no way merited, though your Majesty has been pleas'd to brand me with that infamous title more then once; but I utterly disclame it: for I call Heaven to witness, I never had the least intention to betray you, as you unjustly charge me: nor so much as a thought that tended to the diservice of your Majesty. But if Sir, you object this that I have done in the behalf of the Princess; I have in that, done nothing that you can justly call treachery, or rebellion; since I drew not my sword against you, but against your unjust passion, which transported you beyond all reason, to command things, which if they had been perform'd, your self Sir, would have been the first would have repented it. Had it been my self you had condemn'd to dy (though never so unjustly) I would with my owne hand have become the Exe^c^utioner of your sentence, rather then have opposed your Will though it had been in my power: but you must pardon me Sir, if I could not pay you so blind an obedience upon the Princesses account. If either Prayers, or teares could have prevail'd, I had not been necessitated to make use of Force; which meanes how unwillingly I had recourse too, the Gods can tell. And as I onely^ unsheath'd my sword in her defence, so if your Majesty ^will^ but spare her life (since your anger cannot otherwise be appeaz'd, but by [fol. 47ʳ] the life of an Offender) I'le freely give you mine Sir; shed the remainder of that blood which I have not been spareing of in your service, but let that Vertuous, that Innocent Princess live.

Tis not for you (repli'd the King) to appoint me whom to spare or whom to punish. But that you may have no colour for your treacherous designes, upon condition you, and all your accomplices throw downe their Armes and submit to my mercy she shall live; but let her repaire to her Chamber, and not see my face.

I confess I did not press him to it (hoping since he had condescended she should live, time would obtain that favour which at present he deni'd her) but without delay caus'd all those that adhear'd to me to fling downe their Armes, and submit themselves, whilst I did the like; and with teares of Joy gave the King thanks, never standing to capitulate with him for my selfe, or any of the rest, nor to provide for the security of our lives; which I was not ignorant lay at his mercy when we had disarm'd ourselves: but I supposing he having lost so many of his soldiers in the quarell, that all he had left would be few enough to maintain the siege, would not take away any of our lives unless it were mine; which I valued not at all since I had been so happie (as I thought) to have preserv'd the Princess *Clazomena*'s.

But we had no sooner disarm'd our selves, but my self, and a dozen more of the chiefest of those that tooke my part, were ceaz'd on, and carried to Prison; where the rest of that day, and the next night we were strongly guarded: but early the next morning *Oruntus* sent for me to come to him; which order I obey'd: and being come, he commanded me to follow him to *Clazomenas* chamber. I hearing him say so, began to admire what his intentions were. But being enter'd, and earnestly looking about for the Princess, I spied *Hersilia* (her Favourit) standing by the Bed with her Face so drown'd in teares, that I scarce knew at first whether it were she or no. This sight struck me into a terrible apprehension to think for what intent I was brought thither; but the King soon let me know, for drawing open the Curtains of *Clazomenas* bed. See there *Cydarius* (said this cruell King) behold how well you have employ'd your Valour; didst thou believe fond man (continu'd he) she was secure because I promis'd thee her life: tis true, I did so; but did not promise thee how long I would permitt that life to last. Thou thoughtst because thou ~~hindredst~~ hinderst me from giveing her one death, that I could find no more to make her suffer: but a draught of Poyson is as effectuall as a Headsmans Axe. You have deserv'd death no less then she; but if ^I^ mistake not you would rather esteem that as a favour now then a punishment, and therefore you shall live: but this night depart Issedon, and within five dayes Scythia, and never enter my dominions more I charge you; for if you do, I vow by all the Gods to make you such an example, as shall be a suffucent terrour to all such presumptious Traitors as your self.

Assoon as he had done speaking he left me, and went out of the Roome, giving me no leasure to answer him; neither indeed had he stay'd, could I have repli'd suddenly; for such was my amaze that for a good while it depriv'd me of my speech. At first I confess I onely fancied her asleep, and that *Oruntus* said what he did onely to try how I would resent [feel] [fol.47ᵛ] her death; for it could not sink into my imagination that any Father, how great a Tyrant soever, could so unconcernedly look on his Child when he had murther'd her. But being confirm'd more by *Hersilias* teares then his words that she was but too certainly dead; though who ever had seen her would hardly have believ'd Death had took possession of that faire habitation: for dead as she was, she yet appear'd so exceedingly lovely, as in my life I ne're beheld her look more sweetly. For that vile Theefe though he had rob'd her of her soule, had not dispoyl'd her of those vermilion Roses which Nature had implanted in her Cheeks. But when I had regain'd my speech, and that I was assur'd that what I saw was but too true; my griefe immediatly grew to that height, that I know not whether it may more properly be term'd griefe or madness; for so was I transported with it, that I knew not a long time either what I did, or said.

One while I exclam'd against the Fates, another while against *Oruntus* for deceiving me: then would I change my thoughts, and rave as much against my self, for trusting her so soon in the hands of an incensed Father without some greater assurance of saftie for her. Oh Heavens what did I not say, and think in the height of my fury. I then resolv'd to go and kill *Oruntus*, and so reveng on him his Innocent Daughters death; and questionless in that transported rage wherein I was at that instant, I had done what I resolv'd, though I had been sure to have had my heart pierced with a 1000 swords assoon as I had done it. But when I remembred I was without a sword, or any other Weapon to attempt his life, I was constrain'd to let that resolution give way to one more reasonable, when I call'd to mind how he had commanded me to depart out of Issedon; which was, that I determin'd to come and implore your Majesty (said he to *Achemenes*) to revenge my Princesses death since tis impossible for my self to do it. But first I went to the side of the Bed whereon the poor dead Princess lay; and looking on her a long time, without so much as speaking one word, and indeed my passion was so great, that I knew not in what language so fittly to express the greatness of it as in my sighes and teares. Then taking one of her faire hands I kist it a hundred times, assuming to my self a favour that I durst never have aspired too had she been sensible of my presumption.

Hersilia (finding by the abundance of my sighes and teares, my griefe to be as extreame as the cause of it was lamentable) first brake silence. I perceive sir (said she) by the excess of your sorrow for the untimely end of my deare dead Mistress, that you have perus'd that Paper which she gave you; wherein I suppose you find what a perticuler interest you have in her death, above all others.

No *Hersilia* (I repli'd) I was ever too just an observer of the Princess *Clazo-menas* commands to violate the least of them for the satisfaction of my curios-ity; though I confess I had an ardent desire to know what she had intrusted me withall: but had my desires been much more violent, they should never have tempted me [fol.48ʳ] to disobey her commands in the least perticuler, for since she thought fit to enjoyn me not to look on that Paper till after her death I had not a thought capable of disobedience; and being ignorant that this sad Tragidie was acted till I was brought hither to be a sad spectatour of it, your self can wit-ness I have not had so much command over my passion as to be in a condition to acquaint my self with the contents of it; and therfore know not of any other interest I have in her deplorable death then as she was the Daughter of my King, and might one day have been ^my^ ~~her~~ Soveraign ^her^ ~~my~~ selfe, had not the cruell Fates, or rather a cruell Father depriv'd her of her Life: but having had the honour more frequently to enjoy a converse with her (by reason of my relation to her) then any of her Fathers subjects, I became more perfectly acquainted with those admirable perfections in her, which rendred her the glory of the World: and therefore being highly sensible what an irreparable loss the whole Kingdome in generall sustaines by loosing this inesteemable Princess, I cannot think the greatest griefe, and sorrow I can possibly express to be any other then a just tribute due to her memory.

Since you have not look'd in that Paper (answered *Hersilia*) I could wish Sir you never would; because I know, what it containes will much a^u^gment your sorrow.

That (said I) which you use as an argument to divert me from the sight of it, shall the sooner invite me to it: and the rather because I believe it was the Princesses desire I should see it; or else she would never have given it me with such an Injunction as she did: and I must needs blame my selfe for leaving her Will so long unperform'd which by this Paper (continu'd I pulling it forth and opening it) I may come to understand.

Ah Sir (said she with a flood of teares) you will find nothing there, but the possibility you lately had of being the happiest of men, and an assurance that you are now the most unfortunate, if you have a right resentment [feeling] of the Princesses ^thoughts^.

Be it what it will (repli'd I) I shall soon be resolv'd; with that I open'd it and read these words.

> *I know you have a soule incapable of ingratitude; and therefore I need not enjoyn you to pitty the unhappie fate of the most perfect Friend your Vertues can acquire you: but since nothing but my death could be a sufficent testimony of my Friendship (for other title those severe rules which Vertue prescribes will not permit me to give that esteeme I had for you) I have not declin'd giving you that unquestionable testimony of it, for the preservation of your life; which I was but too well assur'd had been inevitably lost, if the valiant Prisoner by my meanes had not escap'd. Adue forever Deare Cydarius, the dying Clazomena takes her last leave of you, beging no greater recompence for the loss of that life, which for your sake she willingly forgoes, then to live forever in your memory: and which the rather to oblige you too, she permits you to believe that whilst she liv'd you had the intire possession of hers; pardon the expression which no consideration should ere have forced from my Pen, but this, that Deaths cold Hand conceales the blushes of the unhappie*
>
> *Clazomena*

[fol.48ᵛ] Judge Sir [*Achemes*] I beseech you what my resentments [feelings] were when I had read these words: for if meere pity before transported me to such a degree of sorrow; what effects so powerfull a passion as Love when joyn'd with it, must needs produce. For I must confess I had no sooner perus'd those lines, but my heart, which till that instant enjoy'd all imaginable freedome, not once having the least inclination to court anything but Glory; that very instant felt an unknown Fire; which every Line, nay every silable were as so many sparks to kindle a Flame which never can ^be^ extinguish'^d^ but with my life; for from that very moment I became as great an Amorist, as those that for divers yeares have made proffession of the most violentest passion; never considering the impossibility of ever enjoying the Object of my Love: which to any but my selfe had questionless been argument enough to oppose what I willingly entertained. For when I consider'd it was onely for my sake she had lost her dearest life, I thought my selfe oblig'd to love her, or rather to adore her dead as she was, with as constant, and faithfull an affection as ever the loyallest Lover breathing was capable of; or as if she had been living to reward it.

Assoon as I had read over those Words which but now I repeated, I walk'd again to the Bedside; and looking on *Clazomena*, with eyes so overflow'd with teares that I could scarce discerne thorough them the onely Object which I desir'd eternally to behold.

Ah dearest Princess (said I with a sigh as sad as the occation of it) was it for me unhappie Wretch, and for my sake that you have lost that precious life. Oh miserable *Cydarius* (pursu'd I) how accurst art thou, since thou hast liv'd to see thy Princess become thy Victime: to save thy life her owne is sacrificed; and that must willingly by her owne consent: and can I see, and know this, and not in gratitude follow her; ah no, I must not yet, tis fit I first revenge her death on the Author of it, and then upon my selfe as being the occation of it; for live I will not, live I cannot since *Clazomena* does not.

Ah *Hersilia* (said I turning to her) what a Destiny has the Fates ordain'd me; they have shewn me a heaven of happiness, onely to make the resentments [feelings] of my misery the more bitter; why did I not know my happiness when I might have been sensible of it; or why was I now acquainted with it, since tis forever vanish't.

Had you took my advice Sir (she repli'd) you should still have been ignorant of it, since I knew very well how much it would a^d^de to your sorrow, which I saw before was too extreame.

My griefe (said I) is now my onely consolation; therefore if you can informe me of any thing that may make it rise higher, you will more oblige me by telling then by concealing it from me: however favour me so far, as to acquaint me with whatever you knew of my Princesses mind concerning me; for I am sure you were somuch her Favourite that I am perswaded you were not ignorant of her most private thoughts.

Tis very true (repli'd she) I confess it, nor can I deny but that the Princess afforded me that honour in a more perticuler manner then any of her [fol.49^r^] other servants; since I had the honour to be brought up with her from her Infancie, being but two yeare older then herselfe. But certainly I were the unjustest person in the World, if I knew any thing that would be an addition to those sor-

rowes that are allready but too great if I would let you know it; but since I believe
there is not any thing that can give you more tormenting apprehensions then to
behold your Princess lye dead before you, and be assur'd t'was onely on your score
she died; I think I may venture to declare to you all I know, without any injury
to you, or a prejudice to my dear Mistress, seeing she herselfe has thought fit you
should not be a stranger to those resent^i^ments[1] she had for you.

Know then Sir (continu'd she) as soon as the Princess became capable of dis-
tinguishing those admirable qualities which rendred you the glory of our Scythian Court, from those of other mens; she believ'd you had so good a tittle to her
esteeme, that she thought she was oblig'd in Justice to preferre you before all
others, not onely in the Court, but Kingdome too: and as her yeares increased, so
did her knowledge of your vertues; so that at last she dre grew from esteeme to
Friendship; and at length (if I mistake not) that Friendship gave place to affection: but an affection so purely innocent, that I should think it might more properly be term'd Friendship then Love, had she not to the King her Father declar'd
it to be Love; for I could never have imagin'd a passion could ever be so long
conceal'd. But whether it were Love, or Friendship I will not now dispute; but
sure I am it was most violent, as you ^may^ well believe by the sequell, since it
produced such unusuall effects. Oft have I have you were her Brother heard her
wish you were her Brother, or that t'were possible for her to change her sex that
she might more freely enjoy your conversation (which she has many times confest to me, was the onely comfort of her life) and as oft has she most zealously
pray'd to the Gods that none might ever love her, that she might not be put to a
necessity of disobeying *Oruntus* if he should at any time find out a person whom
he should think worthy of his alliance; resolving never to marry, meerly that she
might leave you the Crowne in case she should discease before the King: or if she
should out live him (as in all probability she might have done, had not his inhumane cruelty brought her to this untimely end). She then resolv'd assoon as she
enjoy'd the Crowne to resigne it to you, contenting herselfe to live a private life.
And this (as she said) being the highest testimony of her Friendship which she
could possibly devize to give you, she made it her absolute resolution.

And thus a long time she continu'd seeking all imaginable opportunities
to oblige you; imputing all she did for you at any time to Friendship, not in the
least imagining, or once so much as suspecting it was Love which incited her
to what she did (I am certaine) till that very day you she heard you were taken
Prisoner: but that newes so surpriz'd her and fill'd her with a griefe so excessive, as she began to perceive it had its rise from something of a more passionate
nature then Friendship; which oppinion when she was once confirm'd in, I am
not able to [fol.49ᵛ] tell you Sir (continu'd she) the trouble that these thoughts
created in her; but yet it was not so great, but that a little after it was much aug-

---

[1] The phrase "re" is crossed out and "i" is inserted, thus correcting "resentments" to
"sentiments."

mented by the Kings refusall to accept the King of Persias proffer; and thereby abandoning you to the mercy of an enemie, from whom could be expected nothing but a just retalliation of revenge after the slighting so advantagious an offer. Strang^e^ly were the Princesses thoughts distracted when she knew her Fathers absolute determination; and what to resolve upon she knew not: but since it was some comfort in misery to have some faithfull person to whom to impart their discontents; she was pleas'd to make choice of me, whom as she said, she had ever found faithfully, and cordially affected to her service, that so she might a little disburthen her heart of those cares that oppress'd it. Which when she had resolv'd, she call'd me into her Closet, and fully opening her heart to me, she told me she was affraid she had either thorough folly, or ignorance committed a Fault, which she as little knew how to repent of as to repaire.

I see wonder in your face *Hersilia* (said the Princess) but you will more admire when I shall tell you that I love *Cydarius*. I have alass (pursu'd she with a sigh) mistaken my affection for him when I term'd it onely Friendship.

Indeed Madam (repli'd *Hersilia*) I did admire to heare you impeach your selfe of being guilty of a fault, whereas your greatest enemies have not malice enough to imagine such a thing. But since you are so severe to your selfe as to plead guilty before you are accus'd, I think my self oblig'd to vindicate you to your selfe, and tell you Madam that, that which you terme a fault, ought rather to be accounted a Vertue, then a Vice; considering the Law of this Realme which tyes you from marrying any forreign Prince: then seeing you must of necessity make your choice within your Fathers dominions, where is there a person to be found that you can without injustice prefer before *Cydarius*.

But before I proceed I must humbly intreat your Majesty (said he to *Achemenes*) not to condemne me as guilty of so great a vanity, as to attribute to my selfe any of those advantagious qualities that the goodness of that Incomparable Princess, or *Hersilia* imputed to me.

But that I will not interrupt your relation (repli'd *Achemenes*) I should tell you how much you injure your selfe, if you think you merit less then they ascribe to you: therefore, without any more of these needless Apoligies pray go on with your relation. Something he [*Cydarius*] would have repli'd in answere to the Kings Complement, but he again desir'd him to proceed, which in obedience to *Achemenes*'s commands he did. I know very well (answer'd the Princess) Scythia containes not any person whom I can thinke worthy of ~~Cydarius~~ Oruntus's Daughter but *Cydarius*; nor am I much troubled that I think him worthy of my esteeme; it is not that which I account my crime; but tis because I should be so foolish as to suffer my selfe to love him any other ways then Friendship does oblige me too, since I may very well assure my selfe he has no other affection for me then what proceeds from that cause.

How do you know Madam (said *Hersilia*) but that he may have as great a passion for you, as that [fol.50ʳ] you have for him, perhaps one much more violent, though that respect he payes the Daughter of his King keeps it close Prisoner in his brest; not dareing to presume to lift his eyes so high.

No no (repli'd the Princess) had he more then a common kindness for me, or any other respect then what my birth may chalenge from him, it were impossible but he would at some time or other have given me some testimony of it, considering how highly I have ever favour'd him; and how unlimated a Friendship I have always had for him; and considering the grandure of his quality, which might without presumption have encourag'd him to raise his pretences to me.

That Madam (repli'd *Hersilia*) which you use as an argument to authorize a declaration of his Love, is perhaps the reason that deterres him from it; fearing to loose what he has already gain'd: But admit he has as yet no passion for you, I dare affirme did he but know of yours, his Friendship would soon convert it self to one.

But that he ne're shall know (hastily repli'd the Princess) tis too much I know it my selfe, and that I have to you disclos'd my weakness; but to let *Cydarius* ever come to the knowledge of it, were a Crime I never would out live. I must contente my selfe in continuing to give him more unquestionable demonstrations of my Friendship by endeavouring to procure his liberty; and if I loose my life in that attempt, I shall not grieve, since that onely can assure him I was more (if more can be) then meerly his Friend.

I have oft heard you say Madam (said *Hersilia*) if ere you wore the Scythian Crowne, you would un^de^throne² you[r]selfe to set him in your place: but that you need not do it, if you will but bestow you^r^ person, where you have already given your heart, and do resolve to give your Crowne: and I am fully perswaded you will much more oblige him by that Gift then by the other; since he may receive the one with an infinite satisfaction to himselfe, but not accept the other without an injurious wrong to you.

Oh do not flatter me (answer'd the Princess) rather tell me he may receive the first with Joy, and reject the other with contempt and scorne; should I be so fondly simple as ^to^ make him any such offer.

Ah Madam (said *Hersilia*) how can you say you love *Cydarius* and yet think he has a soule capable of soe meane a baseness, as to be more covetous of your Crowne, then ambitious of your person.

Well (repli'd she) however it be we will dispute no further: go call *Phileno* hither that I may with him consult how to preserve the life of the valiant Prisoner; on whose, as things now stand, depends *Cydarius*'s, that my affection may not be less kind to him then my Friendship.

What ~~was~~ was concluded on between the Princess and *Phileno* the sequell I suppose has enform'd your Majesty, so that I may be excus'd from relating what you are already acquainted with.

---

² The prefix "un" is underlined and "de" is inserted above.

Yes *Cydarius* (answered *Diomed*) the King has been fully enform'd of all perticulers touching my escape; though till now both his Majesty and my selfe have
been ignorant of the cause which excited that most excellent [fol. 50ᵛ] Princess
to conferre on me an Obligation so fatall to herselfe; which misfortune I am so
much concern'd for, that were it possible to recall her from the lower shades I
would again put my selfe into her Fathers power; and rather then he should have
fail'd of his so much desired satisfaction (could I have foreseen what since has
happen'd) I would that very day I left my Prison, have quit^t^ed my life with it
and on my selfe have ex^e^cuted *Oruntus's* unjust revenge, rather then have liv'd
to be the unhappy ^occation^ of that innocent Princesses death.

Your resentments [sentiments] are noble like your selfe (said *Cydarius*) but
alass, what could not be mistrusted [suspected], could never be prevented.

After *Diomed* had beg'd the Kings pardon for this interruption he was silent,
and *Cydarius* went on. *Hersilia* then told me *Clazomenas* disquiets for feare her
designe should be discover'd, or not take effect: but when she saw it had pros-
pered according to her wishes in my returne to Issedon. Certainly (said *Hersilia*) nothing could equall her Joy, but her insuing griefe when she heard you
condemn'd first to the unsufferable torture of a Rack, and then to suffer death,
for that which you were so far from being guilty of that you were not so much
as accessary too. But no sooner was the sentence denounced then she resolv'd to
hinder the ex^e^cution of it, by exposing herselfe to the King her Fathers fury.
What at that present, and since has pass'd, your selfe Sir (continu'd she) hath
been an Acter in, or Spectator of; so that I have nothing more to e^i^nforme³ you
of, but onely the manner of her death, which was thus. About some foure houres
after the Princess was returned to her Chamber; as she was set musing on her late
danger, and by what means she might regain the Kings favour both for herselfe
and you; there enter'd one of the Kings servants bringing with him a silver Cup,
and on his knee presented it to her; telling her, he was commanded by the King
his Master so to do, and not to stirre till he had seen her drink off that which it
contain'd: adding withall that he was charg'd to tell her, it was a Potion to purg
her heart of all traitorous designes.

The Princess hearing him say so, presently conjectur'd what it was; and not
being daunted with the apprehension of death, took it in her hand, and looking on him who brought the fatall Present: tell the King my Father (said she) I
receive his Present with thankfullness rather then regreett and am better satisfied to receive my death in private; where none may know the manner of it (but
such as I shall enjoyn not to publish it) then on an infamous scaffold in the open
view of all world, where all that had seen me so to dye, would (undoubtedly)
either have censur'd me guilty of some horrid, strange unheard of Crime, or him
of barbarous cruelty: for how severe soever his punishments are to me, I would

---

³ The e is underlined for deletion, and "i" is inserted.

not have the World esteeme him cruell. Tell him I beg no mercy for my selfe; for seeing tis his desire I should not live, I will not oppose his Will so much as with a wish to the contrary: I onely beg with my last breath, that when I am dead, *Cydarius* [fol. 51ʳ] may again be restor'd to that place he formerly possess'd in his favour, since he never did anything that could displease him, but onely in striving to preserve the life of an unfortunate Creature. And for my owne offence which was far greater, I a thousand times more willingly receive this punishment then the King inflicts it on me.

With that she drank it off, and gave the Cup again to the man, telling him he might assure the King he had discharg'd his Commission. He having seen her drink it with a low reverence went out of the roome, leaving me and my Companions (continu'd *Hersilia*) to bewaile the ensuing death of our Deare Mistress. I confess I would have taken from her the deadly draught, when I saw she was about to drink it; but she held me off, charging me not to hinder her, unless I inte^n^ded to expose her to something worse: and had it not been for feare of that, I had forced it from her, and thrown it away: but knowing, he that had a heart to be so cruell, might be more so, I found there was nothing for me to do, but to lament what I could not hinder.

For a good while the Princess found no alteration in herself; but at last she perceiv'd a stupid dullness ceaze her spirits, and like the hand of death begin to cloze her eyes: then looking up upon me, come my faithfull *Hersilia* (said she) come and do thy last Office to thy Mistress; and help me to throw off these Clothes which I shall need no more; and put on those upon me, which tis necessary I carry with me to my last bed. Why doest thou weep *Hersilia* (pursu'd she seeing me shed teares, not being able to speak to her in any other language) preethee do not grieve, for thy teares will more afflict me then my death does.

Ah Madam (she repli'd) I should be the most hard heartedst creature in the World if I could be a spectator of your deplorable condition with dry eyes: methinks Madam you should rather condemne me of too much moderation in my sorrow, I am sure I blame my selfe for it, and confess I am too patient when I think I must forever loose you; and yet can live to suffer such a loss.

Something the Princess would have said to comfort me (pursu'd *Hersilia*) but she was not able; for as she was just going to speak her speech fail'd, and her eyes clos'd, just as if she had fallen into a slumber; but alass it prov'd so sound a sleep that I could not awake her, though both I, and the rest of her Wo^e^men did enough by our cryes, and lamentations to have rous'd her from the deepest Lethargie (much more the fastest sleep) had hers been of that nature. When we perceiv'd that Death (instead of his elder Brother) had fetter'd all her senses, and that there was no hopes of recovering her out of his power, we undress't her, and laid her in her Bed, even in that very posture wherein you now behold her.

Hersilia having ended her tragicall story, stept into her owne Chamber, and presently returning again, brought with her ^the^ Princess *Clazomenas* Picture (which not long before she had given her) and presenting it to me, She told me,

though she valu'd it above all things she had [fol. 51ᵛ] in the World, yet she
would give it to me on condition I would promise to send her a Copie of it assoon
as I could possibly procure one to be taken. This Present I receiv'd more thank-
fully then I should a Crowne, had she in the stead of it presented me with one,
and promis'd faithfully to performe what she enjoyn'd me, and that if I chanced
to end my unhappie life before such time as I could get a Copie of it taken, I
then solemnly vow'd to returne her the Originall: with which promise she being
very well satisfied, I took off my Finger a Ring of no small vallue, which I presented to her in token of my gratitude; but she would by no meanes have taken
it; nor would not upon that account: but then I beg'd her to weare it in memory
of that Friendship I should always retaine for her, which after many refusalls she
accepted at last.

Just as I had prevail'd with her to take that Gift (inconsiderable I confess in
respect of that rich Present she made me) there came from *Oruntus* a Messenger
who forced me to go away; so that I had not time to reflect on *Hersilia*s relation
[narration], nor express how great an addition it was to my sorrow: but I would
not obey him till I had first bid adue to the faithfull *Hersilia* with this protestation, that to the last minute of my miserable life, I would preserve a most perticuler esteeme for her, and that I would never loose the remembrance of this last
obligation whilst I had sense remaining in me. Then being hastned by the man
I left that dismall Chamber, and presently after Issedon, with a resolution never
to returne, till I might see the death of my Princess fully reveng'd; which thorow
your Majesties assistance I hope ere long to do.

Cydarius having finish'd his relation, the King gave him a very satisfactory
answer: after which, he desir'd him to let him see *Clazomenas* Picture, which he
pulling forth of his bosome (where he wore it) presented it to the King to look
on. While *Achemenes* was viewing it, *Phasellus* came in; who having heard of
Cydarius's returne, but not of that unhappie accident which brought him back,
came thither to enforme himselfe of the occation of his coming. Assoon as he saw
Cydarius he went to him, and saluted him very civilly; but when he saw him look
so sadly, he conjectur'd, some more then ordinary misfortune had befallen him.
When the King had view'd the Picture of that Unhappy Princess, and given a
very high commendation of it, all those that were there flock'd about *Achemenes*
to have a sight of it too. *Cydarius* perceiving their desires, and being willing to
oblige them, gave it to *Diomed* after *Achemenes* had restor'd it to him. *Diomed*
very much admiring it, gave it to *Phasellus*, who seem'd more earnestly, and with
a much greater attention to look on it then any of the others that had seen it. At
length, turning ^it^ to *Cydarius*, I beseech you Sir (said he) is this Picture the
resemblance of a living beauty:

Ah no (repli'd *Cydarius*).

Indeed I thought so (answer'd *Phasellus*), for certainly no mortall Beautie ere
was [fol. 52ʳ] halfe so faire.

You are mistaken (said *Cydarius*) for that Princess whom it resembles was a thousand times more faire then any Arte^i^st[4] could represent her. Then am not I the most perfectly wretched of all that ever breath'd, that so Excellent a Princess should loose her life for my accursed sake.

With that, in short he told *Phasellus* whose Picture t'was, and her misfortune; after which he took his leave of *Achemenes* for that day, and retir'd to a tent appointed for him; whether *Diomed* waited on him, though he would willingly have dispenced with ~~that~~ him for that civility: but finding him more desirous of solitude than company, he left him, after he had desir'd him to command any thinge that the Campe afforded and appointed *Phileno*, and two of his owne servants to attend him; for *Cydarius* was as yet destitute of his owne: but he continu'd not long so, for two of his men to whom he had given order to follow him to the Persian Campe came accordingly soon after, and were conducted to him.

Celia chancing to cast her eye aside saw *Amena* at a little distance off, and supposing she might be sent by *Ermillia* to seeke them, call'd her to enquire whether the Queen had dispatch'd that Concerne she was engag'd in; which *Amena* assuring her she had not, was going away; but the Sicilian believing she could do no less in civility but invite that Lady to take a seat by them; but she perceiving them ingag'd in a serious discourse would needs leave them; after which *Celia* went on.

---

[4] The correcting hand underlines "e" and inserts "i."

Rivall Friendship

THE FIRST PART

The Fourth Book

As *Diomed* came from *Cydarius* he met *Phasellus* who went with him to their owne Tent; where they had not been long ere they fell into discourse concerning *Cydarius* and *Clazomena*; whereupon *Phasellus* began again highly to applaud her Picture.

Indeed (said *Diomed*) if the substance did but equall the shaddow (I must confess) that Princess was a very lovely person; but yet methinks *Phasellus*, you express't in the Kings Tent, too deep a sense of her beauty, for one who is a profess'd adorer of another; and in my opinion, in seeking to do Justice to *Cydarius*'s Mistress, you have been highly injurious to your owne. I have known some men (pursu'd he) whose Mistresses have been none of the most charming Beautys that ever were beheld, yet to maintain that none on earth were comparable to [fol. 52ᵛ] them; and rather loose their lives then suffer so great a dishonour to be done to the Object of their passion, as for any other to be preferr'd before them: and therefore I cannot but strangly admire, that you, who have profess't so violent a passion for *Artabella* should think any comparable to her, or rather more to be admir'd then she; as you seem'd to inferre, when you made a publick declaration, that you believ'd the Scythian Princess to be rather a Goddess then a mortall Creature. I will not deny, but she was rarely hansome; but were she living, she must pardon me if I think *Artabella* farre excells her, though I am not her servant as you are, and therefore not oblig'd to have altogether so good an opinion of her as you ought to have.

But since I am your Friend (*Phasellus*) I must not flatter you, but tell you, this is not the first time I have found you declining in those accustomed respects you owe her whom you have vow'd eternally to adore: for I have observ'd, you very seldome write to her to assure her of the continuance of your fidelity, and passion; though you cannot but know, that all the confirmations you can give her of it, are no more then what is necessary to comfort her in your absence.

Oh heavens, had I that priveledge of writing to my adored *Oriana*, how joyfully would I embrace all opportunities, to testifie to her the sincerity, and greatness of my love; but you that have that favour slight it: or if you do write, if your Letters in my absence were no more obliging then that you wrote her since my returne, she has more reason to complain of your coldness, and indifference then receive any satisfaction from them. But this is not the onely observation I have made of your change, but have by a hundred severall passages found a strang alteration in you of late; and such an indifferency as I cannot but strangly wonder at: for questionless to a faithfull Lover there cannot be a more afflicting discontent, next to the death, or inconstancy of her he loves, then to be absent from her: yet this misfortune great as it is, you are so little concern'd for, that I never heare you complain of it, or once so much as wish the War were ended, that you might again enjoy the sight of a person who ought to be most deare to you. Did I not know you had not seen the face of any Woman since we left Persia, I should then attribute your alteration to Infidelity; and conclude that some new Object had banish'd the image of your absent Mistress out of your heart; but since I cannot think your change proceeds from that cause, I know not what to impute it too: speak then *Phasellus*, and be ingenious, and let me know what I ought to think of you; and whether I must regard you as an Infidell, or as an unconstant person who can love no longer then whilest in sight.

All the while *Diomed* was speaking, *Phasellus* seem'd much perplex't by his often change of colour; for sometimes (though he strove all he could to hide the disorder of his mind) shame would appeare, painting his Face with blushes; then anon a paler colour would procla^i^me him guilty of some concealed crime: but having a little compos'd his disorder'd spirits, he assum'd a more serious Countenance, and looking confidently on *Diomed*. If I were guilty of perfidiousness (repli'd he) on^r^[1] inconstancy, you had reason my generous Friend to account me the basest man alive; [fol. 53ʳ] but since (as you say) I have not seen any one that could be capable of making me so, I think protestations of my innocence needless. I know not what you have observ'd in me that should make you suspect such an alteration in me as you fancy, but for my owne part I find none in my selfe. As for those Objections you make, I shall in a few words answere them; and as to the manner of my writing I account it rather folly then affection to express so much fond dotage as many Lovers use in expressing their affection to their Mistresses, especially when I have such unquestionable demonstrations of a reciprocall esteeme. And as to my absence which you think me so insensible of, I protest sincerely it has been, the greatest trouble I ever resented ^felt^,[2] but seeing tis vain to complaine of what I must of necessity suffer, methinks you should rather commend my patience, then censure my moderation: but I confess, I should be much more impatient then I am, were I not most certaine of the affection of *Artabella*, which is so high a felicity, that I should feare if I were so ungratfull as to repine at a short absence, I might provoke the Gods to deprive me of that happiness which I can never prize enough.

Tis very well *Phasellus* (said *Diomed* not being able to let him go on) tis very well you are become so wise, as to love with so much discretion; but let me tell you, since you are arrived at this height of perfection, I question not but you

---

[1] The "n" in "on" is underlined with carats indicating that ^or^ should be inserted.

[2] The word "resented" is underlined and carats are inserted to indicate that ^felt^ should replace this word.

will soon grow to indifferency, and at last to scorne. Ah poor unhappie Princess (pursu'd he) how noble a passion have you thrown away, on one unworthy of it.

Phasellus perceiving by *Diomed*'s manner of speaking, that he was rather incensed then satisfi'd with his answere; for a while stood silent as it were to consider whether ~~whether~~ he had best acknowledge his fault, or still endeavour to conceale it. But at last (as it seem'd) he resolv'd upon the first. If (said he) an ingenuous confession may extenuate my fault, I will declare that which I had rather dy then acknowledge to you, since I feare I shall thereby merit your ill opinion; but if you will look on my offence with an eye of friendship, certainly you will find more cause to pitty, then to pass too severe a ~~sentence sen~~ censure on my weakness, since I have done as much as I am able to keep my self from being guilty of it. The truth is, you had reason to say, *Artabella* has thrown away her love on one unworthy of it, for so I am, the most of any one that lives; for I must acknowledge (though I cannot do it, but with abundance of shame) that I am of so strang a disposition, that tis absolutely impossible for me to love in absence, with that passion as I do when ^the^ object of my love is present. I confess I had great hopes that so much beauty, as that Princess is owner of, would have been powerfull enough to keep that fickle heart her Prisoner, which my owne reason, no less then her Charmes rendred her Captive: Yet I am still in hopes, that this rebellious Slave which against my reason and desire has broke its strongest Chaine (and thereby almost reassum'd its former liberty) will no sooner look on those eyes which conquer'd me, but they will make their victory more perfect, and tye my Fetters [fol. 53ᵛ] more fast then ever; for thus much I can say in my justification, and say truly, that though I am a little unconstant, I am not in the least perfidious: for *Artabella* is still the person I love above all others, and ever shall; for I am resolv'd, if when I see her, I cannot put on my Chaines again, I'le weare no others, and abhorre my self for my inconstancy more then she can do. And now, seeing I have with all sincerity disclos'd to you my frailty, which I do more condemne my self for then you can, I hope you will judge favourably of my weakness, which I have not voluntarily ~~submitted~~ (but most unwillingly) submitted too.

I know not (repli'd *Diomed*) what difference you can make between Inconstancy, and Infidelity; but for my part I know not how to distinguish the one from the other; for certainly tis an undeniable Maxime, that he that can be guilty of the one, may be so of the other as well, for he that can without any reason, or just occasion cease to love, or grow indifferent in his passion to a person who never gave him the least cause for it, and such a one as merits more love then the perfectest Lover is capable of bestowing; may much more easily, and with a better pretence love another, if at any time he find one more worthy of his affection then his late Mistress was. And therefore (*Phasellus*) I should sooner excuse you if some greater Beauty, or a Lady of more transcendant excellencies then *Artabella* is Mistress of, had ravish'd your heart from her, then thus unworthily to abandon, and forget her, when you have nothing to alleage for your injustice, but your owne phantasticall humour.

Alass, how poor is that pretence to which you have recourse for your vindication, in pleading your naturall inclination to inconstancy; but if you were indu'd with that vertue which I really thought you were, when I gave you the precedency of all others in my esteeme, and Friendship, how easily might you overcome all such ill inclinations; for what good does our Vertue do us, if we make not use of it to vanquish our vices, whether those which we have contracted by custome, or those whereto we are prone by nature: but since I see you can be capable of two such detestable Crimes, as a base Inconstancy, and a most horrid Ingratitude to your Mistress, meerly out of a fantasticall fancy, you may as well become guilty of infidelity to your Friend, if the humour take you: for seeing those promises you so oft repeated to *Artabella* of an eternall affection, and an inviolable constancy, cannot engage you to the performance of them, without question you may dispence as well, nay more easily, with all those obligations you have to me: therefore resolve to tye on again your fetters which were so glorious, and advantagious to you, and be sure you fasten them so, as nothing (but the irresistable power of Death) may ere unloose them, or renounce your interest in my Friendship and utterly discla^i^me all title to it, or I must to yours: for I declare I ~~nether~~ neither can, nor will be a Friend to any one, that is not so to Vertue. I excus'd your unjust Jealousie, because I thought it might arise from the violence of your passion; but I cannot excuse, much less pardon this fickle humour in you, which carries with it no excuse. No *Phasellus*, you must repent your folly, [fol. 54ʳ] and so repent it, as you may never be guilty of the like, or believe it I shall repent I ever was your Friend, or did esteeme you mine: and till I am very well assur'd of your amendment you must not take it ill, if I live with you after another manner then hitherto I have done, and shun your Company as much as I have hitherto desir'd it, lest your Crime become contagious, and infect me too.

Diomed stay'd not for his answere, but went from thence, immediatly to the King: as he was going, he was met by one of his servants, who told him *Achemenes* was just then in consultation concerning the taking of Issedon; and had sent for him to be present at the councell, wherein there were divers debates: some were of opinion it were best to tyre *Oruntus* out by a long siege; others, on the contrary affirm'd it was much better to take it by storme, of which opinion *Diomed* was; for as he said, though there was more difficulty to winn the Citie by storming it, then to take it by famine, yet there was the more glory in it: and that (said he) is an invitation to noble spirits to attempt the most hazardous enterprizes.

To this opinion the King adhear'd, as carrying the greatest probability of put^t^ing the speediest end to the War, which he ardently wish'd: for, being as he was then somewhat advanced in yeares, he desir'd, rather to end his dayes in the sweet calmes of Peace, then in the rough, and boisterous Stormes of War. But when *Achemenes* had declar'd himself, the discenting Partie compli'd with those whom they before oppos'd; acknowledging there was now a necessity of that, which some few minutes before they thought not convenient: for there came intelligence of a very considerable supply that was coming to relieve Issedon, from the Tauro-Scithies, which of all the other Scythians were accounted the most valiant, and the best Archers. This newes confirm'd the King in his resolve, knowing this recruit would retard his conquest; which to prevent, it was concluded, that the next night all the souldiers, and Officers according to their severall commands, should be in a readiness to assault Issedon; onely 10000 were drawn out to march along with *Diomed* (who was to command them) to meet the approaching Forces, and fight them in case they proceeded in their march. They being not above six days march from the City, *Diomed* would make no delay; but having drawne out his men, immediatly departed.

The ensuing night all the Officers (having receiv'd their orders) put their men in a readiness to begin the assault when ever the word was given. *Barsarnes* who commanded the Susianianses, and the Bactrians gave the first onset on the Backside of the City; but were soon repell'd by a shower of Arrows which were power'd [poured] downe upon them as thick as Hailestones, which forced them to make a little retreat; but t'was onely to returne with the greater force. But for all the valour of *Barsarnes* and his followers, it was more then five houres ere they could approch the Walls so as to plant their Ingins of battery, but whilst they were so busily employ'd on that side, *Achemenes* was not idle on the other; for though his yeares, and Dignity, might have dispenced [fol.54ᵛ] with him from acting in his owne Person, yet would he not be perswaded to be a spectator onely, of those dangers his subjects underwent.

Phasellus fought on that side the King was on, and to give him the praise he merited, he behav'd himself with abundance of gallantry: he was the first that fastned a scalling Ladder to the Wall, though not without a manifest hazard of his life; which he was many times in danger of loosing: but at last, inspight of all opposition he planted a Persian Standerd on the Walls; he was soon follow'd by many others, which made way for ~~other~~ *Achemenes* to ascend in safty: but Fate had otherways decreed it, for just as he came to the top of the Wall, he was mortally wounded in the Eye with an Arrowe: a rumour of the Kings danger being presently spread abroad struck such a damp upon the Persians courages, that they would no longer pursue the taking [of] Issedon, but sounded a retreat ^to^ carry off their wounded Soveraigne, in whose misfortune each man had a part.

When the Chirurgions had search'd his Wounds, their Looks spake the little hopes they had of his life; but yet, they declar'd they could give no certain Judgment till the next dressing, when they open'd it again it seem'd so much better then they expected, that it put them in some hopes: but the Eye being the most tender, and sensible part of the body; the pain was so extreame, that what with the violence of that, and want of sleep, it brought him into a high feavour; which meeting with a body of no very strong constitution, and thereby unable to resist the violence of the Distemper, it was impossible he could continue many dayes, though neither his Chirurgions, nor Phisicians wanted either

skill or desire to recover him, had it been in the power of Art to work his cure.
But whilst he lay in this condition he had yet this satisfaction to know himself
before his death an absolute Conquerour of Scythia; for he had certain Intelligence that *Diomed* had fought the enemy, and won the Field with an inconsiderable loss as to his men, though with the hazard of his owne life; being very dangerously wounded: in somuch, as he was fain to be carri'd to a little Village not
far from the Place where they fought, uncapable of stiring a long time, if he did
at all recover: but though he could not come himselfe, he was sending *Oruntus*
(whom he had taken Prisoner) to the King, as the chiefe Trophie of his Victory:
but the King seem'd rather to grieve, then rejoyce at the newes; for when he had
heard it, he sighing said, the Victory was bought too deare, if *Diomed's* life must
be the price of it: declaring, it would be more trouble to him to loose *Diomed*,
then rejoyce him to win Scythia.

Presently after the Chyrurgions came in to dress his Wound, but when they
had open'd it, they soon chang'd their feare of his cure, into an absolute dispaire of it: he finding by the dejected countenances of all that were about him,
something of a more then ordinary feare, commanded the Chyrurgions upon
their alleigiance to tell him [fol.55ʳ] truly whether there was any hopes of his
life. Having receiv'd such a Command they durst not flatter him any longer,
but answer'd with a sad negative there was not; unless the Gods would work a
miracle in favour of him: which answere when the King had heard, he bid all
should avoid the Roome except *Barsarnes*, and *Phasellus*, and calling them to his
Bedside (while with abundance of Sorrow they approach't to know his pleasure)
he declar'd somewhat to them in private, and as he had done, his speech began
to faulter: *Barsarnes* perceiving his end drawing nigh, and that he had no more
to say, caus'd the Dore to be open'd that those who desir'd it might have liberty
again to enter, which divers of the Nobility did, time enough to see him breath
his last. Never was sorrow express'd to the life till now: all that were present,
seem'd as if their soules had a designe to forsake their Bodies to wait on him
to the other World. The certainty of his death being spread thoroughout the
Campe (as t'was impossible to conceale it) fill'd all places with such cryes, and
lamentations, as would have inspir'd pity into the Rocks could they have heard
them.

The next day *Phasellus* left the Campe to go to *Diomed*, and being arriv'd
there at the Village where he lay, he found him in a more dangerous condition
then report spake him to be. *Diomed* receiv'd him with a great deall of kindness,
but not with those raptures of Joy wherewith he was wont to wellcome him,
before the difference which lately was between them.

I beg your pardon (said *Phasellus*, after he had made some enquiries of his
condition, and express'd much sorrow to find him so ill) for my intrusion into
you[r] presence (from which you so cruelly banish'd me) without your permission: but the occation that brought me must make my Apollogie; tis the death of
Achemenes.

The death of *Achemenes* (said *Diomed* and started) Heavens forbid it.

Tis but too certaine (repli'd *Phasellus*) I saw him dye: but to dispell that trouble which I see this ill newes has excited in you, I have somewhat to acquaint you with, that will bring you as much Joy, as what I have already said has brought you griefe.

Oh tell it quickly then *Phasellus* (said he), or I shall hardly live to heare it, my sorrow is so great for the loss of that good King.

Phasellus then presented him a Ring, and whisper'd something in his eare, not thinking it fit (perhaps) to speak it openly before so many as were in the Roome: and now (said he), since there is no more need of my assistance in these parts, I think it requisit to waite on my Princess [Artabella], and try if by the sight of her, I can again reduce my heart to its subjection. I confess I had rather stay with you till your recovery, then leave you, did I not believe, my company would prove more troublesome then obliging, till such time as I can give you some unquestionable Demo^n^stration of my Conversion.

No (repli'd *Diomed*) I would by no meanes do you, or my selfe so great an injury, as to retaine you with me when tis so necessary that you return to Persia, that you may thereby approve again your fidelity to your Mistress, and by that assure yourself of my Friendship, which you shall possess again with larg advantages [fol. 55ᵛ] when you have once again recall'd that Vertue which you have almost forsaken.

Then giving him some private Instructions what he should say to the Princesse *Oriana*, and charging him not to take notice to her of any thinge that he had told him, adding, he desir'd to be the first that should acquaint her with it at his returne, which (as he said) should be as speedily as the Gods would be pleas'd to restore him to his health, and strength, and that he had took order for the settling of Scythia, and for the establishing *Oriana's* power over her wel new Dominions: after this he most affectionatly embraced *Phasellus*, whilst he bad him farewell, and return'd to the Campe, spake with *Barsarnes*, and deliver'd him a Message from *Diomed*, and without delay began his Journey towards Persia; though *Barsarnes* would have perswaded him to stay, to attend *Achemenes*'s body, which within three dayes was to be carried thither, and waited on by himself and a considerable part of the Armie to the River Araxes, where they resign'd it to the conduct of some of the chiefest of the Nobility to convey it with all Millitary Pompe, and Ceremony to Susa (where the Princess then was) to be interr'd in the Monument of his Predecessors.

I should have told you Madam (said *Celia*) that *Oruntus* was brought to the Campe, the day after *Achemenes* died; where the souldiers were so transported with rage against him, for the death of their King (imputing it wholy to him) as *Barsarnes* had no easie task of it to restrain them from pulling him in pieces. But after he had with much perswasion allai'd their fury, he caus'd him to be brought into that Tent which was *Diomeds*, placeing a strong Guard on him to prevent his escape, if he should attempt it. *Barsarnes* being naturally of a generous temper, could not endure to a^d^de contempt, to misery, nor trample with scorne upon a fallen Crowne; but remembred that *Oruntus* had lately been a Monarch, surpass'd by few in grandure, and therefore caus'd him to be treated with a respect, more sutable to his dignity then his condition.

Assoon as *Diomed* was in a capacity to be remov'd, he caus'd himself to be put into a Litter; and so carri'd by easy Journeys to the Armie, where he knew his presence was exceeding necessary. Assoon as he was come *Barsarnes* waited on him, to give him an account of all things that had past in his absence: but when he related the manner of the Kings death, it brought a new Deluge of sorrow on the soule of *Diomed*, which had like to have overwhelm'd his spirits with its violence; so many were the sad expresions of his griefe for the loss of that good King, that should I stay to repeat them (continu'd *Celia*) I should but tyre your Patience. After this, *Barsarnes* told him, *Achemenes* had left *Oruntus* to his dispose, onely commanded he should dy for his cruelty, but the manner of his death he left to him to determine. The next day he commanded *Oruntus* to be brought before him [fol. 56ʳ] which was accordingly perform'd. *Diomed* was in Bed when he came in, his weakness rendring him unable to see him in any other posture.

King of Scythia (said he to him) I suppose tis not unknown to you that the King of Persia at his death, constituted me to be your Judge; but I could wish he had ordain'd some other to determine your Fate, lest that which Justice will compell me too, should be looked on as revenge: for notwithstanding you have with all imaginable rigour sought my life, yet had your cruelty extended no further then to me, or that I had been the onely person concern'd in it, I should very easily have been perswaded to have wav'd my owne Concerns: but tis that Vertuous Princess (whose onely crime was that she had a being from you so bad a Father) tis that life that you have so barbarously depriv'd her of, that calls so loud for Vengeance that I cannot stop my eares against its cryes, nor (without as high an injustice as that wherewith you acted that cruell deed) pardon your crime. I am sorry you have thorough your obstinacy, or ambition (I know not which to terme it) provok'd a King to pull you from your Throne, who had neither desire, nor design to envade your Dominions, would you have suffer'd him to live peaceably in his owne: but you see (*Oruntus*) the justest sword has been the sharpest; and reduc'd you to a condition which deserves pitty even from your enemies; for my part, you have so much of my compassion, that I should in pitty let you live, though Pollicy, and Prudence both forbid it: yet I say, I should certainly have pass't by both those respects, did not a more pressing consideration (I meane that Justice I owe to your Illustrious, and unfortunate Daughter) force me to pass the sentence of death upon you. But to let you see I am as free from Malice, as you were fraught with it, and with what reluctancy I execute my Office, I give you leave to chuse what death you will dye.

Affliction (answer'd *Oruntus*) oft teaches that Vertue, which Prosperity either suffers us not to learne, or if once learn'd, soon makes to forget: The verity of what I say, I can now prove from my owne experience; for had I still

continu'd in my florishing estate, questionless I had never seen the deformity of
Vice, which now appeares so ugly to me, that I can never enough admire what
blinded me before, I could not see its true shape: but now the Mist is vanish'd I
perceive the greatness of my Crimes which appeare with so much horrour to me,
that Death will rather be a mercy then a punishment, since it will free me from
this Terrour which like a Fury will torment me whilst I live. Had I again that
Kingdome I have lost, and with it all the Crownes on Earth united into one, I
would freely give them all to purchace that life for my Deare *Clazomena* which I
caus'd her to loose: but since that cannot be, that my Punishment may be resembling to my fault, I desire to dy by Poison as she did; that I may become the more
sensible of what she suffer'd.

In my opinion (said *Diomed*) you have made a very good choice, and therefore to morrow you shall have your last draught presented you.

After *Oruntus* was carried back to that Tent which was his Prison, *Diomed*
sent to Issedon to [fol. 56ᵛ] sommon them to yeeld after the example of Sinone
and all the other Cities of Scythia who had submitted; for they no sooner heard
of a certain that their King was taken Prisoner, but they yeelded to his mercy,
whose example he sent them word, if they would follow, they should find his
Clemency as great to them as the other Citties had done; promising them there
should not a man of them, neither souldiers, nor Inhabitants receive the least
prejudice either in their goods, or persons; but if they refus'd, they would through
an obstinate folly, draw on themselves, their Wives, and Children an inevitable
ruine, which he was willing to prevent; for if they rejected so faire a proffer, he
declar'd they must expect nothing but the uttmost of violence from the fury of
a powerfull, and insenced Enemy. To this summons they return'd no positive
answere; onely desir'd security for a young Lady (who they said was then in
Issedon) to come in safty to speak with him; which he having upon his honour
assur'd them of, she came soon after to the Campe, in a Chariot cover'd all with
black, drawn by six white Horses cover'd by the same: she was herself in mourning, and onely accompanied with one Lady, who rode with her in the same sable
habit; and in this equipage she appear'd like the Queen of Night: for thorough
her black her beauty cast such a splendor, that she seem'd to all that saw her, like
bright Cynthia breaking thorow a Cloud. When she was brought into the Tent
where *Diomed* was, she pulled downe her Vaile, so as he could see but very little
of her face; but yet she herselfe could see so much in his as assur'd her which was
he without enquiring: so that addressing herselfe to him with a meen [mien] so
majestick, and with so much humility mix'd with it; as she became no less the
admiration of him, then of all the rest that were present.

The designe Sir (said she) that brought me hither was, to tender you a Ransome for our King whom misfortune has made your Captive; but since the Fates
ordain'd him such a destiny, it was some satisfaction to his subjects, that he was
fallen into the hands of so brave an Enemy, who knows as well to vanquish by
his generosity, as by his Sword: it was this noble Principle in you, that gave us

the hopes you would not refuse that to our Prayers, which without injustice (I confess) you may deny. But that which I have heard since my coming to this place, has forced me to change my sute for his Freedome, into an humble Petition for his life; which on my knees I begge Sir you would spare. Let it suffice that you have taken his Kingdome from him; and that he has nothing left of all that Royalty wherewith he was invested, but the bare title of a King; and let that miserable, that deplorable condition where unto you have reduced him, create some compassion in you towards him: if you doubt his life may any way disturbe the Persians Conquest you have made them, keep him your Prisoner still; do any thing but destroy him by an untimely death.

Cease Madam (he repli'd) I beseech you to importune me to what I cannot grant; for if I could, believe it I had prevented [anticipated] your desires in giving *Oruntus* his life, [fol. 57ʳ] but I cannot do it, being oblig'd to the contrary by two inviolable Obligations, that of the command of the late King of Persia, and that Justice I owe to the memory of that most excellent Princess who most unjustly perish'd by his cruelty.

I think tis more then you can prove (said she interrupting him) that t'was unjust in him to put her to death, though I must needs say it was somewhat too severe; but that it was unjust I do deny; for though she was his Daughter, she was his subject too, then by a double right ^he^ had a power over her, both as her Father, and her King: and her Offence being no less then Treason, which in a subject deserves death, why was she not as lyable to suffer it as the meanest person in the Kingdome.

I confess Madam (said he), your Arguments carry so much of reason in them, that I can hardly find any to dispute against you. But admit she were guilty of what you charge her with; yet none but a Tyrant, but would have given her a Legall Tryall, and not have judg'd, and condemn'd her in his owne cause, without allowing her the liberty to plead in her owne behalf. I am not ignorant Madam of that power which belongs to Kings; I know it absolute, not to be controul'd by any; but I know withall that Good and just Princes never make their Will their Law; none but a Tyrant does do soe, and such your King shew'd himselfe, when he with so much inhumanity murther'd his onely Daughter; had he put her to death Legally, he had been much more excusable.

Whilst you accuse him of cruelty (repli'd she) you are your selfe sir guilty of a greater to *Clazomena* in making her guilty after her death of her Fathers; a Crime so great, as were she living, she would cur^s^e herself for; and will (questionless) if she has knowledge of ought transacted here below eternally disturbe her happiness.

I cannot tell Madam (said he), what interest you may pretend to *Oruntus*, sure somewhat more then common alleigance, that incites you to plead so highly in his behalfe, so much to the prejudice of his Daughter, you show much of Friendship to the one, but you speak no less enemity to the other.

So far am I sir (she repli'd) from being *Clazomenas* enemy, that did you know me, you would confess I were as much her friend as she could be to her selfe; but you must pardon me if I declare I am more my Kings then I am hers: wherefore I once more conjure you sir to grant what I implore; and if no other Argument can prevaile with you, let your gratitude to that Unhappie Princess plead for what I humbly sue; she sav'd your life, which caus'd her death; Oh do not then with such ingratitude requite that favour, as to take away her Fathers.

I should indeed but too ingratfully requite her kindness (*Diomed* repli'd) should I let him live that kill'd her.

Were she living (said she) would you let him live.

Most willingly (said he) on that condition, and more then that, were it in my power, I would (for her sake) freely restore him all that Fortune has taken from him.

Since you have promis'd he shall live (answer'd she) conditionally that *Clazomena* does, I must declare to you she is not dead though you believe her soe.

Tis impossible (he repli'd) *Cydarius* saw her dead.

He was deceiv'd (said she) in what he saw; for on my word she lives if I do so, for I am that unfortunate Princess (continu'd she turning up her Vaile) happie in nothing but in this, that I have liv'd to be a meanes of preserving the life of him, from whom I had my being. If you suspect any thing of ~~fallicy~~ fallacy in what I say; call for any of those Scythians you have taken, and if there be any amongst [fol. 57ᵛ] them that have ever seen me, and let them say whether I am not *Oruntus*'s Daughter or no: but *Diomed* needed no further confirmation then the full sight of her; for having seen her Picture he knew, none but herself could so perfectly resemble that. But being amaz'd at what he saw, he remain'd a while silent, as it were to consider whether he might believe his eyes; but finding they did not deceive him, he rose from his Chaire (though not without much difficulty) and threw himselfe at her Feet, to implore her pardone for his uncivill reception of her (as he term'd it).

Ah Madam (said he), have I been so unhappie to bring that Princess on her knees to me, to whom I owe my life and liberty: but I hope Madam your unparalel'd goodness will make a favourable construction of my rude deportment towards you, and harsh deniall of your sute, and that you will impute what I have done or said, to nothing but my ignorance of your true quality: and if it may any way alleviate the offence I have committed against the most Excellent, and most Obliging Princess of the World, I will assure you Madam on my Honour (which I value above all things) that had I known what now I do, I had ere this sent home your Father Ransomless; or if that had been beyond the extent of my power, I would my selfe have paid his Ransome; for all the designes I had against him, had no other foundation but my gratitude to you; and my hatered I conceiv'd against him was meerly on the account of that violence wherewith he treated you. But why Madam would you no sooner discover your selfe, and so prevent the trouble of a deniall; which you had ne're receiv'd, if I had had the honour to have known you.

The truth is (answer'd she) if I could by any meanes but the discovery of my selfe, have obtain'd my Petition, I would still have remain'd conceal'd, least when *Oruntus* knows he owes his life to my intercession, his hatered of me should make him detest it, and thinke it rather a punishment then a favour ~~of y~~ from you.

Were he the same he was, still possest with a ~~malishi~~ malicious and revengfull mind, you would have some reason Madam for that apprehension; but I'le assure you, you may banish all those feares for he is quite another from what he was, and does as much repent his cruelty to you, as he desir'd before to act it.

May I with confidence (said she) credit what you tell me, if so, I shall not value what Fortune has depriv'd me of, since the Heavens has restor'd me to my Fathers Love.

I tell you nothing Madam (repli'd he) but what I am my selfe perswaded of; but I will not impose that beliefe on you, till experience shall confirme it. I would my selfe waite on you to the King your Father, did not my weakness render me unable to do you that service; but in my stead, *Barsarnes* shall attend you thither (with that he sent one to call him) and in the meane time, while he comes Madam (said he) let me humbly beg the favour to know how you were preserv'd from that death to which *Oruntus* destin'd you; I know already the whole story of your sufferings from the mouth of *Cydàrius*.

At the mention of *Cydarius* she blush't and [fol. 58ʳ] ~~and~~ pull'd downe her Vaile the better to conceale that little redness which his name had painted on her Cheek. That (said she), by which my Father was deceiv'd ~~and I preserv'd~~ (who as really believ'd me dead as *Hersilia* and all that saw me) and I preserv'd, was by a sleepie Potion which I drank instead of deadly Poison for he who made it, being more friendly to me, then faithfull to *Oruntus*; put in it such Ingredients, as might so stupifie the vitall spirits for a time, as it was impossible for me to be thought any other then dead. When they saw this drink had wrought on me the operation he intended; he perswaded the King, that the Venoume of what he had given me was so great, that it would presently corrupt the Body if it were not ~~presently~~ ^instantly^ buried, so that the stench of it would be very offencive to all that came neere me: he found no difficulty in perswading my Father to this, so that he gave him order to bury me privately the ensuing night: which he accordingly perform'd, none following me to the Grave but my owne servants; amongst whom my Faithfull *Hersilia* was one, who never would forsake me; but beg'd (as I afterwards was told) with the greatest importunity imaginable that they would bury her alive with me: but when she saw she could not prevaile in her desire, she vow'd never to stir from my Grave, but to remain perpetually to lament me.

This Phisician (who was call'd *Medicius*) being well enough assur'd of her fidelity to me, made no scruple to discover to her, that what he had done was onely to preserve me from my Fathers fury; telling her withall, that if she would be but a little patient she should see me revive again: but such was her sorrow as she could give no credit to such an improbability. But as I said, the rest being gone, he call'd two of his owne servants in whom he knew he might confide, and caus'd them to take me up again, and carry me to his house (which was not far from that place) where his Wife, and *Hersilia* took me me out of the Coffin, and laid me in a warme bed: after which, the Coffin was carr'd [carried] back again, and put into the Grave, and that made up, so as none could mistrust what had been done.

All that night, and the greatest part of the next day I continu'd in that Trance, to all appearance dead: but he knowing very well that there was something of danger in what he had given me wrench'd open my mouth, pouring downe a certain Spirit which I suppose brought me from my seeming death a little too soon; for presently after I awak'd, so as to open my eyes, and give some symptoms of life, but yet I lay a long time as one senseless: but at length my spirits began a little to come to me, so that I was a little more sensible. But when I came perfectly to my self, (which was not till the next morning) I looking up with admiration, wonder`d where, or in what place I was; well knowing I [fol. 58ᵛ] was not in my owne Chamber: but seeing *Hersilia* standing by me, with her eyes almost swell'd out with weeping, I ask'd her where I was, and what she ail'd that her looks testifi'd so much of sorrow: she in few words made me understand where I was, and how brought thither, and consequently the occation of her griefe. Thus sir you see by what meanes the Gods preserv'd me; and in *Medicius*'s house I remain'd ever since conceal'd, till that very day you sent your summons to Issedon to yeeld, so that I need not tell you what occation brought me hither, being already acquainted with it.

Barsarnes being by this time come, *Diomed* desir'd him to waite on the Princess *Clazomena* to the King of Scythia, and to tell him, since she was living, he freely forgave him all the injuries he had done him; and that he would for the Princesses sake (if he would condescend to some Propositions he would make him) not onely give him his liberty, but restore him his Crowne and Kingdome: which Message *Clazomena* having heard, she express'd a high resentment [regard] of [for] his generosity, and presented her hand to *Barsarnes*; who took it with a respect due to the greatness of her birth, and lead her to the Tent where *Oruntus* was: When they came in, they found him lying on the Bed; but hearing some body enter his Chamber, he arose, believing it was the Messenger of his approaching death which he had many houres expected: but seeing a Gentleman enter, leading a Lady, and another following, he knew not what to conjecture; but as they drew neer him, he thought in the Countenance of the first he saw his Daughters face: and retreating a little back, he gave a sudden start as one affrighted, crying out,

Oh *Clazomena* why have you left that Place of bliss, where your pure soule enjoy'd all true felicity, to come to reproach your unhappy ^Father^ with your death, since he is now about to satisfie for it with his owne. Or if that be not enough, let me, Oh let me (continu'd he with a sigh) know what I may do before

I leave the World to pacifie thy justly incenced spirit; but couldst thou see my heart, thou wouldst behold there so much of sorrow and remorse for my unnaturall cruelty, as thou couldst not but be satisfi'd with what I suffer for the wronge I did thee.

Clazomena perceiving he took her for a Ghost, was not troubled at his mistake; since thereby she found she was in a possibility of being once more happie: but she would no longer let him continue in his errour, but falling on her knees, and taking one of his hands which she kiss'd, washing it with teares. Let these teares, (Deare Father said she) the true witnesses of my repentance for having incurred your displeasure, and of my unfeigned sorrow for your misfortunes, assure you Sir that I am really your Clazomena not her Ghost as you suppose; and if you doubt I am so, let Hersilia witness the truth of what I say (continu'd she pointing to her who came with her) he hearing her speak, and finding by her actions she was no Apparition, as he had fanci'd her, he burst forth into Teares of Joy, and embraceing her with a more Fatherly, and tender affection then ever he had [fol. 59ʳ] express'd towards her, he took her up and set her downe by him.

Have the Gods then my Deare Clazomena (said he) been so undeservedly favourable to me who have oft so wickedly despis'd their power, as by a miracle of mercy to raise you from the dead, and restore you to me again after I had lost you through my owne cruelty. Ah deare Child (pursu'd he embraceing her again) nothing now grieves me, but that I must not live to testifie my thankfullness to them for so great a blessing.

If that be the onely thing that does disturbe your Joys Sir (said Barsarnes) you may cast off all thoughts of Death; for if you can accept of Life from a Generous enemy, Diomed gives you yours.

I will forget he was so (repli'd Oruntus) and from henceforth esteeme him as my Friend.

And more then that (added Barsarnes) he will set you free, and reinstate you in your Dominions again for this faire Princesses sake, upon some Conditions: what they are I know not; but if you please Sir to ^go^ with me to him he will himselfe acquaint you with them.

Come let us go then (answer'd Oruntus) taking the Princess by the hand to lead her with him; whilst Barsarnes did the like to Hersilia; and as Oruntus pass'd by her, he told her he hop'd he should be one day able to requite her fidelity to her Mistress, and so pass'd on. Diomed seeing him come met him at his Chamber Dore; for though he was not well enough to stir abroad, he made a shift to walk a litle about his Chamber.

I am come (said Oruntus to him) in the first place, to beg your pardon for whatever my implacable and revengfull disposition made me injuriously commit against you, and that you would so far forget it, as never to think on those injuries any more; and do me the Justice to believe, I will ever be as much your Friend, as I have hitherto bin your Foe, if you esteeme the Friendship of a distressed Captive Prince worth your acceptance.

As it has been Fortunes fault that you are so (repli'd *Diomed*) so it must be now your owne, if you continue soe; for if you will accept of some Propositions I shall make you, you may then be as happie, as you esteeme your selfe unfortunate. As for my Pardon, tis needless Sir to desire it, since tis already granted; but for my owne part I am oblig'd to beg yours, for not treating you with that respect and reverence, that I should have done, had my prejudice to your Majesty been on any other score then what it was.

The next thinge that brought me hither said (*Oruntus*), was to know of you what those things are, which you have to propose to me touching a Peace, which I earnestly desire may be establish'd between this Kingdome and that of Persia.

The Conditions Sir are these (repli'd *Diomed*) on which I shall venture to restore you your Crown. First that you pay yearly a 1000 Tallents forever to the Queen of Persia and her successors, to acknowledge you hold your Crowne of them. And secondly that you shall aide, and assist the Persians if any other Nation make War upon them, with 10000 of your most valiant Scythians. And thirdly you shall send Ten Children of the Sons of the noblest Families in your Dominions as Hostages, to be [fol. 59ᵛ] educated in the Persian Court; and still at their returne, their number to be suppli'd with others. And lastly that you shall recall *Cydarius* from Banishment (and set out your Manifests to that purpose) and receive him into your Royall favour whensoever he shall render himselfe.

To this last Article *Oruntus* consented very willingly, but to the others not without much repugnancy, being very unwilling to bring those that should succeed him into such subjection: but since there was no remedy, he consented to them, after *Diomed* had promis'd to perswade the Queen of Persia to moderate somewhat of the severity of those Conditions; but of himselfe (he said) he could not exact less, since he conquer'd for another, not himselfe. The Articles being seal'd, *Diomed* told *Oruntus* he was free to go to Issedon when he pleas'd, and that he himself would waite on him there within a day or two, when he had a little setled his owne Affaires. *Oruntus* biding him farewell till then, departed, taking the Princess along with him, and was wellcom'd by his subjects (as many of them as were in Issedon) with great expressions of Joy; and the rather, in regard he brought Peace home with him, which of all other, is the greatest blessing any People can enjoy.

The two Following days were spent in preparation for the reception of *Diomed*, which was with abundance of state, and more Magnificence then could be expected in so short a time. The third day after the Kings returne, *Diomed* came to Issedon, bringing *Cydarius* with him; to whom he had declar'd the Princesses being alive, least the unexpected sight of her might have been prejudiciall to him, being but newly recover'd from a dangerous sickness, which had so weakened him, as he had scarce strength enough to be brought to Issedon, without the danger of a Relaps: but when he had heard this Joyfull newes, he would not be perswaded to keep any longer from the sight of his beloved Princess. At the Gate of Issedon *Oruntus* met them, attended by a great Traine of Nobles with the Crowne upon his head, and invested with all his Royall Ornaments.

Diomed seeing him approach, lit out of his Chariot to meet him, taking *Cydarius* by the hand to present him to the King. I shall see Sir (said *Diomed* to him) how well you will keep all the other Articles by the reception you give the Generous *Cydarius*, though he has not stay'd to be call'd home; but trusting on that favour wherewith you have heretofore honour'd him, returnes to render himself to your mercy.

With that *Cydarius* presented himselfe on his Knees to *Oruntus*, whilst he embraced him with no less kindness then if he had never been displeas'd with him; and told him, he was sorry he had expos'd him to such sufferings, as that alteration which appear'd in him shew'd he had undergone: and turning to *Diomed*, he told him if there ne needed no more to testifie the reallity of his intentions to keep those Articles he had made, then his treating *Cydarius* well; he should ere long have an [fol. 60ʳ] assurance great enough: with that he took the Keys of the Cytie Gates from the man that carried them, and presented them to *Diomed*; and took off his Crowne and laid it at his Feet, in token that he resign'd it to the Queen of Persia: which *Diomed* (^as^ representing her person) having taken of him put it again on *Oruntus*'s head, saying. Though by the right of Warre we might justly weare this Crowne, yet out of our royall bounty we restore it, on condition those Articles you have seal'd be never violated.

This Cerimony being past, they stay'd not, but went on to that house which the King had made his Palace ever since he came first to Issedon. Being come into a very spacious Roome, fit for the reception of such Illustrious Company; the King sate him downe, upon a Throne (which he had caus'd to be erected for some perticuler designment) causing *Diomed* to be seated on his right hand; and sent instantly for the Princess, who soon after came in: but when she saw *Cydarius* standing by the King her Father, she express'd much of disorder in her thoughts, by her often change of colour; not that she was troubled to see him, but since she had made such a cleare discovery of her affection, as neither he nor any else could be ignorant of it, she knew not with what confidence to look on him; especially in her Fathers presence. Faine would *Cydarius* as soon as he saw her come in, have gone to throw himself at her Feet, to tell her the greatness of his Joy, to find himself so happily deceiv'd in the beliefe of her death, had he not fear'd to draw on him the Kings anger again (being but lately pacifi'd) by such an action: but he was forced to content himselfe with onely giving her a very low reverence as she past by him; and let the dumbe language of his eyes express his thoughts.

I sent for you *Clazomena* (said the King) to recompence you for that severity wherewith I treated you; which I can never sufficently do but by placing you on that Throne, to which, Nature (without my aide,) will help you one day to ascend: but that will be no thanks to me, if I then leave you what I can no longer keep, but if I now resign my Crowne, tis my owne free act, which nothing but my love to thee compells me too. Come then my *Clazomena*, let me with my owne hand Crowne thee Queen of Scythia (continu'd he rising up, and taking off his Crowne).

The Gods forbid Sir (she repli'd) that ere you should for me unthrone your selfe; no, long may you live to weare this Crowne which by the favour of our generous Conquerour you once again repossess in Peace: nor need you seek Sir for a recompence for me, I have already receiv'd one great enough for ^more then^ what I suffer'd, in the enjoyment of your love, and favour; which I a thousand times prefer before that Diadem which you would bestow upon me: nor could *Oruntus* [fol. 60ᵛ] perswade her to permit herself to be crown'd by him, till to his perswasions he joyn'd his Commands; and withall declar'd, that what he did, was as well to ease himselfe of a Burthen (wherein he had found more trouble then delight) as to show his love to her: so that seeing her Fathers resolutions were firmly fix'd to execute what he had determin'd, she sate downe on that Throne which (as it seemes) *Oruntus* had caus'd to be erected for this very purpose, and suffer'd him to set the Crowne upon her head (though not without much unwillingness) which when he had done, he kist her, wishing her Reigne might be as prosperous as his had been unfortunate. This being done, all that were present gave a shout, crying with unanimous Voices, the Gods preserve Queen *Clazomena*.

The noise being a little past, *Oruntus* spake again. Though I have given away my Royall authority, yet I have not parted with the power of a Father, that I still retaine; and that I trust Daughter (said he) you will still obey: but I will onely make use of it in one thing; which is, in chusing a Husband for you, which shall be noe other then *Cydarius*, whom I desire you would accept, as him who best deserves you.

Since I have obey'd you Sir (repli'd she) in what was most repugnant to my reason, and desires; you need not question but I will obey you in all things else: but perhaps Sir though you esteeme *Cydarius* worthy of me, he may not esteeme me worthy of himselfe.

Oh Madam (said *Cydarius* with the greatest passion imaginable) do not that injustice to that high respect, and unfeigned passion I beare you, as to make that a question, which needs no answere: can you esteeme me so void of sense, as to look on this honour, and happiness which is design'd me by your Royall Father, any otherwise then as ~~the~~ a felicity so great, as not any thing under Heaven can equall.

Oruntus perceiving he could not more oblige them then in giving them to each other, sav'd his Daughter the trouble of a reply; for taking her by the hand he gave her to *Cydarius*. Here *Cydarius* (said he to him) I do as freely give her you, as Heaven bestow'd her on me; and I will that your marriage be no longer defer'd, ~~then~~ till such time as things may be prepar'd fit for your Nuptiall solemnities; till which time (said he to *Diomed*) I shall intreat your stay here, that you may honour my Daughters Marriage with your presence.

Though my occations are urgent for my departure (he repli'd) yet I will dispence with them, till I have seen the happiness of the Illustrious *Clazomena*, and my generous Friend accomplished, in whose felicities I shall beare a part.

This choice of *Oruntus*'s, was no less satisfactory to the Scythians, then obliging to *Cydarius*, for he was generally belov'd by all; nor could he in all his Kingdome have made choice [fol. 61ʳ] of any person to bestow her on, so much deserving as he, both as to his birth, and those excellent quallities wherewith he was endu'd; which were such as few could parallele; so highly generous, so truly Valiant, so wisely Prudent, so every way accomplish't was he, as none but would have believ'd, he had rather receiv'd his education in Rome, or Athens, then amongst a People so rude, and barbarous, as they scarce knew what belong'd to common civility: then seeing *Cydarius* was such, and far more excellent then I [Celia] have represented him, tis not to be thought but that *Clazomena* will be no less happy in him then he in her; to which happiness I will leave them in a desired expectations of their approaching marriage, and returne to Persia to see what is there is acted since we ~~since we~~ left that sceane.

But *Celia* could proceed no further; for the Queen having been enform'd that *Gentillus* was come, admitted him into her presence and instantly sent for the Sicilian Lady [Arthenia] to give the relation of her misfortunes, which she no sooner understood, but she immediatly went in, and presented her selfe to *Ermillia*, who told her it was now that she expected the performance of her promise.

I shall obey you Madam (she repli'd) though I know I cannot do it without reviveing in my soule those resentments [feelings] which I ardently desire to banish thence; but neither that, nor any other consideration is so prevalent with me, as my obedience to your Majesties commands, and my Lord *Gentillus*'s desires, to whom I must ever acknowledge my Obligations infinite.

To which expression he having made a sutable reply, at the Queens request he took a seat, preparing with attention to hearken to the ensuing discourse, which the Sicilian Lady (after a short silence, to recall some almost forgotten passages of her life) began in these Words.

Rivall Friendship

THE FIRST PART

The ~~Fourth~~ Fifth Book

The History of Arthenia

My name Madam is *Arthenia*, (said she) addressing her speech to the Queen, my Country Sicilia (as you have already heard) there drew I my first breath. An Island it is, famous in former Ages for severall remarkable things; as the punishment of the Giant Enceladus for his attempt against the Gods:[1] the frequent eruptions of Fire from Mount Etna under which he was suppos'd to be shut up. The rape of *Proserpine*, and the birth of *Ceres* to whom the Isle is dedicated,[2] Neer to the Citie Agrigentum (memorable for *Phalaris* his torturing *Perillus* in a Brazen Bull which he had invented for the torture of others)[3] was I born, of a Family noble enough; but as I have ever esteem'd it the greatest of vanities to rifle the Monuments of the Dead, or sift their Ashes for honour if we cannot by our owne proper vertue make good our title to it; So will I not boast the Nobility of my Ancestours, Since I have no further a right unto it then what my vertue gives me,

---

[1] During the battle between the Giants and the Olympian gods, Enceladus, the principal adversary of Athena, goddess of wisdom, was buried under the island of Sicily when she threw it at him. He was believed to be the main cause of volcanic eruptions and earthquakes in Sicily.

[2] Ceres (Greek name, Demeter) is an agricultural goddess associated with the harvest. Her daughter Proserpine (Greek, Persephone), was carried off by Pluto, god of the underworld (Hades). The rape of Proserpine is related in Ovid's *Metamorphoses*, Book 5. It was decided that Proserpine could return to earth if she had eaten nothing in Hades. She had eaten six pomegranate seeds, and so it was decreed that she could spend six months on earth with her mother but had to return to Hades for six months. This myth was used to explain the change of seasons.

[3] The battle of Agrigentum in Sicily in 262 BC was the site of the first battle between Carthage and the Roman Empire and the site of the first pitched battle of the First Punic Wars. The tyrant Phalaris, who was associated with Agrigentum, had a brazen bull fashioned by the artist Perillus in which to torture and roast his enemies and may even have experimented with Perillus (Diodorus Siculus, *Bibliotheca Historica*, 9.19.1).

lest by a deficiency of those qualities which enobled them, I leave a blemish on their memories.

I was yet but an infant, when I beheld my Country cruelly embroil'd in a Civill, and most unnaturall War; and terribly wasted, and destroy'd with Fire and sword, not of strangers, but even of those very People she had bred. I was then too young to enquire the occation of this War; but have since fully enform'd my selfe concerning it: and so much dependance has my owne perticuler story on this Warre, that I cannot give a perfect account of my misfortunes without relating it; since my unhappiness derives its originall from that of my country. Corsica, another Island not far distant from Sicilie was some years since govern'd as a distinct Kingdome of it selfe: but upon the death of *Queen Ericina*[4] [fol. 62ʳ] (who reign'd in Sicilie, and extended her Dominion likewise over Sardinia) the King of Corsica took possession of her kingdome, She dying a virgin, and he being the neerest alli'd to her, by that meanes united those two Kingdomes into one, but Sicilie being much the greater, and more potent, *King Ismenas* soon left Corsica (establishing a Councell there for the managment of affaires) and came into Sicilia to take possession of his new Dominions, where he reign'd many a yeare in peace and great tranquility, both belov'd by his subjects, and fear'd by his neighbour Princes.[5]

After him his son *Clearchus* succeeded (in whose reign I was born).[6] This Illustrious Prince was for Wisdome, Piety and all the vertues that ere concenter'd in any Mortall no less to be admir'd, then lamented for those misfortunes which he underwent. No sooner was he seated on his Fathers Throne but he perceiv'd Sicilie had many foreign enemies that look'd with envious eyes on the tranquill prosperity it enjoy'd, who onely waited for an opportunity to work its ruine; by raising seditions within its owne Bowells. This *Clearchus* prudently forseeing, no less prudently endeavour'd to prevent; seting out his Manifests for the calling of a Senat, by whose advice and councell he might preserve his People in that happie, and serene state wherein he found them at his coming to the Crowne.[7] But as a City without Walls how strong soever the Inhabitants of it are, can make but little resistance if once besieg'd; so likewise if an Iland be not well stor'd with ships, all the opposition it can make against foreign Invaders will be to small purpose, but it lies open on all sides to any that desire to make a conquest of it. This the

---

[4] Elizabeth Tudor (*Ericina*) ruled over England (Sicily) and Ireland (Sardinia) from 17 November 1558 until her death on 25 March 1603.

[5] Upon the death of Elizabeth, James VI of Scotland (*Ismenas*, King of Corsica) succeeded to the English throne on 25 March 1603 and ruled until his death on 27 March 1625.

[6] Charles I (*Clearchus*) succeeded James I on 27 March 1625 and reigned until his execution on 25 January 1649.

[7] Charles I called parliaments in 1625 and subsequently in 1626 and 1628, and, in 1629, after dismissing Parliament, he embarked on eleven years of personal rule.

King considering; and knowing the saftie of his People (no less then his owne) depended on his being potent on the seas, which might render him formidable to his enemies: not that he design'd to molest others, but onely to defend himself. But finding it would too much exhaust his revenue to be at so vast an expence himself alone, as it must of necessity be, first to build, and then to maintaine such a Fleet as might be sufficent to protect his kingdome; he thought it no way unreasonable to require from his subjects some assistance towards it, since they, as well as he would reape the benefit of it.

But having no power without the consent of the Senat to levie Taxes, like a good, and a just Prince he addrest himselfe to them who represented the whole Body of the Nation; declaring to them the necessity of what he demanded, and what a perticuler interest each man had in it:[8] but some amongst them who sought for nothing more then to intraduce innovations both in Religion, and State affaires took this for their rise, strongly opposing him in what he required, with so much insolent impudency as never yet was heard from subjects to their Soveraign; secretly stiring up the People against him (especially the inhabitants of Palermo His Royall City where [fol. 62ᵛ] he resided) telling them he was a Tyrant, and intended to rule by tyranie, and to impose on his subjects such heavie burdens as they would ne're be able to sustaine: but lest their design should be discover'd by that apparant Callumny wherewith they vildly slaunder'd the just-est, and the best of Kings that ever Sicilie was blest with, they added he was not of himself so bad, but that he was too much carried away by the ill advice of some about him, whose Councells he adhear'd too the prejudice of his People.

In fine so did they behave themselves by moveing sedition, not onely in Sicilia, but Corsica too as the ill effects thereof soon after appear'd: for the Corsicans were a People of themselves but too prone to rebellion, and had of a long time been displeas'd with that Government which had been by *Ismenas* establish'd amongst them at his coming to the Sicilian Crowne, insomuch as little incitements were sufficent to induce them to rebell against their King: to which end they first ceaz'd on his revenues, together with all his Castles, and places of defence, and then enter'd Sicilie in a hostile manner; which having intelligence of he set forth to meet them, waited on by an Armie so consider-able to oppose their progress, as he had no cause to doubt their success. But being unwilling (not withstanding so high a provacation) to shed the blood of his subjects unless necessity constrain'd him to it: he first determin'd to treat with them, by some whom he deputed; to the intent he might understand their grievances; which when he knew, he graciously condescended to their demands,

---

[8] Under English law, Parliament levies taxes to generate a subsidy supporting the monarch and his government. Charles I used forced loans and Ship money (a medieval tax traditionally levied only on coastal communities, to generate funds). While unpopular, the imposition of Ship's money was declared legal by the King's Bench in 1637 and not declared illegal until 1641 by the Long Parliament.

though to his prejudice in many things, rather then he would not make up that breach, thorough which he foresaw many ill accidents might happen to disturbe the peace, and tranquility of his other Kingdomes; for so desirous was the good *Clearchus* of his peoples wellfaire that he still prefer'd the publick before his owne perticuler good.[9]

By the mediation of these Deputies, and the Kings consession an agreement was concluded; upon which he disperced his Forces, and return'd to Palermo: but having been assur'd by some of the most considerable in the Corsican Armie that they had been provok'd to this invasion by some of the Sicilian Sennators whose names they perticulerly gave him, and so great proofes of their disloyalty, and disaffection to him as he had not the least reason to doubt the truth of what had been discover'd to him; whereupon at his returne he demands them of the other Senators, to the end they might be punish'd if found guilty after a Legall Tryall, or acquited if found innocent.[10] But instead of being deliver'd, they were by them protected; wherupon *Clearchus* commanded they should no more presume to appeare in Senat, but was in that also disobey'd: for notwithstanding his Command to the contrary they came as before, being for their security guarded by multitudes of the vulgar sort, who knew not the just ground the King had to be incens'd against them; though he protested he had no prejudice to them further then he had discover'd those unlawfull correspondencies they had held, and engagements they had made to embroile his Kingdoms in a civill war.

But this his proceeding (notwithstanding [fol. 63ʳ] the justice, and reasonableness of it) was so ill resented, that his Palace was presently after throng'd with people who came thither in a tumultuous manner, some crying out for Justice ere they had any wrong design'd them; others crying the Senators priviledges were infring'd, others, that they were violated, and that they would maintain them: some exclaming against the King, others against his Councell, insomuch as the whole Cytie was in a confus'd uprore; so that finding the Senat too powerfull, and Palermo by reason of the Tumults unsafe for him to reside in, he abandon'd it; not knowing whether their discontent, and fury might not fly so high as to come to the extreamity of violence against him; especially having no Guards for his defence (as many other Monarchs have) so much did both his royall Father and himselfe relye on the love and fidelity of their subjects; but finding how much he had been deceiv'd by them in whom he had repos'd the greatest trust, he thought it unfit to expose the majesty of his person and Dignity, the safty of

---

[9] Charles convened two parliaments in 1640 (the Short Parliament and the Long Parliament) to levy funds for the Bishops Wars against Scotland. Conflicts in the Parliament led to the outbreak of the first English Civil War.

[10] In January 1642, Charles accused five members of the House of Commons (John Pym, John Hampden, Denzil Holles, William Strode, Sir Arthur Haselrig) and a peer in the House of Lords (Edward Montagu, Lord Manchester) of treason, alleging that they encouraged the Scots to invade England.

his Queen (whom he most passionatly lov'd) and of Prince *Claromenes*[11] his son who was likewise infinitely deare to him; to the insolence of such who are aptest to insult most when they find objects, and opportunities capable of their rudeness. These thoughts made him retire to Messina (a Cytie of great strength in the Province of Mona) where he might (together with those persons who were so deservedly dear to him) be in security till such time as he might make it appeare to his subjects how they had been cheated into rebellion, and that being in a place of safty he might the better find out a way to rectify these disorders.[12]

But it sufficed them not to have drove away their King from them in this manner by their treasonous practices, but they still persisted in them; filling the Peoples eares with stories (especially those of Palermo) which had no other originall then their inventions, and their hearts with suspitions that *Clearchus* intended to rule by the sword, which they adviz'd them to prevent; by affording them their assistance whereby they might be able to raise an Armie, that so they might be in a capacity to defend their liberties, and preserve themselves from being slaves to the will of a Tyrant (as they most ignominiously stil'd their King) this Councell was but too readily embraced; for before such time as *Clearchus* could suspect any such thing, there were severall Forces listed and on foot in divers places in the Kingdome; which having certaine Intelligence of, he went to Milase (another Citie in the same province) where he had a storehouse of Armes, and War Artillery which he had prepar'd for the Warre against the Corsicans: but having as then no occation to use them, he had caus'd them to be laid up there. Of this citty he determin'd to possess himselfe, that he might be in the better condition speedily to suppress this rebellion: but when he came thither, he found the Gates shut, and enterance deni'd him by *Ithagenes* the Governour thereof, who declar'd he would keep it for the Senats service.[13]

From thence he repar'd to another Citty (not far distant) call'd Nicosia, where he found a much civiller reception; and there it was that he first displai'd his Royall Banner, sommoning all [fol. 63ᵛ] his loyall subjects to repaire to it; this sommons was readily obey'd by the greatest part of the Nobility, and many of the vulgar sort: and no sooner was it known where he was, but all those Senatours who had formerly adhear'd to him (in whose generous soules was fix'd a deep sense of their allegiance to their soveraign) when they saw the differences in the Kingdome too great for them to reconcile left their fellowes and hasted to their Kings assistance.[14] For no sooner had he left Palermo, but he found all things were carried on to that height against him, that he had small hopes of

---

[11] Charles I (*Clearchus*) was succeeded by his son Charles II (*Claromenes*).

[12] By March 1642, Charles had left London (Palermo) for York (Messina).

[13] From York, Charles went to Hull (Milase); Sir John Hotham (*Ithagenes*) under orders from Parliament refused him entry.

[14] On 22 August 1642, the royal standard was raised at Nottingham (Nicosia) in what is commonly identified as the beginning of the English Civil War.

restoring Peace to his Dominions but through the Gates of Warre; which he was most unwilling to have recourse too (notwithstanding those high provocations he had receiv'd) till he had made tryall of all other expedients; which prov'd all invallid and to no purpose. For so eagerly were the opposing Party bent to the carrying on their wicked designes, that they would never suffer any Proposition touching Peace (though never so reasonable) to be hearkened too; but still return'd him answere, that they were resolv'd to defend the liberty of the People against such as adviz'd him to enslave them: but if he would be pleas'd to returne to his Senat, and abandon those ill Ministers of State, by whose pernicious Councells he had suffer'd himselfe hitherto to be misguided, and for the security of the Kingdomes wellfare put into their hands the Cittadell of Palermo, with all the others Forts, and Castles in the Land together with the command of all the ships in any of the Ports, they would most readily lay downe those Armes they had taken up for their owne defence, and the Peoples good, and returne to their former obedience.[15]

A demande so full of arrogant impudence was never heard from subjects to their Prince (said the Queen) [Ermilia] and sure, if with their duty, and allegiance they had not laid aside their reason they would have blush'd to have made it. Questionless (continu`d she speaking to *Arthenia*) your King could not but be strangly amazed, and incenst in the highest degree against those that durst presume to propound such things to him.

Tis very certaine Madam, (she repli'd), he was so much displeas'd, that he resolv'd without delay to march directly to Palermo to reduce those to their duty by force, whom a milder course had but rendred more insolent. But in his way thither he was encountred by an Armie more potent then his owne, commanded by *Diocles* who was by the Senat made Generall of it:[16] but although the Rebells were far more numerous then the Royall Party, yet trusting on Heavens assistance and the Justice of his cause, the King gave battell to his Foes with all the courage, and conduct that was requisit in a valiant and prudent Prince: it was thought by severall who were Actors in it, that this Fight, for the time it continu'd was the most terrible that ever was beheld; for certain it is, none fight with greater animosity then those ^in^ whom blood and nature had made the neerest union before such distractions excited divisions in their minds; which renders a civill war of all others most horrible, and destructive to a Kingdome: For here might have have been beheld Fathers tearing out the Bowells of their

---

[15] On 1 June 1642, both Houses of Parliament issued Nineteen Propositions, requiring that all privy councilors be approved by Parliament and declaring that Parliament was to control the forts, ports, militia, and even the education of the royal children. In response Charles issued Commissions of Array directing Lord Lieutenants of each shire to levy troops for the Royalist cause.

[16] The Parliament appointed Robert Devereux, 3rd Earl of Essex (*Diocles*), General of the Parliamentary army in July 1642.

Children, and the swords of sons crimson'd with the blood of those from whom they deriv'd their beings. Brothers sanguin'd with each others blood, and sundry other most dismal [fol. 64^r] objects. But bloody as this battell was it had been much more so if the nights approach had not put an end to it, with the loss of nigh 50000 lives.[17]

Both Parties pretended to the Victory, though *Clearchus* alone had right of it; for though he lost that day the brave *Lysander*, the Generall of his Armie, yet he kept the Field, and clear'd himself a passage to Mazara, into which he tryumphantly enter'd, bearing with him (as the Trophies of his Victory) all those Ensignes he had taken from the Rebells:[18] he having possess'd himselfe of this place, resolv'd to march on to Palermo, but as the Fates would have it, *Diocles* with the Remains of his shatter'd Armie had made such speed, as he got thither ere the King could well determine what course was most expedient for him to take: but notwithstanding, he pursues his first resolves, and advances towards Palermo; and in his way thither forces a little Towne that the Enemy had fortifi'd to obstruct his passage, takeing 500 Prisoners there; which having done, he continues his march: but having intelligence that *Diocles* had drawn together a more considerable Force then that he had defeated; to which were joyn'd many thousands of the Inhabitants of Palermo (who are most of them expert souldiers, being train'd up in a Military Disipline from their youth) he thought it better to return to Mazara whilst he might safely do so, (there to wait the coming of some new supplies which he daily expected) then hazard a second battell, which if lost, he knew too well, it would be impossible for him to raise another. But t'was not long ere those recrutes arriv'd, with which he again leaves Mazara, after he had made *Rizander* (a Prince neer alli'd to him) Generall of all his Forces.[19] And now it was that Fortune seem'd to smile on his affaires; for so prosperously went they on as in a short space he reduced both the Provinces of Mazara (from whence the chiefe City in it took its name) and that of Mona to their former obedience, some few inconsiderable Places excepted.

But before I proceed, (pursu'd *Arthenia*), I cannot pass by one effect of Heavens vengeance which discharg'd itselfe on the guilty head of the disloyall *Ithagenes* without acquainting your Majesty with it. If you remember Madam I told you, this man was the first that oppos'd his Soveraign with a sword in his hand,

---

[17] The first major battle of the English civil war, the Battle of Edgehill, was fought on 23 October 1642 at Edgehill, Warwickshire. Since both armies numbered about 14,000, the claim that 50,000 lives were lost is exaggerated.

[18] Charles's General Robert Bertie, 1st Earl of Lindsay (*Lysander*) died in this battle. Charles planned to march on London (Palermo) but Essex blocked his advance and he retired to Oxford (Mazara).

[19] Prince Rupert of the Rhine (*Rizander*), nephew to Charles by his sister Elizabeth of Bohemia, was made the General of Royalist forces and later created Duke of Cumberland.

declaring himself for the Senat; and well they rewarded that service he did them: for whether it were that they onely suspected his fidelity to them (as with reason they might, since he had been perfideous to his Prince), or that he was really touch'd with remorse for his Crime (which it was reported he endeavour'd to expiate by resuming his abandoned loyalty) I know not, but so it was, that both himself and son were ceaz'd on by the command of those very Senatours he had but a little before declar'd for; and in a short space paid the forfeiture of both their lives; for so had Heaven decreed it, that as he had been an accomplice in his Crime, he should be likewise a sharer [fol. 64ᵛ] in his punishment.[20] But so far was this gracious Prince from rejoyceing at the Destiny of this man, that he was heard to say (when newes was brought him of it) he had more compassion for his death, then satisfaction by it; adding, he was sorry *Ithagenes* was so unfortunate to fall into the hands of their Justice, rather than into those of his Clemency, since he could as willingly have forgiven him, as he could have ask'd pardon of him.

But *Arthenia* having beg'd pardon for this digression proceeded, after the Queen had let her know, she would have needed it much more had she omitted so remarkable a passage. The Kings affaires went on, continued she, so happily, that all those of greatest eminence, and that had been the most violent against him in the Senat, prepar'd to quit Sicilie; and had certainly done so, had he but pursu'd his first design, in marching directly to Palermo: for then he had not allow'd them time to fortifie that Citty against him, as they soon after did: for so terrifi'd were they with the newes of his approach, that they instantly fell to erecting Fortresses, and raising Bullwarks on all sides for the defence of the Citie, in such a manner as rendred it almost impossible to be taken though never so strongly besieg'd. To which good work (as they erroniously stil'd it) divers of their Woemen were so zealously devoted, as they themselves wrought in casting up the Trenches with an incredible diligence;[21] therein imitateing those Spartan Wemen who assisted their Husbands in fortifying their Citty against the common Enemy: in which, if they had likewise follow'd their example, they might have been as justly famous, as they rendred themselves the contrary, by employing their care and industry against their King: but he unhappily declined his first intentions thorough a desire he had to take Drepanum a Citty of great importance, having the command of a very fair Port, but he so long laid siege to it without effecting any thing, that *Diocles* rais'd the siege, bringing them so powerfull a reliefe as put them into a capacity of standing out a long time.[22] But yet the Rebells had not much cause to glory in the advantage they thereby

---

[20] Sir John Hotham (*Ithagenes*) and his son, who together had opposed Charles's entry into Hull, were executed by Parliament for conspiracy.

[21] Approving of the militant stance of these women, but not their political allegiance, Bridget Manningham significantly calls attention to the female brigades.

[22] Essex relieved the Royalist siege of Gloucester.

gain'd; for *Diocles* was constrain'd ere he could returne to Palermo to encounter the royall Armie, which fell out much to his loss; for after a sharp dispute he was forced to march off in great disorder, being so hotly pursu'd, that his Cavallree were necessitated to make they [their] way over a great part of their Infantry to save their lives.[23] The King being now return'd to Mazara with such success, and the season of the year being unfit for action, he resolves there to repose himself till the spring should sommon him abroad again to pursue the conquest of his rebellious subjects.

In the mean time, the Senat perceiving their affaires to grow very ill, and much to their disadvantage, they thought it requisit to sue to the Corsicans for assistance, which at length they obtain'd, and through much importunity, and larg promises enduced them once more to enter Sicilia, which they accordingly soon after did, with an Armie of no less then 20000 [fol. 65ʳ] men; and having gain'd divers places of importance in their march, they besieg'd Messina, being aided by a considerable part of the Rebells Armie under the command of *Faragenes*.[24] Tydings being brought of this to Mazara, Prince *Rizander* was sent away with as many of *Clearchus*'s forces as could conveniently be spar'd, and power given him to raise more in all places as he pass'd along; so that, by that time he arriv'd at Messina he had increas'd his Troopes to the number of 12000, ^with^ which he rais'd the siege, beat the enemy from their walls, and so well suppli'd all their necessities, as he left them in so good a condition as to be able to hold out the siege a long time in case the enemy should again renew it: having done this, t'was thought expedient by some of his Officers who much better understood the carrying on of a War then himself (being as he was then but very young) that it would be far better to keep marching a while, whereby he might increase his strength, then to go instantly to encounter the enemy who were far the stronger.

But this Fiery young Prince (whose excess of courage was his greatest fault) chose rather to follow the dictates of his owne inclination then their both sage, and safe advice. Resolving for the encounter, he drew out his men into Battailia; and having perform'd all the duties of a Generall, he gave the onset, charging so fiercely on the right wing of the enemy, consisting of *Faragenes*'s Cavalrie in the van, and the Corsicans in the Reere, that they fell back in such disorder on their owne Infantry that they broke their ranks, treading many of them under their horses Feet: but *Rizanders* Cavalrie pursuing the execution too farre, and none advanceing to make good their place, *Faragenes* taking hold of that opportunity, once more turn'd back upon them so vigorously, and with such success, as not-

[23] Soon after relieving Gloucester, Essex's army encountered Rupert's cavalry at the important first Battle of Newbury on 20 September 1643.

[24] The House of Commons appointed Ferdinando Fairfax, 2nd Lord Fairfax of Cameron (*Faragenes*), General of the Parliamentary forces on 21 January 1645 and Oliver Cromwell (*Ormisdas*) as Lieutenant-General. Bridget Manningham seems to conflate the father with his son, Sir Thomas Fairfax, later 3rd Lord Fairfax of Cameron.

withstanding the Prince perform'd so many gallant actions in his owne person as will hardly gain beliefe with any, but those who were spectators of, or felt the effects of them, yet he lost the Victory, with most of his chiefe Commanders, who were either kill'd or taken Prisoners: so that being utterly unable to repare his loss, he was constrain'd to march off with much dishonour, and retire to Milase till such time as he receiv'd new orders from the King.

Where I will leave him a while, (continu'd Arthenia), to repent that fault his too rash and precipitate humour had made him indiscreetly runne into; and whereby he contracted such a blot on his Fame, as the lustre of those heroick deeds he afterwards perform'd could hardly efface) and return to the King; who never ceasing to consider the sad condition of his Kingdome even destroyed by those miseries that attend on Warre, and desiring nothing more then a happy composing of those divisions which had already prov'd so fatall, and if not prevented must inevitably be more so, most graciously condescended to sue too, and court those to peace who had been the onely fomentors of those unhappy differences, and still were the maintainers of them; conjuring them by that Duty and allegiance they ought [owed] him as their [fol.65ᵛ] King, to have compassion on the deplorable estate of their unhappie Country; and that they would joyne their sincere endeavours with his to put a speedy period to those miseries Sicilie groan'd under the pressures of: promising, conditionally they laid downe Armes, immediatly to disband his owne Forces, and freely to pardon all past offences, of what nature, or quality soever they had been. It was not onely one, or two of these gracious Messages that these ungratfull and disobedient Senators receiv'd from him, but many; to which, sometimes they would vouchsafe no answere, or else such as serv'd rather to enlarg, then close the breach; falsly imagining all these tenders of grace and favour proceeded rather from *Clearchus's* incapacity to continue the Warre then from that regard he had to his Peoples wellfare.

Soon after *Rizanders* defeat, the Kings affaires grew every day more desperate then other in the Province of Mona; Messina yeelding upon composition, and after that all the other Cities in that province. In the meane time it was generally believ'd that *Diocles* had some designes upon Mazara, as being the place of the Kings residence; upon which it was thought fit, the Queen (being then with Child) should remove to Erix a place of more saftie, from whence she might (if occation were) be transported into Naples; where in the Court of the King her Brother she might remaine till such time as she might return to Sicilia with safty. This when the King had once resolv'd, he comunicates it to his Councell, with those reasons which induced him to desire the Queens absence; which were so pressing, as they had nothing to reply against his determination: whereupon, after a little silence, with a Countenance wherein all the Tokens of a most sensible Concerne was to be seen.

I think (said he) there is none of you but will acknowledge I have just cause to lament the departure of my Dearest Consort; yet does not her absence grieve me somuch, as that necessity that forces her from me: it does afflict me I confess

more then I am able to express, to think that she should by my owne subjects be
constrain'd to abandon me.

Unfortunate *Clearchus* (continu'd he to himself after a little pause) must that
Relation thou hast to so Divine, and Excellent a Princess be the cause of her danger and affliction whose merits are such as doubtless would have been sufficient
to protect her even amongst the wildest Barbarians who have not wickedness
enough to atte^m^pt to injure Vertue in that degree as some men do here, who
make larg pretences both to civility and piety too; though I think there are few
amongst them so maliciously wicked as to hate her for her self whom they can
accuse of no crime, but that she is my Queen:

Justice sure then: no less then affection (pursu'd he directing his speech to
those about him) obliges me not onely to study, but likewise to provide for her
security since she is onely in danger for my sake: Yes, I can be content to suffer
shipwrack so she may be but in safe Harbour; for this satisfaction I shall enjoy
by her security, whatever happens, I can perish but half if she be preserv'd; for I
am sure to live still in her memory, and may yet [fol. 66ʳ] survive the malice of
my Foes though it should be so extreame as nothing but my blood could saciate.

These sad words were deliver'd with so much passion, as they brought teares
into the eyes of all that heard them; and excited such resentments in their minds
as they were unable to express, a resembling griefe sealing up the passage of their
speech leaving them not the power of any other reply then that of sighs. The
Queens departure being thus decreed, the King resolv'd to accompany her as far
as Felinus, which Towne stood about a days journey from Mazara; and there it
was that they took so sad a farewell, as if their hearts had by some secret instinct
told them it must be the last adue they must ever take of each other; after which he
return'd to Mazara, leaving the Queen a suffcent convoy to conduct her to Erix,
where she was receiv'd with as much state as that City was capable of. About two
moneths after her arrivall there, she brought into the World a Daughter, whom
she caus'd to be call'd *Herenia* after her owne name.[25] This wellcome tydings
being carried to the King, brought him as much Joy as the Queens absence, and
the condition of his affaires would permit him to resent [feel]. Assoon as she was
well recover'd again, she committed the young Princess to a Lady of great trust
about her (nam'd *Macaria*) and having receiv'd some instructions from the King,
she took Ship and return'd to Naples with a resolution there to continue till such
time as she might with safty come back to Sicilie.[26]

---

[25] The queen left Oxford in April 1644, and they accompanied her as far as Abingdon (Felinus). Henrietta (*Herenia*) went to Exeter (Erix) where the Princess Henrietta
Anne was born on June 16. The daughter of Henrietta Marie and Charles I was named
after her mother but called Minette at the French court.

[26] Anne (Villiers) Douglas, later Countess of Morton, and known at that time as
Lady Dalkieth, (*Macaria*) was godmother and later governess to the princess. The queen
bequeathed the care of her infant to this Royalist heroine when she departed for France.

I should be but to tedious, and too much presume upon your Majesties patience, (said *Arthenia*), should I recount all the perticuler events of this Warre, which sometimes prov'd favourable to the one side, sometimes to the other; and for a long time so dubious that none could determine whom Fortune had a design to favour; but after many various traverses she seem'd to incline to *Clearchus*, by conferring on him a most Signall Victory, which was compleated by the death of *Diocles*, Generall of the Senats Armie.[27] After which success the King dispatch't a Message to the Senat, in which he laid open to them the sad estate the Kingdome was reduced too, reminding them of those many Messages they had before receiv'd from him upon the same score, desiring them ere Sicilia was quite destroy'd to bethinke themselves of some expedient whereby the effusion of blood might yet be stanch'd; assuring them he took so little satisfaction in his victories that he could not look on them but with sorrow, since t'was ore his owne subjects he obtain'd them. Hereupon they drew up some Propositions which they sent him by some appointed to treat with him; but such strang ones were they, that had he consented to them, he must absolutely have declin'd that power wherewith Heaven had invested him, leaving himself nothing but the bare title of a King

I confess I am not so well acquainted with those Proposalls, (continued *Arthenia*), as to give your Majesty the very words they were express'd in, but this, as I have heard was the sum of them: That the King should disband his Forces, returne to the Senat, and remit the government of the Kingdome into their hands, and give an implicit consent to whatever they should further propound:

When he had heard these imperious demands. Tell those that sent you (said he) such a blind obedience was never yet requir'd of any man, much less of a King, by his owne subjects. They would have me trust to their moderation, and abandon my owne discretion, to the end I might justifie those representations [fol. 66ᵛ is blank and followed by Fol. 67ʳ] they have made of me to the World, as if I were fitter to be their scholer then their King. But though I am not so confident of my owne abilities as not willingly to admit of the Councells of others; so neither am I so doubtfull of my selfe as brutishly to submit to any mans Dictates: for that were to betray the soveraignity of Reason in my Soule, and the majesty of my Crowne and Dignity, which gives me power to deny what my Reason tells me I ought not to grant: they may remember, they set in Senat as my subjects, not superiors; call'd thither to be my Councellours, not Dictators. No (pursu'd he) you may tell them further that as I will not, to gratifie my owne humour, deny any thing that my reason allows me to grant, so, on the other side, I will never yeeld to more then Reason, Justice, and Honour obliges me too in refference to

---

[27] This "most Signall Victory" refers to the Royalist defeat of Essex's troops at the Battle of Lostwithiel on 21 August-2 September 1644. Essex did not die until September 1646.

my Peoples good: I'le study to satisfy the Senat in what I may, but I will never for feare, or flattery gratifie any Faction how potent soever.

This Treaty proving unsuccessfull,[28] as it was not likely but it would, since the Rebells made such Overtures as the King could neither with saftie nor honour consent unto; nor without an irreparable prejudice, both to himself and his Posterity; nor would they agree to anything propounded by him; So that both Parties resolv'd to proceed in the Warre, since there could be no hopes of any accomodation but by being the one a Conquerour, and the other Conquered. Upon the death of *Diocles*, *Faragenes* had his power confer'd on him; but being a person fitter to charge an enemie, then command an Armie, having more of courage then conduct; the Senat joyn'd in Commission with him *Ormisdas*, a man so dextriously subtill in carrying on of a designe, as none could equall him.[29] About the same time did the King confirme the honour of Generallissimo to the Prince *Rizander*, by renewing his Commission. By these two it was then that the Fate of Sicilie came to be desided.

Faragenes hearing that the King had left Mazara (onely leaving in it a strong Garrison for its defence) again betook him to the Field, directing his march towards him, intending to fight him; sommoning together all the strength that he could possibly make, to the intent, this one Battell more might end the controversie: the same design had *Clearchus*, which induced him not to decline the Fight. On a spacious Plaine not far distant from Catana it was that these two Armies met; and having raing'd their men in order, they began the fatall dispute with so much vigour, and resolution, as it might easily be seen, no less then a Kingdome was the Prize for which they fought; *Clearchus* to preserve his undoubted right, his enemies to deprive him of it. [30] But as none ever fought upon a juster score, so none ever fought with greater magnanimity and courage then this poor unhappy Prince; and had his Fortune been but equall to his Valour, treason, and rebellion had (questionless) then receiv'd their due reward.

Tis very true, Fortune in the begining of the Battell seem'd to be propitious to the King, for the greatest part of the day he had the better; for *Rizander* having broke their Ranks, shatter'd their Troops, and routed the left wing of their

---

[28] The Treaty of Uxbridge was an attempt to negotiate peace during the first Civil War. Parliament issued twenty-seven articles generally insisting on control of the military and on the imposition of Presbyterianism throughout England. Charles I's requests were more reasonable, but negotiations failed.

[29] See note 24 above. After Essex's death, Parliament appointed Sir Thomas Fairfax, 3rd Lord Fairfax of Cameron (*Faragenes*) as General and Cromwell (*Ormisdas*) as Lieutenant General. Charles I renewed Prince Rupert's commission, making him General of the Royalist forces.

[30] The battle of Naseby (Catana) was fought on 14 June 1645 and brought to a conclusion the first English Civil War. Arthenia's description is accurate except that Henry Ireton commanded the fleeing troops, not Cromwell (*Ormisdas*).

Armie (which was commanded by *Ormisdas*) might possibly have perfected the victory had he not too eagerly pursu'd the vanquish'd Partie, by which he gave *Faragenes* the opportunity to gain as great advantages on that part he encounter'd, as *Rizander* had goten on the other: which being perceiv'd by *Ormisdas* [fol. 67ᵛ] he suddenly faced about, rallying again his dispierced Troopes, exhorting them by his words, and encouraging them by his example to turn again on their pursuers; and finding his men resolv'd not to desert him, he turn'd back, charging again with so much fury, and was so well seconded by *Faragenes*, as the fortune of the day was in an instant chang'd, the Rebells intierly carrying away the Victory, although the illustrious *Clearchus* performed such prodigies of valour that day in his owne person, as to recite them I must detract from the glory of them.

But alass (pursu'd *Arthenia*) there is no force sufficent against Fate, nor was he able with all his strength and courage to ward off this blow of Fortune, which fell with such a violence on him, as left him no way to escape but by flight; which he rather chose then to become the Trophie of his enemies tryumph, or give theire unequal'd malice the satisfaction of mispending his Illustrious blood invain, to saciate their cruelties which thirsted for nothing more. The Prince *Claromenes* was not in this Battell, having been sent by the King his Father into the Æolian Islands (which belong to Sicilie, though separated from it by some part of the sea) to the intent he there might raise such Force as might be not onely sufficent for their owne defence, but likewise give some addition to his Majesties Armie: [31] but before such time as he could render himselfe master of any considerable strength, report brought him the tydings of the unhappy success of the Battell of Catana; which prov'd a Remora [hindrance] to his designes, inducing him to returne to Sicilie with those Troops he had, that he might hasten to the Kings assistance: but no sooner was he come back but he was met with a letter from the King his Father; wherein he let him understand the almost desperate condition his affaires were in, commanding him to provide for his owne security with all possible speed, since he fear'd ere long Sicilie would be unable to protect him.

Having receiv'd this Command, and instantly after certaine intelligence that *Faragenes* was advancing towards him with his victorious Troops, he resolv'd upon an unwilling obedience, since Nature would not suffer him without an extreame regreet to abandon his Royall Father in his distress: but the consideration of how little availe his presence, or personall assistance would be to him, made him conclude with reason, that it would adde to his misery to have him a sharer in it, though t'was impossible for him not to be so by a reall sympathy, in what place soere he was. But it was not so much his owne preservation, as the

---

[31] In March 1645, King Charles sent Prince Charles (*Claromenes*) to the west of England where he was the nominal leader of the Royalist forces. The Aeolian Islands may refer to the Scilly Isles to which Prince Charles sailed in March 1646 on his way to France.

hopes he conceiv'd of obtaining some powerfull supplies from the Neopolitan King that invited him to retire thither, which he did, after he had recommended those Forces under his command to the care and conduct of the brave *Hortensius*, a man every way meriting that trust impos'd on him;[32] after which he pass'd into Naples to the Queen his Mother, whom he found in that Citty from whence the Kingdome derives its name; where he was receiv'd with such an entertainment as might be expected by so illustrious a Prince.

This last success of the Rebells so encourag'd them in their crime, that they ceas'd not dayly to agravate it by the highest outrages, and Acts of violence imaginable, against all such as had been any way assistant to *Clearchus*, or any way adhear'd to him: nay, if they did but suspect any person of Loyalty, it was enough to expose him to all the evill that a powerful enemy was capable of inflicting. It was [fol. 68r] neither the Dignity, nor the sanctity of any one that could shield him from the violence of those impious men; for if it could, they durst not have presum'd to lay violent hands on the chiefest of the ArchFlamins in that manner as they did; murthering him after a long imprisonment: not secretly, but publickly, in the open view of all that would be spectators of so barbarous an Act. The crime wherewith they charg'd him was no other, then Love, and Fidelity to his Prince which he express't by importuning Heaven by Prayers, and Sacrifices for a blessing on him, and a happie success in all his enterprizes; and for refusing to lay aside the title of ArchFlamine, together with that grandure which had ever attended his high Function, and descend to the qualitie of the inferior Flamines.[33] All the other Flamins were likewise suspended from their Offices, and others, of their owne consecration set up in their steads, who would admit of no superiority, but would all be equalls; intraducing a new kind of worship also, which till then Sicilie had been unacquainted with; nor was it approv'd by any, but the Lovers of Novelties, and those that establish'd it. The Tenets that they taught, were likewise of as late an Edition: for some of them affirm'd, that the Divinity being not confin'd to any place, might as well be serv'd, and ador'd with as acceptable a Devotion in any other place as in a Temple. This soon bred such a disesteeme of holy Places, as they were not onely scarce frequented, but even the very Altars were prophan'd, the Temples violated and defaced; many acounting themselves in nothing more religious then in villifying sacred things: even those very Temples which were formerly Sanctuaries for Offenders, could not now be secure themselves from the violence of prophane persons.

Behold then Madam (continu'd *Arthenia*) the piety which these men pretended too, and the liberty of the subject (they affirm'd) they sought to maintain

---

[32] In January 1646, Prince Charles gave command of his remaining forces to Ralph Hopton, 1st Baron Hopton (*Hortensius*).

[33] Flamin, a term for priest, is used for bishop and Arch Flamin for archbishop. William Laud (7 October 1573–10 January 1645), was created Archbishop of Canterbury in 1633 and beheaded on Tower Hill on 10 January 1645.

though the event prov'd they intended nothing less; since all, but those that had cast off all obedience to their Soveraign were by them reduced to so perfect a condition of slavery, as none could be more absolute Vassalls: for with such an unlimmited Tyranie did they insult ore their fellow subjects, that none could call ought that he possest his owne: for if any one was accus'd but of wishing well to his King, or speak of him with reverence, or respect, it was a Crime sufficent to cause him to be despoil'd of whatsoever he enjoy'd; and if he enquir'd what his Offence might be, t'was answer'd, he was ill affected to the Senat. Multitudes were imprison'd, and compell'd to purchase their liberties at such excessive ransomes, as prov'd the ruines of their families. Many others who might have boasted larg Possessions (either left them by their provident Predessessors, or gain'd by their owne laborious industry) suddenly torne from them, their houses rifled, and their whole estates confiscate to the Senats use: insomuch, as divers who were wealthy to a superfluity, in the space of one poore day have been reduced to such necessity, as that they have not known where to seeke their next nights Lodging. Soon did these calamities spread themselves thorowout Sicilie, nor was there saftie for any but professed Traitors: rebells, indeed might live secure, but Faithful subjects must in this manner be persecuted.

In these Calamities my Parents bare as larg a share as any whosoever; my Father being one of the first in the Province of Mazara (for there we liv'd) who felt the effects of them; being b^e^reav'd of all that he possess'd whereby we were for a while reduced [fol. 68ᵛ] to extreame necessitys.[34] Tis true I confess he might have freed himselfe from this misfortune, as many others did, could his Conscience have dispenced with the meanes conducing thereunto by renouncing his allegiance to his Prince, binding himselfe by a solemne Ingagement set forth by the Senat, to become not onely an Enemy to the King, but to all royall authority; but so firmely was Loyalty seated in his Soule, that t'was not the Frownes of Fortune that could drive it thence, or once so much as make him unresolv'd what he should do, or suffer; nor was he capable of a thought which was able to contest with that duty he ought [owed] him whom Heaven had made his Liege Lord and Soveraign; accounting it rather a glory then a misfortune to suffer for, and with his King: and since he suffer'd on so just a score, he did not doubt but Heaven would provide for him and his, although depriv'd of all things the cruelty of unjust men could rob him of. In his affliction he quickly had many Companions; for to such a condition was *Clearchus* now reduced, as he was not able to defend himself, much less protect his Friends.

Thus it was Madam (said *Arthenia*) that Fortune first began her persecutions of me (in which she has held so long a course, as I cannot but admire she should be stil'd inconstant) makeing me even an Exile in my very Infancie; for

---

[34] This description may be personal because Bridget's father, Richard Manningham, was sequestered during the Civil War, and the Manningham family was forced to sell Bradbourne House in Kent during the Interregnum.

indeed, so very young I was when these things hapned as I was scarce sensible of what I suffer'd in my Parents misfortunes; nor of those wants, and necessities I had questionless been expos'd too, had not Heavens bounty, and goodness transcended Fortunes malice; for though we were not banish'd Sicilie by our enemies, yet by Necessity we were, that part of it which was become most naturall to us by the long aboad my Father had made there; and sent to seek a habitation amongst strangers, and a subsistance in that place which might best afford it us. To Palermo then we went, as being suppos'd both by my Father and Mother the most convenient for their residence in many respects: there liv'd they severall yeares in as much quiet as the distractions of their Country would admit; and though they wanted that splendor and gallantry they formerly liv'd in, yet in requitall in their meane estate they enjoy'd content, and Minds suted to their Fortunes; without which the most prosperous condition is but miserable: never were they heard to complain of their owne miseries; all that they did, was onely to deplore their Kings.

As for my owne perticuler, Fortune in part repair'd the injury she had done me by conferring on me the Princess *Merinza's* acquaintance, who was Daughter to *Gracianus*, Duke of Felinus: with this young Princess I receiv'd my education, being brought up with her. From the first day of our acquaintance she took such an affection to me, as she never would willingly suffer me to be absent from her; testifying by all the demonstrations her childish yeares were capable of that I was deare to her: and as her yeares increas'd, so did her kindness so that I enjoy'd as much felicity in her sweet society as I could then have desir'd had my wishes been granted. I was about two yeares elder then she, but as I outstrip't her in age, she a thousand times exceeded me in all things else; becoming in her early dayes excellently qualifi'd with all vertuous endowments, being of a nature so apt to the impression of all great and generous qualities, as none could be more ready to infuse them into [fol.69ʳ] her, then she was to learn: nor had Nature been less prodigall of her bounties in rendring her lovely, then Vertue had been in adorning her with the beauties of the mind. Time, and a constant converse discover'd to me clearly her admirable perfections; which when once I was sensible of, I thought I could not do better then propose her as a Pattern to frame my Conversation by; which with such a diligence I strove to imitate, as that if I have any worthy quality in me I must acknowled[g]e I derive it from her example.

The onely happie time that ere I knew, was that I spent in her company; which was so sweetly charming as those delights I found in it, kept me much longer insensable of my owne misfortune, and my Countries most deplorable condition then otherwise I should have been: but at length, with an increase of yeares having gain'd more understanding, I could not but with sadness consider both; which would many times appeare legible in my face by an unusuall penciveness: which being observ'd by *Merinza*, her Friendship mov'd her to inquire the cause which when she knew, she made it her design to expell from my thoughts all sad reflections by the most pleasing diversions she could invent; and with the kindest expressions would she still seek to make me as forgetfull of my unhappiness, as I had been before unsensable of it. I confess the reasons she gave me why I ought to be contented with my condition were so convinceing, and the councell she gave me to beare my mishaps with moderation so authentick, as I had nothing to reply against either; nor was it long ere she reduced my mind to its former tranquility by those discreet advices she always suppli'd me with. I must needs say, I could not much regreet Fortunes unkindness, when I remembred what a felicity I gain'd by it, in obtaining the Friendship of so excellent a person as *Merinza* was, whom t'was probable I had never known had I not left the Province of Mazara: but alass the content I enjoy'd in her agreeable conversation was too great still to continue; yet for almost the space of seven yeares were we happie in each others company: after which time we were separated, I feare forever, for we have never seen each other since, nor never shall I believe now, the cruelty of my Destiny transporting me hither, and hers confining her to a certaine place in Sicilia, where she lives in a manner depriv'd of her freedome, by the injurious treatment of an unkind Husband.

But ere I tell your Majesty how we came to be separated, I must beg leave to returne to *Clearchus*; who having escap'd by flight, gather'd together the poor remainders of his shatter'd Armie, but was never able to encounter the enemy again; for such was his ill Fate, that in a short time after he lost so many Citties, and Townes that his whole strength was in a manner reduced to Mazara, and some few Garissons besides. All the Kings hopes now depended upon a recrute [recruitment of soldiers] which he had sent *Istander* (a man of approv'd Fidelity) to raise: but as he was on his march towards Mazara, he was suddenly surpris'd in his way thither, by a greater number of the Rebells, who totally defeated, and took him Prisoner.[35] This last disaster utter[l]y depriv'd the King of all hopes, of keeping Mazara till such time as he could better his condition, and induced him to leave it, since there could be no security for him to stay longer there. This when he had once determin'd, and that he was resolv'd whether to go, he sent one evening for *Theodates* the Governour of the City,[36] and some of [fol. 69ᵛ] the principall Officers (in whom he knew he might confide) to his Chamber: this Command was no sooner receiv'd then t'was obey'd; for immediatly after they came, and with a reverent submission address'd themselves to him to know his pleasure; which (after all his Attendants had by his command quited the Roome, those onely excepted that he design'd to take with him) he signifi'd to them in few words.

---

[35] Jacob Astley, 1st Baron Astley of Reading (*Istander*), traveling with 3000 men, the remainder of the Royalist Army, to join Charles I at Oxford, was intercepted and defeated on 21 March 1646.

[36] In October 1645, Sir Thomas Glenham (*Theodates*) was appointed Governor of Oxford, Charles's wartime capital.

My Generous Friends (said he, directing his speech to *Theodates* and the rest) I must acknowledge I have receiv'd such unquestionable testimonies of your loyalties, as I cannot but further intrust you with a thing wherein not onely my liberty, but perhaps my life may be concern'd. I know I need not enjoyn any of you to be secret, since in leting you understand of what high concernment my design is, I shew you how necessary tis you should be so.

Know then (continu'd he) that I intend to leave Mazara, since in it I cannot stay with saftie in this condition whereto things are now brought. I confess it troubles me to be constrain'd thus to abandon you, but I trust it will be for no long time; nor would I do it at all, could my stay be any way advantagious to you; I know your Courages are great enough not to need my presence to augment them; nor can it be of such availe as possibly my absence may: for I hope the way I mean to take will quickly put me into a capacity to give every one of you that recompence the fidelity wherewith ye have serv'd me merits. But if it be otherwise decreed, and that my ruine be unavoidable, so as I am bereaved of all things but a Will to requite you; yet even then you shall not faile of a reward, if not here, assuredly hereafter you shall receive it, and that, a much more glorious one then I could give, were I sole Monarch of the World: then after a little silence he went on.

Though Heaven has given me three Kingdoms, yet in them all, I have now scarce any place left me where I may reside with saftie; but all humane affaires are changable: and such may be my fate, as my greatest danger may arise from whence I expect the most security; and my saftie from that which seemes most perillous. I must leave you then who have so faithfully adhear'd to me, and retire to the Corsicans who have hitherto oppos'd me.

Heavens forbid (cry'd they all at once) that ere your Majesty should put your Royall Person into the hands of those who have express'd no less disaffection, and malice to you upon all opportunities then these Rebells here in Sicilie.

Tis very true (repli'd the King) I know there is much of hazard in this Designe; but evills when they are once growne desperate, will not admit of any but extraordinary cures. The way then that I take, being of that nature, may possibly produce so happy an effect, as to dry up these Rivers of blood which have so long o'reflow'd this miserable Kingdome; for what Providence denies to Force, it may perhaps grant to Prudence. Necessity obliging me to study my owne preservation, I know no better way to it, then by adventuring on their Fidelities, who first began my troubles; for as they were soe, so haply Heaven may make them as instrumentall towards the bringing them to a happie period; since what they endeavour'd to gain by Force, shall now be given them in such a way, as shall even make them blush not to be really what they ought, and have oft proffess'd to be: and perhaps this unusuall confidence I repose in them, by giving up my self intirely into their hands without any the least conditions, and craving their protection as I intend; may be so powerfull as to vanquish all those ill designes they [fol. 70ʳ] may have against me; and more powerfully engage their affections then by any other obligation I can imagine to conferre on them: this I know it cannot but do, if they have but the least spark of Generosity, or any gratfull resentments [feelings] in their soules. Many a time have they protested they fought for, not against me, therefore I am now resolv'd to give them an opportunity to evince to the World, that they meane not what they do, but what they say; which I must needs say is so hard to be understood, as it may well be term'd the Riddle of their Fidelities which I must now unfould.

But in the course which I intend, I am no less solicitious for my Friends safty then my owne; for I will rather venture to expose my person to further hazards, then your generous Loyalties to those extreamities you must enevitably suffer should I continue longer here; since I can now expect no more recrutes, unless Heaven by a Miracle send me a reliefe; which I have not vanity enough to expect. You know all Sicilie is in a manner brought under subjection by the Rebells, so that I have no place where I can promise my selfe the least security, but here in Mazara; and how short a time this will be a place of saftie for me I believe none of you are ignorant, since *Faragenes* comes on apace with his victorious Ensignes to besiege us; who being once arriv'd t'will then be impossible for me to get hence; where if I stay, I must necessarily be constrain'd to dig my owne Monument under the ruines of this City which has been so cordially faithfull to me, or yeeld to such conditions as the Conquerours shall impose: which by what they have heretofore propounded (when they were in almost as declining, as they are now in a prosperous state) we may easily guess will be such, as it will be much more glorious to yeeld to Death then them: but if I go away, I do not dispaire to find that succour for my selfe, and reliefe for you which I cannot hope for here. But hap^pen^ what may, this is my finall Resolve, to dy a King, not live a slave to Rebells; and if I do fall, this satisfaction I shall have however, to dye a Martyre for my Peoples liberty, which is more deare to me then either Crown or life.

The King in this manner having acquainted *Theodates* and the rest with his Design, which he shew'd them so many reasons for, and those such convinceing ones, as they found none to diswade him from what he intended: but though they were convinced his departure was not onely convenient, but also necessary, yet could they not but resent [feel] it with griefe, great as that loyall affection they bare him. Having embraced them severally, he bad them farwell, whilst they took their leaves of him with eyes o'reflow'd with teares; uttering from their hearts many fervent Prayers that Heaven would vouchsafe to date a happie change in his condition, and bring his enterprises to good effect. They being gone (for he would not permit any one of them to wait on him so farre as to the Citty Gate, lest it might raise a suspition of his departure) he put on his disguise which one of those servants who were to attend him had provided; and about the midst of the night quited Mazara, but with it he could not abandon his miseries; those (poor unhappie Prince) still pursu'd him till they brought him to his Grave.[37]

---

[37] On 27 April 1646, Charles I, disguised as a servant, left Oxford (Mazara).

Within a short time after he safely arriv'd in Corsica; where he was wellcom'd
with all the seeming Demonstrations of Joy, that could possibly be express'd;
the great Councell promising in the name of all their Fellow subjects that they
would to their utmost defend him, and as many of the Royall Partie as would
repaire to him; and that they would serve him faithfully both with their lives and
Fortunes. But with how little sincerity these [fol. 70ᵛ] promises were made will
evidently appeare by their succeeding actions: for scarce had he conceiv'd some
small hope of bringing things to a happie period; when he was urged by the Corsican Senat to command the *Prince of Orestagne* (who commanded for his Majesty
in Sardinia) and all the Governours of his Garrisons in Sicilie to deliver all those
Citties and Castles which as yet remain'd untaken, to those who by the Senat
should be appointed to receive them.[38] This Demand was made so peremtorily as
plainly shew'd they would have no deniall; for withall, they told him, that unless
he consented to what they had propounded, they neither could, nor would continue him longer under their protection. But that which they more perticulerly
press'd him too was, that the brave *Mardonius* Prince of Nebio should lay downe
his Commission.[39]

Indeed (pursu'd *Arthenia*) they had reason (considering what they intended)
more earnestly to desire the suppression of this Hero then any of the rest; for had
he still continu'd his power, it had been questionless much more difficult, if not
impossible for them to accomplish that base unhear'd of treachery, which has
since rendred them so justly hatefull to all other Nations: for so many valourous
exploits did he performe with an inconsiderable Force, as the Fame he acquir'd
thereby, will eternize his Fame to all succeeding Ages. Certain it is, his actions
were so transcendently gallant, as compell'd even his very enemies to look on
them with admiration: for besides severall victories of less consequence; he
twice beat *Argelus*[40] (the most potent and notorious Rebell of that Kingdome)
out of the Field, pursuing him into his owne Territories; vanquishing afterwards
Bilindus another Archenemie of the Kings in a set Battell, which was fought
between them: after which he made himselfe Master of the strong City Bastia (the Metropolis of that Island) giving liberty to many of his Friends who
had been there confin'd emmediately upon his taking Armes: and had but some.

---

[38] The Scottish (*Corsican*) Senate demanded that Charles I order James Butler
(*Prince of Orestagne*), later 1st Duke of Ormonde, his Lord Lieutenant in Ireland (Sardinia) to disband his army.

[39] Under pressure from the Scots, Charles I also ordered James Graham, 1st Marquess of Montrose (*Mardonius, Prince of Nebio*) and King's Lieutenant-General in Scotland, to resign his commission and disband his troops.

[40] Archibald Campbell, Marquess of Argyll (*Argelus*), a Scottish peer, opposed the
Royalists.

supplies come as he expected, he had undoubtedly perfected the conquest of all the Rebells in that Kingdome. [41]

But instead of that aid he look'd for, he was unexpectedly set upon, and his Armie dispers'd by *Diophanes* who was sent out of Sicilie to put a stop to his good Fortune: but not withstanding, he had got together again his Troopes, and was in a faire way of pursuing his former Designe when he receiv'd a Command from *Clearchus* to relinquish his Commission; [42] for to that exigent was the King reduced, as to deny what they demanded would have been but invain, since he was now absolutely in their power, having no liberty to get thence had he attempted it: for under a pretence of guarding him, they set a Guard upon him; not to defend, but keep him there: so that being constrain'd by an unavoidable necessity he at length condescended to give those Commands they had requir'd. But they found not that obedience to them as they expected; for not onely the *Prince of Orestagne*, but divers of the Governours in Sicilie, knowing full well the King was constrain'd to give such Orders, stood still upon their guard, in hopes that in time their endeavours might prove advantagious to his service. But no sooner did *Mardonius* receive his Command, but he obey'd it: but having done so; he bid farewell to Corsica, and put himself into a voluntary exile; but ere he went thence he was heard to say (to some of his familiar Friends)

I have serv'd my Prince with all Fidelity, and would yet [fol. 71ʳ] continue to do so though I were sure to shed each drop of blood remaining in me for his service; but since I am depriv'd of all meanes to act ought [aught; anything] to his advantage, I cannot stay here and tamely look upon his ruine without being able to prevent it. [43]

If I mistake not (said the Queen to *Arthenia*) you told me that Sardinia as well as Corsica was united to the Crowne of Sicilie; why then did not *Clearchus* chuse rather to retire thither then into Corsica, which (by what you have said) appears to be the place from whence his troubles had their originall.

It is very certaine Madam (she repli'd) it was so: but no one could have thought, so high an Act of trust as his so freely puting himself into their power but would have produced in them a resembling Fidelity; and perhaps he thought it safer to relie on the affections of his native subjects (as he would often terme

---

[41] Montrose (*Mardonius, Prince of Nebio*) defeated the Marquess of Argyll (*Argelus*) twice, forcing him to flee Inveraray in December 1644 and then slaughtering his army in Interlochy on 2 February 1645. William Baillie (*Bilindus*) was in command of the Scottish troops who lost to Montrose in a disastrous battle at Kilsyth on 15 August 1645. Shortly afterwards, Montrose entered Edinburgh (Bastia) and rescued 150 Royalist prisoners.

[42] David Leslie, 1st Lord Newark (*Diophanes*), defeated Montrose (*Mardonius*) at Philiphaugh on 13 September 1645.

[43] After being ordered to disband his army by Charles I, Montrose (*Mardonius*) left Scotland for Norway and later joined the Queen's court in Paris.

them) then on that, of those who knew no more of him than the power he extended over them. And besides, there was but little hopes of any security for him in Sardinia; that Kingdome having been anexed to Sicilia by conquest, but never intirely subject to that Crown till *Ericina's* reign, who compleated that which her Predecessors had attempted, but never perfected: after which they remain'd in a quiet subjection till these fatall differences hapned in Sicilie; which encourag'd them to rebell, by throwing off again that Yoke which they had not without reluctancie submited too. And thinking no time so fit as now (that they saw the King wholy taken up with composing those civill discords which had fallen out in Sicilie) to practice what they had long before projected, took this opportunity; unanimously rising in rebellion against him; murthering, and destroying in a most barbarous, and brutish manner all those Sicilians that they could lay hands on, who had come thither to inhabit: puting sundry of them to death by such horible and cruell tortures as till then had ne're been heard of, nor invented; though by many yeares continuance there, they were by the alliances they had contracted with them become as it were one People. In this condition was Sardinia when our King left Sicilie. Judge then Madam (continu'd she) if he had any reason to have recourse for protection to those who were naturally of so merciless and bloody dispositions, as they took delight in nothing more then in the highest Acts of cruelty.

Since it was so (repli'd *Ermilia*) I confess *Clearchus* could admit small hopes of saftie there, but did very prudently preferre Corsica before Sardinia in his choice of a retreat. After this the Queen was silent, and *Arthenia* went on.

Rivall Friendship

THE FIRST PART

The ~~Fifth~~ Sixth Book

In the meane time (said *Arthenia*) Mazara was reduced to great extreamities by *Faragenes*, who had so straightly besieg'd it, as they had not the least hopes left them of a reliefe; especially since the King was under a restraint which being once assur'd of, they thought it would be but a fruitless service to him longer to continue the siege: whereupon, after severall debates, and consultations they surrendred the Citty, together with the Prince *Issomantes* the Kings second son, who was immediatly sent to Palermo to be kept with the Prince *Hiperion* his Brother, and two of his sisters who were detained there as Prisoners.[1] But t'was not long that these young Princes continu'd together, for *Issomantes* in a short time after made an escape in the habit of a Lady, which thorough his youth, and beauty he so well personated as he easily deluded the eyes of his Keepers. *Macaria* likewise, to whose care the Princess *Herenia* had by the Queen her Mother been intrusted at her departure ^out^ of Sicilie, conveide her safely into Naples; though not without much hazard of being surpriz'd ere she could effect her Desig^ne^. These two being thus got free from their confinement, there remain'd onely *Hyperion*, and the Princess *Eluzeria* in the enemies power, who poor Princess never knew an end of Captivity till Death release her.[2]

It might with reason have been believ'd (continu'd *Arthenia*) that the confidence which the King repos'd in these perfidious Corsicans, ^and^ his so gracious condescention to all that they requir'd, would so strongly have engag'd them not onely to protect him as they had promis'd; but also to endeavour to reinstate him in the possession of his just, and undoubted right, which those usurping Traitors had most injuriously despoil'd him of: but instead of that, it gave them opportunity to act the most horrid piece of treachery that ever the most Infernall Spirits could suggest. Which was, not onely to betray him into the hands of his most mortall and implacable enemies, but to make Merchandize of

---

[1] James, Duke of York (*Issomantes*) was sent to London (Palermo) to be kept with Henry, Duke of Goucester (*Hiperion*) and Princess Elizabeth (*Eluzeria*) as prisoners in St. James Palace in London.

[2] On 20 April 1648, James escaped from St. James Palace disguised as a girl. Princess Henrietta of England was conveyed to France, leaving Princess Elizabeth still in captivity where she was to die at Carisbrooke in 1650, a year after her father's execution.

him, as if he had been a slave, selling him to them at the price of 30000 Talents:[3] This in my opinion (pursu'd *Arthenia*) was so horrible a thing, as I should tremble to relate it, did not that which succeeded (whereof my owne Countrymen are guilty) stricke such a horrour into me so oft as I reflect on it, that I have scarce my reason free, to pass so severe a Censure on these Miscreants as they deserve.

Why (interrupted the Queen) can there be a Crime more black then that you mention'd; sure if there be, Divells, not men must act it.

Ah, Madam (repli'd *Arthenia* with a sigh) of such a nature is the crime Sicilie stands branded with, and will do, to all posterity, that Corsica's if compar'd with it seemes [fol. 72^r] but a Veniall sin.

But to proceed (continu'd she) that summe I spake of, was no sooner tendred, but *Clearchus* was deliver'd to those, sent by the Senate to receive him; and by them carri'd to one of his own Castles, being one of the most stately buildings Sicilie can shew; nere to the Plain of Catana was it situated, which perhaps enduced them rather to make choice of that to keep him in then any other, to the end he might be perpetually tortured with the view of that unhappy place where he receiv'd his finall overthrow.[4] Here was he kept under so close a restraint, as none, no not so much as any of his owne Meniall servants were allow'd access to him. In the interim hapned a difference between a Partie in the Senate, and some of the chiefe Commanders in the Armie; whereupon one of their Officers was dispatch't with Commission to ceaze the King, and bring him safe to the Campe, which was accordingly done. He was at first treated with great demonstrations of reverence and affection; and leave given to his servants to repaire to him again, and to any of the Royall Partie that desir'd it, permission to see him: but so had he been deluded by that reception he had in Corsica, that he found but little reason to build his hopes on a little outward semblance of respect, since he had onely chang'd his Guards, and Prison, not his Captive state: but this little civility which he receiv'd much enlarg'd the breach which was between the Senate and the Armie: the Inhabitants of Palermo too began to be somewhat sensible of what they had done, in being Instrumentall in the chaceing away their King from them by their rude deportment; which to repaire, they joyn'd with those in the Senate who desir'd his restoration.

Whereupon, those Senatours who had no mind to see him returne, and had the most highly upheld the war against him, quited their Fellows, and betook themselves to the other part of the Armie (over which *Ormisdas* had the more immediate command) who being encourag'd by their repaire to them, advanced without delay to Palermo with an intention to restore them to their former power: upon the newes of whose approach, the Inhabitants (who before spake high, and

---

[3] The sum 30000 talents would have amounted to approximately 300,000 pounds; most sources suggest that only 100,000 pounds of a sum amounting to 400,000 pounds was paid.

[4] Charles was taken first to Holmby House in Northamptonshire.

had begun to raise an Armie to joyne with those who seemed to favour the King) were so scared, as they no sooner saw an Armie ~~within~~ ^at^ their Walls, but they instantly su'd for Peace, opening their Gates to receive them; who instantly went and placed those Senatours that they had taken into their protection, in their severall seates; suppressing those of the opposite partie: after which they pass'd thorow the Citty in a tryumphant manner, with displai'd Ensignes, and diverse Warlike Instruments resounding, so as ^they^ even made the streets to echo with the sound. Presently after this was the King hurried up and downe from one Place to another; till at last he was brought to one of his owne Palaces, some ten miles distant from Palermo; where long he had not been, ere he was terrifi'd with the apprehension of some dangerous contrivance, which (as he was credibly enform'd) was in aggitation against ~~him~~ his life, by some of the Armie, though he could not make a discovery who they were.[5]

Where upon, he secretly got thence, with onely three of his Attendants; and believing the Governour of Lipara (one of the adiacent Islands) to be devoted to him, he unhappily put himself into his power; but he deceiving that trust he had repos'd in him, no less then the Corsicans had done before, made him close Prisoner in the strongest Castle in the Island. Assoon as it was known w[h]ere he was, the Senate sent some Propositions to him much of [fol. 72ᵛ] the same nature the others were before; to which he return'd like Answere as he had formerly done; which so incenst them to see they could not tryumph ore his mind, by inthralling that, as they had done his body, by compelling him to yeeld to their unjust demands, as they instantly decreed amongst themselves, never more to make any Address to him as their King by way of request, sute, or Petition; but to take upon them the Goverment of the Kingdome. To this procedure they were encourag'd by a Manifest publish'd by the Armie, wherein they engag'd themselves to stand firmly to them in the maintainance of that Decree.

And now it was that his subjects both of Sicilia, and Corsica who had so long united their forces against him, began (when it was too late) to look on his deplorable condition with a very sensible ~~condition~~ concerne; and having invain try'd to obtain his freedome by way of Petition, they resolv'd to try what they could do by force. The Province of Nota (which had ever stood well affected to his service) first express'd their readiness to appeare for him, which they did under the conduct of *Gerandus*:[6] after which ^*Leonitus*^ *Pollidor*, and *Policilus*,[7] who had before serv'd under the Senate, revolted; ceazing on some important

---

[5] Hampton Court was the palace ten miles from London where Charles was kept prisoner, but he succeeded in escaping and fled to the Isle of Wight (Lipara).

[6] Mary Ellen Lamb has suggested that Gerandus is George Goring, 1st Earl of Norwich, because of the allusions to the campaign in Kent and siege of Colchester.

[7] Manningham seems to be summarizing the war in England, Wales, and Scotland. John Poyer, Rowland Laugharne, and Rice Powell, Welsh commanders, initially supported the moderate Parliamentarian position and then became Royalists.

Townes, and Castles in the Æolian Isles, and declar'd against them. And lastly *Merobates Prince of Harvilio*,[8] having rais'd a strong Armie of Corsicans came into Sicilie with pretences of restoring the King to his Crowne and liberty. But as the Ilustrious *Clearchus*, (whose Princely mind was far above the reach of Fortunes power) arm'd himselfe with a heroick resolution against all future events, in the midest of these high hopes, and expectations, that what ever happed he might be prepar'd for its reception; so neither were the Senate wanting in their diligent endeavours, to destroy those hopes, and render those expectations ineffectuall: for the danger alarming ^them^ so on all sides, *Ormisdas* is dispatch'd with some part of the Armie into the revolted Islands, where he but too soon reduced all again under obedience to the Senate. Those three Commanders I lately mention'd, submitted to the mercy of him who was compos'd of nought but cruelty; for no sooner had they yeelded, but he caus'd them all to be put to death.[9] Having in this manner subdued all his opposers in those parts, he returnes; and encounters the Corsican Armie, who were marching vigorously on their way, and were advanced as far as the Province of Mona, but were there stop'd by *Ormisdas* his encounter; who put them to the route, killing, and taking even almost their whole Armie, together with their Generall *Merobates* who was sent Prisoner to Palermo: after which, *Ormisdas* visits Corsica, where he totally subdues all those, that in the least could be suspected of Fidelity to their Prince; and so impoverishes them, as he leaves them in no capacity of puting him to the trouble of a returne to quell them a second time.[10]

But whilst he was busie there, *Faragenes* was no less employ'd in the Province of Nota against *Gerandus*, who finding himselfe too weak to encounter him in the Field, retir'd into Agrigentum to stay the arrivall of some expected supplies; but being alarum'd by *Faragenes's* approach, and knowing that Citty too feebly fortified to maintain a siege quited it; but with what design I know not; but whatever it was he had not time (it seemes) to pursue it, being surpriz'd by the enemy, who stop'd their passage at Enna, forceing ^them^ to take sanctuary in that Towne, where, had their strength [fol. 73ʳ] been but answerable to their Courages, they had doubtless held them play till such time as their expected supplies had come to their assistance: but notwithstanding their inconsiderable number, they kept the Towne the day following, and the ensuing night, ere they

---

[8] James Hamilton (1606–49), 1st Duke of Hamilton (*Merobates*) was an influential Scottish nobleman.

[9] Commanders Poyer, Laugharne, and Powell were defeated at the Battle of St. Fagans by Cromwell (*Ormisdas*), and they were sentenced to death but then reprieved with only one being expected to face a firing squad. They drew lots, and only John Poyer was executed.

[10] Cromwell defeated the Scottish army at Preston Moor in 1648. In October, Cromwell entered Scotland and came to terms with Archibald Campbell, 8th Duke of Argyll.

could be driven thence. Just as *Gerandus* enter'd Enna, he was saluted by a Caval-
liere galantly mounted, and Arm'd Capapied, though he had nothing remarkable
in his Armes; (but seem'd as if he had a designe to make himself known rather by
his valour, then by any Device he had about him) save, on his head instead of a
Casque he wore a Helmet shaded with a stately Plume of Carnation, and White
Feathers curiously intermix't; his Face being almost bare disclos'd a martiall
Countenance, yet spake his age not above 18. This young Gallant being come
up to the Generall, suddely stop'd his horse, and accosted him with a profound
reverence, even to his sadle Bow.

Sir (said he to him with a becoming garbe ^grace^)[11] I have hitherto deem'd
it my highest misfortune that my youth has till now render'd me uncapable of
serving my Prince any otherwise then by fruitless wishes; and that whilst so
many brave men ventur'd their lives in so just a cause, I onely should set secure,
studying the Theory of War, the practick part whereof I suppos'd I could of
none learn better then of so experienced a Commander as yourselfe; which has
enduced me to desire admittance amongst these Gentlemen who have the honour to follow you; and though the addition of one single man can bring but small
assistance to your Troops, yet if my Courage deceive me not, I hope sir to performe something considerable enough for so young a soldier.

This confidence in a person of so few yeares, so well pleas'd *Gerandus*, that
he not onely admitted him, but gave him the honour to command a Troop whose
Captain died that very morning; telling him withall, that if all his other souldiers
were inspir'd but with spirits like his, he should not need to give the enemy the
trouble of a further pursute. In this manner it was that the young *Loreto* (for it
was he indeed as I afterwards learn'd) first signaliz'd himselfe: but although he
made then but a short essay in armes, yet (notwithstanding the prejudice I have
against him, I must do him the justice to afirme) he gain'd so noble a repute, as
Sicilie cannot without Ingratitude bury in Oblivion the memory of those valiant
acts which in that little space he perform'd: for twice by his sole valour he made
the enemy retire; and afterwards for the space of 12 houres (with onely a handfull
of men) defended a Bridge which gave enterance to the Towne. And when the
souldiers under his command wanted Bullets, he instantly caus'd all the mony
he had brought with him for his owne perticuler expences, to be cut in pieces,
and distributed amongst them to shoot against the enemy. This action of his was
esteem'd so highly generous, as all persons that heard it, proclaim'd it with infinite applause: but being at length o'repower'd rather by multituds then Valour,
he lost his liberty; and with it, his Party their hopes of keeping Enna any longer,
which mov'd them to abandon it, though in great disorder; but the darkness of
the night favouring them, with much confusion, though no great loss, they got
over a certaine River which runs thorough that part of the Country, and shut up

---

[11] The word garbe is underlined for deletion, and it is to be replaced with the word
^grace^.

themselves in that Citty which gives name to the Province: where after a long siege, and enduring the highest extreamities,[12] even almost to famishment, they yeelded [fol. 73ᵛ] upon these Conditions; that the Citty should be exempt from Pillage, the Officers and Souldiers to submit to the mercy of the Conquerour. But no sooner was the City surrendred, but two of the chiefe Commanders were instantly put to death; and the galant *Cratander*[13] reserv'd for a Trophie to follow the Conquerours Chariot to Palermo, where soon after he was put to death; which he entertain'd with as undaunted a Brow, as *Merobates* (who was put to death with him) receiv'd his with apprehensions unbecoming a Generous Spirit.

But not withstanding these prosperous successes, the Senate perceiving all Sicilie in generall infinitly desirous that they should treat again with *Clearchus* concerning a peace at length consented, repealing their late Decree; and deputed severall to be sent from them to treat with him. But these men (being before instructed by those who had not onely contriv'd, but absolutely resolv'd the destruction of their King) drew out each perticuler to such a length, and stood so long demurring on things of no consequence, as they gave the Armie opportunity to publish a Declaration wherein they most injuriously affirm'd *Clearchus* to be guilty of all the blood that had been spilt in this unnaturall War; adding withall, that he ought to be depos'd, as being unfit to rule, and that it was necessary for the security, and wellfare of the Nation that Justice should be inflicted on him: to which intent, he was on a sudden ceaz'd on, and brought Prisoner to his own Palace at Palermo; after which, all those that seem'd satisfi'd with his gracious condescentions were expell'd the Senatehouse by their Fellows who held intelligence with the Armie:[14] and then assuming an unlimmitted power they summon'd their King to appear before them, in such an unheard of manner as no Historie ere records the like; nor was it known before, that subjects durst presume to set as Judges to determine the life or Death of their lawfull Soveraign.

But the day for his appearance being come, he was brought from his Palace to the Court of Judicature; where *Brataldo*[15] (who was constituted to be his Judge) and the rest of his Assistants sate expecting his coming, which he could no way avoid being ^under^ restraint; but t'was not the power they had unjustly assum'd could in the least make him owne ^their^ authority, or betray Sicilies liberty (to an unlawfull power) which he resolv'd (what'ere he suffer'd) should never be in the least infring'd by his acknowledging their usurp'd Authority a Lawfull

---

[12] The Royalists surrendered at the siege of Colchester from a shortage of food.

[13] Arthur Capell, 1st Baron Capell, (*Cratander*) asked to have his heart buried with the king. He was executed with Hamilton (*Merobates*).

[14] Labeled Pride's Purge, members of Parliament who voted to continue negotiations with the king were forcibly prevented by members of the army from entering the Parliament.

[15] John Bradshaw (*Brataldo*) was appointed Lord President of the tribunal that tried Charles I.

one. But notwithstanding these audacious Villains proceed in what they had determin'd, unjustly charging him with all the miseries that Sicilia had suffer'd for so many yeares; though Heaven knowes, none but themselves were the occation of them; nor none so innocent of them as he who had from time to time try'd sought, and most earnestly endevour'd by all imaginable meanes, not onely to prevent, but likewise to put an end to his People's sufferings. The best titles these Monsters of impudence in their Charge could conferre upon their Soveraign were no better then Tyrant, Traitor, Murtherer, and the common Enemy of his Country: which when the good *Clearchus* heard, he made no reply, onely smil'd, as scorning to vindicate himselfe from such foule aspersions as all the World knew to be notoriously false. But when they saw that all they could do, could not constrain him to betray his owne Innocence by submitting to their accusation, or the Lawes of the Land, and his subjects [fol. 74ʳ] liberties by acknowledging them a lawfull Power, and that he resolv'd rather to dye his Peoples Martyre, then live their Injurer, they presum'd (after he had receiv'd from them many reproachfull speeches, and much uncivill, and unexpressable rude, and saucie language) to doome him to Death; sentenceing him to loose his head within the Gates of his owne Palace within three dayes.

The fatall day being come, wherein was to be acted the blackest, and most horrid Tragidie that ever was presented to the Worlds view; *Clearchus* spent the morning of it in pious Devotions: which were no sooner ended, but he was hurried to the Place of Execution. The Scaffold destin'd for that purpose was hung round with black, to which being brought he asscended it with a Countenance wherin not the least signe of a troublesome concerne was to be seen; but rather a serene calmnes, intimating his inward quiet. Multitudes of People were gather'd together from all parts of the Citty to behold this dismall spectacle; where though thousands lamented, yet none had the courage to rescue him from those Assasines who were going to destroy him; which if any had been so hardy to attempt, possibly they had found better success then in probability they could have expected: but certainly they were all infatuated, or rendred insensible of what they saw; or they could ne're have stood with Teares bewailing, what with their bloods they ought to have hinder'd, or not have liv'd to have been spectators of. Something he said to the People in vindication of his Innocence, lest (as he said) they might believe, in seeing him so calmly submit to the Punishment, that he likewise acknowledg'd the guilt of those Crimes wherwith he had been falsly charg'd; declaring withall his unbounded Charity which oblig'd him freely to forgive all those who had been either the Contrivers, or Authers of his death: much more t'was thought he intended to have said; but finding the People (to whom he addresst his speach) kept at so great a distance by those Guards which surrounded the Scaffold that he supos'd they could heare but little what he said, he desisted from his intended Discourse, and prepared for the reception of the fatall blow; which after some short, though fervent Prayers he resign'd himselfe to that eternall Being who gave him his; and with a greater Patience then ever

Mortall was before endued with, quietly submitted his Illustrious Head to the cruell hand of a vil<u>d</u>^e^[16] Executioner, who with one blow sever'd it from his body: which being done, he held it up, exposing it to the view of all such as had the heart to behold so dismall, and afflicting an Object.

This, this Madam (continu'd *Arthenia* with a sigh) was that ha^i^nous Crime without example wherewith my Country will stand branded with the blackest Infamie to all succeeding Ages, and has justly rendred the very name of a Sicilian hatefull to all other Nations.

I am ~~most~~ strangly amaz'd (repli'd the Queen) at what you tell me, that I should scarce take this story for any other then a Romantick Fiction, did you not assure me tis a reall truth.

Tis but too known a[s] one (answered *Arthenia*) *Gentillus* here, can I doubt not affirme it as well as I: being in Sicilie not many yeares after this Tragidie was acted; where t'was impossible to be and not heare this, which none there were ignorant of.

I was there I confess Madam (said he addressing his speech to the Queen) and know all that *Arthenia* has recounted concerning the Unfortunate *Clearchus's* disastrous Fate to be certainly true having heard it before from the mouthes of those who had been Eye witnesses thereof: but your Majesty has reason not [fol. 74ᵛ] lightly to credit so great an improbability as that there should spring from humane race such inhumane Monsters as nothing could saciate but their Sovereign's blood. It has been known sometimes I must confess, that Kings have been prively made away by Poison, or some other treacherous contrivance of some bold Traitor; but that ever Prince should by his owne subiects be arrained at a Tribunall as a Malefactour, and under a forme of Law, and Justice be doom'd to dye, and be publickly put to death on an Infamous scaffold before the face of all the World, is that which ne're was heard, nor seen before; and which when I first heard, fill'd me with no less horror and astonishment then that wherewith your Majesty is ceaz'd.

Well (answered *Ermillia*) I shall henceforth deeme nothing strang since this is true. But good *Arthenia* tell me (pursued she) did not Heaven inflict on those bloody Regicides, punishments as unheard of as their Crimes.

Yes Madam (she replied) tis very sure it did on some of the chiefest, and most notorious of them; even then when in appearance they were exempt from all but those which Divine Justice reserves for guilty soules hereafter; nor did the rest go free, though Vengeance was awhile delay'd in their exemplary punishments, it [h]it the heavier at length for that it was so slow: but I must humbly beg you will be pleas'd Madam to give me leave to relate things in order as they hapned, and your Majesty shall fully know the Fate that befell those cruell Murtherers of the Illustrious *Clearchus*; for though (I must needs say) much of that I

---

[16] The MS reads "vil<u>d</u>" with "d" underlined and "e" inserted above.

have already told, nor of what I intend further to declare, has no connexion with my owne perticuler concernes, yet deeming it worthier your attention, then those more triviall Events that relate onely to the Unhappy *Arthenia*, it has enduced me to insist more perticulerly on the great Concernments of my King, and Country then otherwise I should have done, had I made this relation to any other then ^the^ Queen of Delphos.

All Princes in general (said *Ermillia*) being concern'd to look with horror, and detestation on your Countryes offence, are no less oblig'd to commiserate with the highest pitty, and most sensible Compassion the unmatchable sufferings of your King; for which I declare my resentments [sentiments] are such, that if I had a perticuler interest in them, they could not be more afflicting: but yet of such a nature is this trouble, that you have more oblig'd me by giving, then you would, had you exempted me from it, by concealing from my knowledge things of such importance: therefore go on *Arthenia,* and let me know as well all as Sicilias adventures, as your owne mishaps.

She having signfi'd to the Queen her readiness to pay obedience to her commands, proceeded in these words. No sooner was this execrable Fact committed, but it was cellebrated with shoutes of Joy, and with the sound of Drumes, and Trumpets, which loudly proclaim'd the satisfaction they took in what they had done; glorying in nothing more then that, which was Sicilies highest shame, and stain'd themselves in perticuler with eternall Infamie.

Th[e] insolent *Ormisdas* being present at this Execution, no sooner saw *Clearchus*'s Royall head divided from his breathless body, but beholding him with a disdainfull Look (turning to some that were next him) See (said he) where lies the disturber of Sicilies peace.

His Corpes being carried to an appartment in the Palace where he usually [fol.75ʳ] lodg'd, was for some dayes there expos'd to the view of such as desired to behold it: after which he was convei'd to a little Towne, distant from Palermo about 20 miles; his body being attended onely by some few of the most Illustrious persons in the Kingdome, who had courage enough to owne publickly that untainted Fidelity, and unshaken Friendship they had cordially pai'd him to the last minute of his life; nor would they yet abandon him till they had seen him interred in the Monument of *Herelius,* one of the precedent Kings of Sicilie, for there it was he was intomb'd;[17] but without the least solemnities of state due to so great a Monarch were his Obsequies perform'd, nay even those Funurall Rites which the meanest persons were allow'd were to him deni'd. Report soon flew to Naples with the dolefull tydings of his untimely death to his disconsolate Queen, whose griefs, and woefull laments nothing could equall, but Prince *Claromenes*'s and the rest of those Illustrious Orphans; which were such, as being unable to describe, I must pass them by in silence, knowing no words nor expressions sad

---

[17] Charles I was interred at Windsor near Henry VIII.

enough to cloth their sorrows in: nor was the hopes of possessing three potent Kingdoms, with the dazling splendor of a triple Crowne (whereof *Claromenes* was the undoubted Heire) capable of dispelling those dark Melancholy Vapours, which for divers yeares clouded his Princely Brow.

In the meane time the ambitious *Ormisdas* having goten the sole command into his owne hands by *Feragenes* his declining his Commission which had been joyntly devided betwixt them: for he, seeing things carried to that height, and begining to perceive the Design they had upon the Kings life, when it was too late to prevent it; or at least wanting courage enough to hinder the execution of those crimes which he could not approve, though he had been too great an Accessary in by that assistance he gave those Traitours, laid downe his Commission (which was thereupon intierly conferr'd on *Ormisdas*) and retir'd to his owne house; where he has ever since lead a private life.[18] *Ormisdas* (I say) having by this meanes got what he long time had aim'd at, stay'd not there, but quickly arriv'd to the supreame power in the Kingdome, though he alwayes declin'd the title of a King, having before endevour'd to render it so hatefull, as he durst not in Pollicie assume the name, though he presum'd to exercise the Authority; which he did, with so unlimmitted, and uncontroul'd a power, as that if ever Sicilie groan'd under the heavie pressure of a Tyrants armes, now was the time. But as he obtain'd the goverment of the Kingdome by the Foxes subtilty, so he resolv'd to keep it by the Lyons force; making all things bow to his interest; compelling even those very senatours who had been hitherto his Masters, now to become his servants; for since he had the sword in his hand, by having the whole Armie at his devotion, he knew well enough none durst be so hardy as to oppose him. Most of the loyall-hearted Nobility, whether it were that their generous spirits could not descend to stoop so low as to submit to a Usurper, or that they abhorr'd a Land stain'd with Crimes so monsterous as Sicilie was, I cannot say; but so it was, that soon after their King was murder'd, they abandon'd their native Country, and the ancient seates of their Progenitours, and repair'd to him whom they now look'd on, and respected as their Lawfull sovereign, though unjustly kept from ascending his Royal Throne by an aspiring Rebell; chusing rather to follow the [fol. 75ᵛ] Fortunes of their exil'd Prince though exposed to the highest necessities, then without him to enjoy all the delights, and plenties that Sicilie could afford.

It was not long ere the Sicilians found by sad experience, the bad exchanges they had made, in changing a Golden Scepter for an Iron one, and a just, and gracious King for an unjust and cruel Tyrant, who knew no Law but his owne Will; imposing on those who ought to have been his Fellow subjects, not his Slaves, what Taxes he thought fit, to maintain his assumed Dignity, and secure him in that Place of honour to which he had waded thorow a River of his Soveraigns

---

[18] Fairfax refused to take any oath to the Commonwealth which would have meant giving approval to the trial and execution of Charles 1.

blood. Two yeares were not expir'd since the never enough to be lamented Murther of the best of Kings ere the Corsicans consider'd how much they had been
accessary to that most execrable deed, both by their rebellion and their treachery;
and finding how little advantagious those Crimes had been to them, began to
bethink themselves by what way they might in part repaire those past miscar-
riages which they could never sufficently deplore. To which end they concluded
to envite to them their injured Prince, and place him not onely on the Throne of
Corsica, but of Sicilie too, by aiding, and assisting him to regain that which his
Royall Father lost. This being once resolv'd, some of the chiefest in that Kingdome were dispatch'd to Naples to make their applications to him, and to give
him all the assurance that might be of their Countries Fidelitie, and an honourable reception; with promises of all dutyfull alleageance, and loyalty for the
future; upon which, he returnes with them to Corsica, where he was with all the
state, and grandure that Kingdome was capable of exhibiting solemnly Crown'd
King of Corsica in Bastia their chiefe Citty, which had for many Ages been the
Royal seate of their precedent Kings. [19]

These transactions in Corsica *Ormisdas* having certain intelligence of, prepared for a speedy Invasion that he might soon drive thence again their King,
well knowing that if he suffer'd him to establish himselfe firmly on that Throne,
it would be impossible long to detain from him that in Sicilie, to which he had
no less a right then to the other; being by just succession the undoubted Heire
of both. To this intent, he advances with a formidable Armie towards Corsica,
before such time as King *Claromenes* could make any considerable provision to
oppose him; whereupon he thought it best (knowing the weakness of Corsica; and
not being so well assur'd of his subiects fidelities too much to relie on them; since
they had been so treacherous to the King his Father) with those Forces he had,
and as many as he could suddenly leavy to march into Sicilie to hinder *Ormisdas*
from advanceing further towards Corsica: to which he was encourag'd by the
daily repaires of Sicilians to him; and an assurance he receiv'd from some of his
approved Friends, that he should no sooner appear in Sicilie, but many thousands
would declare for him: which intelligence he found the truth of in his March, by
those additions he made to his Armie in all places as he pass'd along: but in all
other parts they were so aw'd by *Ormisdas* tyranie that they durst not stir to the
assistance of their lawfull Prince. [20] But notwithstanding the Loyal *Stertorius* was
doing his utmost in a remote part of the Kingdome to raise [fol. 76ʳ] some forces
to joyne with Corsicas King; and had in a short time got together a considerable

---

[19] Charles II (*Claromenes*) was invited to Scotland where he was crowned king at
Scone on 1 January 1651.

[20] Bridget Manningham errs in suggesting that Cromwell was trying to prevent
Charles II from entering England. Cromwell was in Scotland; he had defeated the Scots
at Dunbar and was marching toward Perth when Charles left Scotland in the hope of
severing Cromwell's communication with the south.

company; but being desirous to increase his Troops to as great a number as possible he could, it was so long ere he arriv'd that *Claromenes* was met by *Ormisdas* and constrain'd to come to a Battell: but the King of Corsica knowing his Fate depended on this first encounter, since his Armie was much inferior to the others both in number and experience, he would willingly have declin'd fighting till such time as he might be in a better capacity to encounter his Enemy by the assistance he expected from *Stertorious*.[21] But *Ormisdas* being too well vers'd in War to loose such an advantage, compell'd him to accept the Battell; wherein though he did such things as future times will scarcely credit, even to the admiration both of his Friends and Enemies, yet (this being not the time wherein Heaven had decreed his restoration, nor Sicilie sufficiently punish'd for its crimes) he so totally lost the Victory, that all his Forces were either kill'd, or taken Prisoners, and afterwards sold most barbarously for slaves into other Countries: himself (poor Unfortunate Prince) constrain'd to seek his safty in his Flight.[22]

This misfortune was by all that wish't him well, and had importun'd Heaven for his good success, resented [felt] with an unexpressable sorrow, to see those hopes, which had so pleasingly flatter'd them into a beliefe that they should speedily see Vengeance excuted on the malicious Murtherers of their late Gracious Soveraign utterly frustrated: insomuch, as one whose heart had been cordially affected to his King (though uncapable of expressing it) when he beheld the wretched Prisoners led fetter'd by his Dore, conceiv'd so great a griefe thereat, as in few days hurried him to his Grave. But though *Ormisdas* won the Battell, yet thought he the Victory imperfect since *Claromenes* was neither dead, nor a Prisoner but had made his escape; whereby he might one day be in a condition to repair his loss. Manifests therefore were emmediatly dispers'd into all parts of the Land for his apprehension, and great rewards promis'd to any person that could either take, or bring certaine intelligence to *Ormisdas* of his being conceal'd in any Place: but notwithstanding the diligent care of those who went in quest of him, yet Heaven preserv'd him in a most perticuler manner from all his enemies pursutes: for though he had been absent from Sicilie diverse yeares, and that the weight of those uncomman griefes which has so long oppress'd his great Soule had wrought such a change in his Countenance as it would have bin no easie thing to know him, (except such as had been the faithfull Companions of his Exile) yet if Divine Providence had not in almost a miraculous manner provided

---

[21] James Stanley, 7th Earl of Derby (*Stertorius*) was raising troops in Lancashire and Cheshire. Charles's army may have been just over 13,000 men while Cromwell's was over 28,000.

[22] The Battle of Worcester was a victory for Cromwell. Approximately 4,000 Scots were taken prisoner. According to Clarendon, whom Bridget Manningham may have consulted, they were sold to plantations as slaves, but accounts differ. See Edward Hyde (1609–74), 1st Earl of Clarendon, *The History of the Rebellion and Civil Wars in England.* 3 vols. (1707; Oxford: Clarendon Press, 1819), 3: 553.

for his saftie, it had certainly been impossible for him not to have been discover'd
by one meanes or another; being a Person so remarkable as he is, both for his stature which he exceeds most men in, and his delicate shape which none can equall:
but if neither his height, nor proportion could have rendred him suspected, his
Face was yet more remarkable, having indelibly imprinted on it such Charactars
of Royalty, and an Aire onely peculier to himselfe so Illustrious and Great, as
was sufficent at once to inspire into the hearts of all beholders both love, and
veneration; nay even then [fol. 76^v] when he was so disguised, as his owne eyes
could scarce believe it was himselfe they saw, there yet appear'd such Rayes of
Majesty in him, as none that had exactly view'd him but would have concluded,
if he were not a King, he was undoubtedly born to be one. Being such, and much
more admirable then my imperfect description is able to represent him; you may
believe Madam (pursu'd *Arthenia*) he ran no ordinary danger of a discovery,
when he was constrain'd together with *Philarchus*[23] (one of the most faithfull of
his Attendants, whose resolutions were firmly fixt never to abandon him) to seek
his security in the midst of a Forrest neer adjoyning to the Field of Battell; where
on a Tree whose Branches were interwoven very thick, he was forced to conceal
himself a whole day, and a Night without either sleep, or sustenance; being perpetually alarm'd with feares of a surprizall in his Silvan retreat by some of those
souldiers who continually coasted the Forrest in search of him; and often in their
traverses pass'd under that very Tree on which he was. But early the next morning, *Philarchus* espi'd thorough the Branches two men whose habits spake them
to be Forresters, who seem'd very earnest in discourse, the subiect whereof (when
they came so neer as to be heard) seem'd to him (who hearkned intentively to
them) to concern the Kings misfortune, which with many sensible expressions
they deplored: which made him fancy; there might probably be found more honesty in such as those, who convers'd with few but the Innocent Inhabitants of the
Woods, then amongst others, whom a more publick conversation might infect
with Covetousness, or Ambition.

Which thought no sooner came into his mind, but he acquainted *Claromenes*
with it telling him, that since those men had testifi'd such a Concerne for his ill
Fate, possibly they might by their assistance find some way to escape: however
Sir (continu'd he) your Majesty shall be sure to run no greater hazard then now
you do, if you will grant me a permission to shew my selfe to them. The King
knowing well both the fidelity, and discretion of *Philarchus,* opposed not his

---

[23] Charles II enjoyed telling the story of his escape by hiding in what came to be
known as the Royal Oak. In 1651, after his defeat by Cromwell at the Battle of Worcester, he was accompanied by James Stanley, 7th Earl of Derby; Lieutenant-General Henry
Wilmot, later 1st Earl of Rochester, and Charles Giffard who owned Bascobel House
where the Royal Oak was located. Giffard, along with William Careless, may have introduced him to the Penderel family. Richard and George Penderel and their family were
instrumental in Charles's escape and received pensions at the Restoration.

Proposall, but readily condescended to it; whereupon he instantly left the Tree, and having mark'd what path they had taken, he posted after them with such speed, as in a short space he overtook them, who were walking on but at a softly rate, traversing the Forrest as it was their daily custome, to view the Deere, and to prevent them from stragling beyond their bounds; so that having overtaken them, he accosted them in this manner.

Friends (said he) that which it was my Fortune even now to heare you say, has created in me a beliefe, that since you have express'd a trouble, for the late disaster of him, whom you have been so just as to stile your King, that you will be no enemies to those who are his Friends: which has encourag'd me to hope, by your assistance to find security both for my selfe and another Gentleman of my acquaintance (who is in no less distress and danger then my selfe) which I can no longer doubt of, if you, can but procure us some such habits as men of your degree and quality usually weare; for which we will willingly exchang our owne, which may be of much more advantage to you, but yet, much less then the [fol. 77ʳ] reward you shall receive, if you will but furnish us with what I now request.

These honest men being more joyfull that they had found an opportunity to serve any that profest love for King *Claromenes*, then to inrich themselves by any recompence they could expect; told *Philarchus*, he should find them most ready to serve him in what he desir'd, or anything that their meane estate was capable of: and that if he pleas'd but to conceale himself in a Thicket hard by, the one of them would stay with him to give him notice of any approaching danger, and the other should soon supply him and his Friend with althings necessary for their disguise: and that afterwards if they pleas'd to go along with them to their habitation (which stood but a little distance thence) they would undertake to secure them for that day, and at night conduct them to a Gentlemans house not farre from that place; of whose affection to the royall Partie they were so confident, that the King himself need not feare to put his life into his hands. *Philarchus* hearing them speak so cordially, had his confidence in them redoubled, which gave him no small Joy. The one of them staying with him, the other went to fetch the Disguises. In the meane time *Philarchus* ask'd *Placius* (for so was the Forrester call'd that stay'd with him) amongst other questions, the name of that Gentleman whom they affirm'd to love his King so well.

He is call'd *Leonishus*[24] Sir (repli'd he.) At the name of *Leonishus Philarchus* no longer doubted he was the same who had been his intimate friend for many yeares; though when he abandon'd Sicilia with the Prince, he liv'd far distant from that part of the Kingdome: but knowing diverse things might happen to

---

[24] One possibility is the royalist Colonel Thomas Lane whose sister Jane (*Ileana*) later accompanied Charles to the coast; Charles II was disguised as her servant. Mary Ellen Lamb has suggested that Thomas Whitgreave of Moseley Hall, Staffordshire may be *Leonishus* and that a daughter of his along with Jane Lane may be *Ileana*. Both Jane Lane and Thomas Whitgreave received pensions at the Restoration.

enduce him to change his aboad, he question'd not but in *Leonishus* to find his ancient friend. *Silvius,* the other Brother was by this time return'd, bringing with him two sutes of Apparell with all other necessaries: the two Brothers helping *Philarchus* to put on one of them; after which taking such a direction from *Silvius* as he might be sure not to miss the way to his house, and with him agreed how to demeane themselves when they came thither; (not thinking fit to let them see the King till he had first enform'd him what he had done) he bid them farewell for a while, promising to be with them ere it were long; and hastens back to *Claromenes,* who began to be in some perplexity for his stay: but when he saw him approach the Tree he knew him not (so strange an alteration had that assumed habit made) till such time as he spake.

I would beg your pardon Sir said he for so long an absence from you, had it not conduced to your preservation by meanes of this disguise which I have procured you, which will I trust, secure you from all suspition of being what you are: and I bless Heaven who inspir'd me with a desire of following those men, whom I have found so honest, and ready to afford me any assistance I can require, that I doubt not now to see your Majesty safe both from the secret treacheries, or open violence of those who are so solicitous for your destruction: descend Sir then I beseech you (continu'd he) and for once follow my example in putting on a Pezants shape.

The King being exceedingly satisfi'd [fol. 77ᵛ] with what he had done, spake his resentments [feelings] in such obliging language, as let *Philarchus* see, he serv'd a Prince who of all others merited from his servants the highest evincements of their duty, by the kindness wherewith he receiv'd petty services. The King having in an instant chang'd his Clothes, *Philarchus* began to bethinke him what to do with those, his royall Master had disrob'd himself of: to leave them there, he deem'd unsafe, lest any chanceing to find them, might through inquisitiveness discover what could not be kept too private: and to carry them to Silvius's house was no lesse inconvenient; so that having a while consulted with *Claromenes* what it were best to do with them, he told him, there was no better way then to hide them in that Tree which had been their Sanctuary, and in the evening send *Placius* thither to fetch them.

This being agreed on, and accordingly done, they hasted to *Silvius* his Lodge, which without much difficulty they found; whether being come, they were met at the Dore by *Silvius* himself, who the better to palliate the disguise, wellcom'd them with as kind a familiarity as if he had of a long time been acquainted with these his new and unknown Guests; telling his Wife, they were two Kinsmen of his whom for some yeares he had not seen; desiring her to provide for their entertainment, whatever their poor condition was capable of; whereby his Cousins (as he said) might see they were wellcome to him, which the Good Woman was not backward to do: geting ready with all expedition such Cates as country people account good Cheere. But now, all the Kings fear was that his hands would betray him, or discover that his Person, and Habit held no correspondence with each other (for indeed they were so delicately white, as few Ladies in Sicilie could boast the like) which having told *Philarchus* he presently called to mind, that there was a certain Tree, the Leaves whereof being boil'd in Water, would so change the skin of any person that wash'd in it, that for many dayes they should not recover their former Complexion: whereupon he desired *Silvius* if possible to get him some of those Leaves; and by good Fortune he had one of those Trees grew on the backside of his house, whereby he quickly satisfied *Philarchus*'s request, fetching him instantly as many as he needed; which having made a Bath of, wherein *Claromenes* washing his hands, soon found the effect by the alteration it produced. Dinner being now ready, it is not to be question'd but the King, and *Philarchus* (having neither of them tasted any manner of sustenance for the space of almost two dayes and a night) fed heartily on that which was set before them; the King protested, he rellished more reall sweetness in that homely Fare, then ever he had done in all those Courtly Dainties which were his usuall repasts: and found by the mutuall love there was in that small Family, and the intire satisfaction they took in that little Heaven had bestow'd on them, that Content was more easily ~~found~~ obtained, and oftner found in Cottages, then on Thrones, and lodg'd more frequently under thatch'd Roofes, then Carved Scielings.

The Evening now approaching (as they [fol.78ʳ] determin'd) they bid adue to *Silvius* with thankes and a reward great as the courtesie they had receiv'd, and with *Placius* for their Guide they took their way to *Leonishus's* house, who by good fortune was at that time at home: but supposing it convenient to send *Placius* to make way for their privat reception, they stay'd in the meane time at a little distance to wait his returne. He being admitted to speake with *Leonishus* told him, there were hard by two Gentlemen (whose names he knew not) one whereof desir'd the favour of a quarter of an houres discourse with him in private.

I suppose Sir (added he) the one of them to be some person of quality by the clothes he had on when I first met him, which he has since exchang'd for some of mine.

Leonishus presently conjectur'd he was one of those Unfortunate Gentlemen who had possibly hazarded his life and fortune in his Prince his quarell, and by this late defeat reduced to seek his security under a disguise, might have recourse to his assistance; which if so, he resolv'd to afford him whatever lay in his power: to which end he instantly went along with *Placius* who shew'd him where they were: no sooner did *Philarchus* see him, but by that light which the Moon afforded he certainly knew him to be the same *Leonishus* who had been for many yeares his intimate, and most familiar Friend: but in that manner had his habit disguis'd him, as *Leonishus* had never in the least mistrusted it had been he, had he not by speaking discover'd himself; but sosoon as ever he heard him speak he immediatly knew him by his voice; and embraceing him with all the demonstrations of a reall amitie,

I know not Dear *Philarchus* (said he speaking something low) whether I ought to blame Fortune for reduceing you to the necessity of this disguise, or my self, for my stupidity in not conceiving you were hidden under it. But I beseech you Sir (continued he) what is become of our poor Unfortunate Prince; for you I suppose (if any man) can resolve me, being (as I was enform'd) the onely person that accompani'd him in his flight after the Loss of the Battell; since which fatall day I have suffer'd such tormenting feares for him, lest he up unhappily fall into the merciless hands of his implacable enemies, that I would give my life to know he were in saftie.

You may have that assurance at a lower rate (repli'd *Philarchus* drawing him at a further distance, being unwilling *Placius* should heare him) since I can assure you he is yet safe, thankes to Heaven for his preservation: and tis to me a Joy beyond expression to find the opinion I had of your Loyalty has not deceiv'd me, but that I may with confidence put my Soveraignes Life into your hands, by bringing him to seek a greater security from your Care, and assistance. But not to loose time by unnecessary discourse; I will tell you *Leonishus* (pursu'd he) this very person whom you see with me, is no other then the Illustrious *Claromenes*.

At which assurance he would instantly have thrown himselfe at his feet, to tender him the humblest of his services and submissions that he could have expected from the meanest of his subiects; but being restrain'd by [fol. 78ᵛ] *Philarchus*'s puting him in mind that, that was neither time, nor place convenient for the payment of those respects which were due to the royall Dignity, he contented himself to lead them silently into his house, thorough a private dore, and up a paire of backstaires which lead into his Chamber; and causing a Candle to be brought him, by its dim light he soon perceiv'd Fame had rather injur'd *Claromenes*, then done him Justice in that report she gave of his brave Majestick Mine [mien], which that unbecoming, and most unfitting Garbe he then was in could not so much obscure, but he could gather from that short view assurances great enough that *Philarchus* had not deluded him ^in telling him^ it was the King; which induced him no longer to defer that reverence he thought due to his Soveraign: so that flinging himself at his Feet;

Pardon Great Sir (said he) this rude reception of your Royall Majesty; which nothing but the necessity of your concealment (of which I am very sensible) can in the least degree render excusable: and believe Sir I beseech you, that though my condition denies me ability to give you such a treatment as I ought, and yours permits me not to give you such a one as I might; yet your Majesty shall find by the zeal I have to serve you, that you have yet one faithfull subject left in Sicilie whose Fidelity remaines immovable, though his age rendred him unable to express his loyalty by a personall assistance in the late Fight; and that I am ambitious of no greater honour then the glory of hazarding my life for your saftie.

Rise *Leonishus* (repli'd the King giving him his hand to kiss) and forget I am your King; and thinke not in this estate whereto I am reduced, that I expect anything of Ceremony, or the least respect that my quality might challenge from you at another time; for such is my condition now, that I can admit of none. No, rather (pursu'd he with a sigh, to think how Fortune had Metamorphos'd him) regard me as no other, then what I personate, and as such henceforth treat me. I have from *Philarchus* receiv'd such a Charactar of you, as makes me know the reverence you beare me is fix'd too deeply in your Soule, to need an externall expression to illustrate it.

After this, some time was spent in consultation how to mannage an affaire of such concerne, with so prudent a circumspection as might best facilitate the Kings geting safe out of Sicilie, as speedily as might possibly be contriv'd. But of all those ways propounded by *Philarchus*, none seem'd so probable to *Leonishus* as one which himself had thought on, though at present he said nothing of it, till he had spoken with his Daughter the Vertuous *Ileana*; but being extreamly impatient to know by what meanes the King had been preserv'd, he intreated *Philarchus* to satisfie his curiosity in that perticuler, which in few words he did: whereby he gave him occation both to commend, and highly value those two Brothers for that sincere honesty, and discretion they had manifested by what they had so well perform'd. A little after quiting the Roome, and calling for *Ileana*, she immediatly came to him, whom he commanded to follow him into his Closet, whether being come [fol. 79ʳ] in this manner he spake to her.

As it has ever been my care Daughter (said he) to infuse into you such Principles of Vertue, and Generosity as might give you a title to a Fame as noble as divers of your sex have deservedly acquir'd; so now I offer thee an opportunity to let me see, my care in thy education has not been fruitlessly employ'd; and to encourage thee to what I now propound, I must tell thee thy duty is doubly concern'd therein; both to thy King, and to my selfe. Know then *Ileana* (continu'd he) that our King the great *Claromenes* has dain'd me the honour to make my house his sanctuary; and is at present here conceal'd with my noble Friend *Philarchus* of whom I am sure you have often heard me speak: but to secure them here for any time will be so difficult, and the danger so great on the Kings behalf that I tremble to think of it. That then that I require of you is, that you will take upon you to convey him (if possible) from all those emenent dangers wherewith his Royall person is threatned; which I trust you may safely do, by pretending a visit to your sister, and giving out in the house, that she being fallen sick has sent one to bring you to her; for that Garbe the King is in, may make his pass amongst ours, for one of your Brothers servants: and for *Philarchus* who I intend shall not be seen by any but your selfe, I will ere the day breakes, send before to *Gonsalvos*, who living as he does but a little distant from the Sea, may against such time as you arrive thither with the King, provide a Bark to transport him out of Sicilie.

Leonishus having in these words acquainted *Ileana* with his Design (she repli'd). If you had an intention to try my Obedience sir, it should have been by something wherein my inclinations were averse from yours; but in this which you have now propos'd, my Glory is somuch concern'd, that had my Duty no share in it, I should not scruple to attempt it. Judge then sir, when I have two such powerfull Motives to envite me to so glorious an Enterprise, with what willingness I shall undertake it: nor shall I once consider the hazard wherto I expose my selfe thereby, since were I sure to loose my life, provided I might be but the happie Instrument of my Kings preservation, I should embrace my Destiny with a higher satisfaction then *Iphigenia* became the sacrifice of Greece, and count my Fate too glorious to be lamented.

Leonishus hearing his Daughter speak so generously, was not a little pleas'd to find her such as he had always endeavour'd to render her. But not to loose time, he left her; and went to give *Claromenes* an account by what way he had contrived his escape; which both to the King, and *Philarchus* appear'd so probable as they could not but highly approve of it. After some other discourse, the King desiring to see her who had determin'd so nobly to expose herselfe to the highest danger for his sake, her Father immediatly went and fetch'd her in. Though *Ileana* had never yet beheld the Face of a King but in a Picture, yet the very name struck her with so awefull a respect, and so profound a veneration, that she had not confidence to approach the presence of the Illustrious *Claromenes* without an inward trembling; but being before enform'd by *Leonishus* which was he, with a modest bashfullness she presented herselfe on her knees before him; but he soon rais'd her [fol. 79ᵛ] with a becoming grace, and charming Majesty peculier onely to himselfe.

I have already told your father (said he to her) that as my condition is at present stated I expect not the least Ceremony from him, much less will I accept any from you to whom I shall ever pay a particuler respect for that generous Vertue you express, in proffering so freely to hazard your Life for my preservation; which Obligation how gratfully I resent [feel], Time which makes althings evident shall I trust sufficently demonstrate.

Terme not that an Obligation Dread Sir (repli'd she) which is so much my duty, as should I neglect it, especially now, that Opportunity puts it into my power to performe, however your Majesty might in Clemency pass it by, I should never pardon my selfe such an Omission.

Many other generous expressions having pass'd on both sides, I shall omit them, and onely tell you Madam (continu'd *Arthenia*) that althings being exactly perform'd as had been agreed on, and *Philarchus* dispatch'd away to *Gonsalvo*'s to give notice of the King's coming thither; *Ileana* so well executed what she had undertaken, as she safely conducted her Illustrious Charge even thorough a whole Squadron of the Enemies Cavallrie, who lay so directly in their way as there was no possibility of avoiding them: but by Heavens particuler care they pass'd as quietly as they could have wish't, none in the least suspecting the Daughter of *Leonishus* to have a Royall Servant waiting on her, and at length arriv'd at *Gonsalvo*'s where they found *Philarchus* who had got thither the day before, travelling at a more speedy rate then they could possibly do. Whether being come, the Loyall *Gonsalvo* had in althings acted like himselfe, in taking care for their transportation to Naples, for thither *Philarchus* had enform'd him the King design'd to go. The Barke being in a readiness, and the Wind seting faire for their intended voiage; *Claromenes* thought it requisit instantly to go aboard, not to slip so favourable an opportunity; to which intent, having bid farewell to *Gonsalvo* with this

assurance, that as he was not ignorant of that Fidelity he had always testifi'd to
his Royall Father, and now expresst a continuance of it to himselfe, so he would
never be unmindfull of his past, nor present services to either. But scarce was *Gonsalvo*'s heart larg enough to containe those sentiments of griefe, and Joy which that
Instant strove for precedency in his brest (of griefe to think to what cruell exigents
his Prince had been expos'd by Fortune (or misfortune rather) and Joy, to see he
was so neer a period of his dangers) so that those two contrary passions left him
not the liberty to wish him a prosperous Voiage in such expressions as he desir'd;
yet said he enough to let *Claromenes* see, he had not a more Cordially Faithfull
subject in his Dominions then himself: whereupon, once more biding him adieu
he embark'd with *Philarchus*, and *Ileana* whom he likewise took with him (having
before promis'd *Leonishus* to take no less a care of her then if she were his sister)
knowing Sicilia would be no safe aboad for her if it came once to be known that
she had been [fol. 80ʳ] instrumentall to his escape.

Having a favourable Gale of Wind to waft them from the Sicilian shore, they
soon lost sight of it; and in as short a space as could be expected they arriv'd at their
intended Haven, landing at the first Port Towne in Naples that they came too;
where they made some little stay, onely till such time as they could put themselves
again into a Garbe fit to appear in the Neapolitan Court in: which in a few dayes
being by *Philarchus's* care got ready, they directed their Journey to Court, where
the Joy that was resented [felt] by Queen *Herenia*, the Princess his sister, and the
Prince *Issomantes* his Brother, and divers others to whom he was deservedly deare,
nothing could parallele but those tormenting griefes they suffer'd for his late misfortune; and heartwracking feares which had even in a manner overwhelm'd their
spirits with dispaire of his life; which with too much reason they apprehended lost
if once he fell into the merciless hands of his cruell enemies. To undertake to relate
the reception that the Generous *Ileana* found from all those Illustrious persons
whom either Nature, or Friendship had interested in King *Claromenes's* preservation, with the Caresses, embraces; and acknowledgments she received from them
all; or how highly she was honour'd by all in generall (being regarded as a person
wholly destin'd by Heaven for so glorious a worke) were for me an impossible Task.

Here did the King continue for some yeares; till at length discovering some
secret practices against his person by *Mallinor*[25] the chiefe Minister of state in that
Kingdome, by holding a perticuler (though private) Correspondence with *Ormisdas*; of which, having proofes too manifest to doubt it, he resolv'd to quit Naples;
not deeming it fit to accuse him being so great in power as none durst question
ought he did: since by the authority of the Queen Regent (whose peculier Favourit
he had alwayes been) he intierly ruled the whole affaires of State during the Kings
minority, who was then but an Infant. This *Claromenes* prudently considering, left
that Kingdome, together with the Prince *Issomantes* (knowing the little security

---

[25] The chief minister of France was Cardinal Mazarin.

there was for either of them there since *Mallinor* was become their enemy) and
went to seek a retreat in the Iberian Court;[26] where they were treated with all
imaginable generosity and granduer for the time they made it their aboad: after
which they pass'd into Celtiberia, the Prince whereof had married their eldest
sister the Princess *Marina*;[27] who having not of a long time enjoy'd the felicity
of seeing either of them, wellcom'd them with the highest demonstrations of an
excessive Joy: with whom I will for sometime leave them, and returne to those
things which more perticulerly relate to my selfe.

---

[26] The Iberian Court is Spain.
[27] Princes Mary Henrietta, daughter of Charles I, married William II of Orange of
Holland (Netherlands).

Rivall Friendship

THE FIRST PART

The ~~Sixth~~ ^Seventh^ Book

Perhaps it may with reason be believ'd that scarce ever any so young as I was then, resented [felt] the misfortunes of their Prince with so deep, and afflict-ing a concerne as my selfe, but yet it would not appeare strange to those who knew what sentiments of Loyalty had even in my Infant dayes been infused into my soule by both my Parents; which had such an Influence on me, that I no sooner learn'd to petition Heaven for blessings on my self, but I sent thither my daily Ori-sons to implore the prosperity and wellfaire of my King and with many teares did I lament his last and greatest misfortune: But no sooner was that fatall blow struck but *Mironides* and *Brecena* (so were my Father and Mother call'd) abhorring a place blasted with the contagious breath of those who had put an untimely period to their Soveraigns, resolv'd to quit it; which in a short space after they did; retireing into the Province of Nota to a little village call'd Causa, where they pass'd away divers yeares in that rurall habitation with as much quiet and content as the mis-eries of their Country would permit, deploring them much more then their owne perticuler losses. That which enduced them to chuce this place for their aboad was a desire my Mother had to enjoy the comfort of her sister *Marione's* society who was married to a certaine Gentleman in that Country nam'd *Arnardo*. But now, Griefe made a new assault upon my heart to think on my seperation from *Mer-inza* who was so deservedly deare to me; in which she so sympathiz'd with me, that it was hard to distinguish which of us were the more concern'd. The Gener-ous *Alsinda* her Mother perceiving our mutuall trouble, to mittigate it, obtain'd a promise of *Brecena* that this absence to which we saw our selves destin'd, should be of no long duration, but that I should ere many moneths were past returne to them again: the effect of this promise I found to my great satisfaction; for Luna had not often chang'd her borerow'd light ere I came back to *Gracianus's* where I stay'd neere half a yeare. But then my Duty sommoning me home, which I thought my selfe oblig'd to prefer before the satisfaction of my owne desires which prompted me to wish I might alwayes enjoy the pleasing society of the sweet *Merinza*, I took a second farewell of her with much less regreet then the first, because I was almost [fol. 81ʳ] confident I should not be long detain'd from her.

In my returne home I made some stay at *Arnardo*'s; which *Mariones* intreaties render'd much longer then I designed: the next day after I came thither, she went to waite on *Crisalda* the Duches of Verona (who was her neere Neighbour) tak-ing me with her. But just as we came to *Crisaldas* Gate we were met by a young Gentleman of a good meen [mien] and pleasing aspect, who saluting my Aunt with a Friendly familiarity, told her he was going to waite on *Arnardo*, but would reserve that visit now to some other time; and so turn'd in againe, leading us to the Duches, from whom I receiv'd a very obligeing treatment. We were no sooner seated but he came and placed himselfe by me; and looking so intently on me as he almost put me out of Countenance, admiring [wondering] what mov'd him so heedfully to regard me: but he soon let me know the reason by saying.

If my fancy delude me not Madam I have seen you in Palermo at *Therasmus* his house. I then instantly call'd to mind that going thither to see another of my Mothers sisters nam'd *Hestrina* whom he had married, whilst I was there this Gentleman chanced to come in; but so little notice had I taken of him, as I knew him not again till he reminded me of our meeting there.

Your memory Sir (said I) is much better then mine; for I confess that I had quite forgot that ever I had seen you, but now I very well remember that I saw you there once.

The defect Madam (repli'd he) is not in your memory, but in the inconsiderableness of the object, which merited not from you any perticuler regard; but I am glad however that I have the honour a second time to see you in a place where I have some little interest, and should think my self extreame happie might I but serve you in any thing:

I onely blush'd him an answere, being releas'd from this discourse by the coming in of a Banquet, of which *Crisalda* (taking me by the hand in an obliging manner) invited me to be a pertaker: Having taken our leaves of the Duchess, we would have done the like of him too, but he would needs waite on my Aunt home, though she would willingly have dispenced with that civility. After our returne, so soon as he was gone, I desir'd *Marione* to enforme ^me^ who this person was that appear'd so extreame civill, and obliging, for as yet I knew not who he was.

She then told me his name was *Loreto*, and that he was *Crisalda's* youngest son; she likewise acquainted me then with all those things concerning him whereof I have already enform'd your Majesty (continu'd *Arthenia*) which rais'd in me a very high esteeme of him. She told me moreover, that being constrain'd to quit Sicilie to avoid being made a Prisoner by *Ormisdas* for serving *Clearchus*, he had travers'd most of the Asian countries, enforming himselfe both of their manners and customes, and learning their severall Languages, which he so perfectly attain'd, as none of those Countrymen, but might have mistaken him for one of their owne natives.

But the place (went she on) where he made his longest, and last aboad was in *Armenia*, where he did *Ariobarzarnes* the King thereof such considerable service in his war with *Tigranes* King of Media, [fol. 81ᵛ] that he profer'd him rewards so glorious as might have satisfi'd the most irreguler ambition, if he would continue still in his service; but no recompence how great soever could court his stay abroad when once he had receiv'd *Crisaldas* commands to returne, with an assurance that he might safely venture home, since she had (though with much difficulty) obtain'd from *Ormisdas* a promise not to molest, or trouble him if he acted no more in publick affaires wherein *Claromenes* might be concern'd: for it was not till after *Clearchus* was murder'd, that *Crisalda* got leave for his returne.

What I have now briefly related to your Majesty touching *Loreto* (pursu'd *Arthenia*) *Marionie* gave me more largly the perticulers of, and thereby very much heightned the esteeme I had for him. The next day he gave us a visit, and fail'd not constantly to do so for severall dayes together; so that no day pass'd wherein we had not his company little or much: at all which times he appli'd himselfe perticulerly to me in all his discourses; and endeavour'd alwayes to divert me by severall pleasant relations he made me of things that he had both heard of and seen in his travells: and indeed, to speak the truth I must needs say I thought him the most civill and complacent [complaisant] person that I had ever seen; nor can I deny but that his conversation was very acceptable to me till such time as *Marionie* rais'd in me an apprehension of that which before I had not the least suspition of: for, for my part, I look'd on his demeanour towards me, no otherwise then on civility which oblig'd him to pay somewhat more of respect to a stranger, then to those that were his intimate acquaintance. But *Marionie* taking notice of his so frequent ^visits^ and that extraordinary respect which upon all occasions he express'd towards me, both by his words, and actions, let me understand what her thoughts were; for one day as we were seting alone together she said to me.

Tis to you *Arthenia* certainly that we are oblig'd for the favour of *Loretos* company. What would you say (added she smileing) if you have brought him into that condition from which *Ormisdas* promis'd to exempt him: really (pursu'd she looking more seriously) tis my opinion Love has made him your Prisoner.

If that be his Fate (said I, displeas'd with this discourse) it had been a more favourable one had he been *Ormisdas's* rather then mine; for I perhaps may prove much more severe: but I cannot admit so ill an opinion of *Loretos* judgment as once to fancy he can be guilty of so grand an indiscretion as to throw away a thought on one who can pretend to nothing that may invite him to it.

I will not stand to justifie the reasonableness of what I fancy (repli'd she) lest you think I flatter you; but onely tell you, that admit it should happen as I conceive; and that he should declare a passion for you, grounded on an honourable designe, you would not I hope be somuch your owne enemy as to reject so advantagious a proffer. [fol.82ʳ]

Doubtless (said I) I shall reject all things that may abrid[g]e (much more deprive) me of my freedome, wherein I have placed the sole felicity of my life; nor will I ever willingly admit ought into my breast that may be capable of disturbing, or perhaps destroying that satisfaction I propose to my selfe in the tranquility, and innocence of a Virgine Life.

I'le not deny (repli'd she) but that Virginity has fewer cares to attend it then Marriage has; but as it has less of care, so has it less of comfort too: for trust me Cousin (pursu'd she) who can assure you by experience, that there is more reall satisfaction to be found in the society of an affectionate Husband, then in that imaginary content you promise yourself in the pursuance of a single solitude.

I was so disturb'd with this Discourse, so contrary to my inclinations, as I hearkned to it with such impatience that all the respect I bare *Marionie* was not able to hinder me from shewing the dislike I had of it by my often change of colour; nor was it prevalent enough to have kept me from returning her an answer (perhaps) as little pleasing to her, as what she had said had been to me: but just as I was going to reply, *Arnardo* call'd her away. No sooner was she gone out of the Roome, but I ris up, and taking a Book with me I went into the Garden, intending to pass away an houre or two with it, to divert the ill humour I was in: but long I had not been there before *Loreto* came; and enquiring for me, he was told by one of the servants (that had seen me go into the Garden) where I was; which he no sooner knew but he came to seek me, and at length found me in the most private Arbour I could find.

But so intent was I on what I read, that I heard him not when he came in, which he imagin'd by ^my^ not looking up, nor taking notice of him, wherefore supposeing he might startle me if he spoke to me before I saw him, he made some little noise, which produced the effect he desired; for at it I suddenly turn'd my head about, and seeing him there, I thought

I could do no less then invite him to take a seat, which having done at my intreaty; I ask'd him how he had done to find me out in that Place; and whether it were design, or accident that brought him thither.

I assure Madam (answer'd he) it was designe, not chance that conducted me where you were: for hearing you were gone into the Garden I came with a resolution to find you; and Fortune (I thanke her) was so kind as not to let me search invain, though I expected not to have found you here; and am sorry to see that she who has been so kind to me should be so severe to you as to give you any occation that may move you to seeke out retirements which sutes not with a person of your yeares.

I had no other cause (repli'd I) then my naturall temper which has ever too much inclin'd me to Melancholy, and oft times made me prefer a private converse with my owne thoughts, before a publick conversation, it need not be thought strange if I indulge in my selfe this Inclination: but when I consider my present condition, and think to what I was born, and to what I am now reduced; I think none can justly blame me if I chuse solitude, where I may silently sit, contemplating the Worlds vanity, and Fortunes mutability; and sometime lament her cruelty to me.

If you have hitherto had cause to complain of her ^said he^ you may now dispise her, since tis in your [fol. 82ᵛ] owne power without out[1] her aide to raise your selfe to as high a pitch as that from whence she forced you to descend: tis

---

[1] The scribe incorrectly writes "without out" [sic].

but accepting the Present I have made you of a Heart which never bow'd to any one before, nor never yet knew what subjection meant till it was Fetter'd by your Charmes, which it had as little the Will as Power to resist. Your victory Faire *Arthenia* (continu'd he) is absolute, be then so generous as to treat your Captive with moderation, and tyranize not by cruelty or disdaine ore him who to your eyes with Joy gave up his liberty; and has vow'd to love, nay to adore you farre above all Mortalls whilst he breathes.

So strangly was I surpriz'd at a declaration I so little expected, that I had not the power to interrupt him, but suffer'd him a great while to go on at this rate: but at last recovering out of my amaze, darting a look at him wherein he might have read the displeasure he had given me.

Cease *Loreto* I conjure you (repli'd I) to pursue a discourse I neither understand, nor ever will approve; nor can I longer lend an eare to it without offending my Vertue. I know tis usuall with persons of your sex to make it their study and employment to screw themselves so far into the affections of poor innocent Virgins as to rob them of their hearts, perhaps their honours; cunningly masking their base designes under a Faire Vizard painted with pretences of the truest love: but having once attain'd their ends, they quickly throw off the disguise, proudly insulting o're those seely [silly] Creatures they have ruin'd by their dissemulations, or else with scoffes deriding them; protesting they lov'd but in sport, and courted them on no other score but for diversion sake.

I confess (said *Loreto*) too many such there are who are unworthy that the earth should beare them; and justly merit to be abhorred by all men that have any true sense of honour in them, being no less injurious to us then you: since let our passions be ne're so great, confirm'd with the truest protestations that tongue can utter, the one is not valu'd, nor the other credited. But Madam, none shall ever find *Loretos* name in that black Lists; for as my passion for you is transcendant, so shall it be endless, and pure as it is perfect: for you would have reason not onely to detest, but fly me as a horrid Monster ready to devoure you, could I so highly sinne against your Vertue, as to admit one thought into my brest, or cherish one single desire that might in the least degree be injurious to that (which I will not scruple to avow) I prize highest in you; for though it was your beauty that first caught my eyes, I had perhaps resisted it no less successfully then I have done that of others; since I have seen the most dazling beauties that Europe, and Asia both can boast, and yet have been unconcern'd; but t'was that Vertue that I am perswaded you are absolute Mistress of which made my heart your willing Prisoner. Then think not Madam that my respects for you are attended with ought but honour; nor that I have any other design then to lay both my self and Fortune at your Feet, wishing no greater glory, nor satisfaction then to make my selfe yours by Hymens sacred tye.

If that passion you pretend (repli'd I) speak no other Dialect I must needs confess I have less reason to be offended with it then I late believ'd; but were it yet more innocent, I must [fol. 83ʳ] conjure you to abandon it lest it disturbe your

quiet, and hinder my repose, by the trouble your perseverance may create me, to
find my selfe reduced to a necessity of becoming ungratfull: for I'le deall clearly
with you, that you may owe your sufferings to your owne obstinacy, not my ~~will~~
severity (as haply you may terme it) I have so great a hatered, and destestation to
that fond extravagance call'd Love, that I had rather rip my heart from out my
breast, than suffer a thought that favour'd it to enter there. Then hope not that I
will ere accept, what I can ne're requite: nor do I prize my liberty at so low a rate
as to exchange it for slavery, or prefer the tyranique yoak of marriage before it;
not that I account all wemen slaves, or think all men are Tyrants to their Wives;
but if they are not they are at least capable of becoming so when ere they please.
Content your selfe then *Loreto* with that esteeme I have for you and seek no more
lest you loose what you have already gain'd.

   With that, not alowing him time to reply, I ris up, complaining of the coldness of the Aire, and quited the Arbour in such hast as I took from him the
opportunity of proffering me his hand to lead me in had he design'd it. With all
the speed I could make I got to my Chamber intending to lock up my self till
he was gone; but he follow'd me not as I had apprehended, but went immediatly
home, as I perceiv'd, looking thorow the Glass of the Window; whereupon so
soon as I had a little composed my selfe I ventur'd downe in hopes I should no
more that day be importun'd with the sight of *Loreto* which I thought of nothing
somuch now as shunning.

   But he still continnu'd his accustomed visits, coming constantly every day
to *Arnardo's* where, though I could not avoid seeing him, yet I took such care as
I was sure he deriv'd but little satisfaction from that advantage; for I so contriv'd
it as I never affoarded him so much as one minutes converse in private for many
dayes that I stay'd there, though I perceiv'd he diligently courted all occasions
of renewing his addresses, which I no less solicitously shun'd; so that he was
constrain'd to let his eyes speak what I suffer'd not his tongue to utter; and make
his sighes the silent Oratours of that passion he had pretended: wherfore to put
an end to that trouble of his which I had innocently created, or at least to my
owne of being a spectatour of it, I thought it requisit that I return'd home, hoping
that when he ceas'd to see me, he might in a little time regaine that quiet which
seem'd to have abandon'd him: but when I motion'd my departure, both *Arnardo*
and my Aunt appear'd so averse to it, and declar'd I would so highly disoblige
them if I would not afford them my Company longer, that in complacence [com-
plaisance] I was forced to resolve to stay with them for the space of ten days more:
but all that time I made my selfe an absolute Prisoner, confining my self to the
house, not dareing to stir out lest I might chance to meet *Loreto*.

   But being one day enform'd that he was to go the next morning to Palermo
with his two Brothers, I thought I might securely venture to take the Aire, which
I design'd to do in a most pleasant Grove *Arnardo* had neer to his house, where
the prety Birds perpetually chanted their rurall Carrolls; and many little Rivo-
lets, on the bankes whereof (cut [fol. 83ᵛ] on purpose to bring Water thither from

a River not far distant) grew all sorts of curious flowers, planted ~~more~~ ^rather^ there by Art then Nature; which rendr'd this place of all that I had seen the most delightfull. And rising more early the next morning then I usually did, not staying to dress me, but in my night Attire taking one of *Mariones* maides (call'd *Ethrea*) with me I went out, intending to pass away an houre or two in that delightfull Place. Having walk'd so long till I had almost tir'd my selfe, I sate downe on one of the seates (which were plac'd there for such a purpose) to repose me; sending *Ethrea* to gather some Violets and other Flowers (such as the Spring yeelded) to make me a Nosegay: but no sooner was she out of sight, but I espi'd a man coming towards me in the Allie where I sate (though at a good distance off) in the posture of a person possest with a deep Melancholy; his pace was slow, his Armes foulded one within the other, his Hat pull'd low over his Eyes, which kept me from knowing him at first sight; but when he came neerer I soon knew him to be *Loreto* whom I believed to have been neer arriv'd at his Journeys end by that time.

I no sooner saw t'was he, but I repented I had sent *Ethrea* away, and would have call'd her back had she been within hearing: Fancying he had not seen me yet, I thought if I could but obscure my selfe behind a Tuft of Trees which grew not far from me I might possibly escape his sight; resolving so soon as he was past to go in with all the speed I could: but hasting to fast to that shelter I had design'd I stumbled so as I could not recover my self but fell downe on the ground; the noise I made in falling caus'd *Loreto* to look up, and seeing me downe, he advanced with all the hast he could make to help me up; but not staying for his assistance, I quickly ris and pursu'd my intention: which he perceiving, instantly guess'd that to avoid meeting him I made such winged speed away; which mov'd him to call to me.

[F]or Heavens sake *Arthenia* (cry'd he) stay, and give me not cause to think you fly me as a Monster that sought to devoure you. If I have done ought that has offended you I am ready to give you my life in reparation of my Crime. I thinking it in vain ^to stir^ since he had seen me made a stope, and heard him proceed in this manner. I'le dye if you command me; and in that Command, believe it you will be less cruell then in compelling me to suffer Torments so great as the severest Death would be much more supportable; without affording me somuch ease as to complain unless it be to these Trees which are as deafe as you are pityless.

Were those torments you complaine of, as reall (repli'd I turning about) as I believe them feigned, or at least to have no other being then what your Fancy, or imagination may create; I know no reason you would have to charge me with them, since I never did any thing that might occation those torments you complain of: if you will suffer your passion to overcome your reason, can I help that: if I have already told you with all imaginable Candor and sincerity, and once again I will repeat it, that [fol. 84ʳ] I was born with an antipathy to Love; then if you will accuse any of severity it ought rather to be those starres that rul'd my birth, then me.

Ah Madam (cry'd he) do not adde injustice to your severity, in believeing me guilty of so grand a dissemulation as to endeavour to create a beliefe in you that I suffer by your cruelty if it were not as great a truth as tongue can utter; yet great as my sufferings are, I would be content to indure them, and that with patience too, were I but assur'd, this aversion you oppose my felicity with would but extend it selfe to all others as well as *Loreto*: then do but promise Madam that if ever Heaven date a change in your inclinations (so that you may be won either by the services or affection of any one to love) I may be onely he who may boast the being happy in yours: assure me but this, and I will vow never more to importune you with my offencive passion, but silently to wait till Heaven daine to be propitious to my desires.

Had I the free disposall of my selfe (repli'd I) so that I might without controule follow my owne Inclinations, I durst, nay would, engage to this which you request, might it any way tend to your satisfaction; but since my Will depends on that of *Mironides* and *Brecena* to whom Heaven has given an absolute power to dispose of me as they think fit; so that perhaps at one time or other they may command me to alter my condition: though if they would give me the freedome to continue alwayes as I am, I should embrace that liberty with a much higher satisfaction then the most advantagious match they could propose to me; yet how much soever I am weded to a single life, I should questionless force my inclinations to comply with their Wills; and then though I might find it difficult, perhaps impossible to affect him whilst onely a lover, yet when once my Husband, my Duty certainly would teach me how to love him then.

But admit Madam (said *Loreto*) they should e[n]joyne you to make one your choice whose humour and disposition were utterly disagreeable to your owne; and for whose person you might have no less aversion then you declare against Love; would you yet pay them so blind an obedience as to submit to such a Command.

I have hitherto found them so indulgent to me in all respects that I have little cause to apprehend any such harsh treatment from them; but if it should so happen that my hopes, or expectations should be frustrate on this account, I should nevertheless pay that obedience which I owe to all the Lawfull Commands of my Parents (repli'd I) and find however that satisfaction in the performance of my Duty, which I could not in the person of him who was so impos'd upon me.

If this be your resolution (said he) give me leave to hope, that if I may be so fortunate as to obtain the consent of *Mironides* to make you mine, that you will not be less favourable to me, then any other he should grant that favour too.

I hearing him say so, repented I had ^made^ so ingenious [ingenuous] a discovery of my mind, fearing he might take advantage of what I had said; which to prevent I answer'd him in this manner.

Though I have so freely acknowledg'd to you my intentions; if you design thereby to circumvent me by endeavouring to incite my Father to force me to confer on you that which you ought never [fol.84ᵛ] to pretend too with^out^ my permission, I declare you would by such a way so far insense me, that I cannot tell whether that respect and esteeme I have for you, may not be chang'd into aversion; and though haply I might in obedience to *Mironides* espouse you, I believe the content you would reap thereby would be but little satisfactory to you; since as little as I know of Love, or its effects, I cannot be ignorant of this, that where the affection is not mutuall there ^can^ ~~call~~ but little felicity be found for either Party.

Must I ~~onely~~ then (cry'd he) be the onely person excepted in the generall; this is no less severe then strange; since you affirme you would receive from your Fathers hand a man that you hated, and yet refuse (though authorized by his permission) to gratifie the affection of one you declare you honour with your esteeme. You have shewne me a Path which might conduct me to happiness, and yet tell me if I pursue it I shall at the end of it meet my ruine.

What I have said (repli'd I) will not seeme so strange if you consider the reason which induced me to spake as I did; for since I have so clearly acquainted you with my resolutions you cannot but think I should have much more cause to conceive a prejudice against you, then any other that were ignorant of my mind in this perticuler; because such a Design in you would look as if you resolv'd to compell me (now that you knew the way) to be yours indespight of me: which I should regard as so high a disrespect as it would be very difficult, if not impossible for me not to hate you.

Farre be the least thought of any such intent from me (answer'd *Loreto*) for though I love you with the greatest passion that ever any soule can be inspir'd with, and that my felicity absolutly depends on a reciprocall returne, yet had I rather be forever the most miserable of men by being deni'd it, then attempt to make my selfe happie by any way you might justly disapprove.

This answere (continu'd *Arthenia*) which some perhaps might have imputed to indifferency, I look'd on as a mark of his respect; being of an opinion, that none love so well as those who are most fearefull to displease, or disoblige them whom they pretend a kindness for.

But (pursu'd he after a little silence, as it were to hearken what return I would make) must so perfect a passion, so sacred a respect as this I pay you insensible *Arthenia* obtaine nothing more then a bare esteeme which signifies little to an almost dispairing Lover. I have given you a heart whereof I was absolute Master till that minute I became yours. I have at your Feet resign'd my liberty, and would as freely give up my life if you command it, as a witness to confirme the truth of what I have protested; and all this the Gods can tell (who only know the sincerity of my soule) without the least designe or hope your Vertue might disallow; for that I beare too high a regard too, to admit a thought which if known to you, you might account injurious to it: but Madam tis so naturall to desire some acknowledgment, as you cannot blame me for desiring to inspire you with some part of that affection to which I have devoted my whole life: but if I must not hope to be so happy as to obtain from you a mutuall esteeme, deny me not your pitty; if you neither can, nor will conferre on me you[r] Love, yet let compassion at least incline you to commiserate the sufferings of him whom your insensibility has [fol.85 r] rendred the most miserable man that breathes.

I have heard (repli'd I) pitty is so neer alli'd to Love, that should I suffer my selfe to be touch'd with the one, I should find it difficult to defend my selfe from the other: but however could I but believe those sufferings you complain of were any other then imaginary ones, I should doubtless run the hazard how great soever, rather then not afford you my pitty.

Oh insensible *Arthenia* (cry'd he) Heaven grant you be not punish'd for this incredulity, and that you never suffer for another what I feel for you.

If I do (said I) I believe I shall never come to make my complaints to you: with that, looking about for *Ethrea* I perceiv'd her hard by, and being resolv'd to pursue this discourse no further, I call'd her to me, and biding *Loreto* goodmorrow I left him though he importunately desir'd leave to wait on me in.

When I saw *Ethrea* so nigh me I presently apprehended she had overheard what had pass'd between *Loreto* and my selfe; at least what was last said, which made me feare she would acquaint *Marione* with it; which if she did, I assur'd my selfe my Aunt would second him in his persecution of me; for so I then counted his Addresses. At first I thought if it were so that she had been privie to our discourse, if I enjoyed her secrecy she might be silent; but then I thought again, that in case she had not heard us I should by that way but discover what I desir'd should be conceal'd; so that at last I determin'd to take no notice to her of it, but to let happen what would. But as I at first conjectur'd, so it was, for soon after we came in she told her Lady so much as fully acquainted her with *Loretos* passion and the coldness wherewith I entertain'd it. For that day she [Marione] took no notice to me of it, but the next, *Loreto* coming thither according to his usuall custome, whether it were that she really perceiv'd more sadness in his lookes then ordinary, or that she onely fanci'd so I cannot tell; but as soon as I had left the Roome (which I did after he had been there some little time) she took notice to him of that alteration she had remark'd in him; pressing him very earnestly to tell her the cause of it: but t'was not all her intreaties could prevaile with him to disclose to ~~him~~ her what she seem'd so desirous to know, but onely procur'd from him this civill, though not satisfactory answere.

I am sorry Madam (said he) my Face should become such a tell Taile as without my permission to publish what I was oblig'd to hide with the greatest care; but seeing it has so contrary to my intentions discouer'd to you that no slight, or ordinary discontent has seated it selfe within my brest, I must beg your pardon if I acquaint you not with the occation of it, which I cannot do without drawing on me the displeasure of a person on whose favour depends all my felicity; then since I am bound by such an indispensable necessity to conceale from all the World (but those who are concern'd in it) what you desire the knowledge of, I hope you will be so just as not to impute it to a distrust of your Friendship that I deny your request; for that I am so far from, that did my life onely depend upon any thinge

I might disclose to you, believe it I would have [fol.85ᵛ] prevented [anticipated] your desires.

She then finding that she could not draw from him a confession which might confirme what *Ethrea* had told her, she resolv'd to acquaint him with what she already knew; and thereby let him understand t'was rather a desire to serve him then an ignorance of what disturb'd him which moov'd her to enquire into his Concerns: having performed what she had design'd, he repli'd.

I am really glad Madam that you know without my haza[r]ding *Arthenia's* anger by disclosing to you that she is the onely Object both of my Love and Griefe; for somuch do I believe you to be my Friend as I cannot once admit a ~~bot~~ doubt that you will ever in the least oppose what in the World I am most ambitious of.

Since you assure me (answer'd she) your happiness depends upon my Nieces gratifying that kindness you have honoured her with, it shall be my endeavour to assist you (as far as it rests in my ability) in the obtaining what hitherto ^you have^ su'd for invain; but in that I am onely sorry I cannot give you a more difficult proofe of my Friendship, since herein I can act nothing that will not look as if I regarded *Arthenias* advancement rather then *Loretos* content.

Those that can have such unworthy thoughts of so high a favour (repli'd he) may he be forever deni'd the fruition of what he most passionatly desires.

The effect of *Marione's* promise I quickly found; for no sooner was *Loreto* gone but she let me know she had been enform'd by her Maid both of his kindness to me, and my severity (as she term'd it) to him; and in this manner reprov'd me for it. Never till now *Arthenia* (said she) did I question your discretion, but now you give me just occation to do so; and not onely me, but all persons that shall heare with what obstinacy you reject *Loreto's* affection, who certainly is every way so well quallifi'd as none but you would be so blind as to refuse him: but say *Arthenia* (went she on) what makes you disapprove his passion; is it any perticuler dislike you have either to his Person, qualities, or estate: but sure your aversion springes from none of these, since he is both young, and handsome (as I believe you will grant) his birth noble, his education resembling; and to pass by all other things in him which may merit your esteeme, I'le onely mind you of his Courage, that being a quallity I have oft heard you say ^you^ lov'd, and admir'd in any man, and hated all such as were not endu'd with it; but of his he has given such notable proofes as Armenia no less then Sicilie can testifie his Valour: and though he has at present no great reason to boast the largness of his possessions, yet you know very well he has the assurance of so plentious an estate in the future, as in the height of your Fortunes you could not reasonably have ^pretended^ to greater advantages then with him you may attaine too.

I'le not deny (repli'd I) but that *Loreto* merits all that you have said of him, and perhaps more; but I have often heard there is no reason to be given for Love; nor can I yeeld any for my aversion, which has onely his passion, not him for its object: for let him but divest himself of that, and I shall not faile to pay him the same respect as formerly I shew'd him.

Methinkes tis strang (said she) that you should conceive a prejudice against him [fol. 86^r] for no other reason but because he loves you. Were his pretences attended with any unworthy or ignoble design, you might justly then not onely slight but hate him I confess; but when he has so seriously protested his respects for you are full of honour, meere gratitude methinkes should teach you to entertaine his kindness with more civility. But perhaps (pursu'd she) you are doubtfull of his reallity, or fearfull he may deceive you through Inconstancy.

I shall never be concern'd (repli'd I) for the truth of that which I care not to believe; nor shall I feare to loose what I desire not to keep.

Well *Arthenia* (said she) time I hope will change your mind, and let you see how much to blame you are to neglect a reall good, to follow a fancied satisfaction, which you propose to your selfe in the pursuance of a single life; but be not altogether lead by Fancy, nor guided onely by the dictates of your Inclinations which makes you preferre Virginity before a married Life; I'le not deny but the first is the happier estate in many respects, but as your condition is now stated, it cannot in probability be so for you: for do but consider Deare Niece (continu'd she) that by the course of Nature you ought to expect the death of your Parents to preceed your owne; and then if Heaven take them from you, as it has already rendred them uncapable of providing for you after their discease, think then I say how deplorable your condition would be, should you be expos'd (young as you are) to the wide World, destitute of Friends, support, or maintainance; subject to all the blowes of Fortune, and miseries that necessity (that cruell Mistress) can overwhelme you with; which without doubt would be the more insupportable to you by reason of that tenderness wherewith you have been always bred by your indulgent Parents who have not onely endeavour'd to render your education agreeable to your birth, but have likewise maintain'd you in a garbe much above their present fortune; in hopes (possibly by that meanes) to preferre you: and now that Fate seemes to condescend to their designe, by puting it in your owne power to advance your selfe, by proffering you the legitimate affections of a Gentleman every way worthy of you; why will you be somuch your owne Foe as to oppose your better Fortune by such a slighting, coy, disdainfull carriage as that wherewith you treat *Loreto*. But I'le leave you (added she) to consider of what I have said, and perhaps if you will but seriously reflect on it, you will find divers reasons that may enduce you to embrace what you have hitherto declin'd:

Finishing those words she left me; and no sooner was I alone but I obey'd her last injunction, by intently pondering in my mind the whole summe of her discourse; which after I had done I found, though all the Arguments she had us'd were not powerfull enough to alter my inclinations; yet my Reason was convinced I ought rather to cherish *Loreto's* Flame then to extinguish it. But this was not the onely time wherein *Marione* became his Advocate; for all the time that I continu'd with her she so incessantly pleaded in his behalfe, that the Fortress

of my heart which had till then held out against the Forces of his importunities
began to yeeld to her ~~his~~ perswasions. But notwithstanding I firmly resolv'd
never [fol.86 ᵛ] to let him know the interest he had in me, till I were as undoubtedly perswaded of his Fidelity, as I was convinced of the reallity of his Love.

But now, my Mother thinking I had been long enough absent, sent for me
home; but many dayes had not pass'd ere *Marione* made my Mother a visit purposly to enforme her and my Father of those Overtures *Loreto* had made me;
how they resented [felt about] this information I know not, but I guess'd it to be
very well approv'd of by them, by the reception they gave him when he came to
our house, as in a short while after he did with my Aunt, pretending he came to
waite on her thither; but after that, he could find the way alone by himselfe, and
needed her no more to introduce him. He was quickly no less favour'd both by
Mironides and *Brecena* in his addresses then he had been by *Marione*, for he never
came but I was call'd to entertaine him, and as great a freedome of converse with
me allow'd him as he could have wish'd; and if he deriv'd not much satisfaction
from those visits he made me, t'was onely to that indifferency wherewith I still
treated him that he could impute it: yet I cannot but acknowledge that I believe
Love began to make some little impression in my heart; for his company was now
less tiresome then it had been of late; nor were the protestations of his Love any
longer offencive: yet nevertheless so reserv'd was my demeanour towards him, as
he would oft complain to *Marione* that I gave him more cause to dispaire then
hope ever to be happy in my favour; however he continu'd his addresses, but with
so respective a perceverance, as had my aversion to Love been as great as ever, I
could hardly have conceiv'd any displeasure thereat.

For sometime he conceal'd his Amour from being taken notice of, by pretending business with my Father; but it was not long it could be hid under that
Cloud: for divers in the Village where we lived (who had observ'd his so often
frequenting our house) began to suspect what drew him thither, in which suspition they were confirm'd by the stay I made at home, so much longer then
usuall. This conjecture no sooner got into the heads of some busy persons who
took delight in creating newes if they knew none to tell: but that which at first
was onely whisper'd soon grew a publick discourse, so that in a short space nothing was somuch talk'd of in Causa ~~then~~ ^as^ *Loretos* love to me; some confidently affirming that we were suddenly to be married; but had they consulted
his opinion, he would doubtless have let them understand the little reason they
had to affirme that was so neer a consummation, which he himself as yet had but
small hopes of ever effecting.

I'le not deny, but that I had now more of kindness then indifferency for
him; yet not somuch as could incline me to a thought of being his till such time
as he was possest of that which he onely enioy'd in expectation. I confess when
I heard what was reported I was not a little troubled for feare lest it might reach
Crisalda's eares, which if it did, I knew how prejudiciall it might (and I belie'd
would) prove to *Loreto* whose present Fortunes depended chiefliest on her; for

though he was intituled to a very considerable estate by an Uncle of his, who at his Death made him his Heire, yet had he not, nor was he to have the possession of it till after the death of *Leonora* his Lady who surviv'd him many yeares: but however the Duke [fol.87ʳ] of Verona (whom till now I had no occation to mention) knowing *Loreto* to be so well provided for, took no further care for him, but dying divided his estate between his two elder sons, bequeathing him nought but a Fathers blessing; leaving both his education, and subsistance to *Crisalda's* care till such time as *Leonora's* death might put him in possession of what by her life he was detain'd from.

Knowing then (as I did) how his condition was stated, I could not but imagine *Crisalda* would be strangly incenced against her son for throwing his affections away so lavishly on one from whom he could derive no advantage: what I apprehended soon after hapned, for *Crisalda* having some little intelligence of it, resolving to know the truth, caus'd one of her woemen that waited on her to suborne a servant of *Loreto's* by the promise of a great reward to betray his Master by discovering to her this secret which he had indiscreetly trusted him with: but this I must needs acknowledge my selfe the occation of, by an absolute prohibition I gave him not to write to me; assuring him if he did, I would not answere his letters: but in this I must confess I was more nice then wise; for hereby he was constrain'd to make his man privie to many things which he had no other way but by him to acquaint me with.

In fine Madam (continu'd *Arthenia*) *Crisalda* was enform'd of all that had pass'd concerning *Loreto* and I; and as I had guess'd she would; so was she extreamly troubled; and the rather in regard she knew not what course she had best take to frustrate his intentions as she resolv'd to do one way or other: At first she thought best to curbe that passion he had for me by that authority she had over him as his Mother; but then she consider'd, t'was probable should she endeavour by violence to stop the current of his Love, it might probably render it more fervent: therfore she fanci'd it best to dissemble what she knew, and procure some person or other whom Friendship had given a perticuler interest in him to disswade him from the pursute of that which she look'd on as his utter ruine: and finding none more fit to undertake this task then *Arnardo* whom she had alwayes found very cordially affected to her; having severall times had occation to have recourse both to his Councell, and assistance in divers matters of concernment since the death of the Duke her Husband; and knowing withall that *Loreto* had a more then ordinary kindness for him, and therefore might the more easily be wrought upon by his perswasions to abandon me, and fix his thoughts upon some other: but when she remembred *Arnardo* was related to me, she had some little doubt whether ~~or no~~ he would serve her faithfully in this Designe: But this scruple was needless, but *Arnardo* was too generous not to prefer his Friendship before the interest of a Relation; especially one who could clame no other of him then what was deriv'd from his marriage with *Marione*. But at length *Crisalda* waving all Considerations sent for *Arnardo*, and imparted to him what she had heard of her sons passion, earnestly conjuring him to use his uttmost endeavour to hinder the Union between him and I; which he promis'd to do, if it lay within the compass of his power.

Of this (pursu'd *Arthenia*) I was as then ignorant; being gone a few dayes before to the [fol.87ᵛ] *Duke of Felinus's*, having in my opinion been absent wholle ages from *Merinza's* beloved company: but besides I̶ ̶w̶a̶s̶ ̶w̶i̶l̶l̶i̶n̶g̶ the desire I had to see her, I was willing to leave Causa for a season to try if my absence would allay those rumours which I could not but think had spread too farre; further it seemes then I imagin'd, since they reach'd Palermo assoon as I, or else *Telamour* could not have told you my Lord (added she looking on *Gentillus*) what he did of my Concerns; for I had not been above two or three dayes with *Merinza* ere I went to my Cousins to see that Funurall you mention'd, where I had the honour to see you: and now my Lord I believe you begin to be of an oppinion that I was not then that happie person you took me to be; for though all I had hitherto suffer'd deserv'd not the title of misfortunes, compar'd with those I have, and still must undergoe; yet had I never sustain'd greater Infelicities ^then^ those my Parents were involved in, I had certainly no great cause to boast of Fortunes favours.

I confess Madam (answer'd he) I was much mistaken in my beliefe concerning you, for I verily thought you had been one whom Fate ne're frown'd on; but I see appearances are oft deceitfull.

With that he was silent, and *Arthenia* went on. I went not into the Country (as *Gentillus* thought when I left *Tellamours*) but back to *Merinza* again with whom I continu'd neer a quarter of a yeare; but in all that time I neither saw *Loreto* nor heard one sillable of him, which I much admir'd [wondered] at; not that I thought it strang he writ not to me, (because I had formerly enioyn'd e̶n̶j̶o̶ him the contrary) but by reason he sent not *Hermis* to enquire of my wellfare, nor came himselfe to see me as he had promis'd when he took his leave of me at my coming from Causa. I knew the distance of 12 miles would have been of no consequence to have detain'd him from me so long, had he no other reason to obstruct his coming; nor could I imagine, since he would not be perswaded to restrain his frequent visits in a place where they were more observ'd then he could have wish'd they might, that he would forbeare my sight now that I was i̶n̶ where there was not a person in the wholle Family but would have taken a perticuler satisfaction (as he very well knew) in any thinge that tended to my good: but it was not long that I remain'd ignorant of what occation'd this neglect (as I accounted it) for *Arnardo* calling one day to see me, as we were talking, amongst other questions, ask'd me when I saw *Loreto*.

Never since I came hither Sir (said I).

And do you not wonder at it (repli'd he) but methinks you should not (added he not giving me time to answere) if you have heard how much he is *Madonas* servant, and with what an assidious diligence he courts her, or her wealth; it will be then no mervaile he cannot spare time to waite on you.

I was something surprize'd at what I so little expected, or suspected indeed; yet I retain'd so much moderation as calmly to tell him t'was newes I had not heard.

You may believe then (said he) I tell you nothing but what I am confident is true; and let me advize you Cousin as a Friend (pursu'd [fol. 88^r] he taking me by the hand) not lightly to credit all that carries a shew of reallity: men are fickle, and oft times make larg promises, which are follow'd by slow, or no per-formances:

I having thank'd him for this friendly Caution, he bid me adue; leaving me in much disorder. No sooner was he gone, but I went to my Chamber, and fast-ning the Dore that none might enter to disturbe me; I sate me downe to think what might occation this so sudden change in *Loreto*: love to *Madona* I was sure it could not be, since she was one to whom Nature had been no less spareing, then Fortune had been prodigall of her bounties; for I never heard that she was counted tollerably handsome in her youth, much less could she now be thought soe; now I say, that she was so far advanced in yeares that had *Loreto* married her, she had doubtless been taken rather for his Grandmother then his Wife, being at that time above three score and ten yeares of age.

But if I had no reason to apprehend such a Rivall; if I reflected on her youth, or beauty, yet when I consider'd the vastness of that wea^l^th that she was mis-tress off, and how that she was not more loaded with yeares then riches, I could not thinke it strang if *Loreto* had swallow'd that Golden Bait which most men in these dayes so eagerly catch at, counting nothing ugly that can but be mask'd with ^a^ gilded Vizard. However I found some pleasure in perswading my self (as I did) that it was *Madonas* wealth, not person that he courted; from which I believ'd he would derive but little satisfaction though he obtain'd her, being so exceedingly Covetous as I was almost confident she would never suffer him to become Master of her estate whilst she herselfe was living to enjoy it. But yet the small content I fancied he would find in his Venerable Mistress afforded me not half the satisfaction, as it gave me a trouble to be so unhandsomely abandon'd by him after so many protestations as he had made me of an eternall Constancy; and immovable affection. I must acknowledge he had at that time a greater interest in me then ere I did designe him; for so well I lov'd him then, as I verily thought it an impossibility for me ever to admit so much of kindness for any other, though I had never had the confidence to owne it to him; but was desirous he should rather gain assurances of my esteeme from my actions then my words. But how-ever I very much blam'd my self then, for being conscious of a passion misplaced on one who by his slighting me I deem'd onely worthy of my highest scorn.

Ah *Arthenia* (said I to my self) how couldest thou be guilty of so great a van-ity as once to fancy that ought [aught; anything] in thee could be capable of fix-ing the wavering affections of a Man, then which thou hast been often told the Wind is not more subject to mutability; but thou (it seemest) wouldest credit no other witness but experience, which sure will now convince thee of it, and make thee see how much a Fool thou wert, to let thy Freedome be blown away by the breath of idle courtship, and Airie protestations which quickly vanish, [fol. 88ᵛ] even in that very Aire that helps to forme them; but I now find (pursu'd I) it is a destiny attends poor Maids to be neglected sosoon as they begin to love: but this comfort I have yet left me, to know *Loreto* has no great cause to boast of mine; and possibly tis for that reason, that he has so slender an assurance of my affection that he takes this course to sound my Inclinations; by a seeming Inconstancy to try if by my resentment of his change he could discover how I stood affected towards him: but this Design, if it were his, I determin'd to countermine; for I resolv'd when I saw him next (as I question'd not but I should some time or other) to let him understand I was not ignorant of his descerting me, but in so unconcern'd a manner, as if I had no interest in his change.

This a few dayes gave me the opportunity to put in practice; for not long after, one Afternoon as I was passing thorow the Hall I was met by a Kinswoman of *Loreto's* call'd *Dionella* (who was the onely person of his owne Relations that he had acquainted with his passion) and her Daughter the Faire *Ardelia*, who for the sweetness of her voice, and excellency of her skill was very much admir'd by all that knew her: this young lady I had never seen, though I had oft desir'd it; but seeing her with *Dionella* I presently fanci'd it might be her (as indeed it was) having saluted them, and going to take *Dionella* by the hand to lead her into the Parlour, she turn'd about to speak to a man who came with them which till then I had not heeded; but casting my eye upon him I knew him to be *Hermis* ~~*Hariga*~~, *Loreto's* man: the sight of him instantly set me into such a trembling, as I could hardly have conceal'd from *Dionella* the disorder I was in, had she not been busied in demanding of ^*Hermis*^ ~~*Hariga*~~ if he had not a message to deliever me from his master: whereupon seeing him coming towards me, I step'd a little back expecting what he had to say; at which bowing his head down to my eare he told me (in a low voice) that his Master intended to wait on me within an houre, and beg'd I would so contrive it, as ^he^ might have the favour of one half houres discourse with me in private.

Having understood he had no more to say; you may tell your Master (answer'd I very coldly) if any convenient opportunity hapens I shall not deny to gratifie his request; but if not, I shall not rack my invention to satisfie his desire: with that, turning from him I pursu'd my first intention, leading the Lady into the Roome where *Alsinda* and *Merinza* were sitting who were very well acquainted with them both. Well was it for me that there were others to entertaine *Dionella* and her Daughter, for I was so taken up with thinking how to carry my self to *Loreto* when he came, that I was thereby rendred altogether unfit for conversation.

My chiefest care was to fortifie that resolve I had made, to appear to him wholly unconcern'd; and not to seem in the least dejected, but if it were possible, so [fol. 89ʳ] farre to master my resentments [sentiments] as to assume a more then ordinary gaiety and mirth both in my countenance and humour; this was to me no little difficulty in regard I could never in my life act a dissemblers part.

An houre was scarce past ere *Loreto* came according to his promise; and as if Fate
had conspir'd to gratifie him *Alsinda* commanded *Merinza* to shew *Ardelia* the
Gardens which she had a great desire to see; no sooner was this command given
but *Merinza* lead her out, and I instantly follow'd thinking it my duty to wait
on them. We had been but a very little while in the Garden, before *Loreto* came
after us, and overtaking me being at a little distance behind them (having stay'd
to gather some Flowers with an intent to present them to *Ardelia*) he ceaz'd one
of my hands, and fixing his lips on it with so much ardour, as made me almost
disbelieve what I had been enform'd concerning him; beging me not to make
such hast to overtake the Ladies in their walk but to allow him that opportunity
to impart something to me that he had an earnest desire to acquaint me with.

To which I repli'd, that I thought there was not any thing that he could com-
municate to me now of such consequence as could excuse the rudeness I should
commit in declining the company of his ~~comp~~ Cousin and the Princess *Merinza*,
(since *Ardelia* was altogether a stranger to me, and therefore ought to be treated
with the more respect) to hold a private conferrence with him: nor should you
(pursu'd I) who know so well what belongs to civility and good manners, desire
me to do a thing so contrary to its rules.

I do not understand (said he) but that we may sometimes without offence
(especially when necessity does in a manner constrain it) dispence with a ceremonious punctilio ~~punilio~~ of civility, for the obtaining a satisfaction of more
importance: but methinkes being so intimate as you are with *Merinza* (pursu'd
he) you need not feare a censure from her; and for my Cousin I dare assure you,
she will rather inpute your quiting their conversation to a constraint impos'd on
you by me, then any will in you to desert them; for she cannot but think I would
willingly lay hold on any occation that may give me the happiness of a private
converse, since she is not ignorant of that passion I have for you.

For me *Loreto* (said I looking on him with a smile) sure you mistake; you are
speaking to *Arthenia*, not *Madona*, to whom that expression would now more
aptly b[e] appli'd.

Extreamly surpriz'd he was to heare me speak in this manner; as I perceiv'd
by his change of colour, but composing himselfe again as well as he could, and
fetching a sigh I see Madam (said he) you are no stranger to those pretences I
have of late made to *Madona*; but do not wonder at it, since I took no care to
conceale them; yet I wish I had been my selfe the first that had acquainted you
with them, that at the same time I might have shewn you the necessity that com-
pelled me to what I have done: but seeing you onely know what I have [fol. 89ᵛ]
done, and not what mov'd me to it, I cannot but admire you should receive me
with so calme a brow, and intimate my falsness to me with the lovely language of
a smile; and not rather contract your brows, and dart from thence such frownes
as might so terrifie me as I should never more presume to appeare before you;
nor had I now assumed the confidence to look you in the face were I but half so
guilty as appearance renders me.

You need make no Apolligie (interrupted I) to excuse your selfe; for since you lov'd me for your owne satisfaction, I shall not take it ill that you quit me to increase it: nor have I any reason to think it strang that you abandon a person to whom Fortune has declar'd herselfe an utter enemy, for one of her peculier Favourits. *Madona* has heapes of Gold and Silver to prefer her to your esteeme, whereas *Arthenia* has nothing but Innocence and Vertue for her dowry.

In having that (he answer'd) you possess more then all *Madona's* wealth (were it trebled) could purchace. But give me leave (pursu'd he) to tell you, that this unconcernedness wherewith you support my change appeares to me more cruell then your anger would in its most formidable dress; for had you express'd ought of resentment against me, I might have flatter'd my self with hopes that kindness excited it, being troubled to loose what you had contracted some little value for; but this calme temper shewes too plainly how indifferent I am to you still; for though you declare you will not be offended with me if I relinquish you for my advantage, yet you must pardon me if I cannot take this as an act of your generosity (as perhaps you would have me) but rather as a testimony of your dis-esteeme; since I am perswaded no person ever lov'd who can on any score what-ever be induced to part willingly with what they love.

If my memory deceive me not (said I) I never told you that I lov'd you.

No Madam I confess (repli'd he) you never gave me that assurance of my happiness; but yet pardon me if I say, you permitted me to hope I had some inter-est in you.

You might with reason have still continu'd those hopes (return'd I) had you not given me cause by your example (in withdrawing that kindness which you so oft have vow'd should never end but with your life) to lay aside that esteeme for you which you had created in me. Would you have me desturbe the serenity of my thoughts with angry resentments [feelings] for your unworthyness; tis you that ought rather to be disquieted that do the injury, then I that suffer it: no no *Loreto* you shall never so much insult over my weakness as to make *Arthenia* sigh, or once put on a discontented look for the loss of that which you have thought her unworthy longer to possess. Goe carry your faithless heart, and make a Pres-ent of it (if you have not already done so) to *Madona*; for know I scorne it now tis stain'd with Infidelity, much more then ere I priz'd it.

You would have reason Madam (he repli'd) not onely to scorn, but hate me too, were I such as [fol. 90ʳ] I have been represented to you; but I have onely appear'd guilty to secure my innocence, and been a Crimenall seemingly, that I might not be really soe: for my Mother, (by what meanes I know not) having been enform'd of my passion for you, whereas she was incenced to that height as to vow with bitter imprecations, if I did not banish you my thoughts, to banish me her favour, and never to regard me but as a stranger to her blood, and utterly to deprive me of all subsistance, which you know (pursu'd he) for the present abso-lutely depends on her. This was I assur'd of by a person who had it from her owne mouth: who told me withall, that though he would not councell me to anything so unworthy of me, as perfideously to desert you; yet as I would take his advice, I should endeavour to appeaze *Crisaldas* fury by seeming to slight you, and making my addresses to some other; then whom he could not think any person more proper to make the Object of my feigned love then *Madona*; both for the satisfaction my Mother would conceive thereat, to see me fix my mind so much on Wealth and because he was certainly perswaded that Lady design'd never to marry; and thereby I was secur'd from the feare of her acceptance of those Overtures I should make her. This Councell (added *Loreto*) I found so weighty, as I believ'd I could not do better then to follow it; which I instantly resolv'd to do, in hopes thereby not onely to pacifie *Crisalda*, but likewise to delude her, so as I might the more securely carry on the Designe I have to be yours, and yours onely.

Though I was satisfi'd with what me thoughts he had so ingeniously declar'd to me, yet I seem'd not to be so; and to that intent, You need not *Loreto* (said I) have studied for this far fetch'd excuse to palliate your slighting me, since my want of merit would have furnish'd you with a much juster pretence for it.

He would not suffer me to proceed, but catching fast hold of my hand which I had withdrawn from him, and pressing it with a most violent transport: for Heavens sake *Arthenia* (said he) be not so cruelly unjust as once to fancy that any thing that I have said, has been spoken by me with an intent to extenuate a guilt, that never yet found enterance into any thought of mine: to slight you, did you say; no Deare *Arthenia*, never think I can commit such a crime as that, wherein I must find a much severer punishment then my most malicious enemy can wish me: but if what I have already told you, does not convince you of the necessity that compell'd me to what I did, let this resolution I have made satisfie you both of my reallity, and Fidelity, which to preserve inviolate I determin'd for a while to leave Sicilie, to avoid all occations of being tempted to violate my faith; not that I distrust my owne stability, but lest *Crisalda* (by whose instigation I believe it was that I was put upon the design of courting *Madona*) may again find out some other (or indeed so many others) for me to make love to, till at last she may possibly discover a defect in my Will to be the cause of those [fol. 90ᵛ] successless Amoures, which if she did it might more provoke her displeasure by imputeing it (as she possibly might) to a designed disobedience: to shun these Rocks it is (continu'd he) that I have made this resolve, which nothing but your commands shall be able to alter; if you disallow it, I shall then renounce it, and make it give place to another resolution (which I long since made, and from which you yourselfe (though in all things else I will with the hazard of my life obey you) shall never be able to perswade me) which is to be intierly at your dispose, and never to owne any other Will then what depends on yours.

For my part (repli'd I) I shall never pretend to any such power over you; but what you give me on this score, I shall resign to you again: you are free *Loreto* to dispose of your selfe as you please; if your conveniency depends on your abandoning Sicilie I shall not oppose it.

As I came to this period I heard *Ardelia* at *Merinza*'s request had just begun to sing, whose voice I had heard so much commended that made me desire to know whether Fame had Flatter'd, or but done her Justice: this desire of mine I having made known to *Loreto*, he presently lead me to the place where they were seated; but *Ardelia* had e'ne finish'd her song ere we came to them; wherefore to oblige me he requested her to sing another to us, which I was so extreamly taken with, as I beg'd the favour of her to give it me in writing, which instantly she did with much civility; happing to have a Copie of it about her. The words whereof (as I remember) were these.

A Song

Illustrious Beauties have you still a care
how you abroad unguarded use to range;
for you shall find Deceivers every where
'mong wandring Lovers who still seek for change.

Trust not their Oathes who sweare your Loves to be
the cause of all their cruell deadly smart;
nor those who sigh, and weep to let you see
their loves, but not their false dissembling heart.

Beware of their inchanting feigned spell
that rifle may your heart, but not there dwell
and wisely set a Guard upon your heart
to Countermine their wanton cunning art.

Believe them not, nor their aluring charmes
they onely live secure that first take Armes
for so you may preserve your honour free
from all designes of Lovers treacherie. . . . [fol. 91ʳ]

She had but newly ended when *Dionella* sent one to tell her she was ready to go, and stay'd for her, which made us hasten in; and having with her Mother together with *Loreto* taken their leaves, he came to bid me farewell; intreating me to banish all ill thoughts of him which his late carriage might have contracted in my mind, and to assure my selfe, I should either heare of him, or see him again very speedily.

Being gone, I began to run over in my thoughts all that he had said to me at that time, in any which I found so great a probability of truth as I could not find one reason sufficent to perswade me to continue the displeasure I had conceiv'd against him; nay, on the contrary when I consider'd how he offer'd to quit his Country for my sake, and expose himselfe to the mercy of the seas, and all those inconveniencies that Travelours are liable too, rather then he would be tempted to forsake me, I found he was far dearer to me then ever he had been, or could have believ'd he ever would. Certainly had he studied to deck his passion with the most florid expressions, he could never have put it in a more lovely dress, or rendred it more charming then that resolution made it appeare to me: but how great soever the interest was that he now had gain'd in me, I determin'd to seeme wholly unconcern'd for his departure, though I could not be really so, when I thought upon those many dangers he might peradventure encounter abroad: but notwithstanding that trouble which began to ceaze my mind, though it had been (as he affirmed it was) in my power to expell it by enjoyning his stay in Sicilie, yet I absolutely resolv'd not once to open my Lips to solicit him to it, though I did Heaven in secret, to raise some obstruction or other to his Designe.

One morning being somewhat earlyer up then usuall, I was told there was a man below to speak with me; and having sent for him up, I found he was one that my Mother had sent to bring me home; somewhat amaz'd I confess I was at so sudden a sommons, and much admir'd [wondered] what might be the occation of it, which I demanded of the man; but he could not resolve me, onely gave me a letter from *Brecena* to *Alsinda*, adding that haply that might enforme me. I was impatient till such time as *Alsinda* awak'd that I might know what it contain'd; but t'was not long my expectations waited before her Chamber dore was open'd, which so soon as it was I went in, and giving her the goodmorrow I presented her my Mothers letter which she having read told me she found I was sent for, and that my Mother beg'd her to hasten me away as soon as possible[.]

[B]ut to what end (said she) is it that I must post you away with such speed; do you know (added she).

[N]o Madam (answer'd I) nor can I guess.

It may be (said she) you are sent for to be married; if so, I wish Deare *Arthenia* (pursu'd she, pressing me in her Armes, and kissing me most affectionatly) all true Joy, and reall happiness may perpetually attend your nuptialls.

Having thank'd her for so obliging, and Friendly a wish, I onely told her, I believ'd whatever Concern it was that call'd me home it was not [fol. 91ᵛ] that, and took my leave of her, having before put my selfe in a readiness for my Journey, and bid farewell to *Merinza* whom I likewise left in bed: but as I was going to take horse, *Alsinda* sent me word, that if I were not sent for on that account she had imagin'd, that I should be sure to make a speedy returne to *Merinza* who was never satisfi'd when I was from her; to which I return'd her answere, that my owne inclinations no less then her Commands would oblige me to that, and so departed.

When I came home I saw great preparations for a more then ordinary entertainment: I could not fancy my self to be the onely Guest that was expected; neither indeed was I, as I quickly learn'd from my Sister, who told me *Loreto* was to sup there that night; and that it was through his desire that I was sent for, that he might take his leave of me before he left Sicilie, which the next day he design'd to do. Though he had given me notice of his intentions, yet I did not think he would so soon have put them in practice; and besides, I had ~~hoped~~ hitherto hop'd, that some accident or other might have fallen out to hinder his Voiage; but when I saw things arrived to this pass, and that I believ'd there was not any thing now would hinder his departure, I was concern'd for it in good earnest; and that somuch, as in my life I had never been before sensible of so great a sadness as that instant ceaz'd my heart: ^but^ I did all that ever I was able to confine it within my owne brest so closely as it might not be perceiv'd, nor taken notice of by any one.

About two houres before night *Loreto* came, and with him a Gentleman (call'd *Rosanor*) who was to accompany him in his Travells. All the evening he made it his business to seek an opportunity to speak with me; not but that he had all the liberty of discourse with me allow'd him as he could desire, but being then to take a long farewell of me, he thought perhaps what he had to say at that time might be too passionate for a publick conference, especially before *Rosanor*: but all his endeavours were to no purpose, for he could not find what he sought till after supper: but whether it were that he were troubled to part from me, or that he was vex'd he could not entertaine me so freely as he wish'd, I know not; but he sat so silent, as I verily think he hardly spoke six words whilst he sat at Table; nor was I much more liberall of my speech then he.

No sooner was supper ended (but finding my self something cold, it being the depth of Winter) I ris, and went to the Fire; which *Loreto* seeing, and perceiving his Friend engag'd in discourse with my Father and my Mother, he left them, and came to me, and pulling a chaire he sate downe by me; and making a sigh the preface to his discourse.

May I my ador'd *Arthenia* (said he) without flattery [fol. 92ʳ] please my selfe with a beliefe that tis rather to your kindness, then *Brecena*'s goodness that I am oblig'd for the favour of your company this night.

If it be a favour (repli'd I) tis to my Mother onely that you are indebted for it, for, for my part I pretend no share in it; for I knew not in the least of you[r] being to come hither till since I came home.

But may I not hope (said he) that if you had known it, you would not have oppos'd my enjoyment of this felicity, that perhaps may be the last I may ever obtain.

You may assure you[r] self I would not (answerd I) for since my Parents have commanded me to esteeme you, I cannot think my self blameable in giving you such a testimony of my friendship.

Ah Madam (interrupted he) why would you not say affection; for if I have been so happy as to move you to accept my passion, be now so kind as not to conceale longer from me soe great a bliss; and lay aside a little of that severe humour of yours which makes you think it a crime to say you Love: consider for Heavens sake too, that I have need of more then ordinary comfort to support my exile, in which I shall be uncapable of all Joy or consolation during this cruell absence, if you do not in pitty give me some assurance of your affection.

I cannot tell (repli'd I) if I had that kindness for you as you desire, and perhaps expect; whether I ought to owne it, or whether it were not fitter for me to let you g^u^ess my thoughts, then plainly to unfould them; since absence does many times slacken the strongest bonds of love, and often quite disolve them; which if it should so hapen in you, I should never more be reconcil'd to my self, if I had once own'd a concern for you.

You may be most certaine (said he) that when I leave off loving *Arthenia* I am no longer one of earths Inhabitants; for Heaven sake let me know then at this instant what you will determine of me, and suffer me not to wander farre off with no other comfort to attend me then that of a groundless hope, which is so faint, and languid, as I cannot but feare it will too soon expire and dye: then give me I beseech you now my finall sentence, and either declare you hate me, or tell me that you love me:

Should I say the first (repli'd I) I might be condemned both of Injustice and ingratitude; and should I affirme the last I know not whether you might take too much advantage of my words: but that I may not seeme too nicely scrupelous, I'le give you this assurance, that if at your returne I find your constancy proofe against those two powerfull enemies Time and Absence, I will as far as it depends on me give you that recompense such a fidelity deserves, and in the mean time to arme you the more strongly to resist them, I give you leave to entertaine any thoughts of me that may conduce to the preserving your Fidelity untainted.

Since you have by so obliging a permission (said he) bound me to be faithfull, may I presume to hope you will your self continue so.

I have not I confess (answer'd I) been very easily perswaded to afford you a place within my brest, but that which I have given you nothing shall be able to dispossess you of unless you youre selfe abandon it.

Which to be sure I never will (repli'd he hastily) [fol. 92ᵛ] till life abandons me.

But so much out of countenance was I at what I had said which methought nothing could render excusable but that which extorted these ^words^ from me as I should not in a long while have resetled that disorder I was in, had not *Rosanor*, and *Mironides* just then risse from the Table and come towards the Fire where we were siting, which put a period to all discourses of this nature; but notwithstanding *Loreto* let me understand as he took his leave of me (which soon after he did) that he went away as well satisfied with that esteeme I had favoure'd him with, as he was the contrary to leave me; and that he had now no trouble remaining, but that of his separation from me, which he said he hoped I would joyne my prayers with his, might be of no long continuance.

Then taking one of my hands and kising it with the greatest ardency of a passionate Love. Adue *Arthenia* (said he with a sigh) be but as kind at my returne as I'le be constant and I will ask no more.

With this he went away, leaving me in no little disquiet to think that perchance this might be the last farewell that ever he might take of me, going as he was to expose himselfe to sundry dangers, and perrills of his life: such thoughts as these so intruded themselves into my mind the greatest part of the night, as they suffer'd me not to take much rest; for though I retier'd to my Chamber assoon as he was gone, and went emmediatly to bed; it was rather to hide my trouble, then for the hopes I had to find there any repose; nor did the succeeding day afford me any: and though I did all that in me lay to conceale my discontent, yet my Face was ever too true an Index to my heart, not to charactar on it what trouble soever at any time was engraven inwardly, so that my Mother quickly observ'd it, and not doubting but that *Loreto*'s departure was the cause of my Melancholly, she thought it might be easier diverted by my return to the *Duke of Tellinus*'s then by my stay at home which induced her to send me back sooner then she intended.

But I had not been there above twelve or fourteen dayes when passing along the Court one morning, I saw come in at the Gate of it a Gentelman so like *Loreto* (as had I not verily believ'd him to be at that instant on the sea) I should have absolutely concluded it was he; however I was ^so^ amaz'd as I remain'd immovable, not having the power to go either forward, or backward, never considering how unfit a garb I was in to be seen by a stranger, being but in my morning dress: but when he came neerer, I found I had not been mistaken in takeing him for *Loreto*; for it was even he indeed; yet could I scarce believe my eyes, but thought they still deceiv'd me, or rather that I walk'd in my sleep (as I have heard some persons use to do) and onely dream'd I saw him:

[B]ut he soon put this fancy out of my head by saluteing me with a smile, and saying, do you not admire Madam to see me here.

Indeed I do (answer'd I) and that somuch as I know not well whether I am awake or asleep:

You are the first without doubt (said he) but though my appearance be unexpected, I hope tis not unpleasing.

I think (repli'd I) I need not declare the contrary since I believe [fol. 93ʳ] you are already perswaded of it. But pray *Loreto* (pursu'd I) tell me what tis has render'd your voyage so short; but tis not that your return is unwellcome, that I enquire the cause:

[W]hich as we went in a dores he told me was occation'd by *Ormisdas*, who having had some intelligence of his intended travells, imagin'd that he was going over to *Claromenes* upon some design or other; wherupon he immediatly sent a Pursevant after him, who overtook him at Tauromenion, and brought him back a Prisoner to Palermo, where he was detain'd till that very morning; but had then his liberty restor'd him on condition he attempted no more to go out of Sicilie.

I was not a little joy'd to see the Heavens had been so propitious to my prayers in crossing *Loreto*'s Voyage, even then when I dispair'd of a returne to those petitions I so oft had made to the Celestiall Powers upon that score; and scarce could I keep my Joy from breaking out into some expression, which perhaps I had ~~after~~ afterwards condemned as undecent.

But after some little silence, may I not (said he) chalenge of you now the effect of that obliging promise you were pleas'd to make me, since I return the same to you I was, unalterable in any thing but in an increase of my passion, which has gather'd strength by this short absence; what would it then have done, had it been of a longer duration.

I have as yet (repli'd I) no additionall proofes of your Fidelity, for the time that you have been absent has not I am confident afforded either yourself or me any tryall of it; for tis not likely (added I with a smile) that you should become enamour'd of Chaines, or Fetters; or fall in love with Prison Walls, and other Objects I do not heare that you have of late encounter'd.

I must confess (said he) I have not been so happy in this I late attempted to meet with any occations that might confirme to you the reallity of that which I so oft to you have sworn; but though I fail'd in my first enterprise, I trust I shall have better fortune in that which I have now determin'd; which is (since *Ormisdas* has not confin'd me to any perticuler place in Sicilie) to make my owne Country the scean of my Travells, and trace Sicilie thorough out, with all the adiacent Islands belonging to it; and in that I think I shall not go beyond those limits to which I am confin'd. This may possibly take me up no less time then that which I intended to spend abroad, and perhaps afford me no less a satisfaction then what I before propos'd to my selfe, and give you no less convinceing testimonies of what as yet you seem doubtful of; since you are not ignorant Madam I believe that Fame has rendr'd our owne Country famous for beauties above all others in the World; and if I can withstand their forces, you need not question the power of others.

Alass (said I) if you love *Arthenia*, for nothing but her beauty, I shall have then more cause then ever to question your constancy; nor need you go far to seek ere you may find many who infinitly surpass her in all outward perfections.

Do not injure youselfe Faire *Arthenia* (repli'd he) so much as to admit any such opinion; but if my memory failes me not, I have already declar'd that there is something more charming in you then the most dazling beauty, which compells me to adore you.

By this time *Gracianus* having been told of *Loreto*'s being there, came downe to him, and saluted him with that civility [fol. 93ᵛ] as he believ'd due to the Duke of Veronas son. To do *Gracianus* right, I must needs say, that I really think no man better understood civillity, and what belonged to all punctillios of Cerimony then himself; nor did I ever know a person of a more affable, courteous, and every way obliging deportment to all persons, then he: besides he had naturally so taking a way in discourse, mix'd with such eloquence as *Cicero* so fam'd at Rome scarce excell'd him in that quallity, which render'd his conversation very agreeable to all company; and being so excellently accomplish'd as he was, I thought I should not transgress the rules of good manners if I took that opportunity to steal away to dress me, since I left *Loreto* ~~him~~ sogood a Companion as *Gracianus* to entertaine him in my absence; yet made I so much hast to dress me that day as I believe he hardly miss'd me ere I return'd again.

All that day (till towards Evening) he spent with me, but then bad me fare-well a second time, with repeated vowes of Love and Fidelity, conjuring me not to be unmindfull of him in his absence. The next day (as I remember) he began his Progress towards the western parts of Sicilie, intending first to visit Leontine the Citty where *Crisalda* drew her first breath, but here it was that all his designes were terminated; for hapning to come acquainted with a Nobleman in that Citty call'd *Issodates*, who had been in his youth a profess'd Adorer of *Crisalda* before she was married to *Flavianus*, he quickly lost all thoughts of *Arthenia*, making a present of that his heart to a Daughter of *Issodates's* (nam'd *Belissa*) which he so oft had vow'd none ever should possess but I: yet if any thing could extenuate the Crime of Infidelity, or make an Appollogie for it, I must confess there was enough in *Belissa* to vindicate *Loreto's* change; since she had much the advantage of me in all respects; both as to her birth, which was more noble, her education much more courtly, and her Fortune far exceeding mine; and as to her person, they must have been very partiall that had not given her the prehemenence of me. Her stature was neither tall, nor low, but of a height most generally approv'd: her complexion indeed was not the purest I have seen, yet had she so sweet an aire, and so winning a look about her eyes (which were so delicately black as nothing could equall except her haire) as he must have been of a firmer temper then *Loreto* was composed of, that could have resisted such powerfull Charmes.

[I]n fine Madam he was caught in them (whether designedly, or unawares I cannot tell) and so caught that he laid so close a siege, as in fewer dayes then he spent moneths in gaining a place in *Arthenias* heart he obtain'd not onely *Belissas* love but person too; being married to her in a very short space. We have a say-ing in Sicilie that those marriages are happiest that are soonest accomplish'd, but the truth of that ascertion *Loreto* could not find; for he quickly began to be dissatisfi'd with his choice, and repent what he had done, either out of remorse for his injustice to me (as he would afterwards have made me believe) or else out of a humour he had (as I rather think) to dislike, or slight whatever he was once possesst of: for it could be no defect in *Belissa* that could be capable of lessning his content, since tis most certaine she was every way worthy of a more deserv-ing person then *Loreto*: but having undertaken my owne story, not his; I shall in [fol.94ʳ] silence pass by those addresses he made *Belissa*, and the way he took so speedily to gain her, together with the state and grandure of their marriage solemnities; and not insist on ought that relates to him, save onely those things that are intervoven with my owne Concernes.

Rivall Friendship

THE FIRST PART

The ~~Seventh~~ Eighth^ Book

Scarce were *Loreto's* Nuptialls consummate ere report brought me word of it; which at first I was so far from crediting, as I look'd on it as no other then a rumour spread by that tatling Goddess Fame who oftner appeares spotted with slaunder, then beautifi'd with truth: for it could not enter into my thoughts, much less into my beliefe, that he who had but a little before offer'd to quit Sicily for my sake, should immediatly after abandon me so lightly. But that resolve of his which I resented [felt] with such kindness, as believeing it to be (as he had protested) assum'd onely on my score, was made meerly on his owne (as I afterwards heard) for happing to have some difference with his Mother for abating somewhat of his usuall allowance, pretending he was too profuse in his expences (though others thought him rather guilty of too much Parcimony) whereat he grew so discontented, as in her presence he solemly swore to leave Sicily, and never more to see it till after the death of *Leonora*.

This Madam was the true cause of his designed Travell, notwithstanding his other pretence. But alass how easily are we poore sillie ones deluded with faire semblances and shews of sincerity; sure (pursu'd she) men are compos'd of nothing but hipocricy and deceite.

Be not so unjust (interrupted *Gentillus*) for the faults of some to censure all men so severely.

Mistake me not (repli'd she) I meane not each perticuler man in the World; but onely the generallity, and greatest part of Mankind: for I know many (and namely your self my Lord who may be put in the first rank) that are of a more Generous, and noble Frame; and questionless there are divers that I ne're heard so much as named, who scorn to betray, or abuse our too easie Credulities (that Originall of our sexes misfortunes) and though I am perswaded there lives not a person that has juster cause to inveigh with bitterness against men then my selfe, yet shall not their injuries so far transport me to resentment [bitter feelings], as to make me condemne the Innocent with the guilty, or involve the guiltless in the Crimes of the Culpable.

But what I at first slighted as a false report, hearing it again confirm'd by the testimony of such as I knew could [fol. 94ᵛ] not be mistaken, I could no longer disbelieve, or doubt the truth of it. I must confess this Infidelity of *Loreto's* surpriz'd me very much at first, and the rather in regard t'was so unexpected: nor will I deny, but that for some few dayes I was very much concern'd; yet great as this trouble was, it deserves not to be mention'd, if compar'd with what I suffer'd since upon

the like score; but so carefully did I conceale my grief as none in the least suspected I was any way concern'd. But t'was not long ere that Passion gave place to
one more reasonable; for anger was quickly more potent in me then sorrow, being
a little heightned too by disdaine to see my self deluded, and so undeservedly forsaken: and this satisfaction I had, to find he had not got such a firme possession
in my brest, but that with no great difficulty I utterly expell'd him thence in fewer
dayes then he had spent weekes in geting an interest there: for since the kindness
I had for him sprung rather from gratitude then inclination, when once the cause
was taken away the effect soon ceas'd; and quickly did I dry my eyes, resolving to
employ them better then to lament by them the loss of a Faithless Lover whom I
could no longer count worthy of a teare.

But how highly soever my resentment [feelings] transported me against him,
I determin'd (if ever it ^were^ my hap at any time to see him) to demeane my
self towards him in such a manner as he should not be able to guess upon what
termes he stood with me: for I thought if I treated him scornfully, he might (perhaps) measure my past kindness, by my present Concerne; and if I suffer'd discontent to appeare in my Lookes, he possibly might thinke I more regreeted his
loss, then resented [felt] his baseness; which I thought might perchance move him
to tryumph in his unworthyness, and rather deride my weakness, then repent his
injustice; so that in fine my resolve was, to carry myself with such indifferency to
him and yet with such civility as might make him not onely sorry, but ashamed
he had injur'd a person who had so litle deserv'd it from him: this resolution how
firmely I could hold too, I had occation not long after to try; for one day, as I had
been with my Father, and Mother at *Arnardo's* as we return'd, they made a visit to a
Gentleman and his Wife of their acquaintance who liv'd in theire way homeward.

[B]ut when we came in, Judge Madam (pursu'd *Arthenia*) whether or no I
was surpriz'd (amongst much other Company that were there) to meet *Loreto* and
Belissa too; to have met him onely would doubtless have daunted me enough when
I so litle expected it, but likewise at the same time to see her, when I was so litle
prepar'd for such an incounter, struck me into such a dampe as I am unable to
express. I had heard indeed that he had brought her from Leontium to a Brothers
of his that dwelt not far from Palermo; but that he was come to *Crisalda's* or had
brought *Belissa* thither was a thing altogether unknown to me. But I no sooner
saw him, but I instantly call'd to mind my late [fol. 95ʳ] determination, which I
so strongly confirm'd my self in, and summoning to my aide all the assistance that
reason could afford me, as in a short time I reseted that disorder the sight of him
had stir'd within me, and prepar'd to receive him with as serene a brow as if I had
been wholly unconcern'd; but so did not he appeare to me, for there was not more
calmness to be seen in my lookes, then there was disorder to be perceiv'd in his: for
he no sooner saw me come into the Roome, but (contrary to my intentions) casting
my eye on him unawares, I saw his blood fly in his face in guilty blushes, and his
eyes instantly fix themselves on the Ground, as if he had been asham'd to look her
in the Face whom his Conscience could not but tell him he had done unworthily

by. But notwithstanding, seeing every one salute me, he thought himself oblig'd to do as others did; though (as I perceiv'd) he had scarce the confidence so to do, fancying (perhaps) I would refuse him that civility: but I did not, lest it might have been taken notice of; and seeing every one (after some time) engag'd in discourse save *Loreto* who stood leaning his Arme on the back of the Chaire on which I sate.

I turn'd me a litle about, and told him, I wish'd him much Joy and happiness (which in *Sicilie* is the usuall Complement to new married persons) and assur'd him I had heard of the accomplishment of his Marriage with no less satisfaction then they had celibrated it that sung his Hymeneus.

O how much goodness have I injur'd (said he with a sigh) but may I Madam believe (went he on) that your heart and tongue holds a correspondence at this time.

If my Tongue were of the temper of yours (repli'd I) you would have reason to question their agreement; but upon my word I alwayes speake as I meane, though I have some cause to believe you never did, at least to me.

You have reason indeed to believe so (interrupted he) and t'was meerly the sense I have of my owne unworthyness that mov'd me to doubt whether you could be soe generous as really to wish Joy to me, who have deserv'd nought from you but scorne, and hatred, and to be no otherwise regarded by you then as the basest man alive; all spotted o're with that black and horrid sin of Infidelity; which I know but too well, is in me (who have so highly declam'd against it) a Crime of that nature, as I dare not endeavour to excuse it by any Apologie.

No *Loreto* (said I) tis needless, since the silent rethorick of *Belissa*'s lovly face does it more powerfully then any thing you can alleadge for your justification, for sure if your Inconstancy can find any Advocate to plead in its defence, it must be the charming sweetness of her Eyes must do you that good Office: but since you have made so advantagious a change, and found a person to bestow your self on every way more deserving then *Arthenia* [fol. 95ᵛ] I shall neither envie your felicity, nor so far distrust my owne good fortune, as not to hope (if ere I marry) the Fates has instore for me, one more worthy of me then *Loreto*.

Being unwilling to hold a longer conferrence with him lest it might be observ'd, I would pursue it no further, but turning from him I called a Gentle-woman of my acquaintance (who was there) to set downe by me, and addressing my discourse to her, I took no further notice of him whilst I stay'd. I confess my last words to *Loreto* express'd something more of sharpness then I intended; and vex'd at my selfe I was that I had said ought that might seeme to intimate my resentment [feelings]; but seeing I could not recall what I had spoken I resolv'd to be ^more^ cautious for the future: after this, I saw him no more again in halfe a yeare; in which time I had heard he was grown the most unkind Husband imagin-able; and was told by severall (who had heard of the probability there once was of his having been mine) that they thought me very happie in missing him.

But that I knew, he that had been guilty of one baseness, might as well be guilty of another; I should have thought it strange that in so short a space he should so much forget his Nuptiall vowes as to treat her who by so sacred a Union was become part of himselfe, not onely with indifferency, but with a careless neglect. This, when I was once assur'd of, it created in me a greater prejudice against him upon *Belissa's* score, then on my owne; and mov'd me to congratulate my owne good Fortune that he fell not to my share; for thought I, if he use a Lady so deservedly admir'd for her perfections, at this rate, how would he have tyraniz'd o're me; and what might I have expected from him, who have not the one halfe of those excellent qualities she has to intitle her to his affection in the highest degree.

The next time I saw him was at my Fathers, whether he took the confidence to come, and a fitter opportunity then this to speake with me he could not have wish'd, for that very day, both my Father, and Mother were gone to Palermo: when he came in he found me sitting in the Parlour onely accompanied with a Cousin of mine nam'd *Amarantha* who hapning to be undresst no sooner saw him but she slipt away, and got her up staires, leaving me alone to entertain this unlook'd for and no less unwellcome Guest; however, I thought civility oblig'd me to treat him as I would any other stranger that came to visit us.

I enquir'd of him how *Belissa* fared and when he saw *Arnardo*, or *Marionie*; and some other questions of the like nature I demanded of him, to all which he return'd sutable answers; and after a short silence (prefaceing what he was about to say with a sigh) he told me, that since the last time he had the happiness to see me, he had diligently waited for an opportunity to see me again; which he hop'd (as he said) to have found some time or other ere that, but since the Fates would not so far indulge his desires he had resolv'd (though perhaps I might look on it (he added) as a great presumption in him unlicenced to intrude into my presence) to come and implore my pardon for that high offence he had committed against so much Goodness and Clemency as could with so great Patience suffer such an Injury from him without once upbraiding [fol. 96ʳ] him with it.

But tis this unequall'd goodness of yours Madam (pursu'd he) that has shewn me as in a Glass my Injustice and vil[e] Ingratitude in so larg and monsterous an extent, that I cannot be more hatefull to you, then I am odious to my selfe: nor need you (were you as revengfull as you are the contrary) wish me a severer punishment then that remorse that hourly torments my soule; from which I must ne're hope for ease, unless you daine to seale my pardon which on my knees I beg (continu'd he falling at my feet) and vow thus to remaine forever unless I may obtaine it.

Rise, rise *Loreto* (said I) your Offence great as it is transcends not my charity; I can, and do forgive you freely: but let me tell you, tis rather of the Gods then me you ought to aske forgiveness; since you have more offended Heaven by invoking it to be a Witness to those violated vowes and faithless promises you made me, to no other end then to cheat me of my freedome, and ruine my content; which you might (peradventure) have done, had not discretion kept me from your snares, by advizing me not to engage in Love past a retreat: yet I will not deny, but that I once lov'd you much better then you deserv'd it seemes (since this was the requitall you prepar'd me) yet not so well, but that when you once broke the bonds of your Fidelity, I could as easily untie those of my affection: but never feare that I'le reproach you with your Inconstancy, I rather pity it in you, since it has dropt a blot upon your Fame which you will find it hard ere to efface, seeing you can never cleare your self from the guilt of betraying the Innocent affection of a harmless virgin who never did, or wish'd you the least hurt; nor shall I ever wish you any, but on the contrary, pray you may be happie in the injoyment of *Belissa* who though she excells me in all things else I might (if I had been your Wife) perhaps have equall'd her in a pure and chast affection.

Ah *Arnardo* (cry'd he) how injurious has thy friendship been to me, and how miserable hast thou rendred me in aiming to make me happie. I must needs say (went he on) *Belissa* is a Lady of no meane perfections, but had they been of a greater magnitude they had never shaken much less throwne downe the Fortress of my fidelity, had not *Arnardo* first batter'd and undermin'd it by his perswasions to abandon you and make a second choice, so as might better sute my convenience, and obtaine *Crisaldas* approbation; without ^which^ he told me I could expect nothing but a certain ruine, in which I would involve you unavoidably if I married you before *Leonora* died; and if I made you waite for a Husband till then, it might be so long, as my owne death might possibly precede hers; so that after a tedious expectation of the performance of my promises, I could no otherwise requite your Love and Patience then by an injurious hinderance of your better fortunes: and though he added much more (pursu'd *Loreto*) to induce me to change the Designe I once really had, to be inviolably yours till Death should make a [fol. 96ᵛ] seperation between us; yet was it onely that which I last mention'd that was capable of prevailing with me to forsake you for *Belissa*, then whom I believ'd I could not fix on any that would be so pleasing to my Mother as she in regard I knew there had been an ancient kindness between her and *Issodates*; so that consulting *Crisaldas* satisfaction more then my owne content (which I could neither expect, nor hope to find in any but you alone) I gave my selfe to *Belissa*, yet so, as I reserv'd my heart, and best affections intire for you (whose of right they only are) though I confess (pursu'd he) I know them to be most unworthy either your value, or ~~assist~~ acceptance, since I have dared to prophane my Offering by permitting any other to share with you in it; but give me leave to assure you, that though *Belissa* does enjoy my person, yet tis you onely that possess my heart, which flames with as great a passion for you as ever; and though I know I transgress the bounds of discretion to tell you so, yet whilst I live, I must affirme, I did, do, and will forever love you above all Woemen breathing, and adore you with no less respect then if you were the Universall Princess of the World, and I your meanest slave. Then since you have been pleas'd to make me cease from being the most miserable of men (as I some few minutes since deem'd my selfe) by remitting my past offence, be but so generous as to recall some part of that kindness for me, which I know you have but too deservedly banish'd your heart, and you will make me as happie, as I must be inevitably forever wretched without it.

But having no patience to heare him further (my eyes being no less inflam'd with anger, then his false heart with base desires, and my cheekes cover'd with blushes mix'd with shame and displeasure) I suffer'd him not to proceed; but interrupted him by a look I darted at him, wherein he could not but perceive with what disdain I receiv'd his last request; which with these words I seconded.

Are you in your Wits *Loreto* (said I) or do you think I have lost mine, that you address such a discourse as this to me: but I am glad I can out of your owne mouth convince you of Flattery and dissemulation, as justly as I may brand you with falshood; since at the same time you protest for me so high a respect, you presume to make me a request, which you could not but know would mortally offend me; which you would ne're have dar'd to do, had you but any value for me, much less so great a one as you would make me believe. But I do not wonder now indeed you should abandon me since you could think so ignobly of me, as that I would entertain the proffer of your dishonourable Love (or rather base desire) any otherwise then with the highest scorn, and horridest detestation a vertuous soule is capable of. Was it for this then (pursu'd I) that you implor'd my pardon, to the intent [fol. 97ʳ] you might injure me on a new score; and do you think t'was not enough to cheat my innocent affection, without endevouring to rob me of my honour too: but thanks to Heaven that is guarded on every side with a vertue strong enough to repell with scorn those Engines you vainly employ against it, and dart them back into your soule; which I now plainly see is so foule and Leperos that I shall henceforth shun you as I would a Basilisk, and dread to draw the Aire that's tainted with your poisonous breath. Is this then the reparation you design'd me; I must confess tis noble, and like your self, to seeke to stain my honour, as you endeavour'd to ruine my content; but as discretion prevented the one, so vertue I trust will protect the other. Your Inconstancy would not allow me to be your Wife, but yet it seemes it can afford me the glory to be your mistress; but I am sure you know me not at all, if you can once imagine I can so far forget Heaven, or my owne Soule to descend so low to be Mistress to any man; no not the Mightiest Prince that ever sway'd a scepter, for even then when he were deck'd with all the glories that attend on Majesty, or glittering with all the splendors of his Crowne I would look on him with scorn, and tell him as I now do you, that I dispise and hate you as Hell.

You have resons more then enough I must confess to abhorre me (he repli'd) since I have merited your hatered in the highest degree; but yet, if touch'd with true remorse, I desire to give you all the reparation I am capable of, why should you think me out of my Wits to desire to regain your affection; since nothing is more naturall to those that love then to desire to live in their favour whom they affect!

Yes (said I) I know tis naturall for all men to be wicked; but when I gave you an interest in my esteeme, I thought you Master of so much Vertue as might have been sufficent to subdue whatever ill Inclinations Nature might have planted in you: but though I have been deceiv'd in you, you shall not be so in me if I can help it; and therefore pray disabuse your self, and no longer harbour so erronious an opinion of me, as to believe you shall e're perswade me to be so unjust as to accept from you as a reparation of your fault, that heart, or those affections which are no longer yours to give, since they of right belong wholly to *Belissa.*

But sure *Loreto* (went I on) you could not be so vain as to imagine that I would e're accept the payment of your Debts to me by your Injuries to her. No no, though she innocently depriv'd me of my right, yet will I never be guilty of such Injustice, as to intrench on her p[r]erogative; for all that I will ever desire of you is onely this, that you will henceforth render her all the love and cordiall affection that is due from a Husband to a Wife, as her merits chalenge, and your obligation to her binds you; and no longer harbour the least thought of me [fol. 97ᵛ] that may be to her prejudice; and if in any thing you will oblige me, let it be I conjure you by that Friendship I once had for you, instantly to leave me, and never more to importune me with the trouble of your sight.

I shall endeavour to obey you Madam (he repli'd) but though you banish me your eyes, you cannot force my heart from hovering neere you; for till life forsakes it, that never can abandon you.

Do not percevere in these extravagant expression (said I) lest you compell me to repeat what I have said, and once more tell you (with an Epith͟i͟t͟e^at^)[1] that I will most horridly hate you; which is all the requitall you shall ever have of me for your egregious Folly.

I could adde no more, nor he returne me any answere, for *Amarantha* supposing I might take ill from her that she left me so long alone, dresst her and came downe; whereupon he thinking it unfit to continue such a discourse before her, bid me farewell, leaving me no less pleas'd with his departure, then I had been the contrary with his Company. I thought I had said enough to discourage him from ever coming neer me more; but notwithstanding I had express'd so much bitterness, and anger against him, yet after this, divers times did he assume the confidence to come to my Fathers, in hope that one time or other, Fortune might be as propitious to him as before, in helping him to a second surprizall of me alone; but in this, she was more my friend then his; for I had still the good hap either to espy him my selfe ere he came within the gates, or else had notice given me of his approach by some of our Family, to each perticuler person whereof I had declar'd the aversion I had against him (though I conceal'd from everyone the chiefest reason I had for it, lest they might judge me guilty of some lightness in my carriage which might have encourag'd him so impudently to affront me in my honour, by making me those Overtures which I could not heare motion'd without offending Vertue: but whatever Censure they might have pass'd on me,

---

[1] The word "Epith͟i͟t͟e" is amended with "ite" underlined for deletion and "at" inserted.

I was secure in my owne Innocence from justly meriting any blame) therefore to shun all troubles of the like nature, so soon as ever I knew he was coming, I conceal'd my selfe in private, so as he could never get so much as a sight of me though he still enquir'd for me when he came; but finding me still deni'd, and no possibility of seeing me, he gave over at length his vain pursutes, and thereby freed me from no slight trouble.

But t'was not long I had been rid of that, ere a new one befell me; and such a one, as till then I had never known any so insupportable: which was not onely the loss of *Merinza's* beloved company, but even the utter deprivation of all hopes of ever [fol. 98 ͬ] enjoying any converse with her again: for being about this time married to a young Nobleman (whose estate equall'd his extraction, both being eminently great) she was no longer at her owne dispose, but oblig'd not onely to leave poore *Arthenia*, but likewise her dearest and neerest Relations to follow her Husband, who in a litle while after their marriage carried her from us all, to the further part of Sicily where he liv'd.

Faine would I have gone with her, rather then my life, and no less desirous was she that I should, would *Irvinus* (for so was he call'd) have consented: but whether it were that he envied me her kindness, or imagin'd I had too great a Friendship for her, or that (as I rather think) he had conceiv'd some prejudice against me for opposing the match between them (as I confess I did) fancying him as unworthy of her as he has since but too well proov'd himselfe: but which of these reasons t'was that moved him to deny me the happiness, and his Lady the satisfaction of having me with her I cannot tell; but so it was that he compell'd us to take so sad a farewell as left us no hopes of ever seeing each other more, but patience was my onely remedy, and to that I had recourse endeavouring to mittigate my discontent with the beliefe I had, that Time would not be able to banish me her thoughts, though distance rob'd me of her sight.

But now as if Fortune had a designe to repaire the griefe she had made me suffer in depriving me of *Merinza*, she confer'd on me in requitall, the acquaintance, and Friendship of a Lady (named *Ianthe*) who for Wit and Beauty most deservedly acquired the admiration of all that ever saw her: and using (as in the spring time of her Youth she did) to frequent Adonis Garden, which is a Place of all other in Palermo the most pleasant and delightfull, being constantly filled every Evening with Troopes of the noblest and best accomplish'd Gallants and choicest Beauties that Sicily could boast, who repair'd thither to take the Aire, and recreate themselves: amongst whom, Faire *Ianthe* bare away the prize for beautie, being justly stil'd the glory of the Adonian Walkes: but I dare not undertake to delineat the charming features of her lovely Face, lest by my dull description I injure her perfections in seeking to illustrate them; therefore I will onely tell you Madam (pursu'd *Arthenia*) that though I knew her not till after her youth had past its Meridian, and her beauty was in its waine, yet even then did I think her Natures Master Piece, and the loveliest person that ever I had seen.

What this most excellent Lady saw in me that could move her to affect me as she did, I know not, but this I am sure of, she lov'd me in so passionate a manner, as no Lover ere doated on a Mistress more then she did on *Arthenia*; and no sooner did she begin to love me, but she espous'd all my Concerns, and made them so absolutely hers, as there could not any thing hapen to me wherein she did not beare an equall part: and besides the satisfaction I found in being [fol. 98ᵛ] belov'd by so admirable a person I deriv'd from her Friendship an extraordinary advantage; for having by the Charmes of her conversation, the sweetness of her disposition, and the pleasantness of her humour (in which she excell'd all the woemen that yet I ever knew) gain'd so powerfull an ascendant over my Mothers heart, that her Friendship to *Ianthe* almost equall'd *Ianthes* to me, which kindness of *Brecenas* to her, she employ'd so well for my interest, as I could not wish for any thing that might conduce either to my content, or happiness, if it were in my Mothers power to grant, but she would obtain it for me. But ~~the~~ so unvaluable a treasure as the enjoyment of such a Friend, was a felicity too great for the unhappie *Arthenia* long to possess; for Experience had but newly rendred me sensible of my bliss, when *Ianthe's* misfortunes (in which I must give her the precedency of me as well as in all things else) ravished her from me, though not her friendship I believe, for I am verily perswaded (if she be yet alive) in what part of the World soe're she is, she still retains for me the same kindness as ever.

My Mother was the first that made a discovery of my loss for having neither seen, nor heard of her in a much longer time then she us'd to be absent from us, was not content to send, but went herselfe to enquire after her; but could by no meanes learn what what was become of her: nor other account could she get (notwithstanding all her diligent enquiries) then that she had on a sudden abandon'd her Lodging, and was gone none knew whether onely accompanied with *Ambracia* (her Maid) who for her fidelity and affection to *Ianthe* deserves to have her name recorded in Fames Golden Book; since no frowns of Fortune could fright her from her service; nay, I rather think they invited her to serve her the more faithfully. For *Ianthe* (by the misery of that War that had wasted our Country, wherin her Husband had been engag'd, which together with his profuse Prodigality beside) being reduced to such a condition, as after his death she was so far unable to keep ~~her self~~ a servant, as she was not able to keep herselfe without the assistance of her Friends, yet even in this sad estate did *Ambracia* (who had been brought up with her to be her Companion in her childish sports) find her out, and proffer'd to serve her freely without so much as the hopes of a reward; nor did she onely serve her gratis, but by her industry, and ingenuity help'd to maintaine her too; with which, together with what assistance she had from her Relations, she made a shift to keep herselfe in a garbe and habit so genteel, and handsome, as those that knew not her condition could not but think her Mistress of a fortune plentifull enough: and so sincerely was *Ambracia* devoted to her, that [fol. 99ʳ] though she often importun'd, and perswaded her to leave her alone to wrastle with her unhappie Fate, yet were her requests invain, for so oft as *Ianthe* perswaded her to abandon her, so oft did *Ambracia* repeat her vowes never to forsake her till Death divided them: and truly I believe she was as good as her word; for I could never learn any intelligence of her since no more then of her Mistress, whose loss to me was a griefe so great, as I resented [felt] not *Loreto's* with halfe so much moderation, as I deplor'd poore *Ianthe's* with excess of sorrow; for I considered, that in him I lost but a faithless Lover, but in loosing her, I lost a Faithfull Friend; which was a Treasure to be priz'd above the World, or ought that it contains.

But now Madam I must beg leave to silence a while my owne concerns (pursu'd *Arthenia*) to returne againe to *Claromenes's* whose establishment on the Throne of his Father was now most earnestly desir'd, not by his Friends alone, but even by his very enemies; those excepted who had been the immediate Murtherers of his Royall Father, for they knew well their Crime to be to great to hope a Pardon, and therefore could not but dread the returne of him from whose Justice they could expect nothing less then an utter exterpation; all else (I say) wisht his return as much as those men fear'd it; for Sicilie had since that inhumane Murther so often chang'd not onely her Governours, but her Goverment also, as the People grew extreame weary of both; especially after the death of *Ormisdas* to whom I must be so just as to acknowledge, that though he gain'd his Dignity and Power by Tyranie, and usurpation, yet when once he was securely seated at the Helme of Goverment, Sicily enjoy'd under him a peacefull and quiet condition enough; but he being dead, there was nothing but an Anarchicall confusion thoroughout the whole Nation, and one Ruler pulling downe another; so as all men began to be more sensible then ever of their want of a King: tis true there had been severall attempts made by divers of *Claromenes's* Friends in *Ormisdas's* lifetime to place him on that throne the other so injuriously detain'd from him; but all their Designs were still discover'd by the treachery of some false Ones amongst them to *Ormisdas*, who by his Pollicy still found means to frustrate their good intentions so as they never came to any thing: But the ways of Providence are too obscure for Mortall eyes to look into, or for humane capacities to comprehend; for when all men even dispair'd of ever seeing any of *Clearchus* his Race sway the Sicilian Scepter, Heaven found out a way altogether unexpected, and almost miraculous to bring the Illustrious *Claromenes* back to his Kingdome, and place him on his Throne, without the spilling of one drop of blood to seat him there.

But to let your Majesty know how this was done ~~how this was affected~~, I must tell you Madam (went on *Arthenia*). There was a Gentleman (nam'd *Meltiades*) that had been formerly an Officer in King *Clearchus's* Armie who hapned to be taken Prisoner by the Enemy, and not being thought considerable enough for his quality to deserve a ransome, was enforced to undergoe a long imprisonment; but questionless [fol. 99ᵛ] had his true worth been but known to the King, he would have bought off Fetters at any rate: but at that time he appear'd but as an unpolish'd Diamond the true value whereof cannot be discern'd till some cunning Artists hand has made a discovery of that excellency which was before conceal'd: and so did Time (the Touchstone of true worth) by *Meltiades*, even display in him such uncommon qualities, and gallant performances as rendred him deservedly deare both to the Great *Claromenes* and Sicily, for being the Instrumentall restorer of the one to his Crown, and the rescuer of the other from ruine and confusion.

Tis true he did for a while desert the Royall Party, but whether it were out of resentment [sentiment], or designe I cannot say, but I am apt to think the latter, since what he did, serv'd but to put him into the better capacity to serve his Prince the more successfully: for *Ormisdas* having been made acquainted with his Valour, and conduct, not onely set him at liberty, but conferred on him great Offices of Trust and at length made him chiefe Governour of Corsica.

But I am perswaded (continu'd *Arthenia*) all these preferments would ne're have tempted him to have laid aside his Loyalty, could it any way have been serviceable to his Soveraign; for *Clearchus* then murther'd, and Prince *Claromenes* litle or no hopes left of regaining his lost Crowne, at least whilst *Ormisdas* liv'd; but death had no sooner remov'd him, but he began to lay a Designe which requir'd some time and much privesie to bring it to maturity. He had found by the intelligence he held in Sicily, how weary all men generally were of their Yoak and how much better they now thought it to have one King, then many Tyrants, and laying hold of the divisions, and ambition of *Ormisdas*'s successors he settled all things in Corsica in such a manner as might best conduce to the accomplishment of that which he had long before projected, and march'd back to Sicily (with a considerable Armie, of whose courages, and fidelities he was well assur'd) whether he had been some time before invited by those who retain'd the chiefest power there for their aide against another Party that opposed them: but upon his approach they disappear'd, and with much Joy was he wellcom'd to Palermo the Keys of the Gates deliver'd him, and the sole power put into his hands; which he might have made use of to exault himself to that Dignity *Ormisdas* arrived at: but he was not so ambitious of grandure, as desirous to approve himself a faithfull Subject, and counted it a much more gallant thing to restore a Crowne, then to weare one.

Presently after his coming to Palermo the old Senatours were dismist, and a new Senat chose; in which Election a perticuler care was taken by him that few or none should be chosen that might oppose his Design which in a short time after he brought to perfection: for when they were all assembled in the Senat house, he stood up in the midst of them, and made an Oration, wherein he so well to the life decipher'd the Crimes of those that preceded them in that Place, and the miseries and distractions [fol. 100ʳ] they had both formerly and of late been Involv'd in; and withall so fully illustrated not onely the convenience, but necessity likewise of their being governed by a single person: whereupon inferring, that since the good, and welfare of their Country depended on their having a King, there was no reason but that they might with less reluctancy sweare alleagiance to him who was born to command them, then to any of their Fellow subjects. What he had said, was so unanimously approv'd of, that without ever staying to deliberate on it, they instantly with a mutuall consent decreed to invite home their native Prince, and impale his Royall Temples with that Diadem which had been too long unjustly detained from him.

No sooner was this Decree sign'd, but my Mother who chanced to be then in Palermo, sent me word of it, well knowing how wellcome newes it would be to me; but scarce had I perus'd her letter ere I felt my heart touch'd with such a transport of Joy, as till then I never knew ought that resembled it; nor is it possible whilst my soule's confin'd within this mortall Frame for it ever to be sensible of a more transcendent Joy, that excepted wherewith I was inspir'd, when in the restoration of my King I saw the accomplishment of all those fervent desires, passionate wishes, and most zealous Prayers that I so oft had offer'd to Heaven on his behalfe. Nor was I singuler in my rejoyceings, for so soon as ever this Decree of the Senate was publish'd there was nothing to be seen, or heard in all places, but signes of a generall, and universall Joy, which in an Instant had difused, and spread it selfe thorowout the wholle Kingdome. The night seem'd to vie splendor with the day, by reason of those innumerable Fires which (not onely in every City and Towne, but in each Country Village too) were made as it were to offer up one generall sacrifice of praise to Heaven for so unexpected a blessing.

Nothing now remain'd to compleat Sicilies satisfaction but the consummation of their desires in the Illustrious *Claromenes*, his returne which was daily expected: for being once resolv'd on in Senat, an order was instantly setled for his reception in such a manner as might befit his Majesty, and best express their dutyfull affections; and perticuler persons chosen to go in the humblest manner to implore his Pardon for all past Offences, and to invite him home; which invitation he accepted, and graciously consented to an Act of Grace and Pardon to all Offenders, of what nature, or quality soever their Crimes might be, such onely excepted who had dipt their murtherous hands in his Martyr'd Fathers blood.

He was at this time in Celtiberia (with the Princess *Marina*) whether daily repair'd many Persons of the highest quality in Sicily (in such crowds as that City could scarce containe them) to pay their earliest Tribute of veneration to their now acknowledg'd King, and to waite on his Royall person back to Sicily; where in a few days after he happily arriv'd, together with the two young Princes *Issodates*, and *Hiperion*, and safely landed at the Port of Taromenion [fol. 100ᵛ] where the generous *Meltiades* waited to receive him, and as he landed falling at his Feet which he bedew'd with teares of Joy tendred him there his Faith, and alleagiance; but scarce had he touch'd the earth with his knee, ere the Great *Claromenes* rais'd him up, and embraced him with all the demonstrations of a most tender Amity, conferring on him the honoured title of Father; which ever after to his death he stil'd him.[2]

Thousands of People flock'd to the seaside to wellcome him on shore, congratulating his return with acclamations of Joy so loud as the very Aire far and nigh resounded with the ecchos of their shouts: for that day he repos'd himself in Taromenion, but early the next morning he took his Journey to Palermo where he was expected with impatient longings; yet how great soe're they were, mine I am sure equall'd, if not exceeded the most passionate of their desires to see him, whom above all things on earth I had a thousand times wish'd to behold; and in such a manner were my thoughts taken up with my Countries approaching happiness, as sleep had scarce the power to close my eyes the night that preceded that so much long'd for day: and so early that morning did I rise, as I left the Sun in bed; though I knew t'was impossible till towards Noon for *Claromenes* to reach the place where I stood to waite his coming that I might have a view of him, though onely in transit, which was all I could hope to bless my eyes with at that time: but soe were all places (nay even the very high ways) throng'd with People who press'd so thick to get a sight of him, as t'was not possible for his Chariot to pass on, but at a very slow rate; so that it was past mid day ere he came by where I was: but Multitudes of gallant Gentlemen bravely mounted on their prancing Coursers did I see pass by, and many Chariots fill'd with the noblest personages in the Kingdome of both Sexes who deservedly enough merited a perticuler regard, yet then I counted them all so inconsiderable as I took litle notice of any of them.

At length appear'd Great *Claromenes* with his two Illustrious Brothers; and the Brave *Meltiades* to whom he gave the honour to ride with him in the same Chariot; but though my eyes were so intently fix'd on *Claromenes* as I minded not any of the rest, yet methought such Majestick Rayes darted from his Princely Brow as even dazled me so, as I could look on him no other ways then as One not of mortall extract, but rather too divine for humane race; which inspir'd me with so sacred a veneration for him that though his Chariot went on so slowly as I might have taken a full view of him, yet I scarce beheld him but by a glance, casting my eyes instantly to the ground as one abash'd: but however, I went home so well pleased as I can never hope an equall satisfaction, and he pursu'd his Journey, still meeting multitudes of People who loudly resounded his Wellcome, and their Iopeans[3] to Heaven for this so Joyfull day; nothing now being to be heard from all mouths but such expressions as these[:] Heaven preserve our King; long may he live. Accurs'd be all his Enemies: [A]nd all the way as he went to Palermo,

---

[2] Charles II, accompanied by his brothers, James (*Issodates*) and Henry (*Hiperion*), was greeted by General George Monck (*Meltiades*). Charles addressed Monck as "Father," echoing the title given to Miltiades, the Athenian general victorious over the Persians at the Battle of Marathon.

[3] Io-paeons are Latin interjections of joy.

the high Wayes in the Country, and the streets in every Towne he came through were strew'd with Flowers and the Dores and Windows of each house adorn'd with [fol. 101ʳ] Garlands, and Boughs of Laurell. He had not gone above a mile or two further, ere he quited his Chariot, and mounted his Horse; to the intent he might the better gratifie those that were desirous to see him, with the more perfect view of his Royall Person. Just at the enterance of Gela (which is a little Towne about foure miles distant from Palermo) he was met by four and twenty young Virgins all in White (resembling the purity, and innocency of their minds) curiously dress't with Garlands of artificiall Roses which might have contended for beauty with those that Nature produces. These Virgins were preceded by a certain Grave Matron (that seem'd to be their Governess) who by a most elo-quent Speech design'd for the purpose congratulated his return to his Kingdome, wishing him a long, and happie life, and a prosperous Reign: which with a grace proper to himselfe alone, having testifi'd his approbation of, he proceeded on his Journey, being Usher'd by those Ladies cleare thorough Gela, who going on, two and two before him, carried between them rich Baskets fill'd with the most oderifferous Flowers that crowns the Spring, wherewith they strew'd him all a long till they had brought him to the further side of the Towne, where with low obeasances they took their leaves in the humblest manner imaginable.

When he drew neere Palermo he was met a little without the Citty by *Bonario*[4] (the chiefe Magistrate thereof) and all the Officers of note belonging to the City in their distinct habits demonstrating their severall employments, attended by a Gallant Troop of young men of the chiefest Families in Palermo, all cloth'd alike, in a rich and gracefull manner. Soe soon as *Bonario* came up to the King, he resign'd him his sword, and Keys, which *Claromenes* instantly return'd him back, thereby confirming his Goverment to him. This Ceremony being over, *Bonario* march'd on Foot bare before him, being preceded by the rest in the same manner, till they had brought him to his Palace: on each side of him rode the two young Princes, and *Meltiades* just before him (to signify t'was he that brought him in) and after him follow'd all the Nobility, and Gentry that had waited on him from Celtiberia, as also those that had met him at Taromenion.

His enterance into Palermo was in all respects as magnificent as the short-ness of the time they had to prepare for his reception would allow; but not being comparable to that state and grandure which was shewn at his Coronation, I shall in silence pass it by, and onely tell your Majesty (continu'd *Arthenia*) that being come to his Palace, it was observ'd by some who were neer him, that a Cloud of Sadness o'respread his Princely brow; which t'was believ'd the remem-brance of that inhumane death his Illustrious Father suffer'd in that place, rais'd in him which silently testifi'd the tenderness of his nature that could in the midst of those Joys, and Tryumphs wherewith he was surrounded, forget his present

---

[4] In 1660, Sir Richard Browne was Lord Mayor of London.

happiness to think on the misfortunes of the King his Father though divers years [fol. 101 ᵛ] since past. The first thing he did after his return was to confirme that Act of Grace which he before had granted; after that he took into his Princely care the rectifying disorders in matters of Religion, reinstating the Flamines⁵and Arch Flamines in their former Dignity, confirming to them those priviledges, and perogatives they had enjoy'd in the days of his Predecessors; leaving it to them to take care for the reedifying of those Temples which had in the late troubles been dimollish'd, and for the beautifying of those that were left standing (none whereof but had sufficently felt the injuries and abuses of the Prophane) that Piety might once more appeare in a splendor bright enough to amaze (if not confound) with the glory of it, all those whom with its beauty it could not atract.

But now your Majesty shall see Divine Vengeance appeare in a most formidable manner to revenge the cruell cruell murther of the best of Kings; which being many years since t'was done, it seemed to some as if Heaven had forgot to call the Acters of it to an account for so execrable a Fact: but though it suffer'd some of the chiefest, (as *Ormisdas, Brataldo*, and *Irvistus*)⁶ to go to their Graves in peace, yet it let them not rest long in quiet there: for the bodies of those three men were by the Decree of *Claromenes* and the Senat, torne out of those stately Monuments which had been set up to perpetuate their memories to after Ages, and drag'd on the Ground from the place of their Interment, to that Place where all notorious Mallefactors were executed; where on a Gibet they were hang'd up for three dayes space, to be expos'd to the view of all beholders; which time expir'd they were taken downe and throwne into a hole made on purpose larg enough to containe their wretched Carkasses.

Soe strange a Destiny as this none could imagine would ever have attended *Ormisdas* that had seen his Obsequies cellibrated with such Pompe and state, as it not only equall'd, but far exceeded the Funurall solemnities of any Monarch that ever reign'd in Sicilie. The rest of those Regicides that were living as many of them as could be taken (for severall of them were escap'd away out of the Kingdome, preferring an eternall exile, before a shamefull death which they could not but expect) were brought to the Barre of Justice; where after a Legall Tryall, being convicted of Treason, Murther, and Rebellion, they were condemn'd, and sentenced to be drawne from their Prisons in the most ignominious manner imaginable, to the Place where they were to suffer death; after which, their heads were to be sever'd from their bodies, which were to be cut in pieces, their Intrales to be burnt, and their heads together with the severall pieces of their bodies to be

---

⁵ The terms flamines and arch flamines refer to priests devoted to the service of a particular deity and here are used specifically for bishops and archbishops.

⁶ John Bradshaw (*Brataldo*) was president of the court that sentenced Charles I to death. Henry Ireton (*Irvista*) was a parliamentary general and Cromwell's son-in-law. Both were posthumously executed along with Cromwell (*Ormisdas*), and their heads were placed on gates.

fix'd on the foure principall Gates of Palermo, there to continue for a terrour to all such as might be inclined to practice the like Crimes.

This signall piece of Justice being performed, nothing more remain'd to render Sicily compleatly happie but to see their Soveraigns head deck'd with his triple Diadem, which he had refused to put on till he had in some degree aveng'd his Dread Fathers death on those who had so barbarously destroy'd him; but now that being done, all possible preparation [fol. 102^r] was made to enthrone him with all the grandure that magnificence could give, or Art devize. All the Nobility, and persons of quality in the Kingdom had left their Rurall Seats, to come and be spectators of his Tryumphall passage thorow Palermo to his Coronation, the Citizens whereof not difficent [deficient] in any thing that might illustrate their Loyall affection to his Royall Person, by the entertainments they prepared him; which to give your Majesty an exact account of in each perticuler (continu'd *Arthenia*) is more then I am able; but as far as my memory will give me leave, I shall endevour to relate it as neer as I can without adding to or detracting from it.

[Blank line left in the manuscript]

The Morning of that Glorious Day very early went *Claromenes* privatly to the Cittadell (which stands a litle without Palermo) whether repair'd all those that were appointed, or had of themselves design'd to attend him thence: and in this manner was he conducted along.[7] First march'd on Prince *Issodates*'s Guard follow'd by the Kings meniall servants; next after them rode all the Nobles glittering in all the height of bravery that Gold or Jewells could give; these were succeeded by the chiefe Ministers of state, after whom follow'd Prince *Issodates* by himself alone, and after him came the two great Officers of the Court (whose titles I have forgot) the one of them bearing the Crown, and the other the Scepter; the next that follow'd was *Cleomedon* (a Prince of the blood) bearing the sword; after whom came the most Illustrious *Claromenes* on as stately a Horse as ever Sparta bred, who seem'd to trample on the earth he trod with scorn, as being proud he was destin'd to so noble a use, his Trapings sutable, being couer'd to the ground with a Crimson Velvet Cloth most richly embroidred with Pearls and Diamonds; a gallant Traine of Gentlemen sumptiously habited, in an equipage sutable to the grandure of the day, follow'd him, and last of all came *Claromenes*'s owne Guard led by the Generous *Meltiades* who had been created Prince of Tarentum, and Generall of all the Souldiers that were at present in pay, or might hereafter be rais'd.

But perhaps your Majesty may wonder *Hyperion* appear'd not in the solemnity of this great day, but alass poor Prince he liv'd not to be either an assistant at, nor spectator of it for he died soon after his returne to Sicily in the prime and

---

[7] Charles II proceeded from the Tower, through the City to Whitehall, and a series of triumphal arches marked this route.

flower of his youth much lamented by all, but especially by the King his Brother to whom he was most deservedly deare.[8]

But to returne from whence I digress'd (said *Arthenia*) I must tell you Madam that all the streets thorough which his Majesty pass'd were hung on each side with Cloth of Arras, and rail'd on both sides; within which Railes stood the chiefe Cittizens in their ranks according to their severall qualities and degrees; to keep the common People from rudely pressing to neer him; which they might have been apt to do, had they not been hindred. [fol. 102ᵛ] And though Palermo could not equall the ancient Romanes, who were wont to honour those who brought home Victory, or acquir'd new Conquests for the enlargment of their Dominions, with erecting Arches of Marble for their Tryumphall returns, yet did they strive to imitate them in those which they set up which for number and largness as farre exceeded them, as they excell'd these in richness of materialls.

No sooner was his Majesty enter'd within the City, but he was saluted by a Consort of Wind Musick; and not farre off stood the first Tryumphall Arch, on the one hand whereof, on the foreside of it, on a Pedestall was placed a Woman personating Rebellion mounted on that many headed Beast call'd Hydra; and clothed in a Crimson Robe torn, with Snakes creeping about her, and her Wast girt round with Serpents, and on her head Tresses of Serpents insteed of haire, and crown'd with a Diademe of Fire: in one hand she grasp'd a sword besmear'd with blood, and in the other she held an Inchanting Rod.[9]

She was attended by Confussion in a terrible shape, cloth'd in a Garment of disagreeable Colours, and put on the wrong way; in her hands she bare torne

---

[8] Prince Henry died of smallpox after returning to England.

[9] Many records of this royal progress survive, and so it is difficult to tell if the author of *Rivall Friendship* wrote from personal notes or consulted one of the many editions of John Ogilby. The description given in *Rivall Friendship* seems quite close to the 1661 edition of John Ogilby's *The Relation of His Majesties Entertainment Pasing through the City of London To His Coronation: With A Description of the Triumphal Arches, and Solemnity* (London: Printed by Tho. Roycroft, for Rich. Marriott in St. Dunstan's Church-Yard in Fleet Street, 1661), the Huntington Library copy of RB 0181.140001. The 1661 edition, for example, lists the following details:

> REBELLION, mounted on a *Hydra,* in a Crimson Robe, torn, Snakes crawling on her Habit, and begirt with Serpents, her Hair Snaky, a Crown of Fire on her Head, a bloody Sword in one Hand, a charming Rod in the other. Her Attendant CONFUSION, in a Deformed Shape, a Garment of several ill-matched Colours, and put on the wrong way; on her Head, Ruines of Castles, torn Crowns, and broken Scepters in each Hand.

The far more elaborate edition of 1662, entitled *The Entertainment of His Most Excellent Majestie Charles II in His Passage throughout the City of London to his Coronation,* ed. Ronald Knowles (MRTS, now ACMRS Press) which includes a history of triumphal arches, classical and contemporary verse, and elaborate descriptions of rivers, does not seem to figure as a source for *Rivall Friendship.*

Crownes, and broken Scepters, and on her head the Ruines of Cities. On the
other hand of the Arch on a like Pedestall stood another Woman representing
Monarchy, upheld by another presenting Loyalty. Monarchy was in a Purple
Robe embroidred with Crowns, and Scepters; over which was a Mantle loosly
cast, edg'd with a Seagreen and silver Frieng [fringe], and on it Sicilia painted,
on her head the City Palermo, in her right hand Bastia, and in her left, Calaris,
which were the principall Cities in those three Islands over which *Claromenes*
extended his Soveraignity. Loyalty was cloth'd all in White, and in her right
hand she held three Crownes, and in her left three Scepters.

 Over their heads was admirably represented in Painting, a Prospect of
Claromenes's landing at Taromenion, with ships riding at Anchore, and a Man,
like *Meltiades* kneeling and kissing his hand; on each side Troops of souldiers,
and multitudes of People looking on: upon the other side (opposite to it) was
drawn on another Tablet severall heads of men newly cut from their bodies and
over it writ in Capitall Letters this Motto

Heavens Vengeance Traitors close pursues.

Intimating the Justice executed on *Clearchus's* Murtherers. And over the midle
of the Arch was painted in another large Tablet the Portracture of *Claromenes*
himselfe, with Usurpation flying before him; which was express'd by a certaine
deformed Beast with many ugly heads, some big, some litle; and one by it selfe
growing out of its shoulder resembling *Ormisdas*; and underneath the mouth
of Hell gaping to receive it. Above this were placed the Statues of *Ismenas*, and
Clearchus; and a litle higher between them [fol. 103^r] the Kings, under which in
Gold was writ these Words.

Claromenes King of Sicily, Corsica, and Sardinia
The best and Greatest of Princes
The extinguisher of Tyranie
The restorer of our Liberty
The Setler of our quiet
And the establisher of our Felicity
Who is not onely worthy to command
These Islands, but the whole World

Behind his Statue in a larg Table was delineated that Tree[10] which with its
spreading Branches once lent him a favourable shelter from the eyes of his pursuers after his overthrow by *Ormisdas*; which instead of fruit was laden with
Crowns and Scepters, as a recompense for that benefit it afforded him.

 On the other side of the Arch was prefigur'd *Bonario* presenting the Keys of
Palermo to *Claromenes*; and in four Niches were placed as many Female Figures.

---

[10] For the story of the Royal Oak, See Book 6, n. 23, page 189.

The first had on her shield a Globe painted, with the Sun rising on it, and Bats and Owls (those Birds of night) flying to the shaddow. The second had on hers a swarme of Bees wheting their stings, the third, an Arme appearing out of the Clouds, and in the hand an unsheath'd Sword. The fourth, on hers a Mountain burning, with Cities, and Vineyards ruin'd. The Musick of this structure was wholly warlike, compos'd of Drumes, and Trumpets, placed on two Balconies within the Arch; which upon his Majesties approach beat the one a Battell, and the other sounded a Charge, whereupon *Rebellion* ris up (at which they both ceas'd) and address'd herselfe to him in this manner.

Rebellions Speech

Stand, stand who e're you are; and know before you further pass; this stage is mine, on which I do forbid you enterance; even I, who am to Kings and Monarchy a Foe ne're to be reconsil'd. But if yet you know me not, I'le tell you further who I am that dare presume to bid you stand, even in the midst [fol. 103ᵛ] *of all your Tryumphs, and in your Regall City too. Know then, that I am Hells First born; and at my birth the Powers of Darkness smil'd, while my Joy'd Father unhing'd the Poles and shook the fixed Earth with ecchoing my name. Rebellion shalt thou be call'd (said he) and by my aide, both Kings and Princes shalt thou overcome, and trample on their conquer'd Diadems: there's no Succession though of ne're so long a date, nor Right, how Just soever which thou shalt not subdue, by Popular assistance. But if you further aske what Interest I pretend too in this Place; I must tell you, all Great Citys are my sphear to move in; where by my Sorcery I fill mens heads with wild C[h]ymeras, and Dreames of Anarchy, and force the Vulgar in tumultuous Swarmes to Court a civill Warre. In fine, t'was I that by intestine strife engag'd your Kingdoms in unnaturall broiles; and hope I shall at last with displai'd Ensignes march and tread downe Monarchy throughout the World.*

At which espying *Monarchy* and *Loyalty*, she started as one affrighted, but recollecting herself again proceeded.

Ah Sicilie (Monarchick Isle) standst thou tryumphant there, are thy Wounds whole again, and on thy Cheeks fresh smiles: is Joy return'd to these late mournfull Isles, ah now I do begin to shake with horrid Feare, since Claromenes in despight of me, and all my Fathers power must enter and a King be Crown'd: his rise, too well I see must be my fall, and I must now pack hence to Hell, from whence I came.

At which *Monarchy* taking the word spake thus

Monarchys Speech

To Hell foule Hag and hide thee there in everlasting night. Now Royall Sir you may securely pass, and march in tryumph through the joyfull Streets. Enter our Life (I say) our Comfort, and our Sun; and with your Glorious beames revive your Peo-

*ple, who will henceforth onely contend who shall in Loyalty surpass each other: May
your great actions, and immortall Name be writ in Fames eternall Book for future
Ages to admire; and may both you and your Posterity be crown'd with Palmes and
Laurell, enjoying a perpetuall Peace; that all men may acknowledge, whilst they
great sir are blest in you, that of all Goverments that be, none can compare with
mine.*

She having done the Drums and Trumpets again entertain him whilst he pass'd
through the Arch; but not much further had he advanced ere he was met by a
Youth in Indian habit (attended by two Negroes) who on his knee bespake his
expectation in these words

[fol.104ʳ] I do beseech you Royall sir one minute stay. See where an Indian
comes bringing with him a Caravan full fraight with perfect Loyalty, and thanks
to pay as your due Tribute. Wherat drew neer another Youth (in the like garbe)
mounted on a Camell (led by two Negroes more) laden with Jewells, and Spices
to be scatter'd amongst the Spectators; who in these words made his Address.

The Mores Speech

*Pearles, Diamonds, Rubies, Saphires Emraulds, and the best of Aromaticks, you
glorious Trifles of the East avant; we are rich enough in our compleated Joys. Your
Sacred Person Sir has brought us home more wealth then Tagus shore affords; the
riches of both Indies are but mean, compar'd with what you bring. Nor can we
doubt to see this Realm, the Magazine of all that's rich or great and your Imperi-
all Title be indeed, what other Crowns boast but in name: which Heaven grant,
and that we ne're may see the Sun set on that Diadem you are going to assume, nor
any Cloud arise to eclips, or darken the splendor of your Majesty.*

He having ended, the King again pass'd on to the midst of the next street, where
was erected the second Arch; on the foreside whereof stood a man personating
Neptune, in a loose Garment of Blew and White, waved like the Sea; and over
it a Mantle like a Saile; his Head Crown'd with Flages like long haire falling
on his shoulders, his Beard (seagreen and white) long and curl'd, a Trident in
his right hand, and in his Left, the Modell of a Ship, and besides him an Urne,
out of which flow'd water. And on the Front of the Arch, in a Shield was this
Inscription

*Claromenes
Sicilias Neptune,
The great Commander of the Sea.*

Above it were placed foure statues representing the foure quartiers of the World;
and within the Arch in Foure Niches were placed a like number of Woemen, by
whom were represented *Arithmetick*, *Geometry*, *Astronomy*, and *Navigation*. On
her Vesture, by whom *Arithmetick* was design'd, were Lines drawn with Musick

[fol. 104ᵛ] Notes on them, and in her Banner a Book open, with a hand pointing to certain Figures. *Geometry* had a Green Mantle cast about her, and in her Banner a pare of Compasses, and a Triangle. *Astronomy* was in a loose Robe of a Skycolour, set thick with Stars of Gold, and in her Banner a Table whereon was drawne divers Astronomicall Figures. *Navigation* was in a seagreen Garment, and in her Banner she bare an Anchore with a Cable wound about it. The Musick of this Arch were Wind Instruments, which plai'd incessantly till his Majesty drew nigh; but then stoping, *Neptune* spake to him thus.

Neptunes Address

> *The Moon (Dread Sir) has oft her silver Cressents fill'd since to Sicilian Shores I wafted you; when mounted on a Billow I then strove to bid you wellcome: but on the Land were Joys So loud, as hindred me from being heard; but now; above my highest bounds I have rear'd my head to say, what could not then reach to your Sacred Eare. Haile Mighty Prince (pursu'd he with a low obeasance) whose puissant hand commands the Ocean. This City (which I serve with neighbouring Flouds) did long lament your absence, but now with Joys rais'd to a perfect height, wellcoms with me your bles't returne; by which she is possest of all the wealth remotest Lands afford. You are Neptunes Neptune Sir, and my Dominions are but your Highway to severall Nations, who though they boast their strength on Land, yet you alone command the Watery World: which that you ever may, is Neptunes wish.*

He having ended, the Musick plai'd on again whilst *Claromenes* pass'd through; the Fountains all the while in every street flowing with Wine instead of Water.

By the next Arch was design'd the *Temple of Concord*, on the Front whereof was Inscrib'd in Golden Characters these words.[fol. 105ʳ]

In honour of the best of Princes
Concord
is once more return'd to Sicily,
in hope,
She shall no more be banish'd thence

On each side were placed a Figure, one whereof represented *Peace*, and the other *Truth*. The first had on her Shield, a Helmet, with Bees going in and out, the Motto whereof was. *Peace is the Child of War*. *Truth* bare on her Shield, *Time* bringing *Truth* out of a Cave; her Motto was *Brought to Light*. Above them stood Foure Figures more representing the Four chiefe Vertues, *Prudence, Justice, Tem[p]erance* and *Fortitude*. *Prudence* bare on her shield, Bellerophon mounted on a Pegasus, runing a Iavelin into the mouth of a Chymera, her Motto, *By Councell and virtue*. *Justice* had on hers, a Woman holding a Sword in one hand, and a Ballance in the other, her Motto was, *Perform'd aright*. *Temperance* had on her shield a Viol, and a Bridle; her Motto ^said Arthenia^ I have forgot: and on *Fortitudes* shield was drawn a Lion holding in his Paw the Armes of Sicilie, his Motto was *Faithfull to my charge*. The inward part of the Temple was round, darke at the Top, but made resplendent by artificiall Lights. The lower part was divided into ten equall parts by gilded Pilasters, and beautifi'd by twelve living Figures, three whereof were seated higher then the rest. The first, being the *Goddess of the Temple*, was in a very rich dress, in her hand she held a Caduceus, and at her Feet lay a Serpent which she trod upon. The second was *Truth*, drest exceeding richly too, bearing in her hand a Banner in which was painted a Book open, fastned by a Chain to a Cloud, and underneath a Fury plucking at the end of the Chaine, about the Banner was writ this Motto *Nothing's so strong a*[s] *Truth*. The third *Love*, no less costly in her habit, and on her Banner was drawn a Cupid with Roses in one hand, and a Fish in the other, and writ round it. *Sweet but Fliting*. A most harmonious Consort of Lutes compleated this Tryumph playing without ceasing (such soft and delicate strains as might have contended with the melody of *Amphions* Harp wherewith he charm'd both irrationall and senseless Creatures) till such time as the great *Claromenes* was enter'd the Temple; at which time, *Concord, Love*, and *Truth* who till that [fol. 105ᵛ] instant had not appear'd by the drawing of a Curtain discover'd them selves; entertaining him with a song, the words whereof (if I remember) were these.

1
Comes not here the King of Peace:
Who the Stars so long foretold,
From all Woes should us release,
Converting Iron times to Gold.

2
Behold, Behold;
Our Prince confirm'd by Heavenly signes
Brings healing Balme, and Anodines,
To close our Wounds, and pain asswage.

3
He comes with conquering Bays and Palme
Where swelling Billows us'd to rage:
Gliding on a Silver Calme:
Proud Interest now no more engage.

Chorus:
Let these Arched Roofes resound,
Joyning Instruments and voice,
To fright pale Spirits under Ground
But let Heaven and Earth rejoyce,
We our happiness have found;
He thus marching to be Crown'd,
Attended with this Glorious Traine,

From civill Broiles
Shall free these Isles,
Whilst he and his Posterity shall reigne.

This song ended, *Concord* herself alone spak to him thus.

Concords Address.

Wellcome Great Sir unto my Fane [Shrine] *which your returne has reedifi'd* [fol.
106ʳ] *and rear'd my Structure to so high a pitch, as the lofty Turrits seeme to touch
the Sky. Wild Tumult, and rude War (my greatest Foes) you have imprison'd
within Ianus Gates; oh may they there remaine forever, and no more break forth
to interrupt the quiet of your dayes, or my repose; may all dissensions henceforth
cease, Peace crown your Life, and Prosperity wait always on your Throne; and
may your Felicity transcend all that the most happie Monarchs ever knew; all this
and more Royall Sir is Concords wish.*

She having with a low reverence finish'd her Address, he pass'd on to the last
Tryumphall Arch; which represented the *Garden of Plenty*: over the Gate whereof
on the south enterance was *Bacchus* setting in a Chariot, drawn by Leopards,
with a Panthers skin thrown about him like a Mantle, his head crown'd with
Bunches of Red, White, and Black Grapes mix'd; a Bough of Ivy in one hand,
and in the other a cup; and over his head was painted *Silenus*, on an Ass, with
Satyres dancing about him in drunken, and Antick postures; and before him
the Prospect of a Vineyard. On the Northside was *Ceres*, drawn in a Chariot
by winged Dragons, and crown'd with Eares of Corne; in one hand she held a
Bunch of Popie, and in the other a lighted Torch, and above her was painted a
discription of Harvest. On the Westside was placed *Flora*, in a Gound as various
for colour as *Iriss* gaudy Bow; in one hand she held Red and White Roses, and in
the other Lilies, and on her Head she wore a Garland of severall other Flowers;
over her was painted a Garden, with Walks, Statues, Fountaines, Flowers, and
Figures of Men and Woemen walking up an[d] downe in it. On the East side
was to be seen the Goddess *Pomona* with a Garland of Fruite on her Head; in her
right hand she held the Sun, and in her left a Wand, and at her Feet all sorts of
Grassing and Gardning Tooles; and above her was drawn an Orcha[r]d.

At the foure Corners of the Arch were placed the foure seasons of the yeare;
and in Foure Niches stood as many Figures representing the Foure Winds. *Eurus*
was prefigured by a Blackmore with black Wings, his Emblem the sun rising,
and a faire plain Country. *Boreas* had instead of Feet, two serpents Tailes, his
Wings cover'd with Snow; his Emblem a Rocky mountainous Country, and the
Pleades rising over it. *Auster* was in a dark colour'd Mantle, with Winges like
Clouds; his Emblem a cloudy Sky, and Showers. *Zephyrus* like a Cupid with
Wings; his Emblem a flowry Plain. At a litle distance before this Structure was
erected two Stages, planted and adorn'd like Gardens; on one of which sate a

woman personating *Plenty*, with a Garland of Flowers on her head, and drest in a green vesture embroidred with Gold, holding in her hand a Cornucopiae; on each side of her a [fol. 106ᵛ] Virgin as her Attendants, who upon his Majesties approach arose, and address't herselfe to him thus.

Plenty's Address.

That Starre which at your Birth (Great Sir) did with his Beames at Noon, at once create both Joy and Wonder in the hearts of all; with its auspitious Lustre then ~~heir~~foretold the glittering Plenty of this Golden Age: The Clouds being now blowne o're which did so long our Joyes ecclips, and the sad Winter of your absence past, see Sir how all the Seasons of the yeare agree at once to bid you wellcome. Flora comes here to tender her due Homage, and to strow your Way with her enamel'd Treasure; Ceres, and Pomona too, most liberally diffuse their bounty over all ~~their~~ your Land; and Bacchus is so free of what is his, that Wine flowes now where Water onely ran before. Thus Seasons, Men, and Gods do testify their Joys to see Great Claromenes Tryumphs, and Sicilias happiness.

But to cleare one thing to your Majesty (continu'd *Arthenia*) which *Plenty* mentions concerning a star, I must tell you Madam; that at the birth of *Claromenes* there was a starre seen at midday, which by thousands of spectators was beheld, who with admiring eyes stood gazing on it, which questionless was that she meant. But to proceed (pursu'd she) so soon as *Plenty* finish'd her Address, the King went on to the *Temple of Ceres*, which was the place where all his Predecessors assum'd their Diadems; and there was his put on upon his princely head by the ArchFlamine with all the Ceremonies due to such a solemnity, which being done, he return'd to his Pallace where in, a most magnificent manner he treated all the Princes, and Nobles of his Realme; where I will leave him to the enjoyment of a happy repose after all those afflictions his Youth had been so burdned with, as a courage less sublime must inevitably have sunk under a pressure so weighty, and returne to my owne affaires.

But perceiving the Evening approach she told *Ermilia* that if she pleas'd, she would reserve them to the next day, because t'was now late, and she fear'd she had already tyr'd her patience; to which the Queen repli'd; she had receiv'd too much satisfaction by what she had related to be wearyed with it: but however since t'was probable (she said) that which was yet remaining might extend to a considerable length she was willing to defer *Arthenias* trouble, and protract her owne satisfaction [fol.107ʳ] till the next Afternoon.

Then turning to *Gentillus* she told him he might then (if he pleas'd) content his curiosity (which she believ'd equall'd her owne) with hearing that which was to insue: upon which he took his leave of the Queen, and bid ad^i^ue to *Arthenia* with thankes for the trouble which at his request she had taken upon her, and went away no less satisfi'd then desirous to know the conclusion of that, whereof the begining had been to him so pleasing. He being gone, *Ermilia* gave command her Chariot should be made ready against such time as she had sup'd, designing to take the Aire, the pleasantness of the Evening inviting her abroad; but she took only *Amena* and *Praxentia* (two of her Ladies) with her. No sooner was the Queen gone, but *Celia* and *Arthenia* got them to their Chamber alone, whether being come, *Arthenia* desir'd her Companion to oblige her with the remainder of *Artabellas* Story; which after she had given order to her Maid to give her notice of the Queens returne, and bethought herself where about she left off, she in these words again pursu'd it.

Finis

Rivall Fri[e]ndship[1]

THE SECOND PART

The First Book

The Continuance of Artabella's Story

If you remember *Arthenia* (said *Celia*) I was travelling in my discourse from Scythia back to Persia; and ere I proceed further, we will turne aside to see what is becoming of *Artabella*, who after *Phasellus*'s departure to the Scythian Warre, retir'd to her Castle in Shiras, where poore Princess she remain'd very sad and pencive; perpetually dreading she should heare he was either dead, or a Prisoner, being she had not for the Space of foure whole moneths heard either of, or from him, which made her suspect one of those two was his condition: the apprehension of which misfortune when it had once possest her fancy, it fill'd her mind with so much sadness, as she could hardly have resented [felt] more, had her doubts been chang'd into a certainty. In this perplexity was she when there came two Gentlemen to the Castle desiring to speak with her; she hoping they might bring her newes of *Phasellus,* instantly admitted them in; who after they had render'd her the respect that was due to her quality, the One of them told her, they were sent by the Queen to waite on her back to Court, who desir'd her speedy returne thither. She having not as yet heard so much as the least rumour of the Kings death, admir'd to heare them mention a Queen; but not to be longer in doubt, she ask'd him who spake, what Queen he meant.

The Princess *Oriana* Madam (said he) who by the death of Achemenes is now our Queen.

Oh Heavens! (cry'd she) is *Achemenes* dead, what ignorance have I liv'd in, that till this instant never heard of it.

He hearing her say so, gave her the relation of the Kings death, which having heard with as true a sorrow as [fol. 109ʳ] so good a nature as that of hers was capable of resenting [feeling], she retir'd a while in private to vent her griefe

---

[1] Two blank pages precede the beginning of *Rivall Friendship*, Part 2, Book 1.

in teares, which she believ'd due as a just Tribute to the memory of her Royall
Uncle. When the height of her passion was a litle over, she sent for those Gentlemen in again, to inquire more perticulerly concerning the state of affaires; but
though she made that her pretence, her chiefe aime was to see if she could learne
what was become of *Phasellus:* many questions did she aske ere she could aske
that which she most desir'd (yet fear'd) to be resolv'd of, doubting her affection might make her betray the concerne she had for him: but at last after she
had made an inquirie after all the Persians of quality that went with the Armie
into Scythia, she demanded what was become of him who went Generall, and
his Friend that came with him into Persia. To which, he that had spoken before
repli'd, that *Diomed* was not yet return'd, but lay dangerously wounded still in
Scythia, but *Phasellus* was come back about ten days since, and was at that present at Court. This somewhat cheer'd up her disconsolate mind, and dispell'd all
her former doubts and feares but new ones immediately after usurp'd their place;
for then she fancied he had forgot her, and all those promises he had made her of
an unchangable fidelity, and unalterable affection, or if at all he thought on her,
she believ'd t'was onely with indifferency, or else she thought it impossible (if he
continu'd still the same passion that he so oft protested to have had for her) for
him to be in Susa ten days, and neither see her, nor send to her to excuse himself
for such a high neglect: but resolving not to pass too severe a censure on him, nor
condemne him meerly upon suspition, she pacifi'd her disquiet thoughts as well
as she could till such time as she arriv'd at Susa; where she question'd not but she
should see him and heare from himself the occation of his disrespective silence;
which if he could not give her good satisfaction for, she determin'd no longer
then to throw away a Love so pure, and innocent, on one who had made himself
unworthy of it, but to treat him answerable to his deserts.

No longer then the next morning would she defer her Journey, and accordingly gave order for her Chariot to be ready very early; but she took none of her
servants with her save onely *Saparilla* and *Admetus* that had been formerly a Page
to *Menzor* (who for his approv'd Fidelity to her Father) was after his Masters
death advanced by her ^to^ the chiefest place about her person: with these two,
and Gentlemen that *Oriana* had sent for her, she began her Journey, leaving a
command with the rest of her servants to follow her with what convenient speed
they could. The day after they left Shiras, at the enterance of a great Wood, they
were suddenly surrounded by twenty horsemen who set upon them [fol. 109ᵛ]
vowing to kill the Charoteer if he drove not whether they should direct. *Artabella*
was so terrifi'd with such an unexpected surprisall, and the menaces wherewith
they threatned those with her, and not being able to imagin their designe, or
what they intended to do with her, as she fell into a swound, and remain'd in it so
long, when she came to herselfe again, she had the misfortune to behold both the
gentlemen that accompani'd her slain, and poor *Admetus* so desperatly wounded,
as he was fallen by her Chariot unable longer to resist; which when she saw, she
exprest much sorrow for him, intreating those that had reduced him to that con-

dition, that they would not be so cruell to leave him so, but that they would put him into the Chariot, till such time as she came to some place where she might leave him to be look'd too by some who might take care of him: but they having as little of civility as pity, absolutely refus'd her request, compelling the Charioteere to drive quite another way from that she was going with all the hast he could make. At last came up to them another, that seem'd to command the others, who by his deportment express'd much more of humanity then any of the rest, for seeing *Artabella* weep excessively, he desir'd her (in very civill language) not to grieve so much since they had no intent to do her any further wronge, nor should she receive any prejudice more then what she already suffer'd; and that what they did was meerly in obedience to the commands of a person whom they durst not disobey.

But may I not know (said *Artabella*) whether you intend to carry me.

You shall know that e're long Madam (repli'd he).

[T]his was all the answere that at present she could get, in which she found but small satisfaction.

The rest of the day they travelled without any let, or molestation; but as night drew on, they enter'd into a vast Desart cover'd all with sand which by reason of contrary winds was driven up and downe in such a manner as no track or beaten rode was to be found. By this time *Artabella* grew very weary, which *Saparilla* perceiving, ask'd those in whose power they were, whether there were any Towne, or Village neer where her Lady might stay to repose herself: but she was answer'd that there was none till they came to the end of that Desart, through which they must travell all night, and rest in the day; or else they might be in danger to be buried alive in that sandy Ocean, having nothing to guide them in their Journey but the course of the Stares: but assoon as the day appear'd they stop'd telling *Artabella,* if she had a desire to repose herselfe, she must rest in her Chariot, ~~on~~ unless she would make the Sand her bed as they must be faine to do. He who seem'd the most civill amongst them, appear'd much concern'd at the sight of her griefe, which may well be thought to be extreame, to see herself forceably carried away by such Fellowes as those into whose hands she was fallen, whose design she could as litle imagine, as learne from them; and though she did whatever she could to [fol. 110ᵗ] fortifie her mind against Fortunes batteries, yet was she not able to refraine testifying by her teares, those Feares that assail'd her: the sight of so much griefe in *Artabella* moved *Ozmin* (for so ^was^ that more civiliz'd person call'd) to tell her that he was sorry for the trouble he had caus'd her, and that he repented he had taken upon him such an employment.

And were it not (said he) that I am ingag'd by such binding Oathes as no consideration can oblige me to dispence with, I should never execute what I have undertaken, but should instead thereof carry you back to Shiras, or conduct you any whither else you should desire.

If you have that sense of my sorrow (repli'd she) as you pretend, do me but the favour to let me know what that is which you have undertook to do, and whether you intend to hurry me with soe much violence.

We are carrying you Madam (said he) to Zarispe, a Citie in the furthest part of Bactria (in which Province we are now) where I am to see you imbark on the River Ochus (which runs by that City) for what Kingdome you like best to spend the rest of your Life in, for into Persia you must never more returne; to which (by an inviolable promise) I am to engage you ere you go thence; or else to keep you a perpetuall Prisoner in a house I have a^d^joining to the City.

For Heaven's sake (cry'd she) who may that unjust, and cruell person be, that is so much my enemy.

For that Madam (answered he) you must excuse me; onely thus much I will presume to tell you, he is One who will ere long have a power in this Kingdom equall to our Queens, and is already so potent, as neither I, nor my Companions durst deny obedience to his commands, had they been more unjust; without pulling on our selves some exemplary punishment.

This answere fill'd *Artabella* with as much astonishment, as she was before with griefe; for who could unless by an unjust usurpation of *Oriana's* p[r]erogative, condemne her to a perpetuall banishment, she could not conceive: and then she reflected on the Queen with no less a concern then on herself; fearing she was fallen into some trouble since the Kings death through the ambitious pretences of some aspiring Rebell; but why his injuries should extend to her she could not imagine.

Then after a litle silence, Oh wicked men (said she) do you feare the punishments of men, more then the Justice of the Gods, who will assuredly revenge the violence wherewith you persecute the Innocent; for so harmlessly and innocently have I spent my days, that to my knowledge I never so much as disoblig'd any person in my life, nor ever did I commit a the least offence against any one that might incite them to injure me in so high a degree, as to force me to take an eternall farewell of my native Country, and to wander forelorn and helpless in a foreign Land, not having any [fol. 110^V^] thing to sustaine or keep me from necessity and want, but what will soon be exhausted.

If that were the greatest of your troubles Madam (said *Ozmin*) you might quickly be eas'd of it; for if you will but let me know where you intend to make your aboad, I have order to send you annually the whole revenue of your estate; or else you have the liberty to sell, or dispose of it as you think best for your advantage, for hither you must ne're ^returne^ again to enjoy it.

After this he took out some Meat which they had provided for themselves, and presenting some of it to *Artabella*, pray'd her she would be pleas'd to satisfy her hunger (which he said, he knew she must of necessity suffer, not having eaten any thing in so long time) with it, till they could procure something more agreeable for her.

Though it were much better (answer'd she) for me to dye here by Famine, then eate to preserve a miserable life to linger it out in an unknown Country, yet will I never merit my misfortunes by any willfull Crime; which doubtless I should, if I became an Accessary to my owne death. No, I will rather by a submission to the Will of the Gods with patience suffer whatever tis their pleasure to permit wicked persons to inflict upon me: therefore were it not that the terrour of so unlook'd for a surprize, and the trouble I have since undergone has so indispos'd me as I am not in a condition to accept your proffer, I should not refuse it; but receive it as a civility from a man, from whom (after what I had seen you do to my prejudice) I expected nothing but the height of cruelty.

He then made the same offer to *Saparilla*, but she, whether it were out of complacence to her Lady, or that she had really the same reason to refrain eating, refus'd it likewise. That evening, just as darkness began to draw his sable Curtain to obscure the brightness of the day, they arriv'd at Zarispe, and soon after at that house which was destin'd for *Artabella's* Prison in case she refus'd to consent to a perpetuall banishment: at first she had some thoughts of confining herself to a Prison, rather then become an Exile; but then, those thoughts gave place to others more reasonable, which made her fancy thraldome more insupportable then liberty though purchaced at no less a rate, then an ad^i^ue [adieu] forever to her Country, Friends, Relations, and Acquaintance; for she considered, that if she stay'd, she was as litle like to enjoy the sight or conversation of any of them, as if she were in the remotest part of the Universe; and besides she hop'd, in what part of the World soe're she was (if she were free) she might find an opportunity to let *Phasellus* know where she was; who inspight of her resentment [feelings] against him, was still dearer to her then all the World besides: and if his affection continu'd with that ardour she [fol.111ʳ] might justly expect, she doubted not but he would abandon all advantages he might pretend to by staying in Persia to come to her; and so much did this hope fortifie her in her last opinion, as she resolv'd to prefer liberty before Captivity.

By this time they were come to the house whether they were to goe; which seem'd to be an old ruinous Castle, built all of stone, very stronge, upon a hill of an indifferent height, from whence one might behold the Caspian Sea not far distant, into which the River Ochus (which ran by the Castle Wall) emptied it self. About some three furlongs from Zarispe, on the further side of it was this Castle situate; whether being come, and alighted, *Ozmin* (to whose custody the Princess was committed) conducted her in, where she found a much better accommodation then the outside of those ruines promist: for though it was gone much to decay, and a great part of it fallen downe, yet there remained enough to entertaine conveniently a far greater number of persons then at present it contain'd. *Artabella*, and *Saparilla* were brought into a very faire Chamber, fitted with all necessaries, and indifferintly well furnish'd; save that the furniture thereof was sutable to the Castle, something old, and decai'd; here she repos'd herself a while on a Bed which was in the Chamber: and conjecturing *Saparilla's* weariness by her owne, she made her ly downe by her to rest her likewise. When they were alone the Princess imparted her resolution to the deare Companion of her misfortunes, with the reasons she had for it; which *Saparilla* could not but approve of.

And when they had a while remained silent, *Artabella* turning to her said. Though the Gods are pleas'd to lay on me this affliction for the punishment of some Offence, which questionless I am guilty of towards them, it would be unjust in me to make thee miserable, [be]cause I am so, in desiring thou shouldst tye thyselfe to the fortune of this unhappie Creature; No, dear *Saparilla* (pursu'd she) though thy company be very pleasing, and the onely comfort indeed that I have left me, yet so well I love thee, as for thy sake to deprive my self of it. Leave me then I conjure thee, if I can obtain so much favour of the man to whose charge I am committed, to send thee safe to Susa, Shiras, or any other place thou lik'st better; that thou mayst no longer follow me who am destin'd to nothing but misery; my Castle at Shiras I freely give thee and all the estate belonging to it, as a reward for thy Fidelity.

But *Saparilla* not being able any longer to lend an eare to [fol. 111ᵛ] the desires of her Lady, burst forth most bitterly a weeping. Ah Madam (said she) what have I done to give you cause to suspect I have so base, so meane a spirit as that I can be tempted by the hopes of gain or advantage to abandon you in your affliction: were I One, who follow'd your Fortune rather then your Selfe, I might then (perhaps) be perswaded to forsake you with it, especially having such an advantagious proffer as that you made me: but Heaven knowes, I never pretended to more, then I already injoy in the honor to be neer your person, and to possess the favour of your esteeme; which till this instant I ne're had the least cause to doubt. But sure Madam (pursu'd she) poor *Saparilla* has but litle share in it, if you can admit such an unjust opinion of her, as to think her so unworthy, as that she will ever forsake you in adversity. No, no Madam, that's too weak (how great soever) to fright me from your service; then if my sight be not offencive, nor my company troublesome, speak no more of banishing me from you; for I am absolutely determin'd never to forsake you neither in life nor death.

With that *Artabella* took her in her Armes, and pressing her with all the ardencie of a most passionate affection. I am not so unhappie (said she) as I late believ'd my self, since in the person of a faithfull servant, I have found a most unfeigned Friend: then seeing thy affection is strong enough to carry thee thorow all those dangers, I may (nay questionless must) encounter, and that I find thee the same in my adverse, that thou wert in my more prosperous condition, nothing but Death shall separate us.

By this time, the Table in their Chamber was cover'd, and a very handsome supper serv'd up by persons to attend the Princess; and so soon as she and *Saparilla* had eaten, and the meat carried away, being exceeding weary they went to bed.

The next day when *Ozmin* thought *Artabella* might be in a condition to be seen, he sent to know whether he might be admitted; she knowing but too well the power he had over her, and finding him much civiller then she expected, gave him the permission he desir'd; and presently after he came in.

I come Madam (said he) to aske your resolution; not that I intend to ~~hastne~~ hasten you away (if it be so that you determine to depart) till such time as you have well recover'd that weariness you have contracted by so incomodious a Journey; but this I will tell you Madam, the person by whose order you are to become either an Exile, or a Prisoner, declar'd he would ^rather you should^ make choice of the latter; being unwilling (as he said) you should be expos'd to the dangers of the sea: nor would he (he protested) have expos'd [fol. 112ʳ] you to what you have already suffer'd could he have deviz'd any other way to secure himself from an inevitable ruine; and therefore Madam in my opinion, he is not so much your Foe, as his owne Friend; and does but what some unavoidable necessity constrains him too since all persons are oblig'd to seek their owne preservations, though by the ruines of others.

Tis very true (interrupted she) some will do so, but a Generous man will rather perish then seek his security by injuring the Innocent.

But Madam (pursu'd he) if you will preferre Imprisonment before banishment, I am commanded to settle you a Family as large as that you left behind you, and to treat you with so much respect, that you may find no difference in the condition you are in now, and that you were lately in (baiting your confinement to this Place) which perhaps hereafter may not be altogether so displeasing as it is at present.

Good Gods (cry'd she) what a strange misterious Fate is mine, that makes me persecuted by One, who in the midst of all his injuries, seemes as if he would have me thinke he meant to favour me, by intermingling with his harsh usage some shew of respect. But if I find (continu'd she) such a treatment as you make me hope, possibly I may prefer captivity before the other to which I am destin'd, though Libertie be exceeding sweet in what condition soever: but however I desire a day or two to consider of what you have said, ere I give you my finall resolve.

To this he consented, and told her she might have the Freedome to walk in the Garden when ever she pleas'd: in which he said, haply she might find some litle diversion: for though at present it be gone much to decay (added he) yet was it once the most beautifull and pleasant Garden in all this Province, and exceeded by few in Persia.

Though I shall never acknowledge my selfe oblig'd (repli'd she) to him who sent me hither, yet I must to you for executing your Commission with so much moderation.

Dinner being now brought in, *Ozmin* would have withdrawn; but *Artabella* invited him to stay and dine with her, that by her courtesie she might oblige him to a continuance of his civility; but he refus'd the honour she would have done

him, saying he knew too well what was due from *Ozmin* to the Princess *Artabella*
in what condition soever she was, not to abuse her goodness, by presuming to
accept a Favour whereof he was altogether unworthy;

[B]ut I will attend you after dinner Madam (continu'd he) or when ever you
please to waite on you into the Garden; with that he went away, after the Princess
had told him she would not walke till toward the evening, lest the Sun might be
offencive to her.

About the time that *Ozmin* thought *Artabella* would take a walk, he return'd
to carry her into the Garden, which she found answerable to what he had said
of it. Many delicate Fountains, pleasant Walks, Arbours, [fol. 112ᵛ] and soli-
tary Groves there were in it, set so thick with Trees as the Sun could never
pierce them; and in those Trees, perpetually resided severall sorts of pretty Birds
chaunting forth their rurall musick with much sweetness and delight: but of all
those places he shew'd her, none so well pleased her Fancy as a Walk which was
set on the one side with Orange trees, and Mirtles intermix't, the other side
being open to the River, and at one end of it a Mount rais'd to a very great height,
in which were steps made for the more easie ascent. This place presented her with
the most pleasant Prospect that could be seen, for it had not onely the full view
of the Sea for many Leagues, but also the prospect of all the country thereabout;
which though some part of it was nothing but a sandy baren Desart, yet that
part of it about Zarispe was the richest, and most fertill soile in Persia, abound-
ing with Corne, and all sorts of Fruits (except Olives) rich Mettalls, and some
precious stones it had in it, as Emralds, Crisolits, and Jacinthes; many delicate
Meddows, and Fields of Pasture well stor'd with Cattell.[2]

But I stand too long on the description of this place, having many things
more materiall to relate (pursu'd *Celia*) therefore I shall say no more of it, ~~well
and~~ onely tell you Madam that *Artabella* was so taken with this Walke that she
spent much of her time in it, attended onely by *Saparilla*; for the Garden Wall
was of such an excessive height as *Ozmin* believ'd there was no danger of her
escaping thence, unless she would throw herself into the River, so that she had
the freedome to walke there as oft as she pleas'd; which priviledge she many
times made use of: and one day as she was upon that Walk she took so much
delight in, she espi'd some Ships saile by on the other side of the Channell; this
sight gave her some litle hope that she might at some time or other find a meanes
to get thence without an engagement ne're to returne to Persia more. This hope
made her feign a much greater content then before, and seem so well satisfi'd
with her imprisonment, that she told *Ozmin,* if he treated her no worse then
hitherto he had done, her Captivity would be much more supportable then at
first she believ'd it would; nor should she much complain of those that sent her

---

[2] I am indebted to William Gentrup for the suggestion that, based upon the details
in this description, Bridget Manningham may have consulted Strabo's *Geography,* Book
11, Chap. 11, Section 1.

thither: and that she was now resolv'd to end her days there rather then expose herselfe to new perills.

At this determination *Ozmin* seem'd very joyfull; and assur'd her, if her usage had not hitherto offended her, she should have no reason to be displeas'd with it for the future; protesting he would make it his business to study how he might make that place (if possible) as delightfull to her as her Castle at Shiras had been: and to that end, he presently set a great many men on work to trime the Garden, and [fol. 113ʳ] repaire the ruines of the Castle, that it might be a fit habitation for a person of her quality. This pretended resolution of *Artabella's*, fill'd *Ozmin* with such securitie as she was guarded less strictly then before; and except liberty to stire out of the precincts of the Castle, she had all the freedome she could wish; which much facilitated her designe, which not long after she had an opportunity of accomplishing: for one evening as she and *Saparilla* were standing on the Mount, they espi'd a Ship sailing towards them, which *Artabella* no sooner saw, but she resolv'd to make use of it to effect her purpose, which she imparted to her Faithfull servant. When it was come so neer as those in it might discerne their actions they both of them together beckon'd to them to come neerer (not dareing to call to them for feare of being overheard) and both of them spreading out their hands, and bringing them together again in a suppliant posture; which was quickly understood by the Master of the Ship, who was the first that took notice of their actions; which assoon as he had seen tack'd about, and in a litle time came so neere, as causing the Long Boate to be cast out, he put himself into it, and came close under the Wall where they stood. When he was come nigh enough to be heard without difficulty, he demanded what it was they desir'd but before *Artabella* repli'd to his question, she ask'd him whether he was going.

I am bound for Bizantium in Thrace (answer'd he) where I live, being a Merchant by proffession; and having been in Egipt am now returning home.

If you have any sensibility of, or compassion for the miseries of the distressed (cry'd she) you will never meet with fitter subjects whereon to exercise your pity then on us, who beg you to free us from miseries as great, as the impossibility we have to escape them if you refuse to receive us into your Ship: but if you will be so generous to grant, what I'le earnestly implore, no recompence you can aske, but I shall account too meane for such a service.

Whilst she was speaking, he heedfully consider'd her Majestick garb, and gracefull manner of speaking, from whence he concluded she was no ordinary person that implor'd his aide; whereupon he stay'd not to consult whether or no he should grant her request, but readily consenting; yes Madam (repli'd he) I will assist you in what you desire: but whether would you be carried.

Any whether (answer'ed she hastily) do but deliver me from this hatefull place, and I care not.

With that he threw her up some Ropes: which he told her must be fastned to some of the Trees, that by them they might slip downe into the Boat, being too high to get downe any other way. She instantly sent *Saparilla* to her Chamber for a Cabinet she had, wherein were many Jewells of great value, being unwilling to leave them behind her; this she might easily enough do, having a paire of staires that went directly out of the Garden up to her Chamber. In the meantime the [fol. 113ᵛ] Princess try'd to fasten the Ropes, which with much difficulty she effected by that time *Saparilla* return'd; and sliding downe by them she got into the Boat though not without much Pain; for her hands being very tender, the hardness of the Ropes had all drawn off the skin: but she thought not of her pain, her Joy was so great to find herselfe so neer regaining her Liberty. When she was once got into the Boat, *Saparilla* stay'd not long ere she got thither too, and presently they came to the Ship, which was but a litle distance off; the Master of the Ship first geting up himself, holpe them so well, as they got into the Shipe much more easily then they did into the Boate: and having hois'd saile they made all possible speed to la[u]nch out into the maine Ocean, and soon lost sight both of Zarispe, and *Artabella*s Prison. How *Ozmin* resented [felt about] her flight I know not, nor is it much materiall to enquire; though without question he could not be very well pleas'd to find himself deceiv'd with so much subtilty at a time when he thought himself most secure of her stay.

All day they sail'd very prosperously, but towards night the Sky, which till then had been very cleare, and serene, began to be o're spread with black and dusky Clouds; and a litle after, the winds began with gentle whistlings to play with the sailes, which fill'd the Sailors with some apprehensions of an insuing storme: but those Feares quickly grew greater by the sight of certaine Fishes call'd Porposes, which began to play upon the water, and never appear'd but to presage some more then ordinary Tempest. Which having seen, without delay they prepar'd for it, repairing with all diligence the defects of their Ship, wherby they might sustaine any prejudice: and because of the nights approach they cast Anchour, resolving there to wait the fury of the Storme, lest in the nights darkness it might precipitate them on some Rock. Their apprehensions were not causeless, for the Sun had scarce left this Hemisphere to go visit the Western shades, when the Windes began from those soft whispers, to blow more rougher Gales; and at last ris to that height, as with its violence it rais'd such Mountains of the Waves, that they seem'd every moment to be o'rewhelm'd with those Billows that rowl'd o're them. The noise of the Winds, the roreing of the Waves, and the clamour of the Seamen calling to their Fellows ~~calling one to the other,~~ made such a horrible din, and such a strang confused noise that the horrour of that, and the apprehension of that danger which threatned them, was able to daunt a stouter courage then *Artabellas,* and therfore it was no marvell if she who had never seen the sea, but since her coming to Zarispe, should be exceedingly terrified with that which was dreadfull enough to those who daily had experience of the deliverances they had from such dangers.

The truth is, feare and horrour had so ceas'd the spirits both of her and *Saparilla,* that they were in a manner senseless of their condition; and besides, the tossings of the ship, and its routing to and froe, made them so very sick, that they could not think of death any other way, then by that indisposition which they felt; though that was nothing [fol. 114^r] but what was usuall with those that never were upon the sea before: but at length the storme increas'd to that height, that the strength of the Waves broke all the Cables which fastned the Ankers to the Ship, and by that meanes left them to the mercy of that merciless Element; where they all that dismall night floated in dispaire, having lost all hopes of safty by the loss of their Ankers; having nothing now to relie on but the Goodness of the Gods, to whom they addrest themselves with as much devotion as those distracting terrours they were ceaz'd with would permit them. At length the day appear'd, if it may be call'd a day which so resembled the night, as hardly any difference could be discerned between them; for so black, and cloudy was the Face of Heaven, that the Sun had but litle power to give them any comfort with its enlightning Rays. For three whole days they remain'd in this hopeless condition; sometimes all cover'd with waves, expecting every minute to be swallow'd by them; then again, carried on the top of others so high, that they seem'd transported even to the very clouds; then suddenly brought downe so low, as they believ'd themselves quite buried in those watery Graves: but on the fourth day this furious storme something abated, and *Neptune* began to tye up again those boisterous Spirits which had rag'd with so much violence since he gave them liberty; and at last the Sun brake forth, dispelling all those Vapours which had so long obscur'd, or rather totally eclips'd his splendour, restoring that hope which had quite abandon'd those poor Wretches.

Serastes (for so was the Master of the Ship call'd) seeing the danger past for that time, went to carry *Artabella* that assurance, which he believ'd, could not but be to her very wellcome newes. Dispell your feares Madam (said he) the storme is over; and I hope the Gods who have been so mercifull as to preserve us from the fury of this Tempest (which to say truth was the greatest I ever yet was in) will bring us safe to the end of our Voyage, though it must be much longer then I design'd it; for I find we have pass'd the Hellespont, and are come into Greece: so that we must be constrain'd to fetch a compass which will cost us many days ere we arrive at Bizantium.

Since there is no remedy (repli'd she) we must be content to suffer the inconveniencies of so long a Voyage; but can you not land me at some Port towne in Persia before you go to Bizantium, for tis to Susa I must go; and therefore if you could do so, you would very much oblige me, and should assuredly receive a reward sufficent to satisfie you for the service I require of you.

That I cannot possible [possibly] do (answer'd he) but if you please Madam, assoon as I [fol. 114^v] have unladed my Ship of her fraight I will then transport you any whither you shall command me; this promise prity well satisfi'd her, hoping her voyage would not be much longer; so he retir'd, leaving her to give thankes to those Powers who had preserv'd her from so manifest a perrill, which she did with a great deall of Piety and Devotion.

But no sooner was *Serastes* come out from *Artabella*, ere he was alarmed with the approach of a new danger, noe less formidable then that they lately scap'd; which was the sight of a certaine Pirat who had of a long time infested those Seas neer Delphos (which they were not many Leagues distant from) finding many rich prizes among those that daily came to consult the Oracle in Del^ph^os; for seldome any came upon that account, but they brought with them great treasures of Gold, and Jewells to offer at Apolls Altar; which oft became a prey to those Robbers; who ceaz'd on the Goods, and made Slaves of the men they took, unless they would redeeme themselve[s] at such excessive rates as they would set upon them; which was to be paid at a certaine place appointed for that purpose, ere they would set them at Liberty. This sight fill'd the minds of the most couragious of the Mariners with mortall apprehensions, knowing there was no way to shun those Pirats who pursu'd them both with Saile and Oare: and not being ignorant to what condition they must be reduced if they yeelded; how that of free men they must become Slaves to those cruell wretches, from whose inhumanity they could expect but litle favour, they resolv'd to fight for their Liberties, prefering death before a Slavery more insupportable. This being once resolv'd, insteed of flying, they tack'd about to meet their Pursuers, and prepar'd for the encounter.

The Pirat very much admir'd to find a resistance so litle expected; but *Serastes* having in it no less then his whole estate, could not be perswaded to part with it upon such easie termes as many others had done; and being of a courage not common in men of his Proffession, he made a stout resistance; and questionless had his men been but as valiant as himself their Enemies had found it no easie taske to vanquish them, though they were by much the stronger. Twice did they bord the Merchants Ship, and were repell'd; but at last *Serastes* fell downe wounded with litle signe of life in him; which so daunted the hearts of all the rest, as they no longer would dispute a Victory they now dispair'd of gaining; but all at once, falling on their knees, cri'd for mercy to their pitiless Conquerours, who puting them into Irons, fell to ransaking of the Ship; where they found wealth enough to have satisfi'd their covetous desires, could anything in reason have satisfi'd those base men who built their Fortunes meerly upon the ruine of others.

All this while poor *Artabella* was ignorant of this new misfortune; some noise she had heard indeed, but that she imagin'd [fol. 115^r^] was caus'd by the Mariners repairing something that might have been broaken by the violence of the Waves: but too soon knew she the truth of it, when she saw severall men rudely rush into her Cabin; who without speaking, ceaz'd on her and *Saparilla*, and binding both their hands, haul'd them forth upon the Deck with a rudeness they had never seen practiced to the meanest Slaves; which so surpriz'd them as they were ready to Sink downe dead: but when they came out upon the Deck where they beheld the dismall Spectacles of dead, and dying men who there lay weltring in their blouds! Oh Heavens; how great was their astonishment at that lamentable sight, and the more because they knew not what too impute that Slaughter too, but casting their eyes about, they espi'd the Pirats Ship, which gave them strong suspitions into what condition they were fallen; which strook such a terrour into them, as it depriv'd them both of life for a long time. After those barbarous Villains had made some essaies to bring them to life again (not with any intention to oblige them, but onely in hopes to make a gain of them) and finding their endeavours ineffectuall, their Captain commanded them to leave them where they were, and to retire to their owne Ship, saying there was litle hopes of deriving any advantage from two Woemen, who were like to bring them more trouble then proffit. This command they readily obey'd, leaving the poor Princess, and her Faithfull *Saparilla* in that most deplorable condition; they having gotten a treasure much greater then they look'd for, hois'd Saile, with an intention to returne home, and there to dispose of their Purchace, that they might the more freely to sea again to seeke for new Prizes.

Saparilla came to herself a good while before the Princess, and seeing her lye streach'd out by her side, she was so afflicted at that sight as she was even ready to fall again into her former Trance: but *Artabella*s danger made her strive as much as possible to keep up her spirits, that she might be in a capacity to assist her deare Mistress; which assoon as she was able, she did: using her uttmost endeavour to fetch life into her again; which with much adoe at last she did. But when *Artabella* had open'd her Eyes, she cast them with a faint, and languishing look on those sad Objects which lay before her; and then turning them on *Saparilla,* she said sighing, ah I see I must live to endure more miseries; and I feare those I have hitherto undergone, are but the Shadows of what I have yet to suffer. Oh how much better had it been, that those cruell Wretches had left me in the same condition these poor Men are in; and how mercifull should I have esteemed them had their cruelty extended to the taking away my life, which is now so miserable as death will be the onely happiness I can hope for, as being that alone which can put an end to all my miseries: these words she ended with a shower of Teares wherin *Saparilla* kept her company and strove, with the most comfortable words she could invent, to mittigate a griefe which she acknowledg'd had but too just a cause. [fol. 115ᵛ]

But that which most diverted her from those sad thoughts for the present, was her hearing *Serastes* give a groan (which spake him not to be quite dead) which she no sooner heard, but puting *Saparilla* from her, prethee leave me (said she) and employ thy care to better purpose, by endeavouring to preserve the life of that Good Man to whom we owe our Liberties: perhaps tis for my sake that he has been plung'd into this misfortune, and that by asisting this unhappy Creature (whom the Gods have destin'd to nothing but misery) he has provok'd them to make him a pertaker of those Punishments I onely have deserv'd. Then leave nothing unattempted (Deare *Saparilla*) to recover him; which if thou canst, it will be not onely a charitie to him, but a comfort to our selves: but she being of a generous inclination, needed not much perswasion to incite her to so good a deed. After she had lead *Artabella* back into her Cabin and laid her on her Bed, as she was seeking for some kind of Linen to teare wherewith she might bind up *Serastes's* wounds, she chanced to espy her Ladies Cabinet, which hapning to stand in a dark corner of the Cabin had been therby (it seemes) secur'd from the sight of those who had made a prey of all things else of any value. This sight gave her some hopes since *Serastes* was not quite dead, that her indeavours would not be invain; for she remembred her Mistress had in it a Powder of most Soveraign effects; and bringing the Cabinet to her, see here Madam (said she) as injurious as Fortune has been to you, she has yet left you something you gave for lost.

Tis very true (reply'd *Artabella*) I did so; and I am more glad for that Powder that is in it, then for anything else that it containes; for all my Jewells will stand us in litle stead in this Place, where nought but Death and horrour dwells. Here take my Key (continu'd she) and take out some of the Powder, and give [it to] *Serastes*, I am confident it will revive him if we can but find a way to cure his wounds as well.

This *Saparilla* did; but having nothing but Water to mixe it with, she was fain to make use of that; and pouring it downe his Throat, it soon produced its ordinary effects; for not long after he began to come a litle to himself, though not so much as to be sensible of that charitable Office that was render'd him: but after some litle time more, he open'd his Eyes, and fixed them steadfastly on *Saparilla* as she was washing off the bloud that was congeal'd upon his Wounds, that she might the better see what to do to them. She thinking he might have sense enough (perhaps) to understand her, though not strength enough to speak; told him, her Lady had commanded her to use the utmost of her skill for his recovery.

Your Lady, and your self (said he forceing himself to speak) are both so obliging, and so charitable that if it were possible I would fain live (notwithstanding the reason I have to desire death) that I might find some way to testifie my thankfullness for the care she is pleas'd [fol. 116ʳ] to take for the preservation of one who has but litle oblig'd her, since instead of freeing her from misery I have envolv'd her deeper in it: but if the Gods spare my life I hope to let her see by that faithfull service I will do her, that it was Fortunes fault not mine that she is so unhappie. But (pursu'd he) since you are so kind as to become my Chyrurgion, if ^you^ please to look in my Cabin you will find there a litle Pot which perhaps may be there still, if it be, you may find something in that to dress my wounds with; this she having search'd for, quickly found in the Place where he had told her t'was; and applying it according as he directed, she bound up his wounds with some of it which were none of them in any dangerous place, which made her hope he would find a speedy cure. But so exceedingly was he weakned with the loss of blood as he was not able to get into his Cabin (though *Saparilla* did all she could to help him) but was constrain'd to lye along upon the Deck, which she believing a very uneasie bed (especially for One in his condition) search'd all about for somewhat to lay him on; at last, after long seeking she found some kind of Sedge which had been made use on by the Seamen for the puting up of their Goods; and with this stuffe she made a shift to make him up a litle Bed, and covering it over with some pieces of old Sailecloth which she likewise found; she help'd him to lye downe upon it, though it was no very easie Lodging, yet was it something better then the bare boards on which he lay before. He then giving her thankes for what she had done for him in very gratfull termes, dispos'd himself to rest, whilst she went to give *Artabella* an account [of] what she had done, and the ^hope she^ had of *Serastes*'s recovery; which gave her some litle comfort in the midst of all her feares, and troubles, but alass it quickly vanish'd by the nights approach.

You may better imagine Madam (said *Celia*) then I represent, those horrours that invaded the mind of this disconsolate Princess when she reflected on her condition, and consider'd how she was left amongst a great number of dead men, wherewith the ship was strew'd, without any to accompany her save *Saparilla* (whose Courage was less then her owne) and *Serastes* whose estate was not much different from that of his Companions. These thoughts, the darkness of the night rendred so terrible, that both *Artabella* and *Saparilla* were like to dye with feare of those gastly Apparitions which their timerous Fancies represented to them. Besides that, she saw herselfe abandon'd to the mercy of the Sea on which they floated, without the least hopes of succour or reliefe, not having so much as a Pilot to steere the ship. All night they neither of them clos'd their eyes, but with impatient longings wish't for the day; which to their comfort they saw at length appear: so that when it began to be a litle light, *Artabella* lost part of her feares, and dispos'd [fol. 116ᵛ] herself to try if she could get some sleep, which she found she had great need of, not having had any of a long time: *Saparilla* perceiving her intent, left her to her rest, and went to see how her Patient did; but finding him fast asleep, she would not disturbe him, but went in again setting down at her Ladies Feet; where she had not sate long ere she fell asleep too: and as she awak'd the Princess did so likewise, and raising up her head, *Saparilla* (said she) know you how *Serastes* does to day.

I was to enquire of him (repli'd she) but I found him in so sound a sleep as I was loath to disturb him; but I will go again, perhaps he may be awake by this. With that, as she was going to the Dore she thought she heard some persons talk, which so amazed her as she turn'd back to tell *Artabella*.

Tis nothing but thy feare (said she) which makes thee think so: but going to the dore again, she was so confirm'd in her beliefe, that she cry'd, Good Madam if you will not credit me, do but step hither and listne awhile: with that the Princess ris up, and went to her, and hearkning, she was soon convinced, *Saparilla* did more then fancy such a thing.

Tis very true (said she) I do hear more voices then one; sure some of those poor wretches that we thought dead, are reviv'd again: but to cleare our doubts, preethee go and see and bring me word; if thou fearest to go out, I will go with thee.

No Madam (repli'd she) I cannot apprehend a worse misfortune then has already befallen us, and if I am in any feare tis onely for your sake.

With that, going out, she found her eares had not deluded her; for she saw two men talking to *Serastes*, who express'd much Joy in his Lookes at their presence. But where said one of them (in the Grecian Tongue which *Saparilla* very well understood, having been taught it with *Artabella* when she learn'd it, as she had done most Languages that were spoken) but where is that Lady to whom I am sent.

Yonder is she that belongs to her (answer'd *Serastes* pointing to *Saparilla*) she will conduct you to her Lady.

No sooner did Saparilla cast her eyes on those men but she knew one of them to be *Eumetes*, Brother to *Serastes* who had been carried away by the Pirats. At first she wondred much by what means he got thither again; but looking about, she espi'd another Ship, fastned to theirs; and now she no longer doubted, but Heaven had sent them a reliefe when they least expected it; and hoping they were neer an end of their miseries, she stay'd not to heare what the stranger had to say, but ran in even transported with Joy to the Princess with this newes, and ~~having~~ in a confused manner gave her an account of what she had heard and seen. *Artabella* hearkned to her with a Countenance wherein the sense of her misfortune [fol. 117ʳ] had imprinted so deep a sadness as was not to be bloted out with a litle vain hope, which she thought might but delude her.

But rising up, I will go see those men (said she) and satisfy myselfe further in this adventure which has brought back *Eumetes;* but as she was going out of the Cabin, she was prevented by his coming in, and bringing with him the other; who being told by him which was *Artabella*, he address't himself to her very civilly in these termes.

I come Madam (said he) from *Alcander King of Delphos* (to whom I have the honour to belong) from whom I receiv'd a command to assure you, that you may expect from him all the assistance, and support your condition requires.

Certainly your King is generous beyond example (repli'd she) so freely, and unsought too, to interess himselfe in the mishaps of the most miserable Woman in the World; and one who is so absolute a stranger to him, as till this very moment never heard so much as of his name.

Tis very true Madam (said he) you are no less a stranger to our King, then he is to you; but having receiv'd an imperfect Character of you, together with an information of your distress, it was sufficent to incite him to afford you a reliefe.

But how could he possibl[y] (demanded she) have an intelligence so soon of my misfortunes.

By this man (answer'd he pointing to *Eumetes*) who with the rest of his Companions he has freed from that slavery to which they were destin'd by those Pirats that had taken them: but this is not the first time those Vile men have display'd their wickedness, for they have of [for] a long time infested this Sea which prov'd at last very prejudicial to our King, by the robberies they daily committed on all

that pass'd this way. I suppose Madam (pursu'd he) you have heard of the Oracle
of *Apollo* in *Delphos* so famous for the truth of what it delivers, that it has excited
many to repaire thither to learn their destinies; who are not permitted to enter
the Port of Del^ph^os without paying a certaine Tribute, which is no mean addition to the Kings revenue: but these Pirats making the resort less frequent, by
reason of the danger People ranne of meeting them (the King sustaining much
damage thereby) resolv'd to rid his Dominions of them; and to that end prepar'd
a considerable Fleet, with a part whereof he design'd to block up Seriphus, where
those pernishous Birds of prey made their Nests (this Seriphus is one of the Isles
of the Cyclades, so call'd because they lye in a circle round about Delphos, being
in number 53, lying so neer together, that in a clear day one may see twenty of
them at a time; for which cause (not without good reason) tis accounted a dangerous Place for Sailors in a storme). This Place being the habitation of the Pirats,
was so strongly fortifi'd by Nature, that it needed not the help of Art to render it
more strong: and therefore, it being impossible to be taken any other ways then
by famine, the King determin'd to block up all the Avenues into it, that those
[fol. 117ᵛ] in it might not stire out, nor those abroad get in again: and knowing
the Island of it self afforded nothing to maintaine the Inhabitants for any considerable time, he knew it could not be long ere they would be forced to yeeld
or starve. The one part of his Fleet he sent thither, and with the other (which
himself commands in person) he resolv'd to scoure the Sea; which Design of his
has been so successfull, as I believe there are by this but few remaining of those
Piratick Theeves: for yesterday he had the good Fortune to encounter the chiefest
of them (being the same who not many houres before had pillag'd this Ship) who
for some time made a stout resistance, being animated by their dispaire of pardon from a King whom they had mortally offended; they were quickly assisted
by many other of their Fellows who came up to them assoon as they heard their
Captain was engag'd, but they serv'd to no other end, but to compleat our victory: for in less then four houres space we totally defeated them, taking that Ship
wherin their chiefe Commander was, and four more of their best Gallies, and
sent some of ours in pursute of the rest, who fled assoon as they perceiv'd themselves worsted. They had no Prisoners aboard any of them, but onely those they
had taken hence who they had already chain'd to the Oare. The King had no
sooner cast his Eye on them, but he guess'd by their Looks how litle they were
pleas'd with their employment; whereupon he commanded their Chains to be
taken off: who no sooner were at liberty, but they threw themselves at the Kings
Feet to give him thanks, vowing to serve him to the utmost minute of their lives.

But (*Eumetes* speaking in the name of all the rest) we are persons so inconsiderable Sir (said he addressing his speech to the King) as you can gain nothing
by the favour you have done us, more then the satisfaction of having perform'd
a charitable action, in freeing poor Wretches from a most miserable Slavery; but
Sir, you will do not onely a charitable, but a glorious Act, if you will but extend
your goodness to the reliefe of the fairest Lady in the World; who is left destitute

of all help or succour in that Ship from whence we were taken by those barbarous men who made a Prey of us and all our Goods; and had questionless brought her into an estate as lamentable as ours, had not she and another that waits on her fallen in a swound upon the Deck, whether they had been haul'd with a most uncivill violence: but seeing them in that condition, the chiefe Pirat (he Sir who with your owne hand you slew, pursu'd he) commanded his men to let them alone, saying they would be more troublesome, then advantagious to them; so they retir'd leaving the poor distressed Lady, and the other, amongst those breathless Carkasses, whom the Inhumanity of those pitiless men had depriv'd of life; amongst whom my Brother (who was Owner of the Ship) was one. [fol. 118ʳ]

It was much (said the King) if that Lady be so faire as you report her that her beauty did not incite them to make a Prey of her.

I verily believe it had (repl'd *Eumetes*) but that her Beauty was obscur'd from their sights by a Vaile she wore, which was fallen over her Face as it was not perfectly to be discern'd.

But ~yo~ we loose time (said the King) and that Lady (who ere she be) stands in too much need of my assistance to defer it a minute longer. Goe *Ferintus* (said he to me) and make all possible speed to bring her from a place so terrible, as presents her no other Objects but those of dead, and dying men: and for the greater speed, take the Pirats Gally; which with the help of the Oares will make more hast then any of our Ships. I assure myself (pursu'd he) now of these men that I have given liberty too, but will be willing to take on them their late employment for a litle while. And you (said he to *Eumetes*) shall go with *Ferintus*, that by your guidance he may the sooner find the Ship wherin the Lady is, and I my self will follow with what convenient hast I may.

Assoon as *Eumetes* had presented *Ferintus* to *Artabella*, he went out again to his Brother, leaving him to tell her the cause of his coming; which having done in these words I repeated (said *Celia*) *Artabella* made him this answere. That generous compassion which has mov'd your King not onely to pity, but to help me out of this misery wherinto I am fallen, is of such a nature as deserves more gratfull acknowledgments then I am able to make him, or I feare ever shall be whilst I live: therefore I will instantly go with you, to throw myself at the Feet of my Generous Deliever (for so I must always stile the King your Master) as well as to render some small part of what I owe him, as to prevent his trouble in coming to me.

With that she left her Cabin, and coming upon the Deck, her intentions were stop'd by *Ferintus*'s saying the King my Master is coming Madam. At his words, she looking about, saw some ships making towards them with full Saile; but when they came a little neerer she perceiv'd the formost (which was much larger then any of rest) to be richly gilt, the Sailes of Tyrian Purple, and the Tackling all of Silk, set out, and adorn'd most sumptiously with Flags, and Streamers of severall colours which made such a gallant shew, as *Artabella* could not but very

much admire it, and conclude it to be that wherin the King was; but she needed
no greater confirmation of that beliefe, then the sight of a man who was standing on the Deck, whom by the respect was given him by those about him, she
knew to be the King. He was apparaled onely in a slight Sea-habit; for having no
more enemies to encounter, he had put off his Armes; but his Clothes detracted
nothing from his brave meen [mien], nor from that Majesty that appear'd in his
Face: he seemed to be about the age of two or three and twenty; and *Artabella*
[fol. 118ᵛ] who till now had been of an opinion that none was ever comparable to
Phasellus for handsomeness and lovely Features, began to believe that this young
King equall'd him, though her passion would not permit her to think he excell'd
~~he excell'd~~ him, as questionless a disinterested person would have done. From
his Lookes she gather'd an assurance that he would performe no less then *Fer-*
intus had promis'd her on his behalf; and from that confidence she deriv'd such
a satisfaction, as brought so great a Joy into her heart, as the effects of it quickly
appear'd in her Eyes; restoring to them such a lively chearfullness, as added very
much to her beautie.

By this time the Ships were come to theirs, and having fastned the Kings to
that where in *Artabella* was, he instantly pass'd out of his owne into it. If *Alcander*
had seem'd worthy of admiration in *Artabella*'s opinion, she appear'd in his far
beyond comparisson beautifull above all that ever his eye could think most Faire;
and in such a manner was he charm'd with the sight of her, as he had almost
forgot for what intent he came thither: but he was put out of this surprize, by
Artabella's throwing herself at his Feet; which she did so suddenly, as he had not
time to prevent her: but taking one of her faire hands (on which he imprinted
a Kiss) rise Madam I beseech you (said he) and forbeare these respects to me
(which can be due from you to none but the Gods) unless you desire to see me in
the same posture.

Pardon me most Illustrious Prince (repli'd she) if I cannot in a more humble
manner express my gratitude to my Lifes Preserver.

If I have been so fortunate to do you som litle service (answer'd he) I am
thank't sufficiently Madam by your so highly overvaluing it; and I shall no longer be concern'd for the Injuries both my selfe, and Predecessors have sustain'd
by our rebellious Subjects, since I have therby been furnish'd with an occation
to serve a person whom *Eumetes* affirm'd with so much Justice to be the Fairest
in the World.

If I had no better a title to your compassions Sir (said she) by my misfortunes, then by that litle beauty which the Gods have given me, I should feare
you would repent the Favour you have done me; but since nothing but your owne
generous Inclinations to pity the afflicted, could excite you to commiserate me,
I'll banish from my mind all such apprehensions, and assume to my self a hope
that by your Majesties assistance I may yet once again be as happie, as I have
lately been the contrary.

You may be certaine Madam (he repli'd) since I assure you of it upon the word of a King (who never yet contracted the guilt of a violated promise) that if my self, or Kingdome can contribute to your happiness, you may from this minute so account your selfe; but that my actions better then my words may confirme to you this truth, I must intreat you Madam to go along with me to Delphos, where you shall see no persons but such as will be dispos'd to serve you as well as I. I make you this request because I think it very requisit you take some repose [fol. 119ʳ] after all those troubles, and inconveniencies you have suffer'd on the Sea: but if your occations are such as press you to a present departure, I will my self waite on you, to convey you safely wherever you design to go.

This proffer of the Kings was so obliging, as she thought she could do no less then go with him to Delphos, as well to exempt him from the trouble of attending her to Persia (as she found by his manner of speaking he was resolv'd to do) as to wait an opportunity to express her thankes more fully then at present she could; and by acquainting him with her quality, let him see he had not misplac'd his Obligations on a person altogether unworthy of them. These reasons induced her to make him this Answere.

Though my occations are very importunate for my immediate departure, yet (were they far more urgent then they are) shall they not force me so farre to forget what I owe a King to whom I am indebted for my life, perhaps my Liberty, or something yet more precious; as so abruptly to leave him without some greater testimony of my sensibility of those Favour[s] I have received from his Royall Goodness. Yes Sir (continued she) I will accept of that retreat you offer me, for some few dayes, as well to seek occations to repay part of what I owe your Majesty, as to let you know the name, and condition of her on whom you have confer'd such signall obligations, as to loose the memory of them, I must loose my life.

I should be too tedious (said *Celia*) should I relate all that past between *Alcander* and *Artabella,* and therefore I will onely tell you Madam that her last words gave the King some suspition that she was of an extract more noble then he had before believed her; and if at first he had given her as much respect as he could have done had her true quality been known to him, it was meerly her most ravishing graces that induced him to treat her soe. He would needs have her leave that Ship (wherin she had pass'd the sadest night that ever yet she knew) and go into his, which she willingly agreed too, and was followed by *Saparilla*, who forgot not to carry with her *Artabella's* Cabinet; which the King seeing, ask't her how she did to secure that from the Pirats.

It was either to their negligence, or their blindness (answer'd she) that my Lady is indebted for it, and not to any favour they intended her in not making a Prize of it, as well ^as^ all things else of value.

Then *Artabella* shew'd *Serastes* to the King, telling him that wounded man was Owner of the Ship, and what a loss he had sustain'd by the Pirats; wherupon, *Alcander* gave order to some that were neer him to take care he might be brought to Del^ph^os, and there carefully looked too till such time as he were well; and withall strictly commanded all his Goods should be restor'd to him again. but *Serastes* had not time to give the King thanks, being already gotten into his owne Ship; and seting saile for Delphos from whence they were not above ten Leagues, where in few houres they safely arriv'd.

The King had dispatch'd away *Ferintus* before, to give notice of his return; so that when they came neer the Port they saw the shore all cover'd with the Inhabitants of Del<u>os</u>^phos,^3 accompanied with the Priests of Apollo [fol. 119ᵛ] who were come thither to meet their King, and to congratulate his Return and Victory. Being landed, he saw two Chariots which *Ferintus* had caus'd to be brought for him and the Princess *Artabella*; unto one wherof the King lead her, whilst some of the Gentlemen which belong'd to him paid the like civility to *Saparilla*, and when they were in their Chariot, the King got into his. When they came to the Palace, he alighted; and seeing the Princess *Delizia* his sister (with a Train of Ladies that were her Companions) coming to wellcome him home, he went to meet her: and after he had embraced her in a most affectionate manner, and receiv'd the expressions of her Joy to see him somuch sooner then she expected, and that he had express'd some civility to all the Ladies with her, he went back to *Artabella*, and helping her out of the Chariot, presented her to the Princess.

Sister (said he) I desire you would receive this Lady with no less affection than that wherewith you wellcom'd me: and though she is as yet a stranger to you, when once you know her (if your resentments [sentiments] resemble mine) you will as well as I, bless that occation which offers you the acquaintance of so admirable a person.

Whilst the King spak thus, the two Princesses look'd on each other with admiration; for *Artabella*s beauty produced in *Delizia's* mind the same effects as it did in all those that beheld her, to wit, both Love and Wonder. Nor was *Artabellas* admiration less for Delizia then that she had for her; for something so infinitly sweet, and taking had she in her Face, as *Artabella* thought her the most lovely Creature that ever she had seen. The Princess at her Brothers request, saluted *Artabella* very kindly; and embracing her with more freedome then is usuall with Strangers, she let her see, she was as full of goodness, as of beauty; and that her Face was a true Index to her mind.

The King my Brothers commands Madam (said she) were altogether unnecessary to enjoyn me to give you a reception worthy of you, since you carry that in your Face which alone is able to compell all persons to honour you; and I hope before we part, to let you see the respect I have for you by something more significant then words.

---

³ In the word Del<u>os</u>, the letters "<u>os</u>" are underlined for deletion, and "phos" is inserted in a darker ink.

I shall from this moment Madam (repli'd *Artabella*) cease to believe my self
unfortunate, and on the contrary esteeme my self most happie since Fortune has
sent me such a recompence for the injuries she has done me, as the sight of soe
Excellent a Princess, and so Generous a King, and affording me the opportunity
both of knowing them, and making myself known unto them, which I shall no
longer defer, lest ye should think the merit of your obligation lost through the
inconsiderableness of the person you have oblig'd; and though I have perticuler
reasons that tye me not to discover who I am; yet I know none prevalent enough
to perswade me to conceal my self from a King to whom I shall ever acknowledge
my self redeuable [grateful] for my life; and from whose magnanimous generosity I hope for a reestablishment of that fortune, from which I was with violence
torn by the hands of unjust, and unknown enemies. But I shall onely tell you
now Sir (pursu'd she to the King) omitting the [fol. 120^r] perticulers of my life
to a mere fiting opportunity, that my name is *Artabella*, and that I am descended
from the most Illustrious blood in the World: being sole Daughter to the late
King of Persias Brother, and by the death of my Father (whose loss was the
begining of my misfortunes) possest of that Principality which belong'd to him.

Pardon me Madam (said the King) that I have not treated you with that
respect and veneration which is due to your birth.

Your usage Sir (repli'd she) has been more noble then I could have expected,
had my true quality been known to you; and therefore if their needs a pardon, tis
Artabella ought to aske it, for giving the Great *Alcander* so much trouble.

If you have given me any Madam (said he) tis in thinking the petty service
I have rendered you deserves that name; no Faire Princess I should esteeme it
my chiefest glory if, in serving you I should loose my life; so as I might thereby
but testifie how much I honour you. The King spake this with such an ardency,
as all those that were present suspected somewhat more then civility mov'd him
to it, and began to thinke the beautie of *Artabella* had made some impression in
his mind.

But not to detaine her longer there, *Alcander* lead her up into that Hall where
you yourself *Arthenia* were brought before the Queen; where he together with
the Princess his Sister entertain'd her with severall discourses; and the King gave
Delizia the relation by what accident he had met with *Artabella*, which lasted till
Supper was serv'd up; but the Princess thinking how necessary it was for *Artabella* to take some rest, so soon as they had sup'd, waited on her to à Chamber
which was prepar'd for her: but ere these Princesses parted, they contracted as
intire a Friendship as if their acquaintance had been of many yeares standing: for
such is the charming power of Vertue that it oft times begets an esteeme in the
minds of persons who ever saw each others face.

That I can witness (interrupted *Arthenia*) it may, since I my self know a person for whom I had a very high esteeme for his generous Vertue long before I saw
him, and have some reason to believe ^he had^ no slight respect for me.

You will not think it strang then (pursu'd *Celia*) that it should so easily unite the hearts of these two excellent Princesses, seeing there appear'd nothing in either of them but what was great and amiable. After they had past some time in a very pleasing converse, *Delizia* took her leave, wishing *Artabella* a good nights rest: she being gone, *Artabella* went to bed making *Saparilla* lye with her though there was another Lodging provided for her. The Princess having understood from *Artabella* in what manner she left Persia, how that she had not had time to bring anything with her more then the Clothes she had on, sent her the next morning all such things as she thought necessary for her present occation, desiring her to accept them till such time as she could better accommodate herself. *Artabella* having return'd her thankes to the Princess for this civility, arose soon after and drest her in those Clothes *Delizia* presented her with, though she thought (being so exceeding rich as they were) they were nothing agreeable to the condition of a Mourner which her owne habit spake [fol. 120ᵛ] her to be; for since the death of *Menzor* she had alwayes worne black, though the Persian custome is never to mourne longer then a moneth for any Relation how high soever; but she had continu'd hers upon the account of *Phasellus*'s absence. But since the Princess had presented her another Dress more sutable both to her youth and beauty she resolv'd, for her sake to lay aside her sable Weedes for the time she stay'd in Delphos.

By that time she was dresst, the Princess came in, and after their first civilities were past, and that *Artabella* had given her thankes again for her last Favour in very obliging Language, they both of them sate downe; and after some litle silence, *Delizia* spake to her in these words. If you esteeme me worthy of the honour of your Friendship Madam, which is a happiness I have so litle title too, as to assure me the possession, I must beg some proof of it from your Goodness; which shall be no other then the relation of your Life and Fortunes, without the least concealment of the most triviall accident. I confess (continu'd she) I should not presume to beg so great a Favour, did not that mutuall Friendship which we have contracted give me an interest in all your concerns, which will not permit me longer to ignore them without a very great restraint upon my desires.

Should I refuse you so slight a satisfaction (repli'd *Artabella*) as this you require for an evidence of my Friendship, you would have reason Madam to question its reallity; and I should thereby render myself utterly unworthy of yours. But Dearest Princess I am ready to satisfy your request whenever you please; though I know I cannot myself give you a true account of my Life, without a great deall of confusion which that recitall will cause in me at the discoverie of some follies so great, as nothing but the cause which made me guilty of them can excuse: and therefore I beseech you Madam accept this relation from the mouth of *Saparilla*, who will perhaps give it you more faithfully then I shall be able to do, since there is not anything that Concerns me, which she is not perfectly acquainted with even to my very thoughts that are of any import; then seeing she can satisfy you in every respect as fully as my self, you will adde much to the rest of your favours if you will but exempt me from that which she can as well as I performe. To this the Princess consented as well to free *Artabella* of a trouble, as because she fancied her modesty would have made her prove injurious to herself; so after she had told *Saparilla* she would ere long give her that trouble the Princess her Mistress had impos'd upon her she took her leave of *Artabella* for a while. But at that very instant came in *Felisarda* (*Celias* Maid) to tell her the Queen was come ~~back~~ in, so that thinking it her Duty to waite on her, she brake off her discourse, and beg'd *Arthenia*'s pardon for leaving her alone, promising to returne so soon as ever *Ermillia* should dispence with her: but as she was going, she met one of her Companions, of whom demanding where she might find the Queen; she told her she need [fol. 121ʳ] not go to her unless she would, for that she had heard the Queen charge she should not be call'd from *Arthenia*. *Celia* hearing this, went back, and acquainting *Arthenia* with the reason of her quick returne (which made her infinitly admire *Ermillia*s goodness) she again reassum'd her discourse.

Rivall Friendship

THE SECOND PART

The Second Book

The Princess was but just gone out when one of *Alcander*s Gentlemen came to demand permission for his Master to waite on the Princess *Artabella*; but he was scarce return'd to the King with his answere ere *Alcander* came in. If *Artabella* had appear'd so charming in a time when the sense of her present afflictions, and her feare of greater misfortunes had detracted much from the liveliness of her beauty, and in a Garbe so negligent as had nothing in it of attractive; but rather darkned that splendour wherewith he now ~~now~~ was wholly dazled and o'recome. If (I say) she had seemed so faire and lovly in so dejected a condition, judge *Arthenia* (pursu'd she) what his thoughts were now, when that by the banishment of all her Feares, and the repose she had taken through the hopes she had conceiv'd that she had seen an end of all her sorrows, her beauty had regain'd its full lustre, heightned something too, by the advantage of her dress, which was much more becoming then the Persian habit. Certain it is, he thought her more faire and Excellent then the Seaborn Goddess, whose beauty mov'd Paris to present her with the Golden Ball; and if the first sight of her infus'd into him some disquiet motions, this second quite b^e^reaft him of his whole repose, and left him no more a command over a heart which was no longer his, but that Faire Princesses: though (questionless) had she known of the Victory she had gained, she would have found rather a trouble, then taken any content in a conquest neither design'd, nor wish'd by her.

As yet *Alcander* was so much Master of his words and actions as he gave her not the least cause to suspect any thing of his passion: but after some complements, and expressions of civility, he made her the ^same request^ as *Delizia* had done a litle before. To which she repli'd, that she had given *Saparilla* a command to enforme the Princess his Sister of all things [fol. 121^v^] that concern'd her, and that if he pleas'd, she would enlarge her Commission to acquaint him also with her adventures. At *Artabella*'s condescention to his request he testifi'd a great content, and turning to *Saparilla*, told her, he would not give her a double trouble, but would stay till his Sister should be at leasure to heare the recitall they had both desir'd: and in the meane time I will go to the Temple (pursu'd he) to render thankes to *Apollo* for the victory he has given me over my enemies, and to implore his assistance in a conquest of more importance.

May the Deity you adore (said *Artabella*) be ever propitious to all that you desire: but if your Majesty please to permit me, I will waite on you thither, to pay my devotions at your Altars for those mercies I ought never to forget.

Most gladly Madam (repli'd he) and I take it as a favour that you will give me leave to waite on you thither, or any whither else.

Then taking her hand he lead her downe the staires into the Great Court, where stood a Chariot ready waiting for the King in which he and *Artbella* were carri'd to the Temple, at the Gate whereof they alighted: but before they went into the Temple he lead the Princess all about to shew her the rarity of its structure; the Walls of it being of that kind of Marble call'd Ophites, the ground whereof it [is] Green, diaper'd with blew or purple spots; the Windows were of the purest Christall Glass set in Gold; but the inside was yet more admirable, adorn'd on all sides with statues of the whitest Parian Marble (so call'd from the Isle of Paros remarkable for those Quaries of it which are found there) and of Alablaster; in which Statues were represented the most remarkable stories of *Apollo* recounted by the Poets; he shewed her there an Altar made of the Horns of Beasts, so artificially contriv'd as it had no thing to cement it; and an Image of *Venus* given by *Thesius*, which he had of *Ariadne*, a Golden Cup given by the Romanes, made of their Wives Jewells which they volluntarily gave to the making of it, and a three-footed stool of massy Gold which was found by ~~the~~ certaine Fisher-men of the Isle of Co and by an Oracle commanded to be sent to the wisest man in Greece; whereupon it was sent to *Thales*, and by him to *Bias*, and by him to another, till at last it was sent to *Thales* again, and by him sent to *Apollo*s Temple here, and many other things too tedious to recount did *Alcander* shew her.

Upon the Great Altar stood the Image of *Apollo*, his Face resembling the sun when he appeares most radiant; and on his head was placed a Coronet of such rich and sparkling Stones, as the lustre which they darted so dazled the beholders eyes, that they were no more able to behold them then the Sunne in his Noontide glory. Before this Altar there was a row of Pillasters so richly gilt, as none but might have taken them to be really what they seem'd, further then which, none but the Priest who pronounced the Oracles [fol. 122ʳ] was suffer'd to come; and there it was, that those who came either to enquire their Destinies, or to pay their Devotions were to performe their Oriasons: here did the King, and *Artabella* prostrate themselves to render thankes for those mercies they had receiv'd; and *Alcander* having first done, arose, and went out of the Temple to wait for the Princesses coming out; but no sooner had she finish'd her Prayer, but the Priest came from behind the Altar (where he always stay'd) to receive the Answers that *Apollo* gave those that desir'd to know anythinge of their Fates. The Princess *Artabella* seeing him was much affrighted at his gastly lookes, never before ^having^ seen any One inspir'd with a Prophetick Fury; but endeavouring to resetle herselfe, and looking about for the King, she perceiv'd he was gone forth which till then she had not minded; so that imagining the Oracle was intended onely to her, she listned very attentively to him, and heard him with a strang unusuall voice pronounce these Words.

The Oracle.

Here stay, and expect th' Destinies Decree
Which never can with Care prevented be:
And Learn with Patience a Loss to beare,
Which if thou wilt, thou quickly mayst repaire.
False Friendship, and ungratfull Love
Will punissh't be ere thou remove.
To Persias Land return no more
But bound thy thoughts within this Shore.

He having pronounced the Oracle came immediatly to himself again, and went back to the Place whence he came out, where he made no stay, but instantly return'd to *Artabella* whom he had left in a strang confusion at what he had deliever'd, not being able to apprehend the meaning of it, and the further she div'd into it, she [the] less she understood it: she desir'd the Priest to unfould the Will of the God more clearly if he could. But he having told her ~~he having told her~~ he knew as little the meaning of what he had deliver'd as she did herselfe; adding that Time would declare it by the event, conducted her out of the Temple.

Assoon as she came out she espi'd the King, who had stay'd for her in that Walk that lead to the Gate where they had left the Chariot in which they return'd to the Palace (after she had given the Priest thankes, and presented [fol. 122ᵛ] him with a Jewell she had brought with her for that purpose). *Alcander* presently found by some visible marks of trouble he observ'd in her Face that she had learn'd from the Oracle something that pleas'd her not, and fain would he have known what it was, but finding her unwilling to discover it, he curb'd his curiosity, and forbare to press her to tell it him. So soon as they return'd from the Temple dinner was serv'd up, and presently after the Princess *Artabella* retired to her Appartment to consult with her thoughts how she might interpret that which she had heard from *Apollo*s Priest. But not without a great deall of trouble could she reflect on that loss where ~~which~~ with she was threatned, nor could she imagine what to impute it too.

I have already (said she to herself) lost almost all I have to loose. I have lost my Father, I have lost the King my Uncle (who was a Father to me in his tender Love and Care he expresst towards me), I have lost my whole Estate, and what have I more to loose: ah (pursu'd she with a sigh) I have yet one thing more dear to me then all the rest; and thats the affection of my Deare *Phasellus*, that, that is it which I have yet to loose; and it cannot sure be anything else that can put my Patience to a stronger tryall, which has been hitherto so great, in all my other afflictions, as I needed not that warning which the Gods seeme to give me if they intended not to overwhelme me with a loss so insupportable. But if I loose him, certainly it must be by Infidelity; or else, what do they meane to speak of punishing ungratfull Love.

Whilst she was thus tormenting herself, the Princess *Delizia* had sent for
Saparilla to performe the promise which *Artabella* had made her. The King, and
Princess were gone into the Garden, and in one of the Arbours waited her coming; but 'twas not long that they expected ere she came, and being told by *Delizia*
for what cause she was sent for, she without delay, began her relation; omitting nothing that I have told you Madam (pursu'd *Celia* to *Arthenia*) of all that
concern'd her Mistress. As her birth and education, the manner of *Phasellus*'s
coming into Persia, his Love to *Artabella*, and her reciprocall esteeme of him,
her Fathers death, her leaving the Court after *Phasellus*'s departure to the Scythian war, her carrying away to Zarispe as she was returning to Susa, her escape
thence, the Tempest she suffer'd; and in fine, all that had hapned to her from
her Infancy, to that very day the King met with her, and brought her to Delphos; all which *Alcander* hearkned too very attentively a great while; but when
she came to those passages relating to the love of *Phasellus* and *Artabella*, he
chang'd colour severall times, insomuch as the Princess observing it, could not
forbeare asking him how he did: to which (the better to conceale the disorder
of his mind) he repli'd he found himself not very well. Which *Saparilla* hearing would have deferr'd the conclusion of her story til another opportunity; [fol.
123ʳ] but he would not permit her, but told her, his Concerns for the Princess
Artabella were too great, to suffer with any patience the recitall of her Adventures
to be suspended till another time. With that she went on, and in a few words
more finish'd her Naration; in which the Princess found a mervellous satisfaction, and gave *Saparilla* thankes for the pains she had taken to satisfy her desires;
and if the King forbore to do the like, it was because he found but little content
in what she had told.

Saparilla having perform'd that for which she was sent for, desir'd leave to
go to her Mistress whom she had left alone, to whom the Princess *Delizia* would
needs go too; but when they came ~~into~~ in to *Artabella*, they found her on her
Bed, and perceiv'd by the redness of her Eyes that she had newly been a weeping: which *Delizia* taking notice of, if I thought Madam (said she) that you had
receiv'd any new cause of displeasure since your coming hither, I should be much
more troubled then you seem to be, and beg you would make me a pertaker of
it by telling me what 'tis afflicts you: but when I reflect on those misfortunes
of yours, wherewith (by your permission) I have been made acquainted, I think
I need not enquire further the occation of your sadness; nor can I justly blame
that mellancholy which clouds the sweetness of your more cheerfull Looks. But
though you have been hitherto unfortunate, yet dispaire not; the Heavens no
doubt have reserved a happiness instore for you, which they will bestow when
you least expect it; they do but give you these present miseries, to make your
future felicity the more delightfull.

I wish you may prove a true Prophetess (repli'd *Artabella*) but I see so little
probability of that happiness you would have me hope for, that I should be as
vain as I have been unhappie, should I look for any felicity but in my Grave. No

no, Dearest *Delizia* (pursu'd she with a new floud of Teares) tis onely there that Unhappie *Artabella* must loose that Epith<u>ite</u> ^et^.[1]

The Princess strove with all the kindest, and most obliging words she could invent, to comfort her, and when she had a little allai'd her griefe, she left her to go to the King; whom she remembred she had left somewhat indispos'd. The Princess being gone, *Artabella* call'd *Saparilla* to her, to tell her the words of the Oracle, to see if her interpretation of it would agree with hers. When she had a great while consider'd it without making any answere, *Artabella* ask'd her what she thought of it; but I charge (added she) speak your reall thoughts, and do not disguise them to flatter me.

Truly Madam (answer'd she) what you have heard seemes to me so obscure, and intricate; as I cannot for my life conceive the meaning of it, nor am I able to give you the least Light to understand it; onely the command of the Gods for your stay here, is so cleare, and manifest, as it cannot be doubted but tis their Will you should obey them.

But what is that (said *Artabella*) which I must loose, that they exhort me to beare with Patience.

I cannot devize (answer'd she) unless he who [fol. 123ᵛ] sent you to Zarispe ceaze on your Estate, and take that from you after he heares of your escape.

Alass (said *Artabella*) that would be a thing so inconsiderable after my other losses, that I should be but little concern'd for it; but I rather feare 'tis *Phasellus* I must be depriv'd off, yes *Saparilla* without doubt he will ungratfully forsake me, and most unjustly rob me of a Heart which can of right be no bodies but mine; and I ought no longer to delude my self with a beliefe that he still continues Faithfull: the Mist begins to vanish, and I now perceive his neglect of me proceeded from no other cause but from some new Conquest he has made, which makes him slight that too too easie victory he obtain'd o're most unhappie me.

As *Celia* was in this part of her story, she saw some Teares drop from *Arthenias* Eyes, which made her break off her discourse, to aske her why she wept.

I cannot chuse (answer'd she) when I think on those misfortunes which forced from ^me^ that very expression of the Princess *Artabella*s which you mention'd last: but I beg your Pardon for this interruption, and desire you would proceed. Soe *Celia* went on.

But if it be so (continued *Artabella*) what can I do to repaire such a Loss, which I shall never be able to beare without dying: no, I will never out live the griefe and shame it would be to me, to see my self so basely abandon'd by that perfideous man.

Do not admit so ill an opinion of *Phasellus* I beseech you Madam (said *Saparilla*) for your owne quiets sake, before you are sure you may justly do it: but suppose he should be so disloyall as you feare, he would be so worthy of your hatered

---

[1] Epith<u>ite</u> with "ite" underlined and "et" inserted above in darker ink.

then, that very disdain should make you scorn to spend so much as a sigh for the loss of that, which you can no longer desire to keep, without a meanness of spirit, wherof I have never known you guilty yet. Pardon Madam my liberty of speech, if I presume to tell you, that his Infidelity (which I see little reason why he should be guilty of) should be so far from making you thinke of dying, that you should rather resolve to live, that you may hate as much as you have lov'd him, and banish him your breast, as far as he has banish'd vertue his; and not conserve the least rememberance of him, that may disturbe your quiet.

No *Saparilla* (repli'd she with her Eyes ready to oreflow with teares) I will to the last minute of my life preserve the memory of him; if for no other end, yet to punish myselfe for loveing so lightly; and for my indescretion, in making so ill a choice.

Ah Madam (said *Saparilla*) be not so unjust, to revenge anothers Crimes upon your selfe; if you will punish any, let it be the guilty *Phasellus*; not the innocent *Artabella*: but that you may know whether you ought to acquit, or condemne him, send into Persia to inquire after him, and let him know where you are, and if he comes not to you, you may then assure your self he is an unconstant man, and by consequence unworthy to hold any place either in your esteeme, or memory.

I am no longer able to live unresolv'd what to conclude (repli'd she) nor can I stay till the return of a Messenger, to expect what the Fates have decreed concerning me, for [fol. 124ʳ] tis some consolation to know the worst of ills: therefore I am resolv'd to go for Persia assoon as I can obtain of the King the Favour to furnish me with a Ship for my Voyage.

This discourse was broken off by one of those W^o^emen *Alcander* had appointed to attend on *Artabella*, who came in to tell her that there was a man nam'd *Serastes* who humbly beg'd leave to speak with her; she seem'd very glad to hear he was so well recover'd, and presently sent for him in; whether being come, he address't him selfe to *Artabella* thus.

I come Madam (said he) to render you my humblest thankes for the care you were pleas'd to take of my Life; which I had certainly lost, had it not been for that assistance the Good *Saparilla* (by your command) afforded me; and as I hold my life meerly from your Charity, and Goodness, so I am resolv'd to employ it wholly in your service, if you will but vouchsafe to retaine me, though as the meanest of your servants: and if the zeale, and fidelity wherewith I will serve you, may but excuse my unworthyness of that honour, you shall have no cause to repent you entertain'd me into your service.

Artabella considering how necessary *Serastes* might be to her in the condition she was, having no servant about her (she could justly call her owne) save *Saparilla*, whose sex rendred her uncapable of undertaking such things as *Serastes* might, willingly accepted his proffer.

And though (said she) I have not as yet done any thing to reward the service you have already done me, if the Gods restore me to my former Fortunes, you shall find *Serastes* you have not serv'd an ungratfull person: but I confess, in the condition I am in at present, I can give you but litle encouragment to hope for any advantage, by quiting your Proffession for my service: but notwithstanding, if you can be content to follow the Fortune of an injur'd Princess, despoil'd of all things by the cruell injustice of her Enemies, if I ever returne to the possession of my just Right, I'll raise your Fortunes to that height, as you shall have all the reason in the World to be satisfi'd. But what do you intend to do with your Ship, and Goods (added she) and how do you meane to dispose of them.

I intend Madam (repli'd he) to send my Brother away for Bizantium there to dispose of my Goods as I shall give him order; that done, he shall returne hither with the Ship that it may be ready to transport you into Persia when ever you please,

[T]hat will be needless (said she) for I believe the King will furnish me with a Ship; nor will my Occasions suffer me to stay so long, as it must of necessity be, ere yours comes back again.

Unless some ill accident fall out (repli'd he) it will not be above ten dayes before it returns.

Nay then (said she) if it will aske no longer time, I'll rather stay, then importune new Favours from a King to whom I am already so far indebted. Goe then *Serastes* (continu'd she) and dispatch your Brother, and enjoyn him to make all possible speed hither again.

Serastes being gone, she left her Chamber to go spend the rest of the day with the Princess in the charmes of whose conversation she found so sweet a consolation, as made her oft [fol. 124ᵛ] wish it were possible she might alwayes enjoy her company in which she took an infinite delight, and could not think of parting from her forever, without a resembling sadness. And as the Friendship of these two Princesses daily increast by the cleerer demonstrations they had of each others admirable qualities, so likewise did the Kings affection for *Artabella*, which grew to that degree, as it insensibly stole from him all his quiet, and in its steed, left him nothing but doubts, feares, and dispaires: which made him appear quite different from what he had ever been.

All the Court began to be concern'd for so apparent an alteration in their King, but more especially the Princess, who took notice of it with a mervellous trouble, not being able to comprehend the reason of it; though after some serious thoughts she partly suspected the truth, which she gather'd from her Brothers constant frequenting the Princess *Artabella*s company; being not a minute from her (but onely at such times, as decency or civilty deni'd him access) his ready compliance to all her desires, his studious seeking out all manner of diversions that might any way delight her, the respect he commanded all those about him to give her, and the state wherewith he had caus'd her to be serv'd; which was such, as if she had been his Queen she could not have expected more then what she already had. But all this she would have imputed meerly to his complacence to a Princess whose Illustrious birth gave her a title to that respect the King paid her, without any other motive to incite him to it: but that which most confirm'd

her suspition was, his often change of colour, whilst *Saparilla* was recounting the
story of her Mistresses love, and his alteration from that very time. But not long
after, when she was alone with him, she took the confidence to aske him the
cause of that sadness she had remark'd in him.

If you have observ'd any such thing in me as you say (answer'd he) I assure
you tis against my will you have perceived it; for I have endeavour'd to conceal from all the World the trouble of my mind; and if I did not except your
selfe Deare Sister (pursu'd he) it was, because I knew you would be more neerly
touch'd with griefe for my misfortune, then any one beside, for I know you make
all my concerns your owne.

Wave those thoughts Sir I beseech you (said *Delizia*) and believe it, my ignorance of what afflicts you, creates me a thousand times more cruell apprehensions, then the knowledge of it can. Though I cannot help you, yet if you will but
discover to me the cause of your trouble, I may perhaps assist you with my advice,
which you have been pleas'd not to disdain upon some occasions of importance;
but if it affords you no benefit now, I shall beare an equall share in what you suffer; and divided griefes (as I have heard) are by much the more supportable.

For that very reason, I will not tell thee (repli'd the King) for I love thee too
well, to load thee with an unnecessary griefe: tis enough to be miserable my self,
it were too much to make thee so.

With that he went away, lest she might by her importunity force from him
that, which he was very unwilling as yet to let her know, for some perticuler reason besides what he alleadg'd. The Princess had now no longer the least doubt
remaining, but that her [fol. 125ʳ] Brothers concerns were for *Artabella*, and that
his trouble proceeded from a dispaire of obtaining her affection; which she found
so deservedly acquir'd already by another, that it would be not onely the greatest
injustice to seek to dispossess him of his Right, but also impossible, should it be
attempted; and therfore she was much better pleas'd that the King had refus'd
her request, since thereby she was exempted from a necessity of disobliging him,
by denying to further him in his unjust pretences, or offending her Friend, by
becoming her Brothers Advocate.

The time for *Eumetes*'s returne was now expir'd, and *Artabella* began to be
troubled at his stay, and resolv'd that if he came not within a few dayes more, not
to wait his coming, but to desire a Ship of *Alcander*, to carry her into Persia, which
the next opportunity she had of speaking to him she determin'd to do. She had
scarce made this resolve, ere he came into the Room where she was set^t^ing all
alone, not having somuch as *Saparilla* with her. And after some discourse, Sir
(said she to the King) my Obligations to your Majesty are already so numerous,
that it might seem ungratfull incivility to aske any thing more, where I already
owe so much; but such is the necessity of my affaires, that they compell me to
beg you will vouchsafe to adde one Favour more to those many I have receiv'd.

You may assure yourself Faire Princess (answer'd he) there is not any thing
within my Power which you may not as absolutely command, as if you were Sov-

ereign here, and I your Subject; nor can you count any thing that I have hitherto had the happiness to serve you in, an Obligation to me, without infinitly
undervaluing your owne merits; which are such, as you deserve to be obey'd,
and serv'd, not by *Alcander* alone, but by all the Princes in the World beside. Say
then Madam, what it is which you desire, and be assur'd whatever you request
is granted.

Your words Sir are no less obliging then your actions (she repli'd) wherfore
I will not feare, after so free and unlimited a promise to make known my desire;
which is onely that you would be pleas'd Sir to lend me one of your Ships to carry
me home; I will not long detain it, if the Gods permit; but will returne it you, full
fraight with gratfull acknowledgments.

This Demand of *Artabella*s exceedingly perplex'd the King, not being able
to resolve to part with her, and as litle capable of denying her so small a request;
without revealing that, which he had resolutely determin'd to keep from her. But
after he had a while remain'd silent, as it were to consider what he ought to do in
such an exigent, he suddenly turn'd his eyes upon her, with a Look which spake
his unwillingness to part from her.

For Heavens sake Madam (said he) do not think of leaving us yet, nor make
us not so unhappy to loose you assoon as we have the honour to know you. I
know my Sisters Friendship to you is so great, as well as mine, that she cannot
without an insufferable trouble dispose herself to loose you so suddenly; at least
Madam stay one moneth longer with us I beseech you, that [fol. 125ᵛ] in that
time we may be a litle prepar'd to bid you farewell: but notwithstanding, that you
may see how absolute you are here; you may command not onely one, but all the
Ships within the Port; or anything else ~~thing else~~ that Delphos can supply you
with, when so'ere you please; and I my self will be your convoy, nor will I leave
you till such time as I have seen you safely arriv'd where you designe to go.

Pardon me Sir (repli'd she) I had rather be reduced again to extreamities as
great, as those you freed me from, then ever permit you should give your self so
great a trouble upon my account. I confess (pursu'd she) the griefe I shall resent
[feel] to leave the Princess *Delizia* (whom I most passionately love) will not fall
much short of what I have felt, for the most weighty of my afflictions; but since
your Majesty, nor that most Excellent Princess are not ignorant of that, which
presses my departure, I hope neither of you will take it ill that I do that which
necessitie constrains me too. Should I stay longer I should but render my trouble
the greater (by increasing my affection to *Delizia*, by a longer enjoyment of her
sweet obliging Society) nor will hers be the less: then seeing cruell Fate will have
it so, tis better for me to go now, then make a longer stay; unless my presence
could be any way serviceable to the Princess or your self.

Though neither she nor I (repli'd the King) ought to expect any thing of
service from the Princess *Artabella*, yet I must tell you Madam, your presence is
absolutely necessary to the establishing, or ruining my happiness, by the advice I
shall desire of you, in an affaire, in which I am determin'd to be guided onely by

your Councell; nor have I discloased that to any One, which I will now to you. Perhaps Madam (continu'd he) you count your self the most unhappy person in the World; but this I can assure you for your comfort (if there be any, in knowing there are others that are more unfortunate then our selves) that I am a thousand times more unhappie (if possible any one can be so) then your selfe.

That would be so far from affording me any comfort (repli'd she) that it would rather afflict me more, could I believe your infelicities held any parallele with mine.

You cannot but acknowledge what I say to be a truth (said he) when I have told you that I love, though you perhaps (as well as others) believ'd me hitherto not in the least touch'd with that passion; but to you Madam who know so well the irresistable power it does assault those hearts with which it once besiegeth, I'll make no scruple to avowe that which I have endeavour'd with the greatest care imaginable to keep secret from all persons else; assuring my self that you will (taught by your owne experience) pitty me; since my condition does aboundantly need it, not because I love, but because I am not belov'd, nor nere can hope to be; nor does she for whom I must languish out my dayes [fol. 126ʳ] in dispaire, so much as know I love her, nor I believe in the least suspect it; for I am sure unless my eyes have betray'd me, my words nor actions never did; for I have let so vigillant a watch over them, that notwithstanding the violence of my passion, I have hitherto preserv'd so high a veneration for her who is the Object of it, as not to give her any mistrust of that which if she knew it, would mortally offend her; and doubtless, change that esteeme wherewith she honours me into hatered, or at least aversion.

Indeed I see but little reason (repli'd she) for you to expect a perticuler kindness from a person who is wholly ignorant of yours, and as little why you should dispaire; since your Majesty may (without presumption) pretend to the greatest Princess whatever, both as to your Dignity, and the merit of your person.

Ah Madam (answer'd the King with a sigh) were that the onely obstacle I had to incounter, I should hope to overcome it and with the greatness of my passion supply all other defects; but I may with *Pigmalion* court a Marble Statue, and expect as good success: not that I think her I adore to be of a nature so hard, and obdurate, but I know her heart is already prepossest; and now what hopes have I, to gain an enterance there.

I must confess (said *Artabella*) you are far more unhappy then I could have believ'd you; and methinkes your condition does exceed[ing]ly deserve my compassion, and really your Majesty has as larg an interest in it as you can desire. But permit me Sir to aske; if you knew this person were engag'd, why would you ~~would~~ suffer your selfe to become passionate for her.

Alass (repli'd he) though I know it now, yet was I ignorant of it till after such time as I was my selfe engag'd past all retreat.

But in my opinion (said she) the impossibility there is of obtaining your desires, should have prevail'd with you to lay aside all thoughts of One, from whom you can expect no other returne but her Friendship; unless by infidelity she render herself more worthy of your disdain then Love. At least Sir methinkes you should endeavour to recover your Freedome, and no longer throw away a heart (most worthy of a better Fate) on a person uncapable of accepting it.

It would be invain, should I attempt it (he repli'd) for till I cease to live, I cannot cease from being a Slave to that Vertue, and that Beauty which has made me soe.

Since your Majesty (said she) is pleas'd to honour me with a secret of this nature, and to aske my advice (though you could never have made choice of a person more unfit to be your Councellour, especially in such an affaire as this, where I see I can give you no advice but what you must needs dislike) to the end I may the more freely speake my thoughts, and be ingenious, I must first desire to know what course Sir you propose to your selfe to take in the management of a Passion from which (in all reason, and probability) you cannot look for any thing but unhappiness.

If I should follow the dictates of my passion (repli'd he) I should have recourse to those wayes that Rivalls use; which is either to remove the obstacle to my Felicity, by taking away the life of my Rivall, or else, receiving death from his hand, be freed forever from the Torments of a hopeless Love. But I'll shun this Path to [fol. 126ᵛ] happiness, and rather chuse to be eternally miserable; if I can find no other way to Felicity then one so contrary to the respect I have for her my Soule adores; for my Flames being of a more pure, and noble substance then ever burnt in any heart before; makes me resolve to dy a thousand deathes (if it were possible) rather then be a meanes of procuring to my Adored Princess so great a sorrow as (questionless) she would resent, to see herselfe depriv'd of a person deservedly deare to her, no not if I were sure to succeed that happie person in her love, yet would I not purchace that Felicity at so deare a rate, as the price of her displeasure: for if there be a necessity that one must dy, tis fit that I do so for the expiation of my Crime, in dareing to harbour a passion which if she knew it (notwithstanding that Innocence, Purity, and respect wherewith it is attended) might perhaps offend her: but as I have hitherto kept it close Prisoner in my breast, so with the same care will I conceale it from her knowledge till the last minute of my Life; and then it is, that with my latest breath, I'le make her a Confession, which if it displease her, shall likewise at the same time assure her I will no more repeat my fault; and haply, the condition whereinto she has seen me cast my selfe, meerly for my love to her, will inspire her with so much compassion, as may fully recompence all my sufferings.

The King had gone on longer with this discourse, had he not been interupted by the Princesses coming in. But assoon as he saw her enter, he ris up, and going to her, took her by the hand, Deare Sister (said he to her) come and joyne your intreaties with mine, to the Princess *Artabella* that she may not leave us yet. Yes *Delizia* (pursu'd he) she is determin'd to forsake us, if your desires be not more prevalent then mine has been to detaine her longer here.

If you cannot Prevaile Sir (repli'd she) I have but little hope to do so, but however, I'll use all the rethorick I have, to perswade her to alter her resolution.

With that the King took his leave of *Artabella*, leaving *Delizia* with her to employ the utmost of that power she presum'd her Friendship gave her with her, to endeavour to make her change her resolve.

I will not beg you Madam (said she) that you should make me alwayes happie in your company, since that would be in me a most unjust request, should I desire, that for my sake you should forever deprive your self of the sight of those whose society ought to be much more dear to you then mine. No deare *Artabella*, all that I will beg shall be, that you will not kill poor *Delizia* with so sudden a departure as the King my Brother makes me feare: let me I conjure you by the love you beare *Phasellus* (or if I knew any spell more charming, I would make use of it) perswade you to defer my sorrow for some little time, and give me not so soon a misfortune so great as I am not able to beare it with any patience, if you do not a little prepare me for it.

If you believe I shall suffer less by this seperation then your self (repli'd *Artabella*) you have but a meane oppinion of my Friendship; but to let you see Madam how deare you are to me, I protest I could with less regreet abandon Persia and all my Concerns there forever, rather then leave you, did not my passion for him who just now you nam'd [fol. 127ʳ] constrain me to it, and seeme to reproove me for so long absenting my self from a place where he is. But how great soever my desire is to see him, I will for a while oppose it, by staying with you some dayes longer if that may give you any satisfaction;

[A]t this promise *Delizia* was even transported with Joy, and forgot no expression that might testify the greatness of it. One would have thought the King had spoke plainly enough to leave *Artabella* no cause to doubt, but that he meant herself in all he had said; but so meane was that opinion she had of her owne worth, and excellencies as she never suspected 'twas she that had made that undesigned conquest, and tryumph'd over the liberty of the Delphian King; ~~did~~ yet did she very much desire to know who she was that had inspir'd him with so respective a passion as made him resolve rather to dy, then offend her who was the cause of it. This Heroick, and generous resolution, made her infinity admire him, and wish he might be as happy in the progress, as he was unfortunate in the begining of his Love; little dreaming she made wishes for his felicity so contrary to her owne; and supposing the Princess might satisfie her in what she desir'd to know, though *Alcander* had said his passion was unknown to all the World, she yet fancied *Delizia* might be excepted in that generall number, and therefore resolv'd to aske her, believing she would not deny to tell her, if she knew: soe after she had promis'd her to stay.

Now Madam (said she) that I have given you this testimony of my Friendship I must likewise beg one proofe more of yours; in resolving me one question I shall aske you, promising faithfully never to reveale to any One what I desire to learn from you.

Were it a thing wherein my life were concern'd in the concealing it (answer'd *Delizia*) I should never distrust the Princess *Artabella*'s Friendship so far as to keep any thing from her which she desires to know.

I know already (said *Artabella*) that the King you Brother is passionatly in love; but that which I would be resolv'd of is, who that charming person is that has enthraul'd him.

To tell you positively who she is (answer'd *Delizia*) perhaps I may deceive you; for to say truth, I am not certaine that I know my selfe; but if you please I'll tell you who I really believe she is: but because tis impossible for me to describe the admirable beauty of that lovely Creature without injuring her by my imperfect description, tis requisite that I shew you her.

With that, taking a little Looking Glass out of her Pocket, and presenting it to *Artabella*, see here Madam (pursu'd she) the Face of her who without all doubt has captivated my Brother.

She supposing it to have been a Picture with hast took it of *Delizia*, but having open'd it, she found nothing in it save the representation of her owne Face; so that claping the glass together, as if she had beheld in it some affrighting object, she gave it her again.

Oh Madam (cry'd she) do not terrifie me with the apprehension of such a misfortune, which I hope the Gods will defend me from, what misery soever else they decree to throw upon [fol. 127^v] me. But should you once perswade me that this little beauty which Heaven has given me has been so fatall to the Kings quiet, how much should I detest it, and soon should I revoke my promise that I lately made you; for rather then stay any longer in a place where I have been so miserably unhappie, as to procure to a Prince to whom I am so infinitly oblig'd, a misfortune I never can repaire, I should (questionless) throw my selfe into the Sea if I could get hence no other way. But good *Delizia* (continued she) tell me what reason you have for your opinion.

I have many (answer'd she) but my chiefest is the knowledge I have of your perfections, which the King cannot be ignorant of, unless he be the most insensible man in the World; for such a commanding Power do you carry in your Eyes, as compells all hearts to do you homage. I speak not this to flatter you ~~this~~ (tis a thing beneath me) but out of a just sense I have of your incomparable beauty; besides, I am so perfectly acquainted with my Brothers temper, as I know he scorns to fix a thought on any subject of his owne, how faire, and lovely soever she may be. No Madam, there is none in Delphos (I am confident) can be capable of being *Alcander*'s Conquerour but the Fair *Artabella*.

The conquest of *Alcander* is so glorious (repli'd *Artabella*) as no Princess need to blush at the obtaining such a Victory; but that, which any but my self would have been proud of, I can look upon as no other then my highest misfortune; even such a One as I would willingly bye off at the price of my life: but all I can hope for is, that when I am gone, those slight Ideas which the King has conceiv'd of me will vanish, and that he will quickly loose those impressions which my ill

Fate (rather then any thing of beauty in me) has imprinted in his mind; and that he will soon regain that repose, which if I have rob'd him of, it has been most unwillingly. Therefore tis absolutely necessary that I stay no longer, lest by my presence I augment the Kings passion, and my owne trouble: nor must any consideration whatever, detain me, I will depart to morrow if the Gods permit: and if you believe Madam that you have reason to complain of my breach of promise, and of my sudden resolve, do me that Justice as to impute it to the cruelty of my Fate which will have it so: and let me Dearest *Delizia* (continu'd she embraceing her) beseech you for the King your Brothers sake, whose quiet ought to be a thousand times more dear to you then the enjoyment of my company for a few dayes: since if this had not hapned, I must within a little time more have taken my leave of you. For his quiet then, I once more beg you would not speak one word to perswade me from my resolution; which is so fix'd as nothing but death shall divert me from it.

No Madam (said *Delizia*) I will obey you, and onely go let *Alcander* know the ill success of my intreaties.

With that she went away with a countenance, which sufficently testifi'd the trouble of her mind, leaving *Artabella* in a discontent nothing inferior to her owne. According as she had said she would go and acquaint the King with *Artabella*s determination, so she did; and thereby so [fol. 128ʳ] heightned his dispaire, as not being able to contain his passion within those limits he had confin'd it too, he beg'd his Sister to retire, and leave him for some few minutes.

Assoon as the Princess was gone from *Artabella*, *Saparilla* came in, to whom she related all the discourse that had pass'd between the King, and her, as also that which she had with *Delizia*: and I am affraid (pursu'd she) the Princess has told me but too true; if so, what will become on me *Saparilla*, or what can I do to avoid this blow of Fortune: nothing certainly (went she on) but onely fly from the affections of a King to whom my obligations are such, as I cannot (without contracting the guilt of Ingratitude) be so severe as my preingagement ought to make me to any One that should presume to tell me that he loves me; especially when he knowes (as *Alcander* does) how far I am engag'd. Tis true he has hitherto preserv'd for me a respect so great, as makes me esteeme him as much as in reason he can expect: but alass, I know how little a bare esteeme is able to satisfy a Lover: and though he has yet so much command over his passion, as not to give me the displeasure of knowing from him that I am the cause of it, yet I question whether he will still retaine the same power; and therefore to prevent the trouble that such an acknowledgment would be to me, I do resolve to morrow to leave Del^ph^os; go then, and send *Serastes* to provide me a Ship to go for Persia, for the King has granted me one, whenever I please to command it.

Saparilla would have oppos'd her so sudden departure with many powerfull reasons; and sought all she could to perswade her to defer her voyage, but till the return of *Eumetes*; but she appear'd so absolutely bent to do what she had determin'd, that *Saparilla* saw 'twas a thing impossible to induce her to change her mind; so that ceasing to importune her further, she went to give *Serastes* order for the performance of her Princesses command. Which he accordingly having done in a short space after, came and told *Artabella* there was a Ship lay ready for her service at the Port, when ever she pleas'd to go aboard: which having heard, she quited her Chamber, leaving it to *Saparilla* to take care to prepare all things in order to their departure the next morning, and went to find out the Princess with whom she meant to spend the remainder of that day.

But long they had not been together ere the King came into the Roome where they were; but with a Face so chang'd and a Countenance so full of sadness, as perfectly shew'd that sorrow wherewith his heart was so o'recharg'd as he was even ready to sink under its weight. *Artabella* could not but perceive it, and as impossible it was for so good, so sweet a nature as that of hers, but must be extremely afflicted to see a Prince suffer for her sake with so much patience, and so profound a respect. There conversation was very different now from what it had been at other times; and both the King, the Princess, and *Artabella* also seem'd so sadly Melancholly, that there pass'd no discourse ~~as to~~ but such, as testifi'd their resentments. But *Alcander* did in so pressing and passionate a manner ^importune^ *Artabella* for a longer stay, as any one might visibly see the [fol. 128ᵛ] interest he had in what he so earnestly desir'd; and *Delizia* so well seconded him, that *Artabella* had nothing to defend her from their excessive importunaties but her Resolve, which was so firmly setled, as not any thing that could be said was able to shake it, much less prevaile with her to alter her mind.

When night came they all went to their severall Apartments to take their rests, though the King took but little; for so violently was he tormented with multitudes of disquiet thoughts, that the night was scarce half spent ere he fell extream ill; insomuch as his Phisicians were sent for, though to little purpose; for he slighting their advice, obstinatly refus'd all their Prescriptions, expressing much anger against the officiousness of those who had sent for them without his order. The next morning, when *Artabella* was ready for her departure, and that she had rewarded the services of those W^o^emen the King had appointed to attend her (during her aboad in the Delphian Court) with the gift of some Jewells of good value, she bid them all severally farewell, whilst they with teares declar'd their unwillingness to be discharg'd from their employment. This done, she went ^to^ the Princess's Chamber to take her leave of her; but not finding her there, she ask'd some of her W^o^emen where she was, who told her she was gone to the King who had been taken very ill in the night: which having heard she sent one of *Delizia*s Maids to give her notice this she was ready to go, and stay'd onely to bid her ad^i^ue and that if she might be permitted without disturbing the King, she would gladly waite on him to take her Leave of him, as also to give him her humblest thankes for all those royall Favours he had honour'd her with.

She who went to tell the Princess this; spake so loud, as the King chanceing to over heare her, started up in his Bed, and pulling open the Curt^ain^, is the Princess *Artabella* then resolv'd to go (said he). He said no more, but calling for his Clothes, and causing his servants to help him on with them, he instantly arose, notwithstanding his Sisters intreaties, and the Phisicians perswasions to the contrary; who assur'd him he would much prejudice his health by rising. But he told them they were mistaken, for he was not so ill as they imagin'd; but if he were much worse, the consideration of his health (he said) would be too weak to prevaile with him to keep either his Bed, or Chamber at that time. He was almost assoon dress'd as up, and going with his Sister to her Apartment, where he heard *Artabella* still was; who admiring to see *Alcander* whom she suppos'd to be in bed, told him she was extreame sorry he should give himself the trouble of coming to her, being (as she had been enform'd) not well.

I am not so ill Madam (he repli'd) but that I both can, and will attend you into Persia, since you are resolved to go; for I will never leave you till I have deliever'd you safe into *Phasellus*'s hands; that I may thereby in part make him amends for the Injury I [fol. 129ʳ] would have done him by detaining you longer from his sight, had it been in my power by prayers, or intreaties to have prevail'd with you.

It were an unpardonable incivility in me (answer'd she) should I suffer your Majesty to abandon the Concerns of your Kingdome upon my account; and expose your Royall Person to the danger of an unnecessary Voyage for my security. I trust the Heavens will take on them my protection; but were I sure to repeat dangers as great as those which by your Goodness I escap'd, nay, were I sure to perish, I had rather do so, then contract a greater Debt, where I already owe so much.

I beseech you Madam (said the King, interrupting her) speak no more of debts, or obligations: for I shall ever deny you owe me any; nor have you any reason so highly to acknowledge that which meere humanity oblig'd me too: and for what I have done since I had the honour to know you, it has been so farre short of what you merit, most Divine Princess, that I ought rather to aske your pardon, then expect any Thankes for ought that I have done: and if I must receive thanks from any One, tis from *Phasellus* onely that I will accept them: but that I may do somewhat that may deserve them, permit me Madam to convey you safely to him.

No Sir (repli'd she) I can never suffer that; and if you think you have not yet sufficently oblig'd me, do but permit me to take my Leave of your Majesty in this very Place, and I shall take that as the highest Favour you can further imagine to confer upon me.

Many other things she said to divert him from the design he had to accompany her home, whereby she let him know she would by no meanes accept his proffer, so that he was fain to resolve to part from her at the Port, whether (conditionally he would stir no further) she consented he should go with her. The Princess likewise would follow her Brothers example, and waite on her thither too, that she might enjoy her company as long as possibly she could: but being come to the Port, where the Ship lay at Anchour, they were told the Wind was so contrary, as there was no possibility of seting Saile till it chang'd. This troubled *Artabella*, as much as it rejoiced the King and Princess, and faine would they have perswaded her to returne to the Palace to stay but till the Wind alter'd; but she was deafe to all perswasions of that nature, telling them she would instantly go abord to take the opportunity of the first faire wind: but the Seamen told her it would be much more convenient for her to stay at Land, promising to give her notice assoon as they had a Wind. With this assurance she retir'd to a little house which stood hard by, intending to stay there till her departure; the King accordingly resolv'd to abide there too, so did *Delizia* till they had seen her imbarke; nor could she prevaile with either of them to leave her till then. The King too soon found the truth of what his Phisicians had told him; for what with the disturbance of his mind, and the little care he took of himselfe, he had not been many houres in that little house, ere he relaps'd into his late indisposition, and in a short space grew so very ill as he was constrain'd to let himselfe be put to bed; which (though the best the house afforded) was a very uneasie one, and far unfit [fol. 129ᵛ] for a King to lye on.

The Heavens seem'd to oppose *Artabella*s desire of quiting Delphos, for the Wind continu'd where it was, so long as was never known before: in which time, the restraint *Alcander* used upon himselfe, to conceale his passion from *Artabella* to the last moment of his Life, or at least that of her departure which he hourly expected (joyn'd to the neglect of all those remedies he might have found from the skill, and care of his Phisicians; had he not with an immoveable obstinacy rejected all they would have done for the recovery of his health.) So increased his Destemper, as it brought his Life into so manifest a danger, as they began very much to feare it; declaring to the Princess their apprehensions, and that they were as far to seek for the cause of his Indisposition, as the reason why he shew'd so much contempt of life, as to refuse all meanes of preservation; beging her to perswade him to be remov'd to the Palace, before such time as his weakness render'd him unable to endure it. Which she accordingly did, representing to him the inconvenience he suffer'd by staying there. But he told her, if she could perswade the Princess *Artabella* to returne with him, he would instantly be remov'd, otherwise he was resolutly determin'd not to stir as long as she was there. She having receiv'd this Answere from him, went immediatly to *Artabella*, and in so pressing a manner beseech'd her to go back to Court, and there stay but till the Wind serv'd, as she had not the heart to deny her: but told her, rather then the King should in any hazard of his life, or sustaine any further inconvenience upon her account, she would condescend to her request, on condition she would not obstruct her departure by any more intreaties; which *Delizia* promis'd faithfully she would not and return'd to the King her Brother, to let him know she has prevail'd with *Artabella* to go back with them; which she having assur'd him of, he gave command a Litter should be instantly brought for himselfe, and a Chariot for the two Princesses.

But all that the Docters could do could hardly keep him from falling into a sowond [swoon] assoon as they had laid him into his Bed again, such was his extreame weakness. The poor Princess stir'd not from him either day, or night, but witness'd by her incessant Teares how infinitly deare he was to her. The King receiv'd an addition to his trouble by the sight of her griefe, and strove all he could to give her that comfort which she was uncapable of, so long as she beheld him in a condition, in which if he remain'd but a few days longer, she apparently found, she must forever loose him: neither could *Artabella* herselfe behold him in so desperate an estate (courting Death by shuning all meanes conduceing to his recovery) and think herself the cause of his dispaire, without a resembling sorrow. She believ'd she was oblig'd in civility to visit him as frequently as with decency she might, lest he should account her ungratfull, [fol. 130ʳ] or believe she had some suspition of his Passion which induced her to refraine seeing him; these reasons made her visit him oftner then otherwise she would have done. He grew every day much worse then other, and was at last so very weak as the Phisicians affirm'd it to be an impossible thing for him to live if he would not use some meanes to preserve his Life; but so far was he from hearkning to their perswasions, as he seem'd exceedingly to rejoyce when they told him he must die.

But his Joy at that assurance was not greater than *Delizia*s griefe, for she appear'd even halfe distracted at it, and weeping most bitterly: ah Sir (said she to him) is Life so inconsiderable a thing as you will take no care to keep it; or which is worse, will you become guilty of your owne death: if you will not live for your owne sake, yet live for mine; since I neither can nor will live without you: be not so cruell then to kill a Sister who has heretofore been very deare to you: but if you are resolv'd to dy, for pities sake command that I be put to death immediatly, that so I may be freed from that tormenting sorrow, which I must suffer else to part from you forever.

Could I be guilty of so horrid a barbarisme (repli'd he) as to take thy life away. I should indeed be cruell even to the highest abstract. No Dearest Sister (pursu'd he taking her by the hand) you must live, and live happy too I hope, though I must dye the most unfortunate of men: nor can you without that cruelty you accuse me of, desire that I should live, since I cannot do so without suffering torments each houre more intollerable then the most rigorous death that ever was invented. Then seeing Death is onely that which can free me from so much misery, why do you grieve to see me have recourse to the onely remedy that is left me; if I deprive you of a Brother, I leave you in exchange a Crowne.

You may bestow it on some other (said she with a new flood of teares) who will with thankes receive it, but for my part I declare I never will; for I'll not live a minute after I have lost you; and if my griefe be too weake to send me to you, I'll send my selfe by the help of my resolution.

She had scarce pronounced these words ere he fell into a fainting Fit, which the Princess seeing, thought verily he was just dying, whereat she gave a great Shriek and fell downe in a swound; but she was presently taken up, and carried

into another Roome, where some of her Wemen being call'd to her endeavour'd
to bring her to life again, whilst those about the King did the like by him.

The Princess *Artabella* being in her owne Apartment (which was not far
distant from the Kings) heard the Princess cry out, which made her apprehend
somewhat of danger in *Alcander*: she stay'd not to enquire, but went herselfe to
see what the matter was; but no sooner was she come in, but she perceiv'd him
to lye pale and senseless, with his Phisicians about him useing their uttmost skill
to fetch him to life again: so great was her trouble to see him in that condition,
as she never mist the Princess, nor ever thought so much as once to aske where
she was. When the King was come perfectly to himself, he beheld the Princess
Artabella standing by his Bedside, leting fall some teares which pity drew [fol.
130ᵛ] from her Fair Eyes; and turning towards her as well as he was able, with
a feeble voice he said. If I am the occation Madam of those precious Teares you
shed my condition is yet worthy of envie; since it has mov'd you to express some
compassion for my supposed death. But alass (pursu'd he sighing) your pity soon
will cease, when once you know what tis that drives me to my death, which I
feare you will account too gentle a punishment for my fault: but that I may not
dye unpardon'd, tis necessary that I confess my Crime, which I will never do to
any but yourselfe. Therefore I beseech you Madam afford me the Favour of some
few minutes in private, that I may have time to make you this Conffession.

With that, not staying for her answere, he commanded all that were present
to retire. She knew already but too well what the King intended, and dreaded
that declaration which she expected, but knew not how to avoid; for so long
was she considering what reply to make, that she was left alone, and thereby
constrain'd to hearken to him: so that seating herself in a Chaire which stood
by the Bed, with a trouble I am not able to represent (continu'd *Celia*) she heard
him say.

Tis not till the last minutes of my Life Madam that I have presum'd to tell
you, that tis the Princess *Artabella* whom I adore with a respect unparallel'd. Yes
Fairest Princess, tis those inevitable charmes of yours, whose power I have not
been able to withstand, that have setled so deep a passion for you in my soule,
that Death it selfe cannot destroy it. I gave you my heart with an intire resignation assoon as I beheld you, I lov'd you ere I knew who 'twas I lov'd; and had
your birth been as ignoble as it is illustrious, yet would not my passion have
been at all thereby diminish'd: but I must confess after I knew your heart was
already dispos'd of, I strove all that I was able to recover mine, and to resume that
Liberty which at your Feet I had resigned; but all my endeavours were invain,
and my resistance serv'd to no other purpose but to enslave me more, and tye my
Chaines so fast, as nothing but Death, or you have power to free me; and thankes
to Heaven, I have now made so faire a process towards the regaining of my Liberty, that I speedily ^hope^ to receive it from the hand of Death, since from you
Madam I never can expect it; unless it were possible for you to become unconstant, and unjust, which I dare not sin so much against you[r] Vertue as once to

wish you might: for though I love you for your beauty, yet tis for your Vertue Divinest Princess that I adore you most. That being then, the chiefest object of my passion, I will never be so unworthy as in the least to tempt you to a violation of that which I prize highest in you: for such is the sacred respect I have for your honour, that I rather chuse to dye then to desire, that for my sake you should condescend to any thing that might in the least degree blemish the purity of your Fame, by a breach of that Fidelity you owe my happie Rivall. All then Madam that I'll implore shall be, that I may not dye hated, since I could not live belov'd; and that when I have seal'd to you with my last breath the greatness of my passion, you will then believe I lov'd you more, then ever any did: and that though I am more unfortunate, I am not [fol. 131ʳ] more unworthy of your esteeme then him whom you are oblig'd to prefer before me.

At these words *Artabella* b̶u̶t̶ burst out into an extreame passion, weeping excessively, not being able to let the King proceed.

If I am so deare to you Sir (said she) as you would have me believe, sure my content, and quiet would have been so too: and seeing you resolv'd to dye, why would you not as well resolve to dye in silence; and thereby have exempted me from that eternall sorrow it will imprint upon my soule to know I am the cruell (though innocent) occasion of your death: for Heaven knowes I never contributed to the loss of that Freedome which you accuse me to have taken from you; which if I have, I would more willingly restore it, then ever you resign'd it me. Then why Sir do you (by a Declaration so full of Love, and Generosity) reduce me to the necessity of becoming the most ungratfull, or the most perfideous Woman in the World. False to *Phasellus* I will never be; and you your selfe Sir have generously assur'd me you never will desire I should; nor would I be ungratfull, knew I but which way to avoid it: for there is not any thing wherein my Honour, or my Fidelity is not concern'd which I would not do to acquit my self in part of what I owe your Majesty, or to preserve your Life; which to save I would most freely give my owne. But alass (pursu'd she sighing) all that I am capable of is onely to confirme to you that Friendship I have already given you; and though I cannot give you the first place in my affection, yet to give you an equall one in my esteeme.

Ah Madam (repli'd the King) I shall derive but little satisfaction from your esteeme (how great soever tis above my merit) if you can give me nothing else; for I know many that esteeme those they mortally hate, though I cannot thinke you so cruell to hate One who never willingly offended you.

But though my Esteeme be so indifferent to you Sir (interrupted she) my Friendship yet will certainly be more considerable, if your Majesty rightly understands what tis to be a Friend; for admit (as you say) One may hate the person of those whom for their vertues they esteeme, yet doubtless we can have no reall Friendship for any, but such as we love in a very high degree; which I will not scruple to acknowledge I do you Sir, as far as Friendship can oblige me: of which, I think I give you no small evincement, since that consideration alone has induced me to give eare to a discourse so offencive to me, and so contrary to that

Fidelity I owe him to whom I have given my Faith, without being transported to an excess of anger; which questionless I had been, had not my Friendship, together with that sad condition, wherein (to my griefe) I behold you, moderated my just resentments, and instead of anger, inspir'd me with that Compassion your misfortune merits: but though I pitty, I can never pardon you, unless you abandon all thoughts, and desire of dying, and endeavour likewise to cast off a Passion so destructive to my quiet, and your owne repose: try Sir, but to oppose it with all the Forces of your Reason, and doubt not but to obtain a Victory, which if once gain'd, will give your Majesty a more reall satisfaction, then if you could tryumph over my Constancy.

That Essay Madam (said he) is not now to make; but my vain, and fruitless endeavours assures me Reasons power is much too weak to overcome my passion; for even that very reason [fol. 131ᵛ] which you would have me oppose my passion with, compells me to adore you, and perswades me to love, what in the World is most worthy to be lov'd (which is yourselfe) so that unless Madam you can become less Lovely, less admirable then you are, tis impossible I should find any reason strong enough to banish an affection from my heart that had its originall rather from Reason, then Passion. Methinkes then Fairest Princess (went he on) you should find little or no cause to be offended with a Love so full of Innocen[c]e, and respect; for great, and violent as it is, it shall never force from me one sillable that justly may displease you, nor ever compell me to request ought from you that *Phasellus* (were he here) would forbid you to grant. For I neither hope, nor will I aske to be beloved, I'll onely beg Madam, you will permit me to love you, without making your hatred, or aversion the reward of that affection.

I must be faine (repli'd she) to permit what I cannot help, from a person to whom I am redeuable [grateful] for my Life; but were your passion yet more blameless then you represent it, I must conjure you Sir for your owne quiet, to cast it off; since you can never hope to reape any satisfaction by it: and live *Alcander* I beseech you, at least so long as till I am resolv'd whether will more afflict me; your death, or the continuance of your Love.

With that, not staying for his answere she ris up, and went out of the Chamber; and finding some of his servants waiting at the Dore, she told them they might go in when they pleas'd: and remembering she had not seen *Delizia* with the King when she came in, nor that she had not been with him since, he fanci'd she might not be well; so that going to see; she found her thoughts had not deceiv'd her, for when she came into her Chamber, she saw her laid upon her bed, in the posture of a person very much indispos'd: and expressing her trouble at it, began to blame her that she had not let her know it.

I had sent for you (said the Princess) but that I was told you were with the King my Brother, who I was unwilling to deprive of such a Felicity as your company; which I know is deare to him at all times, but more especially now; when all the comfort you can afford him is less then his condition does require.

I know not what satisfaction he has deriv'd from my presence, but for my part I found but little in a discourse he made me, which you would have done me an infinite kindness to have freed me from, by sending for me away.

Will you not tell me (repli'd *Delizia*) what it was my Brother said to you.

Yes (answer'd *Artabella*) you may be confident you are too deare to me to keep any thing as a secret from you that concerns my selfe.

But just as she was begining to tell her, she was interupted by *Saparilla*, who came to beg her pardon for something, which (she said) she had presum'd to do without her knowledge, or approbation; but 'twas my zeale to your service Madam (pursu'd she) that mov'd me to it; and it has fallen out so happily to my wishes, that I trust I have rather oblig'd then displeas'd you by it.

Whatever it be you need not doubt my pardon ^(said *Artabella*)^ since I assure my selfe [fol. 132ʳ] you would not willfully do any thing that in reason might displease me.

I must confess then Madam (said she) tis I that have been the occation of your stay in Delphos so much longer then you intended, by giving *Eumetes* privat orders to go into Persia, and enquire after *Phasellus*: he is just now return'd, but what newes he brings I know not, for I had not patience to stay to aske him: but he has brought with him One who will certainly enforme you of all things that has hapned since you left Persia.

Who is it (hastily repli'd *Artabella*)

Mexaris, *Diomeds* squire (answer'd *Saparilla*).

Whereupon *Artabella* not thinking it proper to send for him into *Delizia*s Chamber went to her owne: after she had beg'd the Princess to excuse her if her impatient desire to heare of *Phasellus* constrain'd her to leave her so abruptly, promising to returne to her again ere long, and then acquaint her with the Kings Discourse.

But, *Celia* perceiving *Arthenia* of a sudden to turne extreamly pale, brake off her relation to aske her if she were well; indeed I am not (arswer'd she) for I find all my Spirits ceaz'd in such a manner, as I am not able to tell you how I am: but sure if I continue long so, I shall believe Death will be so kind as to release me of all my miseries, ere many dayes are past.

Oh Heavens Madam (cry'd *Celia*) why would you not tell me that you were ill.

Your Story was so pleasing (she repli'd) as I was willing to endure as long as I was able rather then interrupt you: but if you please I'll go to bed, and if I can sleep, perhaps I may be better.

Faine would *Celia* have sent for the Queens Phisician to her: but she would by no means consent to it.

I am most extreamly troubled deare *Arthenia* (said *Celia*) to see you so ill; and the rather in regard of a custome we have, which permits no person (except our Kings, and Queens) to dy in Delphos; so that if there appear any danger of death in any One, they are instantly remov'd to a little Island not far off (call'd Rhene) where they are to be buried if they dy, or else to remaine there till such time as they are perfectly recover'd: this I could not but let you know, that you may not count us Inhumane Creatures to send you into a strang Place in the condition you are in; since tis one of those Divine Laws instituted by *Apollo* himselfe (to whom I suppose you know this Isle is dedicated) and therefore not to be violated; so that if once the Phisicians doubt your recovery, you must instantly be carried thither. But this for your comfort I'll assure you, you cannot be more carefully look'd too, or more dilligently tended in any place then you will there; for the Inhabitants are onely such as are appointed to attend sick persons, with all conveniencies imaginable: and to be sure I will my selfe waite on you thither, and never leave you, till you leave the world, or Heaven restore your health, as I hope it speedily will.

I should be sorry (repli'd *Arthenia*) you should impose on your selfe so great a trouble, but yet I know not how to refuse your kind proffer, since your obliging company is the onely comfort that is left me in this miserable World. After this she went to bed, but not one wink of sleep that she could get so violent, and raging a pain had she in [fol. 132ᵛ] her head; very hot, and Feavourish was she all the night, and grew still worse and worse; so that the next morning assoon as *Celia* could come to speak with the Queen, she went and acquainted her with what a Violent Distemper *Arthenia* was ceas'd, which she was very much concern'd to heare, and immediatly commanded two of her owne Docters should go to her; and so soon as she was up, gave her the honour of a visit; and hearing the Phisicians speake dubiously concerning her, not knowing well what to make of her distemper, but both concluding it was necessary she should be sent to Rhene ere she grew worse, she gave order that the best house in the Island should be made ready for her reception, with all requisit accommodations; (preventing the request *Celia* was about to make) commanding her and *Amena* to go with her, and see that she were no less carefully look'd too, then if she herself were in the like case: and whilst she aboad in Rhene, *Ermillia* sent daily to enquire of her health, which by the goodness of Heaven and the diligent endeavours of those about her, in the space of twelve, or fourteen dayes she so well recover'd, as she was able to walk out a little to take the Aire, which the Phisicians affirm'd to be very good for her.

But one day as *Celia* and she were viewing the Monuments of those that were there inter'd (which were very num^e^rous as being the onely place of sepulture for all Delphos) amongst them they espi'd one that challeng'd a more perticuler regard then any of the rest, not for the richness, but the strangness of it, being nothing but a heap of rude unpollish'd stones; yet placed in so good order in the forme of a Piramid as requir'd a great deall of ingenuity to fix them so regulerly; on the Top of it was placed a Wreath of Myrtle and Cypress intermix'd, and round about it on the Ground were Flowers strew'd; which were so fresh as they seem'd to have been but newly gather'd and brought thither to adorn that Grave.

About the midle of the Piramid, there was one White stone about a Foot square, and on it engraven in Scielian characters these words

Here rests secure
From Fortunes crueltly, and Love's tyrany
The Fairest
And, most Unfortunat of Woemen.

The Character wherin this was writ, made *Arthenia* conclude, this unhappy One to be of her owne Country, which inspir'd her with a very great curiosity to know who, and what she was; and having seen a woman pass from the Grave as they came towards it, with a Basket in her hand, she fancied that might be she who had strew'd those Flowers on it; and thinking if she could but over take her, she might possibly from her obtain that information she was soe [fol. 133ʳ] desirous of, she made known her desire and opinion to *Celia*, who concur'd with her in it, and praying her to set downe, she told her she would follow the Woman and try if she could overtake her; which if she could, she doubted not but she should perswade her to come back and satisfie her in what she so much wish'd to know: but scarce was *Celia* gone out of sight, ere she perceiv'd that same Woman going on her way, a very slow and leasurly pace, which mov'd her to hasten hers, so as in a little time she overtook her; and demanding if it were not she that had strew'd the Grave of that so Faire, and Unfortunat person with those Flowers; she repli'd she was, whereupon *Celia* intreated her in so c^o^urti̲^e^ous[2] and obliging a manner to go back with her to that Tombe, and resolve a Lady that waited there for her returne, who that person might be, as she could not refuse her request.

But no soon was she come to *Arthenia*, but she instantly knew her to be *Ambracia*; at whose sight she was but too well assur'd that Unhappie One that there lay buried was no other then her so long lost Friend the Faire *Ianthe*; but though she knew *Ambracia*, yet so had her afflictions, together with her late sickness changed her, as *Ambracia* knew not her till such time as she spake; but then immediatly calling her to mind, with wonder to see her in that place, she threw herself at her Feet, and embraceing her knees with Teares that had in them a mixture both of Joy and Griefe. Oh Heavens Madam (cry'd she with precipitation) what Fate has brought you to my Deare dead Mistresses Grave, was it designe or chance.

The last I assure you Faithfull *Ambracia* (repli'd *Arthenia*) for little did I dreame of finding her in Rhene whom I lost in Sicilie: but alass, tis little satisfaction to find her thus as to be assur'd I have now lost her forever, Ah poor *Ianthe* (pursu'd she with a Flood of Teares) I now too well perceive thy miseries ne're knew an end but with thy life; but Oh how dull was I that could not know by the

---

[2] The correcting hand inserts "o" between "c" and "u" and then underlines "i" and inserts "e" above; "curtious" is amended to "courteous."

Inscription on thy Tombe, that thou layst there, for who could be so justly stil'd the most Unfortunate of Woemen as thy selfe. O *Ambracia* (said she to her) how do I admire thee for thy Fidelity, and love thee for thy Constancy, that neither in life, nor yet in death wilt abandon thy beloved Mistress.

No Madam (she repli'd) there is not any thing whatever, can force me from her, and tis my onely comfort that I can each day offer up my Teares upon her Tombe as a testimony of my endless sorrow for a loss I never can repaire, and deck with Flowers this poore Monument (which in memory of her I have erected) which is my daily employment.

But will you not tell me (said *Arthenia*) what mishap it was, that drave *Ianthe* so suddenly from Palermo, and brought her hither.

That would I most willingly Madam (she repli'd) had she not with her expiring breath enjoyn'd me not to discover to any one that knew her the last and greatest of her misfortunes, and therefore I hope you will not take it amiss if I refuse you a satisfaction, which I cannot give you without a violation of my promise.

No (said *Arthenia*) [fol. 133ᵛ] I am so far from taking your refusall ill, that I esteeme you the more for it; for I will never desire you should bleamish your Fidelity to satisfy me by a breach of that Trust my Friend repos'd in you.

Fain would *Arthenia* and *Celia* have perswaded her to have gone along with them; but she beg'd their excuse for that day, promising she would not faile to wait on them ere it were long, and so took her leave after *Arthenia* had told her where she might find her. This accident had infus'd into the mind of *Arthenia* so much sadness, as she seem'd wholly possest with melancholy; which to divert, *Celia* told her that if she pleas'd she would now finish the remainder of *Artabel-las* Concerns; to which she having assented, in these words she reassum'd her discourse.

Rivall Friendship

THE SECOND PART

The Third Book

You may remember Madam (said *Celia*) that the Princess *Artabella* was gone from *Delizia* to her owne Appartment to receive *Mexaris;* whether she was no sooner come, but *Saparilla* brought. Assoon as *Artabella* saw him enter, she perceiv'd so great a sadness in his Lookes, as from thence she drew an Omen of some ill events: but however she gave him a very kind reception for his Masters sake, of whose health and wellfaire she perticulerly enquir'd, and ask't *Mexaris* what occation had brought him thither.

The cause of my coming hither Madam (answer'd he) was to enforme you of some things wherein you are most nearly concern'd; and had I not by accident from *Eumetes* heard of your being here, my search for you must not have ended but with my life, unless I had been asured you had been no longer in the World to have been found; far so was I commanded by my dear Master ere he died.

What is that you say *Mexaris* (interrupted she) is the brave Prince *Lucius* dead; and is it true that I have liv'd to lament the death of the Gallantest of men, and my most generous Friend; sure I was born for nothing but misfortunes. Ah (continu'd she with a shower of teares) how deservedly deare ought his memory to be to all Persia in generall, but to me in a more perticuler manner. O how justly may the Scythians boast of the revenge they have taken on the Persians for all their losses, [fol. 134ʳ] since they have depriv'd them both of their King, and their most Valiant Champion, two men whose lives were each of them more considerable then an Empire.

Though the Scythlans tryumph'd over the life of *Achemenes* (said *Mexaris*) they cannot boast they did so over my Masters; for after he had died their Fields with the blood of thousands of them, subdu'd the whole Kingdome, taken *Oruntus* Prisoner and reduced him to that estate as to impose on him what Conditions he pleas'd, establish'd a perpetuall League of Amitie between both the Kingdomes, and return'd a victorious Conquerour into Persia; he there (instead of those Tryumphs his renouned Valour merited) found his death; not from the sword of a proffessed Enemy, but from the secret treachery of a perfidious Friend.

I had thought (repli'd *Artabella*) he had died of those Wounds he receiv'd in Scythia when the last battell was fought.

No Madam (answer'd *Mexaris*) he died not then, but happie had it been for him if he had, for then had his destiny been as glorious, as his Fate afterwards was lamentable. But I beseech you Madam stope the Current of your Teares a while (continu'd he seeing her weep still), for ere I have finish'd my story I shall

tell you such thing as will but too justly require them from you: but ere I proceed, I must beseech you Madam to summon all your Courage, and arme your
selfe with all imaginable Patience, for all the assistance you can find will be little
enough to help you to support what you must suffer thorow what I am to tell you.
I confess I had much rather you should have learn'd your misfortune from any
one then me, but that my Masters commands (which I dare not disobey) oblige
me to acquaint you with it: nor would he (I know) have laid such an Injunction on
me, could you always have remain'd ignorant of your unhappiness, but believing it could not be forever hiden from you, he thought me fitter then another to
bring you such unwellcome tydings, in regard he knew ^none^ but myself could
acquaint you with the reall truth.

O *Mexaris* (said she) what is it you design by this discourse; and what strange
Tragedie do you intend to represent, that your Prologue speakes so much of terrour: but let me know the worst I conjure you, for come the worst that can, I am
prepar'd to suffer it.

To give you this relation then, tis necessary Madam (said he) that I tell you
things in order as they hapned; which that I may the better do, I must begin from
the time that we left Persia.

This he did, relating all those things I have already told touching the Progress and end of the Scythian War, the Discourse that hapned between his Master
and *Phasellus*, concerning *Artabella*, which inspir'd her with a just anger at his
Inconstancy; but her displeasure was something appeaz'd by his seeming repentance which the conclusion of the Discourse seem'd to inferre: he then went
on to the Princess *Clazomena's* story, all which Madam you have already heard
(said *Celia*) and therefore need not again repeat it, but begin from the Marriage of *Cydarius*, and *Clazomena* (where we left) which was within a few dayes
solemniz'd to the great Joy and [fol. 134ᵛ] content of all Scythia. My Prince
(continu'd *Mexaris*) sent home the remaines of his Armie under the command
of *Astianax* assoon as the Peace was concluded, retaining onely *Barsarnes* and
some few others to attend him back. But no sooner was the Marriage past, and
that my Prince had seen his Generous Friend with his Faire Princess crown'd
King and Queen of Scythia, but he return'd to Persia, litle ~~imaging~~ imagining
how injurious that short stay had been to him. He took his leave of the Queen,
in Issedon who testifi'd a mervellous esteeme of him for treating *Cydarius* so
generously when he was his Prisoner, and even loaded him with gallant expressions of her Friendship, which he was not backward in returning; but the young
King, and *Oruntus* would needs accompany him to the River Oxus which seper-
ates the two Realmes, where they bad him farewell; which *Cydarius* could not
do without teares, as witnesses of his unwillingness to part from him: *Oruntus*
too, whose unjust hatered was converted into as reall a Love, could not bid him
ad^i^ue without regreet; which after he had done, they return'd to Issedon, and
we pursu'd our Journey.

When we were come within two dayes journey of Susa we were met by about some fiftie horsemen, who being come almost to us, the foremost of them rode up to my Master, and bowing to him with much respect.

Sir (said he) may I obtain the favour to speak a word with you in private.

My Prince being the most courteous person in the World, refus'd not his request, but galloping a little from his Company with him, and making a stand, demanded of him what he had to say.

With that he presented him a Little Note saying, it was onely to deliver this to you Sir from Queen *Oriana* that I desir'd you to withdraw. At the name of *Oriana* my Master blush'd, and taking the Paper with an inward trembling (occation'd by a certaine Joy, and Feare which equally possess'd him) he open'd it and therein read these words.

Oriana Queen of Persia to the Illustrious Diomed.

There hath lately hapned some trouble in Susa, which if not prevented may break forth into an intestine Rebellion: my desire therefore is to confer privatly with you, before tis known you are return'd, that as I owe my Crowne, and the peace and tranquillity of my Kingdome to your Valour, so is it by your advise that I would preserve it: to which end I have sent him who brings you this (with the rest of his Companions) to conduct you to me. Bring none with you but Barsarnes, and Mexaris, nor acquaint none with this affaire but they, and make all possible speed to assist with your Councell her who desires to be indebted to you alone for all the happiness of

Oriana.

[fol. 135ʳ] He, having read these words, rid up to us again, calling *Barsarnes* and I aside he gave us to understand the Contents of the Queens Letter; and telling the rest of his company that some business of great concernment oblig'd him to leave them for the present, but he hop'd to overtake them ere they reach'd Susa; however, in case I should not, speak nothing of my returne till you see me: with this Charge they departed, leaving my Master, *Barsarnes,* and my selfe to the conduct of those men.

That night we came to the Castle of Shiras, where we were told the Queen expected us; but we were scarce within the Gates, ere our swords were ceaz'd on, and we disarm'd before such time as we could suspect in the least any such thinge. My Generous Master was so surpriz'd as he had not the power to oppose them; for seeing himselfe betray'd into a Prison as the reward of all his brave achievements; I am not able to represent that rage and astonishment which possess't him thereat; his Face was in an instant o'respread with fiery blushes, and his eyes so sparkled with fury that for my part I trembled to behold him: nor were *Barsarnes*'s resentments [sentiments] more moderate, onely his left him the liberty of speach; which my Masters did not.

For breaking out into a most violent anger against the Queen (more upon my Masters account then on his owne) Is it thus (cry'd he) that the Queen intends to recompence those that have spent the better part of their blood in her quarell, and who would have shed each drop they have left rather then she should not have been absolute in her Dominions; but if Loyalty be thus rewarded, who will henceforth care to be a Faithfull subject. Ah Queen (pursu'd he) unworthy of the Royall house of Persia, and m[o]st unworthy to be Daughter to the Illustrious *Achemenes,* the most Gratfull, and obliging Prince that liv'd: though your Soveraignity gives you a^u^thority to enslave me; yet what right can you pretend over a Prince who depends not on you; nay to whom you owe that very Crowne you weare. But perhaps Sir (continued he turning to my Master) tis because she knowes you have merited more then she is willing to repay, or acknowledge; and therefore has caus'd you to be shut up within these Walles; lest by your presence you should make her blush for her Ingratitude.

At first my Masters rage inspir'd him with thoughts much resembling these, but that passion wherewith he lov'd *Oriana;* soon repell'd them, and in their place intraduced others more reasonable; for loving her with a most perfect affection, it was not possible for him long to suffer so ill an opinion of her to harbour in his mind, nor was he able to let *Barsarnes* go on with his Invectives, but interrupting him. Leave off *Barsarnes* (said he) to inveigh against the Queen, who is (I dare affirme) as ignorant of this ignoble usage of us, as we our selves were free from suspecting that Treachery wherewith we were decoy'd hither. That we are betray'd is most certaine, but that *Oriana* has any hand in it I cannot see the least shew of reason for it; for to what end should she have recourse to stratagemes to make us Prisoners, when she might openly have attach'd our liberties, having the sole power of Persia in her hands. Besides she knew, she retain'd so absolute a [fol. 135ᵛ] Soveraignity over me that had she demanded my life of me I should have given it her without dispute. Therefore I am rather induced to believe upon calmer considerations, that some wicked person, envious of the glory I have gain'd (well knowing I have too great an influence on the Peoples hearts, for them to attempt openly to injure me) have contriv'd with subtelty to undermine me so as they may securely worke my destruction.

I confess (replied *Barsarnes*) there is so much of likely hood in what you say, and so little probability of that which the first impressions of my fury made me believe of a Princess, whom having known from her Infancy (I must needs acknowledge) I never observed in her the least inclination to any thing that was not agreeable to the grandure of her birth: therefore I am most heartily sorry I should so rashly fly out into reproaches against her, and should be more so, did not that Letter leave some scruples in my mind which I know not how to reconcile.

Do you know the Queens hand (said my Prince) for my part I declare I do not.

No Sir (answered *Barsarnes*) I never saw any thing of her writing in my Life.

Whilst they were thus discoursing he that deliever'd the Letter to my Prince came into the Roome, whom he no sooner beheld but he turn'd away his Face for very griefe and anger to see himselfe reduced to such a condition, as not to be able to revenge that Treachery whereof he had been (though not the contriver) yet the Executer: but *Barsarnes* at his sight, new kindleing those Flames of Anger, which were partly before extinguish'd, and darting a furious Look at him.

Tell us base Instrument of Treachery (said he) who that Unworthy Person is, that has employ'd thee to betray us; and think not to deceive us any longer, by making us believe the Queen has any hand in thy fine Cheat: if thou hast any spark, of Vertue in thee confess thy Crime, and no longer endeavour, to bleamish the glory of thy Soveraign, by rendring her suspected of such things as I know she scorns so much as once to let into her thoughts.

Your beliefe is at liberty ^(repli'd he)^ but you are my Prisoner, and therefore think not my self obliged to give you an account of what you demand: onely this I will tell you that if you support your Imprisonment with moderation, it may perhaps neither be so long, nor so intollerable as you believe.

Prisons (said my Master exceedingly incens'd at his imperious reply) were ever insupportable to generous Spirits, but much more when they have such Jaylours as thy selfe. O Heavens (pursued he) have I the heart and courage of a Romane, and can I suffer this and live. No, were it not that I trust the Gods who deliever'd me out of the King of Scythias power, will ere long free me from thine, I would assuredly follow *Cato*'s example, and teare out my owne Bowells (could I find death no other way) rather then endure this vile indignity that is offered me.

You may kill your self if you please (replied he) but I shall look well enough to you, not to [fol. 136ʳ] let you escape, theough my Brother guarded the Princess *Artabella* so ill as she got from him.

What *Mexaris* (interrupted *Artabella*) was it *Ozmins* Brother that was your Princes Jaylour and could that Villain find no other place to make his Prison but my house. I wish it had been liad [laid] levell with the Ground rather then employ'd to so ill a use. But I begin to perceive that those who were the cause of *Diomed*'s misfortune were likewise the occation of mine.

Tis very true Madam (he replied) they were so and tis as true that both your misfortunes are so linked together that I cannot recount the one without the other. But to proceed (went he [Mexaris]on) my Prince was beyond all patience so transported at his Keepers last words that I verily think he would have flown upon him unarmed as he was, had he not that very instant left the Roome and fastned the Dore after him.

No Villain (cry'd he) I will not kill my selfe, I'll live (unless thou treacherously takest away my life as thou hast my Liberty) if for no other end, yet to be reveng'd on thee for those rude disdainfull answers, and to make thee know the difference there is between the Heire of Rome, and such a cative as thou art.

But after a little silence turning to *Barsarnes*. What was it (said he) that the Villain said concerning the Princess *Artabella*; have they imprison'd her as well as me.

Yes Sir (answer'd he) it seemes so by what that Fellow said.

Nay then live (added my Fenerous [generous] Prince) I must live to revenge her injures as well as my owne.

All the comfort my Master had was in *Barsarnes*'s society; for though they were lodged severally, and a guard set upon each of them, yet were they not debared from coming together in the day, onely they were confined to certaine Roomes that open'd one into another. One day as I was alone by my selfe consulting very seriously with my thoughts by what way we might escape; the Walls (as you know Madam pursued he) were so very strong, and the Windows made in that manner as there was no possibility of our geting from thence that way; and our being Lodg'd asunder rendred it yet more difficult. So that I began to think if any one of us could but get away they might find meanes to procure the others liberty. So very intent was I upon these thoughts, as I minded not a Man who had stood by me a good while; but seeing not I took no notice of him he spake to me.

What *Mexaris* (said he) have you forgot your Friend *Tereus*. At the name of *Tereus* I look'd about, and instantly knew him to be the same with whom I had contracted a most particular Friendship while I aboad in Scythia having observ'd in him a more then ordinary vertue which induced me to love him more then any other Persian of my a^c^quaintance.

Was not this *Tereus*, Brother to *Theocrite* (said *Artabella*) whom for her vertue and discretion the Queen prefers before her other Woemen.

Yes Madam (replied he) the very same.

As I turned about he offered to embrace me: but I steping back put him from me: if you are my Friend (said I) what do you here amongst my Masters enemies, and consequently amongst Mine. It is because [fol. 136ᵛ] I am your Friend (replied he) that I am amongst your enemies, and tis onely to serve your Master that I have put my selfe into the company of these that have betray'd him, that I might thereby get an opportunity to reveale to him things so strange as he will hardly credit. I have diligently sought for a conveniency to speak with you ever since your coming, but never could find any till now: but this day it coming to my turne to guard the enterance to your Roomes, I slipt in whilst *Otanes* is at dinner. I dare not now stay to tell you any thing lest I am misst, but tomorrow night I shall guard your Masters Chamber, and then I will discover to him those things which import him much to know; but in the meane time assure him the Queen is innocent. With that I embraced him, a thousand times beging his pardon for my cold reception, which he easily excused considering the reason I had to suspect him. So soon as he was gone, I went to my Prince with this newes, who found a mervellous satisfaction in the assurance I gave him of the Queenes Innocency, and the hopes he conceiv'd of being enformed who it was that was so much his enemy.

At length the wish'd for time came, for about midnight when *Tereus* thought he might securely venture without being surpriz'd he came into my Masters Chamber, who was not gone to bed, but had stay'd up on purpose to expect him. My Prince no sooner saw him, but he presently called him to mind, and remembred he had oft seen him with me.

Tereus (said he to him) *Mexaris* makes me believe you have strang things to tell me; if so I desire you would relate them as briefly as you can that I may know the truth this misadventur into which I am fallen. But before you begin I desire you would resolve me, since you affirme the Queen is innocent of this Plot which drew me hither, who it is that is guilty of it.

You will know it but too soon Sir (repli'd he) for your quiet; therefore I beg you would be pleas'd to give me leave to tell you things in order; which being granted, he went on.

One night as I was walking in one of the Gardens belonging to the Palace, entertaining myselfe with some melancholy thoughts, wherewith my affection to a person who was as then absent from Court had fill'd my mind: as I drew neere the end of the Allie in which I was, I heard two men very earnest in discourse. I was unwilling to interrupt them yet methought I had a very great curiosity to know who they were, and what the subject of their discourse was; which that I might the better do, I crept close under the Juniper Hedge which separated the two Walkes without making the least noise; where I stood attentively listning to what they said, which I could very easily heare, they not speaking very low, supposing (as I believe) the time of night a sufficent security from being over heard. Although (I confess) meere inquisitiveness lead me at first to hearken to them, yet I soon found reason enough for what I did; for the first words I heard were these.

If you can but secure me the person of *Diomed* as you[r] Brother has the Princess *Artabella* (said the One of them) ~~and~~ [fol. 137ʳ] my worke is done; which if you can, no recompence shall be to great for such a service.

Admit not the least doubt Sir (repli'd *Otanes* for he it was indeed) but I will accomplish what you have enjoyn'd me, if you procure me but that Letter which you mention'd.

Here it is (said the other) and so exactly counterfeited, as the Queen her self should she see it would hardly discerne it not ^to^ be her hand. But you must be gone to morrow ere the day appeares, for just now ^I^ receiv'd an intelligence from one I employ'd to give me notice of his arrivall, that, by that time his Letter came to my hands, he would be within two or three dayes Journey of Susa. I confess (continu'd he) I would not have recourse to this extreamity against a person I have many Obligations too, did not the Queens delays compell me to it; for if I cannot prevaile with her to consummate our Nuptialls before such time as he returnes, I shall forever loose all hopes of possessing either her Crowne or Person; for I know he loves her as well as I, and I feare with better success; or else (I am perswaded) she would not have found out so many pretences to defer our

Marriage. But have you any considerable number that will go with you (pursu'd he) to assist you in case he should refuse to go along with you.

There are some Fifty (repli'd *Otanes*) to whom I have given order to attend me whenever I should summon them; whom I enform'd, it was a design of high concernment which the Queen was pleas'd to intrust them with the execution of.

Well (answer'd the other) we will spend no more time in discourse. I see you are intelligent enough, not to need any further Instructions concerning this business: go then, and prepare for your departure early to morrow.

I believing their conference was ended (continu'd *Mexaris*) left the place where I stood, and hasted to another, where I was sure to have my full view of them as they left the Garden, which by the help of the Moon (which shone exceeding bright) I plainly did. By which I knew him that had impos'd this employ upon *Otanes*, to be no other then *Phasellus*; to whom I had heard (from *Mexaris*) you bare the greatest Friendship of any man living.

At the name of *Phasellus*, my Prince chang'd colour severall times, and looking on *Tereus* with a Countenance that declar'd the disorder of his mind. Either you are mistaken (said he) in him you took for *Phasellus*, or else you have fram'd this idle story to delude me, or unworthily to defame a person who can no more be guilty of so black a design, then I, of folly to believe it: but if thou wouldst have gain'd credit with me to believe thy Fiction, thou shouldst have made use of some other name, then that of my Generous Friend: but thy making him the subject of that abuse thou wouldst put upon me, renders the deceit so apparent, and thy Calumny so odious, that I wish I had but a sword, that with it I might rip that heart out of thy body, that could be capable of suggesting to thee such an abominable Lye.

Were it that I had any intention to delude you Sir (repli'd he, nothing daunted with the furious vehemence wherewith my Master spake) I should very hardly have ventur'd my Life to tell you these things, and to procure your Liberty [fol. 137ᵛ] which I have design'd, and hope to accomplish: nor shall that little credit I have with you hinder me from doing you all the service I am able, nor will I desire you should admit any better opinion of me, till you have more convinceing testimonies of *Phasellus*'s guilt, and my integrity then my affirming either.

At this confident, yet civill reply, my Prince became a litle more moderate, and began to loose part of that anger he had conceiv'd against *Tereus*, and admitted some little suspition concerning *Phasellus*. But that he might know the uttmost of this matter, he said to *Tereus*, though I want Faith to believe so great an improbability, yet proceed, and finish what you have begun; and be assur'd that if I find what you tell me to be a truth, and that I do by your meanes regain my Freedome, I will full well reward you for your service.

As for reward Sir (he repli'd) I expect none, nor did I undertake what I have done upon that score; for if I aim'd at any thing besides the glory of serving you, it was onely to vindicate the Queen my Soveraign from that odium which these Mischerents [Miscreants] have endeavour'd to throw upon her. After they had quitted the Garden I stay'd a long time in consultation with my self what I ought to do. What (said I to my selfe) shall I see my noble Generall so unworthily betray'd by the horrible treachery of his perfideous Friend, and become my self an Accessary to the Plot by concealing it. No (pursu'd I) though Persia harbours men of such base mercinary spirits, yet he shall find *Tereus* is none of them. After this I stood a good while considering what course I had best take; at first I thought by the meanes of my sister to acquaint the Queen with what I had heard, but then I call'd to mind the power *Phasellus* had with her, against which I had nothing but my owne single witness to averre the truth of what I should affirme, which I fear'd (considering the Friendship that was reputed to be between you two) would be look'd on by all people rather as some malicious detraction, then any reall thing. Besides, I knew it was too late to speak with *Theocrite* that night, and early in the morning *Otanes* was to depart: so that after severall debates with my selfe, I resolv'd (if it were possible) to get my selfe into the company of those who were to go along with *Otanes,* and to that intent, I presently went to my Lodging to prepare for my Journey on the morrow.

I hardly slept at all that night, but rising ere break of day, I got upon my Horse, and going to that Gate which I knew they must go out at, I enquir'd of the Porter if there did not a company of Horsemen go out there; who answer'd me there did, about half an houre since: whereupon I stay'd not to enquire further, but gallop'd so hard after them, that I over took them by Noon; and seeing *Otanes* in the head of them, I rid up to him; Sir (said I to him softly) I received a command from *Phasellus* the last night after you parted from him, that I should follow you, and tell you from him, that he desires you would entertain me into your company; that at any time if you have occation to send him word of any thing, or desire further order concerning this design you are employ'd [fol. 138ʳ] in you should make me the Messenger.

He hearing me speak so peremptorily never question'd the truth of my words, but without the least scruple admitted me amongst the rest. If I had any doubt remaining whether I might believe my eyes when they told it was *Phasellus* which they saw, *Otanes*'s receiving me assoon as I mention'd *Phasellus* to him, assur'd me I had not been deceiv'd. What shall I say more Sir (continu'd he) your selfe knowing but too well all that has past since, it onely remaines for me to procure you a release from this place, that you may go and execute vengeance on those who have so dishonourably us'd you.

Pray tell me (said my Prince) if you can, whether *Phasellus* be married to the Queen since you left Susa, or no: for I suppose if there be any such report, it will soon spread so far as to reach your eares.

I have not heard that he is marri'd as yet, nor I think shall not very hastily (answer'd *Tereus*) for by what *Phasellus* said, I guess the Queen has no very great kindness for him.

With that *Tereus* went his way, leaving my poor Prince in so great a trouble as he had never till then resented [felt]. He never cloas'd his eyes all night, but had his heart torne with torments worse then *Prometheus* his Vultures: sometimes his Friendship for *Phasellus* represented him to his thoughts full of Innocence, and made him fancy *Tereus* had slander'd him, then suddenly he call'd to mind again his unconstant humour, which if once joyn'd with Ambition, there was no Crime so horrible (he thought) but he might be guilty of it. These were his thoughts when *Barsarnes* came into his Chamber in the morning, who admiring to find him in bed, ask'd me if he were not well; but over hearing him aske that question, he prevented my Answere.

No *Barsarnes* (said he) I am not well; and tis no small part of my misfortune that I am no worse, for such is my condition now, that Death onely can cure my Wound.

Why Sir (repli'd he) has any One hurt you since I was here.

No (answer'd my Prince) the blow was given before, but I felt the anguish of it but this last night. Ah *Barsarnes* (went he on) do you not know, the unkindness of a Friend wounds deeper then an Enemies sword, for that can pierce but the body, at furthest but the heart; but the other pierces thorough both heart and soule: and thus it is that I have been wounded by that very Friend whom I have lov'd more dearer then my selfe. I think I need not tell you tis ~~that~~ *Phasellus* that I meane; he that was late my deare *Phasellus* (pursu'd he weeping) is now the most perfideous, the most ungratfull man that lives upon the earth. Ah *Barsarnes* tis he, and onely he that has so unworthily betray'd us, and sent us hither to the end he may the more securely prosecute the design he has to ruine me: but let *Mexaris* give you the story of his unparalell'd baseness, for my patience will not extend so far as to give it you my selfe.

With that he commanded me to tell *Barsarnes* all that *Tereus* had told him; which I having done, he call'd to me for his Clothes, and taking [fol. 138ᵛ] out the Ring which *Phasellus* had brought him where he lay wounded in Scythia, and kissing it. O deare Pledge of the Illustrious *Achemenes*'s love (said he) how little will it availe me, that he did by this bequeath me both his Crown and Daughter, since I am kept by that most injurious Usurper from the possession of them.

As my Prince was looking on the Ring, *Barsarnes* cast his eye upon it, and presently knew it to be one which the King gave *Phasellus*, not that which he injoyn'd him to deliver my Master; which so soon as he saw, he cry'd, O Sir you are no less abus'd in that, then other things. That's none of the Ring ~~of the Ring~~ that *Phasellus* was to deliver you, but one that *Achemenes* gave to him; and had I sooner seen it, I had sooner discover'd his deceit. Now I no longer wonder why his treachery extended to me, for now I see it was because he knew none but my selfe could disclose his villany.

At *Barsarnes*'s words my Master let fall the Ring with a careless action, and remain'd in a deep silence a good while; but at length, coming out of his profound study. Oh *Barsarnes* (cry'd he) I am undone; there wanted but this to raise my misery to the highest extream. Must *Oriana* be deluded as well as I, by that perfideous man; and must that which her Royall Father design'd as a testimony of his love to me, crown his presumption. I was in hope (pursu'd he) that it had been something in the beautious perfections of that incomparable Queen, which had committed a rape on his affections, and thereby have left him some excuse (though but a weak one) to extenuate his Crime: but now I see (by what you say) his was a premeditated designe to ruine me, and injure his owne Princess, even then when he seem'd most penitent for his Offence.

All this while (said *Celia*) *Artabella* hearkned to *Mexaris* with an unconceiveable trouble, yet had she till now supported herselfe with some little hopes that *Phasellus* might be wrong'd in what had been said of him; but now alass (poor Princess) she visibly saw it was too great a truth that he was the Injurer both of her and *Diomed*, and that it was he alone that had occation'd all those Miseries she had suffer'd; which forced her to cry out

Great Gods what have I done to deserve such punishments as these which you inflict upon me: my strength's too great since I can beare these heapes of miseries and live, but my patience is too little since I cannot suffer them without complaining. O you Divinities that rule our Destinies (continu'd she) pitty me yet at last, and be so mercifull as to put an end to all my sufferings by ending of my dayes, and grant that I may find a period of them both, in the conclusion of *Mexaris*'s story.

These words she finish'd with a Flood of Teares, which the rememberance of so strange an[d] ungratfull cruelty, no less then Infidelity as she had found from *Phasellus*, forced from her eyes: but assoon as she could, she summon'd all that little courage she had left, to her aide, and endeavour'd to resetle herselfe so as she might be able to attend to what was yet remaining: and after some little silence, perceiving him silent too.

Goe on, go on *Mexaris* (said she) pursue what you have begun, and let me know the conclusion of my woes; for I feare not now what you can tell me further: for since *Phasellus* is false, since [fol. 139ʳ] he is disloyall, since he is ungratfull, there remaines nothing more to heighten my misfortune, nor any thing that can render me more perfectly wretched then I am. With that she stop'd, whilst he proceeded in these words. My Prince went on with his complaints a long time in the sadest words that the most passionate griefe could put into his mouth.

O unkind *Phasellus*, (said he) how ill hast thou deserv'd the title of a Friend from me. Was it for this that I intended to bestow on thee my onely sister, that by that alliance I might tye the knot of our Friendship the faster, and to divide with thee the Emperiall Throne, by making thee my Partner in it; and when thou wert my ~~friend~~ Rivall, did I, to make thee the happie *Phasellus*, make my selfe the unhappy *Diomed*, by abandoning to thee the Princess *Artabella*, when I could with less regreet have given thee my life; but such was my Friendship, that I could deny thee nothing. Was it not enough that I resign'd my first Mistress to thee, but that thou must rob me of my second choice.

O cruell, O unjust *Phasellus*, could not thy ambition be satisfi'd with a Princess, unless thou hast a Crowne to boot; if so, thou mightst have divided with me

Achemenes his legacy; taken his Crowne, and left me his Daughter; but thus cruelly to deprive me of her too, after all I have done for thee, is an ungratfull Injury beyond example. O Heavens (pursu'd he) why was the Princess *Artabella*s Fate so link't with mine, as that to render me most miserable, she must be made so too.

O Monster of Ingratitude, and Infidelity (went he on) art thou from her Vassall, and her Slave (which thou so many times in my hearing hast profess'd thy self) become her Jaylour; and wilt I feare (if not prevented) become her Murtherer; but the Just Gods will revenge her of thee by my hand, if *Tereus* keep his promise: for though my Friendship (notwithstanding thou hast broken all its bonds) should yet retaine such power with me, as to induce me to forgive the wrongs thou hast done me, yet no consideration whatever can prevaile with me to pardon those thou offerest to that Excellent Princess. No false Traitor thou shalt dy (pursu'd he with a furious Tone) not all the Powers on earth shall shield thee from my just Vengeance; for I my self will send that black and hellish Soule of thine to receive the reward of all thy periur'd O^a^thes, and violated vowes to *Artabella*, and of all thy treacherous practices against thy Friend, from those Infernall Fi^e^nds who are prepar'd to punish such as thou art.

In this manner did my poor Master a little vent that griefe which (questionless) else would have been intollerable. He did all that he was able to support himselfe under the weight of his misfortunes by the assistance of his courage; but great, and heroick as it was, it was too weak to defend him from the violence of a high Fevour, which ceaz'd on him within a day or two. He seem'd almost as much troubled at his Distemper as *Barsarnes* or my selfe; for though his Life was now become a torment to him, yet he desir'd to cherish it a while, so as it might conduce to his revenge; which was the passion that at this time flam'd highest in his heart. I seeing the condition wherein he was, requir'd a [fol. 139ᵛ] Phisician, sent word to *Otanes* (for he came not at us himselfe) how ill he was by some of those he appointed to bring us our necessaries, and desir'd him to let a Docter be sent for. After he had a while consider'd on it, he return'd me answere by him that brought him the Message, that if any of those in the Castle had any skill in Phisick, he would command them to employ it to the uttmost for my Masters recovery; but if not (he said) he must be his owne Phisician, for he durst not admit of any man to come neer him but such as he knew he might confide in: this cruell answere let us see the little favour we were to expect from this base Fellow.

But a little after he call'd every one of his Companions about him, and demanded whether any of them had any skill in Phisick, but they all repli'd they understood nothing of it, saving onely *Tereus* who (having heard the answere he had sent me) told him he had some little skill, which if he pleas'd he would make tryall of for the recovery of my Prince: this he said, onely to have the liberty of coming to us as often as he desir'd, which before he had not. He never came neere my Master, but he comforted him with the hopes that his Imprisonment drew neere an end, beging him to contribute all he could to his owne cure ~~that~~ by his Patience, that he might the sooner be in a capacity of leaving that Place. But notwithstanding both his endevour and ours, his Fevour increas'd to that height, as we even dispair'd of his Life: sometimes in his Fits he would talk extreame Folly, and fall into such strang ravings, as made me many times affraid his wits had quite forsaken him. The generous *Barsarnes* express'd an infinite trouble to see him in so deplorable an estate, and manifested a singuler kindness for him, by the continuall care he took of him; never did he stire from his bed, but was as diligent in his watches with him as my selfe, and would by no meanes be perswaded to go to his owne Bed; but when necessity constrain'd him to take a little rest, he would lye downe on a little Pallet I had in the Chamber. But when our dispaire was absolute, and that we had lost all hopes of his recovery, we (to our comfort) had them restor'd to us again by a favourable Crisis,[1] after which, the height of his Distemper abated; and in a short time after he began so visibly to amend, as it fill'd our minds with a Joy resembling our late sorrow; and had his Mind, but held a correspondence with his Body, we might have hop'd to have seen his cure perfected in a little time: but alass those tortures of his mind were such, as could admit of no ease, no cessation during his aboad in a place where he was forced to spend his dayes in Womanish Complaints, whilst the Usurper of all his Joyes in depriving him of *Oriana,* rob'd him of the sole happiness of his life.

A long time it was ere he could leave his Bed, and so much longer it would have been ere he could have got strength enough to undergoe a Journey, that he fear'd it would too much advance *Phasellus's* wicked contrivances; whereupon he consider'd, that if *Tereus* could but set *Barsarnes* free, he might go and enforme *Oriana* privately of what *Phasellus* had done, and further yet design'd to do, and thereby prevent the accomplishment of his ill Intentions, if they were not already perform'd. This he imparted to *Barsarnes,* who had nothing to object against it but his unwillingness onely [fol. 140ʳ] to leave my Master, not knowing (as he said) what misfortune might befall him in his absence. But to that my Prince repli'd, that the greatest as could hapen to him would be inconsiderable in respect of what it would be to him should he loose the Queen, which to prevent, *Barsarnes* consented to what he had propos'd.

The next time they saw *Tereus,* they told him what they had concluded upon, which he very well approv'd of, promising the ensuing Night to set *Barsarnes* at liberty. Since my Masters sickness, he was permitted to be with him continually, so that he was with him now, waiting for *Tereus*; but 'twas not long that he expected ere he came, and desiring *Barsarnes* to follow him, which he did after he had taken his adue of my Prince, with many reall expressions of a very sensible griefe to leave him there behind him. *Tereus* led him downe the staires without the least noise, where they found the Guards all fast asleep, and so they left them; and going into the Garden through the little private dore that open'd into it, by the help of a Ladder on the one side, and Ropes (which he had provided) fastned

---

[1] The word "Crycess" is underlined for deletion but not crossed out and is replaced by "Crisis."

on the other, they got over the Wall, but yet they were not free, for coming to the
Castle Gate thorow which they were of necessity to pass, they found it so strongly
fastned with bolts and chaines, as rendred it impossible to get out, without making so great a noise as must needs waken those who kept it: which mov'd *Tereus*
to perswade him to kill them as they lay asleep: but *Barsarnes* abhorring any thing
of cruelty, would not consent to murder men unable to resist, adviz'd him rather
to use perswasions, then have recourse to that which they could not do without
the imputation of Cowardice. With that *Tereus* call'd to one of them, commanding him in *Otanes* his name instantly to open the Gate; telling him, they were
sent about business that requir'd hast: he whom *Tereus* spake too, knowing his
Voice, was about to do as he had commanded him; when the other, starting up,
stay (said he) if their business require never so must hast, I will go know of our
Master whether he gave order we should let any body out at this time of night.

With that, he was going to do as he had said, but *Barsarnes* quickly stay'd
him, for laying hold of him, you may spare your paines (said he) and either open
us the Gate quietly, or dy by our hands; I have been Prisoner long enough, and
am resolv'd to be so no longer.

He hearing him say so, began to cry out aloud for help, but *Barsarnes* soon
stop'd his outcry, by running him thorow (for *Tereus* had goten him his sword
though he could procure him no other of his Armes). The other of them stood
trembling, not daring to open the Gate, nor to cry out, as his Fellow had done;
but seeing him kill'd, he fell upon his knees beseeching *Barsarnes* to spare his
Life: which he promis'd to do, conditionally he let them out quietly. But assoon
as he had let them out, he betook him to his heeles, leaving the Gate open. This
he did (as they suppos'd) for feare of *Otanes,* from whose fury he might well
expect the loss of that Life which they had spar'd.

About half a mile from Shiras, dwelt *Tereus*'s Father, to whose house he conducted *Barsarnes*, and making himself know[n] to the Porter, they were instantly
let in; and causing him to call up some other of the servants to let them in a dores
he [fol. 140ᵛ] carri'd *Barsarnes* to a Chamber where he alwayes us'd to Lie himself when he was at home.

Now Sir (said he) you are as free as you can wish your selfe, and as secure
as you can desire; for neither *Otanes,* nor any of his Accomplices know that I
have any Relation, or so much as any Acquaintance in these parts, so that there
is no feare they will ever seek you here: but if they should, there is so many
secret places in this house, that none knowes of, but my Father and my selfe;
that should a hundred search for you, tis impossible they should find you, unless
^they^ will pull down the house: so that here you may repose your selfe in safety
till I can provide you a Horse, and Armes; for I could not get yours out of the
Castle, though I oft attempted it.

Barsarnes having embraced him, and given him those thankes so important
a service merited, he left him a while, to go and acquaint his Father with what
he had done: yet thinking it not convenient to let him know the whole truth, he

onely told him, that *Barsarnes* was a Gentleman who had done such good service against the Scythians, as he had thereby procur'd to himselfe the envy of
some great men about the Court; who to hinder him from receiving the reward
which they knew would be confer'd on him, had caus'd him by a Stratagem to
be drawne into the Castle, and there detain'd a Prisoner as by the Queens order,
which I knowing to be false (continu'd he) and having been infinitly oblig'd
to him for many civilities during the Wars, have set him at liberty. The Good
old Gentleman commending his son for what he had done, arose, and went to
Barsarnes, and giving him a very civill reception, he offer'd him his house as a
safe retreat, assuring him (as *Tereus* had done before) that he need not doubt his
security in that Place, and instantly sent a command to all his Servants, that they
should not be^make^2 known to any One whosoever, that either his Son, or any
Stranger was in the house.

But *Barsarnes* resolving to be gone the ensuing night, desir'd *Tereus* (if he
could possible) to procure him a Horse and Armes; which the old Gentleman
hearing, told him he would supply him with both out of his owne store if he
pleas'd to accept such as he had, assuring him they were better then any that
could be gotten there about. So courtious a proffer *Barsarnes* refus'd not, but
returning him thankes, took leave of him so soon as it was night; and getting
on Horseback, in a little space lost sight of Shiras, and all apprehension of a
reprizall. *Tereus* being his Guide, conducted him through such bye places as he
came into no Rode for many miles together; but towards the Morning they came
to a little Village, where they stay'd all the day to rest themselves, determining
for the more security to travall in the Night.

The second day after, being arriv'd at their Journeys end, *Barsarnes* desiring to conceale himselfe from being known kept on his Casque; and entering
the Citty at one of the least frequented Gates (intending to go that way to his
house) he saw the streets hung with rich Sydonian Tapestry, and the Pavements
all strew'd with Flowers, each house adorn'd with Garlands; and as they pass'd
into the next street (which was that which led to the Temple) they saw all the
Glass was taken from the Windowes, and [fol. 141 ʳ] Multitudes of People gazing
in them, as it were expecting some unusuall sight; and all the street so throng'd
even to the Temple gate that they could hardly get a long, which mov'd *Barsarnes*
to enquire the cause, whereof he was soon enform'd; being told that the Queen
was gone to the Temple of the Sun, to be married to *Phasellus.*

Is the Ceremony yet begun (said he to one who told him on it).

Yes Sir (answer'd he) and ended too I believe by this, for tis neere an hour
since they went.

He having heard more then he desir'd, enquir'd no further, only looking on
Tereus fetch'd a sigh. Fain would he have gone on, but the crowde being exceeding

---

² The word "be" is underlined for deletion but not crossed out and "make" is inserted.

thick, he was constrain'd to make a stand, not being able to pass either backward, or forward. But it was not long he stay'd, ere he saw severall Chariots pass by, after which came an open one, wherein sat *Oriana,* and on her head the Crowne; which was so exceeding weighty with Gold and Jewells, that being unable to beare it without a trouble, she had on each side of her a young Lady to support it. Her dress was such as became the Majesty of so great a Queen; about her Neck she wore a Chain of Diamonds, the fairest (I believe pursu'd *Mexaris*) that ever was beheld; but that, and all those other Gems wherewith she was adorn'd, she seem'd to give a Luster too, rather then to receive any from them; for as *Barsarnes* afterwards protested, there was never seen any thing so beautifull on Earth as the Queen then appear'd; which made him a thousand times to curse *Phasellus* for robing my Prince of such a happiness, as the possession of so Faire a Princess.

Oh (said he to himselfe) could poor Prince *Lucius* but see what a Loss he does this day sustain, what griefe would he resent [feel].

But one thing more he remark'd in the Queen, which was an extreame sadness in her Lookes; which seem'd silently to demonstrate the little Joy she took in what she had done. Her Chariot being past, that wherein *Phasellus* was, follow'd next, whose sight excited in *Barsarnes* such a rage, that if he had follow'd the resentments [feelings] it inspir'd him with, he had inevitably perish'd, without the least advantage to my Prince: for his first thoughts were immediately to run him thorough, and kill him even in the midst of his Nuptiall Tryumphs, so to turne his Bridall Bed into a Grave; but this it had been impossible for him to do, had he attempted it, by reason the People stood so very thick as he could not come neere his Chariot by many yards: beside, he was sure to have found his death from the swords of those who attended *Phasellus,* and then, he consider'd, my Prince might forever remaine a Prisoner, and *Oriana* ignorant of those Injuries they had both of them sustain'd through *Phasellus*'s baseness; which made his rash resolve give place to one more reasonable: which when he had assum'd (assoon as the people had a little dispierc^ers^ed[3] themselves) he got to his owne house, where puting off his Armes, and clothing himselfe anew, and causing *Tereus* to do so likewise, they instantly went to Court, and going up the backstaires to the Lodging where the Queens Woemen u'sd to Lie, but not finding any of them there, he sent *Tereus* to tell his sister that he desir'd to speak with her immediatly, [fol. 141 ᵛ] about something that neerly concern'd the Queen.

It was a great while ere he could come to the speech of her, but at length he did, though not without much difficulty. *Theocrite* no sooner heard *Barsarnes* nam'd, (whom she knew very well to be a Faithfull subiect, and a discreet person) but she believ'd his business to be of consequence, so as she stay'd not to aske her Brother any questions, but presently went with *Tereus* to her Chamber where *Barsarnes* stay'd for her. She no sooner saw him, but she perceiv'd a very great

---

[3] The letters "<u>ierc</u>" are underlined for deletion and "ers" is inserted.

trouble legible in his Face, and was about to have ask'd him the cause of it, had he not prevented her by speaking first; after he had saluted with that respective civility he thought due to a Person so highly in the Queens favour as he knew she was.

Deere *Theocrite* (said he) for Heavens sake obtaine for me a private audience from the Queen speedily; for I have things of such importance to enforme her of, that a Minutes delay may render her the most Unfortunate Princess in the World, if she has not already made herselfe so.

Tis impossible my Lord (repli'd she) for me to speak with her Majesty till Dinner be past, but that being over, I know she will retire to her Chamber (for she gave me a perticuler command to attend her there) and then you may have that Liberty you desire. But my Lord (continu'd she) where in the name of Goodness have you been ever since you left Scythia, and where have you conceal'd your selfe all this while that you were not to be heard of; for I verily thinke the Queen has sent into every Province of the Kingdome to enquire for you, and admir'd you would absent your selfe in a time wherein she stood ^in^ so much need of your Councell of late she has done. And what I beseech you is become of *Diomed*, that brave Champion of our Countrey.

Ah *Theocrite* (answer'd he with a sigh) he is a Prisoner (and so was I my selfe till within these three dayes) by the treachery of that Villain the Queen has married: he has unworthily delud'd her with Lyes, which I come now to discover to her.

Good Heavens (cry'd *Theocrite*) can *Phasellus* be capable of such baseness.

Yes (repli'd *Barsarnes*) of much more then I am able to express, or you imagine. With that, setting downe, he gave her in short, a Narative of all his wicked practices; and had just ended when they heard some persons coming, whom *Theocrite* thought might be the Queen; which mov'd her to intreat *Barsarnes* to stay there a while, promising assoon as her Majesty was alone, to bring him to her. She was not deceiv'd, for she had no sooner got into *Orianas* Appartment ere she came in; and having sent away those who waited on her thither, she went to a Cabinet which stood upon her Table, and took out of it a little Dagger, and plucking off her Chaine of Diamonds she gave it to *Theocrite*; there (said she) I give thee that, as the reward of that Faithfull service thou hast done me: thou shalt ere many minutes pass, be free to seek another Mistress.

Theocrite being amaz'd at *Oriana*'s action, but more, at her words, threw herselfe at her Feet. For the Gods sake Madam (cry'd she) what do you intend to do with that Dagger.

I meane to kill my self with it [answer'd [fol. 142^r^] she] (with an undaunted look) but I meane to do it before the Face of *Phasellus*; for since neither my teares, nor intreaties could prevaile with him to free me from that engagement *Achemenes* laid upon me, I'll free my selfe from him. I have as far as I was able, satisfi'd my duty, by giving him my person, but seeing it is impossible to give him my heart;

or bend it once to love him, I'll pierce it with this Dagger, for its disobedience to the King my Fathers Will.

Tis the heart of a Traitor Madam (said *Theocrite*) you ought to pierce, not that of an innocent, and an injur'd Princess; but if you please to stay one minutes space, I'll fetch a person who will acquaint you with things I tremble to relate; yet such they are, as I trust, will soon perswade your Majesty to lay aside your fatall resolution.

Just as she said so, *Barsarnes* came in, for in the Roome where he was, he could both see, and heare all that was done or said in the Queens [chamber]; so that he stay'd not to be call'd, but came in of himselfe: and presenting himselfe on his knee to the Queen, who much admir'd to see him, but more did she wonder what he had to tell her, which *Theocrite* intimated [illegible cross out] to be so terrible. Ah Madam (said he, not giving her time to say any thing to him) what has your Majesty done: you have not onely render'd your selfe Unfortunate, but ruin'd forever the bravest, and most Illustrious Prince in the World, whose passion, and respect for you ne're knew an equall.

That I have made my selfe unhappie (repli'd the Queen) is but too true, but as for *Diomed* (whom I suppose you meane) if he be ruined, tis the Ingratitude of *Achemenes* you ought to accuse for it rather then me.

O blemish not the sacred memory of your dread Father with Ingratitude (cry'd *Barsarnes*) for certainly no Prince that ever liv'd was freer from it.

What mov'd him then (said she) so partially to preferre *Phasellus* out of a Maxime of state pollicy, before a person whose birth was more Illustrious, and from whom he had receiv'd services far more considerable then any *Phasellus* had rendred him.

Do you believe then Madam (he repli'd) that the King your Father prefer'd *Phasellus* before *Diomed*.

I have no reason to believe otherways (answer'd she) since he gave me to him by giving him this Ring (continu'd she shewing one to *Barsarnes*) by which he had engag'd me to marry whosoever presented it to me from him.

Ah Madam (said he sighing) how have you been deluded by the False *Phasellus*. *Achemenes* deliever'd him that Ring, tis true; but with no intent that he should be the presenter of it to your Majesty (as I my selfe can witness) but with a strict injunction to deliver it to Prince *Lucius* with his owne hand: who at that time lay wounded far distant from the Campe.

O heavens (cry'd the Queen with exclamation) how have I been betray'd, but go on *Barsarnes* (pursu'd she) and let me now know the truth, for I have been too long abus'd with Lies.

After your Royall Father found that he must dy (said he) he caus'd all persons to avoid the Roome save onely *Phasellus* and my selfe. *Barsarnes* (said he to me) you are now to change your Soveraign for another; my Daughter I mean, who [fol. 142ᵛ] by the right of succession is to be your Queen; but knowing by experience what cares Thrones are attended with, I ~~foun~~ find a Crowne too weighty for a Womans for head alone to beare: therefore has it been long my aime to find out One to bestow her on, that might help her to support its burden, without depriving her of that power which Heaven and Nature give her by my death. I will not question your Obedience so much as to doubt you will either dispute, or oppose my Will when I have once declar'd it, I'll onely then leave this charge with you (as him who of all my subjects have the strongest influence of over the hearts of all my Armie) to oppose any one that shall refuse to obey him as King, whom my Daughter shall accept for a Husband. If you will promise me this upon your Fidelity *Barsarnes* (continu'd he) I shall leave the World with a high satisfaction.

Your Majesties commands (repli'd I) I have alwayes esteem'd as sacred Lawes which I dare not violate; and sooner will I loose my life, then suffer any One to hinder the execution of your Majesties Will.

I expected no less from you (said the King embraceing me) and as a recompence of your Loyalty, and the service you have done me in this Warre, I create you Prince of the Sacans, and give you the Province of Bactria as an addition to your Principallity, onely paying some small trybute as an acknowledgment that you hold it of the Crowne.

I having with all humility, and thankfullness receiv'd this honour from the King (went on *Barsarnes*) he turn'd to *Phasellus*. And now (said he to him) I am in a more perticuler manner to acknowledge the benefits both my selfe and Kingdome have received from you and your Generous Friend; who being no way oblig'd to serve me, have notwithstanding hazarded your lives as far in my service as any subject in my Dominions; for which, lest my reward should fall short of your deserts, ask any thing for your selfe within my power to grant, and be assur'd you shall not be deni'd.

Your royall Favours Sir (reply'd he) have already transcended my merits so farre, that I should render my selfe altogether unworthy of those I have already receiv'd, should I ambitiously sue for more.

Since your modesty will not permit you to make me any request (said the King) I'll leave you to him whom I designe to succeed me; who will (I doubt not) find out a more ample recompence for you, then I can imagine to bestow: onely as a testimony of that value I have for you I give you this Ring (continu'd he pulling two off of his Finger) which I desire you to weare for my sake; and the other you must deliver to *Diomed* (if he live) with your owne hand, for he it is whom I have chosen for my Successour, as being the onely person whom I can think worthy of my *Oriana,* and in whom I believe she will be farre happier then if I had made choice of the greatest Prince in Asia for her: but if he dye (as Heaven forbid it) I leave her then at Liberty to make her owne choice, knowing her too discreet to make an ill one. This Ring then *Phasellus* (pursu'd he) you must give him, and tell him I bequeath it him as the Legasy of my Love, and with it my Crowne on condition he marry *Oriana*; from whom he need feare no refusall, since she has promis'd me on the duty of a child (which I know she will not violate) to accept him for a [fol. 143ʳ] Husband who shall from me present her with this Ring.

O wicked *Phasellus* (cry'd out the Queen, amaz'd at what *Barsarnes* told her) with what cunning had he contriv'd his owne story to abuse me; but proseed *Barsarnes* (pursu'd she) and let me know how he did, to carry on his Designe so long undiscovered, and by what meanes you came to know it at last.

After the King your fathers death Madam (went on *Barsarnes*) he posted away to *Diomed* to carry him the Ring (as he pretended) but in its steed deliever'd him that which *Achemenes* gave him for himselfe (yet did he tell him the reall truth in all things I confess) which having done, he desires leave of him to returne to Persia to waite on the Princess *Artabella*, whose Votary he had long before proffess'd himselfe; but as it seemes his passion for her was the least cause of his returne; for he had been but a little while in Susa before he caus'd her to be made a Prisoner, but in what place she is detain'd, I am as yet wholly ignorant.

O Gods (said the Queen interrupting him) what Progidies of baseness is this man guilty of: was it not enough to betray me, but must he injure poore *Artabella* too. I heard indeed how that she had been surpriz'd and strangly carried away as she was returning hither from Shiras after I had sent for her, but by whose meanes I ne're could learne till now, nor know I yet whether she is convey'd, though I have caus'd the most diligent enquiries imaginable to be made for her all over Persia.

When he had rid her out of his way (pursu'd *Barsarnes*) he then had none to apprehend a discovery of his baseness from save *Diomed*, and my selfe; well knowing none but we were privie to what the King had done; which to prevent, he caus'd us to be drawn from the rest of our Company as we were coming to Susa, by a pretended Letter from your Majestie, wherein we were commanded to meet you Madam at that place whether the man who brought the letter was to conduct us; we accordingly follow'd him to the Castle of Shiras, whereinto we were no sooner enter'd, but we were disarm'd and made Prisoners by a Brother of his who made the Princess *Artabella* so.

He further told the Queen how all these things came to be discover'd by *Tereus*, *Theocrite's* Brother, and how by his assistance he had escap'd out of Prison: all which, she having heard, with a most horrible detestation of *Phasellus's* crimes, a while remain'd Silent, with her eyes fix'd on the ground, her thoughts being full of various resolutions; but after sometime, of a sudden turning her eyes upon *Barsarnes*. It was not without reson (said she) that I have had so strange an aversion to this perfideous man, who is now so justly odious to me, that I abhorre to name him; but would it had pleas'd the Gods *Barsarnes* (pursu'd she) that you had come but one day sooner; for then you had prevented me from being the most miserable Woman in the World, which I have made my selfe, by a blind obedience to my Fathers Will (as I suppos'd) but now alass what remedy have I left, for as horrid a Monster as *Phasellus* is, he is my Husband; and though I have the power to inflict on him punishments great as his offences, yet would it ill become me being as I am, his wife.

What then [fol. 143 ᵛ] remaines *Barsarnes* (continu'd she) for me to do in this condition whereto I am reduced; for my part I know no better way then to pursue my first resolve which was to kill my selfe, so shall I be in some sort reveng'd on him by depriving him of my Crowne (the fairest of his hopes) which I am perswaded he was more ambitious of, then my person.

Heaven forbid (repli'd he) you should be so cruell to your selfe because he has been unjust and treacherous to you. No Madam, rather resolve to make void this Marriage, which you may do with Justice enough.

Alass how can I disanull my owne free Act said she.

You cannot call that free (answer'd he) which is done unwillingly, or by constraint, and by your owne confession Madam you us'd violence upon your selfe, meerly out of obedience to the King your Fathers Will which till now you never rightly understood.

But I do not desire Your Majesty should be wholly guided by me (pursu'd he) but call your Councell, and confer with them, and see if they advize you not the same: The marriages of Princes Madam (went he on) are not like those of Vulgar persons, especially of Queens, the wellfare of whose Kingdomes are concern'd in their Matches; and so will your Peoples be (doubtless) so much in yours, that when *Phasellus*'s notorious Crimes come once to be divulg'd, it will go neer to set your Kingdome in a Flame, by embroiling it in a civill War; beside Madam, we may assure our selves, if we punish not *Phasellus* for that most injurious affront he has offer'd *Diomed*, the Emperour *Augustus* will on us endeavour to revenge it by a powerfull invasion, which we have much more cause to apprehend then that of the sci Scythian Kings.

I know not what would have been the result of this discourse (pursu'd *Mexaris*) for it was interrupted by *Theocrite*, who staying in the Antie-Chamber to give notice of *Phasellus*'s approach, lest he should come and surprize the Queen ^and *Barsarnes*^ in their conference; she hearing his voice, knew he was coming thither, which made her hasten to acquaint them with it: whereupon the Queen desir'd *Barsarnes* to withdraw into the next Roome, not being willing he should be seen as yet. No sooner was he gone out, but she seated herself in a mellancholy posture, which *Phasellus* marking, went to her, and took her by the hand; but she darting an angry look at him instantly snatch'd it from him: whereat seeming to be very much troubled.

Can it be Madam (said he to her) that neither the passion wherewith I have ador'd you, nor the services which I have render'd you, should be able to convert your unjust aversion into some little sentiments of affection for me, but if neither of those Considerations can prevaile with you to affect me, yet give me leave to tell you, that now methinkes the obedience you owe your Fathers will should move you to it; for certainly you cannot but think he did design I should enjoy your heart as well as person.

Had I obey'd the Will of *Achemenes* (repli'd she breaking out into teares, exceedingly incens'd) I had been as happie, as I am now unfortunate; but as for your services, you had need upbraid me with them: they have been indeed very considerable to your selfe, not me. But though your perni<u>ssius</u>^cious^⁴ practices have been hitherto so prosperous to bring your Designes to this effect, as to compell me through a mistaken obedience to [fol. 144ʳ] confer on you the title of Husband, believe it, they shall proceed no further; for if I lov'd you not before, I declare I mortally hate you now. Content yourselfe with my Crowne (pursu'd she) if my People will suffer you to enjoy it after the knowledge of your horrid Crimes which I will publish to the World; but let alone my person, for I vow by all that's sacred, you shall never come within my Bed. And if at any time you attempt (by that authority you think you now have over me) to force me to a violation of this Vow, I'll kill my selfe that very moment to free my selfe from your embraces, which are to me more terrible then Death.

These words gall'd *Phasellus* to the heart, his Conscience telling him he had deserv'd them; nevertheless, he resolv'd to seeme unconcern'd: and looking upon *Oriana* with a confidence proporti^o^nate to his Crimes. Good Heavens Madam (said he) what moves you to this passion against me.

Those notorious Crimes (repli'd she) whereof thou art accus'd, which thy owne Conscience cannot but condemne thee as guilty of. Yes false man (continu'd she) thou hast betray'd me, Ungratfully rob'd thy Prince (and which is more, thy Friend) of that which ought to have been his, both by his merits, and the Will of *Achemenes,* and most treacherously imprison'd him, as thou hast my dearest Cousin the Princess *Artabella,* whose innocent affection thou hast no less perfideously abus'd. These, these *Phasellus* art thy monsterous (and till now unheard of) crimes, which have rendred thee so justly hatefull to me, that unless thou canst cleare thy selfe of them, I am resolv'd to flee to the furthest part of the Earth, e're I will endure thee in my sight.

With that, she ris up, and went into her Closet, locking the Dore after her, leaving him in a strang perplexity, and amazment to see that all his wickedness should now be brought to Light. The Queen being gone, he look'd about to see who was in the Roome; but seeing none there save onely *Theocrite.*

Who, where is that Villain (cry'd) he that has presum'd to slander me to the Queen. At that, *Barsarnes* was no longer able to forbeare, but coming in, and presenting himselfe before *Phasellus* who was struck with an astonishment I am not able to express (pursu'd *Mexaris*) to him there whom he believ'd securely shut up within the Castle of Shiras.

Tis I (said *Barsarnes* to him) that have disclos'd your wickedness, yet scorn the title of a slanderer; and for that, of a Villaine I returne it to thee: but I do not wonder since thou couldst act such base unworthy things, that thou shouldst have the impudence to deny them; but did not the [four words blotted] reverence I beare to the Majesty of my soveraign restrain me from staining her Chamber

---

⁴ The letters "<u>ssius</u>" are underlined for deletion and "cious" is inserted.

with thy blood, I would force thee to acknowledge what I have told, to be truths, not slanders.

That Consideration is too weak (repli'd *Phasellus*) to hinder me from being reveng'd on thee for the injurie thou hast done me by thy officious information: draw then, or dye (pursu'd he unsheathing his sword, whilst *Barsarnes* did the like).

Let the World be judge (said *Barsarnes*), whose Injuries are greatest, mine, or yours: the Queen I hope will pardon this disrespect you force me to in my owne defence.

With that, *Phasellus* made a pass at him which he [fol. 144ᵛ] put by so as it onely glans'd upon his Arm making some little impression. *Barsarnes* not being altogether so much blinded with fury as his Antagonist, having put his bye, pass'd his sword quite ^thorow^ *Phasellus*'s body, yet not so as to kill him; but as he was going to repeat what he had done, the Queen who had been drawn from her Closet by *Theocrites* outcry, caught hold of his Arme.

Hold *Barsarnes* (said she) you have done enough; for how great a Crimenall soever *Phasellus* is, tis not from your hand he ought to receive his punishment; nor ought I (as much Monster as he is) to suffer any of my subjects to draw a sword against him as long as I am his Wife; find but a way lawfully to discharge me of that title, and then let him receive the reward due to his deserts.

Theocrite can witness Madam (answer'd *Barsarnes*) he drew upon me first; and that what I did, was to defend my owne life, not assault his: but by his defeat Heaven sufficently declares his guilt.

Whilst *Barsarnes* was speaking in this manner to the Queen (continued *Mexaris*) *Phasellus* who was fallen to the ground; weltring in his blood which ranne out of the Wound he had receiv'd, was got upon his Legges again, and coming behind him [*Barsarnes*], gave him a Wound in the back; but having with a good part of his [*Phasellus's*] blood, lost part of his strength also, the Wound was not deep, nor did it hinder him [*Barsarnes*] from turning about to repay his courtisie; which doubtless he had done, had not the Queen step'd betweene them whilst she sent *Theocrite* for some to part them. This action of *Orianas* prevented *Barsarnes* from pursuing his intention, but could not hinder him from saying.

I had thought *Phasellus* thou hadst not quitted thy Courage with all thy other good quallities, but I now see, that likewise has abandon'd thee, or else thou would'st never have assaulted me so cowardly, when I was neither in a posture to offend thee, or defend my selfe; but thou needst not thirst so greedily after my Life, since it can be no advantage to thee to take it away; for hadest thou kill'd me, as thou aimed'st to have done, there are others in the World that will charge thee with the same things that I have, and convict thee of them too.

By this time the Queens Chamber was full of Princes, and other persons of the highest quallity that were then in the Palace; who having been enform'd of this quarell, but not of the occation, throng'd thither to know the cause; whose swords were instantly unsheath'd and bent all against poor *Barsarnes*'s Breast (who had no Defender but the Gods and his owne Innocence) thinking to oblige the Queen by what they did: but she soon let them understand their errour, by speaking to them in his behalf.

Stay (said she) and enforme your selves of the occation of this quarell, which is of a much higher consequence then you imagine; but let *Barsarnes* give you an account of it, I am too much concern'd to tell it you.

Strike (cry'd *Phasellus*) he is a Villaine, and a Traitor.

Believe him not (repli'd the Queene) tis nothing but his Malice makes him speak so.

Kill him I command you (said *Phasellus*)

Touch him not I charge [fol. 145 ͬ] ye (answer'd the Queene).

They all stood suspended with admiration at this event which made the Queen appear rather an Enemy then a Friend to a person whom she had given herselfe too but that very day: but thinking, of the two, they were oblig'd to obey her rather then him, they put up their swords and began to enquire the cause, whilst *Oriana* gave command *Phasellus* sh^o^uld be carri'd thence to his owne Chamber, and Chirurgions call'd to dress his Wound: which having done, she retir'd again into her Closet, leaving it to *Barsarnes* to give them that information they demanded. But thinking it unfit to stay longer in the Queenes Chamber, they agreed to withdraw into the Councell Roome, intreating *Barsarnes* to go with them, and there to let them know the reason of this strange difference which had hapned between *Phasellus* and himself. This he promis'd to do assoon as ever he had got his Wound dress'd, which began to pain him very much.

Accordingly so soon as the Surgion had dresst him, he went to them, and at larg gave them an account of each perticuler thing he had acquainted the Queen with but a little before; which having listned too with wonder, and amazment, they presently fell to consult what was most expedient to be done; the greater part declaring they would sooner dye, then submit to the Goverment of a man stain'd with such horrible Vices. But yet, there were some few amongst them (whom *Phasellus* had won by his insinuating Flatteries) who blam'd the others for so lightly crediting what *Barsarnes* had affirm'd. Your Charge is full (said they to him) but what Witness have you to attest the truth of these things you accuse *Phasellus* of.

I confess (added one of them, whose name was *Praxaspes*, who had ever born a spleen to my Prince (pursu'd *Mexaris*) since he was made Generall of the Armie) there is something of probability in your Accusation, but no certainty. You say the King gave that Ring on which the Queens marriage depended, to *Phasellus* to deliver to *Diomed*; but how do we know, whether he did, or no; since we have nothing but your word to proove it.

Circumstance (answer'd one of the other Partie) proves many times no less then Witness, and circumstance there is enough to testifie the truth of that which *Barsarnes* has affirm'd: for if *Phasellus* had not known himself culpable, to what end did he so privily emprison both *Diomed* and *Barsarnes*, but onely to the intent, the one should not come to claime his right, nor the other come to empeach him for depriving him ~~for~~ ^of^ it.

They might be both imprison'd (repli'd *Praxaspes*) and yet *Phasellus* have no hand in it.

That may soon be known (answer'd *Barsarnes*) if you examine but *Tereus*, who over heard him contrive that treacherous Designe with *Otanes*, in whose custody our Valiant Generall yet remaines. But if [fol.145ᵛ] *Tereus*'s evidence be not sufficent, tis but sending for *Otanes*, and shewing him the Rack, and questionless he will confess the whole Plot. But for my owne part (continu'd he) since I have not credit enough with you to be believ'd in what I affirme, grant me but the Combate against *Phasellus* (if he recovers) and I'll force the truth concerning the Ring out of his owne Mouth, since tis impossible for me to produce any other Witness of that then my selfe, by reason (as most of ye know very well) the King commanded all persons but us two, to leave the Roome.

There was so many apparances of truth in all *Barsarnes* said, that there was none but believ'd him; onely *Praxaspes,* and one or two more, ^who^ oppos'd him rather out of malice, then diffidence. But yet, supposing they could not be to cautious in matters of so high concernment, they sent for *Tereus*, who satisfi'd them so fully in all perticulers, as they had not the least doubt remaining of the reallity of that which *Barsarnes* had affirm'd; so that they left disputing, and fell to consulting in what manner *Phasellus* should be punish'd for his enorm^o^us Offences: Severall were their Debates, onely in this, the major part agreed he had worthily deserv'd to dye, but with what forme of Justice to proceed against the Husband of their Queen they knew not; and for her to condemn him, they deem'd it much more unfit.

But some affirm'd (in which number was *Barsarnes*) that they ought to look on him as no other then a Traitour, and as one that had usurp'd a title which belong'd not to him; for the Queen being given before to *Diomed* by *Achemenes*, she had no right to dispose of herselfe to *Phasellus* though she had design'd it. Besides, the Queen really intending to marry him onely to whom the King her Father gave her, intentionally marri'd *Diomed*, though *Phasellus* by his subtilty frustrated her intentions, by deceiving her, and imposing himself on her; so that she might very lawfully be absolv'd from all tyes of marriage, and be free to dispose of herself according as *Achemenes* had design'd. They added moreover, that it was requisite (the better to exempt the Queene from all Censures) ~~that~~ the Marriage being made void, that *Phasellus* should be sent to the Emperour Augustus (since he was born his Subject) to receive from him the punishment he had deservedly merited. But before they concluded of any thing, some of them mov'd *Phasellus* might be permitted to speak for himself; saying it was but Just to heare what he could plead in his owne Justification. This was thought a thing so reasonable, that they all agreed it should be so, and this business deferr'd till such time as *Phasellus* should be able to appeare in person before the Councell. This was all that was ~~all that was~~ then concluded on, save onely the voting my Prince (pursu'd *Mexaris*) to be immediately freed from his Prison, and a Tryumphall entery into Susa prepared for him, that the Injuries he had sustain'd might in part be repair'd thereby: after which, the Councell broke up, and *Barsarnes* went instantly to the Queen, to enforme her of their Debates, [fol. 146ʳ] and ^what^ was decreed both concerning *Phasellus* and my Master, all which she seemed very well satisfi'd with.

He then beg'd Leave to go along with them who were to fetch my Master (went on *Mexaris*) which she granted, and the next day those that were appointed for that employment began their Journey; but when they came to the Castle, instead of that opposition they expected, they found all the Gates open, and not one person appeare within to make resistance; which made them extreamly wonder: but *Barsarnes* taking some halfe a score of them, hasted to my Masters chamber, but not finding him there, nor any other person in, or about the Castle, he concluded, *Otanes* had either convey'd him to some other Place, or else made him away since his departure. This beliefe made him almost distracted, insomuch that when he came downe to those he had left below, he could scarce speak sense, or give a reasonable answere to any thing that was demanded of him. But after the height of his Fury was a little quallifi'd, Gentlemen (said he to those who came with him) you have liberty to returne to the Queen when you please, and pray let her Majesty understand how we have been disappointed of what we came for, but for my owne part (pursu'd he) I am resolv'd to range the World about, but I will find *Diomed* alive, or dead, and when I know what is become of him I will returne, and not before.

But *Tereus* (who was one of them) disapproving this resolution, took the liberty to represent to him how much he might prejudice both my Prince (continu'd *Mexaris*) and himself by it. For my Lord (said he) you are not ignorant that *Phasellus* has a Party in the Councell, who may (possibly) by your absence take occation to raise some false reports: as that *Diomed* was never in Prison, but that you fram'd it as a story of your owne inventing, purposly to defame *Phasellus* who'm the giddy Multitude will be (perhaps) but too apt to believe Innocent; therefore in my opinion, it behooves you to returne with us if you cannot find him in some short time.

This advice was not so inconsiderable but *Barsarnes* determin'd to take it; onely [word blotted] resolv'd first to coast all about that part of the Country in Sea^r^ch of him, which he did, enquiring of all he met, if they could tell him any tydings of my Prince, or *Ortanes*; but to no purpose, for neither their names, nor persons were known to any there about. At last, One of the Company call'd to mind, that *Ozmin*, *Otanes*'s elder Brother had a Castle of his owne in Zarispe, whether (he said) 'twas possible *Otanes* might be gone. This he no sooner enform'd *Barsarnes* of, but he steer'd his course thither, and riding with hast proportionate to his desires to heare newes of my Prince, he arriv'd there in two dayes space, though they were in great danger of being swallow'd by the sands thorough which they pass'd; whether being come, they lost not all their labour, for there they found both *Otanes,* and his Brother *Ozmin,* whom *Barsarnes* (both by *Phasellus*'s mentioning him in the garden to *Otanes* when *Tereus* overheard them there discoursing, and by *Otanes*'s owning him to be his Brother, in his hearing [fol. 146ᵛ] to *Diomed*) assur'd himself was the same that had made you a Prisoner Madam (pursu'd *Mexaris* to *Artabella*.) Very much Joy'd was *Barsarnes* that he had so happily met with them both together; and instantly caus'd them to be ceaz'd on; assoon as ever *Otanes* cast his eye upon *Barsarnes* he knew him, and looking on him with a bold and confident Countenance.

Is it thus (said he) that *Diomed* performes the promise which he made me, of obtaining my pardon of the Queen, when I gave him his Liberty.

Thou give him his Liberty (repli'd *Barsarnes*) thou hast rather basely murther'd him, and now thinkest to delude me with this Lye; for had he been free, his concernes at Court (I am certaine) would soon have brought him thither, but there he had neither been seen, nor heard of when I came thence; which is not above six dayes since.

I know not that (answer'd *Otanes*) but tis a certain truth, I set both him, and *Mexaris* free the day after you made your escape.

Well (repli'd *Barsarnes*) you shall go with me, and if I find what you tell me to be true, I will engage he shall make good whatever he promis'd you. But as for you base man (said he to *Ozmin*) you shall assuredly receive the recompence of your Fidelity to your Noble Master, who is now married to the Queen, thankes to you, and your treacherous Brother, yet neither he, nor you shall have much cause to boast of your Acheevements; but in the meane time tell me I charge you in *Oriana*'s name where the Princess *Artabella* is.

Alass Sir (answer'd he with a sigh) you demand that of me which I am not able to resolve you (would to Heaven I could) for all that I can tell you of her is, that she and her Maid, either threw themselves into the Sea, or else escaped hence by meanes of some ship which pass'd by this Chanell, as I rather believe. But that you may not think me of so mercinary, and low a spirit (continu'd he) to be tempted to injure so innocent a Princess by the hopes of Gain, I will to you Sir declare that, which I have hitherto conceal'd from all the World (my Brother here not excepted) which was, that I had a passion for her, as far above all other mens, as her birth transcended mine. It was this alone that perswaded me to listen to *Phasellus* when he tempted me to surprize her in her way toward Susa; which I did, as well to hinder others from being employ'd in that Design, who possibly would not have shewn her that respect (which I am confident how much soever she may hate me, she would be so just (were she here) as to acknowledge) she found from me, as to make my self happie in her sight.

Indeed (said *Artabella*) I have more cause to commend his Civility, then blame his disrespect; and oft (I confess) I have wondered at it, but little suspected the cause; which if I had, I am certaine I should have thrown myself into the Sea indeed, rather then have endur'd him in my sight.

These were the onely reasons (continu'd he) that induced me to become her Jailour, I say her Jaylour, since I know she so accounted me, though I should scorne so ignoble a title on any other score. Thus Sir have I been ingenuous (pursu'd he) [fol. 147ʳ] and confess'd to you the reall truth, but not with any desire or hopes of pardon, which know I have not deserv'd; for since I have forever lost the hope of seeing the Princess *Artabella*, the Queen will do me a greater favour in taking away, then in sparing my Life.

Her Majesty will do that which Justice requires you need not feare it (repli'd *Barsarnes*) who made no longer a stay there; but with his two Prisoners return'd to Susa, in hopes to heare newes of my Master (pursu'd *Mexaris*) but his hopes still deceiv'd him, for he could be as little satisfi'd there where he was, as in any of those other Places where he had been to seek him; however, he went to give the Queen an account what he had done, and how that he had brought with him *Ozmin*, and *Otanes*, the two Instruments of *Phasellus*'s wickedness; but she would not see them, onely commanded they should be put into the Dungion where the most notorious Offenders u'sd to be put, till it was determin'd what punishment should be inflicted on them. After which *Barsarnes* desir'd permission to renew his search after my Prince, which was granted assoon as demanded (and severall others appointed like wise to go into all parts of Persia to enquire for him) whereupon he determin'd to be gone very early the next morning, and to that end took then his Leave of *Oriana*, and went instantly home to give order concerning some affaires of his owne.

All this time *Phasellus* lay very ill of his Wound; continually raving, and exclaiming against his Fate, and the Queens cruelty (as he termed it) who would not so much as once vouchsafe to look on him in that condition wherein he was.

If I am guilty (would he say) why is my punishment suspended; if Innocent, why does she use me thus. Divers times did he attempt to kill himselfe by tearing off his Plasters, and other violences he us'd against himselfe: and doubtless he had effected his desires, had he not been prevented by the care, and watchfullness of those about him.

That very night which preceeded the day that *Barsarnes* was to renew his Progress after my Prince, came I to Susa (continu'd *Mexaris*) and sending a Messenger to the Palace to enquire for him, he brought me word, he was gone home a little before. Without delay, I went immediately to his house, where I accordingly found him; who no sooner saw me, but with a great deall of kindness he embraced me, demanding newes of my Master: to which I answer'd, that I had left him in a little house some twenty miles off in so deplorable a condition, as I much fear'd I should scarce find him alive at my returne.

What is the cause of his indisposition (said he seeming much concern'd.)

Ah my Lord (answer'd I) do you aske that, and know the Queen is married. It was that Fatall newes which has thrown him back into his former Fevour with a greater violence then before. I confess, I left him not without an extreme repugnance; nor could either his intreaties, or commands force me till yesterday

to leave him; but having then but little hopes of his Life, I could no longer disobey that charge he laid upon me to come hither, and if I could find you to bring
you to him.

These sad tydings, strook *Barsarnes* to the heart with [fol. 147ᵛ] a most sensible griefe, which he testifi'd by the teares he shed. Yes *Mexaris* said he, I will
go with you immediatly, but I must first go let the Queen know what you have
told to me, who will I am sure beare a larg share in my sorrow. But first tell me
whether your Master was set free by *Otanes,* or got free by some other meanes.

It was he Sir (I repli'd) which set us free, for which my Prince engag'd to
procure his pardon. With that he left me, and went instantly to the Palace, and
enforming the Queen of what I had told him; she gave Command a Litter should
be sent for my Prince, with her owne Phisician to waite on him to Court: with
these we presently (that very night) left Susa assoon as the Litter could be got
ready; and as we rode along, *Barsarnes* ask'd me how *Otanes* came to free us,
which I resolv'd him of in these words.

After *Otanes* found you had made an escape (continu'd *Mexaris*) and saw it
impossible to get you into his power again; he came the second day after your
departure into my Masters Chamber, and saluting him after a much more civill,
and submissive way then [then] he had us'd before. Sir (said he to him) I know
Barsarnes is escap'd, and I am not ignorant, that you will within these few dayes
be rescu'd out of my hands if I permit you to continue longer here; which rescue
I can easily prevent, by carrying you a place far remote from hence, where none
will ever come to seek you: but what I have already done has been too much, and
I am too sensible of my Offence to endevour to contract a greater guilt. I come
not therefore now into your presence as at first with treacherous designs against
you, but with remorse for what is past, and to submit to your mercy, which I confess I have not deserv'd; and withall to declare you are free, either to stay here, or
to depart when you please.

If you ^are^ as sensible of the wrong you have done me (repli'd my Generous
Prince) as you would perswade me, and that I find the effects of it in your restoring me that freedome you so injuriously depriv'd me of, I will not onely forgive
the wrong you have done me, but obtain your pardon too of the Queen, if I ever
am so happie as to see her again.

At this, *Otanes* fell upon his knees, giving my Prince a thousand thankes, for
a favour he acknowledg'd himself utterly unworthy of, in termes which testifi'd
the sense he had of my Masters goodness, and his owne vileness, and presenting
him the Keyes of the Castle, vow'd he would undertake much more for him, then
he had done for *Phasellus* if he might thereby but blot out of his mind the memory
of his past offence.

You need not feare (repli'd my Prince) that ever you shall be employ'd by me
on any such dishonourable designes as those you have of late been destin'd too,
for all that I'll desire of you shall be, onely that you would freely acknowledge
what moov'd you to undertake such unworthy things.

I protest seriously Sir (answer'd he) twas meerly the reall love I bare *Phasellus* which induced me to execute whatever he injoyn'd: never weighing the Justice or Injustice of his Commands; for retaining the same Obedience that I paid him when I fought under his Command, I thought my self oblig'd to serve him with the same Fidelity, having receiv'd from him larg [fol. 148ʳ] testimonies of his favour in Scythia, but more especially since his returne.

Were you then (said my Prince) one of those five hundred Gentlemen he commanded.

Yes Sir, (repli'd he) and I think I may say without vanity that my Brother and I were for our births of the most considerable quality amongst them; though either the misfortune, or prodigallity of our Ancestours (which oft brings a ruine on the greatest Families) reduced ours to so low an ebbe, that though by [my] Brother still possesses a considerable part of that estate which he was born too, yet for my owne part I had nothing left me but my sword, many times the onely Patrimony of a younger Brother.

Had you had but Vertue too (answer'd my Prince) you had had enough, but wanting that, though you had been born to a Crown, you would have been more contemptable then a Beggar; but go, and learn to be vertuous, and you may defie Fortune in the meanest condition: so taking his Leave of my Master, within a while after he left the Castle: but before he went, he told me where I might ^find^ our Horses and Armes (pursu'd *Mexaris*) my Master instantly causing me to help him on with his, we got on Horseback and bid adue to our Prison. All that day we rode without so much as meeting with one Passenger of whom we might enquire our way, with which we being unacquainted, ~~we~~ rode many miles about and could not come to either Towne, or Village; so that we were constrain'd to lye in a wide Forrest the first night, not neer any house, nor could we find any shelter save the Trees, under which we were forced to take up our Lodging: which I really think (went he on) is one cause of my Masters being so ill as he is; for not being perfectly recover'd, it was impossible, but lying on the cold earth, in the open Aire must of necessity prejudice his health through he had not bin any way indispos'd before.

Assoon as the day began to dawn we got on horseback again, and by that time the Sun was an houre high we made a shift to get out of the Forrest; and about Noon we came to a little house where my Prince allighted, intending to stay there a while and refresh himselfe a little with what that poor Cottage afforded; for (as he said) he found himself not very well, and exceeding faint for want of Food, not having eaten any thing since the night before he left Shiras. The Entertainment we found there, though it was plain, yet was it much better then we expected; the Goodman of the house biding us very heartily wellcome after his rustick manner with very hearty expressions; and hearing my Prince say what an ill Lodging he had had that night, he would have had a Bed made ready for him, that he might a while repose himself a little more easily. My Prince thanking him for this courtious proffer, refus'd it, telling him he hop'd he should be well enough able to hold out to the end of his Journey now; and demanded of him how far it was to Susa: to which *Criton* (for so was the old man call'd) repli'd. It was not above twenty miles, but a way so difficult to find, that without a Guide Sir (said he) you will go nigh to loose your way.

How may I do to procure One (ask'd my Prince)[?]

I will go see, and get you one (answer'd he), Whereupon he left us, but soon after return'd again.

My [fol. 148ᵛ] Son Sir (said he) is just now come from Susa, and if you please to accept of him he shall go with you to direct you in your Way: the young man who came in with his Father then approach'd my Prince, and proffer'd him his service, who hearing *Criton* say he came lately from Susa, thought haply he might enform him whether or no the Queen were married; yet did he tremble to demand it, well knowing how exceedingly the assurance of what he fear'd to aske would trouble him; nor was he able to aske that question, though he earnestly desir'd to be resolv'd of it. But at last (after much strugling with himself to over-come his Feares) he call'd me to him, commanding me to make that enquirie.

Assoon as I knew his mind, pray Friend (said I to *Critons* son) what newes is stirring at Susa.

I know none (answer'd he) but that of the Queens being married to one *Phasellus* who came hither with him who commanded the Armie against the Scythians.

How know you (demanded I) that she is married.

Very well (answer'd he) for I saw her both go, and come from the Temple.

I could aske no further (continu'd *Mexaris*) for this fatall newes had no sooner reach'd my poor Masters eares, but it pierced his heart; for ere I could turne about, I heard him drop downe behind me, where he lay streach'd out upon the Ground all palle and sensless; at which sight, I cry'd out so loud, as all in the house, came running in to see what the matter was: but perceiving my Prince in that condition, they thought it but an impertinent question to aske what ail'd me, but insteed thereof did their uttmost to bring him to life again. *Critons* Wife employ'd all that little skill she had, about him, having recourse to all those things which Country People use to persons in the like condition; but seeing they wrought not their usuall opperations, they concluded him rather dead, then in a swoon; but I thinking it impossible for his griefe (how excessive soever it was) to kill him so soon, beleiev'd it was rather his former weakness which rendred it so difficult to revive him: this I told them, desiring a Bed might be made ready for him; which was accordingly done, and assoon as I could I got him into it by the assistance of the people of the house; where after the tryall of severall remedies, at length he began to come to himself; and within a while after when he had regain'd so much sense as to know what had been done for his recovery, casting his eyes about, with a wild distracted kind of Look.

Cruell People (said he) why will you not let me dye.

I fearing his griefe might force from him some words which might betray the cause of it, beg'd all those that were present to retire; telling them I hop'd the worst was past; and that if I could but get him to take some rest, I did not doubt but he would do well again; this I spake onely to get them out of the Chamber, for never were my words and thoughts so contrary. Scarce had they left the Roome, but fixing his eyes on me as I stood by him.

And you *Mexaris* (said he) are crueller then they, since you know how exceeding necessary death is for me, and yet will keep me alive on purpose to suffer torments so great, as I should esteeme it a Crime to [fol. 149ʳ] wish them even on *Phasellus* himself though he be now my greatest Enemy: but tis the onely comfort I have left me that I shall frustrate all your hopes, and render all your endevours fruitless; for I find my end drawes neer, and Death a pace approaches; which word he had no sooner spoken but he swounded again, thereby reduceing me almost to my wits end. I was sorry then that I had sent every One away; but running to the Dore I gave a call, whereat they presently came in again, and seeing it was but invain any longer to dissemble his condition ~~but~~ told them I sadly fear'd it would prove past cure if I could not procure some skillfull Phisician to undertake him. They told me there was none nearer then the next Towne (which was five miles off) but if I pleas'd they would send thither for one, which I desir'd *Criton* he would with speed; whereupon he sent his son away instantly, with a strict charge to make all the hast as possibly he could; and truly I thinke he did (went on *Mexaris*) for before such time as I thought he could be got thither, he was return'd and brought with him the Docter; but alass to little purpose, for my Master (when he came to himself) absolutely refus'd to take anything that he prescrib'd.

I knowing how just a cause he had for his dispaire, could not blame that in him, which (I confess) had I beene Prince *Lucius* I should have done myselfe: however, I did all that I was able to divert him from the resolution he had to dye; for throwing myself upon my knees, I beg'd him both with sighs, and teares not to be guilty of his owne death.

Call up that generous Courage sir I beseech you (cry'd I) which has hitherto so nobly assisted you even in the greatest difficulties, and yeeld not to imaginary Torments, which are no other then what your Fancy inflicts upon you.

Call you those Torments I suffer, but imaginary [word blotted out], what then is reall (said my Prince). Oh *Mexaris* you are u^i^nsensa^i^ble[5] of my sufferings, if you imagine my courage is able to support me under them; for sure it must be more then humane, that can vanquish such a misfortune as mine without dying.

If you are determin'd to dy (said I) yet at least Sir lay aside that resolve till such time as you have reveng'd your selfe on him who is the cause of all your

---

⁵ The word "unsensable" is amended to "insensible"; the "u" and "a" are each underlined for deletion and "i" is inserted in each case.

miseries, and leave not that Insolent Rivall behind you, to tryumph in your ruine, and boast he has destroy'd the most Illustrious, and the most Generous of men.

I confess (repli'd he) I should dye much better satisfi'd could I but give death to that cruell murtherer of all my hopes, and most unjust Ravisher of all my Felicity; but as my case now is stated, I can seek no revenge against him but will procure me *Orania*'s hatered, at least her displeasure: for can I think she will admit one charitable ^thought^ of me, if once she see me crimson'd with the blood of him who (how vile, and wicked soever he be) is now her Husband: therefore tis farre better for me to dy now, when I may assure my selfe my death will be lamented by her, then live longer for no other end but to render my selfe more miserable by incurring her displeasure. No (pursu'd he) I never will do that; the Queen shall rather find by the respect I beare her, the greatness of my Love which moves me to dye rather then offend her.

Many other things did I say after this, to perswade him to live, by all the powerfullest Arguments I could use, but all invain; for he was deafe to whatever I said, and remain'd immovably bent upon his desire of dying. [fol.149ᵛ] His Feavour was now more violent then ever, and in a few dayes it so well seconded his desire, that I began with a sorrow I am not able to express (continu'd *Mexaris*) to dread his approaching death: seldome, or never did he sleep, but when he chanced at any time to fall into a slumber, it was so interrupted with [word blotted out] sighs, and terrifying Dreames, that it did him more hurt by the disquiets it caus'd him, then it procur'd him good. He oft commanded me to go and seek you out, and bring you to him; but twas not all the power he had over me, could force me from him till the last extreamity; yet to satisfy him, I sent to enquire after you, but the Messenger not finding you, I was at last constrain'd to come my selfe.

In the meane time (continu'd *Mexaris*) whilst we were going to *Critons* house to fetch my Master thence, the Queen had caus'd her Councell to be summon'd again, to take the examinations of *Ozmin*, and *Otanes*, who being brought before them and examin'd, they were both found worthy of death, and accordingly condemn'd: their sentence was, to be chain'd to the tops of two Trees opposite one to the other, and there to remaine till they were ste^a^rv'd⁶ to death. But the Queen having been assur'd by *Barsarnes* that my Prince had promis'd *Otanes* to obtain his pardon, for his sake made good that Promise, pardoning him as to his life, and chang'd the sentence of death, into a perpetuall banishment. The Evidence of these two men made so ill for *Phasellus*, as the Councell no longer deferr'd to pass sentence on him; but first denouncing the Marriage between him and *Oriana* to be void, and of no effect, they sentenced him to be sent back to Rome (assoon as he was capable of being removed) there to receive his Doome from *Augustus Cæsar*.

---

⁶ The word "sterv'd" is corrected to "starved" with the "e" underlined for deletion and an "a" inserted.

Rivall Friendship

THE SECOND PART

The Fourth Book

As soon as we arriv'd at *Critons* house (pursu'd *Mexaris* to *Artabella*) I conducted *Barsarnes* to my Masters Chamber, with a trembling heart, lest I should find him dead; and demanding of those about him how he had done since I went, they answer'd me, they saw but small hopes of amendment, for in their opinions he was rather worse then better. I spake but softly (continu'd he) lest I might disturbe him if he were asleep; but as low as I spoke he overheard me; for puting aside the Curtain with his hand, *Mexaris* said he, where is *Barsarnes*.

I am here Sir (answer'd he presenting himselfe to my Prince) who raising himselfe a little in his Bed, strove to embrace him as well as his feeble strength would permit him.

Deare *Barsarnes* (said he) you are now the onely man I can thinke worthy, of my Friendship, and tis on that account I have so earnestly desir'd to see you ere I dye, to take my last farewell of you.

O Sir (repli'd *Barsarnes* after he had wip'd away [fol. 150ʳ] some teares which my Masters condition extracted from his eyes) why would you precipitate yourself to dispaire before you knew whether you had reason to do what you have done so much to your owne prejudice.

What reason could I have more pressing to dispaire (interrupted my Prince) then to know I have lost forever my adored Queen, and with her all the Felicity and comfort of my Life, and nothing left me but miseries my patience cannot bear.

Were your Misfortunes but as great as you believe them (repli'd *Barsarnes*) you would have much more reason for what you have done, then I to blame you for it: but as wretched as you thinke your selfe, you have yet a possibility of being happie; if you can but live to enjoy your happiness; nor have you lost the Queen as you suppose: and more then that, I dare assure you Sir for your comfort, you have a more perticuler interest in her esteeme then ever you possest before.

Is it not true then (demanded my Prince) that she is married.

That report is but too true (answer'd *Barsarnes*).

Why do you then so cruelly delude my griefes with feigned hopes of impossibilities (said my Master) for alass, what happiness can I expect if she be married.

You may expect her (repli'd *Barsarnes*) and that without an impossiblity, as I can make it appeare, if you will but give me the hearing.

Most willingly (cry'd my Prince) and with more Joy receive such an assurance then ever condemned Malefactor did his pardon.

Then seting downe by my Masters bedside, he gave him an account of all things that had pass'd (wherein he was concern'd) since the day he parted from him, till the time I [*Mexaris*] came to him to his house in Susa.

Now Sir you see (continu'd he) you have no obstacle to your Felicity save your present indisposition, which if Heaven permit you to recover, you may yet be as happie as your wishes can contrive.

My Prince (continu'd *Mexaris*)'who but a few minutes before was about to dye with griefe, was now even ready to expire through an excess of Joy; but I perceiving him begin to faint, call'd to (the Phisician who came with us) for something to prevent his falling into a swoone; he presently giving him a strong Cordiall so well kept up his Spirits, as he quickly reviv'd, and Looking on *Barsarnes*. Though I am beyond measure joyfull at what you tell me (said he) yet can I not resent [feel] these glad tydings you bring without a mixture of griefe, since my Weakness assures me I cannot live to enjoy the felicity you promise. O Death, O Fate (pursu'd he) how cruell are you to me: you would not let me dye when I esteem'd my self the most miserable of men: and now I know I may be happy, you will not suffer me to live.

But deare *Barsarnes* (continu'd he) you have done all for me that I could either expect or hope from your Friendship; for which if I could leave you a Crowne in requitall, it were less then you have merited from me: but since in this condition whereunto my misfortunes have reduced me, I have onely the will, but not the abillity to requite you, I can onely leave you this assurance that I shall dye with a heart as repleat with gratfull acknowledgments, as your owne is full of nobleness and generosity.

That Friendship Generous Prince (repli'd *Barsarnes*) wherewith you have been pleas'd to honour me is a sufficent recompence for more then I have beene able to do for you; therefore I beseech you Sir speake no more of that which deserves not to be mention'd but endevaur to regain a little strength that you may be in a capacity to be carri'd [fol. 150ᵛ] to Susa where you may be both more diligently tended, and more carefully look'd too then you can possibly be here.

If I stay for an increase of strength (said my Prince) I must never be remov'd, for you will suddenly see me worse; but never better: therefore as you love me *Barsarnes* (pursu'd he) let me presently be put into the Lytter, for if I can but live to see my Dearest *Oriana,* and in her Armes breath out my Soule, tis all that I will beg of Heaven, or all I can expect; for I find myself much weaker then you can imagine.

Fain would we have perswaded him (continu'd *Mexaris*) to stay a day or two ere he remov'd, in hopes his Fevour might abate; but neither our perswasions, nor the Phisicians advice could prevaile with him for a longer stay: for renewing his request to *Barsarnes* in such pressing, and passionate termes, as being not able to deny what he so earnestly desir'd, he caus'd him to be put into the Lytter

in his Bed as he lay, his weaknes being such, as rendred him unable to put on
his Clothes: but ere he stir'd, he commanded me to call the People of the house
about him, whom he perticulerly bad farewell, after he had gratifi'd, and thank'd
them for all their hospitable kindness, promising if he liv'd, more liberally to
reward them. The poor people were even amazed at his bounty, and falling on
their knees, beg'd of the Gods to restore him to his health. The Lytter went so
very slow as it was almost night the next day ere they entered Susa, but I hasted
away before to give notice of my Masters coming, that a Bed might be made
ready for him; but the Queen had prevented my care, having caus'd all things to
be prepar'd fit for him, though not in his owne Chamber, but in those Lodgings
where King *Achemenes* us'd to lye.

My Masters coming was no sooner known but all Persons of quality in the
City rode forth to meet him, and to waite on him to Court; but being enform'd
by *Barsarnes* how dangerously ill he was, they forbore to salute him with those
wellcomes they otherwise would have given him, and contented themselves to
ride silently by his Litter lest they might disturbe him. Being in this manner
brought to the Palace, he was immediatly carri'd to his Lodging, and laid into his
Bed; and presently after his Chamber was fill'd with Visitants, some out of Ceremony, but most of them out of that respect and love they beare him: but their
civility was very prejudiciall to him at that time; for with striving to answere
their kindnesses in the like returnes, he spent his spirits so much with speaking
to them severally, as he had hardly enough left to sustaine his life withall.

Barsarnes perceiving the injury he did himselfe by speaking, desir'd them to
leave them till such time as he was in a better capacity to receive their Visits: no
sooner had he seen the Chamber emptied, but he went to wait upon the Queen,
who having been enform'd how much Company had been with my Master, fear'd
he had done himself hurt by his complacence to them; and thought if she should
visit him so soon after; it might prove rather an injury then a kindness till he had
a little recover'd his weariness: this she told *Barsarnes*, after she had made a perticuler inquirie in what condition he was; which he assur'd her to be in a manner
hopeless.

But I approve very well Madam of your Majesties not seeing him to night
(said he) [fol. 151 ʳ] if he will be so contented; but I feare he will not.

You may tell him (said she) tis not out of any neglect that I forbeare to see
him, but meerely out of a Feare it may prejudice his health, which is as deare to
me as he can wish it.

With this message he return'd to my Prince (pursu'd *Mexaris*) but as *Barsarnes* had said, he was so little satisfi'd with it, as he was constrain'd to go back
again to the Queen with intreaties not to defer that Favour she design'd him till
the morrow; for he protested to *Barsarnes* that he knew, he should not then be in
a condition to receive it: this he having told the Queen. If it be so (said she with
her Eyes ready to o'reflow with teares) I will no longer delay what I owe both to

my owne Inclinations, and Prince *Lucius*'s merits; with that, she gave him her hand, to lead her to my Masters Chamber.

I seeing her come in, undrew the Curtain of his bed, and told him the Queen was come to see him. At which, he gave a sudden start, as one newly awak'd from sleep, and seeing her by him, he was so transported with Joy as he could find no words patheticall enough to express the greatness of it: for without speaking; he took one of her hands, and kissing, and embraceing it with all the raptures of a most ardent passion, he at length cry'd out. Ah my Adored Queen I am no longer miserable, since I enjoy a Felicity which within these few dayes I utterly dispair'd of ever obtaining.

You see Generous Prince (repli'd she) the goodness of the Gods, who when your misfortunes (in all appearance) were past redress, found out a way to free you from them, if you have not frustrated the care they have taken of your Concerns, by reduceing your selfe to this deplorable estate wherein to my griefe I behold you.

Tis that alone I confess Madam (repli'd he) which has power to disturbe my present Joyes; since such is my weakness as it threatens to drage me from you to my Grave, and ere many houres run out, by death to close my eyes forever, from beholding the onely Object for which I prize them.

Banish those apprehensions (said she) and hope, since Heaven has preserv'd you in such a Sea of miseries (whereinto your Enemies, and mine had plung'd you) that it will still extend the like goodness to you, and not let you suffer ~~you~~ Shipwrack in the Port: speak not then, nor think of dying, unless you desire to inspire me with a trouble resembling such a misfortune: the Destinies sure cannot be so cruell to make you find a death among your Friends, which the Heavens preserv'd you from amidst thousands of your enemies. No *Diomed* (continu'd she) you shall live I trust, to take possession of that Crowne which *Achemenes* left you.

Were his other gift no more considerable to me (repli'd he) then that, I should not part from my Life with such regreet as now I do; nor would the sorrow I should have resented [felt] for its loss, brought torments on me so intollerable as I was forced to have recourse to Death to release me of them.

Were I not sure you beare a noble soule (said the Queen) I should feare you might esteeme me guilty of some part of those sufferings you have endur'd, and think my selfe oblig'd to protest my Innocence; but being perswaded you have no such unjust thoughts of me, I think it onely necessary to let you know the probability of that cunning story [fol. 151ᵛ] wherewith I was deluded; which I confess I had not subtilty enough to dive into the depth of.

O Madam (cry'd my Prince, said *Mexaris*) you would infinitly injure the reverence I beare you, if you can imagine me capable of believing you guilty of any thing the most sublime vertue dare not owne. But if you vouchsafe to enforme me of what you say, I beseech you do it onely to satisfie my curiosity, not with any intention to remove doubts which never found admittance into a thought of mine.

Well (repli'd she) let it be on what score you please, but I desire to be oblig'd to your reason no less then to your inclination; tis requisit therefore you should be no longer ignorant by what means *Phasellus* deceiv'd me (which in these words she let him know). He arriving here (said she) some foure dayes before the Corpes of my Royall Father, brought me the first tydings of Persias misfortune, and my own irreparable loss: how I resented [felt] it, I thinke I need not tell you, since the affection I bare so deare a Father is not unknown to you; onely thus much I will say, that the griefe I suffer'd had almost cost me my life: but when the Funurall Obsequies were past, and that the great Concernes of my Kingdome constrain'd me to appeare in publick, *Phasellus* came to me one day, desiring I would give him the Favour of a private Audience, adding, he had something to acquaint me with, which the King a little before his death commanded him to let me know, but the time of my mourning (he said) had been improper to tell it me ^in^.

With that I instantly withdrew into my Closet, commanding him to follow me. Now (said I to him) what is it you have to tell me.

With that he presented me a Ring, on which I had no sooner cast my eye, but I knew it to be the very same on which my marriage depended. I was presently strook with a trembling, and so strange a coldness ranne thorough all my Veines as I thought verily I should have sunk downe dead: I was faine to set downe in a Chaire which stood by me, to keep my self from falling, and striving all I could to conceale my disorder, I ask'd him how he came by that Ring.

I see Madam answer'd he (seeming something troubled) the sight of it sur-prizes you, but I feare you will be more surpriz'd when I assure your Majesty, the Great *Achemenes* thought me worthy of his Alliance: and that I might find no opposition in what, I confess (how great soever my Ambition was) I had not somuch Presumption in me to aspire too, he gave me this Ring as an assured Pledge of that invaluable happiness he bestow'd on me.

My thoughts (pursu'd the Queen) were so distractedly divided between griefe and resentment [sentiments] that I had not power to interrupt him, but let him go on at this rate.

I confess (continu'd he) I did not at first resent [feel] the Felicity of pos-sessing so Divine a Princess with those raptures of Joy, as I have since, because I could not look on my owne happiness, without beholding my Friend's mis-fortune, which I but too well knew was included in it. I am very sensible (went he on) it was not any worth in me which moov'd the King to prefer me before *Diomed* (who had a thousand times more oblig'd him then ever I had) but onely the grandure of his birth, which I freely acquainted *Achemenes* with (upon his Demand) [fol. 152ʳ] though not with any intent to disoblige, or prejudice my Friend, not in the least mistrusting what the King intended when he ask'd that question. For having from the mouthes of his Phisicians, and Chyrurgions been assur'd of his approaching death, he gave a Charge to all that were present to depart his Presence. I supposing my selfe included in that number, was going too; which he perceiving, call'd me back, telling me, it was to have the liberty to speak with me in private, that he had commanded the rest away.

I have hitherto *Phasellus* (said he) ^been ignorant^ who I have been oblig'd too for those considerable services I have receiv'd both from you and your Generous Friend; and have contented my self to know ye Valiant, to know ye Generous, and to know ye worthy of more honour then Persia can confer: but though in my life time I have been satisfi'd with such a knowledge, yet now at my death, I have a great desire to be enform'd of your true qualities, and extractions which hitherto you have conceal'd.

I knowing *Diomed* (pursu'd he) had an intention to discover himself at the end of the Warre, knew no reason why I might not a little anticipate that discovery by resolving the King now what he desir'd to know: whereupon, I ingeniously told him, that *Diomed* was of an Extraction, the most Illustrious in the World; being no other then Prince *Lucius*, Nephew to *Augustus Caesar*, and Heire to the Emperiall Crowne of Rome. My self I likewise told him was descended from *Mark Anthonie* who was my Grandfather by my Fathers side.

The reason why I ask'd this question (said the King) is because I design'd to bestow on *Diomed* my Crowne and Daughter, but finding (by what you tell me) the greatness of his Birth an obstacle to my intentions, and most contrary to a resolution I long since made, never to give her to any One that is born to a larger Dominion, or a more puissant Scepter then her owne; but being thus disappointed of my First election, I cannot make a Fitter Choice then your self (continued the King) since *Diomeds* Friendship to you, will (I doubt not) induce him to be a Friend to *Oriana*, by strengthning her with his assistance against any that shall presume to disturbe the Peace of her Kingdome.

Here then *Phasellus* (pursu'd he) take this Ring, and from me, deliever it to my Daughter, and feare not but she will without dispute make you her Choice, as I have made you mine; for she has bound herselfe to me by a promise (from which there is not any thing that can o^a^bsolve[1] her) to marry him who should present her with this Ring from me.

I was not able (pursu'd the Queen) to let him proceed, but interrupting him. When I made that promise to the King my Father (said I) I did believe he would have made such a Choice for me as I should have no reason ^to^ dislike; and still I am perswaded his intentions extended not so far, as to ~~ippos~~ impose on me a person I never had more then a civill respect for, nor perhaps never may. I know my Crowne is considerable enough to move you to accept his Gift, but I question whether or no, had he excepted that, my person would have been of any value with you; and therefore till I am assur'd you have a greater kindness for me, then

---

[1] The word "o̲bsolve" is amended with "o" underlined for deletion and "a" inserted.

ambition for my Crowne, you must excuse me if I [fol. 152ᵛ] deferre the performance of what you believe I am oblig'd too.

Many things he repli'd whereby he endevour'd to intraduce a beliefe in me, that he had a long time ador'd me with a most transcendent passion, though his respect forced him to conceale it; but I so little minded what he said (though he made me a long discourse to that purpose) as I have forgot his words; but I remember (pursu'd she) I answer'd him in these. I could not but expect you should speak after this manner, but if you will have me believe you to be really passionate for me, as you pretend; you must convince me of it rather by your Deeds, then Words.

What proofe Madam can you aske (repli'd he) I'll give you my Life if you demand it.

No (said I) I shall desire nothing more of you, then to prefer my content, and satisfaction before your owne; and if you truely love me, you will find reason enough for it, since I ingeniously declare, I neither do, nor ever shall affect you, and consequently if I become your Wife, I must thereby be rendred most miserable, and unhappie. Be then so generous *Phasellus* (continu'd I) as to disengage me from that promise which I made *Achemenes*, since tis in your power to do it; for though I am (I confess) oblig'd by that Promise to marry you, yet you are no way bound to exact of me the performance of it: and by this way still po you may possess that place you have in my esteeme, and purchace to your self the highest in my Friendship; whereas otherwayes you will enevitably deprive your selfe of both, and in their stead procure my aversion, perhaps my hatered.

You are more just sure Madam (he repli'd) then to hate me meerly because I love you; and me thinkes you should not be so cruell, to demand so strang a testimony of my affection, as that to give you an assurance of it, I must give up that right in you which the King your Father gave me. But admit I could for the Love I beare you consent to my owne ruine (however, Madam you may look on it as an Argument of the greatness of my passion) the World would questionless count it the highest piece of Folly imaginable, to bye a fanci'd Felicity, with the price of a reall one: for if it be so, that I must ne're enjoy your affection, it will be happiness enough for me to possess your person.

Not somuch (said I) perhaps as you imagine; for if you compell me to pay obedience to my Fathers Will, I shall endevour to render you as unhappie as you desire to make me.

Not staying for his Answere I ris up and went immediatly out of my Closet to my Chamber, where I threw my selfe upon my Bed; revou^lv^ing² in my mind a thousand severall confused thoughts. I confess (continu'd the Queen) till now I had esteem'd *Phasellus* very much, as I thought I was oblig'd to do, both by those noble Qualities I really believ'd him endu'd with, and those services he

---

² The word "revouing" is amended with "u" underlined for deletion and "lv" inserted.

had rendred my Country; but more especially as he was your Friend (said she to my Prince, pursu'd *Mexaris*) but in an instant, that esteeme was chang'd into so strang an aversion as I beheld him with Eyes quite different from those where-with I look'd on him but a few minutes before: for now, all that had seem'd com-mendable in him heretofore, appear'd to me cleare contrary; and those thinges which before I accounted Vertues in him, now bore the shape of Vice. His Valour (methought) seem'd rather rashness, his [fol. 153ʳ] Generosity, Pride, and Osten-tation; his Civility and Complacence, base Flattery, and dissemulation; so that I could not (in fine) see one quality in him, which did not render him a Fitter Object of my Scorn, then Love. Then did I break out into many sad Complaints against the severity of *Achemenes.*

Ah cruell Father (cry'd I) to exact of me a proofe of my Obedience after your death, which your Indulgence assur'd me you would never have requir'd from me had you liv'd. Many other things the extreamity of my griefe forced from my mouth, which nothing but the sense of that unavoidable misfortune I saw my selfe confin'd to suffer, by the Decree of my Father (as I thought) from whence I had no appeale could render pardonable. I tormented my self day and night in that manner, as it has been my Wonder I did not loose my Wits; and the rather, because I kept my griefe close Prisoner in my brest, not imparting it to any one, no not so much as to *Theocrite* who in all things else was perfectly acquainted with my Thoughts. As long as I could, I avoided both the sight, and conversation of *Phasellus:* but when I found I could do so no longer, I sent for him one day into my Chamber, whether he presently came with much Joy in his Looks, hopeing (as he said) the Fates had made a happie change for him in my Inclination; but I soon let him understand his errour.

For after a little silence, *Phasellus* (said I to him) I sent for you to let you know, I have endevour'd all that I am able to conforme my selfe to what my duty obliges me; but after all, I find it so impossible to give you my heart (though I should give you my person) that you may as well hope to extract Fire out of Water (which of all Elements is the most contrary to it) as ever create in me such an affection as is due from a Wife to a Husband; without which, there is little hopes of any happiness to be found either for you or me: therefore I conjure you by all that you esteeme most deare, to exempt me from that engagement the King my Father laid upon me, and in requitall I'll promise to obtain you the affection of *Artabella,* who is a Princess of whom I can claime no precedency in any thing, my birth excepted; seting that aside, there's nothing but she equalls me in, and in beauty far excells me: and more then that, I will engage never to alter my con-dition, but to lead my life in perpetuall Virginity, that so after my decease my Crowne may descend to you (To this intent it was that I sent for *Artabella* back to Susa) I made him this advantagious proposall (pursu'd she) in hopes he would accept it; and out of a beliefe, that if your passion for me Generous Prince were such as you had represented it, you would chuse to dispence with the loss of the Persian Crowne, rather then *Oriana.*

O Madam (cry'd my Prince [*Diomed*]) how infinitly obliging was your opinion, and how much Justice was there in those generous thoughts of yours. Yes my Dearest Queen (pursu'd he) had there been truth in what *Phasellus* affirm'd, that *Achemenes* had really given him that right to you which he pretended; I should indeed most willingly have dispenced not onely with the loss of the Persian Crowne, but of the Romane too (had I been possess'd of it) nay of all the Crownes on Earth rather then I would have foregone so invaluable Treasure as you Divinest *Oriana* are.

With this he was [fol. 153ᵛ] silent and the Queen went on.

Your proffer Madam is not so inconsiderable (repli'd *Phasellus*), but that perhaps I might accept it, were not my passion greater for you then my ambition for your Crowne or Kingdome; for I know well the Princess *Artabella* is a person of those perfections, as no Prince but would be proud to weare her Fetters; but were she yet more excellent I should disdain her affection in comparrisson of yours.

I have already told you (said I) that mine you never must expect, and therefore you are in my opinion very unreasonable to refuse a Princess who possibly may requite your passion with a reciprocall one, for One who declares she neither can nor will, and who cannot admit of so much as one obliging thought of you, so long as you continue your pretences to her; which I can never approve of for severall reasons.

How weighty soever they may be Madam (replied he) methinkes you should find one more prevalent to accept, then you have to reject me, since the Great *Achemenes* deem'd me worthy of you: but perhaps this undeserved aversion you express for me proceeds not so much from my want of merit, as from *Diomed's* having prepossest your heart.

You are not so deep there (said I) to know my Inclinations; but however, I shall not scruple to avow it, that if the King my Father had pursu'd his first intentions, I should have obey'd him with as high a satisfaction, as I shall now with repugnance; sin^c^e *Diomeds* merits no less then his birth gives him the precedency of you in all respects.

I knew in this, I spake more then discretion alow'd me, but so highly offended was I that he should take the boldness to upbraid me, with what he had no assurance of more then his owne suspition, as I car'd not what I said so that my words might but disoblige him, as much as he had displeas'd me: but finding my anger rise to that height, as I fear'd it would in despight of me break out into some expressions, which (possibly) I might afterwards have repented, I quitted my Chamber, not vouchsafeing to heare what he would reply, onely I left him a scornfull Look as I pass'd by him, to ruminate upon; hoping he would interpret it as an effect of his Presumption: which the next time he saw me, he on his knees beg'd my Pardon for, in the most submissive language he could invent.

I still continu'd to perswade him by all the most prevalent arguments I could devize to relinquish his pretences to me; but he remain'd inflexa^i^ble,[3] still urging me with my Duty, and my Engagement to *Achemenes,* which (he said) if I would have a Dispensation from, I must fetch him from the Dead to absolve me. When I saw no remedy, I at last consented (as far as I was able) to be his, though I still defer'd it as long as I could find any pretence, in expectation of your returne; hoping your Friendship might worke more on him then my Intreaties. But at length, hearing you had suddenly left your Company as you were returning hither, I fanci'd you had some Intelligence of what had pass'd which I believ'd you resented [felt] so ill, to be so slighted, and another unjustly prefer'd before you, as I really thought you had abandon'd this ungratfull Country (as I term'd it) and gone back into your owne. Soe that having no way left me to evade [fol. 154ʳ] *Phasellus's* pursutes, I marri'd him, but with what resolution I suppose you have already heard.

Yes Madam (repli'd my Prince) I have and know not whether was greater, my griefe, or my amazment at that so cruell a resolve; and I really think my trouble would have been greater (if possible) to have known you had di'd by your owne hand, then to have seen you live *Phasellus's.*

The Queen (pursu'd *Mexaris*) doubting she had disturb'd my Master by the length of her Discourse, would no longer continue it; but wishing him a good night she took her leave of him and retir'd to her rest, which was much disturb'd with her feares for my Prince's life. So soon as she awak'd the next morning, she sent to enquire how he had rested, and an Answere being returned that he had had so violent a Fit that night as it was fear'd he could not live many houres, she arose and causing herselfe to be dress'd in her Morning At^t^ire, (with all imaginable speed) she came with hast into my Masters Chamber; but finding him newly fallen into a little slumber, she sate downe in a Chaire by his Bedside; and puting by the Curtain a little with her hand, she beheld him as he lay, with such a Mortall Paleness spread o're all his Face, that had she not heard him breath, she would (questionless) have thought Life had forsaken him, which touch'd her with a very sensible compassion to thinke what he had done and suffer'd for her sake, and that now, when as he might have tryumph'd over all his misfortunes, he was even ready to expire.

Twas not long she sate reflecting on these sad thoughts ere he awak'd, and casting his eyes upon the Queen. Ah Madam (cry'd he with a sigh) my time draws on and Death apace approaches to summon me away: but Madam (continu'd he) I must humbly beg from you ere I dye, a confirmation of that Peace which I concluded with Scythia.

You may assure your self Generous Prince (repli'd she) it shall be done; for I receiv'd from *Barsarnes* so high a Character of the Vertues both of *Cydarius,* and

---

[3] The word "inflexible" is amended with "a" underlined for deletion and "i" inserted.

Clazomena, and the generous Friendship they testifi'd to you, that I resolv'd for your sake (though you had never mention'd it) to acquit them of the trybute, and send back their Hostages; desiring rather to oblige them to assist me as Friends, then Tributaries.

As they were in this discourse *Phasellus* came into the Roome; and approached the Bed where my Master lay, with a Fearless and undaunted Look. The Queen was much surpriz'd at his coming, and the more, in regard she knew not to what violence against my Prince, his malice, and dispaire might transport him: which moov'd her to speak to him after this manner.

Wicked man (said she) hast thou the Impudence to bring that guilty Face into my presence, and carry on it no mark of shame, or of repentance for those notorious Crimes thou hast commited; but say, what is it that you came for, and what Designe bringes you hither.

I come with no other Madam (he repli'd) then to reproach you with your cruelty to your Husband; for though (I confess) I attain'd that title by injustice, yet none without a greater can now deprive me of it; for since by so sacred a tye as that of Marriage you made yourselfe mine, no Mortall Power can disolve the Knot: they may take away my life, but cannot [fol. 154ᵛ] lawfully take you from me; for none but the Gods can now divorce us by the hand of Death. I know my Crimes are such as will render my memory justly odious to poster-ity; but yet, great as they are, you ought rather to look on them as the effects of that violent passion wherewith I was inspir'd, then the products of my inclina-tion. Yes Madam (pursu'd he) I acknowledge, through an excess of Love I have betray'd you, violated all the Lawes of Friendship, abused the innocent affection of a most Vertuous Princess who honour'd me with more Love then ever I could have deserv'd, had I continu'd constant; yet am I so far from repenting, that (I declare) I would act o're my Crimes again, rather then not enjoy you: and could so great, so strange an affection be capable of producing no returne, not so much as pitie. Cruell woman (went he on) though you had so intirely given your heart to another, as you could afford me no place in it; yet methinkes, Decency, and the sense you ought to have of your owne honour, should have restrain'd you from confering Favours on your Lover, you deny your Husband. I know this is the second time you have honour'd him with a visit, though you would not once vouchsafe as so much as to cast an eye on me in this misfortune and disgrace whereinto I am fallen meerly for my affection to you.

So strongly amaz'd was the Queen to heare him speak in this manner, as she had not the power to interrupt him, but let him go on a long time at this rate. But at last, casting a disdainfull Look on him. I know too well (said she) what I owe to my honour, to be put in mind of it by you who have no spark of either verture, or honour remaining in your soule. But know Unworthy Man (continu'd she) had I not been satisfi'd as to my Conscience that I ought no longer to regard thee as a Husband, but as a Traitour that has sought to deprive me of my Crowne, and Dignity; and that I am suffcently dispenced with from all tyes, and obligations

I have to thee, how great soever my respect had been for Prince *Lucius,* it should ne're have made me shew him any other Favour then what Civility, or Gratitude exacted of me; and I think that kindness wherewith you have twice taken the liberty to upbraid me, has not transcended those limits: but get you instantly out of my sight, or you shall dearly repent your Presumption in coming into my Presence unsent for.

I will immediatly obey you Madam (he repli'd) but permit me first I beseech you, to speak a word to him who once honour'd me (though most undeservedly) with the title of his Dearest Friend. With that he addresst himselfe to my Prince (pursu'd *Mexaris*) who had all this while hearkned to him with an unconceiveable trouble, caus'd by the rememberance of his Offences, and of that most affectionat Friendship he once had born him.

Assoon as he saw him enter the Roome he turn'd away his Face, as unwilling to look on him, but perceiving by his last words to the Queen, he had an intention to say something to him, which he [fol. 155ʳ] desiring to prevent said to him.

Oh Heavens *Phasellus* still will you persecute me; have you brought me even to my Grave by your Wickedness, and will you not suffer me to enter it in quiet; methinkes after all those miseries you have made me suffer, you should not be so cruell to desturbe the last moments of my life with your sight, which ^you^ cannot but think is now most hatefull to me.

I know it but too well (repli'd *Phasellus*) that I have rendred myselfe deservedly hatefull to you, by those Crimes wherof I cannot but acknowledge my selfe guilty, and by those Injuries I have done you: but yet I come not with repentance to implore your Pardon, for I know they have been too great for any remorse of mine to expiate, and tis rather by my blood, then by my teares I ought to give you a reparation for them; but that I may not dy in your opinion more guilty then I really am, tis fit I let you know I had no intention, no not the least thought of deceiving you when I gave you the contrary Ring, but did it meerly through a mistake, which I never perceiv'd till after I came hither, where I beheld again the fatall beauty of this cruell Queen (pursu'd he looking on *Oriana*). But had I (as I expected) found the Princess *Artabella* here, I am perswaded I had been still innocent, and you both happie: for missing at my return, the Object of my Love, my heart soon took the impression of a new affection, and I instantly became more passionate for *Oriana,* then ever you had known me before for *Artabella*; and nothing was so great a wonder to me then, as that I had so long been blind to the perfections of the Queens admired beauty, so that I had not before given it the preheminence of *Artabellas* in my fancy: yet I must needs say, I oppos'd this crimenall passion with all the Arguments, my Friendship, my Vertue, and my Reason could furnish me with; but they were all too weak, for it soon forced an enterance into my brest in despight of all the resistance I could make; where once having took possession, it rul'd with so much Tyranie as it utterly depriv'd me of the liberty to act by any motion but what it inspir'd me with. But yet I had not so absolutely lost my reason, but that I saw, if I would be happie, I must be wicked, nay superlatively so, by becoming guilty of the vildest Ingratitude to you that ever yet was practic'd towards any; of treachery, and Injustice to the Queen, of black and horrid Perjury, and Infidelity to *Artabella*; yet these powerfull Considerations were insufficent to deterre me from the Guilt I have contracted.

And now if you believe you still have reason to upbraid me with the wronges you have by my meanes sustain'd, I have some cause likewise to reproach you: for if I depriv'd you of a Mistress, you more injuriously rob me of a Wife, and of those affections of hers, which ought to be no bodies now but mine: for which Injustice since I cannot hope for a reddress on Earth, I will go and complain to the Gods. Prince *Lucius* farewell (continu'd he) may you live to enjoy a happiness I was unworthy [fol.155ᵛ] of, and which I will no more disturbe by presenting to your view an Object so detested. Madam (pursu'd he bowing to the Queen) I ^wish^ ~~beg~~ your felicity may equall my Offences, which I will onely beg, the rememberance of may be buried with me in my Grave. I can but dy to satisfie both your resentments [sentiments], and my owne dispaire. Accept then Madam (cry'd he) the onely reparation I can give, or you receive. Just as he pronounced these words, he strook a Dagger (which he had secretly conceal'd so as none perceiv'd it) soe deep into his heart, as in an instant he fell dead at the Queens Feet.

Hitherto (said *Celia*) *Artabella* had preserv'd some sentiments of kindness for *Phasellus*, notwithstanding those misfortunes he had caus'd her, but now in a moment, they all forsooke her, leaving in their place a perfect hatered, and an utter detestation of him, and was so far from conceiving the least sorrow or compassion ^for^ ~~at~~ his death, that she declar'd if she had any thinge of trouble for it, it was because his punishment proportion'd not his Crimes.

Base perfidious man (said she) were all those miseries he has made me suffer, so little considerable with him, as not to stirre up in his soule some slight regret for all my wrongs; he testifi'd some repentance for the Injuries he had done his Friend, and *Oriana*, but shew'd not the least remorse for any thing he had done against me.

After this she was silent, and *Mexaris* went on. My Prince (said he) hearing the noise *Phasellus* made with his Fall, look't out of his Bed to see what the matter was, and seeing the tragick part which he had acted on himselfe, he was struck with so much horrour at what he had done, and so reall a compassion for him, that I really believe (pursu'd *Mexaris*) it was a meanes of shortning his Life: for beholding him as he lay weltring in his blood, he could not refraine from teares, and deeply sighing.

Ah most Unhappie *Phasellus* (said he) to what a disasterous Fate has thy Inconstancy (that spring, and originall of all thy Crimes) brought thee: but would to Heaven I could as easily restore thy Life, as I could have forgiven thee the Wrongs thou didst me, had not the Princess *Artabellas* been included in them.

The Queens enmity ceas'd likewise with his Life; for him that a few minutes before she could not look on without hatred, she now beheld with pitty;
but except her Majesty, and my Generous Master, I [*Mexaris*] really think there
was scarce any that did not repine that he had so slight a punishment for such
notorious Offences. The Queen perceiving the sight of him was a trouble to my
Prince, caus'd his body to be carried away; which being done, she sate a while in
silence reflecting on the Justice of the Gods, who although they had permitted
Phasellus's treachery so long to remain undiscover'd, yet had so timely brought it
to light as he could not attaine the accomplishment of his desires; and that as he
had contriv'd the ruine of two persons, whose preservations, and felicities ought
to have been no less deare to him then his owne, so with his owne hand he had
reveng'd them on himselfe, by becoming his owne Executioner.

Whilst the Queens thoughts were thus employ'd, my Prince began to find
so great an alteration in himselfe, as believing he must take an eternall Farewell
of her, he put those thoughts out of her mind by saying. I must dye [fol. 156ʳ] my
Fairest Queen, my Dearest *Oriana,* I must dye (pursu'd he) but that affects me
not, for I know I was not born immortall, but onely as it is the cruell occation of
seperating me from you: tis that Madam, and that alone which makes me receive
my death with more regret then ever any did; since I am constrain'd so soon to
leave you, and to leave you too, before such time as you are wholy mine: had I but
liv'd till I had obtain'd that happiness, Death would rather have been a satisfaction then a trouble to me.

While he spake in this manner, the Queen was so o'recome with griefe, as it
stop'd the passage of her words; but her Eyes supplying the office of her Tongue,
sufficently express'd the sad resentments [sentiments] of her mind.

But yet my death would be the more supportable (continu'd he) could I but
obtain an assurance that I shall live forever in your memory.

You cannot but assure yourselfe you shall (repli'd the Queen) unless you
thinke *Phasellus* has infected me with his Ingratitude. Yes my deare *Lucius*
(pursu'd she with a new Flood of teares) you shall ever live in my rememberance,
nor shall a second affection ever deprive you of that interest you have in my heart,
which I am resolv'd to bury so deep within your Tombe as it shall ne're revive
with any future Flame, for though cruell Fate would not suffer me to live yours,
it is not in its power to hinder me from dying so.

Faine would my Master have made some reply (went on *Mexaris*) but his
speech began to faulter, as he could not pronounce his words so as to be understood; but though he could not speak, he fix't his dying eyes upon the Queen a
little while, and of a sudden clos'd them up forever; his Generous Soule in an
instant abandoning its noble Dwelling, took its flight to a more glorious sphear.

How unconcern'd soever *Artabella* was (said *Celia*) for the death of *Phasellus,*
yet could she not refraine from deploring *Diomed's* with all the demonstrations
of a reall griefe. Ah Generous Prince (said she weeping most bitterly) how worthy were you of a better Fate: but Heaven (I doubt not) has given you the full

reward of all your unequall'd Vertues, and all those sufferings to which you were expos'd; by exalting you to those Regions of Felicity, where Vertuous soules do live in endless Joys; where they, secure above the reach of Fortunes power, look downe upon their past misfortunes with contempt.

Then being silent, *Mexaris* went on again. To tell you Madam (pursu'd he) all those expressions of sorrow the Queen utter'd upon this sad occation is more then I am able; my griefe for my Deare Master being so extreame, as I was uncapable of minding tha anything that was said: but I remember after a little time she was carri'd to her owne Chamber in a condition little different from my Masters; but though it was not long she remain'd so, yet for many dayes she continu'd such excessive weepings, as it was the wonder of all those about her, that she did not weep herself to death. All that could be said to comfort her, serv'd but for greater aggravations of her sorrow; which was such as she dispair'd to find a cure even from Time (Griefes best Phisician.) The whole Court put themselves in mourning, as they had done not long before for *Achemenes*; and truly I thinke [fol. 156ᵛ] their Habits spake not more sadness then their hearts resented [felt]. As for *Oriana*, she cloister'd up herselfe in a darkness resembling the blackness of that Melancholy which had ceaz'd ^seized^⁴ on her disconsolate spirits; for, for many dayes she suffer'd not one glimps^e^ of Light to be seen in her Chamber more then what one single Taper afforded.

All the Concerns of the Kingdome she intrusted to *Barsarnes*'s care, leaving it to him likewise to prepare for my Princes Obsequies (continu'd *Mexaris*) which some ten dayes after his death were perform'd with the same state, and solemnity that *Achemenes*'s had been. The day of his Funu^e^erall⁵ being come; the streets were hung with black from the Palace to the place of Buriall, and no person permitted on pain of death to appear in the street that had not on the habit of a Mourner. The Hearse was cover'd with black Velvet, and the Horses with the same downe to the Ground; and both the He^a^rse and Horses adorn'd on every side with the Empieriall ^Imperiall^⁶ Armes. After his He^a^rse follow'd *Barsarnes*, and another Persian Prince bearing between them the Crowne, and Scepter, wreath'd about with black Cypress; after them came all the other Princes that were resident in Susa, two, and two on foot, their severall Chariots following in order according to their qualities next after the Queens (for though she was not in it, she commanded it should attend my Prince to his Grave). In this manner was he brought to the Tombe which was prepar'd for the reception of his body, where they left him to the enjoyment of a quiet repose after all his miseries.

The next day was *Phasellus* buri'd, but without that least shew of any Pompe, or Funu^e^rall⁷ solem^n^ities: but assoon as the Queen was in a condition to

---

⁴ The word "ceas'd" is underlined for deletion and "seiz'd" is inserted.
⁵ The word "funurall" is amended with "u" underlined and "e" inserted.
⁶ The word "Emperiall" is underlined for deletion and "Imperial" is inserted.
⁷ The word "Funural" is amended with "u" underlined and "e" inserted.

consider of anything, she gave order for a stately Monument to be erected for my Prince, which was neer finisht when I left Persia.

The night before my Deare Master di'd (after the Queen had left him) he call'd me to him, commanding and conjuring me by all the Love and Service I had for him to go in quest of you Madam (pursu'd he to *Artabella*) and never to cease my search till I had found you, and given you an account both of his misfortunes, and your owne. And assure that Excellent Princess (said he) that I dy as constant in my Friendship to her, as in my passion to *Oriana*; and that I hate *Phasellus* much more for his disloyalty to her, then his Infidelity to my selfe. Then calling for those Jewells, and that Gold which he had left, he took from among them a Bracelet of Diamonds (which the Princess *Juliana* his sister had given him the night before he left Rome) and presenting it to *Barsarnes* he beg'd him to accept and weare it for his sake; the rest he divided between *Tereus,* and my self, telling us it troubled him that Fortune would not suffer him to reward us with other recompences then those inconsiderable tryfles. For my part, I thought *Tereus* so well worthy of what my Master gave him, that had he given him too what he bestow'd on me, I should not have look'd on my Princes's bounty to him with [fol. 157ʳ] an envious eye.

The Queen the better to manifest her kindness to the memory of my Prince (continu'd *Mexaris*) express'd a singul<u>e</u>^a^r[8] respect to all those that had any way oblig'd him, or that she thought he had any affection for. She confirm'd *Barsarnes* in that Principality which *Achemenes* had given him, and confer'd on him diverse other honours; she took no advice but from him, nor could others obtain any Favour from her but by his mediation: and as he had the honour to possess the Queens favour in a higher degree then any other, so was he more worthy of it: for with that moderation did he still demeane himselfe in that high estate to which he was exalted, that he was not in the least puff'd up with it; but alwayes employ'd the credit he had with her for her advantage, or the benefit of her subjects (as a worthy Favourite ought to do) *Tereus,* and my selfe had both of us considerable Places in Court given us within a few dayes; but I soon after abandon'd mine, to accomplish what my Prince had enjoyn'd me.

The day before I intended to begin my Progress, I was accidentally talking with *Tereus,* in the Palacegate concerning it. But which way do you intend first to steere you[r] course (demanded he) or in what part of the world do you imagine to find the Princess *Artabella* in, I am perswaded (pursu'd he) she is not in Persia.

I am of your opinion (answer'd I) for that, but wheresoe're she is I must seek her out (if she be in the World to be found) or never end my search but with my life: I know I have undertaken a difficult taske, but were it yet more difficult it should not in the least dismay, or hinder me from performing the last service my Dearest Master impos'd upon me.

---

[8] The word "singular" is amended with "e" underlined and "a" inserted.

Whilst we were talking thus, I took notice of a man (whom by his Habit I knew to be a stranger) who stood earnestly looking on me, which moov'd me to ask him whether he had any business with me. That which I heard you say but now (answer'd he) induces me to believe you belong to *Phasellus*; which if you do, I intreat you favour me so farre as to help me to the speech of him.

I having a great desire to know what he had to say to him confirm'd him in his opinion; telling him it was impossible for him to speak with *Phasellus,* but if he had any business of concernment with him if he would intrust me with it, I would let him know it.

Pray tell him then (said he) the Princess *Artabella* is in Delphos.

Are you sure she is (repli'd I overjoy'd at this wellcome newes which I so little expected).

I think so (said he). I am sure she was when I came thence, which was not above ten dayes since.

Did you come from her to *Phasellus* (demanded I).

No (answer'd he) she sent me not, but one *Saparilla* who attends her, did.

Friend (said I) *Phasellus* is dead; and happie had it been for that Princess he had been so ere she had seen him; but I was just going to begin a Journey in quest of her, which for ought I know might have been endless, had you not thus happily come to enforme me of the place of her aboad. I then told him upon what designe I went to seek you that I might engage him the more freely to acquaint me with all he knew concerning you Madam (continu'd *Mexaris*). He then told me his name was *Eumetes*, and how it was in his Brothers ship that you had made an escape [fol. 157ᵛ] from Zarispe, as also what a lamentable condition you had been reduced too by Pirats, and how you had been carri'd to Delphos by the King thereof, and then been treated by him with all the respect due to your quality, and that you stay'd onely for y his returne to bring you back to Persia. I then carri'd *Eumetes* to my ~~Cha~~ Chamber, where I stay'd him till the next day, that being tw^o^o[9] far spent to begin our Journey.

I had certainly given the Queen this Intelligence (pursu'd *Mexaris*) had she been in Susa; for I could not but believe it would be most wellcome newes to her after she had lamented you as dead to be assur'd you were yet alive: but having much impair'd her health by her excessive Griefe, by the advice of her Phisicians (in hopes to recover it) she chang'd the Aire; removing to Elymais which is reputed to be the purest Aire, and the most healthy place in all Persia: but this Citty being many miles distant from Susa, I could not perswade *Eumetes* to stay my returne: for being (as he said) confin'd to a certaine time which was already expir'd, he was oblig'd to make all possible hast back again to Delphos lest Madam you might be come away ere his returne. I then consider'd if it would rejoyce the Queen to heare you were alive, it would much more rejoyce her to see

---

[9] The word "two" is amended with the "w" crossed out and "o" inserted.

you were soe; whereupon I resolv'd to depart with *Eumetes* the next day to waite
on you back to Persia. The fourth day after, we imbark'd, and had as prosperous
a Voyage as we could wish, landing here the thirteenth day after we set saile.

Mexaris having thus ended his sad story, *Artabella* gave him many thankes
for taking on him so great a trouble to oblige her; after which he took his leave
of her for that time, going along with *Saparilla* who carried him to some of
Alcanders Gentlemen who treated him with aboundance of kindness and civility.
When she had brought him to such good Company, she left him with them, and
return'd to the Princess her Mistress, whom she found reflecting on her owne
misfortunes, *Diomeds* mishape, and *Phasellus*'s ungratfull Infidelity to both.

But after some serious thoughts of these things, she fix'd her Eyes (being
wholy drowned in teares) on *Saparilla*. Ah (said she) tis onely unhappie *Artabella*
that has been the cause both of her owne misfortunes, and poor Prince *Lucius*'s
too; for had I not so blindly ty'd my heart to a fond dotage on *Phasellus*, I had
not (questionless) oppos'd my father^'s^ will, but given my selfe to that brave
Prince who would (perhaps) have found a satisfaction in this little beauty which
Phasellus so much disdain'd. Ah Foolish *Artabella* (continu'd she) how indiscreet
a choice didst thou make, in preferring so worthless a man, before two of the
bravest, and most Generous Princes in the World, whose noble passions were as
reall, as his was counterfeite: but although I have rejected those whom I could not
refuse without ingratitude, *Alcander* shall see, though I know not how to requite
his affection, yet I know how to punish my owne Ingratitude; which I will do, by
inflicting on my selfe a Pennance most severe: for I am resolv'd ne're to see Persia
more (that Land of my misfortunes) but I will fly from hence, into some desolate
and unfrequented place, where in the horrour of [fol. 158ʳ] some dismall Cave,
I'll spend the remainder of my miserable Life: there will I set till Death shall put
an end to my Laments, incessantly bewailing my owne Folly, and the misfortunes of my Dearest Friends. Ah now too well I see the truth of that prediction
foretold me by *Apollo*, since Divine Justice has made *Phasellus* punish on himselfe
his Ungratfull Friendship, and his Faithless Love: But by what way (pursu'd she)
can I repaire the loss of his Affection, and my owne which I have fool'd away so
long on One unworthy of it.

Methinkes (answer'd *Saparilla*) you need not Madam study much to find a
repe͟e^a^ration[10] for that Loss, ~~sinse~~ since Heaven seemes in requitall to proffer
you the affection of the Brave *Alcander*, a Prince so every way accomplish'd as
his equall cannot be found, since *Diomed* is gone, who onely could stand in com-
petition with him; what then should hinder you Madam (continu'd she) from
quit^t^ing that Resolution you lately made so prejudiceall to that Felicity you
may yet enjoy, and assuming one more reasonable, as well as Just: For pardon
me Madam if I say, you cannot without a high Injustice thinke of punishing on

---

[10] The word "rep̲e̲ration" is amended with "e" underlined for deletion and "a" inserted.

your selfe the offences of another. Because *Phasellus* abandon'd you (with a baseness beyond example) will you therefore be so unjust, and cruell to your selfe
to decline all the comforts of Life, and entombe your selfe ere you are dead, by
abandoning all society. No Madam (pursu'd she) rather thinke how you may
erect a Trophie of Felicity upon the ruines of your former Love; which you may
(undoubtedly) do, if you can but once resolve to make the Delphian King happie,
by conferring on him an affection you cannot but acknowledge him most worthy
of; since he has ador'd you with so pure, and perfect a Flame.

The Princess *Artabella* was so displeas'd with *Saparilla* for offering to perswade her to entertaine a second Love˙into her Bre^a^st (after the enduring so
many miseries as her first had procur'd her) as she turn'd away her head, commanding her not to speak a word more, for she was no longer able to lend an Eare
to a Discourse so offenc̲^s^ive[11] to her. All the rest of that day she stir^r^'d not
out of her Chamber, but remain'd in a deep sadness, and a silence as great; making no other expressions of her Griefe then sighs, and teares which softly trickled
downe her Cheekes.

The Princess *Delizia* admiring she saw her not again that day, the next
morning after she had been with the King went to her, to e̲^i^nforme[12] herselfe
of the cause; but when she came to her, she perceiv'd she was dress'd in those
very Clothes she came into Del^ph^os in, which moov'd her to say to her. What
new misfortune has befallen you Deare *Artabella* that you put on again this sable
dress; or is it for poor *Alcanders* death that you weare this anticipated Mourning.

I hope (answer'd *Artabella*) I shall ne're have cause to put on black on that
account you mention'd last. No *Delizia* (continu'd she) tis my misforutnes (which
are such, as there is not any thinge that can render me more perfectly wretched
then I am) that have e̲^i^nduced[13] me once to put on a Habit su^i^table to my
mind: but to tell you how unhappie I am, I need say no more than that I have lost
Phasellus eternally.

How have you lost him (demanded *Delizia*) by Death, or Infidelity.

By both (answer'd *Artabella*) but you will think it strange if I assure you that
his death, and Infidelity to me, are the least occat̲^s^ions[14] of my sorrow; and
that I am much more concern'd for his Injuries to others, then to my selfe. But
set downe, [fol. 158^V^] Deere *Delizia* and I will tell you such a story as you shall
be amaz'd to heare.

With that she gave her in short a recitall of all *Phasellus*'s Villanie, which
having done, *Delizia* repli'd. You had reason to say I would be amaz'd at what
you had to tell me; indeed I am so, and that so much as I shall never think any

---

[11] The word "offenc̲ive" is amended with "c" underlined for deletion and "s" inserted.
[12] The word "e̲nforme" is amended with "e" underlined for deletion and "i" inserted.
[13] The word "e̲nduced" is amended with "e" underlined for deletion and "i" inserted.
[14] The word "occat̲ions" is amended with "t" underlined for deletion and "s" inserted.

thinge strange that I shall henceforth heare. But say *Artabella* (pursu'd she) can you retaine any spark of kindness for a man so base unextinguish'd in your heart.

I should count my selfe well worthy of my sufferings (answer'd she) if I had so poor, so meane a spirit as still to continue the least sentiments of passion for him who died without remorse for all those miseries he had heap'd on me. No *Delizia,* believe it, hatred Flames now within my heart as high as ever Love has done.

Both then (said *Celia*) continuing a while in silence, *Delizia* at last broke it in these words. Since the greatest Obstacle to *Alcander's* happiness is now remoov'd, and that you have no longer your Fidelity to oppose it with, permit me Deare *Artabella* (continu'd she) to implore your Favour for him; which you know I never did before, nor would not now, were I not sure you may (without the least fault) grant my su^i^te: for how deare soever the King my Brother is to me I would have suffer'd him to dye, and died my selfe to testifie that kindness I have for him, ere I would have open'd my Lips with a desire ^to obtain^ the least thing in his behalfe injurious to your Vertue: but now I trust, your Friendship will excuse me if I beg you to save my Brothers Life, since tis onely in your power to recall him from his Tombe to which he hastnes^ens^.

Though the Infidelity of *Phasellus* (repli'd *Artabella*) has disengag'd me from that affection I ought to have preserv'd inviolable to the last minute of my Life, had he been Faithfull to me, yet I know not any thing that can free me from what I owe my selfe, or set my heart so far at liberty to make a second choice; tis enough that I have once submitted to that tyran^n^ick passion, it would be too too much should I be twice conquered by it. If then you wish your Brothers Felicity, employ that power you have with him, to perswade him to give over all thoughts of forever of a person whose misfortune has rendred her most unworthy of him; and beg him Deare *Delizia* I beseech you to permit me to enjoy in quiet this poor forsaken heart, since tis impossible for me to part with it any more.

Ah cruell *Artabella* (cry'd *Delizia*) tis no longer of Fortune, but of you, I must complain, since tis on you *Alcanders* destiny does now depend; and in your power alone to create him the happiest of men; seeing he hast bounded all his happiness in your affection, which you cannot without the highest Ingratitude deny him, having no justifyable reason to the contrary; but admit you had, and that he were a person more indifferent to you then he is; yet sure if you have so reall a Friendship for me, as I have hitherto believ'd, you would a little do violence ^on^ your humour and inclination (especially when you may safely do it, without the least prejudice to your Vertue) rather then expose to death a Friend who loves you dearer then her selfe. Yes *Artabella*, for my sake methinkes you should mittigate somewhat [fol. 159^r^] of that severity which (I dare assure my selfe) that inviolable passion wherewith *Alcander* does adore you, would at length wholy divest you of, could he but live to continue it. But if you neither can, nor will crowne his affection with a mutuall one, yet I conjure you for my sake, shew him onely somuch kindness as may secure both him, and me from a death so certaine as nothing but your Favour can rescue us: for if he dies, I have vow'd to sacrifice my Life upon his Tombe; and then, you will be the cruell occa̲t^s^ion[15] not onely of *Alcanders* death, but of *Delizia's* too; and by that meanes deprive your selfe like-wise of the Faithfullest Friend, as well as of the most passionatest servant your Vertues (great as they are) can ere acquire you.

You are more cruell (repli'd *Artabella*) then you think me, to heape more misery on my oppressed Soule. O *Delizia* why do you terrifie me with such a Fatall Vow, I will do all that I am able to preserve you that Deare Brother, whom my ill Fate (rather then that cruelty you unjustly accuse me of) exposes to death: but to do it, would you have me turne dissembler. No *Delizia* I am so much *Alcanders* Debter for that noble passion he expresses for me, that I cannot without the highest ingratitude imaginable, repay it with a counterfeit kindness; allow me then at least some little intervall, some little time to race [erase] out of my Soule, the Ideas of my former Love, before I entertain any new impressions: nor will it be so easie a taske as haply you imagine, to perswade my heart (after so cruell, and injurious a treatment as it receiv'd from *Phasellus*) to become anoth-ers, le^a^st it should be expos'd to new, and greater sufferings; not that I ques-tion *Alcanders* Vertue, but doubt my owne ill Fate; and the malice of my Starres, which have hitherto had so strang^e^ an influence on me, that I have reason to feare, (if it be in their power) they will change the Kings Inclinations (as I am perswaded they did *Phasellus's*) on purpose to make my unhappiness compleat: for I really think, *Phasellus* once was noble, once was generous and Faithfull to his Friend; but when he once became mine, all that was great, and noble in him abandon'd him, and he became wicked, that I might be unhappie. But in the meane time, you may give *Alcander* this assurance, that if ever I am capable of a second affection, it shall be onely for himselfe: and that I will never prefer any other before him upon no account whatever, whilst I live.

Exceedingly was *Delizia* rejoyced that she had obtain'd so much from *Arta-bella*, and thinking it imprudence to press her further at that time, left her (with as much Joy in her Looks, as she late had sadness in her heart) to go to the King, whom she found in the same weak condition wherein she left him. After she had sate silently a while by him, as it were to consider in what manner she should let him understand she was not ignorant of his Love, she spak^e^ to him thus. The little confidence you have in me sir (said she) has not been able to deter me from taking a most perticuler interest in that misfortune of yours, whereof you refus'd to acquaint me with the cause. I know it for a certain truth, though not from you (but meerly from bare conjectures at the first, which have been since confirm'd by many pregnant testimonies that [fol. 159^v^] my observation has furnish'd me with) that those mortall disquiets under which you languish, has no other origi-nall then your passion for the Princess *Artabella* and though I cannot promise

---

[15] The word "occa̲tion" is amended with the "t" underlined for deletion and an "s" inserted.

you an absolute felicity; by engaging you shall obtain a reciprocall affection from her, yet this can assure you, you may repeall your banish'd hopes, since you have now no Rivall to oppose you[r] happiness; for *Phasellus* lives not, nay more then that, he is deservedly dead too in *Artabellas* esteeme; and has left her heart free for you to take possession of, if you can but make your title to it good by a Fidelity himself was uncapable of.

Ah *Delizia* (cry'd the King) what do you meane, you may by this delusion a while delay, but cannot hinder my death a minute after I find you have deceiv'd me.

If I have said ought with a design to delude you (repli'd *Delizia*) inflict on me the severest punishment you can invent: but Sir I tell you nothing but the reall truth, of which I am my selfe convinced; and if you are not so, it shall not be my fault, since I will e^i^nforme[16] you of all I know concerning *Phasellus* if you please but to give me the hearing.

Most willingly Deare Sister (said he) for I can never have too great an assurance of such an unexpected Joy.

The Princess then in short told him all that she had heard from *Artabella*, as also the discourse she had with her concerning him, and the promise she had made her, never to prefer any before him in her choice; all which he hearkned too, with a farre greater satisfaction then ^he^ believ'd a few minutes before, he could ever be capable of; instantly giving over all desires of dying, and on the contrary embraceing all meanes conduceing to his recovery, with as much willingness as he late with obstinacy oppos'd it.

To see (pursu'd *Celia*) how great an Influence the Mind has o're the Body; for in a few dayes after the Princess brought him those Joyfull tydings he began to mend, and in a little space more, regain'd so much strength as to waite on the Princess *Artabella*, who could not but express a great deall of Joy for his recovery, though she was sensible how much she should be persecuted both by him and *Delizia*; nor was she deceiv'd, for the hopes *Alcander* now had, that his passion would not be forever unsuccessfull, daily augmented it, which rendred his importunities proportionable to the greatness of his Flame; yet were his Addresses still attended with so profound a respect, as she could find no just reason to be offended with them. But not being able to think of coming neer that Rock where she had so lately scap'd a wrack, and being no longer capable of defending herselfe against the Kings u^i^ncessant[17] importunities, with all the reasons, and perswasions she could use to enduce him to change his passion into Friendship, she bethought herselfe of an expedient which she resolv'd to have recourse too, in hopes it might be a meanes to move him to lay aside his affection without a further prejudice to him; but if it wrought not that effect she wish'd, but that (contrary to her expectation) he still persever'd in it, she then determin'd to requite

---

16 The word "enforme" is corrected with the "e" underlined and an "i" inserted.

17 The word "uncessant" is amended with "u" underlined and "i" inserted.

it by intirely resigning to him that heart, which his Faithless Predecessor had ungratfully [fol. 160ʳ] relinquish'd.

This being ~~ones~~ once resolv'd on, she arose one morning exceeding early; and calling for Pen, Inke and Paper she wri̲t^ote^[18] two letters; when she had done she caused her Chariot to be made ready, pretending to *Saparilla* that she was going to the Temple to enquire something more pe^a^rticul̲e^a^r^l^y[19] concerning her destiny; and sending for *Mexaris* to go with her, as she was going downe the sta^i^res she gave *Saparilla* one of the Letters, charging her if she did not returne within two houres to deli~~e~~ver it to the Princess. Assoon as she was without the Palace-gate she commanded the Charioteer to drive to the Hill Cynthus.

This Hill (pursu'd *Celia*) stands some halfe a mile distant from this Citty, and on the top of it stands a House dedicated to *Diana;* where certain Virgins devoted to that Goddess devoutly spend their dayes in honour of her. The Lawes of this Nunnery are, that any of those that come in, have seven yeares of Freedome (as they call it) in which space, they have liber^t^y to depart when half that time is expir'd, and at the seventh yeares end they have the same priviledge but if they stay beyond that time, they are not suffer'd to go out, but are confin'd to reside their whole lives there. To this Place *Artabella* directed her steps after she alighted out of the Chariot, being lead up the hill by *Mexaris,* but when she came to the Gate, she told him she would no longer detain him there, since she was resolv'd never to returne into her owne Country, but to lead the remainder of her miserable dayes in Delphos.

But if you go back to Persia, take with you this Letter I entreat you (continu'd she, giving him the other she had writ^t^en) and present it from me to *Oriana,* I have at large declar'd in it the reason of my stay, which I trust she will not be dissatisfi'd with; and desiring him to tell *Saparilla* if she could be contented to lead such a recluse life as she intended to lead she should come to her on the morrow, she bid him farewell, wishing him a Fortune worthy his Fidelity to his Prince. Assoon as she had acquainted those who kept the Gate what designe had brought her thither, she was instantly admitted in, which she no sooner was, but *Mexaris* return'd to the Chariot which waited for *Artabella,* in which he went back to Court, and deliever'd his Message to *Saparilla* who was extreamly troubled because the Princess her Mistress had not permitted her to go with her; however she resolved to follow her on the morrow; whereupon she went immediatly to the Princess, and presented her the Letter she was to deliver her (with teares in her eyes) which *Delizia* took notice of, yet fear'd to aske her the reason of her trouble; but taking the Letter and hastily opening it, she found it contain'd these Words

---

[18] The word "wri̲t" is corrected with "it" underlined for deletion and "ote" inserted.

[19] The word "pe̲rticul̲e̲ry" is amended with "e'" underlined twice and "a" is inserted each time; "l" is also inserted.

The Unfortunate Artabella
To the most Excellent Princess Delizia

     If your Friendship Madam can but extend so far as to pardon my uncivill
departure; I shall never need a greater confirmation of it: time will assure you it
was no disaffection to Alcander made me chuse this retreat, but rather my feares
[fol. 160ᵛ] *Deare Delizia that your importunities would have prov'd too potent*
to be resisted, though both reason, and discretion tell me I ought never to yield to
them, having so lately learn'd by sad experience the little trust there is to be repos'd
in those who make the largest proffessions of Fidelity. I have no reason to question
the reallity of your Generous Brothers Love, I must needs say, nor had I any to
doubt Phasellus's till absence prov'd it to be counterfeit; which tryall if Alcander
can withstand, and that I am once as thoroughly convinc'd of his Constancy, as
I am perswaded of his present affection, I shall no longer refuse to gratifie your
Friendship, and the Kings passion, then till the time wherein I may be permitted
to leave this place: but tis my hopes, and shall be my constant wishes, that ere that
time be halfe run out, the King will discover the errour he commits against his
Judgment, in cherishing a passion for One unworthy of it, and find some fairer,
and more deserving Object to fix his thoughts on then the most Unhappie

                                              Artabella

Delizia having read this Letter with an extreame trouble, as well knowing how grievously the King would resent [feel] *Artabella*s departure, told *Saparilla* she could not have believ'd the Princess her Mistress would so unkindly have left her without so much as once bid^d^ing her farewell. But pray tell me (said she) whether tis she is retir'd; this *Saparilla* e̲^i^nform'd[20] her of, as also the permission she had sent her by *Mexaris* to come to her the next day.

The King having (according to his usuall custome) been to waite on *Artabella*, but not finding her in her owne Appartments came to *Delizias*, supposing she might be there; where looking about, and not seeing her, he ask'd *Saparilla* where she was; who not knowing whether she had best tell him the truth or no, was so long ere she answer'd, that the Princess repli'd, she is gone this morning to *Dianas* Nunnery.

How (cry'd *Alcander* in a strange amaze) to *Diana's* Nunnery; upon what account.

This will e̲^i^nforme[21] (answered *Delizia*) giving him *Artabellas* Letter, which he having intentively perus`d, gave it her again; and remaining a great while in a penc̲^s^ive[22] silence, his mind being confus'd with sundery resolutions; but at last turning his eyes upon the Princess.

---

   [20] The word "e̲nform'd" is amended with "e" underlined for deletion and "i" inserted.
   [21] The word "e̲nforme" is amended with the first "e" underlined for deletion and "i" inserted.
   [22] The word "penc̲ive" is corrected with "c" underlined for deletion and "s" inserted.

Ah *Delizia* (cry'd he) how unjust is *Artabella* to punish me for the offences of another; but great as those sufferings are to which she does expose me, I shall undergoe them without regret if she will but keep her word, in giving me at last that glorious recompence she seemes to promise if I continue unchang^e^able. I will not dye to witness my affection (as I late resolv'd) but I will live on purpose to let her see, my Constancy is proofe against both time, and absence; nor shall that Severity wherewith she treates me once shake that immov^e^able resolution I have made to adore her to the last minute of my breath, or Life. But since I know, tis impossible to get her from that Place where [fol. 161ʳ] she has taken Sanctuary against my Love, till she herself vouchsafe to quit it: tell her *Saparilla* (continu'd he) tell my Deare (though cruell) *Artabella,* that since she has thought fit to exile^banish^²³ me her presence for the tryall of my Constancy, I will likewise banish my selfe from Delphos, and am resolv'd to spend the time of my Exile, in visiting the Courts of all the Princes in Asia, where possibly I may behold the greatest beauties that the World can boast: that I may thereby convince her, that a heart once vanquish'd by her eyes, can dread no other Conquerour.

Nor was this Resolution of his to be alter'd, by any thing that *Delizia* could say to divert him from it; for constituting her Queen Regent till his returne, he began his Travells within a few dayes after, leaving the Princess in so great a griefe as she had ne're been sensible of till now, that she saw herselfe necessitated to undergoe so long a separation from a Brother she had ever lov'd more dearely then herselfe; but Patience was her onely remedy, and to that she had recourse.

Alcander took with him a considerable ^quantity^ of Gold and a great many rich Jewells to defray his expences till his returne, but being unwilling to be taken for what he was, he put on a Disguise, taking onely *Ferintus,* and one Gentleman more with him. The first Voyage he made was into Persia, where he saw Queen *Oriana*: but could see nothing in her (as he afterwards protested) that could in the least excuse *Phasellus*'s change, but (as he said) he believ'd, it was the dazling splendor of her Crowne, rather then her beauty which had blinded him. From thence he went into Media, to the Court of King Tygranes, where he beheld *Verania* (the Kings yo^u^nger Daughter) a most delicate, and beautious Princess. From thence he took his Journey into Cap^p^adocia, thence he went into Cilicia, then into Armenia, where he made a longer aboad then in any of those other Courts he visited; being infinitly taken with the conversation of King *Tyribasus*'s Sister, the Princess *Piramena,* who had a Face so full of Innocence, and a deportment so sweetly obliging, that he found more difficulty (as he afterwards confest) in defending himself from her assaults then any other of those Faire Ones he saw, whose beauties carried such a commanding power, as if they would compell all hearts to do them homage: but so indissolubly were his

---

²³ The word "exile" is underlined for deletion and "banish" inserted.

affections knit to *Artabella* by the strong Chaines of an unshaken Fidelity, that, all that these Beauties could produce in him, was onely admiration, and esteeme. From Armenia, he went into Parthia, where he saw the so much admir'd *Lucaria*, who had been su'd for by six of the greatest Princes of the World, before she had attain'd her fourteenth yeare. Thence went he into Thrace where he had a sight of the Princess *Orithia*, who was reputed the Wonder of the World for Wit, and Beauty.

Here 'twas he put an end to his Travells, returning from thence to Delphos, whence he had been absent full three yeares. Though he made but a short stay in any of those Places thorow which he pass'd, yet stay'd he long enough to procure the Pictures of all those severall Beauties he had seen, causing them to be taken by the most skillfull Arte^i^sts²⁴ [fol. 161ᵛ] in the Kingdomes; onely *Orianas* Picture he could not possibly procure although he endeavour'd it very much. Being safely arriv'd at Delos^phos^²⁵ he was wellcom'd with all the demonstrations of a reall Joy, by all in generall, but more especially by the Princess; whose Joy nothing could equall but the sorrow she suffer'd at his departure.

The first question the King ask't his Sister was, whether she had seen Artabella since he went (for that prive^i^ledge²⁶ was allow'd to those who were not professed Votaries, that they might one day in every yeare, be permitted to see any Virgin of their acquaintance that would favour them with a visit) to which *Delizia* answer'd, that she had seen her as often as she could be suffer'd.

And is she still determin'd to be inexorable to my affection (said the King) and may I not yet hope to be happie in hers.

I dare not promise you any thing (repli'd she) lest I deceive you with vain hopes, but if I may freely speak my thoughts, I really thinke you will have no cause to complain of her cruelty any more.

Ah Deare Sister (cry'd he embracing her) may I credit what you say.

I do not desire Sir you should (said she) till you have spoke with *Artabella* your selfe.

The three yeares and a halfe being now expir'd since she put herself amongst *Dianas Nunns*, *Alcander* sent the Princess to try if she could perswade her to returne to Court again; for he knew if he had gone himselfe he should not have been suffer'd to speak with her. Readily did *Delizia* embrace the Kings command, in going to her, and had the good Fortune to work so powerfully on her, by the assurance she gave her of an *Alcanders* constant perc^s^everance²⁷ in his

---

²⁴ The word "Artests" is amended with "e" underlined and "i" inserted.

²⁵ The word "Delos" is corrected with "os" underlined for deletion and "phos" inserted.

²⁶ The word "priveledge" is corrected with "e" underlined for deletion and "i" inserted.

²⁷ The word "perc^s^everance" is corrected with "c" underlined for deletion and "s" inserted.

passion, that finding she could no longer refuse to recompence it without deserv-edly purchaceing to herselfe the Epith<u>ite</u>^et^28 of Ungratfull, she at last con-sented to quit her retirement; which she did, after she had chang'd her Habit, and taken Leave of the Governess, and the rest of that Society, who could not part from her without much lamenting the loss of so sweet a Companion.

About the time that the King suppos'd his Sister might be coming back, he commanded his Chariot to be made ready, that he might go meet her, in hopes he might with her also meet the adored Mistress of his Heart; and causing himselfe to be carried to the foot of the Hill, he there alighted, and begining to walk it up, he espi'd at a good distance, some Woemen coming downe the Hill over against him, whom he quickly knew to be *Delizia*, *Artabella*, and *Saparilla*; this so agree-able sight made him hasten to meet them; which he no soon did, but he threw himself at *Artabellas* Feet, and embraceing her knees with a transported Joy, he let her see his passion was rather augmented then diminish'd since he saw her.

My Divinest Princess (said he) what do you determine of me; may I yet hope, or must I still dispaire of a Felicity I know I am unworthy of yet cannot cease to beg. My passion Madam (if possible) is greater now then ever, and for Fidelity, I dare vie with Constancy it selfe.

It is not just (repli'd she, giving him her hand to raise him up) that so noble a constancy as you have shewn, should perpetually remaine unrewarded. No, Generous Prince (pursu'd she) though I have hitherto [fol. 162ʳ] retain'd power enough to resist the testimonies of your Love, yet have I none to defend me any longer from the Demonstrations of your Fidelity, tis those alone that have o'recome me, and taken so large a possession of my heart, as none could ever plead a Fairer title to it then your merit gives you: and though I have found so high a content, so perfect a satisfaction in my solitude, that I would freely quit the Empier of the World were I possest of it, rather then abandon my retirement, yet have I chosen to forgoe it (how pleasing soever it has been to me) rather then I would lye under the just imputation of Ingratitude.

Whilst *Artabella* spake thus, the King was even ravish'd with Joy, and taking one of her faire hands on which he printed many ardent kisses, he cry'd out even in an Extacie Ah my Dearest Princess how gloriously have you recompenced me for all my sufferings; what can I be ever able to do that may deserve so blest a condition as this whereto your goodness has rais'd me.

If you count it so (said *Artabella*) you may by the same way you took to attaine it, preserve your selfe in it; for as not anything but your Fidelity could have given you an interest in me, so nothing but Inconstancy can deprive you of it.

Then Madam I shall be forever happie (he repli'd) for since my passion is now tryumphant over your severity, and that my Constancy has been hitherto

---

28 The word "epith<u>ite</u>" is corrected with "ite" underlined and "et" inserted.

invincible when I had little or no hope for its foundation, it cannot now but eternally continue so.

By this time they were come to their Chariots, and the Princess to oblige the King her Brother took *Saparilla* with her, leaving *Alcander* to go alone with *Artabella,* that he might have the greater Freedome to entertain her with the assurances of his passion, of which he gave her so many convinceing testimonies, as she repented she had expos'd him to such tedious sufferings for the tryall of his Love; and in fine, gave him as intire an interest in her affections as he could wish.

And certainly (continu'd *Celia*) Love never made a perfecter Union of two hearts then now; for whereas the passions of Amorists usually take their rise from Fancy, theirs had reason for its Foundation, on which it rais'd the Structure of a love so lasting, as had their Lives been lengthned to Ages, it never had admitted the least diminution. The King being now al^l^ow'd a freer converse with his Princess, daily made such new discoveries of the beauties of her mind, as made his happiness (in his opinion) transcend all that the most happie persons ere enjoy'd, by knowing how great a share he had in the heart of her who was Mistress of such rare perfections.

One day, as they were walking in a Gallery which Joyn'd to her Appartment, she took notice of certain Pictures which hung there, which she had never seen ~~there~~ before; and viewing them very heedfully a good while, she at last ask'd the King whose Pictures they were, or whether they were onely Fancies.

No Madam (answer'd he) they are not Fancies, but the reall Resemblances of certaine Princesses fam'd thorow the World for their beauties, which has gain'd them many Adorers; but they are such as never saw my Princess, for if they had, doubtless they would as well as I thinke nothing lovely in comparisson of her.

Though I cannot pretend to the least of those incomparable beauties those Princesses so plenti^e^iously[29] possess, (*Artabella* modestly [fol. 162ᵛ] repli'd) yet I confess I should be very well satisfi'd to appeare such in your eyes as you perswade me; but I beseech you Sir tell me perticulerly their names, and who they be.

That Lady which hangs the lowest (said the King) is the Princess *Elusina,* Daughter to the King of Cilicia. The next her, who has on her head a Murrion shaded with White Feathers, and a La^u^nce in her hand, is the Princess *Timandra* the King of Cap^p^adocias Daughter; by her Mother desended from *Thalestris* Queen of the Amazones, and therefore I caus'd her to be drawn in an Amazonian garbe.

In my opinion (said *Artabella*) you could not have given her a more becoming Dress; for her beauty having in it something Masculine, her habit is the more proper, and agreeable. But who is that (continu'd she) whose Eyes, and Haire are so delicately black as nothing can equall but the purity of her Complexion, which

---

[29] The word "plenteously" is corrected with the "i" underlined and "e" inserted.

is so fine a mixture of Red, and White as I never saw any thing yet comparable to it.

She is *Orithia* (answer'd he) Daughter to the King of Thrace, who is no less admir'd for her wit, then beauty.

She may indeed be term'd the Wonder of the World (repli'd *Artabella*) as I have heard she is esteem'd, if her inward perfections equall but her externall graces.

The next below her (went on *Alcander*) is *Verania*, the youngest of the King of Medias Daughters, who falls not much short of the Fairest ^of those^ with whom she is placed. And she whom you see Madam (pursu'd he) with the Crownes at her Feet (whereon she seemes to look with disregard) is the King of Parthias Daughter, the so much admir'd *Lucaria*, who young as she is, has had the glory to extend her conquest over the hearts of no less then six puissant Princes, who have at her Feet resign'd their liberty, proffering for their ransome each of them his Crown; but amongst them all you cannot see *Alcanders* there: for as great, and excellent as her beauty accounted, I yet can boast I serve one more transcendent.

Leave off your Flatteries *Alcander* (said *Artabella*) and think not to perswade me that your passion has so far blinded you as not to see the advantage that Princess has over me; but if you are so vain as to equall me with her, you cannot but acknowledge the other (whose name you have not told me yet) excells not onely me, but all that the Earth can shew of Lovely; for sure the hand of Nature never drew anything so exactly prety, as that sweet innocent Face.

Did you behold the Princess *Artabella* with those eyes wherewith I do (repli'd he) you would questionless Madam have the same opinion of her as I have, which obliges me not onely to prefer her before the Princess *Piramena* (as I do) but all the Beauties that the World containes. Yet this I will confess, that had not my heart been prepossesst, I should have found it no easie task to have defended it from her asaults; and certainly if it had been possible for anything to have rivall'd you in my passion, or startled my unalterable Fidelity, the Charmes of her Conversation had gone the neerest to the performance of such a Miracle; but all that ever her rare perfections produced in me was onely an assurance [fol. 163ʳ] I gain'd by the knowledge of her who own'd them, that my Constancy was invincible.

Tis meerly your Vertue, not any worth in me (said *Artabella*) that has oblig'd you to so generous a Constancy as will render you justly famous to succeeding Ages; and will questionless ^invite^ all Vertuous Lovers to make you their Pattern, striving to imitate what they can ne're transcend.

The Princess *Delizia* coming in that instant, chang'd the discourse to other theames: but nothing now was wanting to render *Alcander*'s happiness as perfect as Felicity it selfe could make it (since he saw himself securely enthron'd in the Heart of his Adored Princess) save only the consummation of all his Joys which remain'd to be compleated by *Hymen;* for which when he had once obtain'd *Arta-*

bellas consent, his Nuptialls were no longer deffer'd then was requisite for the preparation for so grand a solemnity.

All the Nobles, and Ladies of the Kingdome (not onely those in Delphos, but all likewise that inhabited any of the adjacent Islands) were summoned to Delos^phos^[30] to attend the Nuptialls of their King; the day for the solemnizing where of being come, his Marriage was cellibrated with as much state as Magnificence it selfe could invent. The Princess *Artabella* was dresst that day in a Goun[e] of White Velvet so richly embroidred with silver, as the ground of it could hardly be discern'd what it was. Her haire wound round with Ropes of Pearle (the fairest the Orient ever saw) and bound up in the forme of a Coronet, on the top whereof was fastned a Jewell of inesteemable value all of Rubies, and Emralds; about her neck she wore a rich Carkanet of Diamonds which *Alcander* had presented her with not long before; but the other Jewells were her owne which she had brought out of Persia with her: nor was the Kings Habit anything inferior to hers for richness, his Clothes being silver Cloth of Tyssue, on the which he wore a loose Robe, which was fastned before with two Diamond Clasps, and reach'd from his shoulders trayling many yards after him on the ground.

The Princess being ready, the King came to fetch her from her Chamber to lead her ^to the^ Chariot wherein she was to be carried to the Temple. The Chariot which she rode in was cover'd with thine [thin] Plates of Silver, curiously cut into Flowers, and drawne by six white Horses, cover'd with cloth of silver, with Harness su^i^table to it. One each side ran Foure Pages attir'd in White Saten^sattin^[31] richly laced with silver: but the Chariot in which the King rode was all enamel'd Blew, stud^d^ed with Starres of Gold; the furniture of it being Watched [Watchet] Velvet embroidred in like manner; a like number of Pages to attend him as *Artabella* had, in a Livery of Watched [Watchet] Saten^ti^[32] laced with Gold.

They were no sooner come without the Palace Gates ere they were met by the Priests of *Apollo* (in their Robes, wearing on their heads wreathes of Laurell) who were come to waite on them to the Temple, to which they led them the way, going on before the Kings Chariot two and two in order, singing with curious Voices, an Hymeneus, or Marriage Song. Being come to the outward Gate of the Temple they all alighted, *Alcander* going first, was led by the Princess *Delizia,* and the Princess *Beltizera* (Daughter to his Uncle Prince *Cleophantus*) his Traine being carri'd up by six Pages of [fol. 163ᵛ] honour appointed for that purpose. Then came the Princess *Artabella,* led by *Anaxiles,* and *Nearchus* Brothers to *Beltizera,* being follow'd by four and twenty of Virgins, of the noblest Families

---

[30] The word "Delos" is corrected with "os" underlined for deletion and "phos" inserted.

[31] The word "saten" is underlined for deletion and "sattin" is inserted.

[32] The word "saten" is corrected with "e" underlined for deletion and "ti" inserted.

in the Kingdome, attir'd all a like in cloth of Silver; six of the Fairest of them (amongst whom *Saparilla* was one) carried up her Train. In this manner enter'd they the Temple, where *Alcander* and *Artabella* mutually gave their Faith to each other, having their Hands united by *Flaminius* the chiefest of the Priests; where, after having receiv'd his Benediction, and a prophetick promise of much happiness to befall them, *Alcander* took off his Crowne and set it on *Artabella*s head, in token that she was now his Queen; which she taking off again, and kissing it, with much respect return'd it back to the King.

This Ceremony done, in the same equipage as they came, they return'd to the Palace, where all things were prepar'd with a su^i^table grandure, their meat being usher'd up by the Musick of severall Wind Instruments, which continu'd playing all the while they were at Dinner; but that being ended, those louder soundes gave place to ~~straines~~ softer strains, from Instruments more sweet. The diversion for the rest of that day was a Mask presented with much curiosity by some of *Alcanders* servants; after which a Ball began, which lasted till the Night was far advanced, summoning them to rest; which after they had participated of a Banquet, the most profuse, and costly one that ere was seen, the Virgins convey'd the Bride to her Chamber, where they disrob'd her of her rich Attire, and having laid her into her Brideall Bed, they retir'd, leaving the Roome free for the Illustrious Bridegroom who came in soon after to assume to himself that priviledge which *Hymen* had that day confer'd on him. The next day ^renew'd^ their entainments with Maskes, and Dancings which lasted for the space of thirty dayes; which time expir'd, every one that had been assembled thither, took their leaves of the King, and his beautei^o^us Consort, leaving them in the plenary possession of the highest, and most perfect Felicity that ever Mortalls enjoy'd. Nor was *Alcander*'s passion like that of other mens, which usually ceases when once they have enjoy'd the Object of their desires, degenerating into a kind of indifferent Love, which hardly merits the name of affection; but his still continu'd with the same ardour as when it first began, till cruell Death made a divorse between those Hearts which nothing else could separate.

A year and a half being expir'd since their marriage, the Queen brought into the World a Daughter (the same pursu'd *Celia* who is now our Queen) of whose beauty I need give you no discription, your owne Eyes Madam (said she to *Arthenia*) better enforming you of her admirable perfections then I can. About a yeare after *Ermillia* was born, the Queen was deliever'd of a Son, to whom she gave a Persian name, calling him *Orsodates*. Never was anything beheld so lovely as this young Prince (unless the Faire *Ermillia* might be said to equall him) for all that was admirable both in *Alcander* and *Artabella* was to be seen in [fol. 164^r^] him, with so perfect a resemblance of both as was scarce to be believ'd. When he was about seven yeares of age, he was sent to be educated in the Persian Court, that being brought up there, he might be perfectly acquainted with the Laws and Customes of a People he might one day come to rule, if *Oriana* still perc^s^ever'd[33] in her resolution of living perpetually a Virgin. The Queen of Persia having alwayes had an intire Friendship for *Artabella*, receiv'd *Orsodates* with a most tender affection, which she testifi'd by the care she took in his education, caus-ing the World to be sought for Masters to instruct him in all noble, and excellent qualities which it was requisite he should be skill'd in. With the like care was the Princess *Ermillia* bred up in Delphos being to succeed her Father by a Custome we have here (which I believe pursu'd *Celia* is not to be found in any Kingdome of the World but this) which gives the scepter in succession to the eldest Child, prefer^r^ing the Daughter before the Son, if she be born first.

   Queen *Artabella* considering the many miseries, and misfortunes she had undergone by meanes of a conceal'd affection to an unknown person, and being perswaded that if *Phasellus* had been of Royall birth he could not have been guilty of such base, degenerate, and ignoble things; and with all thinking 'twas possible *Ermillia* might be in danger to run the like misfortunes as she herself had done, if care were not taken to prevent it: that the like ill Fate therefore might not hap-pen to her, or any of her Posterity, she prevail'd with the King to establish that Law which prohibits all Strangers, or Unknown persons from coming within the Palace, or any Place belonging to it; as Gardens, or Walkes, or that Park (wherein we were hunting that Morning we met with you *Arthenia* continu'd she which is likewise within the precincts of the Palace) without speciall leave from the King, or Queen then reigning; which after they have obtain'd they change their habit (of what Nation or Country soever they are) into such as is worn here (for so they are injoyn'd by their Warrant) and by that they are known to be priviledg'd persons. None are excepted in this Law save onely Princes, and Ambassadours because they represent the persons of those Princes from whom they are sent; but though they are in their owne persons al^l^ow'd this liberty, none that come with them are, no not so much as any of their Attendants, till such time as they have given a perticuler account what they are to an Officer deputed for that pur-pose; nor are any but Princes suffer'd to come into the presence of the Queens, or Princesses of this Kingdome unless by any unavoidable accident, except they have Concerns of high consequence to e^i^nform[34] them of, which in the pres-ence of six Witnesses they must declare; otherwise on pain of death they are to hold no conferrence with them. This Law being thus dictated by the Queen, was in like manner enacted by the consent of the King and his Councell, and has ever since remain'd inviolate, none infringing the least perticuler of it.

   Never had *Artabelia* any disaster to check that perfect happiness she enjoy'd after she was Queen of Delphos, nor the least discontent, till she was constrain'd [fol. 164ᵛ] to part from the Princess *Delizia*, who two yeares after the King her

---

   [33] The word "perᴄevered" is corrected with the "c" underlined for deletion and "s" inserted.
   [34] The word "ᴇnform" is corrected with "e" underlined for deletion and "i" inserted.

Brothers marriage, was herself likewise married to the Prince of Cypr^us^ess. About that time also was *Saparilla* marri'd to *Ferintus* with the consent of the King, and the Queen her Mistress, from which marriage (went on *Celia*) I had the honour to proceed, and no sooner was I capable of it but I was given to the Princess for a Companion, as divers other young Ladies were; but of them all I believe I may say without Vanity, or Ostentation, that I have still been so happie as to possess her Favour in the highest degree. *Serastes*'s services were not forget, nor yet *Eumetus*'s neither; for *Serastes* was by *Alcander* made Admirall of all his Ships, and his Brother ViceAdmirall. Many yeares did the ~~Queen~~ King and his Faire Queen live in a Felicity none could equall, till at length, Death, envious of their happie state, made a short Divorce between them, taking *Artabella* from her Deare *Alcander*; but so sadly did he resent [feel] that disunion that he liv'd but six dayes after her; and was (as he had commanded) entomb'd in the same Monument with her. After which, *Ermillia* was crown'd Queen, since which time tis now nigh two years. Thus Dear *Arthenia* (said *Celia*) I have given you an exact account of the misfortunes, and succeeding happiness of our late Queen.

You have indeed (repli'd *Arthenia*) for which favour I do most humbly thanke you; and must acknowledge the relation you have give[n] me of the Life of the Illustrious Queen does suffcently justifie the reasonableness of that Opinion you owne in the begin^n^ing of her story: for sure no One could have more cause to dispaire of happiness then *Artabella* had, and yet I find she ended her dayes in so perfect a Felicity as left her no reason to complain of Fortunes severity, or unkindness: but yet from her example I can derive to my selfe but little hope, since I have known some who ne're knew a period of their miseries (and perticulerly *Ianthe*, who from her Cradle to her Grave was never happie, but as she liv'd (so it seemes) she died the most unfortunate of Woemen as *Ambracia* can testifie who knew her from her Childhood) and therefore have more reason to feare a like Fate attends me then to hope the contrary. But however (pursu'd she) since Dispaire is the worst of ills, I'll not be guilty of it; nor dare I indeed charge Fortune with my greatest sufferings, but rather my owne Folly; for I must do her the Justice to confess she has oft proffer'd to make me happie, had I not willfully refus'd it, and obstinatly courted my owne ruine.

You do well to resolve against Dispair (said *Celia*) seeing it may render you more miserable, but can avail you nothing. But Good *Arthenia* (continu'd she) oblige me so far as to let me know the story of *Ianthe's* mishaps.

That I would most willingly ^said *Arthenia*^ but since *Ambracia* can more exactly then I enforme you of them, I'll send for her who will I am sure (at my request) gratifie your desire more fully then I can, and may perhaps acquaint you with those things whereof I my selfe am Ignorant; being you [fol. 165ʳ] were altogether a stranger to her.

To this proposall *Celia* having consented, *Arthenia* was just about to send but was prevented by *Praxentia's* coming in, who brought her word *Ermillia* desir'd she would returne to Court if she were able; this summons she no sooner heard, but she obey'd, going immediatly back with *Praxentia* to the Queen into whose presence she no sooner came, then with all due respects she render'd her thankes for that concerne she had exprest for her Indisposition, and princely care she had been so graciously pleas'd to take for her recovery in termes that spake sufficently the deep sense she had of her Royall Favours.

It rejoyces me very much (said the Queen) to see you so well again; and if it may be without a prejudice to you I now desire to heare the conclusion of your adventures. I confess I would willingly have dispenc^s^ed[35] with giving you this trouble so soon, but that *Gentillus* here (pursu'd she pointing to him) tells me his occat^s^ions[36] are so urgent for his departure as will not permit him to stay above a day or two longer, and I was very desirous I confess to oblige him with the knowledge of your stories period, as he has been acquainted with the begin^n^ing.

My obligations Madam (she repli'd) are so exceedingly great both to your Majesty and this noble Lord, as I can never think my Debt sufficently discharg'd though I gave my Life for the payment of it; and therefore I should never value a thing so inconsiderable as the impairing of my health, did I believe speaking much might do it; but thankes to Heaven and your Majesty I find my self so well as I do not in the least apprehend any prejudice by it; so setting downe upon certain Cushions which were laid for her at *Ermilias* Feet (who would not suffer her to stand) she after a short silence as it were to prepare their attention began in these words.

---

[35] The word "dispenced" is corrected with "c" underlined for deletion and "s" inserted.

[36] The word "occations" is corrected with "t" underlined for deletion and "s" inserted.

THE CONTINUATION OF ARTHENIA'S STORY[1]

[fol. 165 ^r]

[fol. 165 ʳ]

Ihad some reason to beleive I had pass'd over all my unhappy dayes when I had once seen my Father quietly possess'd again of that which had for many yeares been wrongfully detain'd from him, which he was immediatly after *Claromenes's* returne, for no sooner was he seated on his Throne but all Usurpers of other mens estates either vanish'd of themselves, or else were by a lawfull power thrown out of their unjust possessions: but alass a little time too well convinced my mistake in vainly presuming my selfe above the reach of Fortunes power; for miseries now befell me a thousand times more insupportable then ever yet I had known any; wherein I must do Fortune the right to affirme, Love was the cheifest Instrument of my undoing.

About halfe a [fol. 165 ᵛ] yeare after our returne to Himera (for so was the place call'd where we then liv'd) I chang'd the Cuntry solitudes for the various delights, and severall diverssions Palermo abounded with; which since the restoration of our King was become an absolute seane [scene] of pleasure. I confess I had formerly rather an aversion, then any love for that Citty; but now it was honour'd with the presence of the most Illustrious *Claromenes*; I delighted in no other place save that, nor desir'd nothing so much as to be allwayes there: and so kind was *Brecena* to my wishes, as ^I^ soon obtain'd leave not only to visit Palermo but likewise to stay there as long as I pleas'd. But far better had it been for me had I prefer'd the Flowry Meddows, the sweet Aire which perfumes the Fields, the melodie of the purling streames, and the chirping of the prity Birds those innocent rurall delights, before the noisefull pleasures of the Citty; or ruffling braveries of the Court with all its perfum'd Gallants who spend their time in nought but in debauching each other, or else in studying which way they may easiest beguile poor woemen by their triffling courtships; pretending much of love but intending nothing save their delusion or abuse.

When I came first to Palermo I went to *Therasmenas's* house but both he and *Hestrina* being gone to *Eugenias* (another of my mothers sisters who liv'd

---

[1] The "Continuation" is written by a different hand, and it is probably not that of the correcting hand that underlines letters or words for deletion. In the "Continuation," the spelling of names changes, and names are frequently not distinguished by italics. For the sake of consistency, names will continue to be italicized and regularized; parentheses also are added when necessary to indicate the speaker, e.g., (she replied).

about a mile out of the Towne) I stay'd there onely that night, and early the next morning I design'd to go to *Eugenias's* too, but first I went to see a Brother I had who liv'd constantly in Towne (call'd *Melliantes*) but being told by the mistress of the house where he lodg'd that he was gone abroad a little before; I went on to *Eugenias's* where I found him who was no less surpriz'd to see me then any of the rest, inregard he had not heard of my coming to Palermo nor could I indeed have given him notis of it my Journey not being resolv'd on above a day or two before I began it; but however I found I was not the less wellcome for coming so unexpectedly, for they all express'd much joy to see me. My stay there was not long, for so soon as *Therasmenas* and my Aunt went home, they carried me with them though *Eugenias* was very unwilling to part with me so quickly, but promising it should not be long ere I would wait on her again she was at last content to let me go, yet much longer was it then I intended ere I could be as good as my word for so infinitly kind was both *Therasmenas* and *Hestrina* to me as twas impossible to leave them without hazarding their displeasure which I confess I was unwilling to do in regard it was very agreeable to my inclinations to stay still in Palermo especially so neer the Palace as they liv'd, where there was no kind of diversion but either I was or might have been a pertaker of it.

I had not been long at *Therasmenas's* [fol. 166ʳ] ere I took notice of a lady that liv'd on the other side of ^the^ way just opposite to us who when ere I chanced to be at any of the windowes looking into the street as I often did for my diversion on those severall people that pass'd a long, I still saw that Lady either stand in her Balcony or set at one of the windowes of her Dining Roome and with intentive Eyes so heedfully to view me as if she had taken some great content in the sight of me, though I could not conceive from whence she could derive it; and many times I observ'd after she had look'd on me a good while she would retire and set her downe and weep; this I could easily perceive the windowes being very larg, and the distance being not so great but that one might plainly see whatever pass'd in that Roome, I confess I very much admir'd what should be the reason of her concern but was not able to imagine the cause of it; but t'was not long I continu'd ignorant of it for hapning one day to have some discourse with a young Gentlewoman (call'd *Mettella*) who liv'd at the next house to us I ask'd her whether she knew what Lady that was that liv'd over against us. Where upon she told me her name was *Perinissa Perizana* and that she was wiffe to a noble Lord nam'd *Persides* who was linially descended from King *Acestes* who was fam'd for the Princely entertainment he gave *Aeneus* and his wandring Trojans. This *Persides* (pursu'd she) is the one who has suffer'd as highly for his King in the late troubles as any person in Sicilia having all his whole estates ceaz'd on by the Rebells, and himselfe inforced to fly for his Life to *Claromenes* with whom he continu'd tell his returne and ever since has liv'd in Palermo, to try I suppose (pursu'd she) if he can get any reparation for all his great losses.

I then told her (went on *Arthenia*) what I had observ'd in *Perizana:* to which she reply'd, that she had heard she very much desired my acquaintance, fancying me extreamly like a Daughter she had that di'd not long since, whom she passionatly doated on, as the Love she had for any of her other Children (which are two sons and one Daughter more continu'd she) was not comparable to what she had for *Mizalinda*: and without doubt (added she) tis the resemblance you have of her which moves *Perisana* to look on you so concernedly: therefore since she so much desires to know you, methinks you would do well if you went to waite on her and give her that satisfaction.

Not (answer'd I) but that I would willingly gratifie the desire of any person in so triviall a thing, but alass with what confidence can I press uninvited into the presence of a person of her quallity without some or other to intraduce me, for I should be so very much out of countenance to appeare of my selfe before her as I shall never presume to attempt it; not but that I believe she may ~~give~~ be so obliging to give me a much civiller reception then I can expect. But if I could perswade my selfe to assume the confidence to wait on her it must be at such a time as I might be sure to find her alone: but when (pursu'd I) can that time be found, for they are never free from company, nor is there any house in Towne I believe, so much frequented as that.

Nay (said she) if you stay for an oppertunity to find *Perisana* unacompani'd twill be impossible for you ever to give her the satisfaction of knowing you since there is scarce an houre in a day wherein some person of quality or other comes not to pay their respects either to her or the Noble *Persides*.

But not long after this I tooke ~~notice~~ a particuler notice of a young Lady that came lately thither who by the stay she made, I concluded to be some way related either to *Persides* or his lady. This Excelent person (for such indeed she was) seem'd to me so well worthy of a particuler regard, that I never saw her (as I oft did at *Perisana's* chamber [fol. 166ᵛ] window; or in the Belcony) but then despising all other objects I intirely ti'd my eyes to her alone; and soon did I become as ambitious of her acquaintance as *Perisana* was desirous of mine; for at that distance I not onely admir'd her, but found in my heart a strong inclination to affect her above all the wemen that ever I had seen, even before I knew so much of her as her name; but I could not be satisfied tell I had inform'd my selfe of it which by *Mettella* I did, for I intreated her to inquire it; which she accordingly did, and told me her name was *Bellamira*, and that she was Daughter to a Kinsman of *Persides's* call'd *Blesarius*, and how that she had some yeares liv'd allmost constantly with *Perisana* who was so extreamly fond of her company and lov'd her so dearly well as she could never willingly endure she should be from her. She had come with her to Palermo (added *Mettella*) but that some accident fell out which hinder'd her, but she engag'd *Blesarius* to bring her to Towne as soon as possible he could, and now she is come I do not heare but she intends to keep her here as long as she herselfe stays.

This was to me very pleasing newes (continu'd *Arthenia*) in regard I hop'd Fate might at some time or other be so kind to give me a more particuler knowledge of so admirable a person as she appear'd to be. But twas not without some

hidden cause that I so passionatly wis[h]'d to be acquainted with her, since 'twas
from her alone that I deriv'd the sole felicity of my life and (that which seemes
a paradox) my greatest misiry I may say too for had I not known *Bellamira* I had
questionless never come to the knowledge of him who has rendred me the most
miserable of wemen, but 'twas not not in the least her fault but my owne ill Fate
which made me so; for never did any one do more to make another happy then
she did for me: but since my future fortunes are so intermixt with the faire *Bellamiras* as to tell my owne, I must relate hers too; I'll give your Majesty some
little Character of her ere I pass further though I confess it will be so imperfect
a one as when I have said all I can it must needs fall infinitly short of what she
deserved, or I ought to say of her.

Not without reason then did I stile her the Faire *Bellamira* for so deservedly
was that Epithite her due, as the Queen of beauty herselfe could not shew a fairer
title to it; and questionless had she been by when *Paris* gave the golden Ball to
Venus[2] he had declin'd her to make his Present to the more beautious *Bellamira*
since no Carnation was ever comparable to that wherewith Nature had died her
Lips [and] cheeks with which was mix't so pure a white to embellish her lov'ly
face as nought but new fallen snow could equall: nor was her beauty alone that
challeng'd my admiration for the innocent sweetnes of her eyes clamed no less
a share, in which was seated so commanding a power, joyn'd with a modesty no
less sublime, which made her though she dayly vanquis[h]'d Hearts, yet never
owne her conquests, but alwayes blush'd when she was told how larg her Empire
was and whereas other[s] by the help of time, and by degrees orecame, she did so
the first minute she was seen: but still when e're a Ray shot from her eye threw
fire into the brest of her adorers, that very instant she enkindled it, she did refine
it too and purify it by the charming vertue of her lookes, no dull or smoaky fire
durst any one presume to offer at her shrine. Her Haire which requir'd not the
help of Art to put it into curious Rings was (though not a perfect Flaxen) yet of
a very bright colour, her stature tall, her shape exactly well proportioned and so
exceeding gracefull was her deportment, as her carriage and behaviour was no
less taking then her person.

But what I have hitherto said of her (pursu'd *Arthenia*) was so visible that
^none^ had eyes to see her but must acknowledge that truth of it, and therefore it
need not be thought strang that I (though at a distance) admir'd her as I did but
when I once [fol. 167ʳ] became so happy as to know her, I dayly made such rich
discoveries of [her] generous mind as I no longer regarded her externall perfection (how great soever) but as the Cabinet wherein was contain'd a Jewell of that
Luster as even dazled me with the brightness of it, the purity and innocence of
her soule was such as only Angels could paralele, the Charmes of her conversa-

---

[2] Paris was selected to judge the beauty of Athena (Minerva), Hera (Juno), and
Aphrodite (Venus) and award an apple to the fairest. Venus won the contest by promising
him the fairest woman in the world, Helen of Troy.

tion such as cannot be express'd, her humour the most gay and pleasant in the world: yet such her Modesty as scorn'd so meane a Guard as Pride to protect her Honour which her eyes alone were sufficent of themselves to do. The gentle sweetness and eveness of her temper such, as adverse Fate could nere depress, nor a more prosperous one exallt, but still in all conditions she enjoy'd so serene a calme, as if she neither fear'd the frowns of Fortune, nor valu'd her smilles: and alwayes were her thoughts employ'd upon some great and noble Theame ne're on the Follies, and trifles of the world, unless to pity, or despise them: nor did she in anything resemble the Ladies of her age who were much more solicitus to beautify their bodies then to deck their soules, but her chiefe care was to adorn that part of her which she well knew must still survive when the other was crumbled into dust; nor did she ever make it her designe to surprize a heart meerly to try how far her power did extend, nor was she ever heard to glory in her victories (though they were great and many) but often wish her Empire were confin'd to narrower limits. In fine such a One was the admirable *Bellamira* as Envie herselfe could never find an errour in her except her indulging for me too great a kindness which was her onely fault: but tis rather the recitall of her actions then my dull discription must let your Majesty see the generosity and galantry of this unparalel'd person whom to know, and not to love was as impossible as 'twas for any but the Princely Eagle with undazled eyes to gaze upon the sunne.

But if before I courted all occasions that might bring me to the honour of kissing *Perisanas* hands, I ^now^ much more diligently sought for an oppertunity to waite on her, since with hers I hoped to obtain the acquaintance of that beautious Lady from whose very sight I deriv'd so high a delight; but when I even dispair'd of finding what I so long in vain had sought, Fortune presented ~~me~~ it to me when I least expected it: for having been abroad, at my returne home I found there *Marione* (who was newly come to towne) and abundance of other Company amongst whom was *Blesarius* and his Faire Daughter who had not appear'd so lovly to me at a distance but that she seem'd a thousand times more so now that I had a perfect view of her. Having saluted her, I paid my respects to *Marione* (whom I had not seen since my coming to Palermo) then turning to *Bellamira* I took her by the hand and led her to a seat, and though I confess I ought in civility to have given the first rise for discourse since I was to entertain her, yet in such a manner was my mind taken up with admiring those many perfections she seem'd repleat with as my tongue gave up its office wholly to my eyes: but she had the goodness to excuse that which any less obliging would have been apt to have term'd rudeness, or country simplicity, counting it rather a modest bashfullness that hindred me from speaking; and breaking silence first herselfe.

Though I was wholly a stranger to you Madam (said she) I could not but enquire for you, and hearing you were gone abroad I extreamly regreated my ill Fortune which I fear'd had disapointed the hopes I had conceiv'd of being acquainted with you, which I assure you was the chiefest inducement that brought me hither.

The misfortune Madam (reply'd I) would have been mine should I have mist so great a happiness as tis to see you here, which is an honour I have [fol. 167ᵛ] been long ambitious of; many the like expressions having pass'd between us, I quickly found her temper was not in the least reserv'd neither indeed is mine to any that I find desirous to be acquainted with me; so that ere we parted we became so well known to each other as we scarce needed the help of time to perfect our acquaintance; and when she went away she told me it was her hopes we should be no long straingers to each other, assuring me it should be no fault of hers if we were, and beg'd me to oblige her with a visit, which she promised doubly to repay, telling me withall that *Perisana* was the most obliging person in the world, and her Daughter *Elesena* so very good as I could not but think it no meane felicity to know them.

This invitation so well suted with my wishes as I could nere have met a fairer occation of gratifying *Perisana's* desire, so that about two dayes after I took the confidence to go thither where I was most civilly receiv'd by all, but more especially by *Perisana* whom I found to be the very abstract of courtisie. She was as then somewhat advanced in yeares which yet had left her so many visible markes of an eminent beauty, which the rude hand of Time (the enemy of all good Faces) could not destroy, as I could plainly perceive she had once equall'd the Fairest of our Sicilian Dames: but though Time had been something injurious to her Beauty, it had not in the least detracted from her good humour, for that she had still preserv'd amidst her highest misfortunes, of which she had sustain'd some sad and insupportable enough to produce a change in her inclination which was wholly dispos'd to an innocent mirth, and a gay free temper, which rendered her infinitly belov'd by all persons that were permitted the honour of her converse: this temper of hers would not suffer her to treat me with that ceremonious reservedness as is usuall with persons at the first enterview, but with so free, and unconstrain'd a kindness did she deport herselfe towards me as made me repent I had not sooner given her occation to express it, and inspire[d] me with an extraordinary affection for her mix'd with a very high respect and veneration. But so intirely did she ingross me to herselfe for all that day as I could converse but little with *Bellamira* which I should have been very much concern'd for had I not hop'd I might now often find oppertunities to renew our mutuall endearments. *Elesena* too I found no less good and obliging then *Bellamira* had spoken her to be, so as I could not without injustice denie her a larg share in my esteeme.

One morning (not long after this) just as I was out of my Bed came one from *Bellamira* to intreat me to go with her to the Palace, I stay'd not to examine whether she intended a visit to any one there, or what other designe carried her thither, return'd her answere I would not faile to waite on her immediatly; and instantly dressing me with all convenient speed I could I went to her; but as much hast as I made she was ready ere I came, and *Perisanas* Chariot waiting at the Gate to carry us to court. Having given the good morrow to each other, she ask'd me if I had ever seen *Claromenes*.

Yes (answer'd I) I saw him that day he enter'd Palermo after his returne but never since, nor had I then any other then an imperfect view of him as he pass'd by me.

Well (reply'd she) you shall now if you please have a full sight of him as he sits at Dinner, for to that entent ~~tainment~~ it was I desir'd your company.

You have extreamly oblig'd me in it (said I) for that is a sight I have been very ambitious of ever since I came to Towne, and *Therasmus* has promis'd me that favour but has not yet been so good as his word.

Whilst we thus stood talking on the top of the staires (where she met me as I was coming up) two young Gentlemen came out of the Dining Roome and both of them saluting me, the one of them tooke me by the hand and turning to the other, *Herminio* (said he to him) take you care of *Bellamira* this lady shall be my charge; will you not Madam (pursu'd he to me)

[T]hat's as you please Sir (answer'd I)

I am very well pleas'd you should be so (reply'd he) so briskly as made me conclude him to be of an excellent pleasant humour, and that mirth and gayetie was his [fol. 168ʳ] chiefe composure, in which opinion he sufficently confirm'd me by the pleasant discourses he entertain'd us with all the way we went; but when we came to court we were enform'd that the King was gone that morning abroad and would not returne till night, so that by this meanes our designe was frustrate, yet could I not think my time ill spent in such good company, nor my labour altogether lost, since this Gentleman (whose name as yet I knew not) to oblige me shew'd me all things remarkable or worthy to be seen in the Palace; but since *Claromenes* was not there to be seen by us we made but a short stay.

That afternoon I went to waite on the Princess *Alsinda* (who being now a Widdow liv'd altogether in Towne) with whom I spent the remainder of that day; but when I came home *Hestrina* told me I was but newly gone out when *Bellamira* and a Gentleman came to call me to go with them abroad again, who by the discription she gave of him I knew to be the same brisk Gallant that was with us in the morning. Divers times after this had I the satisfaction of seeing *Bellamira* either at our house whether she often came or else at *Persides's* which I no less frequented, but I never saw her but I still discover'd some new charmes either in her person or conversation which were as so many chaines to tye me more firmly to her in an inviolable Friendship which in a short while grew so strong between us as nothing had ere the power to slacken much less disolve it, nor could Death it selfe put a period to it. The Friendship too of the generous *Perisana* honour'd me with, was so great, as I have reason for ever to cellibrate that happy minute wherein I attain'd the knowledge of a person so excellently qualifi'd with all things that were great vertuous and noble. The prity *Elesena* too acted by her mothers example in the expressions of her kindness to me, nor was *Persides* himselfe less civill, then the rest were kind, insomuch as really I thought it was impossible to find in the wholle world more good obliging persons then that Family was repleat with, nor was I ever contented in my mind but when I was amongst them.

One day as *Perisana* and I were sett talking together of severall things; after some little intervall of silence. Ah *Arthenia* (said she with a deep sigh and teares redy to break from her eyes) the more I look on you the more do I find in you of my *Mizalinda* who was so deservedly dear to me as I must needs confess I was so partiall as to treasure up in her my chiefest love, and sole delight; but too too cruell Death not many moneths since ravish'd her forever from my eyes leaving me with fruitless teares to deplore her loss. [B]ut I think Heaven commiserating the bitterness of my griefe has sent me her Picture to looke on, to please my fancy, or at least a little to divert my sorrows. I say her Picture sweet *Arthenia* pursu'd she for so sure you are, since such is the resemblance of her you beare as no one can be more like another then you are to my poor dead *Mizalinda* nor do I see more of her in your Face, then in your humour, disposition, and all your actions represent to me; but seeing I cannot hope for the satisfaction of having you ever in my view, I must beg the favour of you to permit me to have your Picture drawn by some skillfull hand, that when Fate shall be so unkind to deny me a longer enjoyment of your sight, I may then please my selfe with beholding the Pourtrait not onely of my Dead Daughter, but also of my absent Friend which will give me a very great content and satisfaction.

I shall esteeme my selfe extreamly happy (repli'd I) if I may any way contribute to your satisfaction: and Ill assure you madam I take it as a signall token of your Favour that you will [fol. 168^{v}] vouchsafe to command me to serve you in any thing and am sorry you demand not a proofe of my obedience in something less advantagious for myselfe, since this cannot adde so much to your content, as it will to my glory to be thought any thing like so excellent a person as I have been enform'd *Mizalinda* was.

Within a short space after this I went to *Arnardos* where I spent the remainder of the summer with *Marionie* who told me so oft as she saw *Loreto,* he was alway[s] cursing his inconstancy which him made him (in his owne opinion) the most unhappy of men, but perceiving all discourses of him to be very unpleasing to me, she ever after wav'd them, and forbeare to mention him to me any more while I aboad there. But hoary headed Winter (which renders the country unpleasant) approaching I went back to Palermo again whether I was joyfully wellcom'd by all my new acquaintance, but more especially by *Bellamira* who enjoyn'd me to afford her as much of my company as possibly I could; this I having promis'd, thought my selfe oblig'd to make good; and believing the evenings would be the fittest time to find *Persides's* house freest from company I chose still to go thither then to the end we might the more undisturbedly enjoy the conversation of each other, and whereas the long winter evenings had been formerly tedious to me, on the contrary now me thought time flew so fast away, as the houres seem'd but minutes when spent with my beloved *Bellamira* but seldome, or never after I came to Town again did I go to *Persides's* but I still met that same

brisk Gallant there that went to court with *Bellamira* and I who always appear'd
so jocose and pleasant yet so exceeding civill and courtly withall as I could not
but think him not onely the best humour'd but the most perfectly accomplish'd
man in Sicilie, yet knew I not a long time who he was, nor did I so much as once
enquire, onely I heard him call'd *Issodorus* which assur'd me that was his name;
but chanceing one time to speak something in commendation of him to *Elesena*,
I confess (reply'd she) my Brother is one who is very acceptable to all persons.

How Madam (interrupted I) is *Issodorus* your Brother, I ~~thought~~ had thought
you had had none save *Theander* (for I had forgot (pursu'd *Arthenia*) that *Mettella*
had told me *Perisana* had two sons).

Yes (answer'd she) this is my youngest Brother.

I did indeed believe (said I) that *Issodorus* was some way related to you by
the priviledge I have observ'd he takes here, and the familiarity wherewith ye all
treat him, but I should ne're have guess'd him to be Brother to *Theander* they are
so much unlike either in person or favour, though I confess their carriage and
deportment are very resembling:

[F]or *Theander* madam (said *Arthenia* to the Queen) was of a midle stature,
neither so high as to be counted a[s] tall, nor so low as to be term'd a litle man;
his complexion very faire, his haire of the same colour, his eyes purely black,
and all the Features of his Face form'd to a perfect semetry, his humour pleasant
enough, though not altegether so light and airy as his Brothers, but of temper
much more constant and sollid; his disposition sweet, mild, and obliging, and
indeed so admirably quallified, and excellent a person was he, as it would puzzle
a more discerning judgment then mine whether of the two Brothers was ~~the~~ most
to be admir'd. As for *Issodorus* he was very tall, exceeded in height by few men in
Sicily and exactly well proportion'd to his height; his complextion sanguine; his
eyes of a dark grey cleere and sparkling, his haire of an Abourn colour which fell
in long curles upon his shoulders, and though his birth was noble enough being
the son of *Persides* and *Perisana,* yet in all the linaments of his Face there appear'd
something so sublime and high as he has oft been taken by such as knew him not
to be of a desent much above [fol.169 ʳ] [t]hat, and in his lookes too might be seen
an Aire so firce and haughty as plainly shew'd his mind to be elevated above the
degree and quality of a younger brother, and seem'd to tell the world he design'd
to force that from Fortune which nature had deni'd him, his gesture, and carriage was noble, each action of his becoming, having in them a charming grace
proper onely to himselfe; and for his humour (as I have already said) it was the
most agreeable, and the fullest of diversion in the world, and in short such a one
he ~~was~~ is tis absolutely impossible for any hearts (though ne're so well fortifi'd)
long to resist his assaults where once he besiges it.

I have presum'd to give your Majesty this little Charactor of these two
Brothers (continu'd *Arthenia*) to the end Madam you may the better know them
whenever I bring them on the stage of my discourse.

I must confess ingeniously (said *Ermillia*) I cannot tell which to prefer in my opinion, for if *Theander* appeares so sweet and gentle as to invite ones esteeme, *Issodorus* seemes by his brave, and heroick mind no less to command an equall place in it.

For my part (said *Gentillus*) I am clearly of your Majesties mind, for I cannot determine whether of the two is the more deserving person.

It will not be so hard to guess (went on *Arthenia*) who to give the Palme too, when in the progress of my story I have delineated their internall quallifications, and shewn you that the one is no less true observer of his promises, and faithfull to his Friend, then the other was falce to both, and of a nature so strangly given to chaing change, as I have oft admir'd his soule has not found some way to quit his body, or transmigate it selfe into some other as being weary of being so long confin'd to one.

At the same time *Elesena* likewise told me *Issodorus* was suddenly to go over into Sardinia a long with the Prince of Orestaign (whom the king had made vice-roy thereof)[3] who being related to her Father had in kindness to him confer'd on her Brother some considerable Places (that were in his dispose) both of honour and advantage, which (as she said) *Persides* hop'd would be a good addition to his sons present fortunes and a way to raise them to a future grandure which (she afirm'd) was her Fathers chiefest aime, as well knowing *Issodorus* had a soule too great to be confin'd within the narrow limits of a younger Brothers Patrimony. I was a litle concern'd (I confess) to heare this, in regard I was very unwilling to loose so much mirth as I perpetually deriv'd from *Issodorus* good company before such time as I left Palermo my selfe: but his departure which was suppos'd would so soon happen was not till many moneths after.

In the meane time 'twas my chance to be envited to a Ball by one *Diophantus* a Friend of *Melliantes's* (who made it to treat a certain lady whom secretly he ador'd) and Tickets sent me for any other two persons whom if I pleas'd I might bring with me; whereupon I instantly pitch'd upon *Elesena* and *Bellamira* and was more glad that permission was granted me (since I thereby hop'd to oblige them) then for the perticuler Favour in relation to my selfe. In order hereunto I instantly went to give them the like invitation as I had receiv'd but being both of them otherwayes engag'd before, they refus'd my civility (as they term'd it) with many thankes, beging me not to take it ill, which I assur'd them I did not.

But to let me see you do not (said *Bellamira*) you must promise to dine with us the day after your Ball at Lavernus's, (which was a house of publick entertainment (continu'd *Arthenia*) as there is in Palermo divers of them where any persons may treat their Friends who have not houses [fol. 169ᵛ] of theire owne convenient for it) for there is severall of *Elesenas* Friends and mine to meet there (pursu'd *Bellamira*) without a designe to be very merry, and therefore you must

---

[3] The *Prince of Orestaign* refers to the Marquess (later Duke) of Ormand, Lord Lieutenant of Ireland (Sardinia), 1660–1669 and 1677–1685.

be sure not to faile us; which ~~being not~~ having engag'd not to do I took my leave after I had told *Bellamira* that if the Ball were ended late I should not come home, but did intend to stay and ly with *Sillindra* (who was a lady *Melliantes* was to marry) however I would assuredly meet them at the place appointed. As I had suppos'd, so it fell out, for so very late was it ere the Ball was done, that if I would have come home I durst not being unsafe venturing thorow the streets at that time of night since I was at the furthest part of the Towne distant from that I then liv'd. But the next morning reminding the promise I had made to meet *Bellamira* I sent to my Brother to go with me, deeming it unfit to go alone to any such publick house lest I might chance to come there before such time as any of the rest were come that were appointed to meet there as indeed I did; but it was not long ere *Elesena*[,] *Bellamira* and *Issodorus* came in, and were imediatly Follow'd by *Reallus*[,] *Bellamiras* Brothe[r,] and a Brother of her fathers nam'd *Theano*, and his lady, with *Merinda* and *Melissa* their two faire Daughters, with severall others. After my Brother had saluted *Elesena* and *Bellamira* (having been by me enform'd who they were) you see ladies (said I to the[m]) how punctuall an observer of my word I am, since rather then not be so, I have presum'd to increase your company by bringing my Brother with me.

You have doubly oblig'd us Deare *Arthenia* (reply'd *Bellamira*) in giveing us thereby the oppertunity of being acquainted with *Melliantes* who I assure you is no less wellcome upon his owne account then yours.

This she might affirme since 'twas *Reallus* that gave the entertainment, though as then I knew not to whom I was to pay my thankes for that share I had in it. But whilst we were talking in this manner, the Gentlemen were caressing *Melliantes* each striving who should be the most civill to him, especially *Issodorus*, and after some little time coming to me.

This was the kindest thing Madam (said he) that you could have done, in obliging us with your Brothers company to day, in which high favour every one here has an interest but perticulerly my selfe who have been long ambitious of his acquaintance[.]

I can assure you Sir (repli'd I) he is no less ambitious of ~~yours~~ the honour of yours, and I am extreamly glad I thought of bringing him with me, though 'twas meerly my owne convenience that enduced me to it; but I could hardly I confess prevaile with him to come by reason you are all strangers to him;

It shall not be any fault of mine (said he) if we are so any longer; for I declare for my owne part I shall never willingly be a stranger to any person so neerly related to *Arthenia* as to claime a Brothers Interest in her: but in this litle time I find him to be a person of such worth as needs not your merit to introduce him into the esteeme of all that have but once the honour to converse with him; and in mine I must needs say he has already got so larg a share as I know none save his Faire Sister that can dispute the place with him.

If none but I can do it, the dispute shall soon be ended (repli'd I) for I love my Brother too well to pretend to any advantage above him, and honour tis enough for me if the Generous *Issodorus* alowes me but onely a civill respect, which is all I shall ever pretend too from any man.

They are not rationall Creatures sure (repli'd he) that can denie you that.

He could ~~nadd~~ adde no more, had he design'd it, Dinner being brought up, and [fol. 170ʳ] usher'd in with Musick, and after we had din'd, every one dispos'd themselves to a severall diversion as best suted their genious, some danced, others play'd at dice, and some there were that pass'd away the day onely in discourse. The danceing being about to begin, *Issodorus* came and proffer'd to take me out, but being unwilling to dance so soon after I had eaten, (having been very ill not long before) I beg'd him to excuse me and make choice of some other; telling him withall the reason I had to decline his civility lest he might thinke me rude in refusing it.

I like my choice so well madam (said he) as I shall never be induced to make an another; but since you suppose it may [be] prejudicially to you to dance as yet, I'll waite your leasure till you may securely grant me the honour I desire; ~~which~~ with that bowing very low, he went and engag'd himselfe amongst those that were at play.

I confess I could not but admire that *Issodorus* who was so good humou[r]'d should shew so little of it as he did that day especially among such pleasant company as there was; nor did I remember I had ever heard him speak in a serious manner before; for still so full of mirth, and ralliry was all he said as I verily thought he could not at any time be serious, yet I did not much concern my selfe to enquire into the cause: nor never till then had I had the least mistrust that there was anything of a pertculer kindness between *Herminio* and *Elesena* but seting by them as they were discoursing together, I chanc'd to heare him say to her.

Be not so much concern'd for that Deare *Elesena* things may fall out much better for us then we expect.

What had proceeded this I know not but hapning to speak this a little loud I over heard him against my will, for I ever counted it the greatest piece of rudness imaginable to listne to any thing another sayes wherein one has no interest, wherefore lest I should be guilty of it I rose from my seat, and went and sat me downe at a good distance from them. But what I onely conjectur'd, *Bellamira* not long after confirm'd, assuring me he had been some yeares a passionate servant to *Elesena* though privatly and unknown to any of her Friends, unless to *Issodorus* who she believ'd favou[r]'d him in his addresses to his sister.

Those that had danced giving off, and a new company going to begin, *Issodorus* was call'd for, who thinking he had given me a sufficent time for digestion came to me again with the like request as before, which I could now no longer refuse. *Herminio* took out *Elesena*, *Melliantes Bellamira*, and another Gentleman (whose name I know not) took out *Merinda* the elder of the two sisters. But in that manner did the most excellent *Bellamira* dance as I could scarce mind what I did my selfe for looking on her, for such a charming Grace had she in every step as I had ne're seen any that could equall her, unless 'twere *Issodorus* but to do him right I must needs say he danced with such agility and nimbleness of Body yet with so gracefull an address as my admiration was equally divided between them; and pitty me thought it was that two such admirable Dancers should have been parted. But so had my late illness weakned me as I was weary before any of the rest, and often wish'd they would give off, or that *Issodorus* would relinquish me and take some other, but when I motion'd it to him he seem'd to take it ^so^ ill of me, that rather then I would dissoblige him I resolv'd (if possible) not to give off till the rest did so which was not till lights were brought in, to supply the absence of the day which had now given place to the approach of night. My Brother supposing it might be late ere we parted company, was unwilling to stay [fol. 170ᵛ] longer being to go out of Towne early the next morning and therefore took his leave, *Issodorus* would needs waite on him downe to the Dore, where as they parted (as *Melliantes* afterwards told me) he pass'd so many Complements on him and made him such high expressions of Friendship as he was even amaz'd thereat, and could not but admire what should move him at first sight to treat him in so perticular a way of kindness, nor did he leave him without an ardent desire of a more perfect knowledge of a person the most civill and obliging of all that ever he had been.

Whilst *Issodorus* was complementing *Melliantes* they had again begun to dance so that when he came in I was setting by my selfe at one corner of the Roome looking on them, all the other Ladies being taken out, and so might I too (had I not refused it) by *Herminio* but being before extreamly tir'd I beg'd his excuse, presenting *Mellissa* to him (who had not danced at all). No sooner had *Issodorus* spi'd me but he came and siting downe by me he told me he was sorry my Brothers occations should be so injurious to him as so soon to deprive him of his good company, but he would not quarell with them so much as otherways he should have done, since his absence allow'd him the liberty to entertain me the more freely.

Why *Issodorus* (said I) do you imagine my Brothers presence layes any restraint on me.

No Madam (answer'd he) I speak in refference only to my selfe, since he being the greater stranger to me I should have been oblig'd to act contrary to my inclinations in sacrificing a good part of that time to civilty which I had wholly devoted to your service; for though *Melliantes* is a person I infinitely honour, and his company very deare to me upon the account of that worth (which in this short enterview) I really find in him; and much more so for your sake, yet can I willingly at this time dispence with the deprivation of it, since your converse is to me far more acceptable.

I should very much question that respect you pretend for my Brother (said I) if I did fancy you could preferre my conversation before his which certainly of all that know him was ever judg'd more desirable then mine.

I dare assure you then (repli'd he) none ever had those sentiments of you that I have or they could never have conceiv'd so injurious an opinion of you.

I know not what your thoughts of me are (interupted I) nor I am I very curious to [blot] enquire; but I am perswaded there are many in the world that think of as well of me as I deserve.

If they did (answer'd he) they would as well as I not onely preferre you before *Melliantes* but before all persons living.

Good *Issodorus* (cry'd I) do not complement me so much to the prejudice of your judgment, you cannot sure be so blind as I should count you did I believe your words held any correspondence with your thoughts.

If I am blind (said he) tis love has me me so, but since all obiects appeare to me the same as formerly I cannot mistrust there is any defect in my sight, much less can I think my eyes have forsaken me though I have lost my heart.

Alass poor *Issodorus* (repli'd I) laughing I pitty your misfortune; why do you not send hue and cry after the Theefe.

That's needless madam (answer'd he looking more seriously,) since [fol. 171ʳ] I have her in my view.

Why do you not lay hold of her (said I) and compell her to restore what she has taken.

It is not in my power to retrive it (he repli'd) but if I should, it would be in vain, since in her eyes lies couch'd a secret force which would not let me long enjoy it, yet however seeing you advize me to ceaze the Theefe I'll take your councell (pursu'd he taking one of my hands and pressing it in his) now Madam you must either render me my heart again (went he on) or give me in exchange your owne, which I much more desire, for I declare tis you, and onely you who have depriv'd me of it. Yet I confess I have done you wronge in charging you with taking it from me, since I rather freely gave it you the first time that I beheld you and have hitherto made a shift to live without a heart, but can do so no longer.

Had I mistrusted (continu'd *Arthenia*) I had been concern'd in this discourse I had questionless put a stop to it ere it had arrived to that it did; but I endeavou[r]'d to turne it into rallery. I am resolv'd (said I) I'll ask *Bellamira* when she has done danceing whether she thinks 'tis possible for a man to live without a heart the space of halfe a yeare for so long 'twas (pursu'd *Arthenia*) since he first saw me.

Do you suppose *Bellamira* then so great a Judge of love (ask'd he)[?]

I know not (answer'd I) how well she may determine of that, but I believe none is better able to Judge of Reason then herselfe; and this which you aver is so irrationall a thing in my opinion that you must pardon me if I can give no credit to it.

Why are you incredulous *Arthenia* (said he) have you no Faith,

[Y]es (answer'd I) for Divine Misteries but not for such impossible Fooleries: for I well know I have no heart save that which I was born with, and that I'll keep, no Flatteries of your False sex shall ever tempt it from me, but if you can

find any other pray take it home to you again, for I desire not to be troubled to
lodge a stranger in my Brest which may perhaps create me more disquiet than I
would willingly sustain, for I have heard the heartes of men are such unhospi-
table Guests as they oft set their lodging on a Flame and then with scorn returne
[returne repeated] to some secure retreat pittilessly tryumphing ore those ruines
they have made.

I should be more vain and Foolish then you believe me (he reply'd) should
I go about to perswade you that I had vertually given you this little piece of
Flesh that beates within my brest, no madam that was not my intention; nor
do I believe you understood me so, what ever you pretend; but in affirming you
have my heart I meane the entire affections, thoughts, and desires of it. But
though you scorne me your selfe yet make me not the subject of *Bellamiras* mirth
I beseech you by acquainting her with what I have said to you, for so insensible
of all that love inspires is her soule as she will wish no better sport then to deride
and laugh at me.

Well well said I you need not feare that I'll trouble my self with speaking
of that which I shall never think on more. But I admire how we fell into this
unpleasing discourse which is to me so troublesome as I must intreat you to be
silent or to talk of something else.

I'll talke of whatsoere you please (reply'd he) provided you will believe I love
you more then ever any did, and must and will to my death continue so to do;
nor can I madam ceace to tell you of my passion tell I may be so happy to gain an
assurance that tis not unpleasing to you.

You have propos'd to your selfe (said I) a harder [fol. 171 ᵛ] task perhaps then
you imagine, for though I want many of those good qu[a]llities wherewith ~~many~~
divers of my sex are beautified, yet believe it you may chance to find me as severe
as the most perfect of them, but tis probable I may have no occation to trouble
you with anything of that nature since tis like you may be possest with the fancy
of some men in these dayes who imagine wemen count them deficent in point
of breeding if they should pass halfe an houre in a perticuler converse without
entertaining them with some piece of Amorous Folly; but if there be any such
vain creatures in the world (as I can hardly think ther are) that can take pleasure
in such feign'd addresses which are made meerly out of custome, or either to shew
their wits, or to prove that of others, I do assure you *Arthenia* is none of them.

No Madam (repli'd he) my respects for you is too honourably attended to
suffer so injurious a thought of you to enter my brest; and so far am I from offering you a pretended passion that though my heart vow'd it selfe your votary
from the first moment that my eyes beheld you, and that it has e're since burnt
with a Flame so ardent as the highest disdain you are capable of exhibiting can
never quench it, yet had I not the confidence to owne it, nor should not yet have
presum'd to disclose the resentments [feelings] of my soule had not my unkind
Fate threatned to drag me sooner from you then I expected, but though it has
that power over my person it shall never force my heart one minute to abandon

you: be kind then madam I beseech you in my absence to my poor heart and treat it not with rigour when I am not by, to plead in its behalfe; for by Heaven I swear nothing in nature ere lov'd anyone more then that does you.

The hearts of men (interrupted I) are generally so falce, disloyall, and ungratfull that I am resolv'd nere to have ought to do with any of them, lest it should be my hape to meet with such a one, not that I can say yours will prove so, yet being fram'd of the same mettle that others are, it may be subject to the like ill inclinations. But whether (pursu'd I) is it you are going in such hast.

Into Sardinia (answer'd he) along with the ViceRoy who has honour'd me with an employ there so considerable as may in some short time I trust raise me to a condition not altogether so unworthy as I am at present to declare my selfe *Arthenias* Servant: for I know madam you are not ignorant Fate has made me a younger Brother and therby exposed me to seek for that from the hands of Fortune which *Theanders* birthright has given him; but however though he be born to a Fortune considerable enough, yet if my hopes prove not Flatterers I do not question but to attaine if not equal yet not much inferior to that which he will be one day master of; but infinitly would it quicken my endeavours, and render my industry much more solicitous might I be happy in obtaining a perticular interest in your esteem which though I dare not pretend the least merit too, yet can I not but most ambitiously sue for: but yet pardon me Madam if I say that methinks tis but just since I have freely resign'd to you the intire and absolute possession of my heart, that you if it were but in gratitude give you me some litle share in yours; and that seeing I love you with the truest and most unalterable affection that any mortall can be inspir'd with, you should not be so cruell to let me languish without the hopes of a returne.

I know not (said I) what opinion you may have of me in generall, but sure I am you have but a very ill one of my discretion if you can think me so unwise to engage in a perticuler Friendship for a person whom tis probable after some litle time I may never see [fol. 172ʳ] more, but were it as likely as tis the contrary, and that the Passions you pretend were as reall as I believe it feigned, yet I must tell you I shall neer be perswaded to accept from you what I must be so ungratfull as never to reward.

Never *Arthenia* what never (cry'd he) O recall that fatall word and date some period to my sufferings which else must be as endless as my Flame which tis impossible for anything to extinguish,

[N]e're Feare it *Issodorus* (said I) the Sardininian aire (whenre once you come thither) no question will quickly put it out or else inspire you with new inclinations more advantagious for you, and less troublesome to me.

I am sorry Madam (repli'd he) my kindness should prove your [annoyance], yet would it be in vain to beg your pardon, since at the same time instant I did so I should resolve to percevere in my offence; but perhaps you would not count me so great a Crimenall in presuming to harbour a passion in my soule the most honourable and respective passion imaginable were not your affections preingag'd to some more happie person.

Did any one tell you that they were (interrupted I) upon my word if they did they were mistaken and so are you in believing any such thing; and though tis more than I am oblig'd too yet for my owne satisfaction, I'll assure you I am not engag'd to any man breathing neither by promise nor affection.

Then will I not conclude my selfe totally miserable (said he) nor yet dispaire (since you are not already gain'd) but by the vastness of my love and that Fidelity which shall ever be its constant attendant to plead a better title to you than any he that dare adore you.

Much more did he say (continu'd she) to which I either lent no eare, or else made him such displeasing answers as I am perswaded he deriv'd but little satisfaction from them and as small hopes of any better success in the future: but notwithstanding I endeavour'd all I could to decline a further converse with him yet could I not avoid it tell such time as they had given over dancing, which they had no sooner done but I call'd *Bellamira* to me and would not suffer her to stir an inch from me all the rest of the time we stay'd which was not long, for I did all I could to hasten our departures home whether soon after we went though much against *Issodorus's* mind who highly importun'd our longer stay. I could not so much as fancy that there was the least of truth in what he had protested; but thought rather he had made me that address either for his diversion, or else to try whether I was of a humour to be taken with a few insignificant expressions of kindness which oft vanishes even in that very Aire that formes them; which if so I hop'd I should then receive no further disturbance from him on that score since I had said enough to discourage him from attempting the like: but what ever his intent might be, I thought it best to absent my selfe for some dayes from *Persides's* supposing I might thereby avoid his sight, but I was mistaken for the second day after he made me a visit and as it hapned found me all alone, for *Therasmus* was gone that afternoon to Court and my Aunt kept her chamber being something indispos'd. I was somewhat concern'd I confess that he had found me wholly unaccompani'd in regard I had no way left to shun his pursutes however I resolv'd to treat him with that respect which I believ'd due from me to a son of the most obliging *Perisanas* but withall to decline all [those] things as nigh as possible I could that might give him a rise to prosecute what he late began; but I was not more solicitus to avoid then he was on the contrary to seek for [fol. 172^v] an oppertunity to compleat the declaration of his passion; but when he perceiv'd how I evaded him, he told me after some litle silence this was a happiness he did not expect to find me so alone, and could I find Fate but so kind to my wishes (pursu'd he) as to have produced no less favourable change in your inclinations for me I should have reason to esteeme myselfe the most fortunate of men; but if you still determine to be as incredulous, and as inexorable as to my unspeakable torment I lately found you I must inevitably be miserable without all hopes of redress. You told me then madam that you pittied me, O had that which you then spake ironically been meant really I should not be altogether so disatisfied as I am; but if you will afford me neither love nor pitty I cannot beare my Fate without complaining or sinking under the pressures of it.

Sure *Issodorus* (interrupted I) you are not in earnest.

By Heavens but I am (answer'd he) and I swear by all that's good at that rate I love you as I must be yours, and as such own'd by you, or not be at all.

Why (said I) you will not kill your selfe I hope.

I need not madam (replied he) your cruelty will assuredly do it for me, and force me to dy the Martyre of my love, and then perhaps you will be convinc'd I was in earnest.

Not a jote the more (said I) for I should questionless impute your death to any cause rather then love; for I must tell you I have a better opinion of you then to believe you have so little wit to dy for love of any one, much less for me: but seeing you have made such a serious protestation of kindness for me, I'll onely beg one proofe of it.

Ordaine me anything but ceasing to adore you (cri'd he) and I'll pay you an implicit obedience to whatever you command, but never expect that I can consent to that since both your power and mine are not strong enough to effect it for tis as impossible for my body to survive the departure of my soule as for my heart to quit its passion for you.

Do but silence your passion then (said I) and I will aske no more.

Should I use so great a violence on my selfe (repli'd he) as to impose an etternall silence on my tongue I might perchance offend you more, since the Fire that is kindled in my Brest (would by my seeking to smoother it) ere long burst forth into a Flame so visible as must inevitabl[y] be obvious to all eyes.

Nay (said I) if I thought there were any danger of that I should rather chuse still to be importun'd with your love how displeasing soever tis to me, then that you should give the world so clear a demonstration of your weakness as your having misplac'd it on one so unworthy of it as *Arthenia* from whom you cannot expect to derive the least advantage.

I call the Gods to witness (answer'd he) I pretend to ~~noon~~ nor wish no greater then a reciprocall returne; that madam is the onely thing my soule is most ambitious of, and for which I must never cease to sue till [I] have obtain'd it.

Alass *Issodorus* (said I) such expressions as these I have been ere now acquainted with but found so litle verity in them as you must pardon me if I cannot credit or believe you, for more then I have already had said to me you nor none can say, and seeing I have once been mistaken I'll not be so a second time.

Nor shall not ~~upon~~ in me upon my honour (he repli'd) would you but repose that confidence in me that you did in that perfidious One who ere he was.

Indeed I dare not (answer'd I), for I but too well know the hearts of all men, you may perhaps dessemble more dextrously then other men: or else tis like that at that very instant you declare your passion your heart may be a little affected with somewhat of that nature, but for all that I am perswaded you are liable to the same imperfections that other men are, [fol. 173 ʳ] who begin to love and nere consider why, continue their kindness onely for a while through custome and then relinquish it meerly out of a humour; nor can it possibly be otherwise since the love thats generally pretended by the most of your sex proceeds but from their lips not from their heartes, and tis onely an idle divertsment, no reall resentment [sentiment]; and though tis frequent with these Amoriests to talke of nothing more then of dispaire, to utter such direfull imprecations as oft makes the ~~hear~~ hearers tremble and to invoke Death (the Deity of lovers) each minute to put a period to their sufferings, bitterly inveighing against our honours which they terme cruellty and yet for all these specious pretences who is there that performes the least of what they promise for all their Oathes are onely writ in sand apt to be blotted out by every litle puff of Aire; and by their vowes (which ne're so firmly made) they do as by their clothes value them whilst new, but once grown old they neglectedly lay them aside and soon forget them leaving those credulous Fooles as had so much Faith, ^as^ to believe them, with teares to lament the credit that they gave to the delusive protestations of their Faithless lovers, who on those at whose Feet they have lately lain beging for pitty and reliefe look now with scorne and disregard, and onely make their boast how many feminine conquests [to] embellish their stories with.

Be not so uncharitable *Arthenia* (cry'd he) to tax our whole sex with crimes whereof onely some are tainted; do you not think there are wemen every way as guilty of inconstancy and Infidelity as men.

Yes no doubt (answer'd I) and therefore to secure you[r] selfe from any prejudice you may sustain by incountering a person of that temper take my advice, and do as I resolve, never love any, and then you need not feare to be disceiv'd.

I had rather run that hazard (he reply'd) then Follow your advice, for could I but obtaine your love though I were certain afterwards to loose it; it would be to me a greater satisfaction that I had once enjoy'd your heart then never to possess it.

Believe it (said I) I am not of your mind for I should rather chuse never to have my love accepted, then afterwards to be betray'd, or unworthyly deserted: but such a usage you nere shall find from *Arthenias* hands; for what ever interest you had once gain'd in me, nothing could ere be able to deprive you of unless I found you guilty of Inconstancy which is a thing I so highly abominate, and am such an implacable enemy too, as I shall allwayes take a perticuler care to preserve my selfe from receiving any prejudice by it; which whilst I can but keep my selfe from loves ensnareing Nets I need not apprehand.

More I could not adde, for at that instant came in *Therasmus* who seeing a stranger with me demanded of me who he was; which I having told him, he saluted him with much civility and when he went away told him he should think himselfe very much oblig'd to him, if he pleas'd to afford him the favour of his company sometimes. This invitation it was needless for *Therasmus* to repeat for *Issodorus* soon accepted it missing few evenings of coming to our house if I had not in the day been at his Fathers; making his visits pretendedly to *Therasmus* but really to me; at all which times he never left me without some demonstration of his passion; which 'twas as long ere he could perswade me to think it reall: yet I must needs say I could not keep my heart from secretly wishing it might prove as sincere as I fear'd it counterfeit: for never in my life did I see that person whom I had so great an inclination to affect as *Issodorus*, nor any man so well worthy of my Friendship as I thought him, yet seeing I had been so much mistaken in *Loreto*, I was extreamly fearfull of being a second time disceiv'd; and to that [fol. 173ᵛ] end I might not I summon'd together all the arguments I could devize that might best fortifie my Brest again[st] loves assaults; but alass they avail'd me nothing since my inclination too soon betray'd me to its tyranick power; yet so much command I still retain'd ore that unruly passion as firmly to resolve never to give *Issodorus* the least hopes till such time as he had given me such unquestionable evidences of his fidelity as it should be a sin to be longer doubtfull of it; nor was the esteeme I had for him a little heightned by that extraordinary respect *Melliantes* had for him, and that which in like manner he had for my Brother, for he seldome came nigh me but he proffess'd almost as much of Friendship for him as affection for me; and that which confirm'd me the more, was to find (as I did) those kind thoughts I had for him were so far from being dissalow'd by *Melliantes* that he rather encourag'd me to percevere in them, which I confess I needed not much incitement too; but if already he had gain'd no slight interest in my favour, the generous refusal I heard him make of a Fortune the most advantagious for him as could be imagin'd abundantly justified the preferrence I gave him before all others in my esteeme, and sufficently in my opinion made good his title to it.

For going one day over to his Fathers I found none of them within save *Bellamira* and *Issodorus* who were set by the Fire side talking very seriously together; but she seeing me come in rise up and taking me by the hand with an obliging freeness placed me by her. What do you think *Arthenia* (said she) I have been perswading *Issodorus* too.

I cannot guess (answer'd I).

Rather to make ~~to make~~ his Fortunes here at home (pursu'd she) then to go seek them in Sardina, since I dare almost assure him he may acquire a nobler here then any he can hope to find else where if he will but follow my advice in making his addresses either to *Valeria* or *Euridice,* which if he has but courage to attempt I am perswaded he needes not question his success; and fairer oppertunities he cannot wish then he may find by the meanes of his Uncle *Boetius* who has married the Princess *Victorina* their mother.

These two young Ladies madam (pursu'd *Arthenia* to the Queen) were Daughters and sole Heires to the disceased *Prince of Drepanum*, and reputed two of the greatest matches in the Province of Mazara where they for the most part liv'd though at present they were resident in Palermo.

But of the two (continu'd *Bellamira*) I had rather he should chuse *Euridice* because I know her to be of a humour the most agreeable to his owne of any person in the world.

What think you Madam (said he to me) ought I to follow my cousins councell (for so he oft still'd [styl'd] her):

Tis not for me to determine what you ought to do (answer'd I) but I must tell you ~~think~~ that I think the advice she has given you is so much for your good as none that are your Friends will wish you [not] to take it.

Pardon me madam (said he) if I cannot comply with your opinion in that perticuler, since those who are my Friends certainly will not wish I may do any thing but what may conduce to the making me happie; which I confess if my Felicity depended ~~upon~~ wealth I might tis like find enough in either of those two sisters to render me so, but I declare I am not so covetous to purchace riches with the price of my content which will be far greater in the enjoyment of another person who though I cannot hope from her those rich revenues *Valeria* and *Euridice* may entitle me too, yet my passion for her (may it be but once requited) will create me a more substantial happiness then wealth can give, since I believe you will grant one may be happy without riches but ne're without content.

I'll not deny (interupted *Bellamira*) but there are some that may enjoy content [fol. 174ʳ] even in a mean condition, but you are none of them I am perswaded, for were your passion (if you are inspir'd with any such thing) gratifi'd even to the fullest satisfaction of your wishes, it would in some short time I verily believe expire and dy, if a full confluence of plenty be not the fuell to maintain it.

That is your opinion Cousin (repli'd he) but I'll assure you none of mine.

Well be it how it will (said she) I am resolv'd to set your Mother on to perswade you to what I know will be both all honourable and advantagious for you.

I cannot tell what answer he would have made her (went on *Arthenia*) for just then came *Persides* in and chang'd the scean of the discourse.

For 6 or 7 dayes after this I saw not *Issodorus* again which made me conclude he was caught with the Golden Bait which *Bellamira* had laid for him though not with any intention of with drawing him from me (for I verily believed her utterly ignorant of those pretences he had made to me) but rather with a Friendly design of doing him good. However this conclusion did not a litle disturbe my rest, yet I resolv'd to dissemble it and to hold on my usuall course of going to *Persides's* lest he might think I refrain'd the house upon the account of some prejudice I might conceive against him: but just as I was going thithere one afternoon I was stay'd by his coming to see me and having given him to understand my intention of waiting on *Perisana*.

Though your company I dare assure you Madam (reply'd he) be at all times very acceptable to my mother, yet I must be so ingenious with you as to tell you I believe you will more oblige her if you ~~will~~ reserve the favour of that visit you designe her till some other day since there is a little kind of disorder hapned in our Family by a discovery which is newly made of my sisters being married.

Married *Issodorus* (interupted I much surpriz'd to heare it) to whom.

To *Herminio* (answer'd he) to whom she has been married this halfe yeare though till now she has conceal'd it, but not deeming it convenient to do so any longer, she desir'd a Friend of hers to acquaint my Father with it; but to that height is he insens'd against her for what she has done, as I feare it will cost some time to reconcile him to her, but from *Perisanas* indulgent affection I hope better things; for I well know she cannot long retaine anger to any of us, but *Persides* will not be perswaded so much as to see her but has commanded she should this night avoid the house, so as poor *Elesena* must be constrain'd to seek a new lodging, nor is *Theander* less unkind then my Father is severe; but for my owne part I'll not forsake her in her trouble.

You will in that shew your selfe a kind Brother (said I) yet I must needs blame *Elesena* for doing that which she could not but think she should incurre the displeasure of her Parents [by] in a very high degree, which I am really sorry she should be so unfortunate to do.

Passion madam (repli'd he) is seldome guided by reason or by duty, and if you once come to be acquainted with its power, and bow to loves controuling scepter you will then know no other law save that which it imposes.

If it should ever go about to oblige me to any thing contrary to that Duty I owe my Parents (said I) it would be enough to make me disowne its athoritie, and never more submit to so blind and irrationall a Deity.

You may boast your strength (repli'd he) as long as you are free, but were your heart once fetter'd in those bonds that *Elesanas* was, you would not then perhaps find so much cause to condemne her as now you do.

You have reason (interupted I) to vindicate her having your selfe been guilty of the like failing.

This I spake (continu'd *Arthenia*) [in] refference to his having married a Lady nam'd *Artelinda* unknown to [fol. 174ᵛ] his Parents, and no less disapprov'd on by them both when known, then his sisters match now was; for at this time he was a widdower and had been so for the space of neer seven yeares, yet had he not as yet attain'd to more then the age of 27.

But (pursu'd I to him) you will questionless make amends for the indiscretion of your first Amour by following that Friendly advice *Bellamira* gave you the other day, which I believe upon second thoughts you have found so much conducing to your advantage as I hope it has enduced you to lay aside all thoughts of me from whom you can neither pretend too nor expect any. But whether of the two (went I on) have you made your choice.

Neither of the two I'll assure you madam (answer'd he) for to your selfe alone is my choice confin'd, nor can those Golden Baites (which some vulger spirits perhaps might greedily catch at) ever have the power to take me, or once withdraw me from that unalterable resolve ne're to be any ones but yours. So far am I then from taking *Bellamiras* councell (as you unkind *Arthenia* injuriously suppose) as I never troubled my mind so much as with one thought of it since, for such full employment does my passion for you find my thoughts as I have no leasure to remind ought save what may render it acceptable, at least not offencive to you as I have but too much reason to conclude it: and though I have not been so happie as to receive from you the least encouragment for my perceverance, yet till death I am determin'd never to decline that unequall'd love my soule has for you. I am not ignorant I confess (pursu'd he) there was much of truth in my cousins ascertion (for so Madam he oft call'd *Bellamira* continu'd *Arthenia* to the Queen) in affirming it would be both honourable and advantagious for me if I could obtaine either *Valeria* or *Electra*,[4] as tis possible I might would I make it my endeavour: but were both their Fortunes united into one, and as much more added to it, I do declare it should not startle my fidelity, or tempt me to forgoe *Arthenias* vertue for their mines of treasure. But what mov'd you I beseech you madam (added he) to charge me with a fault resembling my sisters.

Methinkes you need not aske that question (answer'd I) since you are not ignorant how displeasing your match with *Artelinda* was both to *Persides* and *Perisana*.

I do confess it madam (repli'd he blushing) but did believe my having been married might to you have been unknown, as I could wish it had, lest you esteeme that offering I have made you of my heart the more unworthy your acceptance for having been formerly devoted to another. But perhaps we may be yet on equall termes, for if I have lov'd once, I am mistaken if you have hitherto been absolutely exempted from that passion.

I know not from whence you should draw that conclusion (said I) yet will I not deny but that I have lov'd; yet was it onely on the score of gratitude, and when the cause was taken away, the effect soon ceas'd: but never did I know as yet affections power upon the account of inclination.

So have I (repli'd he) I must acknowledge: and seeing my marriage is to you no secret, I will not scruple to avow that I so well lov'd my deare *Artelinda* that had I been sure to run greater hazards of my ruine then I apparently knew I did, I should not to shun them have deviated from the least title of that engagement whereby I had bound my selfe to be hers alone till death should make a seperation between us, which alass (pursu'd he with the teares ready to start from his eyes) too soon he did, suffering me to enjoy but one poor yeare what I for the space of seven before most passionately lov'd [fol. 175ʳ] and though by her death I was free to make a second choice yet so deservedly dear was her memory to me, as I ne're entertain'd a thought of any one till that minute I first look'd on you; 'twas then my heart lost those impressions my love for poor dead *Artelinda* had still preserv'd undefaced, and in an instant, in their stead ingrav'd those never fading Charactors of a no less intire and perfect affection for the admir'd *Arthenia* which nothing but the hand of Death shall ere race out.

---

[4] *Electra* seems to be a mistake for *Eurydice*.

I am sorry (said I) it should be my Fate to be so injurious to *Artelinda* as to blot her out of your heart, but tis however my satisfaction that she has no reason to complain of me since I never contributed to the depriving her of that Monument which questionless she deserv'd eternally to possess.

She has indeed no reason (repli'd he) to complain of you, nor yet of me, since none but will acknowledge I have sufficently evinced both the greatness and constancy of my affection by my continuing to love her, as long after her Death, as before it I did adore her: but I am perswaded if it were possible for her to know what is transacted here below, she would be so far from taxing me with unkindness, that she would rather rejoyce to see I have design'd her a successour so deserving as your selfe: He could adde no more, nor I returne him any answer by reason *Melliantes* came just then in, and testifi'd a very great satisfaction to meet *Issodorus* there, who did the like to see him, and when he went away took my Brother with him but whether they went together I know not, nor was I much curious to enquire.

This generous refusall made by *Issodorus* of two such advantagious proffers, either of which I was perswaded would have been a thing feasable enough for him to obtain had he but made it his business, joyn'd with that sincere kindness, and contancy of affection he had testifi'd to his *Artelinda* both in her life and since her death, made on my heart so strong an asault as I had as little the will as the power any longer to deny him the intire possession of a heart I could not but think him of all men living the worthiest of; nor did I now look on *Loretos* deserting me as any other then the effect of my good Fortune which had deni'd me the less Felicity but to confer on me the greater, nor could I any more complain of that inconstancy which I had hitherto consider'd as an invitation to detest the whole race of mankind, since it had much more oblig'd then prejudiced me; for I could not but account it a far nobler happiness to possess *Issadorus's* love then *Loretos*; which I thought 'twas possible I might still have been mistress off had I not my selfe contributed to its loss by that coldness and indifferency wherewith I receiv'd it. Which that I might not on *Issodorus's* score procure to my selfe a resembling Fate I determined to give him some hopes of a mutuall esteeme; and the rather in regard of a declaration I had heard him openly atteast occation'd by a discourse which at *Persides's* was begun by severall Ladies and ^young^ Gentlemen which one night were met there together concerning the severity wherewith some wemen treated their servants, some declaming against it, and others no less earnestly pleading for it, saying there was nothing so distructive to love as to have it gratifi'd by a reciprocall one, for love having its origine from Desire, and that once obtain'd it must needs Follow that the cause must cease having attain'd its end; whereas Feares Jealousies, and dispaires do rather heighten and increase the vehemence of the passion by the opposition it finds to thwart its attainment.

Tis very true said one of the Ladies (nam'd *Philotheta*) love can be never [fol. 175^{v}] be violent or lasting but when the desires are so; and tis certainly impossible for them to be so when whatever they ~~desire~~ require is granted; it must necessarily follow that then to render a passion durable a woman must never grant those Favours she designes to bestow but with much importunity to the end the higher value may be placed on them, for else they will be receiv'd without delight, or at least with a meane acknowledgment; for tis too often seen men slight and scorn those favours which they lightly and easily obtain'd, and I must tell you tis much more easie to revive that Flame which is extinguish'd by an excess of severity then one that is stifled by too many and continu'd kindnesses.

I cannot but acknowledge madam repli'd one of the company (called *Doristus*) that there is much of reason in what you affirme since experience often shewes that enjoyment takes of[f] from the value of what before we highly priz'd, so when any man has obtain'd the affection of his mistress it soon becomes much less considerable; for when was it ever known that any Husband contin'd to love his wife with that ardency and passion as when he was her servant.

I will not go about to confute these opinions of yours (answer'd *Issodorus*) how erronious soever I think them, since I question not but time will sufficently convince you, and experience teach you how much more satisfactory tis to have ones affections crown'd with a mutuall one then alwayes to ly under the tyranie of a cruell and rigorous mistress; for my owne part I declare I do so far discent from what you maintain, that should I ever love, and find no other requitall but severity or disdain, how great and fervent so ere my Flame might be, it would not faile in a short time to expire and dy where there was no Fewell to feed it with: bare imaginations, faint hope, tormenting and heart wracking Jealousies would nere afford me any: I must have love for love I do declare, for nought save that can make my Flame endure, and as for all you (pursu'd he) that are of a contrary mind, I wish it may be your destinies to encounter wemen of such Flinty and obdurate tempers as may make you repent you believ'd such ill treatments necessary to the augmenting or (at least) continuance of your passions.

This which *Issodorus* affirm'd of himselfe, whether it were with a designe to prepare me for the reception of his love when once he should declare it, and withall to let me understand with what resentments [feelings] I must ~~intertainit~~ entertaine it if I desir'd to render it permanent and lasting, or whether he spake his reall thoughts I cannot say (went on *Arthenia*) but this it was I confess which mov'd me to resolve not so long to defer (as otherwise I should) the owneing of that conquest which never was intire till *Issodorus* made it so.

The next evening came *Bellamira* with him to our house who told me they were going to see *Elesena* and ask'd me if I would not oblige them with my company, to which I readily assented, assuring *Bellamira* I had an intention to wait on *Elesena* very speedely, but since she was dispos'd to go now I would imbrace this oppertunity of paying her my respects. Divers times after this did I accidentally mee[t] *Issodorus* there, but one time above the rest abundance of other company hapning to be there too when he had long sought for an oppertunity to entertain me with a private converse but could find no plausible occation conducing to his desire, he demanded of me a loud (to the end all there present might heare) when I saw my Brother.

[T]wo or three dayes agoe (answer'd I)[.]

[A]nd did he say nothing to you (added he) of that concern I spake to him about when I last saw him.

No (said I) he did not tell me any thing wherein [fol. 176ʳ] you had an interest.

Tis possible you have forgot it (repli'd he) but if you please madam to afford me your care one minute I'll tell you what it was (pursu'd he taking me by the hand and drawing me to a window at a good distance from the rest of the company whilst I willingly follow'd him, never mistrusting his designe, but verily thinking he had some weighty matter to acquaint me with) but he soon undisceav'd me by saying I have not any thing to tell you madam ^in^ refferance to *Melliantes*, but in relation to my selfe I must again repeat what I so oft have vow'd, though you are still so incredulous as not to believe me when I protest and swear I love you with the highest passion imaginable, and till I dye shall never cease to do so; for since your severity has not been able to allay the ardour of my Flame there is nought else you need to apprehend. For the gods sake Deare *Arthenia,* I conjure you moderate somewhat of your cruelty and be no longer so obduratly determin'd to render me totally miserable when you may so easily by one kind word create me the happiest of men.

Alass *Issodorus* (said I) what would you have me do, I would do anything that I am capable of to render you as happy as I really wish you.

Then you must love me madam (answer'd he hastily) for any thing less then an absolute enjoyment of your affection will be utterly unable to make me so.

Admit I should (repli'd I) and that (not withstanding those weighty reasons I have nere to believe there's truth to be found in any of your sex) I ~~shoull~~ should credit you so far as the Faith I gave to your protestations (which carry with them a Face of reallity I must confess) might convert that aversion I have justly conceiv'd against all men in generall into a perticuler kindness for you, yet tis possible you will derive but small satisfaction from it, as not being such a one as perhaps you may require, having rather Friendship then affection for its root, for though I may give you an interest in the former, it is not in my power to intitle you to the latter till authoriz'd by the consent of *Mironides* and *Brecena* to whose will I ought to confine my choice.

O Madam (repli'd he) why will you be so cruell to lay such an obstruction in my way to felicitie as tis impossible for me to remove; not that I do in the least dispaire of gaining your Parents consents to make you mine had I but time to importune that favour from them, but alass that time for my departure is too nigh for me any way to attempt what in so short a space I cannot hope to accomplish: but with how deep a sadness I shall leave Sicilie I am not able to represent nor you conceive, when I consider that ere I come back you may be dispos'd on to another.

That may be *Issodorus* (said I) but I'll assure you this, I'll do whatever lies in me to avoid, what cannot be more your trouble then my misfortune; and that if those to whom Heaven and Nature has given a right to bestow me on whosoere they please should command me to marry another I should obey them with no less a reluctancie then with satisfaction I should embrace their permission to make me yours. Nor will I scruple to avow (though perhaps I may go some-what beyound those strict limits which decency prescribes in leting you know so much) that were I free to make my owne choice I would not onely prefer you before all men in Sicily, but even all that the world contains of either rich or great within the compass of its vast extent.

At this assurance I perceiv'd so lively a joy to sparkle in his eyes as no one but would [fol. 176ᵛ] have conceiv'd his heart to be deeply affected with that passion, and taking me ~~by~~ by the hand (which he press'd with a most transported ardency) oh Dearest *Arthenia* (cry'd he) that the place were void of witnesses that I might have the liberty to throw my selfe at your Feet in the humblest posture imaginall [imaginable] to pay my thankes for this obliging assurance and acknowledgment you have made so highly conducing to my unspeakable happiness; be as kind then, as you are generous I beseech you (~~said~~ pursu'd he) and compleat my felic-ity by giving me leave to derive that intirely from your owne goodness and free condescention which I may one day hope from the confession of *Mironides*.

For heavens sake *Issodorus* (said I) tempt not my Friendship to injure my Duty which if you move me to transgresse against, I shall doubtless repent the interest you have in me.

Your pardon madam I humbly beg (repli'd he) if the ambition of my passion-ate desires cannot be content to be confin'd within those limmits wherewith you have bounded them, but aspires to more then you are willing to grant, yet since you are pleas'd to mittigate my sufferings by the hopes you give me that I am not indifferent to you, I will endeavour to rest satisfi'd with that esteeme which you vouchsafe me.

I then reminding him that it was possible our privacie might be remark'd which to prevent; feigning to have inform'd me of some concern relating to *Mel-liantes* he said to me (as I turn'd about to go from him) loud enough to be heard by all there present. You will very much oblige me madam to put your Brother in mind to get this affaire dispatch'd with what expedition he can.

You may be confident (repli'd I) my Brother is too much your servant to neglect any concern of yours.

You are very subtill *Issodorus* (said *Hermino* to him smiling and speaking so low as I am certain he was not heard by any save my selfe) but all your cuning is not enough to secure you from some concerned eyes which pierce far deeper then you imagine.

But *Issodorus* seem'd to take no notice of what he said, nor could I conceive on what account 'twas spoken unless any of the company should mistrust that passion he had own'd for me; which if they did, I could not think what concern they could have in it, since the Gentlemen were all strangers to me, and the Ladies every one of them married except *Bellamira*. Though I had acquainted my Brother with *Issodorus's* pretences, yet had I never taken the least notice either to *Therasmus* or *Hestrina* not withstanding that I found by severall words they let fall that they had conceiv'd some Jealousie of it: but at last *Hestrina* gave me more intimation of her suspition by her cautioning me to take heed I did not in *Issodorus* encounter a second *Loreto*:

I know not madam what you meane (said I) but this I will presume to tell you that I am perswaded had *Loreto* been of so ~~well~~ generous and well compos'd a temper as *Issodorus* is, I had certainly been but too happie in him.

I perceive (repli'd she) he has had the good fortune to produce in you a very advantagious opinion, but ~~how~~ let me advice you Niece (continu'd she) not to suffer it to prevaile too far in favour of him to your prejudice. I am not so blind nor *Therasmus* neither as not to perceive these visits which he makes you has something more in them then common civility.

That may be (answer'd I) since tis probable he may come to see me so oft as he does rather out of complacence to *Perisana* who he very well knows does me the honour to allow me no meane place in her Friendship, then out of any perticuler respect he has for me.

Come, come *Arthenia* (cry'd she) don't dissemble with me I know you do not think so, though perhaps it were better, and more for your quiet that you did; for when once the Sea has devided you, [177ʳ] and that he is gone into Sardina I dare pass my word he ne're thinks on you more whatever he may now pretend, or yet admit he did, and that you find him no less constant then at present you (it may be) believe him kind, yet I say, what advantage can you hope for by placing your affection (as I feare you have already but too far) on a person who has not one foot of land (as far as I heare) to endow you with, but must be constrain'd to build his Fortunes on the Vice-roys favour, and how totering a foundation great mens favours are to lay the stress of ones whole Fortunes on experience dayly shewes; and besides, do you believe your Mother who so dearly loves you will ere consent you should wholly abandon her to spend your dayes in a forreign land.

I am not about it madam (I repli'd) nor need you fear, had I that esteem for *Issodorus* which you onely fancy, yet should it never move me to any thing in favour of him inconsistent with my duty which I shall always prefer before my owne or any other bodies satisfaction.

You will do well (answer'd she) to percevere in that resolve, but since you are with me I cannot but think my selfe concern'd to take a perticuler care of you; for should you do any otherwise then well, you know my sister would be apt to charge it on me as a neglect of your wellfaire; which none I'll assure you more sincerely wishes then my self: then seeing I am certainly assur'd *Issodorus* (notwithstanding all his good qualities) is no fit match for you, nor you for him, I must intreat you to refrain his company, or not to take it ill if I acquaint *Brecena* with my apprehensions.

If it will give you any satisfaction Madam (repli'd I) I will so farre comply with your commands as to request him to forbeare seeing me here any more, but you must pardon me if I cannot promise you not to let him see me elsewhere; for then I must absolutely decline waiting on *Perisana* and his sister, and deprive myselfe of the conversation of the excellent *Bellamira* who would questionless think it very strange that without any the least shew of reason I should with so high an incivility abandon their society which I confess I should be most unwilling to do. But methinkes you need not be anyway concern'd since I declare I never will yeeld to any thing my Parents shall have just cause to charge on me as a breach of that obedience I am obliged to pay them.

I knew there was but too much of truth and reason in what *Hestrina* said to me (continu'd *Arthenia*) not to be convinc'd how disadvantagious my passion for *Issodorus* might prove to me, and no less injurious to him, since I could bring but a slight addition to his Fortunes, which I could not but believe would be as ill resented [felt] by his Parents as mine; but alass I found my selfe engag'd too far to retreat, and though I knew I had embark'd for a voyage wherein I foresaw I must inevitably encounter many stormes, yet was not the danger that they threatned able to perswade me to retire ere I proceeded further. I did not designe to make a secret of *Issodorus* love, but did intend assoon as I could find out a convenient way to make it known to *Mironides* and *Brecena* yet was I not willing (I confess) *Hestrina* should be the first Intelligencer of it to them, because I very well knew her to be of so capricious and suspitious a humour as I had reason to doubt she would make the worst of all things in her information which might tend very much to both our prejudices; which to prevent I thought it best (as I had told her I would) to desire *Issodorus* to forbear coming any more to see me, and withall to acquaint him with the reason that induced me to make him that request the next time I saw him, [fol. 177ᵛ] which hapned to be in the Princess of Erix's ~~walk~~ Gardan where having the priviledge of walking as often as I pleas'd most commonly every morning I us'd to walke for my health which I en[j]o'd not long together having almost ever since I was seven yeares of age for the most part been very sickly. I usually walk'd alone but one morning chanceing to have *Bellamira* with me, we had not been long there ere we ~~sp~~ espi'd *Issodorus* and *Melliantes* at the further end of the Alie that we were in who no sooner saw us but they hasted to meet us, and having given ^us^ the good morrow.

Do you not want company ladies (said *Issodorus*) I'll assure you we came on purpose to waite on you and proffer you ours:

No indeed (answer'd *Bellamira* somewhat tartly) we wanted none of yours.

Well (repli'd he) since you did not I will ~~try~~ not give you the trouble of it, but try whether *Arthenia* will be so kind as to accept it (pursu'd he presenting me his [arm] to lead me whilst *Melliantes* did the like to *Bellamira*).

Tis possible she may be so complacent (said she) but I wish her civilitie prove not her prejudice,

I was a litle startled (I confess) to heare them talke to each other at this rate, in regard I always thought they had held a very friendly correspondence, but supposing there might of late have been some picque between them which might be unknown to me, I thought it improper for me to enterest my selfe in anothers concernes so far as to make any enquirie, and therefore pass'd on without taking the least notice of what had past. But *Issodorus* walking something faster then they, ere I was aware, he insensibly drew me a good distance from them; which I perceiving, and thinking I might venture to speak without the danger of being overheard. Pray *Issodorus* (said I) take it not ill if I intreat you to see me no more.

No more (interupted he) for heavens sake what have I done to deserve so severe a punishment; and what accursed starre is it that has so malicious an influence on you in so short a time to worke on your inclinations such a strang and unexpected alteration.

I am not chang'd at all since last you saw me I'll assure you (answer'd I) nor is it unkindness that moves me to make you this request; neither do I intend (as you conceive) to banish you my sight, but onely to desire you to see me no more at *Therasmus's* (as I would have told you ~~wou~~ would your impatience have allow'd me time to speak) since my Aunt is become suspitious not onely of your respect for me but believes I favour you more than I ought.

She would have but little reason to judge me so happie as she takes me to be (repli'd he) did she but know what hard conditions you have impos'd on me for the attainment of my ~~chiefest~~ felicity. But I hope madam (pursu'd he) though you deprive me of the priviledge of seeing you at *Therasmus's* you will be so kind as to allow me else where.

You may assure your selfe I will (answer'd I) nor I compli'd with *Hestrina's* humour so far as I have, had I not the convenience of giving the satisfaction (if such you esteeme it) of seeing me either at your father's or *Elesena*['s] as oft as you desire.

Do you believe, *Arthenia* (he hastely repli'd) it would be a satisfaction to me to be happie.

Yes without ^question^ (answer'd I)

[T]hen believe it for a certain Truth (said he) there is not any thing that can make me so (next to the enjoyment of your heart) save onely your sight and conversation. But are you still determin'd madam to oppose my supream felicity (went he on) with that severe duty you arme against me: and may I not importune from your owne free grant what the transcendency of my passionate desires will not suffer me with any patience or content to expect from the favour of your [fol.178ʳ] Parents to ~~which~~ whom (I beseech you) be not so scrupelously severe as absolutely to referre my Fate since tis on you alone it does depend, and in your power (were your will but correspondent to it) to render me the happiest of men by making your selfe the reward for what I have given you. And let me tell you Madam (continu'd he) any thing less can never gratifie the Present I have made you of my Heart which is so intirely yours, as it would enevitably pine away and dy but for the hope it has of so close and neer a union with that you carry in your Brest as nought save Death may ere be able to seperate, or divide them.

I am sufficently blamable (repli'd I) in [blot] not taking the first sentiments of my kindness from the command, or at least the permission of those to whom my birth has subjected me; desire not then to render me more faulty by importuning to what I neither ought, nor ever will consent too, since the lawes both of heaven and Nature oblige me to the contrary.

If this be your finall resolve (said he with a countenance where in all the tokens of a visible discontent might be seen) as neer as the prefixed day design'd for my departure is, I shall not live to see it. Ah (pursu'd he sighing) how little reason had I to conclude my selfe that happie person as I late believ'd since I now too plainly find, that affection you were pleas'd to owne for me is so ~~clo~~ cold and indifferent as I have far more cause to dispaire then hope; but Death is the universall cure of all misfortunes and to that I'll have recourse for mine.

Do not terrifie me with so fatall a threat (repli'd I) nor wrong not the sincerity of my love by thinking it so indifferent; for so far from that it is as I protest there is not any thing under Heaven dearer to me then *Issodorus* nor any thing (my Duty and my honour preserv'd unblemish'd) which I would not do for his satisfaction. And cause you shall have no justifiable reason to complain of ~~my~~ me I will assure you this, that if I may not be yours (as I confess I feare I shall not) I will never be any others mans, if by any imaginable meanes I can avoid it; but if all should faile me, and that another should be impos'd on me by those whom heaven has invested with a power to dispose of me as they think fit, I should accept him with such resentments [feelings] as some happie amidst the confluence of all Earthly delights and pleasures would welcome the tortourous and most painfull of Deaths that the witiest of Tyrrants ere invented for the punishment of them they mortally hated.

O Madam (cry'd he) how kind and cruell are you both at once; the first by shewing me so sweet a Prospect of felicity as this most obliging assurance is to me; the later, by cuting off in a manner my hopes of reaping any benifit by it, in declaring you feare you never must be mine: but why do you think so, and what reason have you for your apprehension.

I'll tell you *Issodorus* (answer'd I) tis this, I am most certain *Brecena* will rather chuse to see me dye and with more content Follow me to my grave, then ever yeeld I shall marry any man that shall be oblig'd to carry me so far from her as Sardina is.

Methinks tis strange (repli'd he) she should prefer your death before your absence, since to whatever distance you were remov'd she had still a possibility of seeing you again sometimes though not so oft (perhaps as she might wish) but if dead, she would then utterly loose all hopes of ever seeing you again. But would I could as easily and as soon remove all other difficulties as this I should not doubt of obtaining what my soule is most ambitious of: for tis not my designe absolutely to quit Sicily: no Madam, upon my word I have too great a kindness for my owne

Country to abandon it for ever though I must necessarily for some time; but I question not in some few yeares so well to settle my concernes there as I may live if not altogether yet for the most part here at home.

If you can do so (said I) the greatest nay indeed the onely obstacle to your desires on my account will be remov'd; make good your tittle to me then by a constant [fol.178ᵛ] fedelity and rest confident that if a truly sincere, vertuous, and innocent affection may requite your passion you shall ne're have cause to terme me ungratfull. But I beg and conjure you *Issodorus* (pursu'd I) by that kindness you have for me require nothing more at my hands till such time as I may without offending my duty gratifie your request.

I will obey you Madam if I am able (repli'd he) but if I cannot you must charge my passion not me with disobedience.

I deeming it not convenient any longer to decline *Bellamira's* conversation lest she might take it amiss that I quited her company for *Issodorus's*, told him what I apprehended and thereby obliged him to walk so as we might [o're take] them; which we no sooner did, but assuming his usuall briskness,

I hope Cousin (said he to *Bellamira*) you will not say but that I have been very obliging.

To your selfe perhaps (repli'd she) but not to me I'll assure you.

I have fail'd in my designe then (return'd he)

I believe not (answer'd she) you would not be so pleasent if you had.

But not seeming to take any notice of what she said last. Come *Melliantes* (cry'd he to my Brother) since they are no better humour'd let us leave them: with that biding us adue they went away leaving us to pursue our walk which we continu'd not much longer; for soon after they were gone we repair'd home, but as we went I could not forbear asking *Bellamira* the reason of that difference that appear'd to be between her and *Issodorus*.

Nay no great matter (answer'd she) but onely I design'd to carry my selfe a little crossly to him, on purpose to be reveng'd on him for vexing me the last night with something he said to me concerning *Melliantes*. but what it was I perceived she was unwilling to tell me and therefore forbeare to press her further. But whether it were that I had caught any colld with walking, or what other cause to impute it too, I know not, but so it hapned that I was in a short while after ceas'd by an indisposition which not onely confin'd me to my Chamber, but my bed also for some time. I had not been ill above two dayes when *Melliantes* knowing nothing of it came to see me, and told me he came just then from *Issodorus* whom he had found in a condition resembling mine.

I think (pursu'd he) you sympathize with each other.

But too much concern'd was I to heare this unwellcome newes to make any reply to what he spake in rallery, onely demanded how long he had been ill, and what it was he ail'd.

He has not been well above this three or four dayes (answer'd *Melliantes*) though not so very ill as now he is till yesterday, but what his Distemper may be I cannot informe you since it puzells his Phisician to determine of it, but conclude Mellancholly to be the chiefe cause from whence it proceeds.

Of all men living (said I) I should ne're have judg'd *Issodorus* to be of that humour.

So one would have thought (repli'd he) but if he be tis certainly accidently, not natural to him[.]

I should have told your Majesty (pursu'd *Arthenia*) that *Issodorus* was now altogether at the *Prince of Orestagns* that he might be in a readiness to attend his departure for Sardina which was dayly expected, and therfore I thought it ~~was~~ not strang that I heard no sooner of his being ill since I believ'd they scarce knew it as yet at his Fathers. No sooner was my Brother gone, ere *Bellamira* came to see me, and finding me in that condition seem'd to take it unkindly that I did not let her know of it assuring me she would have been with me every day had she in the least mistrusted I had not been well. She then confirm'd what my Brother had told me concerning *Issodorus* saying *Perisana* was gone that afternoon to see him, and that if she found any appearance of danger in him she intended to have him remov'd home again to the end she might take a more perticuler care of him then she thought strangers would.

This I wish'd she might (pursu'd *Arthenia*) in regard I hop'd to heare oftener of him then I could expect to do in the place where he now was, for I confess I was much ^more^ concern'd for him then for my selfe; but [fol.179 ʳ] 'twas not whilst I continu'd in Towne that he came back to his Fathers; for the Doctor having once declar'd that nothing but good Aire would recovery me, *Melliantes* would not suffer me to rest til he had got me out of Towne, and carried me to *Eugenions;* where long I had not been, ere I felt the good effects of the Country Aire very prevalent towards the recovery of my health; which assoon as I could perfectly regain I meant to go back to *Therasmus's* again, for not one minutes quiet could I enjoy in such a manner did my feares torment me for *Issodorus,* seeing I had no way left to enforme my self of his condition without making too clear a discovery of that kindness I had for him: but ere I could execute this resolve, he sent *Filoret* (his Lacque) to me with a letter (both to inform me of his owne condition, and to enquire of mine) which as I remember contain'd these words.

> *I have rather chose Madam to hazard your displeasure by this presumption, then merit it by a longer silence since my present condition denies me both the honour, and happiness of waiting on you in person, which nothing save this strang Indisposition that makes me its absolute Prisoner could have laid such a restraint on me; but much more willingly could I submit to it, had not Fate been doubly cruell in not onely depriving me of my health but of your sight and conversation at a time when both are so exceeding necessary for the preservation of a life which I cannot value but for the interest you have in it, and by a way too, no less afflicting then the deprivation of what my soule most passionatly wishes: it is not possible for me to express the satisfaction it would be ^to^ me to receive from your Faire hand the assurance of your regaining that which I so much want, and then*

should I presume to beg you would by a speedy returne mittigate those pains which
nothing renders so intollerable as your absence; but if otherwise, be assur'd madam
assoon as ever I am in any capacity of stiring I'll waite on you to tell you once more
ere I dy that none can be more yours then

Issodorus

These lines inspir'd me at once both with joy and griefe, the first to see him not unmindfull of me at a time when the violence of those paines (as by *Filoret* I understood) he minutely endur'd might have excus'd him from any thing of this nature: and the later to find rather an increase then a Diminution of his Distemper. I nere consulted with ought save my passion whether or no I should answere his kindness in the like manner, and without delay taught my Pen to reply, but in what words I have now forgot, not counting them worthy to be retain'd still in mind; onely I remember I told him in my letter that if my returne might afford him any reliefe it should not long be deni'd him, for the morrows sun should not run halfe his course ere he might to expect to see me.

This Promise I was not more free to make, then puntuall in performing, for the next morning by 9 of the clock I was got to *Therasmus's* but both he and *Hestrina* were gone from home, and were not to returne that weeke, whereupon I stay'd not there, but went instantly to *Persides's* but being so early *Perisana* was not drest wherefore thinking it unfit to press into her chamber till she had notice of my being come to Towne, I took that oppertunity of paying my first visit to *Bellamira* who testifi'd much joy for my recovery and returne. I had scarce answer'd the expression of her kindness when *Issodorus* came in, but so alter'd as (que[s]tionless) had ~~else~~ I seen ^him^ else were [elsewhere] I should ^ne're^ have believ'd 'twas he, so pale and thin was [fol.179ᵛ] his Face grown; his eyes dull hollow and languishing, yet (whether it were onely my opinion that flatteringly made me conceive so) me thought he no sooner saw me, but a more gay and spritly Aire diffus'd, and spread it selfe ore all his Face; however he gave me onely such a salutation as any other person of his acquaintance might have expected; but 'twas not long ere we enjoy[ed] an unrestrain'd converse; for *Bellamira* being call'd to come to *Perisana* left me alone with him who assoon as she was gone out came, and taking me by the hand, kissing and embracing it with all the ardency of a passionate love.

Though the early performance of your promise Dearest *Arthenia* (said he) has prevented my expectations, yet my impatient desires has made this morning seem to me as tedious as the longest day, and forced me often to travell to the window to see if my longing eyes could be rewarded with the sight of your approach as indeed they were, for I saw you enter *Therasmus's* and when you pass'd over hither, which I was a joyfull spectatour of, though I should feare you would scarce believe me to be so, by reason of that cold reception I was confin'd to give before *Bellamira* but I know Madam (pursu'd he) you are to ingenious not to acknowledge that oft times our actions are necessitated to run counter to our inclinations; but time is precious with me, and therefore I shall not wast it in imploring a pardon for that which I am perswaded your goodness does not charge on me as a fault; and imploy it more necessarily in beging you to consider whither you think I am not yet reduced to an estate that deserves your pitty.

I need not study to resolve you that (answer'd I) but must needs confess that the condition wherein, to the greife of my soule I do behold you, not onely merits, but has my pitty in the highest degree: for I should be no less unjust then you are unkind to question it, should I deny him my compassion who has so larg an interest in my love.

Tis rather reason (repli'd he) then unkindness that moves me to doubt it, for how can I believe you pitty me, since you will chuse to see me dy rather then afford me a reliefe; for what I have allready said I must again repeat that I neither can nor will live to leave Sicily if you will not condecend to be absolutely mine ere I go.

Wrong not the sinceritie of my affection *Issodorus* (said I) by these groundless fancies; Heaven knowes I would do anything to convince you of its reallytie that did not intrench upon my duty which I am resolutely determin'd to preserve inviolate to my death; but if my prayers may have any influence on you, I do not onely intreat, but conjure you by all the love you have protested for me, not to cast a way a life far dearer to me then my owne meerly out of a willfull humour, since what you now require may better be much better obtain'd at your return.

I do confess it Madam (cry'd he) but how can I be certain you will be then in a capacity of being mine.

Endeavour a recovery I beseech you (said I) and if it be possible I'll find out some way to give you that assurance without prejudicing my duty.

Bellamira having in this time made known my being there to *Perisana* she contented not her selfe to send for me in, but came and fetch'd me into her Chamber causing me to set by her all the while. She was a dressing and knowing *Hestrina* to be absent, she not onely invited [me] to dine with her that day, but also injoyn'd me to eate with her every day till she came home. This extraordinary civility merited a proportinate returne of thanks, which I gave in the most gratfull and respective language I could invent; for though with a seeming unwillingness I at first declin'd it lest I might be troublesome, which she having assur'd me to the contrary, with an inward joy I accepted it as most agreeable to the desire I had of being neer *Issodorus,* and enjoying his company as much as [fol.180ʳ] possible which I had the satisfaction to do whole dayes together; yet was this content mix'd with an equall trouble to see him (as I dayly did) to strugle with so strang a Distemper as neither before, nor since did I ever see, or heare of any one to be in the like manner: he was indeed for the most part all the mornings indifferent well, but in the Afternoons especially towards the evenings so ill as he was constrain'd to go either into his Bed, or Lye downe on it. Upon the first approach of his Fits he would in an instant grow so excessive cold as if the Icie hand of Death had spread it selfe o're all his body, his very hands, and Nailes seem'd absolutely dead, his Face cover'd over with a mortall paleness, and all the Joynts and Limbs of his Body torne as on a Rack by most violent, and tormenting paines; and many times would he lye for the space of an houre, or more streach'd out seeming quite depriv'd of life, or motion; and when he came began to come to himselfe again, the first symtomes of life he gave, were such deep fetch'd sighs as one might have apprehended that each of them would have rent his heart in sunder.

I confess (pursu'd *Arthenia*) I never saw him in the height, and extreamity of his Fits, for soon after midnight was the time th[e]y excercis'd their greatest severity on him, and so continu'd till neer break of day, at which time they would of a sudden abate, and become more moderate. But though I saw him not in this deplorable condition 'twas terrible enough to me (me thought) to heare the relation of it; and often (though in vain) did I wish it had been possible for me to be a constant attendant on him invisible to all eyes but his; that by my solicitude and care about him I might have given him an unquestionabl[e] testimony of my sincere affection; but that being impossible I was fain to rest contented onely to afford him my company at such times as decency would allow. Assoon as his Distemper summon'd him to his chamber *Perisana* would still injoyne *Bellamira* and I to go with him to try if we could by any meanes divert him; for he was allwayes at those times most desperatly mellancholly.

Your Majesty may believe I was not backward to performe what agreed so well with my wishes; but *Bellamira* (as I oft observ'd) after we had set awhile together by him would still pretend some occation or other to call her away, so as she would leave us alone for some considerable time; but these pretences which call'd her thence I many times perceiv'd to be so triviall as I knew not well what to impute them too; yet at last I concluded she had an absolute knowledge, or strong opinion suspition of our loves, which mov'd her to withdraw to the end she might oblige us in leaving us at liberty to entertain each other with the greater freedome in her absence: nor was it onely now, but oftentimes before that she had given me cause to fancy her a furtherer of *Issodorus*'s addresses to me. But not long after I had some reason to change my opinion and to conclude it to be rather some litle sentiments of Jealousie mix'd with a kind of high Generosity that prompted her to what she did.

One night *Issodorus* having had a more terrible Fit then usuall, so bad indeed as had put the wholle Family into teares with a beliefe that 'twas impossible his death could be far distant, I came in just as his Mother and *Bellamira* (both of them having set up with him all night) were newly laid downe to sleep, and being told (upon my inquirie) how more then ordinary ill he had been, I step'd into his chamber to aske how he did where I found onely *Filoret* waiting on him; but no sooner did *Issodorus* see me but commanding *Filoret* away he beg'd me to come and sit downe by him (which at his request I did) and fixing [fol.180ᵛ] a languishing eye on me, Ah dearest *Arthenia* (cry 'd he) tis now that I am more unhappie then ever, for I am now uncapable not onely of requiring what I have hitherto so passionately desir'd of you (I meane your consent to marry me ere I leave Sicily) but likewise of accepting that favour should you so far gratifie my passion as to condescend to it; for *Persides* (for what reason I know not, unless he has heard of, or is become suspitious of my designe to make my selfe yours) has not been content alone to enjoyne, and strictly charge me on my duty and Obedience to him but also on pain of his mortall displeasure, and irreconsilable hatered never to marry any more whilst he lives without his consent which tis as impossible for me to obtain should I indeavour it, as tis for me to live without the hopes of being yours at last. To importune you (continu'd he) to stay for me till Death has put a period to my cruell Fathers dayes (and thereby freed me from this engagement) would be so highly injurious to your better Fortunes that it would be both unjust and unreasonable in me to make you any such request; yet if you do not ~~promise~~ make me such a promise I must dye, as it is fit I should rather then live to prejudice what I so dearly love.

These words did he pronounce with such a sad, and mournfull accent as the pitty they infus'd into my Soule forced the teares to fall from my eyes: but concealing them as well as I could I said to him. If it be so *Issodorus* (as you suppose) that your Father has any knowledge of your passion, his so apparent~~ly~~ disapproving it as his absolute prohibiting [blot] your marriage does import; should induce you to relinquish it; which if you ^do^ upon the score of Obedience to his will, believe me I will never quarell with you, nor complain of you nor yet of any other but of my owne hard Fate which rendred me unworthy to be yours in the opinion of those who cannot but wish you well.

I would be no less oblig'd to your Justice, then your good nature Madam (cry'd he) in not complaining of me, which I can never be, should I be guilty of such baseness as to abandon you for wealth as I but too well know it is my Fathers aime I should; but when I do let all felicitie forsake me, and eternall horrour ceaze my soule: yes Faire *Arthenia* (pursu'd he) I will obey *Persides* but it shall be in such a way as it shall make no breach in my fidelity; for though this injunction utterly debarres me from marrying you for some time, yet will I love you and you alone till the last minute of my life; nor shall all the power he has over me, compell me to violate the least title of this resolve.

I believe he had gone longer at this rate had he not been interrupted by one of the servants coming in, to bring me a letter, which opening I found to come from *Brecena;* and having purus'd it I saw my selfe reduced to a necessity of leaving Palermo (and consequently *Issodorus*) the very next week, for so had my Mother in it injoyn'd me: this command troubled me not a litle, in regard I was not able to think of quiting *Issodorus* (as long as he continu'd so extreamly ill as at present he was) without resenting [feeling] a most unspeakable griefe. The disturbance that this letter gave me, was too legible not to be read in my countenance, which mov'd *Issodorus* to say as I was about to fould it up. If you would not count me too inquisitive Madam, I would beg to know what that Paper containes that can be capable of ~~making~~ producing such disorder in your lookes as I perceive it has.

You may see it if you ~~will~~ please (answer'd I giving it to him) and thereby satisfie your selfe, for ther's no secrets in it I'll assure you; or if there were, I should
not make them so to you.

He having read [fol.181ʳ] it, return'd it to me again with a sigh, sure Fate
(said he) does conspire by all imaginable wayes to render me miserable: is it not
enough for *Persides* to conspire against my happiness, but that *Brecena* must joyne
her commands to make me more unfortunate, and can it not suffice cruell Fate
to hinder me from injoying your person, but must I be depriv'd both of your sight
and presence too. But are you determin'd (pursu'd he after a little pause) to obey
this severe command, and leave me in this sad condition.

No *Issodorus* (answer'd I) I am absolutely resolv'd the contrary, for rather
then go and leave you thus, I'll frame a thousand excuses to detaine me; but you
must promise me then to endeavour your recovery, assoon as possible that I may
not by too long a stay discover the fallacie of my pretences; yet I confess I would
not stay to see the day of your ~~arrive~~ departure arrive since it would be a much
greater satisfaction to go first and leave you here then stay to see you go before
me; for if I leave you in Palermo I may (perhaps) a little delude that greife your
absence will cost me by fancying you still are here, when I do not see the contrary; but try if you can sleep, and I'll go answer *Brecenas* letter.

With that I ris up, and as I went out of the Chamber I met one of *Perisanas*
Maids who at my request furnish'd me with Pen and paper; and going in to the
Dining Roome I there wrote my letter, by which I obtain'd permission to stay the
space of 6 weeks longer, for then *Melliantes* was to go downe into the Country
as I writ my mother word, beging her with the greatest importunity imaginable
she would be pleas'd to permit me to stay till then (and come home along with
him) by reason (I said) I had a very great curiosity to have a sight of the new
Queen whose arrivall was dayly expected; for *Claromenes* had by proxie been not
long before affianced to the Princess *Celestina* Daughter to the King Numidia.
For about Fourteen dayes after this, did *Issodorus* continue very ill, though not so
extreame bad as he was that precedent night; but then, upon the advice of divers
of his Friends having chang'd his Phisition, he found a speedy, and present remedy though not a perfect cure; for often afterwards upon any high discontent he
relaps'd into the like distemper.

But as I was telling your Majesty (continu'd *Arthenia*) I had some apprehension that *Bellamira* was my Rivall, so I must now tell you now Madam what gave
me the occation to suspect it, which was this. As I was seting by her one morning
as she was dressing her selfe (after *Issodorus* began to recover) I have had a quarell
to you *Arthenia* said she ever since you went out of Towne, but did not think to
tell you of it till now, and I am resolv'd not to forgive you unless you sue out your
pardon in a letter to me; which if you do, I shall easily be induced to grant it.

First let me understand my fault (repli'd I) for as yet I'll assure you I am
wholly ignorant of any thing that I have done that could be capable of displeasing you.

Think you not I had reason (answer'd she) to take it ill that you could be so unkind as not to bid me adue when you went out of Towne, nor send me word of your departure that I might have come and taken my leave of you.

You would have reason deare *Bellamira* (repli'd I) to chide my incivility had I been willfully guilty of it: but *Melliantes* was more to blame then I, for hurrying me away on such a sudden as I had not time [to] render those respects to any I ow'd them too: but however since you charge this omission on me as a fault, give me but Pen and Paper and I'll instantly beg your pardon for it; with that she reach'd me them, and I assoon dispos'd my self to execute what she had injoyn'd [fol.181 ᵛ] me in these words.

> *The least Crime committed against so transcendent a Goodness as yours Divinest*
> *Bellamira merits the severest punishment, but since I know your clemency equalls*
> *your other vertues, I cannot doubt but that your mercy will extend it selfe so far*
> *as to forgive an accidentall, not design'd offence; in confidence whereof I presume*
> *not onely to implore your pardon but an absolute abandoning all misapprehen-*
> *sions of the innocent.*
>
> *Arthenia*

Just as I had concluded she snatch'd away the Paper saying tis enough *Arthenia* I would not have you turn that into really which I onely design'd for rallery.

I was afraid you ~~were angry~~ had been angry with me in earnest (said I).

Indeed I could find in my heart to be so (repli'd she) for conceiving such a thought of me who love you at that rate as never to admit the least displeasure against you, though you should be guilty of that towards me which any other would account the highest injurie.

That I ne're will be (cry'd I) you may be assur'd.

Not willingly I do believe (said she).

Then runing over with her eye what I had writ, sighing she foulded it up and put it in her Pocket; and kissing me, let that assure you (said she) that your pardons granted.

Assoon as she was dress'd we went downe together into the Dining Roome and finding no body there, we took each of us a chaire placeing our selves at a Window that look'd into the street. For my part my thoughts at that instant were taken up with none but triviall things such as the several obiects I saw, presented to me; but as for *Bellamira* I believe hers were more seriously employ'd: for a good while she sate silent, but of a sudden rousing her selfe from that Mellancholy dump which had ceaz'd her, she fell asinging a piece of a song which I had oft heard sung before though not by her: the words as I remember these.

> *T'was not his Person nor his Parts*
> *Though ne're so faire that wone me*
> *He swore he lov'd and I believ'd*
> *And that Faith hath undone me.*

But never let it undoe you *Arthenia* (cry'd she claping me on the hand where by she made me start)

[W]hat would [you] have me not undone by (said I).

Not by believing what that impious creature call'd man protest[s] and sweares (answer'd she) since there is not any thing that they speak though confirm'd with the most fearefull imprecations that can be uttered that they will stick to violate for the satisfaction of their weathercock Inconstancy. For my part (went she on) I am grown so great an Infidell within these few dayes in matters of love, that should I heare my owne Brother courting a woman I should be so far from crediting what he said, as I would rather swear he went about to abuse and disceive her.

There are but too many in the world (replied I) I confess that make it their business or at least their recreation to delude our too crudulous sex.

Too many (interrupted she) say rather that the ~~world~~ earth beares none but such, for such a thing as truth their ~~tongues~~ tongues are wholly unacquainted with. But were I doubtfull whether the Gods had prepar'd rewards for vertue, or punishments for vice in the other world: it were sufficent to convince me of it, to see such perjur'd soules go on prosperously in their wickedness as oft they do: but [fol.182ʳ] there is a secret Judgment certainly reserv'd for them hereafter, or else questionless Heaven would immediatly dart downe its loudest Thunderbolts upon their guilty heads.

What moves you to this passion Deare *Bellamira* (said I) so contrary to your naturall temper.

That which would raise your anger possibly to as great a height (answer'd she) did you but know what I could tell you; but tis not for me to undeceive you, since the errour you are in is (I am perswaded) so sweetly pleasing to you, that I am shure you had much rather continue in it your whole life time, then be convinc'd of your mistake.

If you know me to be in an errour (said I) you ought not (if you are my Friend) to suffer me to percevere in it.

I must confess I ought not (repli'd she) neither would I, did I not believe a litle time will help to unceale your eyes which are at present blinded with counterfeit shewes of verity and besides I cannot do it but by such a way as will give you occation to believe selfe enterest rather then Friendship mov'd me to it. But mind not what I say (pursu'd she) think onely that I rave, and talk I know not what; for as People in distraction fancy all others like themselves so perhaps may I and because I have been deceiv'd, imagine you are so. Your charmes may prove so powerfull perchance as to teach Constancy to the most unconstant person in the world, and confine that heart (which knows no other limmits then these of fancy) within the bounds of Fidelity.

More I believe she would have said, and thereby possibly have made a clearer discovery of her meaning had not *Issodorus's* coming prevented her, for she no sooner saw him but she fell a talking of something far distant from her late discourse: But if what she had said gave me a rise to suspect her my Rivall, or rather my selfe to be hers, her deportment to *Issodorus* all the rest of that day would no longer let me doubt it; for not one word would she speak to him, or once so much as look on him unless with anger in her eyes.

To represent the trouble this apprehension gave me is more then I am able. I was impatient to be gone home where I might have the liberty without any disturbance to reflect on what had pass'd; but not withstanding all my excuses 'twas evening ere I could get away: so soon as I came home I went to bed, but it was rather to have my thoughts free and uninterrupted then for any rest I expected there to find, for not one wink of sleep that night ere clos'd my eyes; but with many a bitter Teare, and Heart rending sigh did I deplore my strange unhappy Fate, to see that Fortune should be so maliciously injurious as to make me Rivall to my best beloved Friend; and One who could tryumph over me by all manner of advantages, as well by the merit of her person as by the enterest she had with *Issodorus's* Relations to whom I knew she was deservedly deare. Fain would I have concluded my selfe mistaken, and believ'd I had not rightly understood her meaning, and that what she had spoken had refference to some other not *Issodorus,* for (thought I) how can it be that she can have a perticuler kindness for him herselfe, and yet, not onely propose *Victorina* or *Electra*[5] for a wiffe for him, but also perswade him seriously to make his Addresses either to the one or other of them upon that score: but knowing her to be generous beyound examplle I then fancied the high effects of that might transport her to that noble pitch of gallantry as to prefer his advantage before her owne satisfaction; which if so, she appear'd (in my opinion) the more worthy to possess what her merits gave her so just a title too.

But all the reasons, and Argument I could rally to relieve me from this misadventure, were insufficient, since I had more to convince me 'twas fallen to my lott: for divers things came then into my mind, which before I had not regarded, as namely *Issodorus's* perticuler injunction to me not to discover to *Bellamira* his [fol.182ᵛ] Passion for me, lest (as he pretended) she might enforme *Perisana* of it. As also *Herminios* saying (as he did when he was talking to me at his lodging) that he was observ'd by interested eyes. As likewise that of *Bellamiras* wishing (when *Issodorus* and ~~Mellian~~ *Melliantes* met us walking together in the Garden) that my kindness might not prove my prejudice. These, and sundry other passages on which till then I had not bestow'd the least reflection, but too fully now confirm'd my feares; which if true (as I saw small reason to doubt) I found my selfe reduced to the miserable necessity of injuring a person I lov'd equall with my selfe, or of hating another no less deare to me: as well worthy of my hatered will he be (thought I) if he once stands convicted of that Cryme whereof *Bellamira* seemes to intimate him guilty.

---

[5] *Electra* seems to be a mistake for *Eurydice.*

For admit (said I to my selfe) he can commit so great a perfidie as to abandon her, though with an intention to be more just to me (as that is the best I can hope) yet sure I cannot be so ignoble as to accept him on such dishonourable termes; or yet, suppose I could, what assurance can I have from One who has broke his Faith with so Excellent and Incomparable a person as the divine *Bellamira*. No Dearest Friend (pursu'd I) my chaines will certainly prove too weak to retaine that captive whom thine far stronger could not hold. I now rememberd too, what *Balario* (an intimate Friend of *Issodorus's*) not long before had said to me: for as he was talking to me one day this Gentleman being by, but he upon some occation or other (what I cannot ~~absolutely say~~ possitively say) going out of the Roome, *Balario* came and assuming his place with a smille he said to me.

Give me leave Madam too advize you not to repose too much confidence in this *Issodorus* lest he deceive your expectations, for I must tell you madam I feare he is become so great a Bankrupt in the trade of love, as he has already taken up so much on trust as he will ne're be able to pay the use, much less the Principall, but must be forced ere long to break with all his Creditors. O would to Heaven (pursu'd he with a sigh) I were but as much your Debtor as he is, and I would assuredly never faile to repay what ere you lent me with a trebled interest.

Issodorus may soon pay me all he owes (repli'd I) but if he could not, I should questionless forgive him.

You are very charitable madam (answer'd he) but I am perswaded he will scarce meet with another so kind amongst those he deales with.

I had not time to reply by reason *Issodorus* came in again, which *Balario* seeing rose to resigne his Place, ^that^ he had taken up in his absence and in rising up said softly to me,

[T]is fit, the unhappie give place to the more fortunate.

I had hitherto believ'd *Balario* so highly *Issodorus's* Friend as I could not but admire he should speak so ill of him; yet I must needs say this was not the first time he had given me some litle suspition that he was become his Rivall, which what he last said so absolutely confirm'd as I no longer doubted it; and therefore concluded it to be meerly selfe interest that had induced him to say what he did on purpose to ruine him in my opinion; which mov'd me not onely to regard him as an envious Detractor but to slight the caution [he] ~~gave me~~ he had given me; which doubtless from any person I had thought unconcern'd I should with thankfullness have receiv'd and made a much better use of it then I did.

I had certainly acquainted *Issodorus* with it, had I not fear'd it might beget a mortall quarell, which twas probable might prove fatall to one, or both of them, for which reason I chose rather to silence the injurie I believ'd *Balario* had done him, and to expect his justification from the hand of Time then give him the oppertunity of vindicating himselfe by so dangerious a way as I but too well knew his courage would prompt him to take: [fol.183^r] being (as he was) the most impatient person in the world of any affront. This though questionless spoken by *Balario* with a designe to work *Issodorus* out of favour with me, to the end he might the easier introduce himselfe into my esteeme; yet since *Bellamira* joyn'd with him in declaming against his Inconstancy, I could not upon second, and more serious thoughts but believe ~~Balaroi~~ *Balario* would ne'er have ventur'd so openly to accuse a person of a crime unless he certainly knew him to be guilty of it in some measure, especially to me, from whom he might rationally apprehend a discovery of what he had aver'd.

Yet not withstanding all this, I would fain have justifi'd *Issodorus* in my thoughts, but could not, yet would I not absolutely condemne him, but resolv'd first ere I pass'd sentence on him, to heare him speak in his owne deffence; which I esteem'd but just to allow him that favour since the greatest Crimenall that were; had still that priviledge granted them. In fine, ^I pass'd^ that whole night in such afflicting disquiets, as till then I had never resented [felt]; and no sooner did the day appeare then I arose with impatient longings for a convenient opper-tunity to disburthen my Heart of that which lay so heavy on it, to the Auther of my disquiet; for not one minutes rest could I enjoy till I knew what I ought to determine of him: but when I went over to *Persides's* in hopes to speak with him, I understood he lay that night at the *Prince of Oristagnes*, and that his returne home ~~would~~ was uncertain which when I had heard [which when I had heard: repeated in the manuscript], I stay'd not long, onely step'd up to *Bellamira* and told her I had some thoughts of going back to *Eugenia* that day (as indeed I had) and an intent no more to returne, (in case he should not give me good satisfaction upon the charge I should bring against him) and lest you should challenge me of unkindness a second time (said I) I am come to take my leave of you ere I go.

This is a sudden a motion (repli'd she) sure you did not think of going yes-terday.

Indeed I did not (answer'd I) but there is something hapned since that I sup-pose will oblige me to it, for I am not as yet certain whether I shall go or no, but if you see me not tomorrow conclude me gone.

But when may I hope to be so happie to see you here again (said she)

In earnest (answer'd I) I cannot tell whether I shall come back ^again^ to make any stay; but however I will be sure to waite on you to take my finall adue ere I leave Palermo for altogether.

So leaving my service with her to present to *Perisana* I went home again wholly unresolv'd what course to take, nor had I any to advize me, but was fain to be guided onely ^by^ the dictates of divers disorder'd passions, which being contrary to each other, made me incline to the pursute of as many severall Pathes no less different the one from the other. Assoon as we had Din'd I writ a Note to *Issodorus*, wherein I desir'd him to meet me in the Garden of Adonis which was but a litle distance from the *Prince of Orestagnes* meaning to leave it with the Por-ter as I went by, but when I cam to enquire of him for *Issodorus*, he told me he was gon forth about an houre before, and had left word he should not be within till Night: so as I had no hopes of seeing him that day, which did not a litle heighten my impatience.

I stay'd not to make any new resolve, but returning to *Hestrinas* I demanded of her if she had any service to command me to *Eugenia* for thither I told her I intended presently to go; (she no less admiring at my so sudden a resolve then *Bellamira* did not long before) would fain have perswaded me to stay till the next day adding that it was so far [fol.183ᵛ] spent as it must infallibly ^be^ night ere I could get thither: but I was too much bent on what I had determin'd to be perswaded to stay a minute longer, instantly took my leave of her, adding that if I found the night approach I would stay at my Brothers till the next morning (which I intended to do not withstanding). He was gone abroad when I came thither, but soon after me he came in, and remarking an extraordinary sadness in my lookes, he with no less concerne enquir'd the cause; which I confess I was unwilling to tell him the truth lest I might ruine *Issodorus*, in his good opinion, which I was loath to do, till I was sure he deserv'd to be deserted mine, and therefore fram'd the occation of my discontent to be this: that *Issodorus* had so pressingly importun'd me to marry him, as I must either condesend to his desire, or resolve to break off with him.

This hard choice (pursu'd I) to which I am ~~inclin'd~~ confin'd is that which reduces me to so great a trouble as I am not able to express: for to think of parting with him forever is that I cannot with Patience undergoe, and to keep him on such termes as my Duty disallows I can with no less unwillingness yeeld too.

I know not Sister (said *Melliantes*) what construction you may give this Proposall of his, but for my part I can think no otherwise of it, then that he has a desire to quit you, and therefore propounds what he believes you will not grant, on purpose that he may find a pretext to do it fairly.

I am but too much of your opinion for my owne quiet (repli'd I) but however I'll make him one Overture more, which I am sure cannot but satisfie him unless it be so that he intends to abandon me; which I shall guess by his accepting or rejecting it; which if he does the latter I am fully resolv'd then never to see his Face again.

Just as I had past the precedent night, even so did I that, in restless, and disquiet thoughts, for sleeps powerfull Charmes could not make me so much as one moment to lay aside my inquietudes, but with unclos'd eyes did I behold the dayes approach. The first thing I fix'd on, was to send for *Issodorus* thither to me that afternoon; which I did, writing two or three lines to him to that intent, wherein I so earnestly conjur'd him to let me see him, as I thought if he had onely common civility for me he would not refuse to gratifie so easie, and reasonable a request. This Note being dispatch'd away to him fail'd not to produce the desired effect; but coming to his hand ere he was out of his Bed, he onely sent word he would bring me an answere himselfe at the time appointed; as indeed he did,for instantly after Dinner he came; but so indispos'd was I with watching, and the trouble of my mind as I was forced to keep my Chamber all that day, and was laid upon the Bed when *Melliantes* brought him in. Very much concern'd did he seeme to find me so ill, and demanding the occation of my Distemper, I onely answer'd that I knew not well what to impute it too. But as I ~~speak~~ spake that, a deep sigh forced its passage from my Brest to his Eares, which he taking notis of (after my Brother was gone out)

That sigh madam which you endeavou[r]'d even now to smother (said he) induces me to believe your illness to be rather an indisposition of your Mind then Body.

You judge not much amiss *Issodorus* (repli'd I) but would you could as readily devine the occation, you might then exempt me from the trouble it will be to me to tell ~~you~~ it you; and yet I must, since tis onely your selfe that can cleare my doubts; which to do, I'll onely aske you one qu[e]stion, and I beseech you be so ingenuous as to deal sincerely with me; and if my intreaties be not sufficent, I do conjure you by all ~~you~~ that you esteeme, or hold most deare to tell me true.

Good gods (cry'd he) what can it be that you can demand of me that I will denie to tell you.

You may perhaps (said I) returne me such an answere as you I suppose will afford me the best [fol.184^r] satisfaction, though perchance far distant from the truth, but though you leave me never so much dissatisfi'd by it yet I beg you would deall Faithfully with me and confess to me the reall truth without any the least disguise or falacy.

By Heaven I will (repli'd he).

Then I must tell you (said I) I am either the most mistaken person that ever was, or you are falce; falce *Issodorus* to me or *Bellamira* but to which of us is that which I would be resolv'd of; for I am but too well assur'd you have either made your feighned Addresses to me whilst you paid her your reall ones, or else declin'd her to fix your love on me, which at that rate I will never accept: for to injure my Friend innocently thorough ignorance is what may easily be forgiven; but knowingly, nay but suspectedly to intrench upon her right, and make my selfe an Accomplice in the wrong you offer her, is that which I can nere expect, or hope a Pardon for, nor so much as pardon to my selfe should I be guilty of it. Tell me then what I ought to conclude you whether an unconstant or a Treacherous person, for I feare tis but too sure you are either the one, or the other.

I hope Time will convince you if I cannot (repli'd he) that I am neither, though you are so unkind to judge so hardly of me. I know not what *Bellamira* may have told you concerning me, but this I dare aver, 'twas her owne interest rather then her Friendship for you that mov'd her to it: for this I must confess, I do believe she honours me with more kindness then I desire or deserve from her as of late I have had some reason to conceive.

Peace *Issodorus* (interrupted I) unless you will force me to harbour a worse opinion of you then ever yet I gave admittance too, by your so unworthily ~~dect~~ detracting from *Bellamira*s discretion, which I am very confident she can never so far forfeit as to be guilty of that folly which you charge her with: no, no she is none of those Amorous Ones that fall in love they know not why with those that ne're su'd for the favour of their affections. But sure you have forgot (yet though

you have, believe it I have not) what you said to me concerning her insensibility which (as I might sooner have consider'd) you could not so peremtorily have
affirm'd, had you not experienced it.

   Since (said he after a short silence as it were to think him what to say) it is
so necessary for my vindication, I will with all imaginable candour and sincerity
make you an ingenuous confession, that some yeares since *Bellamiras* charmes
inspir'd me with some impression of a reall passion for her; but with such a per-
cevering disdain, and rigorous coldness did she reject the proffers of my love as
quite extinguish'd, and put out my Flame, long before I saw, or knew there was
such a person in ~~the~~ being as *Arthenia*. [N]ay further I will yet declare, that had
she given me any incouragment to serve her, I had continu'd as faithfully hers,
as I now am your[s]: but so cruelly, so severely did she treat me as I endeavourd
not unsuccessfully to quit my Chains; and if I have again assum'd them, for One
whom I have found more favourable, she has certainly small reason to challenge
me of Infidelity, or inconstancy: for if I vow'd for ever to be hers, 'twas in hopes
to make her mine, but when those hopes were utterly frustrate, and turn'd into
Dispaire, it would have been an Argument of my folly rather then my stability
to have percever'd in proffering that which she as often ~~deu~~ declar'd she ^never^
would not accept.[6] I know not then, nor can I guess what now should move her
to clame a right in me, (as I am apt to think she ~~does~~ has) or to confer on me a
kindness which I no longer wish, unless the Jealousie she has conceiv'd of you (of
which I confess she has given me severall intimations) incite her to it, [fol.184ᵛ]
envying to see that Heart anothers which (perhaps) she could have been content
should still have worn her Fetters, and laine prostrate at her Feet the Trophy of
her scorn; but *Issodorus* Heart (I must needs say) was too proud long to brook
such an uncivell usuage; which *Arthenias* more gentle treatment has absolutely
redeem'd it from.

   I cannot but repent that kindness I have shewn you (said I) since it occations
Bellamiras trouble who it may be now repents her severity and is (perhaps resolv'd
to be more kind); reassume then your former passion, and divest your selfe of that
which you have own'd for me; and if one of us must be a sufferer, tis just it should
be the worthless *Arthenia* not the most deserving *Bellamira* to whom I ought to
yeeld precedency in all things, and whose Friend I ~~am~~ so much am as to refuse
all interest in what she has any the least title too, and let me tell you *Issodorus*
(pursu'd I) twill be more generous as well as just in you to leave me now, then
further to engage my affections and then abandon me.

   For whom I beseech you Madam (cry'd he) do you imagine I should desert
you.

---

   [6] It is likely that "not" would have been canceled after the insertion of "never" in
order to maintain the sense.

For *Bellamira* (answer'd I) whose invinceable charmes having already captiv'd you may prove again so powerfull as all the strength which you can make will not be able to resist them.

I am not ignorant of their power (repli'd he) but yet as potent as they are, arm'd with that firme and unalterable resolve I have made of being yours, I dare withstand their united force, and never feare to be orecome. ~~from my fidelity to you.~~ Do not give way then I beseech you madam to any such thought that I can be withdrawn by *Bellamira* or any other ~~what~~ whosoever from my fidelity to you. No Dearest *Arthenia* when once you find me falce spit in my Face, and brand me with the most hatefull and ignominious terme of villiane; nor need you fancy your esteeme for me, to be in the least ~~to Bellamira~~ injurious to *Bellamira*, since I'll assure you, had you nere dain'd to accept, or gratifie my Passion, nay should you from this minute renounce me, and deprive me of all hopes of being yours, she would reap no satisfaction by it; for so far is my Heart disingag'd from the resentments [sentiments] it had once for her, as I can ne're be hers whose ere I am.

If that (said I) which you have now attested may justifie you in point of Fidelity, yet does it not cleare you from the guilt of inconstancy; for you have lov'd *Artelinda*, you have lov'd *Bellamira* and now love me, at least pretend so.

I do confess it Madam (repli'd he) but had the one liv'd, the other lov'd, I had doubtless not been liable to that change which you charge on me as a fault, but may more fittly be counted my misfortune; though I cannot call it by that name seeing I have by it acquir'd an enterest in your affection more deare to me then any thing under Heaven. But if you yet question my constancy, methinks a seven yeares tryall which my *Artelinda* had of it ere I married her, should be a suffcent demonstration of it; for if I continu'd my Passion so long for her; why should you not believe my constancy as immovable now as then.

Because perhaps (answer'd I) you lov'd *Artelinda* better then *Arthenia*.

No I'll assure you Madam did I not (repli'd he) though *Artelinda* was the first that ever taught me the power of love; yet if there be a difference in my kindness tis on your side who have the advantage of her in my being ^more^ sensible of my passion for you then ere I was for her when it had attain'd its greatest ardency: but if you will have a firmer security for my perceverance it must be founded on the duration of your [fol.185ʳ] owne affection for as long as that endures, ~~must~~ mine must remain unalterable: for 'twas no less on the assurance of *Artelind*[a]*s* love, then on my engagement to her that I founded my fidelity, for as I will acknowledge to you (being sensible as I was that in marrying her I weded my owne ruine) I have oft left the country, coming hither to Palermo with no other intention or designe, then by the various diversions that this Place affords to try if I could withdraw and wean my heart from affecting her; yet when I had done all I could, there was a certain litle thing within me call'd conscience which so strongly took her part as it would not suffer me to act so base, and treacherous part, as to abandon one whose innocent affections I knew I had the intire possession of; nor will it be less your Friend (I dare answere) then it was hers, should I with an unpardonable ~~just~~ injustice go about to rob you of that which by so many reitterated vowes I have made absolutely yours. But I heare your Brother comeing and therefore cannot adde much more for the confirmation of that which I have to you so oft repeated, which if I ever violate, or prove faithless or unjust to you, may this hand (continu'd he streaching forth his right Hand) rot from my Body, and may I never enter that Place of ~~bliss~~ bliss and happiness where vertuous soules shall dwell in endless Joyes.

Say no more *Issodorus* (said I claping my hand on his Mouth) I had rather rely on your integrity then heare you bind your selfe by such direfull imprecations to Fidelity.

With that came in *Melliantes* again, and by his presence silenced our present discourse; but if what *Issodorus* had said left me not perfectly satisfi'd, yet did it remove much of that trouble which sate so heavie on my heart. But O the weakness of a soule once vanquish'd by the power of love (pursu'd *Arthenia*) and how easily alass are we perswaded to credit any thing from those we love that carries with it but a specious shew though never so far distant from verity; and how willingly do we close our passion blinded eyes; and stop our Eares to althings save those which help to conserve our errour: for me thought all that *Issodorus* had spoken in his justification appear'd to me in such an innocent, and undisguised dress as I could no longer apprehend him guilty; nor could I see any reason why *Bellamira* should charge him with infidelity (if it were so as he affirm'd) that she had utterly refus'd his affection, nor could I conceive why she should be disturb'd to see another accept what she herselfe with scorn rejected.

All that I could conclude then was that she had a secret passion for him, and had yeelded up her heart to his invinsible armes, though she was loath to owne herselfe vanquish'd by him, and no less unwilling to be abandon'd which mov'd her to endeavour to create in me so ill an opinion of him as might incite me to cast him off; which if I did, she thought (perhaps) she might retrieve him by her charmes. But O how injurious were these erronious conjectures of mine to the Divinest *Bellamira* whose Unmeritable Friendship sought rather to preserve me from a precipice, whereinto her prudent, and more discerning Judgment perceiu'd me falling: yet however so well satisfied was I (though I seem'd the contrary to *Issodorus* for when he parted from me I left him doubtfull what Place he held in my opinion) as by the rest I took the insuing night I so well [fol.185ᵛ] repair'd my health which the disquiets of the two precedent ones had prejudiced as I was able to go the next day to *Eugenias* where I had not been but a few dayes, when as she and I were talking together at her chamber window we saw a chariot stop at the gate, and out of it allight two Gentlemen and a Lady whom I had no sooner cast my eye on ere I knew them to be *Issodorus*, *Bellamira* and her Brother the generous *Riallo*; and having told *Eugenia* who they were, I went immediatly downe to meet them with abundance of joy; nor knew I whether was the more wellcome *Issodorus* or *Bellamira* for Friendship had render'd the one no less deare to me then affection had the other. But if in the private recesses of my heart he had the precedency, yet Decency oblig'd me to give *Bellamira* the greater publick demonstrations of my gladness to see her; and renewing my thankes in a more perticuler manner to every one severally for the favour of this visit, but I am doubly oblig'd to you *Issodorus* (said I to him) in not onely coming your selfe to see me, but for bringing *Bellamira* with you.

Nay I'll assure you (cry'd she) 'twas I brought him, not he me; and therefore you need owne no obligation to him, for I was fain to use all that little Rethorick I am mistress of to court him to come with me: not that I could not have come alone with my Brother without him, but that I thought his company might render ~~might~~ mine the more acceptable.

You infinitly detract from that high Friendship I have for you dear *Bellamira* (repli'd I) if you conceive the presence of any other necessary to enduce me to set a higher value on yours.

Is this the requitall Cousin, you give me (interupted *Issodorus*) for dispencing with my more then ordinary occations to waite on you to complain of me to *Arthenia*: but I am ^in hopes^ she is ^perswaded^ so charitabl[y] as to believe I had some perticuler reason that would have made me decline paying her ~~that~~ at this time that respect which she merits from all that have the honour to know her.

Dont think to excuse your selfe with a complement (said I smilling) but since you came with so ill a will to see me, to be reveng'd I'll not so much as tell you that you are wellcome.

Tis no matter Madam (he repli'd) whether you tell me so, if you will but permit me to think so.

With that came downe *Eugenia* to us, and chang'd our perticuler conversation to a more generall one. But whether it were that I were really more reserv'd in my behaviour that day then usually I was at other times, or that he onely fancied so I cannot say; but when he took his leave to go away, as *Eugenia* was complementing *Riallo* and his faire sister he took the oppertunity to say to me: I hope madam you are more just then to reflect on any thing that *Bellamira* said to my prejudice, so far as to believe I would not joyfully ^embrace^ all opportunities of waiting on you, which if I would have denied my selfe that satisfaction, 'twas meerly upon the account of that which lately hapned lest you should apprehend what I did, to be rather out of complacence to *Bellamira* then in kindness to *Arthenia*.

No *Issodorus* said I, I am none of those who are apt to consture things in the worst sence: but to let this pass, I will onely tell you, there is somewhat come into my mind since last I saw you which you formerly said to me (which I thought not on then) so apparently false, as I have reason to believe whatever else you have aver'd to be no less untrue.

What may that be Good Madam I beseech you (demanded he).

Meet me to morrow at *Melliantes's* (answer'd I) and then you shall know, but now I have not leasure to informe you; which having faithfully promis'd to do, he took his leave of me till then.

Much did *Bellamira* perswade me to go back with them that she might (as she said) have the satisfaction to enjoy my company that litle time I had more to stay in those parts: but I beg'd her to excuse me that I [fol.186ʳ] could not gratifie her request having already engag'd my promise to *Eugenia* to continue with her till my returne to my Fathers.

But I hope I shall have the happiness to see you ere you go said she: which assuring her she should, they went away.

The next day when I came to my Brothers I found *Issodorus* there, but *Melliantes* gone abroad, not knowing any thing of our intention to meet there.

You see Madam (said he after his first salutations) how punctuall an observer of your commands I am, but the truth is I could not rest in ^any^ quiet till I knew what new charge this is which you have drawn up against me.

You may remember *Issodorus* (answer'd I) you once told me, that after *Artelinda* died, you never entertain'd a thought of love for any one till you saw me, and yet acknowledged to me the other day that *Bellamira* preceded me in your affection; and finding by that confession, your first affirmation to be falce, I have reason to question the verity of althings else you have at any time protested; for if you would publish a falshood without any reason to incite you to it, I may rationally conclude, you will not stick to do so when it may tend to the furtherance of that designe which perhaps you may have to betray my innocent affection.

Far from my thought (repli'd he) is any such unworthy intent, for when I go about by treachery to injure what I prize so deare, let Heaven inflict on me some strange unheard of punishment. But why Madam should you count that so crimenall in matters of love (continu'd he) which in War is daily practiced uncondemn'd; for you well know tis allow'd to those who besiege a Towne to have recourse to strategems to get, what by force, or treaty they cannot hope to gain, and using that litle artifice to inhance the value of my love, by endeavouring to perswade you 'twas sacred to your selfe alone without any others having had an interest in it since *Artelinda* left me the disposall of it, I can see no reason; nor need you methinks on so slight a ground [to] build a suspition of the candour, and sincerity of what I have oft by such binding protestations confirm'd to you the truth of.

Ah *Issodorus* (said I sighing) you know too well the power you have to perswade me to any thing you would have me credit (though never so unlikely) yet I must tell you I still very much feare you have either unhandsomely deserted *Bellamira* for me, or else hold a mutuall correspondence with us to the prejudice of us both.

As for my deserting *Bellamira* (answer'd he) you need not be any waye concern'd for it, not being in the least the occation of it; since (as I before told you) I had long ere I saw you quitted all pretences of, or thoughts of passion for her;

but tis not possible for me to express the trouble tis to me to see you so doubtfull of my reallity, which seeing you are so ~~ere~~ incredulous of, and that I cannot (by the reason of that engagement which *Persides* has laid upon me to the contrary) give you any other then a verball Testimony of it, I'll make you one Overture more which I trust will absolutely convince you of my sincerity. I protest then by all the Gods in whose presence we alone are and make a solmne vow to you, such as no consideration whatever shall compell me to violate, and on it give you both my hand and Faith to performe what now I promise (pursu'd he giving me his hand) to be yours for ever, and to make you mine by Hymens sacred tye, and never to marry any other, nor so much as think of any woman breathing (save your selfe) upon the score of love. Will [fol.186ᵛ] you not Deare *Arthenia* (went he on) make me the like engagement; that by so firme and mutuall tye we may for the future prevent all unkind disputes, or needless distrusts, and secure me by such an assurance from all feares of loosing you when I am gone.

Yes *Issodorus* (repli'd I) I do not onely accept this Promise you now have made, but engage my selfe in the like manner (giving him my hand) to be yours, and onely yours so long as you are mine.

Give me leave then my deare *Arthenia,* (said he) to seale this mutuall engagement we have made to each other with a kiss, which till now I ne're had confidence enough to beg the favour of from your Faire lips.

But not staying for my permission he took that liberty which tis probable I had else refus'd him. By this time *Melliantes* was return'd and seeing *Issodorus* there he assur'd him if he had dream'd of finding such good company as himselfe he would have made more hast home. I stay'd that night in Towne at *Issodorus's* request who promis'd he would on the morrow come again and waite on me back to *Eugenia,* I confess I was willing to embrace all opportunities that might afford me so pleasing a satisfaction as the enjoyment of his company and therefore readily consented to his request, lying that night with *Sillindra* at her lodging which was not far distant from my Brothers.

According to his promise *Issodorus* came the next day, and went with me home; whether having brought me he stay'd not long being recall'd by some urgent occasions; but to make me amends he assur'd me he would not faile to see me every day as long as I stay'd there: and truly I think he did not miss above once all the time, which (as I remember) was about 14 dayes. At which times he was treated by *Eugenia* with so much freedome and civilitie as it produced in him no less a respect, then he had conceiv'd a prejudice against *Hestrina* for interesting her selfe so highly in that wherein he thought her not concern'd. *Eugenia* had at this time sojourning with her an antient Lady (nam'd *Serena,*) and her son who was call'd *Silisdes*; and one day as this lady and I were sitting together she took an occation to begin a discourse of *Issodorus* and amongst many other questions which she ask'd me concerning him, beg'd me at last to resolve her whether he did not make his Addresses to me on the score of love and profess himselfe my servant.

Come do not blush (pursu'd she) perceiving me to do so, I'll take it for granted that he does, and not put you to the trouble to confirme it. But if I were worthy to councell you, I should advize you (as one too who perhaps wishes you much better then you imagine) not to engage your selfe past a retreat in a perticuler kindness for him, since he is going so far, that tis probable ere he returnes he may have laid aside his passion, or make some other the obiect of it.

If he should prove of so unfix'd a temper (I reply'd) I shall without doubt count him better lost then found.

But believe it (said she) if once you love him you will not so easily dispence with his loss: and beside, tis possible, in his absence you may have those offers made you, so much more to your advantage, as you would be to blame if you refus'd them in expectation of what might never happen.

I should esteeme my selfe far more blameable (repli'd I) should I for the highest advantage imaginable abandon a person I am oblig'd to esteeme, by the greatness of that passion he declares for me, on no other score then a bare apprehension that he may violate his Faith, which I confess I have a better opinion of *Issodorus* then to believe he will.

How good thoughts soever you may have of him (said she) yet I must beg, and earnestly conjure you, not to bestow all your affection [fol.187^r] on him, but reserve some litle kindness to gratifie anothers passion, who adores you with one so transcendant, as nothing save his respect, and feare to displease you can equall; and of that I think you will acknowledge he gives no slight testimony, since he has firmly resolv'd rather to dy in silence, then by speaking, declare what may offend you. But if you denie my first request, yet however grant me this which I now beg; that you will not bind your selfe by any perticuler promise to be Issodorus's.

Perhaps Madam I have already done it (answer'd I) how can I then condesend to that which you desire.

Then poor *Silisdes* (said she) must be inevitably unhappie. Yes *Arthenia* (pursu'd she) tis onely the tender affection of a Mother to an onely child which has mov'd me to such an unseasonable importunity which if I cannot succeed in, I must lament his hard Fate in placing so true a love on one from whom he must never expect any returne; but tis my hopes, Dispaire will worke his cure; not that I am less desirous you should call me Mother, then he is ambitious to be stil'd your Husband: and should esteeme my selfe happie in a Daughter of your incomparable worth and goodness, which I have been oft an admiring observer of.

I wish Madam (reply'd I) there were that reall worth in me to merit that too advantagious opinion you have of me; and that I were capable of accepting that honour *Silisdes* and your selfe design'd me: but I must ingenuously confess I am too much *Issodorus's* both by promise, and affection ere to be anothers. I am not ignorant Madam (continu'd I) of those advantages your son has of *Issodorus* in point of Fortune yet were they far greater then they are, I should refuse them, and chuse rather to spend my dayes with *Issodorus* though in a Cottage, then with any other on a Throne.

Tis pitty (said she) such a disintressed love should meet with any unkind returne, as I am afraid it will.

Good Madam what moves you to think so (cry'd I)[.]

I can not tell (answer'd she) but I have a strong conceit this Gentleman will not answer your expectations; for methinks, he lookes as if he knew better what belongs to Ambition then love.

It may be so for ought I know (said I) but till I am convinc'd he does, I'll be sure to teach him no ill by my example.

Loath was I to continue so unpleasing a discourse any longer, but whilst I was studying to evade it, came in *Eugenia* and by her presence releas'd me from it: however (I must needs say) I was not a litle satisfi'd that I had so faire an opportunity offor'd me of retalliating *Issodorus's* generosity in refusing (as had done) for me the *Duke of Drepanum's* Daughters, since *Silisdes* was reported to be so vastly rich, as I could scarce think it credible what Fame spake of his wealth; nor was I less surpriz'd with wonder to think what should move *Serena* to court me for her son, especially having heard it said, that she had refus'd severall considerable Matches which he might have had: insomuch that it was generally believ'd she would never willingly suffer him to marry whilst she liv'd: and for *Silisdes's* part, it was beleiv'd he had rather a naturall aversion to our sex, then otherwise, for of such a reserv'd temper was he, it was suppos'd love would never find much employment in his mind; yet I cannot deny, but that he alwayes shew'd me so great a respect, as I had no reason to charge him with a want of complacency, or civility, as many others did.

You see Madam (interrupted *Gentillus*) how powerfull your Graces are, that they change even Nature it selfe, and turne aversion into inclination.

Had I been capable of performing anything so strang as that (reply'd *Arthenia*) I should questionless have extended my power to the retaining what I had already gain'd: which how litle I was able to do, the sequell of my story will enforme you, and let your Lordship see how litle I deserve [fol.187ᵛ] that high Complement you have pass'd upon me. But beging *Ermillias* pardon for this digression she went on.

In a short time after this, going to the Gate one afternoon to look if I could see *Issodorus* coming, it being something later then he usually came, just as I open'd it he alighted, but methought he did not throw himselfe from his Horse with that nimbleness and agillity as he was wont; and coming towards me I perceiv'd him to hault a litle in his steps, which I demanding the cause of, he told me he had hurt his Thigh with a fall from his Horse but 'twas a mercy (pursu'd he) I had no more hurt, for I might as well have broke my Neck.

The Gods defend you (cry'd I extreamly frighted) how came you by such a dangerous fall; the way from *Palermo* hither being so levell, one would hardly think a Horse could as much as stumble in it.

No (a^n^swer'd he) 'twas not in coming hither that I fell, but in the morning as I rode a Hunting with some of the *Prince of Oristans* Gentlemen who would needs have me accompany them to that diversion; but I was like to have paid deere for my sport, for Following the Game a litle too eagerly, and being willing to take the shortest way, I would fain have made my Horse leap from a Bank which was on the side of a very deep Ditch to the opposite side; but leaping short, he not only th[r]ew me, but fell upon me, whereby he bruis'd me so extreamly as I could scarcely rise: but 'twas well there was no water in the Ditch or else I might have run the hazard of being drown'd too; but at last (though with much difficulty) I got out of that steep Precipice, but was not able to get on Horse-back again till some of the Gentlemen came and holp me up.

Finding him no less tyr'd then hurt, I gave order to one of *Eugenias* Maids to make ready a Bed, into which I very much perswaded him to go, and to resolve to stay all night, in hopes (as I said) that he would be better after he had rested himselfe.

I am of your opinion Madam that rest would do me much good (reply'd he) and willingly would I accept your proffer were it not that I am engag'd ere sun-set to be at the Viceroys, because *Claromenes* is to sup with him, and tis requisite that all those Gentlemen who have any dependance on him be in a readiness to attend the King.

I [Aye] but you have so just an excuse (said I) as when the *Prince of Oristan* shall heare what disaster has hapned to you, he will no question dispence with your absence.

Tis probable he may (reply'd he) but being I sent word by my companions (when I parted from them) that I would not faile my attendance at the appointed houre, I will not if possible, be worse then my word.

But if you will not go to Bed (said I) yet methinks you might lye downe for an houre or two to refresh your selfe.

That I would (answer'd he) did I not find my selfe sleepy as well as weary (having been up ever since 4 of the clock this morning) which if I ware once laid at my ease, I should soon fall a sleep, and might perhaps o're sleep my selfe.

If that be all your feare (said I) I'll be sure to wake you at what time soever you would be call'd.

I dare not trust you (reply'd he smiling) yet I care not much if I take a Nap for one halfe houre in this Chaire as I sit, if you will promise to call me then, not that I intend to run a way from you so soon, but am loath to rob my selfe of the pleasure of your Society any longer.

Nay (said I) if you will I not lye downe, you shall not setle your selfe to sleep here because One or other may chance to come in and disturbe you: but if you will go along with me, I'll carry you into another Roome less frequented, where you may repose your selfe in quiet, with that taking him [fol.188ʳ] by the hand I made him follow me into another Parlour (a pritie way distant from that wherin we were) which was seldome us'd but for the entertainment of Visitants of more then ordinary quality; thither having brought him, and call'd for a Pillow for him to rest his head on, I fastned the Dore that open'd into the Garden through which we enter'd because I would have no person come in to molest him; and when I had seen him compos'd himselfe to sleep I would have left him, but as I was rising up to go away, he caught hold of my hand [:]

[N]ay my *Arthenia* (said he) if you will have me sleep, you must be content to undergoe the Pennance of setting by me the while.

Do not think (answer'd I) that I count that a trouble; which I esteeme so much my satisfaction, as I would wish no greater, provided I might never be depriv'd of this; for to enjoy your sight and conversation is the uttmost bounds of my desires: beleive not then I would have left you upon any other score, but out of feare I might disturbe you: so siting downe by him, he would not lay his head on the Pillow as I would have had him, but on my lappe, clasping his hand in mine, and in a very litle space fell fast asleep.

The still silence in which I sate, made me follow his example, so as I was just fallen into a slumber when *Silisdes* rous'd me out of it again by the noise he made in opening the other Dore which I suppos'd had been fast lock'd, I had scarce open'd my eyes when I saw him enter with another Gentleman and two ladies who were wholly strangers to me, but so much abash'd was I to be seen by such as knew me not (with a man all alone in that posture) as I scarce knew what I did; nor was *Silisdes* less surpriz'd not dreaming that any one was there: but ere they had advanced many steps into the Roome, I had snatch'd my hand from *Issodorus* and laid his head from off my lappe upon the Chaire on which I sate, and made such hast away, as scarce any save *Silisdes* had a sight of me, the Roome being of that largness as one could not readily discern at the one end what was done at the other.

As I ris up, (I cry'd) *Issodorus* here is company come in I know not, but whether it were my removing his head, or my calling to him that wak'd him I cannot tell, but so it was that he instantly awaked, and looking up, missing me, and seeing strangers in the Roome he guess'd the cause of my sudden flight; whereupon, arising from his place, and giving the Ladies a civell respect as he pass'd by them came forth, and perceiving the blushes still upon my cheeks he could not refrain laughing to see me look so concernedly.

Do you think (said I) that I have not suffer'd vexation enough already, but that you must laugh at me too.

You cannot sure Madam count me so rude (answer'd he assuming a more serious look) as to laugh at you, but rather to think how pritily we were surpriz'd.

Pritily (cry'd I) do you call it, it was not ^methinks^ so pleasing to deserve that stile but I verily thought we had been secure enough from any bodies coming to us; yet had they not been strangers I had not car'd.

Nor need not now (said he) since the innocence of our intentions will be sufficent to protect us from any unjust suspitions.

Tis like they might if they were known (reply'd I) but not being so, we may
be liable (as many other innocent have been) to injurious censures.

For my part (said he) I value not what they think of me, since tis probable
they may never see my face again, and for yours Madam I dare answer [fol.188ᵛ]
there is none that knows you that will admit a thought to the prejudice of your
vertue: make it not then a matter of vexation but turne it into rallery, as I do. But
who are those (continu'd he) that came in as it were on purpose to disturbe my
rest.

I cannot tell indeed *Issodorus* (answer'd I) but I guess them to be some ^of^
Silisdes's Friends whom he has brought with him from Palermo for thither he
went this morning: but if I am not mistaken he blames himselfe more then I do,
for bringing them in; for I know him to be civiller then to have attempted any
such thing had he in the least thought of our being retir'd thither; therefore the
servants are more faulty in not giving him notice of it; but seeing it cannot now
be remedied, I'll frett my selfe in vain no longer.

Assoon as *Issodorus* was gone, *Silisdes* came to plead his excuse supposing he
had displeas'd me by pressing so rudely as he said on my retirement; protesting
'twas meerly his ignorance that made him guilty of so high an incivility.

I do believe it *Silisdes* (answer'd I) for I have alwayes found you so civill, and
obliging, as I have no reason to judge otherwise of you; nor had I been troubled
in the least, had you chanced to come alone, but I must be very much oblig'd to
those with you, if they conceive not some sinister opinion of me.

That I'll assure you Madam (reply'd he) I took a perticuler care to prevent,
by telling them the Gentleman with you, was your Brother, and I wish for my
owne sake that what I affirm'd had been as true, as I knew it was the contrary.
But O how much do I condemne *Issodorus* in my thoughts (went he on after a litle
silence) that could so lavishly mispend those precious minutes in drousie slum-
bers in your presence, which had they been allow'd to others with that freedome
as to him would have been employ'd to a more noble use, and serv'd to inspire
them with so ravish[ing] a satisfaction as would have been enough to banish sleep
forever from their eyes at least at such times as they were blest with the felicity
of gaizing on yours.

But being unwilling to engage in a discourse of this nature with *Silisdes*
I made him no answere, nor seem'd to mind what he said, but fell presently a
talking of something else, that I migh[t] wave [have] a clearer intimation of his
passion, which I very much desir'd he should think me ignorant of. The next day
Issodorus came not; at which I was extreamly troubled lest his fall might occation
his ~~fall~~ absence, but the day following he did; and by his presence discipated all
my feares.

I am sorry Madam (said he) that I should make the least breach in that
promise I made to wait on you every day whilst you continu'd here; but I trust
that interest I presume now to challenge in your kindness will plead so effectu-
ally in my behalfe as to obtain your pardon when I have assur'd you 'twas not any

willfull neglect that detain'd me from you, but rather that obedience I owe to the commands of *Perisana* which she impos'd on me to go yesterday to a Brothers of hers on some very urgent business from her which could not be dispenced with.

Think not (reply'd I) that I am so rigourous an exacter of every litle punctilio that you promise, no *Issodorus* provided you faile not in the maine, I'll never quarell with you for such slight omissions.

But observing a kind of sad Aire to ore shaddow that gaiety which at other times sparkled in his eyes, I could not be satisfi'd till I had enquired the cause, demanding whether his fall still troubled him, or whether he had any new mishap befallen him.

No Deare *Arthenia* (answer' d he) tis not any new misfortune that dejects me, since tis but what I long since knew I must undergoe; though I [fol.189ʳ] confess I hop'd it would not so soon have hapned. But cannot you guess, and spare me the trouble of telling you what tis has rais'd this Melancholy cloud that appeares so visible in my face.

There are such various causes of trouble in the world (reply'd I) that should I beat my Braines to find out yours, I might sooner light on the wrong then hit upon the right.

Methinks (said he) it should not be so difficult for you to conceive it, for what can you imagin can be of any afflicting concerne to me now that I am blest with the assurance of your deare affection save onely my seperation from you; which sad time within a day or two will come.

Must you then leave me so soon (reply'd I sighing).

No madam you must leave me it seemes (answer'd he) for calling on *Melliantes* as I came, and telling him whether I was coming, he enjoyn'd me to let you know that he desires you not to faile to be with him to morrow in order to [begin] your Journey, and assur'd me two dayes more would be the uttmost date of his stay; but I hope you will give me leave to waite on you one dayes Journey.

You need not aske me leave (said I) to do anything so much conducing to my happiness, which I must bid farewell to when I part from you.

I would as willingly waite on you home (reply'd he) would my extraordinary occasions permit, or my absence be dispenced with for so long a time; but however I am resolv'd to venture all things rather then not enjoy your company for the space of one poor day. Many ~~expressions~~ passionate expressions did he utter of his griefe to part ~~with me~~ from me, so piercing as they infus'd as great a measure of sadness into my heart as his seem'd repleat with.

In order to [abide by] *Melliantess* desires the next day I bid adue to *Eugenia* and in her presence took my leave of *Serena* and her son, that thereby I might shun, all opportunities of a private discourse with him in case he had design'd any such thing; so that he onely told me, he fear'd his company would prove but troublesome or else he should have importun'd my permission to waite on me to Palermo[.]

[B]ut however Madam (pursu'd he) my cordiall wishes shall not faile to attend you thither, and where ever else you go, that you may find a felicity great as your merits in whatsoever you most desire, or that can render it compleat and perfect; and may *Issodorus's* passion continue unchangable as *Silisdes's* should have done, had he had but the least glimps of hopes to sustaine it with; but tis Dispaire alone must kill, what a too high Pr[e]sumption gave life too.

For these obliging wishes I gave him my due thankes, and bid him farewell; but *Eugenia* would not part from me so, but went with me to the very enterance of Palermo and there with many teares kiss'd and embraced me when we parted, as if we had been to take an everlasting far[e]well of each other ne're to meet again. Assoon as I had seen and spoken with my Brother I went to *Therasmenes's* and lay there that night; and the next day after Dinner bid adue both to him and *Hestrina*, from thence I went to *Persides's* where I spent the remainder of that day and towards the Evening took my leave of *Perisana* and *Bellamira* with many gratfull retributions for all those unmerited favors I had at any time receiv'd from them.

I'll assure you my Deare *Arthenia* (said *Perisana* pressing me in her Armes with all the Demonstrations of a most tender Amitie) those testimonies of my Friendship which I have given you has so little express'd the reallity and greatness of that value I have for you which is such as I know not any thing that can sufficently illustrate it, nor shall Time, or absence be capable of lessening my Friendship: and fain would I put on you a Spell that you might ne're be able to forget me though by distance far remov'd. Weare this then for my sake (continu'd she puting a Ring upon one [fol. 189ᵛ] of my Fingers) and each time you cast an eye on that think on the Giver.

Your goodness Madam (reply'd I) had questionless been a Charm strong enough to fix you too deeply in my thoughts, for Time ever to blot you out; but seeing you have been pleas'd to confer on me this additionall Obligation, I shall think my selfe bound no less by Duty then Inclination to devote the kindest of my Thoughts to the memory of a person I infinitly honour; and rather would I loose my life then ever part from this Deare Pledge of your inesteemable Friendship (pursu'd I kissing the Ring she gave me).

To *Bellamira* I renew'd my Vowes of a perpetuall Amitie; which she reciprocally return'd; beging me to make her happie in my letters now that she must be so no longer in my Company: which, having accordingly promis'd, we once more embraced and bid farewell to each other with so great a trouble on my part as nothing could transcend save that which insu'd at my seperation from *Issodorus*.

Thence went I to *Sillindras* with whom I lay that night, and geting up early the next morning I went to my Brothers, taking her with me, whose Griefe to part from *Melliantes* fell not so much short of that which I resented [felt] on *Issodorus's* score; yet she endeavour'd to conceale it all she could, masking it with her concern for my departure.

Ah (thought I) to my selfe, if *Sillindra* so much lament a short absence from *Melliantes* which a litle time will repair, what may I do, who am to part with from my *Issodorus* not for some few dayes, or weeks onely, but for yeares, nay perchance forever. The sadness of these reflections were a litle discipated when I came to my Brothers, and found *Issodorus* there, who (as it ~~smeer~~ seem'd) had been his Bedfellow that night, as I had been *Sillindras's*.

When we came thither we found him in Bed, (but *Melliantes* up, and puting all things in order for our Journey) but he immediatly arose, and dressing himselfe almost in an instant, we went soon after altogether in a chariot to the other end of the Towne where our Horses waited in a readiness for us; we there bid adue to poor *Sillindra* who with weeping eyes took her leave of us, and seem'd by her Teares to tell me, I was shortly to act a part in that sad sceane. I was to have rode behind *Melliantes* but *Issodorus* would needs carry me himselfe so far as he went with us, and my Brother rode on his Horse. Never did I think time flew away so fast as now, and oft (though) in vain did I wish that day might have been le[n]gthen'd to an age; but the vanity of those fruitless wishes I too soon perceiv'd, by the approach of that time of the night which sommond us to our Beds, I cannot say our rests, for if *Issodorus* took no more then I, he found that night but litle; for Teares instead of sleep found full employment for my eyes all that wholle night long. I ris early the next morning, yet *Issodorus* was gotten up before me, and a knocking at my Chamber Dore to see if I were sturring, and assoon as I was drest I caus'd the Dore to [be] open'd.

Ah *Issodorus* are you come (said I sighing, with teares ready to start from my eyes) to take your last farewell of your poor *Arthenia*.

Heaven forbid it madam (cry'd he) I hope we shall meet again and with more Joy then now with Griefe we part, and in a shorter space too then either you, or I expect: but if Death should be so cruell as to take my life away ere I see you again, as a witness of my passionate affection for your Dearest self, I'll leave you sole Mistress of that litle fortune I can justly call my owne.

Ah *Issodorus* (interrupted I) think not if ^you^ should dye that I can live to enjoy ought that is yours; for I am most certain if that dismall day should once arrive, it would prove no less fatall to me then you, or if for some short time I should be so wretched as to survive you, it should be onely so long to melt away my life in Teares.

Do not afflict your selfe my Deare *Arthenia* before [fol. 190ʳ] hand with an unnecessary griefe (reply'd he) for that which Fate may possibly prove kinder then to permit, I onely spake of my Death as a thing that might happen. But to put these sad thoughts out of your mind which I have rais'd, pray tell me where you had this Ring (pursu'd he looking on that his Mother gave me).

Twas *Perisanas* present to me (answer'd I) when I took my leave of her yesterday, and a happiness beyond expression should I count it were I but sure she would make good what the Motto of it promises.

What may it be (demanded he).

Nothing shall move my constant love (I repli'd) but I doubt when she once comes to the knowledge of yours to me, it will be a meanes to deprive me of hers, which I so highly value as I can never quit the interest I have in it without an infinite concern.

Never feare you shall be put to that trouble (said he), since I dare assure you, the kindness she has for you is so firmly rooted in her heart that there is not any thing that can be capable of depriving you of it.

If that I mention'd does not (reply'd I) I am certaine nothing else ere shall.

By this time my Brother being ready call'd on me to go, which summons I obey'd with a heavy heart, as supposing the time of our seperation to be come; but *Issodorus* resolv'd to let me be [blot] happy in his company a litle longer, telling me he would go with me to the next Towne which was that ~~we~~ where we design'd to rest at Noon. It was nigh two houres that we stay'd there; and having Din'd, *Melliantes* to give us the more freedome of converse left us alone, saying he would go and give order for the Horses to be brought forth; but no sooner was his back turn'd ere I burst out into a most violent passion, weeping most bitterly, though I did all I could to fetter up my griefe within the confines of my Brest; but so unruly was it, that the more I thought to restrain it, with the greater violence did it break forth.

This *Issodorus* being a spectator of; for a while follow'd my example, but assoon as his passion would suffer him to speak (he cry'd) for the Gods sake Deare *Arthenia* do not break my heart with greife to see you wast so many of those precious teares in vain, in deploring what necessity confines us too; I shall leave you with the pressure of such a heavy weight of sadness on my soule as ~~litle~~ needs not yours to be an addition to my Burthen: Then since tis so decreed that our persons must ~~unad~~ unavoidably be seperated, let not our sorrows be united, suffer the whole load then to remain on me, who am fitter to sustain it then you are.

Ah *Issodorus* (said I) how great an argument of my Discretion it might be counted I ~~know not~~ cannot tell, but sure it would be but a litle one of my love if I could part from you with dry eyes, when I consider to how long an absence I am doom'd.

I must confess this testimony of your kindness is very obliging (repli'd he) yet would I rather choose to have been deni'd this satisfaction then to read it in your Teares; which I once more beg you to dry up, and no longer suffer those watery cloudes to eclips the luster of your eyes.

It would have much aleviated my trouble (said I) had you been as good as your word in giveing me your Picture ere I went out of Towne (for your Majesty must know (pursu'd *Arthenia* to the Queen) he had a good while since promis'd it me, but had so long delay'd to set for it as it could not possibly be finish'd though it was begun before I came away) That I might have found a pleasing diversion for my eyes (continu'd I) in viewing your shaddow, when they had lost the satisfaction of beholding the substance any longer. But tis no matter (went I on with a sigh) you cannot hinder me from bearing away your Image so deeply engraven in my heart as no length of time shall ere be able to deface it.

And there forever shall I weare yours (repli'd he) but though I have been very much to blame in so long neglecting to get it dispatch'd (as not thinking your departure would so soon have hapned) yet by my future diligence I hope to make amends for this my first offence which I am.[7]

---

[7] See Figure 8. I am indebted to William Gentrup for the suggestion that since the manuscript concludes at the very bottom of the folio page, rather than mid-page, that may indicate that the final pages were separated or lost from the rest, rather than simply not finished.

APPENDIX 1
THE ELLIS FAMILY

The Ellis family figured significantly on both the parliamentary and the royalist sides during and after the Civil War and Restoration.[1] Even a brief overview of the seventeenth-century history of this colorful family underlines the difficulty of assuming that every branch of an ostensibly royalist family was loyal to the king. Reverend John Ellis descended from a branch of the Ellis family that had settled in York. He graduated from Cambridge where he became a Fellow of St. Catherine's Hall and, subsequently, a chaplain to Archbishop George Abbot and a Rector of Waddesdon in Buckinghamshire. Ellis was a famous figure in religious debates. At the beginning of the Civil War, he was an advocate for Parliament against the king but then retracted his republicanism and changed his allegiance back to the king. He had six sons and two daughters, and his four elder sons were also famous for their differing political and religious allegiances. His eldest son and namesake John Ellis, born in 1645, became an Under Secretary of State to King William. The next and second eldest son, William Ellis, became Secretary to the Duke of Tyrconnel, when he was Lord Lieutenant of Ireland. William Ellis later followed the Catholic James II into exile; he was Secretary of State to him and later Treasurer to his son the old Pretender. The third son became a Roman Catholic bishop and the fourth an Anglican bishop in Ireland.

---

[1] *The Ellis Correspondence. Letters Written During the Years 1686, 1687, 1688, and Addressed to John Ellis, Esq. Comprising Many Particulars of The Revolution*, ed. Hon. Agar Ellis, 2 vols. (London: Henry Colburn, New Burlington Street, 1829), 1: xii–xxiii. The original letters are preserved in the Birch Collection at the British Library.

APPENDIX 2
FICTIONAL NAMES OF HISTORICAL FIGURES AND PLACES

Argelus   Archibald Campbell, 1st Marquess of Argyll (1607–1661)

Bilindus   William Baillie (d. 1653), Commander of Scottish troops at the Battle of Kilsyth

Bonario   Sir Richard Browne, Lord Mayor of London, in 1660

Celestina   Catherine of Braganza (1638–1705), wife of Charles II

Claromenes   Charles II (1630–1685), King of England, Scotland, and Ireland

Clearchus   Charles I (1600–1649), King of England, Scotland, and Ireland

Cratander   Lord Arthur Capell (1604–1649)

Diocles   Robert Devereux, 3rd Earl of Essex (1591–1646), Commander of Parliamentary troops

Diophantes   David Leslie, 1st Lord Newark (1601–82)

Eluzeria   Princess Elizabeth, daughter of Charles I (1635–1650)

Ericina   Elizabeth I (1533–1603), Queen of England and Ireland

Faragenes   1) Ferdinando Fairfax, 2nd Lord Fairfax of Cameron, General of the Parliamentary forces on 21 January 1645; 2) His son Sir Thomas Fairfax, 3rd Lord Fairfax of Cameron (1612–1671) also served as Commander of the Parliamentary forces. Bridget Manningham conflates the son and father.

Gerandus   George Goring, 1st Earl of Norwich (1585–1663); Goring's son also served as a prominent Royalist general.

Gonsalvo   Possibly a fictional character or Colonel George Gunter of Racton, Sussex

Herelius   Henry VIII (1491–1547), King of England and Ireland

Herenia   Queen Henrietta Maria (1609–1669), wife of King Charles I; Princess Henrietta (1644–1670), the youngest daughter of Charles I and named after her mother

Hortensius   Lord Ralph Hopton, Baron Hopton (1596–1652)

Hyperion	Prince Henry, Duke of Gloucester, son of King Charles I (1640–1660)
Ileana	Jane Lane of Bentley Hall, who received a pension from Charles II
Ismenas	King James I of England and VI of Scotland (1566–1625)
Issomantes	Prince James, later King James II (1633–1701)
Istander	Jacob Astley, 1st Baron Astley of Reading (1579–1652)
Ithagenes	Sir John Hotham (1589–1645)
Leonishus	Possibly a fictional character or Thomas Whitgreave (fl.1651) of Moseley Hall, Staffordshire
Leonitus	Commander Rowland Laugharne (1607–1675) participated on the Royalist side in the Battle of St. Fagans, sentenced to death but reprieved after lots were drawn
Lysander	Robert Bertie, 1st Earl of Lindsey (1582–1642), leader of the Royalist forces at the Battle of Edgehill
Macaria	Anne (Villiers) Douglas (1610–54), later Countess of Morton. Known as Lady Dalkieth after her marriage to Robert Douglas, Lord Dalkeith and later Earl of Morton; godmother and later governess to Princess Henrietta, the daughter of Charles I
Mallinor	Cardinal Jules Mazarin, Duke of Rethel, Mayenne, and Nevers (1602–1661)
Mardonius	James Graham, 1st Marquess of Montrose (1610–1688)
Marina	Mary Stuart, Princess of Orange (1631–1660)
Meltiades	George Monck, General of both Royalist and Parliamentary armies. Charles II raised Monck to the peerage in 1660 as 1st Duke of Albemarle (1608–1670). Bridget Manningham names him Meltiades after Militades, the Athenian general and stateman who led the victory of Athens over Persia at the Battle of Marathon
Merobates	James Hamilton, 1st Duke of Hamilton (1606–1649)
Orestagne, Prince of	James Butler, 1st Duke of Ormonde (1610–1688). Known as the Earl of Ormonde (1634–42), Marquess of Ormonde (1642–1661)
Ormisdas	Oliver Cromwell (1599–1658), Parliamentary General and Lord Protector of England (1653–1658)
Philarchus	Henry Wilmot, 1st Earl of Rochester (1613–1658)
Placius	William or Richard Penderel; see also Silvius below (fl. 1651).
Policilus	Colonel Rice Powell was condemned to death after the Battle of St. Fagans but reprieved after lots were drawn
Pollidor	Colonel John Poyer (d.1649) participated on the Royalist side at the Battle of St. Fagans and was executed after lots were drawn

Rizander   Rupert, Prince and Count Palatine of the Rhine and Duke of
               Cumberland (1619–1682)

Silvius   William or Richard Penderel; see also Placius above (fl. 1651).

Stertorius   James Stanley, 7th Earl of Derby (1607–1651)

Theodates   Governor of Oxford in 1646

Places

Aeolian Islands Scilly Isles or Wales

Agrigentum   a city near Maidstone (Enna); Manningham family home was
               in East Malling, near Maidstone. See Illustration 6

Bastia   Edinburgh

Calaris   Dublin

Catana   Naseby

Celtiberia   Holland

Corsica   Scotland

Drepanum   Gloucester

Enna   Maidstone

Erix   Exeter

Felinus   Abingdon

Iberia   Spain

Lipara   Isle of Wight

Mazara   Oxford

Messina   York

Milase   Hull

Mona   Yorkshire

Naples   France

Nicosia   Nottingham

Nota   Kent or Wales

Palermo   London

Sardinia   Ireland

Sicily   England

Taromenion   Dover

APPENDIX 3
IDENTIFICATION OF FICTIONAL CHARACTERS

Acestes	A prince famed for his lavish entertainments of Aeneas
Achemenes	Oriana's father and King of Persia
Admetus	Artabella's attendant
Adrastus	Cydarius' friend, who aids in Clazomena's rescue
Alcander	King of Delphos, who loves and marries Artabella
Alsinda	Princess and widow, Merinza's mother whom Arthenia visits in Palermo
Amarantha	Arthenia's cousin
Ambracia	Ianthe's attendant
Amena	A lady from Queen Ermillia's court
Anaxiles	Beltizera's brother and Alcander's cousin
Ardelia	Loreto's kinswoman and Dionella's daughter
Ariobarzarnes	King of Armenia
Arnardo	Arthenia's uncle by marriage to Marione
Artabella	Menzor's daughter and Oriana's royal cousin, later Queen of Delphos and mother to Queen Ermillia
Artelinda	Issodorus' deceased wife
Arthenia	Narrator of the history and battles of the English Civil War, described initially as Mellidorus or "fair unknown" when washed ashore in Delphos
Astianax	Commander of Persian troops under Diomed (Prince Lucius)
Balario	Issodorus's close friend
Barsarnes	Friend to Diomed and lieutenant general of Persian troops
Belissa	Loreto's wife
Bellamira	Blesarius's daughter, resident with Perisana
Beltizera	Alcander's royal cousin and daughter of Prince Cleophantus

Blesarius	Persides's kinsman and Bellamira's father
Boetius	Issodorus's uncle and Princess Victorina's husband
Brecena	Arthenia's mother
Celestina	Claromenes's wife and Queen of Sicily (England); see Appendix 2
Celia	Queen Ermillia's attendant and narrator of Artabella's story
Claromenes	King of Sicily (King Charles II of England, Scotland, and Ireland); see Appendix 2
Clazomena	Daughter of Scythian King Oruntus and love interest of Cydarius
Crisalda	Loreto's mother and Duchess of Verona
Criton	Old man who offers Diomed refuge in his cottage
Cydarius	Scythian general who loves Princess Clazomena, later King of Scythia
Delizia	Alcander's sister and Princess of Delphos
Diomed	Love interest of Oriana, friend of Phasellus, the assumed name of Prince Lucius Octavius, grandson of Augustus Caesar and heir to the Roman throne
Dionella	Loreto's kinswoman
Diophantus	Friend of Arthenia's brother, Melliantes
Doristus	Gentleman present at Persides' house who agrees with Philotheta that requited love destroys a lover's desire, cf. Philotheta
Drepanum, Duke of	Deceased and wealthy father of Valeria and Euridice (Electra)
Electra	Possibly a mistake for Euridice
Elesena	Perisana's daughter who marries Herminio
Elusina	Cilician princess
Ermillia/Ermilia	Artabella's daughter and Queen of Delphos
Ethrea	Marione's maid
Eudora	Artabella's deceased mother
Eugenia	Sister of Arthenia's mother who lives outside of Palermo
Eumetes	Serastes's brother
Euridice	Daughter and heir of Victorina and deceased Prince of Drepanum, a recommended love interest for Issodorus
Felinus, Duke of	See Gracianus below

Felisarda	Celia's maid
Ferintus	Alcander's servant who later marries Saparilla, Artabella's attendant
Filoret	Issodorus's servant
Flaminius	Chief priest at Delphos
Flavianus	Loreto's father and Crisalda's husband
Gentillus	Thracian ambassador to Delphos
Gracianus	Merinza's father and Duke of Felinus
Herminio	Elesena's husband
Hermis	Loreto's attendant
Hersilia	Clazomena's attendant
Hestrina	Arthenia's aunt and wife to Therasmenas, who hosts Arthenia in Palermo
Ianthe	Arthenia's close friend who is buried on the island of Rhene
Iros	Diomed's keeper in the Scythian prison
Irvinus	Merinza's husband
Issodates	Belissa's father
Issodorus	Arthenia's love interest in Part 2, son of Perisana and Persides, Elesena's brother, younger brother of Theander
Julia/Juliana	Sister to Diomed (Prince Lucius)
Julius Antonius	Grandson of Marc Antony, assumes the name Phasellus
Leonora	Loreto's wealthy aunt to whom he is heir
Loreto	Arthenia's suitor and the Duchess of Verona's youngest son, cavalier supporter of Clearchus (Charles I)
Lucaria	Parthian princess
Lucius Octavius	Grandson and heir of Augustus Caesar, assumes the name Diomed
Madona	Wealthy elderly woman wooed by Loreto
Marcellus	Julia's deceased husband
Marione/Marionie	Sister of Arthenia's mother Brecena
Medicius	Scythian physician to Clazomena
Melissa	Theano's daughter and Bellamira's cousin
Melliantes	Arthenia's brother who lives in Palermo
Mellidorus	Assumed name of Arthenia after she washes up on Delphos in masculine disguise

Menzor	Artabella's father and brother to Achemenes, King of Persia
Merinda	Bellamira's cousin and Theano's daughter
Merinza	Arthenia's childhood friend and daughter to Gracianus, Duke of Felinus
Mettella	Neighbor of Therasmus and Hestrina with whom Arthenia stays in Palermo
Mexaris	Narrator in Part 2, Diomed's servant, who reveals to Artabella what has transpired since she left Persia
Mironides	Arthenia's father
Mizalinda	Perisana's deceased daughter, whom Arthenia resembles
Nearchus	Beltizera's brother and Alcander's cousin
Octimasdes	Oriana's rejected suitor and King of Scythia
Orestaign/Orestan, Prince of	James Butler, 1st Duke of Ormonde and Lord Lieutenant of Sardinia (Ireland) in 1661–1669 and 1677–1685; see also Appendix 2
Oriana	Artabella's cousin and daughter and heir of King Achemenes, succeeds her father as Queen of Persia, Diomed's love interest
Orithia	Thracian princess
Orosmades	Scythian god
Orsodates	Son of Artabella and King Alcander of Delphos, Queen Ermilia's brother, successor to Queen Oriana
Oruntus	Clazomena's father and King of Scythia
Otanes	Diomed's jailor and Ozmin's brother
Ozmin	Artabella's kidnapper on Phasellus's orders and Otanes's brother
Perisana/Perizana/ Perinissa	Persides's wife
Persides	Perisana's husband
Phasellus	Diomed's friend, suitor to Artabella, tricks Queen Oriana into marriage, grandson of Marc Antony, assumed name of Julius Antonius
Phileno	Clazomena's attendant who aids in rescuing Diomed
Philotheta	Lady present at Persides's house and proponent of the view that requiting love destroys a lover's desire, cf. Doristus
Piramena	Sister of King Tyribasus of Armenia
Praxaspes	Persian Prince who envies Diomed's leadership